The Forties
in America

DELPHI PUBLIC LIBRARY

222 East Main Street
Delphi, Indiana 46923
765-564-2929

The Forties in America

Volume I
Abbott and Costello—Germany,
Occupation of

Editor
Thomas Tandy Lewis
St. Cloud State University

SALEM PRESS
Pasadena, California
Hackensack, New Jersey

Editor in Chief: Dawn P. Dawson

Editorial Director: Christina J. Moose
Project and Development Editor: R. Kent Rasmussen
Manuscript Editors: Tim Tiernan, A. J. Sobczak,
Christopher Rager, Rebecca Kuzins
Acquisitions Editor: Mark Rehn
Editorial Assistant: Brett Weisberg

Research Supervisor: Jeffry Jensen
Photo Editor: Cynthia Breslin Beres
Indexer: R. Kent Rasmussen
Production Editor: Joyce I. Buchea
Graphics and Design: James Hutson
Layout: Mary Overell

Title page photo: *One of the most popular vocal groups in world history, the Andrews Sisters are cultural icons of both World War II, when they performed before countless military audiences, and the entire decade of the 1940's, when they were a constant presence on the radio. In this mid-1940's publicity shot, Maxene Andrews is seated in front, with Patty and LaVerne behind her.* (Michael Ochs Archives/Getty Images)

Cover images: (pictured clockwise, from top left): Hiroshima atom bomb blast, 1945 (The Granger Collection, New York); Joe DiMaggio, 1947 (Time & Life Pictures/Getty Images); Betty Grable, pin up girl, 1942 (The Granger Collection, New York); U.S. bombers formation, 1942 (The Granger Collection, New York)

∞ The paper used in these volumes conforms to the American National Standard for Permanence of Paper for Printed Library Materials, Z39.48-1992 (R1997).

Library of Congress Cataloging-in-Publication Data

The forties in America / editor, Thomas Tandy Lewis.
  p. cm.
Includes bibliographical references and index.
  ISBN 978-1-58765-659-0 (set : alk. paper) — ISBN 978-1-58765-660-6 (vol. 1 : alk. paper) —
ISBN 978-1-58765-661-3 (vol. 2 : alk. paper) — ISBN 978-1-58765-662-0 (vol. 3 : alk. paper)
  1. United States—Civilization—1945—Encyclopedias. 2. United States—Civilization—1918-1945—
Encyclopedias. 3. Canada—Civilization—1945—Encyclopedias. 4. United States—History—
1933-1945—Encyclopedias. 5. United States—History—1945-1953—Encyclopedias.
6. Canada—History—1945—Encyclopedias. 7. Canada—History—1914-1945—Encyclopedias.
8. Nineteen forties—Encyclopedias. I. Lewis, Thomas T. (Thomas Tandy)
  E169.12.F676 2011
  973.91—dc22
                                                                                    2010028115

PRINTED IN THE UNITED STATES OF AMERICA

■ Table of Contents

■ Publisher's Note

The Forties in America is an encyclopedic work offering comprehensive coverage of the most important people and events and developments of all types in the United States and Canada from the year 1940 through 1949. With this publication, Salem Press's Decades in America series now encompasses every decade from the 1940's through the 1990's, and the series will soon add sets on the 1920's and the 1930's. Librarians have acclaimed this series for its ability to help students grasp significant aspects of each decade's history—precisely the goal of each set.

Articles in the *Forties in America* are written primarily for high school students and college undergraduates, but the set's clear and innovative approach to the 1940's should also make it useful to advanced students and scholars. Its more than 650 alphabetically arranged articles cover the full breadth of North American history and culture, and its supporting features include 17 appendixes and such helpful finding aids as end-of-article cross-references, detailed indexes, and a category index.

Scope and Coverage

Each twentieth century decade is closely identified with at least one landmark event or major turning point. The key event of the 1940's was, without a doubt, World War II. The greatest military conflict in world history, the war not only fully preoccupied the United States and Canada through nearly half the decade but also left both nations and virtually the entire world fundamentally changed: It rearranged the balance of political and military power throughout the world, introduced the threat of nuclear weapons, and set the stage for the Cold War. No other twentieth century event had an impact on its decade comparable to that of World War II.

Although *The Forties in America* devotes a great deal of its space to the war, it does not do so at the cost of neglecting other subjects. Indeed, the set makes a special effort to treat the war primarily within the context of its impact on other aspects of American and Canadian life. Hence, while the set contains many articles on essential military details of the war—major campaigns, selected battles, important weapons, the military services, principal military commanders—it places even greater emphasis on the ways in which those and other aspects of the war affected government, business, culture, and daily lives throughout North America.

One of the most fascinating aspects of a reference set such as *The Forties in America* is what it reveals about its decade's many unique contributions to history. Readers will find articles on such subjects as the invention of aerosol cans, microwave ovens, instant photography, and transistors; desegregation of the U.S. military; discovery of the "big bang" theory of the creation of the universe; the first purported sightings of "flying saucers"; the rise of the National Basketball Association; and the origins of the Cold War.

The breadth of the set's 654 articles can be seen in the variety of some of the categories under which they fall:

- African Americans
- art and architecture
- Asian Americans
- business and economics
- Canada
- courts and court cases
- crime and scandal
- diplomacy and international relations
- disasters
- education and scholarship
- environmental issues
- film
- government and politics
- health and medicine
- journalism and publishing
- labor
- Latinos
- laws and treaties
- literature
- music
- Native Americans
- popular culture
- radio
- religion and theology
- science and technology
- social issues
- sports
- theater
- transportation and travel
- women's issues
- World War II

The end of volume 3 contains a complete list of specific category headings, followed by the articles to which they apply.

As with Salem's other decade sets, *The Forties in America* mixes long overview essays on broad subjects with shorter articles discussing people, books, films, fads, inventions and scientific discoveries, and other events and important topics representative of the decade. Every article focuses on its subject within the context of the 1940's, devoting only such attention to the subjects before and after that decade as is needed to place the subjects within their fuller historical contexts.

Organization and Format

Ranging in length from 1 to 6 pages, each article in *The Forties in America* begins with a concise title followed by a brief definition or description of the person, organization, work, concept, or event. Headwords are selected to help users find articles under the titles they expect, but extra help is provided in the form of textual cross-references. For example, users looking for an article under the heading "Hockey" are referred to the article titled "Ice hockey." Additional help in locating topics can be found in the extensive Subject Index in volume 3.

After their titles, the articles provide a variety of ready-reference top matter tailored to the individual topics. For example, articles on individual persons provide brief identifications and their subjects' birth and death dates and places. Articles on events give brief descriptions of the events and their dates and places. Other types of articles provide similar information. Under the subheading "Significance," all articles provide summary statements about the importance of their subjects within the context of the 1940's.

The main body of each article concludes with an "Impact" section that reviews the subject's broader importance during the 1940's. "See also" cross-references following every article direct readers to additional articles on closely related and parallel subjects. Every article also offers bibliographical notes, which include annotations in articles of 1,000 or more words, and every article is signed by its contributing author. The affiliations of the contributors can be found in the list following this note.

Special Features

A rich selection of more than 320 evocative photographic images illustrate the articles in *The Forties in America*. The subjects of these photographs are listed in a special index in volume 3. In addition, 25 maps and nearly 100 sidebars—lists, time lines, tables, graphs, and excerpts from speeches—highlight interesting facts and trends.

Volume 3 contains 17 appendixes providing additional information about major films, Academy Award winners, major Broadway plays and theatrical awards, major radio programs, best-selling books and major literary awards, popular musicians and top-selling recordings, winners of major sports events, major U.S. legislation and U.S. Supreme Court decisions. The appendixes also include a glossary of new words and slang that arose during the 1940's, a detailed time line, and an annotated general bibliography. Finally, *The Forties in America* contains lists of U.S. wartime agencies, major World War II battles, and top wartime military leaders.

The encyclopedia also contains a number of useful tools to help readers find entries of interest. A complete list of all essays in *The Forties in America* appears at the beginning of each volume. A list of entries sorted by category appears at the end of volume 3. In addition to a photo index, volume 3 also has personage and comprehensive subject indexes.

Online Access

Salem now offers users access to its content both in traditional, printed form and online. Every school or library that purchases this three-volume set is entitled to free access to a multifeature and fully supported online version of its content through the SALEM HISTORY DATABASE. Available through an activation number found on the inside back cover of this first volume, access is both immediate and unlimited, so it is available to all the purchasing library's patrons—on site or in their residences. Online customer service representatives, at (800) 221-1592, are happy to answer questions. E-books are also available.

Acknowledgments

The editors of Salem Press would like to thank the more than 340 scholars who contributed essays and appendixes to *The Forties in America*. Their names and affiliations are listed in the front matter to volume 1. The editors especially wish to thank Professor Thomas Tandy Lewis of St. Cloud State University in Minnesota for serving as the project's Editor and for bringing to the project his special expertise on North American history.

■ Contributors

Randy L. Abbott
University of Evansville

Michael Adams
City University of New York, Graduate Center

Patrick Adcock
Henderson State University

Linda Adkins
University of Northern Iowa

Richard Adler
University of Michigan, Dearborn

Peggy E. Alford
State Bar of Arizona

Emily Alward
Las Vegas, Nevada

Nicole Anae
Charles Sturt University

Corinne Andersen
Peace College

Carolyn Anderson
University of Massachusetts, Amherst

David E. Anderson
Seymour, Indiana

Jermaine Archer
State University of New York College, Old Westbury

Erica K. Argyropoulos
University of Kansas

Charles Lewis Avinger, Jr.
Washtenaw Community College

Charles F. Bahmueller
Center for Civic Education

Amanda J. Bahr-Evola
Southern Illinois University, Edwardsville

Jane L. Ball
Yellow Springs, Ohio

Carl L. Bankston III
Tulane University

Rosann Bar
Caldwell College

David Barratt
Montreat College

Bijan C. Bayne
Washington, D.C.

Pamela Bedore
University of Connecticut

Keith J. Bell
The Citadel

James R. Belpedio
Becker College

Raymond D. Benge, Jr.
Tarrant County College

Alvin K. Benson
Utah Valley University

Milton Berman
University of Rochester

Anthony J. Bernardo, Jr.
Wilmington, Delaware

R. Matthew Beverlin
Rockhurst University

Margaret Boe Birns
New York University

Nicholas Birns
Eugene Lang College, The New School

William C. Bishop
University of Kansas

Ami R. Blue
Eastern Kentucky University

Devon Boan
Belmont University

David Boersema
Pacific University

Gordon L. Bowen
Mary Baldwin College

William Boyle
University of Mississippi

Susan Roth Breitzer
Fayetteville, North Carolina

Kathleen M. Brian
George Washington University

Norbert Brockman
St. Mary's University

Howard Bromberg
University of Michigan

Richard R. Bunbury
Boston University

Michael A. Buratovich
Spring Arbor University

Michael H. Burchett
Limestone College

William E. Burns
George Washington University

Susan Butterworth
Salem State College

Joseph P. Byrne
Belmont University

Jennifer L. Campbell
Lycoming College

Kimberlee Candela
California State University, Chico

Byron Cannon
University of Utah

Russell N. Carney
Missouri State University

Sharon Carson
University of North Dakota

Paul J. Chara, Jr.
Northwestern College

Frederick B. Chary
Indiana University Northwest

Allan Chavkin
Texas State University, San Marcos

Michael W. Cheek
Kennett Square, Pennsylvania

Douglas Clouatre
North Platte, Nebraska

Kathryn A. Cochran
Longview Community College

Susan Coleman
West Texas A&M University

Jo Ann Collins
Arts Junction

Michael Conklin
College of New Jersey

Brett Conway
Hansung University

James J. Cooke
University of Mississippi

Raymond D. Cooper
Eckerd College

Laura Cowan
University of Maine

David A. Crain
South Dakota State University

Robert L. Cullers
Kansas State University

Michael D. Cummings, Jr.
Madonna University

Amy Cummins
University of Texas—Pan American

Marsha Daigle-Williamson
Spring Arbor University

Eddith A. Dashiell
Ohio University

Anita Price Davis
Converse College

Jennifer Davis-Kay
Education Development Center, Inc.

Randee Dawn
Jackson Heights, New York

Frank Day
Clemson University

Bruce J. DeHart
University of North Carolina, Pembroke

William K. Delehanty
University of Kansas

James I. Deutsch
Smithsonian Institution

Joseph Dewey
University of Pittsburgh, Johnstown

Thomas E. DeWolfe
Hampden-Sydney College

Jonathan E. Dinneen
Bridgewater, Massachusetts

Marcia B. Dinneen
Bridgewater State College

Paula C. Doe
Ypsilanti, Michigan

Cecilia Donohue
Madonna University

Thomas Du Bose
Louisiana State University, Shreveport

William V. Dunlap
Quinnipiac University School of Law

John P. Dunn
Valdosta State University

Val Dusek
University of New Hampshire

Darius V. Echeverría
Rutgers University

Wilton Eckley
Colorado School of Mines

Kelly Egan
Ryerson University

Howard C. Ellis
*Millersville University of
Pennsylvania*

Mark R. Ellis
University of Nebraska, Kearney

Robert P. Ellis
Worcester State College

Victoria Erhart
Strayer University

Sara K. Eskridge
Louisiana State University

Jack Ewing
Boise, Idaho

Kevin Eyster
Madonna University

Dean Fafoutis
Salisbury State University

Thomas R. Feller
Nashville, Tennessee

Dennis E. Ferguson
Boston University

Ronald J. Ferrara
Middle Tennessee State University

Keith M. Finley
Southeastern Louisiana University

Paul Finnicum
Arkansas State University

Gerald P. Fisher
Georgia College and State University

Jane Brodsky Fitzpatrick
*City University of New York,
Graduate Center*

Dale L. Flesher
University of Mississippi

Anthony J. Fonseca
Nicholls State University

Joseph Francavilla
Columbus State University

Alan S. Frazier
University of North Dakota

Gary Galván
LaSalle University

Janet E. Gardner
Falmouth, Massachusetts

June Lundy Gastón
City University of New York

Camille Gibson
Prairie View A&M University

Priscilla Glanville
Manatee Community College

Richard A. Glenn
Millersville University of Pennsylvania

Sheldon Goldfarb
University of British Columbia

Ursula Goldsmith
Louisiana State University

Raymond J. Gonzales
California State University, Monterey Bay

Michele Goostree
Southern Illinois University, Carbondale

Nancy M. Gordon
Amherst, Massachusetts

Johnpeter Horst Grill
Mississippi State University

Larry Grimm
University of Illinois, Chicago

Richard L. Gruber
Xavier University

Scot M. Guenter
San Jose State University

Larry Haapanen
Lewis-Clark State College

Michael Haas
California Polytechnic University, Pomona

Jasmine LaRue Hagans
Northeastern University

Irwin Halfond
McKendree University

Jan Hall
Columbus, Ohio

Fusako Hamao
Santa Monica, California

C. Alton Hassell
Baylor University

P. Graham Hatcher
Shelton State Community College

Leslie Heaphy
Kent State University, Stark

Bernadette Zbicki Heiney
Lock Haven University of Pennsylvania

James J. Heiney
Lock Haven University of Pennsylvania

Michael Hennessey
Texas State University, San Marcos

Mark C. Herman
Edison State College

Michael Hix
Troy University

Matthew Hoch
Shorter College

Paul W. Hodge
University of Washington

Samuel B. Hoff
Delaware State University

John R. Holmes
Franciscan University of Steubenville

Shaun Horton
Florida State University

John C. Hughes
Saint Michael's College

Ski Hunter
University of Texas, Arlington

Mary Hurd
East Tennessee State University

Raymond Pierre Hylton
Virginia Union University

Margaret R. Jackson
Troy University

Ron Jacobs
Asheville, North Carolina

Ramses Jalalpour
University of Wisconsin

Jeffry Jensen
Altadena, California

Bruce E. Johansen
University of Nebraska, Omaha

Sheila Golburgh Johnson
Santa Barbara, California

Yvonne J. Johnson
St. Louis Community College, Meramec

David M. Jones
University of Wisconsin, Oshkosh

Jeffrey Daniel Jones
University of Kentucky

Ramonica R. Jones
Austin, Texas

Karen N. Kähler
Pasadena, California

Steven G. Kellman
University of Texas, San Antonio

William E. Kelly
Auburn University

Lisa Kernek
Western Illinois University

Baris Kesgin
University of Kansas

Paul E. Killinger
Indiana University

Leigh Husband Kimmel
Indianapolis, Indiana

Paul M. Klenowski
Clarion University of Pennsylvania

Bill Knight
Western Illinois University

Gayla Koerting
Nebraska State Historical Society

Grove Koger
Boise State University

David B. Kopel
Independence Institute

Beth Kraig
Pacific Lutheran University

Jean L. Kuhler
Auburn University

P. Huston Ladner
University of Mississippi

Wendy Alison Lamb
South Pasadena, California

Timothy Lane
Louisville, Kentucky

Eugene Larson
Los Angeles Pierce College

William T. Lawlor
University of Wisconsin, Stevens Point

J. Wesley Leckrone
Widener University

Joseph Edward Lee
Winthrop University

Margaret E. Leigey
California State University, Chico

Jennie MacDonald Lewis
University of Denver

Leon Lewis
Appalachian State University

Thomas Tandy Lewis
St. Cloud State University

Roy Liebman
*California State University,
Los Angeles*

Roberta L. Lindsey
*Indiana University—Purdue University,
Indianapolis*

Victor Lindsey
East Central University

L. Keith Lloyd III
McMurry University

M. Philip Lucas
Cornell College

Alex Ludwig
Brandeis University

R. C. Lutz
CII Group

M. Sheila McAvey
Becker College

Joanne McCarthy
Tacoma, Washington

Roxanne McDonald
Wilmot, New Hampshire

Daniel McDonough
Lynn, Massachusetts

Roderick McGillis
University of Calgary

Elizabeth A. Machunis-Masuoka
Midwestern State University

S. Thomas Mack
University of South Carolina, Aiken

Robert R. McKay
Clarion University of Pennsylvania

Richard L. McWhorter
Prairie View A&M University

David W. Madden
*California State University,
Sacramento*

Paul Madden
Hardin-Simmons University

Rachel Maines
Cornell University

Martin J. Manning
U.S. Department of State

Andrew R. Martin
Inver Hills College

Victor M. Martinez
*University of Illinois, Urbana-
Champaign*

Sherri Ward Massey
University of Central Oklahoma

James I. Matray
California State University, Chico

Laurence W. Mazzeno
Alvernia College

Joseph A. Melusky
Saint Francis University

Scott A. Merriman
Troy University, Montgomery

Eric W. Metchik
Salem State College

Michael R. Meyers
Pfeiffer University

Matthew Mihalka
University of Minnesota, Twin Cities

Dodie Marie Miller
Fort Wayne, Indiana

Timothy C. Miller
Millersville University of Pennsylvania

Randall L. Milstein
Oregon State University

Christian H. Moe
Southern Illinois University, Carbondale

Andrew P. Morriss
University of Alabama School of Law

Daniel P. Murphy
Hanover College

Alice Myers
Bard College at Simon's Rock

Jerome L. Neapolitan
Tennessee Technological University

Steve Neiheisel
St. Mary's University

Leslie Neilan
*Virginia Polytechnic Institute
and State University*

Elizabeth Marie McGhee Nelson
Christian Brothers University

Caryn E. Neumann
Miami University of Ohio

Norma C. Noonan
Augsburg College

Myron C. Noonkester
William Carey University

Eric Novod
Morganville, New Jersey

Elvy Setterqvist O'Brien
Williamstown, Massachusetts

James F. O'Neil
Florida Gulf Coast University

Arsenio Orteza
World Magazine

Elizabeth Whittenburg Ozment
University of Georgia

William A. Paquette
Tidewater Community College

Robert J. Paradowski
Rochester Institute of Technology

Alyson Payne
University of California, Riverside

David Peck
California State University, Long Beach

Mark E. Perry
North Georgia College & State University

Mark A. Peters
Trinity Christian College

Barbara Bennett Peterson
University of Hawaii

Thomas F. Pettigrew
University of California, Santa Cruz

John R. Phillips
Purdue University, Calumet

Christine Photinos
National University

Allene Phy-Olsen
Austin Peay State University

Richard V. Pierard
Indiana State University

Julio César Pino
Kent State University

Troy Place
Western Michigan University

Marjorie Podolsky
*Pennsylvania State University, Erie,
Behrend College*

Michael Polley
Columbia College of Missouri

Mark D. Porcaro
University of Dayton

David L. Porter
William Penn University

Judy Porter
Rochester Institute of Technology

Tessa Li Powell
University of Denver

Victoria Price
Lamar University

April L. Prince
University of Texas, Austin

Maureen Puffer-Rothenberg
Valdosta State University

Aaron D. Purcell
Virginia Tech

John Radzilowski
University of Alaska Southeast

Steven J. Ramold
Eastern Michigan University

Jonah Raskin
Sonoma State University

John David Rausch, Jr.
West Texas A&M University

Christina Reese
California State University, Chico

Kevin B. Reid
Henderson Community College

Rosemary M. Canfield Reisman
Charleston Southern University

H. William Rice
Kennesaw State University

Mark Rich
Cashton, Wisconsin

Betty Richardson
*Southern Illinois University,
Edwardsville*

Alice C. Richer
Norwood, Massachusetts

Robert Ridinger
Northern Illinois University

Edward A. Riedinger
Ohio State University

Gina Robertiello
Felician College

Russell Roberts
Bordentown, New Jersey

Chris Robinson
University of Kansas

Carol A. Rolf
Rivier College

Carl Rollyson
City University of New York,
Baruch College

Joseph R. Rudolph, Jr.
Towson University

Concepcion Saenz-Cambra
Newport Harbor Nautical Museum

Virginia L. Salmon
Northeast State Community College

Daniel Sauerwein
University of North Dakota

Timothy Sawicki
Canisius College

Richard Sax
Lake Erie College

Elizabeth D. Schafer
Loachapoka, Alabama

Beverly Schneller
Millersville University of
Pennsylvania

Lisa Scoggin
Saint Anselm College

Shawn Selby
Kent State University, Stark

Brion Sever
Monmouth University

Chrissa Shamberger
Ohio State University

Emily Carroll Shearer
Middle Tennessee State University

Martha A. Sherwood
Eugene, Oregon

Wayne Shirey
University of Alabama, Huntsville

R. Baird Shuman
University of Illinois, Urbana-
Champaign

Julia A. Sienkewicz
Smithsonian American Art Museum

Narasingha P. Sil
Western Oregon University

Charles L. P. Silet
Iowa State University

Donald C. Simmons, Jr.
Dakota Wesleyan University

Paul P. Sipiera
William Rainey Harper College

Amy Sisson
Houston Community College

Emilie Fitzhugh Sizemore
California State University, Northridge

Douglas D. Skinner
Texas State University, San Marcos

Billy R. Smith, Jr.
Anne Arundel Community College

Joanna R. Smolko
University of Pittsburgh

Jingyi Song
State University of New York,
Old Westbury

Staci A. Spring
Abilene Christian University

Brian Stableford
Reading, England

Mark Stanbrough
Emporia State University

Arthur Steinberg
Salisbury, North Carolina

Robert E. Stoffels
St. Petersburg, Florida

Theresa L. Stowell
Adrian College

Eric S. Strother
University of Kentucky

Cynthia J. W. Svoboda
Bridgewater State College

Roy Arthur Swanson
University of Wisconsin, Milwaukee

Patricia E. Sweeney
Shelton, Connecticut

Glenn L. Swygart
Tennessee Temple University

James Tackach
Roger Williams University

Abram Taylor
Mount Vernon, Kentucky

Jeremiah Taylor
Mount Vernon, Kentucky

Cassandra Lee Tellier
Capital University

Rebecca Tolley-Stokes
East Tennessee State University

Kelly Amanda Train
Ryerson University

Paul B. Trescott
Southern Illinois University, Carbondale

Andy K. Trevathan
University of Arkansas

Marcella Bush Trevino
Barry University

Monica T. Tripp-Roberson
Anne Arundel Community College

Charles L. Vigue
University of New Haven

William T. Walker
Chestnut Hill College

Shawncey Webb
Taylor University

W. Jesse Weins
Dakota Wesleyan University

Henry Weisser
Colorado State University

Cheryl H. White
Louisiana State University, Shreveport

George M. Whitson III
University of Texas, Tyler

Thomas A. Wikle
Oklahoma State University

LaVerne McQuiller Williams
Rochester Institute of Technology

Megan E. Williams
University of Kansas

Tyrone Williams
Xavier University

Raymond Wilson
Fort Hays State University

Sharon K. Wilson
Hays, Kansas

Scott Wright
University of St. Thomas

Susan J. Wurtzburg
University of Utah

Heather E. Yates
University of Kansas

Tung Yin
Lewis & Clark Law School

William Young
University of North Dakota

Philip R. Zampini
Westfield State College

■ Complete List of Contents

Volume I

Volume II

Volume III

A

■ Abbott and Costello

Identification   American comedy acting team

Bud Abbott
Born   October 2, 1895; Asbury Park, New Jersey
Died   April 24, 1974; Woodlands Hills, California

Lou Costello
Born   March 6, 1906; Paterson, New Jersey
Died   March 3, 1959; East Los Angeles, California

Abbott and Costello were a very successful comedy team on stage, radio, film, and television. Apart from a brief separation in 1945, the duo performed together from 1936 through 1957. Their skit "Who's on First?" became their signature routine, making them one of the most popular comedy teams in history.

It is believed that Bud Abbott and Lou Costello first met in New York City in 1933, crossing paths on the burlesque circuit. In 1935, while performing separate acts, the two comedians officially met at the Eltinge Theatre in New York City. They joined their acts in 1936 and soon found themselves atop the entertainment world, where they remained for twenty-one years.

In 1939, the team accepted roles in the Broadway musical *Streets of Paris*. After receiving noteworthy reviews for their work, they were contracted by Universal Studios for the comedy *One Night in the Tropics* (1940), in which they played minor roles. Recognizing the star power of the young team, Universal quickly signed them to a long-term contract. First starring in the 1941 film *Buck Privates*, the comedic duo made a total of twenty-five films during the 1940's, including *Hold That Ghost* (1941), *Ride 'Em Cowboy* (1942), *Pardon My Sarong* (1942), and *Abbott and Costello Meet Frankenstein* (1948).

Abbott and Costello were not limited to the silver screen. It was during this same time period that they also took their act to radio. In 1940, they hosted a summer show for the National Broadcasting Company (NBC) in Fred Allen's absence. The following year, they were regulars with Edgar Bergen and Charlie McCarthy on *The Chase and Sanborn Program*. Then, in 1942, they presided over their own half-hour program on NBC. The show peaked in 1944 at number six and was consistently ranked in the top ten. In 1947, the duo took the program to the American Broadcasting Company (ABC), where they also hosted *The Abbott and Costello Children's Show*, which aired on Saturday mornings.

During World War II, Abbott and Costello were supportive of the war effort. Their comedy was uplifting not only to the general public but also to the

Publicity still of Bud Abbott (above) and Lou Costello made to promote the radio program they launched in 1940. (©Bettmann/CORBIS)

troops. In an effort to raise funds for the war bond drive, the comedians funded their own cross-country tour and continuously played to full houses. At one point, they raised $89 million in three days.

Impact   Best known for the skit "Who's on First?," in which the suave and smooth-talking Abbott describes to a confused Costello a baseball team including players named Who, What, Tomorrow, and I Don't Know, the duo was hardly a one-act show. The 1950's saw the comedy team starring in their own television program and films, until they amicably parted in 1957. In 1941, Abbott and Costello were honored at Grauman's Chinese Theatre in Hollywood, California, where they left their hand- and footprints in the cement outside the landmark venue. In 2005, they were inducted into the National Radio Hall of Fame in Chicago.

Michael D. Cummings, Jr.

Further Reading

Costello, Chris, and Raymond Strait. *Lou's on First: A Biography.* New York: St. Martin's Press, 1981.

Cox, Stephen, and John Lofflin. *The Abbott and Costello Story: Sixty Years of "Who's on First?"* 2d ed. Nashville, Tenn.: Cumberland House, 1997.

Thomas, Bob. *Bud and Lou: The Abbott and Costello Story.* Philadelphia: Lippincott, 1977.

See also   Berle, Milton; Film in the United States; Hope, Bob; Radio in the United States.

■ Academy Awards

Identification   Annual awards given to actors, directors, producers, and other filmmakers by the Academy of Motion Picture Arts and Sciences

Academy Awards tend to reflect popular tastes in films, and Oscars usually increased winning films' exposure and their box-office revenue. During the 1940's, American film studios devoted large portions of their output to war films and the dark films that later came to be called films noirs. It is for these two genres of films that Hollywood of the 1940's is perhaps best remembered and the distribution of Academy Awards reflected that fact. Such films came to characterize the temper of the times both during World War II and after.

The Academy Awards, or Oscars, are given by Academy members to acknowledge achievement in vari-

ous categories of technical and creative fields in the motion-picture business. The awards given out by the Academy during the 1940's were for the most part given to productions of the big studios, which financed the awards ceremonies. Although comedian Bob Hope was never nominated for an acting award himself, he hosted or cohosted the awards ceremonies eighteen times between 1940 and 1978, including five ceremonies during the 1940's.

In was only after the war that smaller-budget films such as *The Lost Weekend* (1945) were among those recognized by the Academy. Many of the decade's nominated films focused on World War II; these can be separated into films devoted to combat and those focusing on the impact of the war on the home front. The noir films were a mix of melodramas and crime films. The war films were often quite problematic, especially the earlier ones that were made when the outcome of the conflict was far from certain. Postwar films, such as *The Sands of Iwo Jima* (1949), on the other hand, celebrated the Allied victory with a mix of pride and jingoism. What remains curious are the noir films, with their dark portrayals of the underside of American life, which seem to contrast with the postwar return to normalcy.

Prewar Academy   The United States did not enter World War II until the end of 1941, after the Japanese attack on Pearl Harbor. Consequently, the Academy Awards for 1940 and 1941 were dominated by prewar productions: In 1940, *Rebecca* and *The Philadelphia Story* both received multiple nominations, as did *Sergeant York, How Green Was My Valley,* and *Citizen Kane* in 1941. In 1940, Alfred Hitchcock's *Foreign Correspondent* was about a prewar peace conference in Europe with typical Hitchcockian villains, and Charles Chaplin's *The Great Dictator* spoofed Adolf Hitler and Benito Mussolini. It now seems almost ironic that when Chaplin's film came out, it irritated the U.S. State Department because the U.S. government was still officially neutral regarding the developing European war. *Sergeant York*, a biopic of World War I hero Alvin York, was a patriotic film that celebrated the common man as soldier. Many of these films touched on the coming war in various ways, preparing the way for Hollywood's wartime films. As a sign of the times, Bette Davis suggested that the ceremony be held in a theater and tickets sold to the public with the proceeds going to British war relief. However, the Academy declined.

Academy Award Winners for Best Picture and Best Director, 1940-1949

Year	Best Picture	Best Director
1940	*Rebecca*	John Ford, *The Grapes of Wrath*
1941	*How Green Was My Valley*	John Ford, *How Green Was My Valley*
1942	*Mrs. Miniver*	William Wyler, *Mrs. Miniver*
1943	*Casablanca*	Michael Curtiz, *Casablanca*
1944	*Going My Way*	Leo McCarey, *Going My Way*
1945	*The Lost Weekend*	Billy Wilder, *The Lost Weekend*
1946	*The Best Years of Our Lives*	William Wyler, *The Best Years of Our Lives*
1947	*Gentleman's Agreement*	Elia Kazan, *Gentleman's Agreement*
1948	*Hamlet*	John Huston, *The Treasure of the Sierra Madre*
1949	*All the King's Men*	Joseph L. Mankiewicz, *A Letter to Three Wives*

Wartime Academy Awards By the time of the 1942 awards ceremony, the first major war-era films were being recognized with nominations and Oscars. The film most celebrated at that time was *Mrs. Miniver,* starring Greer Garson, Walter Pidgeon, and Teresa Wright. It portrayed the trials of an English family at the time Great Britain was beginning to fight Germany. Both Garson and Wright won acting awards, as did director William Wyler and the film. *Wake Island* and its director, John Farrow, were also nominated. The film highlighted the heroic efforts of American forces defending an island in the Pacific in the early years of the war.

In response to wartime conditions, the Academy had the Oscar statuettes cast from plaster, rather than metal, and it increased the number of nominations in the documentary category to accommodate more documentaries with war themes. Following the suggestion that Bette Davis had made, the Academy's 1943 ceremonies were held in a theater and two hundred tickets were given to servicemen. Nominated films with wartime themes that year included *Casablanca, For Whom the Bell Tolls, In Which We Serve,* and *Watch on the Rhine.* Humphrey Bogart, Ingrid Bergman, and Paul Henreid are pitted against Nazis and Vichy France in North Africa in *Casablanca,* which featured MGM's crew of émigré actors, many of whom had fled war-torn Europe. *For Whom the Bell Tolls* was based on Ernest Hemingway's best-selling novel set during the Spanish Civil War, a prelude to the wider European conflict. *In Which We Serve* fol-lowed the military activities in the North Atlantic of the British Royal Navy, and *Watch on the Rhine,* adapted from a play by Lillian Hellman with a script by her lover Dashiell Hammett, was set in wartime Washington, D.C., where Nazi agents menace Bette Davis and Paul Lukas—who won an Oscar for his performance.

Since You Went Away was one of the highlights of the next year's nominees. Featuring a family facing the absence and loss of loved ones, it was one of the more poignant films about the trials of the home front and the pain they experienced. Alfred Hitch-cock's *Lifeboat,* with an ensemble cast, places people in a lifeboat after their transport ship is torpedoed by a German submarine. However, by this time, the film industry was already returning to peacetime production. A Bing Crosby picture, *Going My Way,* was the most nominated film in 1944, and the Academy also nominated Otto Preminger's *Laura* and Billy Wilder's *Double Indemnity*—both films later regarded as noir classics.

In 1945, Billy Wilder won a directing award for *The Lost Weekend,* a film about an alcoholic. Although it was a small production about a dark subject, it also won the best-picture Oscar and a best-actor award for its star, Ray Milland. Hitchcock's *Spellbound,* about an amnesiac who thinks he is a murderer, and Joan Crawford's comeback film that won her a best-actress Oscar, *Mildred Pierce,* added to the gloomy, if socially relevant, list of films that dominated the awards. Although such war-themed films as *Thirty Seconds over*

Tokyo (1944) and *They Were Expendable* (1945), both made from best-selling wartime books, continued to be released, the shift away from the heroics and emotionally wrenching wartime films presaged Hollywood's swift transition in the postwar years.

Postwar Academy Awards The 1946 Academy Awards were dominated by *The Best Years of Our Lives*, a film about three war veterans returning home to the same small town and their adjustments to civilian life. Fredric March won the best-actor award, and a double amputee Navy veteran, Harold Russell, won for best supporting actor. Eight nominations went to British films, and screenplay nominations went to the Italian film *Open City* and the French film *Children of Paradise*.

Gentleman's Agreement won best picture in 1947, and director Elia Kazan also won an Oscar. Another film nominated for an Oscar was *Crossfire*, a noir feature about returning soldiers with an anti-Semitic theme. However, its producer, Adrian Scott, and its Oscar-nominated director, Edward Dmytryk, were then under investigation by the House Committee on Un-American Activities (HCUA), whose hunt for communist influence in the entertainment industry had a chilling effect on Hollywood during the postwar years.

In 1948, Laurence Olivier was nominated for best director for *Hamlet*, which won, as did Olivier himself for best actor. Two of the year's noir offerings, *Key Largo* and *Sorry, Wrong Number*, also garnered nominations. That year was also notable for the stu-

Navy veteran Harold Russell (center) at the 1947 Academy Awards ceremony with the two Oscars he won for his performance in The Best Years of Our Lives. *To the left is the film's producer, Samuel Goldwyn; to the right is director William Wyler.* (©Bettmann/CORBIS)

dios' refusal to fund the ceremonies because of the large number of nominations that went to foreign films: *Hamlet* and *The Red Shoes* alone received a total of eleven nominations. In response, the Academy moved the event to its own theater.

The last awards ceremony of the decade, in 1949, honored two more war-themed films, a combat film, *Battleground*, and *Twelve O'Clock High*, a film examining combat fatigue. However, by this time the Hollywood film industry was trying to return to some sort of normalcy. That year's nominations were dominated by serious dramas, a political film *All the King's Men*, *The Heiress*, based on a Henry James novel, and *A Letter to Three Wives*. Once again, foreign productions stood out. Two neorealist films from Italy, *The Bicycle Thief* and *Paisan*, were nominated for screenwriting. Despite these nominations, the studios returned to paying for the awards ceremony.

Impact During the 1940's, the Academy Awards combined the patriotic and the professional, the selfless and the self-serving. The major studio films continued to garner the most nominations and awards, but smaller films and films made abroad were making inroads into the world of Hollywood's awards. This trend mirrored the changes that were looming in the studio's future, as television was about to undermine Hollywood's profits, and it presaged the gradual decline of the studio system. In addition, foreign-made films also attracted increasingly large audiences and presented a challenge to the American film industry. While both these trends were in their infancy and represented only a minor irritant during the 1940's, they did indicate the direction the film industry was going.

Charles L. P. Silet

Further Reading

Dixon, Wheeler Winston, ed. *American Cinema of the 1940s: Themes and Variations.* New Brunswick, N.J.: Rutgers University Press, 2006. Essays on war films, national identity, postwar recovery, Cold War politics, communist subversion, and the American family.

Harkness, John. *The Academy Awards Handbook: Winners and Losers from 1927 to Today!* New York: Pinnacle Books, 1999. Handy listing of all nominees and winners by year.

Jewell, Richard. *The Golden Age of Cinema: Hollywood, 1929-1945.* New York: Wiley-Blackwell, 2007. Chapters on historical events and social phenomena that have shaped Hollywood films, the studio system and how films were distributed, the role of censorship, narrative and style, genres, and stars and the star system.

Levy, Emanuel. *All About Oscar: The History and Politics of the Academy Awards.* New York: Continuum, 2003. Offers a thorough, but sometimes almost tedious, behind-the-scenes look at the awards.

Matthews, Charles. *Oscar A to Z: A Complete Guide to More than 2,400 Movies Nominated for Academy Awards.* New York: Doubleday, 1995. Listing of all films, studios, and individuals nominated and winners by category.

Osborne, Robert. *Seventy Years of the Oscar: The Official History of the Academy Awards.* New York: Abbeville Press, 1999. Authoritative history of the Oscars written by one of Hollywood's insiders.

Pickard, Roy. *The Oscar Movies.* New York: Facts On File, 1994. Comprehensive look at the films that have been nominated for and won Oscars.

See also   *The Best Years of Our Lives*; *Casablanca*; *Citizen Kane*; Davis, Bette; Film in the United States; Film noir; Films about World War II; Garson, Greer; *The Great Dictator*; *Laura*.

■ Acheson, Dean

Identification   Secretary of state of the United States, 1949-1953
Born   April 11, 1893; Middletown, Connecticut
Died   October 12, 1971; Sandy Spring, Maryland

While Acheson served as undersecretary of the Treasury and assistant secretary in the Department of State in President Franklin D. Roosevelt's administration, it was as undersecretary of state and then secretary of state under President Harry S. Truman that Acheson shaped American foreign policy during the postwar era that involved the Truman Doctrine and the Marshall Plan and his leadership of American diplomacy during the Korean War.

During the 1940's, Dean Acheson served in the administrations of Presidents Franklin D. Roosevelt and Harry S. Truman. In 1941, Roosevelt appointed Acheson as assistant secretary of state. In that capacity, Acheson formulated the American oil embargo against Japan that contributed to the Japanese rationale for the attack on Pearl Harbor on December 7, 1941. During World War II, Acheson contributed to

President Harry S. Truman (left) with Dean Acheson, who has just taken the oath of office as U.S. secretary of state from Chief Justice Fred M. Vinson (right). (AP/Wide World Photos)

In 1949, Acheson was appointed secretary of state by Truman; he led in the formation of the North Atlantic Treaty Organization (NATO) that year. By entering this defensive alliance, Acheson altered the traditional American foreign policy of following an isolationist position during periods of peace; NATO was directed against Soviet expansion in Europe. Also in 1949, Acheson was concerned with the success of the communists in China; under Acheson's direction, the State Department developed an analysis of the Chinese situation and concluded that the United States should not intervene militarily against the Chinese communists. However, in June of 1950, Acheson did urge Truman to commit American troops to defend South Korea from North Korean aggression. During the same year, Acheson was attacked by Senator Joseph McCarthy for being "soft" on communism and for employing communist sympathizers in the State Department.

Impact As Truman's undersecretary of state and secretary of state, Acheson shaped American foreign policy during the post-World War II era. Through the Truman Doctrine, the Marshall Plan, the establishment of NATO, and his call for Truman to use force to defend South Korea, Acheson formulated American Cold War policies directed against the Soviet Union and communist China. After his tenure as secretary of state, Acheson served as an adviser on foreign policy to Presidents John F. Kennedy and Lyndon B. Johnson.

William T. Walker

the establishment of organizations (including the World Bank and the International Monetary Fund) that were designed to maintain world peace after the war. Acheson's most significant achievements in foreign policy were associated with the Cold War against the Soviet Union. Acheson aspired for a postwar world in which the United States and the Soviet Union would maintain a constructive alliance in which they would pursue the goals of the new United Nations. However, before the fall of 1945, Acheson, distressed at the Soviet Union's aggression in Eastern and Central Europe and its retention of the Baltic states (Estonia, Latvia, and Lithuania), became convinced that Soviet expansion had to be contained.

Between 1945 and 1949, Acheson served as undersecretary of state in the Truman administration. During that period, Truman and Acheson developed a close working relationship; Acheson was the primary author of the Truman Doctrine in 1947, in which the president requested congressional support to assist Greece and Turkey in combating the forces of totalitarianism that threatened to seize control of those countries. Acheson advanced the containment policy (originally argued by George Kennan) in 1948, when he designed the European Economic Recovery Program (the Marshall Plan).

Further Reading

Beisner, Robert L. *Dean Acheson: A Life in the Cold War.* New York: Oxford University Press, 2009.

Chace, James. *Acheson: The Secretary of State Who Created the American World.* New York: Simon & Schuster, 1998.

McMahon, Robert J. *Dean Acheson and the Creation of an American World Order.* Washington, D.C.: Potomac Books, 2008.

See also Berlin blockade and airlift; Cold War; Foreign policy of the United States; Kennan, George F.; Marshall Plan; North Atlantic Treaty Organization; Truman, Harry S.; Truman Doctrine.

■ Advertising in Canada

Canadian advertising—as separate and distinct from American advertising—came into its own during the 1940's. This effort was promulgated to a large extent through the auspices of the Canadian Broadcasting Corporation, which via radio brought to the farthest corners of the country sponsored informational, educational, and entertainment programs reinforcing national identity.

At the dawn of the 1940's, Canada as a Commonwealth member was already engaged in World War II, following Nazi Germany's September, 1939, invasion of Poland. As with many countries locked in conflict, Canada found its culture quickly transformed. The last vestiges of the decade-long Great Depression vanished in a sustained burst of production inspired by patriotism and the needs of war. Women and minorities were recruited to replace former workers now serving in the military, both as manufacturers of consumer goods and in factories retooled to produce military material. Commodities became scarce, and rationing was imposed.

Advertising, by necessity, changed its focus during the war years because production of many consumer items was suspended or cut back for the duration. Instead of selling products and services no longer available, advertisers complied with the government's request to sell ideas related to Canadian welfare—in other words, propaganda. Both independent advertisers and government-sponsored marketing played a large role in disseminating relevant news and engendering participation in the national war effort across the vast and sparsely populated Canadian landscape. In a cooperative effort between corporations and the government (in the form of the Wartime Information Board, known as the WIB), a variety of means was employed to get a series of messages across to the public.

Together, the WIB and the National Film Board produced war documentaries to be shown in Canadian and American theaters, especially in population centers clustered in a narrow band on either side of the border. A government speakers' bureau served local clubs and women's groups, with speakers specifying what individuals could do on the home front to assist the war effort. Government-produced pamphlets were distributed that explained in detail the purpose of various programs. Bold, bright posters—often employing caricatures of the beaver, the national symbol, standing shoulder to shoulder with the British lion—exhorted men and women to enlist, or warned against "loose talk" that could be of benefit to the enemy, or worked to boost morale. Print ads in magazines and newspapers encouraged conservation of foodstuffs, urged greater productivity, and highlighted the benefits of investing in Victory Bonds during ten successful drives conducted over seven years.

Radio contributed significantly to the overall advertising/propaganda endeavors throughout the war. The government-backed Canadian Broadcasting Corporation (CBC), established in 1936, along with its French-language counterpart, Radio Canada, brought immediacy to advertising that other media could not match. Radio commercials brought a uniquely Canadian quality to popular broadcasts that often originated in the United States, such as *Amos 'n' Andy* and *Fibber McGee and Molly.* By the mid-1940's, the proportion of original Canadian material had greatly increased, thanks to broadcasts of hockey games, variety shows (such as *The Happy Gang* from Toronto), big band music shows (such as Mart Kenney from Vancouver), dramas (such as *The Craigs, Soldier's Wife,* and *Theatre of Freedom*), and talk shows (including *Let's Face the Facts* and *Arsenal of Democracy*).

Impact Following the end of the war, manufacture of consumer products slowly increased, and advertising across all media returned to the prewar concern of convincing customers to buy tangibles. CBC Radio and its national identity-enhancing ads became a driving force in building on the postwar portrayal of Canada as a unique entity. During the early 1950's, television became the dominating medium of entertainment and persuasion, and the focus of advertising turned to that medium.

Jack Ewing

Further Reading

Johnston, Russell Todd. *Selling Themselves: The Emergence of Canadian Advertising.* Toronto: University of Toronto Press, 2001.

Rose, Jonathan. *Making Pictures in Our Heads: Government *Advertising in Canada*. Santa Barbara, Calif.: Praeger, 2000.

Tuckwell, Keith J. *Canadian Advertising in Action*. Toronto: Pearson Education Canada, 2008.

See also Automobiles and auto manufacturing; Business and the economy in Canada; Canadian nationalism; Demographics of Canada; Radio in Canada; Television; Wartime propaganda in Canada.

■ Advertising in the United States

At the dawn of the 1940's, the American public, after a decade of the Depression, had a deep distrust of business, and corporate advertising was guilty by association. After American entry into World War II, however, confidence in business was restored through coordinated efforts of government agencies working in conjunction with the independent, nonprofit War Advertising Council, which helped unify the United States through effective promotional campaigns dealing with issues of vital concern to society.

The decade of the 1940's was a divided time for America and American advertising. The decade began on a promising note for business, despite the war in Europe and the threat of American involvement, as the economy began to recover from the effects of the long Depression. Employment was on the rise, consumers could again afford products they had done without because they lacked money, and advertising rose in tandem with the recovery.

With 30 million households possessing radio sets in 1940, broadcast was the dominant national medium of the era, running more than $216 million worth of commercials while providing news, music, and entertainment in the form of soap operas, quiz shows, children's programs, mysteries, dramas, and sporting events. Single advertisers sponsored most popular programs (featuring such stars as Kate Smith, Arthur Godfrey, Red Skelton, Jack Benny, and Bob Hope), a marketing model that would continue during the early years of television. The catchy and hugely successful "Pepsi Cola hits the spot" ditty, introduced in 1941, launched a renewal of the use of advertising jingles that would peak during the 1950's.

Wartime Changes American entry into World War II in December, 1941, changed everything. Suddenly, many manufacturers stopped turning out items for consumers—especially such large items as refrigerators, washing machines, automobiles, television sets, and other objects requiring large amounts of metal or mechanical components—and converted under government contracts to wartime production for the military. Other businesses cut back production as the result of shortages of supplies that were diverted toward the war effort. The publishing industry, for example, suffered from restrictions on civilian use of paper. Elements of the population that had formerly been underemployed or excluded from various jobs (notably minorities, married women, recent immigrants, non-English speakers, and the disabled) were given jobs to replace workers who had left to serve in the military. Commonplace goods often were in short supply and/or rationed, such as sugar, gasoline, coffee, meat, cheese, shoes, and canned goods. Salvage drives were conducted to collect what once was considered trash, including tin cans, fat, wastepaper, and iron and steel scrap.

With the U.S. military reeling from setbacks in the Pacific early in the war, and with deprivation and uncertainty reigning on the home front, advertising stepped in to pull the population together and to give meaning and direction to the American war effort. The nonprofit War Advertising Council (WAC), conceived in November, 1941, was a collection of volunteer ad agencies, corporate advertisers, and media representatives that worked with various government boards, such as the Office of Public Information and the U.S. Treasury's War Finance Committee, to plan and execute a series of national campaigns explaining policies and persuading the public to participate in government programs.

In July, 1942, the WAC coordinated the United We Stand campaign, in which five hundred national magazines displayed the American flag on their covers to rally support for the war effort, to celebrate Independence Day, and to establish the benefits and necessity of buying war bonds (called savings bonds before and after the war). Utilizing donated radio time and space in magazines, in newspapers, and on billboards, the first of the major war bond drives (alternately called war loan drives) was launched on November 30, 1942. In slightly over three weeks, almost $13 billion worth of bonds were sold, surpassing the goal of $9 billion. Seven additional war/victory bond drives would be undertaken through early 1946, each of them exceeding stated objectives by considerable amounts. More than $180 million worth of radio, print, and outdoor advertising (and countless hours of volunteer work) was donated to the cause, resulting in investments from 85 million Americans who purchased more than $150 billion in bonds to help finance the war.

Other WAC Campaigns Another successful multimedia campaign conducted by the WAC, in conjunction with the Office of Price Administration and the War Finance Committee, was to educate the public on the dangers of inflation. The campaign explained that economic disaster was a real possibility as more consumer money became available from increased employment; that money, competing for fewer consumer goods, could lead to rapidly escalating prices (inflation). Americans were encouraged to put excess cash into bonds, to begin payroll savings plans, to shop carefully, to observe price caps, to conserve, to consume less, and to recycle.

To boost morale and instill pride in workers, the WAC promoted government agency and armed services awards that recognized achievements in productivity or bond sales. Pennants, pins, and other symbols—the Army-Navy *E* for excellence, the Maritime *M*, the Minute Man Award, the Service Flag, the Star for repeatedly meeting production goals, the War Food Administration *A* for outstanding achievement—were proudly promoted in both government-sponsored and independently produced ads for corporations, some of which would have little but goodwill to sell to the public until the war ended. The Lucky Strike cigarette brand, for example, promoted its efforts via the memorable slogan "Lucky Strike Green has gone to war" to explain that its usual green packaging had been changed to white to conserve green paint for camouflage.

A particularly memorable wartime campaign conducted under the auspices of the WAC was undertaken to recruit women for war jobs. Symbolized by a colorful "Rosie the Riveter" graphic, the print campaign drew two million women into the

Advertisement appealing to American women to help the war effort by taking jobs in industry. (Getty Images)

workforce between 1942 and 1945, and it legitimized the role of women as contributors to the national economy. Other WAC campaigns that ran until the war's end involved the necessity of keeping war information secure ("Loose Lips Sink Ships") and the need for conservation (such as "Meatless Tuesday" and "Use it up, wear it out, make it do or do without"), recycling, and avoiding waste. The Office of War Information (OWI) assisted these efforts by subsidizing the production of morale-boosting, war-related radio series. *This Is Our Enemy, Uncle Sam, An American in England, Passport for Adams,* and *Hasten the Day* dramatized the value of various governmental policies. The OWI also inserted information into scripts for commercial radio programs, produced many newsreels about the war, and founded the Voice of America as the official broadcasting service of the U.S. government.

As the war's outcome became seemingly inevitable and hostilities began winding down, the OWI's participation in public information lessened and the WAC shifted toward public service advertisements (PSAs) not directly associated with the waning battle overseas. The famous "Only You Can Prevent Forest Fires" campaign, featuring the iconic Smokey Bear, was begun in 1944. In 1945, a public awareness-raising campaign began to recruit blood donors for the American Red Cross.

Postwar Advertising After the war ended in 1945, American society gradually returned to a consumer basis, though it would never be the same as before the war. The Nazis, the Italian fascists, and the imperialist Japanese had all been vanquished, but now there was a new, potentially more malevolent enemy—communism—to be fought in the Cold War.

In the meantime, Americans weary of World War II reveled in the relative peace, prosperity, and plenty of the late 1940's. Certain essential items, sugar and meat in particular, remained in short supply, but most consumer goods and foodstuffs became abundant and available. Millions of veterans with cash in their pockets came home to be reabsorbed into the workplace. Many took advantage of the G.I. Bill (Servicemen's Readjustment Act of 1944) to obtain unemployment compensation, to take out home or business startup loans, or to acquire college or vocational education. They joined millions of wage earners who had worked hard at home, who had scrimped and saved to do their part in the fight, and who now were ready, willing, and eager to buy with their earnings and savings.

Manufacturers were eager to oblige them and quickly converted from wartime production. Cars, refrigerators, radios, and a cornucopia of goods soon flowed off assembly lines. Consumer advertising, relegated for four long years mostly to institutional "image" ads, blossomed across all media, from the standard radio and print to illuminated billboards to sky typing, a type of skywriting that employed multiple planes. Magazine ads touted amazing new products, such as the ballpoint pen (introduced in the United States in October, 1945) and the Toni home permanent. Standbys such as Coca-Cola, seen around the world in wartime, experienced a new renaissance, aided by advertising in a variety of forms.

Although radio enjoyed the boom (advertising revenues nearly tripled between 1940 and 1950, to more than $600 million), its long run as the leading entertainment medium was coming to an end. A new, powerful, imagination-captivating force sprang up: television. Although television had debuted in 1939, there was a freeze on the manufacture of television sets during the war. In 1945, only a handful of stations existed, and only a few thousand households owned television sets. By the early 1950's, more than four hundred stations were on the air to accommodate millions of viewers, and advertisers were spending twice as much (more than $1 billion in 1955) on television than they were on radio.

Impact Never before World War II, or since, has the nation been as unified for a cause. Appeals in newspapers and magazines, radio commercials, billboards, and posters sold citizens on the value of participating in the national war effort, and they responded by buying billions of bonds, salvaging tons of scrap, and taking jobs or volunteering as needed. Because of advertising, it became acceptable, even desirable, for women to work outside the home. Advertising also opened the door for different types of workplace contributions from minorities and other underrepresented groups, who made further gains during and after the Civil Rights movement. Advocacy advertising, particularly in the hands of the Ad Council (the name taken by the War Advertising Council after the war), has prodded millions to action through memorable campaigns concerning polio, pollution, the Peace Corps, the United Negro College Fund, crime prevention, and AIDS. Television, the medium that eclipsed radio during the 1940's, continues to hold the American public in thrall, with stations supported primarily by advertising.

Jack Ewing

Further Reading

Hill, Daniel Dellis. *Advertising to the American Woman, 1900-1999.* Columbus: Ohio State University Press, 2002. Informative overview of advertising aimed at women. Takes a marketing, rather than a consumer, point of view. Contains many examples of print advertisements.

Jackall, Robert, and Janice M. Hirota. *Image Makers: Advertising, Public Relations, and the Ethos of Advocacy.* Chicago: University of Chicago Press, 2000. Examination of the art of marketing ideas from

World War I to the end of the twentieth century. Illustrated with many examples.

Jones, John Bush. *All-Out for Victory!: Magazine Advertising and the World War II Home Front.* Lebanon, N.H.: Brandeis University Press, 2009. Using examples of actual ads, shows how advertisers and ad agencies switched the emphasis from selling products to supporting the war effort by encouraging conservation and volunteerism.

Levenstein, Harvey. *Paradox of Plenty: A Social History of Eating in Modern America.* Berkeley: University of California Press, 2003. An entry in the California Studies in Food and Culture series, this book studies America's eating habits from the Depression through the end of the twentieth century. Includes a section describing the economic, political, cultural, and marketing factors affecting domestic diets during World War II.

Sickels, Robert. *The 1940s.* Westport, Conn.: Greenwood Press, 2003. This entry in the Daily Life Through History series examines the many cultural shifts that occurred during the 1940's. Includes bibliographies, a time line, and cost comparisons.

Yang, Mei-Ling. "Creating the Kitchen Patriot: Media Promotion of Food Rationing and Nutrition Campaigns on the American Home Front During World War II." *American Journal* 22, no. 3 (Summer, 2005): 55-75. Deals in depth with the cooperative effort between the government and the media to inform the American public about the necessity of rationing foodstuffs and to educate people about how to achieve proper nutrition despite cutbacks.

Young, Dannagal Goldthwaite. "Sacrifice, Consumption, and the American Way of Life: Advertising and Domestic Propaganda During World War II." *Communication Review* 8 (January-March, 2005): 27-52. Study of the combined government and advertising industry efforts to inform, educate, and motivate the American public to follow various wartime programs and policies.

See also Automobiles and auto manufacturing; Ballpoint pens; Business and the economy in the United States; Economic wartime regulations; Radio in the United States; "Rosie the Riveter"; Wartime propaganda in the United States; Wartime rationing; Wartime salvage drives.

■ Aerosol cans

Identification Pressurized containers that dispense fine liquid particles

The introduction of aerosol cans led to the development of numerous aerosol products such as disinfectants, hair spray, and spray paint. During World War II, scientists from the U.S. Department of Agriculture developed a portable aerosol spray container for insecticides.

In an aerosol spray system, fluid expands under high pressure to dispense another fluid through a nozzle or actuator, creating an aerosol mist of particles or droplets that evaporate quickly once the liquid is sprayed. Erik Rotheim, a Norwegian engineer, invented an early version of the aerosol can and valve during the late 1920's. Julian S. Kahn received a U.S. patent in 1939 for a disposable spray can, but the invention was never developed. However, during World War II the U.S. government funded research conducted by Lyle Goodhue and William Sullivan, who developed a small aerosol can pressurized by liquefied gas. The refillable spray can was patented in 1943 and was largely used by soldiers to fight against malaria-carrying mosquitoes in the Pacific.

By the late 1940's, Robert Abplanalp had invented a valve crimp that allowed liquids to be sprayed from a can under the pressure of an inert gas. The can was constructed of lightweight aluminum and a clog-free valve, making it possible to dispense liquid foams, powders, and creams practically. The use of spray paint in aerosol cans was developed by Edward Seymour. He founded the highly successful Chicago-based company Seymour of Sycamore, which is still in business today, to mass-produce the product.

Impact Aerosol cans were indispensable during World War II, as U.S. servicemen used aerosol insecticide products to defend against disease-carrying insects in the Pacific. However, concern over the use of fluorocarbons and the depletion of the ozone layer during the mid-1970's caused companies to substitute environmentally friendly water-soluble hydrocarbons in aerosol cans.

Gayla Koerting

Further Reading

Acton, Jimmy, Tania Adams, and Matt Packer. *Origin of Everyday Things.* New York: Sterling, 2006.

Ikenson, Ben. *Patents: Ingenious Inventions—How*

They Work and How They Came to Be. New York: Black Dog & Leventhal, 2004.

Slocum, Ken. "New Magic with Pushbutton Sprays." *Science Digest* 42 (December, 1957): 23-26.

Zark, Bob. *The Aerosol Can.* New York: Panic Button, 1997.

See also Air pollution; Inventions; Science and technology; Wartime technological advances.

AFL. *See* **American Federation of Labor**

■ African Americans

Despite suffering from segregation and other forms of discrimination, African Americans made important contributions to the Allied victory in World War II, and the goals of the Civil Rights movement began to take shape during the early postwar years.

Although the "Great Migration" of African Americans from the South to the North began early in the twentieth century, the expansion of industrial jobs during World War II spurred the migration to an unprecedented degree. From 1940 to 1945, approximately 1.5 million African Americans settled in northern cities. Even though the migrants often encountered virulent racism, many of them were nevertheless able to earn decent wages for the first time in their lives. At the same time, African Americans entered the armed forces in large numbers, demonstrating great competence and courage. Recognizing the opportunity for advancement, black activists and intellectuals commonly referred to the "Double V," by which they meant victory over oppression both overseas and in the United States.

Military Service in the War Although the Selective Service Act of 1940 continued the traditional racial segregation in the military services, it prohibited racial segregation in recruitment and training. When African American leaders protested the segregation policy, President Franklin D. Roosevelt announced that administrators of the draft would seek to admit black soldiers in numbers equal to their proportion in the general population—about 10 percent. To promote this goal, he appointed Judge William H. Hastie as civilian aide to the secretary of war. About the same time, he promoted Colonel Benjamin O. Davis, Sr., to brigadier general, which made him the first African American to reach this rank.

During the four years of the war, about 1.2 million African Americans served in the military—approximately 7 percent of the total membership. The underrepresentation of African Americans was primarily due to disparities in education and health, which resulted from historical discrimination and oppression. More than half of the black servicemen served abroad. Denied equal opportunity for combat and administrative roles, they were disproportionately assigned to support services, particularly mess duty and loading/unloading supplies. Walter White, secretary of the National Association for the Advancement of Colored People (NAACP), following a fact-finding inquiry, reported that black soldiers resented the necessity of performing mundane, backbreaking tasks that provided little prestige or opportunity for promotion, even though the work was often as dangerous as fighting on the front lines.

Despite discrimination, large numbers of African Americans participated in active combat, often with great distinction. More than twelve thousand citations and decorations were awarded to the 92d Infantry Division, a traditional all-black infantry division whose members had long been called "buffalo soldiers." The 761st Tank Battalion participated in some of the fiercest fighting in the Battle of the Bulge, and it received the Presidential Unit Citation for "extraordinary heroism in military operations." The Navy usually assigned its 150,000 black sailors to duty on shore or near coastal harbors, but two vessels—the USS *Mason*, a destroyer escort, and the submarine chaser *PC-1264*—were both manned by predominantly black crews. One hero of the December 7, 1941, attack on Pearl Harbor was mess attendant Doris (Dorie) Miller, who was awarded the Navy Cross for shooting down three Japanese planes with an anti-aircraft machine gun. In 1942, the Marine Corps finally ended its 167-year exclusion of African Americans, but most of the 17,000 African American Marines were assigned to service units.

In the early 1940's, most commanders in the Army Air Forces assumed that African Americans were incapable of flying aircraft. Responding to pressure, nevertheless, Secretary of War Henry Stinson authorized the training of some 992 black aviation cadets in Tuskegee, Alabama. Organized into the 332d Fighter Group and the 99th Pursuit Squadron, the Tuskegee Airmen flew some 15,533 sorties, and they were credited with destroying 261 enemy planes. Almost one hundred of the Tuskegee men were killed in action. They were awarded 150 Distinguished Flying Crosses, eight Purple Hearts, and numerous other decorations. In 1945, the 332d Fighter Group, commanded by Colonel Benjamin O. Davis, Jr. (later promoted to general), received a Presidential Unit Citation. In 2007, President George W. Bush awarded 350 of the surviving airmen and their widows with a Congressional Gold Medal.

Members of an African American Marine battalion serving in the Pacific in 1945. The men nicknamed their gun "Lena Horne" after the popular singer. (National Archives)

Frequently, the efforts of African Americans to oppose discriminatory treatment resulted in clashes on military bases. At Freeman Field, Indiana, for instance, more than a hundred Tuskegee officers were arrested in 1945 for having attempted to integrate a club reserved for white officers. Three of those arrested were subjected to court-martial, and one of them, Lieutenant Roger Terry, was convicted and fined $150 for having shoved a white officer. In a similar event, Army Lieutenant Jackie Robinson was court-martialed for having refused to obey a command to sit in the back of a bus at Fort Hood, Texas. Robinson was acquitted because of the Army's antidiscriminatory policies in transportation.

The so-called Port Chicago mutiny was a vivid illustration of the unequal treatment faced by African American servicemen. In 1944, when black soldiers were loading ammunition and other supplies at Port Chicago, California, the cargo of two ships exploded, killing 320 men, including 202 African Americans. When ordered to resume the loading several weeks later, 258 black sailors refused to obey and demanded improved safety precautions. The Navy charged fifty of the sailors with mutiny. Despite the best efforts of Thurgood Marshall, chief counsel for the NAACP, all fifty were found guilty and were given dishonorable discharges as well as prison sentences of between eight and fifteen years. The incident, nevertheless, resulted in a number of changes, including better safety precautions. After the war,

the fifty sailors received amnesty, but they were denied veterans' benefits.

Late in 1944, General Dwight D. Eisenhower approved a limited experiment in racial integration. About five thousand black soldiers volunteered for the experiment. Of these, twenty-five hundred were selected and organized into thirty-seven platoons of forty men each, which were then attached to white units of some two hundred soldiers. The integrated units fought in the Battle of the Bulge as well as on German soil. Although white officers reported an unqualified success, the experiment was quietly discontinued at the end of the war because of concern that it would undermine white southern support for the postwar draft.

Home Front During the War   By early 1941, employment opportunities in defense industries were rapidly expanding in anticipation of U.S. involvement in the war, but few employers were willing to hire African Americans for the higher-paying jobs. Hoping to bring about change, A. Philip Randolph and other black leaders organized the March on Washington movement, which was preparing to bring about 150,000 protesters to the nation's capital. In a meeting with Randolph and Walter White, President Roosevelt argued that the protest march would be harmful for the nation's image. In exchange for canceling the event, Roosevelt issued Executive Order 8802, also known as the Fair Employment Act, which formally prohibited discrimination in defense industries because of "race, creed, color, or national origin." To implement the policy, the executive order further established the Fair Employment Practices Commission (FEPC), which was the first federal agency devoted to combating racial discrimination.

Although the FEPC lacked enforcement powers, the growing demand for labor in the booming defense industries allowed many African Americans to obtain factory jobs. Whereas black employees constituted only about 3 percent of U.S. defense workers in 1942, their proportion grew to 8 percent by the war's end. Their percentage of the members of the United Auto Workers in Detroit, Michigan, grew to about 12 percent. More than a half-million African Americans moved from the South to take jobs in the North and California. With so many men serving in the military, about 600,000 black women, including 400,000 former domestic workers, were able to obtain industrial jobs for the first time.

A great deal of racial violence occurred during the war years. According to Tuskegee University records, there were at least ten lynchings of African Americans, including two soldiers. Researchers at Fisk University documented that racial fighting took place in forty-seven cities in 1943 alone. In the most destructive of these events, which occurred in Detroit, a minor skirmish on a bridge escalated into a race riot that resulted in the deaths of at least twenty-five African Americans and nine white Americans. A few weeks later, in Harlem, a disagreement between a black soldier and a white police officer set off an angry riot that resulted in six deaths, 550 arrests, and five million in property damage.

The wartime struggle against Fascism and Nazism promoted the growth of an intellectual movement opposing Jim Crow and other forms of racism. Numerous scholars, writers, and activists pointed out the extent to which the racial policies of Nazi Germany resembled those of the southern states. In *Man's Most Dangerous Myth: The Fallacy of Race* (1942), Ashley Montagu framed the war as a struggle between "the spirit of the Nazi racist" and the "spirit of democracy." The most influential treatise on this topic was Gunnar Myrdal's *An American Dilemma: The Negro Problem and Modern Democracy* (1944), which emphasized the contradiction between the treatment of black Americans and the ideals of the Decla-

ration of Independence, which he called the "American creed."

Postwar Developments   As the war ended, a wave of racial violence broke out as white southerners confronted returning black veterans who believed that they had earned respect and equal treatment. Between June, 1945, and September, 1946, at least fifty-six African Americans were killed. In January, 1946, the race riot of Columbia, Tennessee, began with an altercation between Navy veteran James Stephenson and a white clerk, and it quickly developed into a street battle between the Ku Klux Klan and black citizens. The riot finally ended after a hundred blacks were arrested and two were killed while being questioned by the police. In South Carolina, Army veteran Isaac Woodward, following an argument with a white bus driver, was brutally beaten and blinded by the police while held in custody. In July, 1946, another returning veteran, Maceo Snipes, was shot to death by several white men the day after he became the first black citizen since Reconstruction to vote in Taylor County, Georgia. That same month, near Monroe, Georgia, the lynching of two black couples by a white mob prompted seventeen-year-old Martin Luther King, Jr., to write to the *Atlantic Constitution:* "We want and are entitled to the basic rights and opportunities of American citizens."

Black leaders of the period can be divided into two major groups. Liberal gradualists accepted capitalism and believed in the necessity of compromise and piecemeal reform. In contrast, left-wing leaders demanded an uncompromising push for full equality without delay—often coupled with goals of socialism and Black Nationalism. Prominent liberals included Walter White of the NAACP and Ralph Bunche, a State Department adviser who helped write the charter for the United Nations. Significant left-wing leaders included historical sociologist W. E. B. Du Bois and singer-actor Paul Robeson. In 1947, Du Bois went to the United Nations Human Rights Commission with an "Appeal to the World," calling for international pressure to end racial discrimination in the United States. When Du Bois's tactic was widely condemned, White removed him from the NAACP.

President Harry S. Truman was the first president of the century to take a strong position in favor of expanding civil rights. In 1946, he issued Executive Order 9808, which established the fifteen-member

President's Committee on Civil Rights. In December, 1947, the committee issued a report, *To Secure These Rights*, which recommended several reforms, including federal protection against lynching and discrimination in employment. In the summer of 1948, when Truman advocated a civil rights bill at the Democratic National Convention, states' rights southern Democrats, led by Strom Thurmond, walked out to form the States' Rights Democratic Party, whose members became known as Dixiecrats. Two weeks later, prompted by A. Philip Randolph, Truman signed Executive Orders 9980 and 9981, which effectively ended segregation in both the federal civil service and the armed forces.

At the Supreme Court, moreover, civil rights lawyers, led by Charles Houston and Thurgood Marshall, won a number of important legal victories. In *Smith v. Allwright* (1944), the Court held that white primaries violated the Fifteenth Amendment. In *Morgan v. Virginia* (1946), the Court ruled that states could not discriminate on the basis of race in interstate bus and rail transportation, but the ruling was limited insofar as it did not apply to intrastate transportation. The Court was not ready to condemn segregated schools, but it decided in *Sipuel v. Oklahoma* (1948) that states must allow qualified African Americans to attend all-white graduate schools if no comparable black schools were available. In *Shelley v. Kraemer* (1948), moreover, the Court held that it was unconstitutional for the courts to enforce racially restrictive covenants that had prevented African Americans from purchasing housing in white neighborhoods.

Impact   By participating in World War II, many African Americans earned the respect and gratitude of the nation. The Fair Employment Practices Commission became a precedent for promoting equal opportunity. The second half of the decade was a time for several progressive reforms, including the desegregation of the military and several favorable Supreme Court rulings. In 1948, a large portion of the Democratic Party supported legislation to outlaw segregation. By then, moreover, a significant number of African Americans had managed to enter the socioeconomic mainstream. This combination of developments helped prepare the way for the civil rights victories of the next two decades.

Thomas Tandy Lewis

Further Reading

Berman, William C. *The Politics of Civil Rights in the Truman Administration*. Columbus: Ohio State University Press, 1970. A standard work concerning ideologies, leadership, and political rivalries during the beginning of the Civil Rights movement.

Dudziak, Mary L. *Cold War Civil Rights: Race and the Image of American Democracy.* Princeton, N.J.: Princeton University Press, 2000. An excellent study of the relationship between racial issues and the Cold War diplomacy, with an especially good discussion of Truman's civil rights policies.

Moore, Christopher Paul. *Fighting for America: Black Soldiers: The Unsung Heroes of World War II*. New York: Random House, 2004. A comprehensive account of the African American contributions toward victory in World War II, based on original documents, letters, photographs, and oral histories.

Morehouse, Maggie. *Fighting in the Jim Crow Army: Black Men and Women Remember World War II*. New York: Rowman & Littlefield, 2002. The story of the 92d and 93d Infantry Divisions, based on personal interviews and exhaustive research in archival sources.

Takaki, Ronald. *Double Victory: A Multicultural History of America in World War II*. New York: Little, Brown, 2000. A readable account of the problems, goals, and achievements of minority groups during the war.

Wexler, Laura. *Fire in a Canebrake: The Last Mass Lynching in America*. New York: Scribner, 2003. A poignant account of the 1946 lynching of four victims in Walton County, Georgia, demonstrating that extreme racism continued after the war.

See also   American Negro Exposition; Civil rights and liberties; Davis, Benjamin O., Jr.; Desegregation of the U.S. military; Fair Employment Practices Commission; National Association for the Advancement of Colored People; Port Chicago naval magazine explosion; Race riots; Racial discrimination; Randolph, A. Philip; Tuskegee Airmen; Tuskegee syphilis study; White, Walter F.

■ Agriculture in Canada

For years, Canada had been described as a natural-resources, or staples, economy, and it remained substantially so during the 1940's. In 1941, agriculture was second only to manufacturing in Canada's gross domestic product, but during the decade Canada's economy began to change from one based on natural resources to one that was predominantly industrial.

The first half of the 1940's in Canada was dedicated wholly to Canada's participation in World War II; the second half was focused on the conversion to a peacetime economy. The changes that took place in agriculture during that decade were profound. Canada's agriculture in 1940 was the major source of export earnings, but it was still troubled by the dislocations that had occurred during the 1930's, especially the impact of severe drought that had afflicted the Prairie Provinces of Manitoba, Saskatchewan, and Alberta. With the outbreak of World War II, Canadian agriculture became a major source of supplies for Great Britain, the mother country of the majority of Canada's citizens. Canada supplied a critical portion of Great Britain's agricultural imports, without which the island nation would not have survived.

Geographical Distribution The primary determinant of Canadian agriculture is the varied climates of the country. The eastern provinces (Nova Scotia, New Brunswick, and Prince Edward Island) were heavily wooded but had sections that were important producers of agricultural products. The central provinces, Quebec and Ontario, contained the bulk of Canada's population but had interspersed with a variety of urban centers agricultural activities that were well suited to the temperate climate of those provinces. Moving westward, Manitoba, Saskatchewan, and Alberta contained vast stretches of relatively flat land easily cultivated for grain production but hampered by low rainfall and a harsh climate, with a short growing season. At the western end of the country lay the province of British Columbia, whose climate was mild and suitable for agriculture in the valleys but whose rugged terrain had limited farming potential.

The immigrants who came to Canada brought valuable agricultural skills. The earliest immigrants, the French peasants who settled in Canada under the Old Regime, brought a community approach that evolved from the French manorial system. The holdings they had created along the St. Lawrence River periodically redistributed allotments to ensure that all farmers had a land base to support their traditionally very large families. The British immigrants who arrived in the nineteenth century favored individual holdings that the family inherited and could enlarge if the owner was prepared to invest in it. Some radical religious communities, notably the Hutterites who settled on the great plains, brought a system of cooperation that promoted the welfare of the group. In the immediate postwar years, Canada's willingness to accept refugees brought a number of eastern Europeans into the country.

Crops The most important Canadian field crop was grain, chiefly spring wheat (planted the preceding fall) and fall wheat—mostly the former. At the beginning of the 1940's, Canada's average wheat production was slightly less than 4 million bushels per year. Canada was one of the world's top producers of wheat, along with the United States, Argentina, and Australia. During the war years, a substantial portion of the wheat crop was exported, chiefly to Great Britain. Prices went up substantially for agricultural products, especially wheat, as the entire wheat crop was sold.

In 1943, the marketing of wheat was wholly entrusted to the Canadian Wheat Board (created in the 1930's to dispose of unmarketable grain surpluses), which modulated the fluctuations in the price of wheat that had formerly battered producers. In 1946, the British agreed to the Anglo-Canadian Wheat Agreement, which set wheat prices for four years. The British government committed itself to buying around 1.5 million bushels of Canadian wheat annually through 1950 at fixed prices between $1 and $1.55 per bushel. In 1949, Canada also committed to the International Wheat Agreement and promised to supply at least 2 million bushels of wheat annually to the world. The marketing of barley and oats was also turned over to the Wheat Board in 1949.

The production of livestock increased substantially during the 1940's. The number of cattle on Canadian farms went up by about 20 percent during the early 1940's, rising from about 8 million in 1940 to more than 10 million by 1944. The number of hogs also rose, from 6 million in 1940 to about 7.5 million by 1944. Livestock and grains were the major sources of farm income in the 1940's. The number of dairy farms increased during this period, serving primarily the growing population of Canada's cities. The mechanization of agriculture during the late 1940's and thereafter made possible further expansion of the beef cattle industry because feed was no longer needed for horses formerly used to power agricultural equipment.

Truck produce, especially potatoes grown both on the prairies and in the central and eastern provinces, was also important, as were dairy products, eggs and chickens, honey and maple syrup, the latter produced chiefly in Quebec. Apples were produced in British Columbia, and leaf tobacco was grown primarily in southern Ontario.

Technological Change   A process of technological change began in Canadian agriculture in the immediate postwar period that was to continue into the following decades. Mechanization really took hold: During the early 1940's, there was one tractor for every two farms, but by 1976, there were two tractors for every farm as well as additional mechanical equipment, especially combines. Whereas before the 1940's a single farmer could handle three hundred acres at most, the growth in number and size of farm machinery made it possible for a single farmer to handle several thousand acres. The result was a consolidation of farm holdings and a striking drop in the number of farmers and farm families, especially on the prairies. At the same time, the number of grain elevators decreased, and many railroad lines that had previously served the more numerous, smaller farms, were abandoned. Agriculture became big business.

Impact   During the postwar period, Canadian agriculture began to shift to a highly mechanized operation, especially in the Prairie Provinces in the production of grains. During this time, Canada, along with the United States, provided Great Britain with food that the nation could not produce itself. As Canadian farms grew larger, the labor needed to operate them decreased, and the rural population declined. Canadians moved from the farms to the cities and earned their living by other means.

Nancy M. Gordon

Further Reading

Bothwell, Robert, Ian Drummond, and John English. *Canada Since 1945*. Toronto: University of Toronto Press, 1989. Contains some good introductory material on the 1940's.

Dominion Bureau of Statistics. *Canada in 1940*. Ottawa: Bureau of Statistics, 1940. An annual volume that contains useful statistics and descriptions.

Friesen, Gerald. *The Canadian Prairies: A History*. Lincoln: University of Nebraska Press, 1984. Surveys the development of the Prairie Provinces—Manitoba, Saskatchewan, and Alberta.

Smith, P. J. *The Prairie Provinces*. A broad survey of the prairies and their history.

See also   Business and the economy in Canada; Canada and Great Britain; Canadian participation in World War II; Canadian regionalism; Demographics of Canada; Foreign policy of Canada; Gross national product of Canada; Urbanization in Canada.

■ Agriculture in the United States

U.S. agriculture underwent a transformation during the 1940's, beginning with peacetime surpluses of agricultural products and labor, then abruptly adjusting to the need for higher yields and more workers to cultivate and harvest crops to meet wartime demands for food and raw materials. Political and socioeconomic factors shaped the agricultural workforce during the war and after. Wartime activities influenced demographic, technological, and scientific changes that altered farming by the end of the decade.

When the 1940's started, the U.S. Department of Agriculture (USDA) personnel oversaw efforts to curb agricultural excesses that had accumulated in the previous decade. Dire economic conditions resulted in many people moving to farms during the Great Depression. New Deal legislation discouraged increased agricultural activity, but the number of American farmers expanded by an estimated 980,000 people during the 1930's. Farmers planted too many crops, which lost value. USDA secretary Henry A. Wallace led efforts to create a federal granary for surplus crop storage. In 1940, the USDA's Bureau of Agricultural Economics stated that 2.5 million farmworkers were unable to secure agricultural employment. Approximately 30.5 million farmers resided on the nation's six million farms, which averaged 174 acres in size.

Agricultural Leadership and Changing Policies During the 1940's, four men filled the cabinet position of secretary of agriculture to assist presidents with agricultural policies. Wallace, who had been serving as USDA secretary since 1933 in President Franklin D. Roosevelt's cabinet, resigned in September, 1940. Claude R. Wickard replaced Wallace and held that position until June, 1945, serving under both Roosevelt and President Harry S. Truman. Clinton P. Anderson, a member of the House of Representatives during the war, became USDA secretary in June, 1945, and guided policies for Truman through May, 1948. The next month, Charles F. Brannan started work as USDA secretary for the remainder of the decade.

The 1940 USDA Yearbook of Agriculture, titled *Farmers in a Changing World*, acknowledged the impact of international conflicts on U.S. agriculture. Roosevelt and Department of Defense officials emphasized that reinforcing U.S. military resources was a higher priority than resolving agricultural problems. They moved researchers from a USDA site in Arlington, Virginia, to build the Pentagon. Government officials, monitoring the war in Europe, sought to fill industrial manpower deficiencies with American farmers. Agricultural Adjustment Administration director Chester Davis suggested in November, 1940, that approximately five million farmers could perform defense industry jobs. At that time, officials were not concerned about creating a farm labor shortage by transferring workers between employment sectors. During the next year, however, increased demand for U.S. agricultural products and farmworkers occurred.

Congress passed the Lend-Lease Act in March, 1941, to provide protein-rich food and agricultural goods to Allied forces. Reversing previous crop-control policies, USDA secretary Wickard urged farmers to increase yields to supply both domestic and foreign populations. The federal government sold farmers cheap corn from the federal granary to use as livestock feed to increase yields of dairy, poultry, and meat products. As a result, U.S. agriculture experienced its historically largest overall yield of agricultural goods in 1941, including setting records for the amount of eggs and milk produced. A total of 2,240 million pounds of food arrived in the United Kingdom by the year's conclusion. Starting in 1943, the War Food Administration shipped and distributed agricultural products overseas.

Wartime Production and Labor Supply The USDA intensified its demands for production of agricultural goods when the United States entered the war after the December 7, 1941, Japanese attack on Pearl Harbor. The Emergency Price Control Act, passed in January, 1942, assured farmers that they would receive profitable prices for their agricultural goods. Roosevelt demanded that Congress limit price amounts, and an October, 1942, amendment sponsored by Representative Henry B. Steagall outlined maximum prices and stated that farmers would receive price supports several years after war production ceased.

The USDA expanded 1942 production plans to achieve such yields as 48 billion eggs and 83 million hogs. Farmers were told to plant more cotton, peanuts, and soybeans. Officials requested that agriculturists grow flaxseed to process for vegetable oil and cane and beets to attain sugar because of disrupted imports of those staples. Wickard wrote a chapter highlighting farmers' wartime contributions that was published in the book *America Organizes to Win the War: A Handbook on the American War Effort* (1942). He stressed that U.S. agriculture provided raw materials and fibers useful to manufacture military equipment. He described agricultural products as munitions, saying that vitamins and minerals were crucial for reinforcing soldiers' health so they could fight effectively.

Despite increased agricultural production, economic incentives led many farmers to work in factories instead of tending livestock and fields. In summer, 1942, workers earned wages averaging $5.08 per day in industries compared to $2.45 on farms. Many African American sharecroppers hoped to leave agricultural jobs for industrial employment but were often denied those positions and continued farming. Despite industries luring many farmers from fields, Roosevelt and Paul V. McNutt, head of the War Manpower Commission (WMC), thought that enough agricultural laborers were available to attain desired production levels and did not consider the possibility of a farm labor shortage.

At a June, 1942, WMC meeting, Wickard noted that farmers said they would lose crops unless enough workers helped them, and they suggested that Mexican workers could temporarily assist with harvesting tasks. As a result, approximately 50,000 foreign laborers were employed as agricultural workers in the bracero program. Other wartime

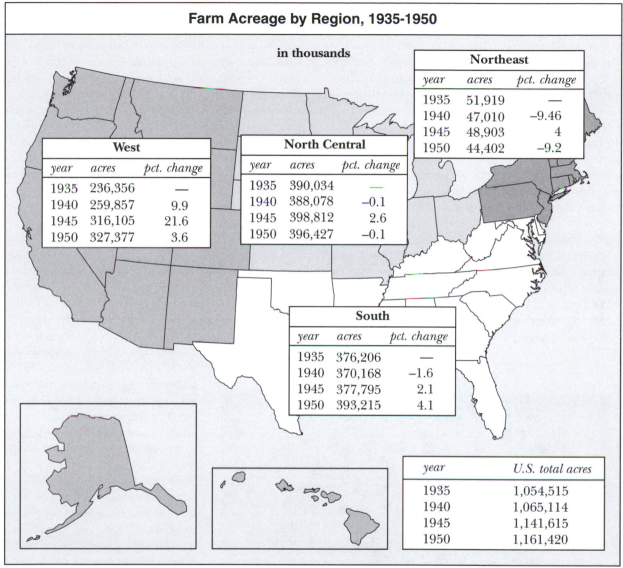

Farm Acreage by Region, 1935-1950

in thousands

Northeast

year	acres	pct. change
1935	51,919	—
1940	47,010	−9.46
1945	48,903	4
1950	44,402	−9.2

West

year	acres	pct. change
1935	236,356	—
1940	259,857	9.9
1945	316,105	21.6
1950	327,377	3.6

North Central

year	acres	pct. change
1935	390,034	—
1940	388,078	−0.1
1945	398,812	2.6
1950	396,427	−0.1

South

year	acres	pct. change
1935	376,206	—
1940	370,168	−1.6
1945	377,795	2.1
1950	393,215	4.1

year	U.S. total acres
1935	1,054,515
1940	1,065,114
1945	1,141,615
1950	1,161,420

Notes: The West region includes Alaska and Hawaii; data are not available for either region for 1935 and 1945. Percent change is from the previous represented year.

sources of farm labor included convicts, Japanese Americans from relocation camps, and German and Italian prisoners of war.

Deferment Legislation and Volunteer Farmers By late summer, 1942, several state leaders had expressed worries regarding insufficient numbers of agricultural workers to harvest the increased amount of crops planted the previous spring. North Dakota governor John Moses asked Roosevelt to approve a ninety-day military deferment for males in

that state so they could work on farms. Edward A. O'Neal, American Farm Bureau Federation president, estimated that 1.5 million agricultural workers had been diverted to military service by 1942. He wanted Roosevelt to recognize that agricultural work represented a form of defense labor. O'Neal suggested that the Selective Service defer farmers.

Dismissing deferment talk, Roosevelt stated that farmers above draft age could perform more agricultural tasks to free younger for service. Roosevelt noted such groups as the Victory Farm Volunteers alleviated labor shortages. He encouraged children and their teachers to help farmers after school and in summer. County agents and the United States Employment Service (USES) assigned those volunteers to farms needing laborers. In 1942, an estimated one million 4-H club members assisted with livestock production.

By late 1942, agricultural lobbyists intensified their efforts to keep farmers from being drafted as more American soldiers were deployed to foreign battlefields. Many congressmen valued agriculturists' contributions and agreed with lobbyists' requests for a blanket deferment of all farmers. They prepared a bill for widespread deferments because they realized that Selective Service legislation did not permit mass exemptions. Worried that legislators would quickly pass this deferment law, War Department officials stressed that U.S. military forces lacked enough troops and needed all available men, including farmers.

Paul V. McNutt, in an attempt to provide stability

to agricultural businesses, issued a November 6, 1942, WMC directive stating that laborers for poultry, dairy, and other livestock farms were ineligible to be drafted, enlist in military service, or accept employment with contractors. On November 13, Congress passed the Tydings Amendment to the Selective Service Act. This amendment stated that male citizens crucial to the agricultural sector were qualified for deferment from both military and industrial service. McNutt created a system of assigning credits for various factors, such as types of crops grown, which local draft boards consulted to assess laborers' deferment eligibility, with decisions often being arbitrary according to examiners' biases. By December, 1942, 192,364 farmers had been deferred.

Women performed agricultural labor on their farms when their husbands, sons, or hired hands were drafted, enlisted, or went to work in the factories. In 1940, women composed 5.8 percent of the farm laborers according to the Bureau of Agricultural Economics. By April, 1942, they represented 14 percent of the agricultural workforce. The Emergency Farm Labor Program, which included such agencies as the United States Crop Corps, oversaw the Women's Land Army, established in 1943 to encourage women ages eighteen and older to assist farmers in their communities, especially in harvesting fruits and vegetables. Groups of coeds volunteered to help on farms near their college campuses. These workers helped prevent many crops from spoiling in the fields. By December, 1943, approximately three million women were involved in agriculture.

Farmworkers posing with all the equipment they will use to harvest potatoes on a family farm in 1949. (Time & Life Pictures/Getty Images)

Labor Shortages and Political Strategies In January, 1943, McNutt transferred to Wickard his authority to secure agricultural labor. Fears of shortages persisted, and some farmers declared that they would not plant their fields until they were confident that sufficient workers would be available to harvest crops. Thirty-nine percent of farmers responding to a February 14, 1943, Gallup poll said that they supported agricultural workers being deferred and soldiers furloughed for harvests. House Agriculture Committee chairman Hampton P. Fulmer supported furloughs to obtain agricultural laborers. Roosevelt resisted and then agreed because farmers had said that cotton, an essential raw material for parachutes, was at risk if there were not enough workers to pick it.

Politicians discussed the farm labor shortage and proposed legislative solutions. Senator John Bankhead stated that if one million farmers were not discharged from service, severe food shortages might occur. In March, 1943, the Bankhead-Johnson bill demanded that every farmworker be exempt from the draft. Although the Senate passed the bill, the House defeated it, primarily because public opinion indicated that many Americans resented farmers receiving deferments. Some people called farmers draft dodgers and painted mailboxes at farms yellow to suggest cowardice. McNutt and General Lewis B. Hershey had assured representatives that they could publicly appease their constituents by voting against the bill but privately encourage draft boards to defer more farmers. In 1943, almost four million farmers received deferments.

That spring, government investigators concluded that Wickard was an ineffective farm labor administrator, and General Hershey oversaw agricultural worker procurement until the war ended. Defense officials pressured Hershey to draft farmers, but he supported deferments. The peak of agricultural worker deferment occurred in January, 1944, when 1,667,506 men were exempted from service. During World War II, the Selective Service drafted approximately two million farmers despite deferment efforts.

Postwar Agriculture   Twenty percent of the U.S. population lived on farms when the war ended in 1945, reflecting demographic shifts from rural to urban areas. As the war concluded, farmers revised wartime production goals to provide food relief through such international organizations as the United Nations to countries where agricultural resources had been damaged. The USDA focused on the transition of agriculture from wartime production to peacetime production. Agriculturists resumed most prewar farming methods and also incorporated new techniques, crops, and machinery that became available after the war.

Soybeans had filled many fields during the war and continued to be a favored crop afterward. Southern farmers grew nine million bushels of soybeans on one million acres in 1945. Soybean farming increased during the remainder of the decade. Fish farming became a significant agribusiness, with farmers building ponds to raise catfish, bream, and bass. Some scientists inserted pituitary hormones in captive fish to encourage reproduction. During the 1940's, many farmers started growing trees, particularly fast-maturing pines, to sell to lumber companies. The 1949 USDA Yearbook of Agriculture, titled *Trees*, examined how forests provided farmers with income and strengthened the nation's economy, but it also expressed concern that U.S. timber was being harvested faster than it was being replaced.

Postwar agriculture also experienced changes in animal husbandry. Many farmers accepted veterinary assistance to combat cattle, swine, and poultry diseases. Livestock breeders developed strains of animals that were more resistant to diseases transmitted by insects and that could withstand climatic extremes. They enhanced breeds of dairy and beef cattle, which produced better-tasting milk and meat. Poultry farming was industrialized, with commercial farms building barns to house large groups of chickens or turkeys and using automated devices to feed and water them.

Many farmers and agricultural workers who had been employed as defense workers in factories or served in the military decided not to return to farms. Patriotism no longer motivated many women and children to perform agricultural labor. To fill these labor gaps, some minorities sought agricultural employment. Migrant workers, mostly Hispanic and Japanese Americans, traveled through the United States to find work harvesting crops or processing livestock for agribusinesses, which expanded after the war.

The Agricultural Act of 1949 adjusted maximum price supports that farmers could receive from the federal government and established enduring agricultural policies. That year, USDA secretary Charles F. Brannan, who wanted to protect small farmers from commercialized agriculture, proposed revising policies regarding agricultural price supports by having prices set by markets instead. Farmers and agricultural groups expressed varying views supporting or rejecting Brannan's plan. The American Farm Bureau Federation and other organizations lobbied for legislators to oppose the changes Brannan suggested. Surpluses in 1949 resulted in prices dropping 26 percent. Simultaneously, consumers protested high food prices, which they blamed on agricultural price supports. Farmers encountered economic problems that would continue into the following decades.

Science and Technology Agricultural researchers conducted scientific investigations and developed technology throughout the 1940's. USDA experts provided agriculturists with scientific resources such as the 1941 Yearbook of Agriculture, titled Climate and Man, a reference book containing data useful to farmers in all regions of the United States. During the war, scientists and agricultural specialists at land-grant institutions such as Iowa State College printed informational bulletins to help farmers cope with wartime shortages of rubber, burlap, and chemicals—materials often used in agriculture. State and county USDA War Boards assisted farmers to secure supplies they needed for wartime agricultural production.

When the 1940's began, U.S. farmers had approximately 1.8 million tractors. After the United States entered World War II, implement manufacturers stopped making most agricultural machinery and their components because an October, 1942, War Production Board directive stated that steel was needed for defense industries. Within communities, farmers often shared machinery or learned how to repair and maintain equipment that could not be easily replaced until after the war. Limited gasoline supplies during World War II forced many farmers to return to using mules and other draft animals. Demand for farmworkers increased as farmers lost mechanized agriculture options. When war production ceased, steel became available for tractor and implement production, and the use of farm technology expanded. The development of farm equipment for specific tasks such as picking cotton reduced the need for many human laborers.

Veterinary scientists pursued animal disease control and educated farmers about medical care for livestock. The 1942 USDA Yearbook of Agriculture, titled Keeping Livestock Healthy, emphasized public health and how veterinarians helped prevent epidemics. Experts described parasites and insects associated with spreading diseases. They stressed that more preventive measures should be developed (noting previous cattle tick eradication and hog cholera serum successes), calling such work patriotic because it contributed to safer meats for soldiers to eat. The yearbook noted that farmers might not be able to secure some of the suggested pharmaceuticals for livestock because of the war.

Scientific and technological advancements for agriculture accelerated after the war. Extension Service and Experiment Station personnel assisted farmers by demonstrating how to use new equipment and tools appropriate for various types of agriculture. They also alerted agriculturists to improved seeds and chemical products, including fertilizers and pesticides. Farmers read USDA publications describing enhanced agricultural methods to increase yields and obtain higher quality crops. In 1947, the USDA released its Science in Farming yearbook, which discussed USDA scientists' research during the war in diverse agricultural subjects, ranging from animals and plants to chemistry and machinery. Sections featured new products and practices, many related to mechanization.

Impact War shaped U.S. agriculture throughout the 1940's. Farmers responded to government requests to boost production of specific agricultural goods that nourished troops and civilians. In the process, farmers became increasingly dependent on government price supports and funding to provide financial security, establishing an often politically controversial reliance. Shortages of labor and supplies resulted in innovative ways for farmers to practice agriculture. Many farmers who left farms during the war because they were drafted or worked in defense industries decided not to resume agricultural pursuits. Instead, they remained in urban settings, where they enjoyed better, more consistent incomes than agriculture offered. Some veterans pursued education with G.I. Bill funds and selected nonagricultural professions.

U.S. farm demographics experienced significant changes during the decade. The nation's farm population continued to decline in all regions as commercialized agriculture began to spread and average acreages grew. For example, in 1940, 16 million southerners inhabited 2.9 million farms, with farmers making up 43 percent of the region's workforce. Five years later, about 13 million southerners lived on farms, and farmers represented one-third of the region's laborers. In the early twenty-first century, fewer than 5 percent of southerners resided on farms, and farmers accounted for almost 2 percent of the region's workforce.

Elizabeth D. Schafer

Further Reading

Carpenter, Stephanie A. *On the Farm Front: The Women's Land Army in World War II.* DeKalb: Northern Illinois University Press, 2003. Comprehensive account of American female volunteers who performed diverse agricultural work to ensure adequate food supplies during wartime. Compares with female agricultural workers in other wars and countries. Illustrations, appendix, bibliography.

Chamberlain, Charles D. *Victory at Home: Manpower and Race in the American South During World War II.* Athens: University of Georgia Press, 2003. Examines African American farmworkers' experiences and industrial aspirations, other minority migrant workers, and how labor events during the 1940's shaped civil rights strategies.

Hurt, R. Douglas. *The Great Plains During World War II.* Lincoln: University of Nebraska Press, 2008. Several chapters address agricultural issues specific to this region, such as ranching. Photographs depict agricultural workers, including prisoners of war. Bibliography.

_____. *Problems of Plenty: The American Farmer in the Twentieth Century.* Chicago, Ill.: Ivan R. Dee, 2002. Places agricultural events occurring during the 1940's in context with demographic shifts, legislation, and labor and economic issues in other decades.

U.S. Department of Agriculture. *Yearbooks of Agriculture.* Washington, D.C.: Government Printing Office, 1940-1949. Each yearbook summarizes the USDA's annual activities. Articles focus on a specific topic such as climate. The years 1943 through 1947 are included in one volume.

Wessel, Thomas R. "Agricultural Policy Since 1945." In *The Rural West Since World War II,* edited by R. Douglas Hurt. Lawrence: University Press of Kansas, 1998. Describes how new American Farm Bureau Federation leadership in 1947 aided western agriculturists, particularly farmers raising livestock.

Winters, Donald L. "Agriculture in the Post-World War II South." In *The Rural South Since World War II,* edited by R. Douglas Hurt. Baton Rouge:

Louisiana State University Press, 1998. Analyzes how farming in the South dramatically changed during the 1940's. Examines labor, types of crops, socioeconomic factors, and technology. Provides statistics.

See also Agriculture in Canada; Bracero program; Food processing; Income and wages; Lend-Lease; Science and technology; Wallace, Henry A.; War Production Board; Wartime industries; Wartime rationing.

■ Air Force, U.S.

Identifcation Branch of the U.S. military responsible for most air operations
Date Became an autonomous organization in 1947

As the military impact of air power increased during the early decades of the twentieth century, advocates within the U.S. Army pressed their claim for an independent Air Force. The Army Air Forces, after demonstrating its usefulness during World War II, received its wish to become autonomous in 1947. The new United States Air Force became a major factor in the emerging Cold War with the Soviet Union.

The U.S. Air Force evolved out of several organizations established during World War I. The U.S. Army reorganized its air assets (created as the Signal Corps) into the U.S. Army Air Service during the war, reflecting the offensive role that aircraft could play. The Air Service remained a subordinate service until 1926, when Congress permitted the creation of the U.S. Army Air Corps. With recognition that air power could do more than simply support ground combat, the Army Air Corps earned elevation in status. Air power remained under the control of a subordinate branch of the army, however, until the threat of World War II forced reorganization.

First Steps Toward Autonomy With World War II looming, the army changed the status of the Air Corps to reflect the growing influence of air power. Observing the impact of air power on the war in Europe and in Asia, the War Department elevated the Air Corps to a service equal to the Army and Navy in June, 1941, when the Air Corps became the United States Army Air Forces (AAF). Although still nomi-

Army Air Forces training planes flying in formation over Randolph Field, near San Antonio, Texas, in early 1942. (Getty Images)

by the chief of staff, the AAF directed its own operations during World War II, independently of the Army and Navy. Having developed the tactic of strategic bombing during the prewar years, the AAF engaged in massive bombing operations, with mixed results. In Europe, the AAF joined with Great Britain to conduct around-the-clock bombing of German targets. The bombing was not always accurate, and the bombers suffered significant losses of aircraft and personnel. The AAF could not employ bombing against Japan until the capture of the Marianas Islands in the summer of 1944 put that country within reach of the new long-range B-29 Superfortress bomber. Even then, conditions forced the AAF to switch from high-altitude precision bombing to low-level area bombing with incendiary bombs, which caused massive civilian casualties. The AAF also conducted the first atomic bombings, on Hiroshima and Nagasaki, Japan, in August, 1945. These two atomic explosions effectively brought the war to an end.

The AAF operated fleets of fighter planes, notably the long-range P-51 Mustang and P-47 Thunderbolt, capable of escorting bombers into hostile airspace. It also operated a wide array of light (A-20 and A-26) and medium bombers (B-25 and B-26) to provide tactical support for ground forces, as well as a large training establishment and transport service.

Staking Its Claim for Independence Based upon the AAF's performance during World War II, many air power enthusiasts and officers within the AAF believed they had proven themselves worthy of a separate and fully independent branch of the U.S. military. Great Britain had organized an independent air force, the Royal Air Force (RAF), during World War I, and the AAF pressed for independence along the lines of the RAF. As evidence of the potency of air power, the AAF conducted the Strategic Bombing Survey, a series of studies that sought to determine the impact of strategic bombing upon enemy forces, industry, and morale. Although the Strategic Bombing Survey revealed some shortcomings, the report generally was favorable (critics would say biased) regarding the effectiveness of strategic bombing, a task that only air power could achieve. The AAF also claimed that it was the only military service capable of delivering

nally part of the U.S. Army, the AAF had a large degree of autonomy. Officers of the Air Corps answered to senior commanders in their respective operating areas, but the AAF, commanded by General Henry Arnold, reported only to the Army chief of staff. Freed from the restraints of supporting land forces, the AAF had full control of its own personnel, planning, and equipment. Its only obligation was to conduct operations directed by the senior political leadership; beyond that requirement, the AAF developed as it saw fit. As war loomed, the Army Air Forces grew rapidly. In 1940, the Air Corps had about 50,000 personnel; by the outbreak of war in December, 1941, the AAF had more than 150,000 members.

Although occasionally restrained and redirected

nuclear weapons at the time, and that the specialized nature of that task required a separate branch of the military to ensure that atomic bombs were used properly and effectively.

Politics also supported the drive for an independent air force. On the domestic front, Congress was eager to cut defense spending after World War II ended, and the AAF made an appealing claim that an independent air force could reduce the numbers of Army and Navy personnel needed to defend the country from distant enemies. On the international front, the growing Cold War between the United States and the Soviet Union meant that atomic weapons might be used against America's communist enemies in the near future. After President Harry S. Truman initiated his Truman Doctrine in a speech to Congress on March 12, 1947, committing the United States to containing the expansion of communism, the flexibility of air power as a Cold War weapon argued forcefully toward giving the AAF the freedom it sought. As part of the National Security Act of 1947, Congress created the fully independent United States Air Force (USAF) on equal standing with the Army and Navy, with all three services under the political authority of the secretary of defense, a newly created position.

Initial Obstacles of the USAF   The new USAF faced a series of issues during the late 1940's. The USAF's first clash with the Soviet Union came during the Berlin airlift (1948-1949). Soviet forces, in an attempt to force the capitalist powers out of occupied Berlin, cut the city off from the outside world. Instead of resorting to force, President Truman ordered a massive airlift of supplies into the city. For a year, the USAF and Allied air forces kept Berlin supplied, although the mission seriously taxed the USAF's transport capabilities.

The USAF also faced internal rivalries. With nuclear weapons dominating future war plans, the USAF received the majority of the limited postwar defense spending, forcing the reduction of Army and Navy units and the cancellation of several projects. The Navy, for example, had its first supercarrier, the USS *United States*, canceled to fund USAF expansion. The Army and Navy fought for budget funds by creating nuclear delivery systems of their own and by protecting their control over their own air assets (helicopters for the Army and aircraft carriers for the Navy).

The USAF also had to deal with technology issues. The USAF found it difficult to acquire aircraft because of the rapid evolution of aircraft technology. Jet engines became available at the end of World War II, rendering the USAF's fleets of propeller-driven aircraft obsolete. Other wartime breakthroughs, such as in electronics, radar, and radical aircraft configurations, meant that aircraft might become obsolete within a few years of their construction and purchase.

The USAF also had problems creating a jet bomber that could deliver atomic bombs effectively. The massive B-36 Peacemaker, which dwarfed all wartime aircraft, needed a mix of six piston engines and four jet engines to get into the air. Although the aircraft had global range, its top speed of barely 400 miles per hour made it vulnerable to jet fighters.

Impact   The USAF continued to be a major element of American defense. Throughout the Cold War and into the twenty-first century, air power remained one of the deciding factors of nearly every military campaign. The ability to strike targets at long distances without involving large numbers of ground troops added flexibility to military operations. This flexibility required large numbers of diverse aircraft, but the USAF adapted to changing combat conditions.

Although originally organized to wage nuclear war, the USAF has taken on additional missions since the 1940's. Its tactical aircraft still support U.S. ground operations, its fighter planes maintain control of vital airspace, and its transport aircraft supply U.S. forces around the world. When ballistic missile systems became the primary means of delivering nuclear weapons during the 1960's, the USAF operated these new systems as replacements for nuclear-capable bombers. When the Space Age began, the USAF became responsible for monitoring U.S. defense interests in orbit as well.

Steven J. Ramold

Further Reading

Boyne, Walter G. *Beyond the Wild Blue: A History of the United States Air Force, 1947-1997*. New York: St. Martin's Press, 2007. Written by a career Air Force officer, the book is a good general history, although with a somewhat partisan slant.
Cherny, Andrei. *The Candy Bombers: The Untold Story of the Berlin Airlift and America's Finest Hour.* New

York: Putnam's, 2008. An account of the USAF's efforts to keep the Berlin crisis from escalating and of how dropping candy to Berlin children became a major public relations victory over the Soviets.

Coffey, Thomas M. *Hap: The Story of the U.S. Air Force and the Man Who Built It, General Henry A. "Hap" Arnold.* New York: Viking, 1982. A biography of the leading proponent of an independent Air Force, who led American air power in the European theater during World War II.

MacIssac, David. *Strategic Bombing in World War II: The Story of the United States Strategic Bombing Survey.* New York: Garland, 1976. A well-researched account of the AAF's study of the effectiveness of strategic bombing as justification for an independent air force.

Perret, Geoffrey. *Winged Victory: The Army Air Forces in World War II.* New York: Random House, 1993. A broad history of U.S. air operations in World War II, with comparisons of the application of air power in the European and Pacific theaters.

See also   Army, U.S.; Arnold, Henry "Hap"; Berlin blockade and airlift; Bombers; Department of Defense, U.S.; Doolittle bombing raid; *Enola Gay*; Jet engines; National Security Act of 1947; Strategic bombing.

■ Air pollution

Definition   Noxious chemical and biological substances and particulates found in the air

Industrialization has been blamed for causing air pollution, but much of the air pollution created during the 1940's resulted from burning of coal and fossil fuels to provide heat and power, both for businesses and for homes, as well as from activities of railroads, water cargo carriers, and electricity generating facilities. The resulting pollution had negative impacts on the health of all living organisms as well as the aesthetics of the environment.

Air pollution comes from both natural and artificial sources, but the term refers primarily to the artificial sources. Common pollutants include sulfur and nitrogen oxides, which contribute to acid rain, and carbon oxides. Artificial pollution is generated by industries, agriculture, and motor vehicles, among other sources.

Smoke was one of the major pollution problems of the 1940's. It came from burning coal, as emissions from coke ovens, as the result of mining activities, and from burning wood for fuel. Many manufacturing facilities, such as those producing steel, operated at maximum capacity during the war, so that their output of pollution was high. After World War II and the use of atomic warfare, along with atomic testing, many nations also became concerned about radioactive fallout, which can be considered an air pollutant. Air pollutants do not stay in one place, and radioactive fallout brought that fact into sharp focus. The United States was instrumental in generating air pollution that negatively affected Canada during the 1940's. The industrial heartland of the United States was built in its sulfurous coal regions to be near to the fuel, and wind currents blew the pollution from burning it north into some of Canada's most populated regions.

Most of the serious air pollution during the 1940's surrounded big cities. Urban centers such as Pittsburgh and St. Louis adopted successful smoke control policies, some of which were employed to control railroad smoke. After World War II, the number of automobiles began to increase, and their emissions further degraded the quality of the atmosphere.

Effects of Air Pollution   Air pollution had many negative impacts during the 1940's, some of which were unknown at the time. Soot and dirt particulates were a general nuisance. Laundry hung on clotheslines took longer to dry because not as much sunshine came through, and it would rarely stay clean in heavily polluted areas. In addition, the reduction in sunlight caused by smoke affected the ability of humans to absorb vitamin D, which is important for reducing rickets and for other health reasons, and scientists were beginning to recognize that air polluted with smoke seemed to correlate with deaths from lung cancer, tuberculosis, and cardiac diseases. The darkness and visibility problems generated by urban air pollution, which caused some cities to burn streetlights day and night, may have also caused depression in many people and contributed to an increase in urban crime rates because it was easier for criminals to remain hidden or obscured.

Air pollution also affected the economy of the 1940's, including losses in food and plant production. Dirt deposits choked plant pores, and chemicals in the air generated acid rain that destroyed plant tissues and settled into the soil, thus reducing its fertility.

Fog exists because of particles in the air, and fog polluted with smoke is known as smog. Not only was smog a health hazard during the 1940's, especially in cities such as Pittsburgh and Los Angeles, but its corrosiveness also was a factor in damage to buildings and other property.

Collaboration with Canada   The 1940's saw substantial increases in both population and chemical air pollution in the United States and Canada. In 1940, the United States and Canada entered into the Ogdensburg Agreement, which established a Permanent Joint Board on Defense. Although the board was concerned mainly with defense issues, one of its mandates was to study air problems, including the smog and air pollution that were affecting the economies of both countries and creating potential problems in physical defense for both nations.

In 1909, Canada and the United States signed a treaty to regulate water pollution. The treaty created the International Joint Commission, which by the 1940's had also become involved in air pollution issues, including what became known as the Trail Smelter arbitration (1939). After many years of cross-border negotiations, the commission adopted an agreement that required polluting smelters to pay damages to United States farmers.

Impact   As a result of air pollution caused by burning coal, many new technological advances were adopted. These included more efficient furnaces, gas-cleaning devices, clean coal technology, and conversion from coal to oil and natural gas as fuel sources. In addition, many of the harmful materials generated by coal were turned into smokeless fuels, and new synthetics, including nylon, plastics, and pharmaceuticals, were produced by making use of chemical coal by-products that previously had been emitted into the atmosphere.

The federal Air Pollution Control Act of 1955 provided federal funds for air pollution research, and the 1963 Clean Air Act, which Congress has subsequently amended several times, was the first com-

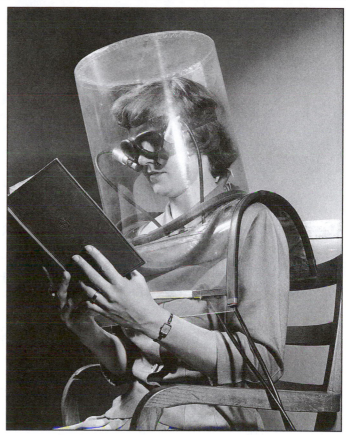

Assistant at California's Stanford Research Institute wearing an experimental device for testing the effects of air pollutants on human eyes in 1949. The plastic helmet contains measured amounts of smog; photoelectric cells in the subject's goggles record how often her eyes blink—an indication of eye irritation. (AP/Wide World Photos)

prehensive federal law to control air pollution in the United States. In addition, the United States and Canada have continued their cooperative efforts to control cross-boundary air pollution, especially acid rain, through the Air Quality Agreement of 1991.

Carol A. Rolf

Further Reading

Jacobson, Mark Z. *Atmospheric Pollution.* Cambridge, England: Cambridge University Press, 2002. Provides a historical review of the development of air pollution science and discusses the successes and failures in controlling atmospheric pollution.

National Academy of Sciences. *Air Quality Management in the United States.* Washington, D.C.: National Academies Press, 2009. Up-to-date scientific resource on air quality management with input from multiple scientists, government officials, and research organizations.

Seinfeld, John H., and Spyros N. Pandis. *Atmospheric Chemistry and Physics: From Air Pollution to Climate Change.* 2d ed. Hoboken, N.J.: Wiley-Interscience, 2006. Good reference on atmospheric science and its processes, especially chemical aspects and climate change.

Tarr, Joel. *Devastation and Renewal: An Environmental History of Pittsburgh and Its Region.* Pittsburgh: University of Pittsburgh Press, 2005. Good resource concerning some of the first attempts by a city in the United States to overcome severe air pollution caused by industrialization, including the Pittsburgh steel mills.

United Nations. *Clearing the Air: Twenty-five Years of the Convention on Long-Range Transboundary Air Pollution.* Geneva: United Nations Publications, 2005. Discusses the United Nations' successes in facilitating international treaties to protect the environment.

See also Aerosol cans; Atomic bomb; Automobiles and auto manufacturing; Business and the economy in Canada; Business and the economy in the United States; Congress of Industrial Organizations; Nuclear reactors; Wartime industries; Wartime technological advances; Water pollution.

■ Aircraft carriers

Definition Military ships with the ability to allow aircraft to land on and take off from them

British, Canadian, and American aircraft carriers helped defeat German U-boats and played critical roles in the Pacific campaign. Carriers also figured prominently in post-1945 American military policy.

By size and service, aircraft carriers were one of the most recognized weapons systems of the 1940's. British and Japanese victories at Taranto, Italy (November 11-12, 1940) and Pearl Harbor (December 7, 1941) demonstrated clearly that the carrier, not the battleship, was the key technology for winning naval battles. Carrier design was typified by the USS *Shangri-La*, an *Essex* class ship named in honor of the Doolittle raid of April, 1942, the first to strike a Japanese home island. At 27,200 tons, it could travel at thirty-three knots and carry one hundred aircraft. At

the opposite end of the scale was *I-25*, a Japanese submarine that carried a single float plane. Between August and September 1942, the *I-25* launched the only World War II aerial attacks against the continental United States, attempting to start fires in Pacific coast forests.

Between these extremes, World War II carriers performed myriad duties. They delivered waves of dive and torpedo bombers to sink enemy warships and submarines, scout planes for reconnaissance, and fighters, which both escorted the bombers to target and protected their own warships from enemy air strikes.

Some of the largest carrier battles of World War II were at Midway (June 4-7, 1942), the Philippine Sea (June 19-20, 1944), and Leyte Gulf (October 23-28, 1944). Every post-Midway carrier battle ended in an Allied victory, as a result of a combination of superior technology, such as radar; superior military intelligence via code breaking; superior pilot training; and leadership.

Although carriers such as the *Shangri-La* come to mind when thinking of the big Pacific naval battles, much smaller ships also played important roles. These were the escort carriers, also called "jeep carriers" or "baby flattops." Intended to protect convoys from submarine attacks or provide tactical air support during amphibious operations, these ships were found in nearly every theater. The 7,800-ton *Casablanca* class was a good example not only of the escort carrier but also of America's tremendous industrial power. Fifty were built between 1942 and 1944.

Carriers were very much part of post-1945 American Cold War strategies. This was epitomized by the USS *United States.* A "supercarrier" of 65,000 tons, it was designed to launch fifty-four jet fighters and twelve heavy bombers, the latter capable of delivering nuclear weapons. The *United States* cost $190 million, at a time when President Harry S. Truman wanted to reduce military spending.

Considerable interservice rivalries existed over access to shrunken revenues and the roles of the Army, the Navy, and the newly independent Air Force. The sometimes bitter controversy of 1949 between Navy admirals and high-ranking civilians, on one hand, and the president and secretary of defense, on the other, has been dubbed "the Revolt of the Admirals." As its conclusion, the *United States* was scrapped, while the Air Force had obtained funding for B-36 bombers. The admirals had their revenge a year later, when the Korean War demonstrated the tremendous utility of carriers in providing tactical air power at great distances.

Impact Aircraft carriers played a critical role in the Allied campaigns against Japan. For the United States, their post-1945 value was one of "force projection." This allowed a roving military punch that was quickly available to back up foreign policy. Carriers remain significant naval assets into the twenty-first century.

John P. Dunn

Task force of American aircraft carriers headed for the Philippines in December, 1944. (Digital Stock)

Further Reading

Friedman, Norman, with ship designs by A. D. Baker III. *U.S. Aircraft Carriers: An Illustrated Design History*. Annapolis, Md.: Naval Institute Press, 1983.

Ireland, Bernard. *The Illustrated Guide to Aircraft Carriers of the World*. London: Hermes House, 2005.

Y'Blood, William T. *The Little Giants: U.S. Escort Carriers Against Japan*. Annapolis, Md.: Naval Institute Press, 1987.

See also Aircraft design and development; Atlantic, Battle of the; Doolittle bombing raid; Forrestal, James; Great Marianas Turkey Shoot; Midway, Battle of; Navy, U.S.; Pearl Harbor attack; Submarine warfare; World War II.

■ Aircraft design and development

The development of aircraft technology in the United States, which had slowed during the 1930's, accelerated during the 1940's because of World War II. New designs, engines, and technologies made planes larger and faster, a trend that continued in the postwar era fueled by the Cold War and the growth of civilian aviation.

Aircraft development during the 1940's began under the influence of World War I. Given the antiwar sentiment of the 1930's, military spending was minimal, and American aircraft technology lagged behind European standards. While European air arms adopted aluminum-skinned monoplanes during the early 1930's, the United States retained fabric-covered biplanes well after they had become obsolete. European aviation technology received subsidized funding from national governments, but military aviation in the United States received only limited funding and support from the government. The National Advisory Committee for Aeronautics (NACA) ran a government-funded research facility in Virginia, but without firm budget support NACA's breakthroughs rarely found their way into production. Civil aviation, however, enjoyed wide public popularity thanks to heroes such as Charles Lindbergh and entertainment such as traveling barnstorming pilots. Surplus military aircraft permitted many Americans to own airplanes, and civil aviation was a popular pastime for those who could afford it. Flying was still possible for those who did not own aircraft, as a number of commercial airlines began operating during the 1930's, including Trans World Airlines (1930) and United Airlines (1934).

Aircraft Development in Wartime World War II reinvigorated American aircraft development. The German air force was a formidable force, while the Japanese Zero was technologically superior to any American fighter aircraft. The American reaction was a crash program to produce a large number of technologically superior aircraft. The first new aircraft were improved versions of those already on the design board or just coming into service when World War II broke out in 1939. The Grumman F4F Wildcat, introduced in 1940, was a good example. The Navy's first all-metal monoplane fighter, the Wildcat could not match the Zero's agility, but its heavy firepower and rugged construction allowed it to counter the Zero's advantages. Other new American aircraft, however, were without peer. The Boeing B-17 Flying Fortress, the first American four-engine heavy bomber, first flew in 1937. Capable of carrying six thousand pounds of bombs, the B-17 gave the United States the ability to strike enemy targets at long distance, but it was produced in only small numbers before the war. By 1945, however, the United States had produced nearly thirteen thousand of them.

By 1942, a new wave of aircraft was coming off the assembly line, airplanes designed and manufactured after the war began and benefiting from new technology and production methods. Supplementing the B-17 in the long-range bomber role, the Consolidated B-24 Liberator could carry more bombs at a higher altitude to a longer distance. Featuring a long, slender laminar wing, the B-24 became the most-produced aircraft in U.S. history, with more than eighteen thousand airframes produced in bomber, transport, and maritime reconnaissance versions. Even more advanced was the Boeing B-29 Superfortress, first flown in 1944. With a range and bomb load twice that of the B-17, the B-29 featured an aerodynamic shape, fully pressurized interior, and remotely aimed gun turrets. The most advanced bomber of World War II, the B-29 remained in service until the 1960's.

Engine Technology and Propulsion   One of the features of the B-29 was its massive engines. Powered by four Wright R-3350 piston engines, each producing 2,200 horsepower, the B-29 had twice the power of the B-17. The configuration of the engines was a traditional radial design, with the pistons arrayed around the drive shaft so that passing air could cool the engines. It was an effective, but bulky, setup that created drag. For aircraft that required speed and maneuverability, a new range of in-line engines appeared during the 1940's. Instead of ringing the shaft, the pistons of the in-line engine were in banks along the aircraft centerline. This produced a more compact power plant but also meant that air cooling was not possible. Instead, in-line engines used liquid cooling, which was efficient but also added another complexity to the engine. The most successful fighter of World War II, the North American P-51 Mustang, used the British-developed Merlin in-line engine that produced 1,600 horsepower. By comparison, the engine of the Curtiss P-40 Warhawk, the primary U.S. fighter at the start of the war, produced only 1,200 horsepower.

Propulsion advances during World War II also included the introduction of the jet engine. Frank Whittle, an officer in Great Britain's Royal Air Force (RAF), first tested a jet engine in 1937, but only prototypes were operating by the time World War II began. The sole American wartime jet was the Bell P-59 Airacomet, but it proved to be disappointing, being less maneuverable than existing piston engine fighters and barely faster. Development during the late 1940's, however, improved the performance of jet engine fighters. Lockheed produced the P-80 Shooting Star in 1945, a jet capable of 600 miles per hour (mph) propelled by an engine that put out 5,400 pounds of thrust.

By 1949, the North American F-86 Sabre, powered by a 6,000-

A U.S. Navy Grumman F4F-3 in early 1942. (Courtesy, U.S. Navy)

pound thrust engine, reached nearly 700 mph in level flight and exceeded the Mach 1 in a dive. While useful for lightweight fighters, jet engines were unsuitable for larger aircraft because of their limited thrust. Bombers and transport aircraft still relied on piston engines for propulsion. Several large aircraft, most notably the Convair B-36 Peacemaker bomber, used both types of propulsion. The B-36, which dwarfed the B-29, employed six 3,800-horsepower piston engines and four 5,200-pound thrust jets. Even with that power, the massive aircraft had a top speed of only 420 mph. There were efforts to merge the two forms of engines, resulting in the turboprop engine, a power plant that uses a jet engine to turn a propeller. Consolidated tried a turboprop in its XP-81 fighter prototype in 1945, but the technology was unreliable and offered little advantage over conventional piston engines.

Civilian Aviation in the Postwar Era   The same limitations that restricted the use of jet engines on large military aircraft applied to postwar civilian aircraft. Air travel boomed during the late 1940's thanks to the large number of wartime airfields being converted to peacetime use. Also, the general prosperity of the late 1940's meant that more Americans could afford to fly than before the war, when flight was a relatively expensive mode of transportation. Passenger airlines, however, had to employ piston engines because the new jet engines lacked the thrust to lift large aircraft and burned fuel at a prodigious rate. Instead, manufacturers concentrated their production along two broad design concepts. Some companies, such as Douglas and its DC-6 aircraft, opted for large fuselages capable of carrying many passengers (up to 102) at a relatively slow speed (315 mph), while others, such as Lockheed and its Constellation aircraft, preferred slim aerodynamic fuselages that flew faster (380 mph) but carried fewer seats (62 passengers). The war also proved a boon to private aviation. The military sold off thousands of trainer and observation aircraft, such as the Piper Cub, that were inexpensive for the private pilot to own. Capable of operating from small airfields, these planes aided in making aviation a common experience during the 1940's and beyond.

Impact   Aircraft developments of the 1940's influenced subsequent decades. The Cold War led to technological races with the Soviet Union to perfect military aircraft lest the rivalry turn into full-blown war. Massive nuclear attack bombers, such as the Boeing B-52 Stratofortress, became the symbol of the Cold War era and its threat of nuclear annihilation. Improved jet engines and sophisticated design layouts, such as the delta wing and variable geometry, found their way into production to offset Soviet numbers with advanced technology. Civil aviation benefited from Cold War technology, as improvements in engines led to larger and faster airliners. Advances in turboprop engines led to larger passenger planes, such as the Lockheed Electra, but they were quickly supplanted by jet airlines. The arrival of the de Havilland Comet and Boeing 707 allowed large numbers of people to travel long distances at high speeds. This, in turn, lowered the relative cost of flying, making air travel even more accessible to the average person.

Steven J. Ramold

Further Reading

Anderson, John D. *The Airplane: A History of its Technology.* Reston, Va.: American Institute of Aeronautics and Astronautics, 2002. A broad evaluation of the first century of powered flight. Covers developments in both military and civilian aviation.

Bowers, Peter M. *Boeing Aircraft Since 1916.* Annapolis, Md.: Naval Institute Press, 1989. An examination of the most influential American aircraft company from its inception to the late twentieth century. Examines the company's early aircraft, its wartime contributions such as the B-29, and its emergence as the world's preeminent designer of large aircraft.

Eden, Paul E., and Sophearith Moeng, eds. *Aircraft Anatomy of World War II: Technical Drawings of Key Aircraft, 1939-1945.* Edison, N.J.: Chartwell Books, 2003. An insider's view of the technical demands of creating new aircraft. Provides good explanations of the reasons why certain elements are integrated into a design and how a plane is shaped for a specific purpose.

Gunston, Bill. *The Development of Jet and Turbine Aero Engines.* London: Patrick Stephens, 1997. Contains a thorough history of jet aircraft technology, especially the early experiments, wartime applications, and use in civilian aviation.

Solberg, Carl. *Conquest of the Skies: A History of Commercial Aviation in America.* Boston: Little, Brown, 1979. Although the book generalizes on post-

World War II airline development, it includes good discussions of the origins of civilian aviation and the expansion of private aircraft ownership.

See also Bombers; Doolittle bombing raid; *Enola Gay*; Jet engines; Strategic bombing; Trans World Airlines; Wartime industries; Wartime technological advances; World War II.

■ Alaska Highway

The Event Construction of a road connecting Alaska with the contiguous United States
Also known as Alaska-Canada (ALCAN) Highway
Date March 8-October 28, 1942
Place From Dawson Creek, British Columbia, to Delta Junction, Alaska

The Alaska-Canadian highway provided a World War II supply route connecting Alaska with the contiguous United States.

Proposals for a road route connecting Alaska to the contiguous United States were made as early as 1905, but the Canadian government saw little value in funding a project that would benefit few of its own citizens, even though the bulk of the road would pass through Canada. However, in December, 1941, after the Japanese attacked Pearl Harbor, such a route became an urgent need.

Prior to the Pearl Harbor attack, much of the population of North America felt safe from the war, even though Canada was an active combatant. A direct threat to North America became recognized with the attack on Pearl Harbor, increased Japanese presence in the Pacific, and the realization that the Japanese were operating a base only 750 miles from Alaska's Aleutian Islands. Before construction of the highway, a series of airfields was used as a supply route through Canada to Alaskan military bases. This system was inadequate because it left U.S. military outposts in Fairbanks, Alaska, isolated and vulnerable to attack.

In order better to secure the United States mainland, President Franklin D. Roosevelt authorized construction of the Alaska Highway on February 11, 1942. The U.S. Army Corps of Engineers would have one year to build the highway, then known as the Alaska-Canadian Highway (ALCAN Highway). As part of an agreement with the Canadian govern-ment, the United States was to fund the entire project and the Canadian sections of the route were to be relinquished to Canadian authority after the war ended.

Construction Begins The U.S. Army Corps of Engineers began construction of the highway on March 8, 1942. By late March, more than 10,000 workers had been sent to the route, creating temporary population booms. Dawson Creek, in British Columbia, the southern starting point, saw its population of 600 explode to more than 10,000.

Up to this point, American military policy had dictated that African Americans not be sent to northern climates or active duty. Faced with a shortage of officers because of the war, the Army was forced by the secretary of war to put black officers in Alaska. Of the more than 10,000 American soldiers sent north, 4,000 were African Americans. The total number of workers, including officers, ordinary soldiers, and civilians, numbered approximately 20,000.

April 11, 1942, was the official groundbreaking of the Alaskan Highway. From the beginning of the project, troops faced unfamiliar conditions. They were greeted by harsh winter weather, for which they were inadequately prepared. Many of the men lacked experience operating heavy equipment, necessitating on-the-job training. Shipments of building supplies and machinery did not always keep up with needs.

On June 3, the Japanese attacked American forces at Dutch Harbor in the Aleutian Islands. Within two weeks of the attacks, the Japanese captured the islands Kiska and Attu. With the Japanese now in the Alaska Territory, the urgency to complete the route was even stronger.

Problems and Progress Spring rains brought new problems. As the ground thawed, muskeg (wet decayed vegetation) became a serious problem for the builders. Once-frozen wetlands proved treacherous. Bulldozers and dynamite were used to clear the route in shallow areas of muskeg, but larger sections could swallow equipment. Realizing it was best to avoid these sections, they were forced to build a less direct route. When building around the muskeg was not an option, they used trees in a process of corduroying to create a floating road surface across the muskeg. The warmer weather, however, allowed construction to proceed at various portions of the route, rather than only the south- ern end. By the end of June, 360 miles of road were complete.

The summer months saw tem- peratures rise, and the drying mud allowed construction to pro- ceed more quickly. In July, 400 ad- ditional miles of the route were completed. The northern sun- light was seemingly endless, and workers took twelve-hour shifts. Mosquitoes forced the men to wear long-sleeved shirts, long trou- sers, and netting.

By the end of August, with less than 500 miles to go, the troops struggled with permafrost (ground that has remained frozen for two or more years). As the troops re- moved vegetation from the land, the hard surface would thaw and turn to mud. Without guidelines for building on permafrost, the troops spent six weeks of trial and error before settling on a process of cutting trees and immediately corduroying the land. Although the solution worked, it slowed progress.

October began one of the cold- est winters on record. Groups working from opposite ends of the final gap worked feverishly to complete the route. They struggled with the bitter cold, sometimes tens of degrees below zero Celsius, which could result in rapid onset of frostbite and cause machinery breakdowns.

The route was completed on October 28, 1942, with a northern linkup at Beaver Creek. The 1,390- mile highway was dedicated on November 20 at Sol- diers Summit, Alaska.

Impact   The Alaskan Highway was a major engi- neering accomplishment. Overcoming adverse con- ditions, the Army Corps of Engineers oversaw the completion of the route in a little more than seven months. The highway not only provided security to North America but also boosted morale on the mainland and paved the way for postwar immigra- tion to the Alaska Territory. The successful perfor- mance of African American troops on the project contributed to the U.S. military's integration of its armed forces.

Michael D. Cummings, Jr.

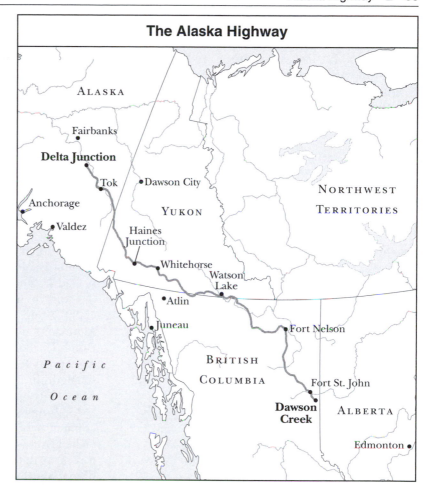

The Alaska Highway

Further Reading

Brown, Tricia. *The World Famous Alaska Highway: A Guide to the Alcan and Other Wilderness Roads of the North.* Golden, Colo.: Fulcrum, 2000. Practical travel guide to the Alaska Highway and other ma- jor Alaskan and Canadian roads.

Coates, Ken. *North to Alaska: Fifty Years on the World's Most Remarkable Highway.* Fairbanks: University of Alaska Press, 1991. Explains the technical, logisti- cal, and human factors of working in the high- way's isolated locale. Evaluates the road's impact on the postwar far Northwest.

Haigh, Jane. *The Alaska Highway: A Historic Photo- graphic Journey.* Rev. ed. Whitehorse, Y.T.: Wolf Creek Books, 2009. A history of the highway's construction, use, and cultural effects. Many photographs.

Krakauer, Jon. "Ice, Mosquitoes, and Muskeg—Building the Road to Alaska." *Smithsonian* 23 (July, 1992): 102-111. Provides stories of human interest relating to the building of the highway, with glimpses of travelers, tourist attractions, and day-to-day life in the region.

Olsenius, Richard. "Alaska Highway: Wilderness Escape Route." *National Geographic* 180 (November, 1991): 68-99. Combination of travelogue and history of the highway, presented in the magazine's usual vivid style. Spectacular color photographs and an excellent bound-in map of the road.

Twichell, Heath. *Northwest Epic: The Building of the Alaska Highway.* New York: St. Martin's Press, 1992. A definitive account, covering actual field work and living conditions, political background, the major players, and the related Canadian Oil Road (Canol) and Northwest Staging Route operations. The author is a winner of the Allen Nevins Prize in American history and the son of Colonel Heath Twichell, who commanded several engineering regiments during the project.

See also Aleutian Island occupation; Army, U.S.; Canadian participation in World War II; Lend-Lease; Pearl Harbor attack; World War II; World War II mobilization.

■ Aleutian Island occupation

The Event Japanese attacks on, and occupation of, the Aleutian islands of Attu and Kiska during World War II

Date June 3, 1942-August 15, 1943

Place Aleutian Island chain, North Pacific Ocean

The recapture of Attu and Kiska was the first American theater-wide success in World War II and meant the end of Japanese occupation of American soil.

The Aleutian Islands became United States possessions with the purchase of Alaska from Russia in 1867. American military opinion was divided on whether to garrison the territory's Aleutian Island chain until December of 1934, when Japan repudiated the Washington Naval Treaty of 1922. That treaty regulated the tonnage and numbers of ships in its five signatories' navies as well as regulating na-

val bases and fortifications. By the late 1930's, seaplane stations were established at Sitka and Kodiak, and the U.S. Army had small installations at Anchorage, Unalaska, and Dutch Harbor.

By the time of the attack on Pearl Harbor on December 7, 1941, the total Alaska garrison numbered about 22,000 people, under the command of Brigadier General Simon Bolivar Buckner, Jr. The U.S. Navy, under Rear Admiral Robert A. Theobald's command, had four surface vessels, two submarines, and half a dozen aircraft. Theobald also commanded the Army's Eleventh Air Force, with bases at Anchorage, Cold Bay, and Umnak Island.

During the early summer of 1942, about 850 native Aleutians were removed from their homes in the Pribilof Islands north of the Aleutian chain and interned in southeastern Alaska for the duration of the war. By June, 1942, the War Department had 45,000 troops in Alaska, but only about 2,300 in the Aleutians, at a naval base on Unalaska Island at Dutch Harbor, and a newly constructed Army facility, Fort Glenn on Umnak Island. Peak Allied strength in Alaska, in August, 1943, was about 144,000 troops.

On June 3, 1942, a small Japanese fleet under the command of Vice Admiral Boshiro Hosogaya attacked Dutch Harbor as part of a plan to draw Allied forces north to defend the Aleutians, while the Japanese main fleet attacked Midway. American casualties were 43 killed and 64 wounded; 10 Japanese aircraft were brought down by Allied fire and weather conditions. While returning south two days later to rejoin Admiral Isoroku Yamamoto's diminished main fleet, now headed home for Japan, the Northern Area Fleet was directed to return to the Aleutians. Hosogaya took Attu and Kiska islands on June 6.

When Allied forces retook Attu in May, 1943, they were hampered by inadequate intelligence, harsh terrain and climate, inappropriate field clothing and gear, and weather that made effective reconnaissance nearly impossible. Japanese resistance was both tragic and heroic: 2,350 Japanese were killed and 29 taken prisoner. American casualties were 529 killed, 1,148 wounded, and about 2,100 victims of frostbite, hypothermia, and trench foot.

The recapture of Kiska, however, was thoroughly planned and conducted with appropriate gear. After four weeks of bombarding the island from both the sea and the air, the Allied invasion force landed on

August 15. After several days, it was discovered that the more than 5,000 Japanese who had occupied it two months previously had departed in late July. A harbor mine, friendly fire, and other accidents resulted in 91 Allied dead on Kiska and 168 sick or wounded.

Impact   The recapture of Attu was one of the most costly U.S. victories in World War II in terms of U.S. casualties relative to the number of opponents, with seventy-one American casualties for every one hundred Japanese encountered on the island. The island also was the last significant threat to American home territory in World War II.

Rachel Maines

Further Reading

Chandonnet, Fern. *Alaska at War, 1941-1945: The Forgotten War Remembered*. Anchorage: Alaska at War Committee, 1995.

Conn, Stetson, Rose C. Engelman, and Byron Fairchild. *Guarding the United States and Its Outposts*. Washington, D.C.: Army Office of the Chief of Military History, 1964.

Perras, Galen Roger. *Stepping Stones to Nowhere: The Aleutian Islands, Alaska, and American Military Strategy, 1867-1945*. Vancouver: University of British Columbia Press, 2003.

See also   Alaska Highway; Midway, Battle of; Pearl Harbor attack.

Alien Registration Act of 1940. *See* **Smith Act of 1940**

■ All-American Girls Professional Baseball League

Identification   Women's baseball league
Date   Operated from 1943 until 1954

The All-American Girls Professional Baseball League changed the role of women in American sports. No longer were women seen simply as softball players because they were the weaker sex but proved that they could participate more equally on a level playing field.

After the United States entered World War II at the end of 1941, Major League Baseball rosters shrank, decimated as players went to serve their country. In an effort to keep baseball alive and to continue providing Americans with sports entertainment during the war years, business mogul Philip K. Wrigley decided to start a women's baseball league. It was intended to be merely a temporary measure to fill a defined need during the war, but the growing popularity of the league and the desire of the young women on its teams to continue playing kept the league going through the 1954 season, when it finally folded.

Business Opportunity   As a businessman, Wrigley saw an opportunity during World War II and he took it. He believed that America needed baseball and if the major and minor leagues could not fill that need, then perhaps a women's league could. Following on the idea of the cultural icon Rosie the Riveter, a temporary change for women in the workforce, Wrigley expected his league to operate through the duration of the war, and then its players would return to their prewar responsibilities. When Wrigley began the league, it was called simply the "All-American Girls Baseball League." The word "Professional" was added later.

Wrigley believed that with careful recruiting of players, a league could operate throughout the Midwest. He sent out scouts and announcements to hold tryouts in selected cities. Of the hundreds of young women who showed up, sixty-four were assigned to four teams. Women were chosen for beauty as well as for their baseball skills. Wrigley wanted people never to forget the players on the field were women. He even required the league's initial players to take charm-school classes.

More than six hundred women played in Wrigley's league between 1943 and 1954. The number of teams each season varied from four to as many as ten. In addition to its players, each team also had a female chaperon to help the players deal with the press, keep an eye on them on road trips, and generally keep things in order. With the exception of Mary Baker, who managed the Kalamazoo Lassies through most of the 1950 season, the league's managers over the years were all former Major League Baseball players. The numbers of games and competitive formats varied from season to season, but every year the teams played at least ninety games and sometimes more than 110.

After the 1945 season ended, Wrigley sold the

league to Arthur Meyerhoff. Meyerhoff directed the league until 1951, when he sold control to the team owners, who operated it until it was dissolved in 1954. Meanwhile, the league went through a variety of rule changes. For example, the size of ball was reduced, pitching motions shifted from underhand to overhand delivery, and the distance between the pitcher's mound and home plate was lengthened. Overall, the trend was toward making the game more similar to traditional, male baseball.

Teams and Players Teams such as the Rockford Peaches, South Bend Blue Sox, and Racine Belles enjoyed many seasons with the league. Other teams such as the Peoria Red Wings, the Milwaukee Chicks, and the Muskegon Lassies either folded

quickly or moved their franchises around because their markets were small. Every year, the league held both an all-star game and a championship series, which the Racine Belles won in the league's inaugural season. The Rockford Peaches eventually held the league record with four championships.

In addition to those chosen as all-stars, the league had numerous standout players. One of the best was Dottie Kamenshek, who played from 1943 to 1953 and led the league with 1,090 hits. Sophie Kurys led the league in stolen bases with 1,114—including 201 during a single season—and batted .260. Jean Faut pitched two perfect games during her outstanding pitching career, while pitcher Connie Wisniewski had a 107-48 career record with a 1.48 earned run average and earned the nickname "Iron Woman" for her durability. These and other stars helped keep the league going. However, as American social and economic conditions changed, interest in the league waned, and the league eventually had to fold. Competition with television broadcasting, advances in travel, new leisure opportunities, and changing images of women in society all contributed to the league's demise. As marriage and home took on increased popularity in the 1950's, the league could not compete.

Marie Mahoney of the South Bend Blue Sox reaches first safely as the throw to first base goes high in a 1947 game. (Getty Images)

Impact For the more than six hundred women who got the chance to play, the league offered them opportunities they never would have gotten otherwise. It opened a world of travel, paid them livable wages, and gave many the confidence to then go on and try other things. Over the years the league and the players have become an inspiration to other women not only in baseball but also in life. In 1988, the National Baseball Hall of Fame dedicated an exhibit honoring the league. In 1992, Penny Marshall directed a fictional film about the league's first year, *A League of their Own* (1992). Tom Hanks played the former Major League Baseball star who managed one of the teams, and Geena Davis portrayed the league's star player.

Leslie Heaphy

Further Reading

Brown, Patricia I. *A League of My Own.* Jefferson, N.C.: McFarland, 2003. Memoir written by a woman who pitched in the All-American Girls Professional Baseball League.

Browne, Lois. *The Girls of Summer: The Real Story of the All-American Girls Professional Baseball League.* New York: HarperCollins, 1993. History of the league published shortly after the film *A League of Their Own* came out.

Hammer, Trudy J. *The All-American Girls Professional Baseball League.* New York: New Discovery Books, 1994. History of the league written for middle school readers.

Johnson, Susan E. *When Women Played Hardball.* Seattle: Seal Press, 1994. Memoir written by a sociologist recalling her excitement being a fan of the All-American Girls Professional Baseball League during her youth.

Madden, W. C. *The Women of the All-American Girls Professional Baseball League: A Biographical Dictionary.* Jefferson, N.C.: McFarland, 2005. Profiles of more than six hundred women who played in the league, with their statistical records, brief biographical sketches, and many previously unpublished photographs.

See also Baseball; Negro Leagues; Recreation; "Rosie the Riveter"; Sports in the United States; Women's roles and rights in the United States.

■ All the King's Men

Identification Novel about American politics
Author Robert Penn Warren (1905-1989)
Date First published in 1946

Winner of the 1947 Pulitzer Prize, All the King's Men *remains an important piece of literature for its depiction of American politics and the corruption that can surround it.*

Robert Penn Warren asserted that he never intended for *All the King's Men* to be about politics; nevertheless, it has been interpreted as a political novel. The book took nearly ten years to write and is a sweeping saga that follows two main characters—the narrator, Jack Burden, and the rising political figure, Willie Stark. Burden, Stark's assistant, relates Stark's swift rise from backwoods Louisiana lawyer to governor. Along the way, Burden watches as Stark becomes increasingly entwined with nefarious elements that allow him to rise to power while facilitating a corrupt government. One of the central themes of the novel is that all actions have consequences: Stark's time in power is short-lived, a downfall precipitated by his own makings. Although Warren denied the connection, many critics believe that the book follows the events of former Louisiana governor Huey P. Long.

Impact Two years after winning the Pulitzer Prize, *All the King's Men* was made into a film, debuting in 1949 and garnering seven Academy Award nominations, for which it won three. The epic novel was also turned into several stage adaptations, the first of which was written in 1947. The book is now considered a classic and is regularly listed as one of the great novels of the twentieth century. In 2006, the work was again adapted to film.

P. Huston Ladner

Further Reading

Beebe, Maurice. *Robert Penn Warren's "All the King's Men": A Critical Handbook.* Belmont, Calif.: Wadsworth, 1966.

Chambers, Robert H., ed. *Twentieth Century Interpretations of "All the King's Men": A Collection of Critical Essays.* Englewood Cliffs, N.J.: Prentice-Hall, 1977.

Perkins, James A., ed. *The Cass Mastern Material: The Core of Robert Penn Warren's "All the King's Men."* Baton Rouge: Louisiana State University Press, 2005.

See also Book publishing; Film in the United States; Great Books Foundation; Literature in the United States.

■ America First Committee

Identification Noninterventionist pressure group
Date Established on September 4, 1940

The America First Committee was the largest pressure group opposed to U.S. intervention in World War II. It included a number of prominent businessmen, politicians, and reli-

gious leaders among its supporters. Many of these individuals, such as Charles Lindbergh and Norman Thomas, spoke at national rallies in support of nonintervention. The group was variously attacked as being anti-Semitic, communist, fascist, and anti-American.

Founded on September 4, 1940, the America First Committee (AFC) became the primary voice of opposition to U.S. intervention in World War II. The widespread concern over the role of the United States in the European war became the burning issue of the period. The organization was founded by R. Douglas Stuart, a Yale Law student, along with Kingman Brewster, Jr., editor of the *Yale Daily News*. It soon merged with the Keep America Out of the War Committee. Support for the noninterventionist policies of the organization attracted well-known and influential individuals such as Charles Lindbergh, Sinclair Lewis, Potter Stewart, and Gerald R. Ford. Others, such as John F. Kennedy, financially supported the organization. By December, 1941, it boasted of a membership exceeding 800,000, with more than 450 semiautonomous chapters and subchapters. The principal strength of the organization lay in the Midwest, primarily Illinois, where sixty chapters existed. The AFC initially refused to allow membership or accept donations from the German American Bund, communists, and anti-Semitic groups such as Father Charles E. Coughlin's Christian Frontiers.

The organization evolved into the most influential pressure group in the country and attempted to influence public opinion through pamphlets, radio addresses, and public appearances by well-known speakers. Charles Lindbergh became the most popular speaker, drawing thousands to anti-intervention rallies. As a result, he was virulently attacked as a Nazi sympathizer, an anti-Semitic, and as anti-American. Lindbergh's often radical statements alienated supporters such as Norman Thomas, the presidential nominee of the Socialist Party, who refused to appear at AFC rallies for a time.

As the organization continued to grow, it came under attack from the press and President Franklin D. Roosevelt's administration. The AFC was accused of being helpful to the Nazis as well as being anti-Semitic. Ironically, the AFC had a number of Jewish members, some of whom served in leadership positions. In spite of these attacks, polls indicated that the majority of Americans opposed intervention. The AFC attempted to compel administration adherence to the Neutrality Acts. It opposed Lend-Lease and the Atlantic Charter and went so far as to propose that the question of war and peace be formally submitted for a congressional vote. Not a pacifist organization, the AFC advocated a strong national defense to prevent any European power from threatening the country. Some supporters, such as Thomas, objected to this position, which he labeled "armament economics." Internal disagreements such as this accounted for the high turnover in both membership and leadership throughout 1940 and 1941.

Impact The Japanese attack on Pearl Harbor on December 7, 1941, ended the nonintervention debate. The AFC voted to disband immediately after the attack. In spite of its efforts and success in bringing the debate before the American public, the AFC was unsuccessful in preventing passage of Roosevelt's initiatives. Ultimately, it was unable to prevent American entry into the war. In 1942, a grand jury identified the AFC as an organization that had been used to spread Nazi propaganda.

Ronald J. Ferrara

Further Reading

Coles, Wayne S. *America First: The Battle Against Intervention, 1940-1941.* Madison: University of Wisconsin Press, 1953.

Lindbergh, Charles H. *Autobiography of Values.* New York: Harcourt Brace Jovanovich, 1976.

Sarles, Ruth. *A Story of America First: The Men and Women Who Opposed U.S. Intervention in World War II.* Edited by Bill Kauffman. Westport, Conn.: Praeger, 2003.

See also Atlantic Charter; Isolationism; Lend-Lease; Pearl Harbor attack; World War II.

■ An American Dilemma: The Negro Problem and American Democracy

Identification   Sociological study that exposed the stark contrast between the restrictive lower status assigned African Americans in the America of the 1940's and the pervasive American belief in equal opportunity and justice

Author   Gunnar Myrdal (1898-1987)

Date   First published in 1944

Renowned Swedish economist Gunnar Myrdal documented the inferior status of African Americans in American society. By presenting a stark contrast between the American creed of equal justice and the constricted opportunities offered black Americans in segregated America, Myrdal brought the dilemma to the attention of opinion leaders and effectively undermined the rationalizations for racial segregation.

In *An American Dilemma: The Negro Problem and American Democracy*, Gunnar Myrdal points out that ideals of equal justice and liberty are widely shared in America as an "American creed." However, black Americans during the 1940's were relegated to a lower caste in society. The vast majority of "Negroes" were poor, either seeking out a marginal existence as southern farm laborers or sharecroppers or employed in cities as unskilled laborers. Black professionals and small-business people were comparatively few in number and economically marginal. By being excluded from Democratic primaries in the one-party South, African Americans were effectively excluded from any real political influence there. In the southern states of the Old Confederacy, racially segregated schools, churches, social clubs, hotels, and restaurants minimized genuine and spontaneous interactions between black and white Americans. Myrdal notes that the norms supporting segregation were differentially enforced. A violation that might be overlooked if initiated by a white person would be followed by threats and legal sanctions if initiated by a black person.

Americans dealt with the glaring discrepancy between their ideal of equality and the reality of inequality in several ways. Since most large rural states in the North and West had few African Americans, this dilemma was not very salient to many Americans in these states. A common belief in the segregated South was that black people were by nature, simple, undisciplined, and unintelligent. Therefore, segregation saved the races from embarrassing conflicts and preserved harmonious relationships. Myrdal observed the almost visceral fear advocates of racial segregation had of interracial marriage, which would, they feared, lead to the degeneration of the race. Myrdal noted the speciousness of these assertions, which, he argued, use the results of segregation to justify it. Denied educational and economic opportunities, a black person might appear poor and uneducated. This lack of education was then employed to attest to the black person's "low intelligence" and this lack of economic opportunity to "laziness." Even the expressed horror of defiling "racial purity" by interracial marriage was, Myrdal argues, based upon a fiction since a lot of interracial mating, often instigated by white planters, had already occurred.

Impact   The first edition of Myrdal's book sold some 200,000 copies. Myrdal's arguments became familiar to such opinion leaders as presidential advisers and Supreme Court justices. The book was assigned in many college social science classes. In the late 1940's, African Amercans could never forget their color, but, beneath the surface, the laws supporting racial segregation had already begun to erode. In 1948, President Harry S. Truman desegregated the U.S. military. In the late 1940's, Heman Sweatt, an African American applicant to the University of Texas Law School who was denied admission because of his race, argued in Texas courts that segregated education by its very nature prevented African Americans from being afforded equal opportunities. In June, 1950, the Supreme Court agreed in *Sweatt v. Painter.* The ferment that was to explode into the Civil Rights movement was already gaining momentum. Guiding that movement were the ideals of the American creed articulated by Gunnar Myrdal.

Thomas E. DeWolfe

Further Reading

Clayton, Obie. *American Dilemma Revisited: Race Relations in a Changing World.* New York: Russell Sage Foundation, 1996.

Myrdal, Gunnar. *An American Dilemma: The Negro Problem and American Democracy.* New York: Harper and Brothers, 1944.

Wahl, Ana-María González. "From Old South to New South? Black-White Residential Segregation in Micropolitan Areas." *Sociological Spectrum* 27, no. 5 (2007): 507-535.

See also African Americans; Civil rights and liberties; Fair Employment Practices Commission; Jim Crow laws; Lynching and hate crime; National Association for the Advancement of Colored People; Racial discrimination; Social sciences; Supreme Court, U.S.

■ American Enterprise Institute for Public Policy Research

Identification Conservative think tank
Also known as AEI; American Enterprise Association
Date Established in 1943

The American Enterprise Institute, the first conservative American think tank, espoused free market principles during the New Deal and World War II, when such ideals seemed outdated. At the same time, however, the think tank reflected the apprehensions of many Americans about rapid government expansion.

The American Enterprise Institute for Public Policy Research (AEI), originally called the American Enterprise Association, began its official life in 1943 as the first conservative think tank, promoting the ideals of the free market and limited government. Its founders, including business executive Lewis H. Brown and economic writer Henry Hazlitt, long distrusted the growing centralization of the American economy; the acceleration of this trend during World War II prompted the AEI to challenge New Deal policies. The AEI's early studies focused on the economic consequences of proposed legislation or policies such as the Bretton Woods system. Though the think tank's efforts were well intentioned, these modest studies had little impact during the 1940's.

Impact The AEI would become more influential, particularly under the directorship of William J. Baroody, beginning in 1954. The scope, quantity, and quality of its research grew, attracting luminaries such as economist Milton Friedman, future president Gerald R. Ford, and neoconservative intellectual Irving Kristol. The organization officially changed its name to the American Enterprise Institute in 1962.

Anthony J. Bernardo, Jr.

Further Reading
Nash, George H. *The Conservative Intellectual Movement in America Since 1945.* Wilmington, Del.: Intercollegiate Studies Institute, 1996.
Wiarda, Howard J. *Conservative Brain Trust: The Rise, Fall, and Rise Again of the American Enterprise Institute.* Lanham, Md.: Lexington Books, 2009.

See also Bretton Woods Conference; Business and the economy in the United States; Conservatism in U.S. politics; Economic wartime regulations; Rand, Ayn; Taft, Robert A.

■ American Federation of Labor

Identification Federation of labor unions
Also known as AFL; Federation of Organized Trades and Labor Unions
Date Founded on December 8, 1886

The American Federation of Labor (AFL), founded in reaction to the extensive unionism of the Knights of Labor to focus on promoting the interests of skilled craftsmen, was forced during the 1940's to compete for worker loyalty with its more inclusive and militant rival, the Congress of Industrial Organizations (CIO). By the end of the decade, however, organizational and political changes brought the AFL and its rival together to form the AFL-CIO.

The American Federation of Labor (AFL) grew out of the Federation of Organized Trades and Labor Unions (FOTLU), which was founded in 1881. The AFL was established five years later, rising to prominence as the power of the Knights of Labor (KOL) was waning in the wake of the Haymarket Square riot. For decades, the AFL, under the leadership of Samuel Gompers (1886-1924) and William Green (1924-1952), successfully promoted itself as the sole legitimate labor organization and its focus on craft-based organization and limited political organization as the most effective way to organize. Although there were always some AFL unions that included unskilled workers, there was little effort to organize them. Additionally, while the AFL officially condemned racial discrimination, in practice it did little to stop constituent unions from refusing to organize

African Americans or maintaining segregated locals.

By the 1930's, the Great Depression, the increased deskilling of industry, and the renewed labor militancy brought about by the New Deal had inspired increased challenges to the exclusive craft focus of the AFL, as well as challenges (after 1924) to the halfhearted practice of creating "federal locals" by industry with the intention to assign skilled workers to the appropriate craft unions, with little concern for the fate of unskilled workers. In 1935, John L. Lewis, the head of the United Mine Workers, promoted the formation of a Committee for Industrial Organization, but continued disputes led to the expulsion of the organization and its transformation to the independent Congress of Industrial Organizations (CIO) by 1938. The rise of the CIO led to a decline in the AFL's numbers and influence in American mass-production industries, but the AFL proved adaptable enough to make new organization inroads into the transportation, communication, and service sectors.

During World War II, the AFL also gradually abandoned its traditional adherence to voluntarism and "pure and simple trade unionism" to become more closely connected with the government and more openly politicized. The AFL did this even while promoting itself as a more conservative alternative to the CIO—a strategy that would preserve its standing while the CIO was under political attack in the immediate postwar era. On one hand, the AFL refused to take action on issues of race and gender and rejected government intervention on issues such as shop-floor safety. The AFL also largely resisted Franklin D. Roosevelt's effort to bring it together with the CIO. On the other hand, during the war, the AFL's traditional emphasis on bread-and-butter issues was transformed and politicized into the theme of shared wartime sacrifice; the labor federation gave its effective, if qualified, support for Roosevelt's postwar plans to continue and expand the New Deal provisions. Finally, the AFL joined with the CIO in opposition to the Smith-Connally Act of 1943 (also known as the War Labor Disputes Act), which placed severe restrictions on the circumstances under which unions could call strikes and attempted to restrict organized labor's political activities.

Impact Even as the AFL continued to reject government pressure to merge with its rival, as a result of wartime common causes the AFL began to become closer to the CIO both organizationally and politically, discussing the possibility of a merger as early as 1942. The AFL also expressed increased militancy through its support for a 1941 transportation workers' strike in New York City and promoted increased political involvement through its Labor League for Human Rights, which raised money to support oppressed labor movements and workers during World War II. In the late 1940's, the AFL leaders successfully weathered the political fallout from the postwar strike wave and accepted the 1947 Taft-

AFL president William Green putting up posters exhorting union members to support the war effort in Washington, D.C., on December 9, 1941, two days after Japan bombed Pearl Harbor. (AP/Wide World Photos)

Hartley Act anticommunist affidavit requirement with little dissent. By the end of the 1940's, the AFL had signed a mutual no-raiding pact with the CIO, paving the way for the 1955 merger of the two organizations.

Susan Roth Breitzer

Further Reading

Kersten, Andrew Edmund. *Labor's Home Front: The American Federation of Labor during World War II.* New York: New York University Press, 2006.

Sinyai, Clayton. *Schools of Democracy: A Political History of the American Labor Movement.* Ithaca, N.Y.: Cornell University Press, 2006.

See also Business and the economy in the United States; Communist Party USA; Congress of Industrial Organizations; Income and wages; Labor strikes; National War Labor Board; New Deal programs; Smith-Connally Act; Taft-Hartley Act; Unemployment in the United States; Unionism.

■ American Negro Exposition

The Event Cultural event celebrating the achievements of black Americans since the 1863 Emancipation Proclamation

Date July 4-September 2, 1940

Place Chicago, Illinois

The exposition showed the diversity and vitality of black America at a time when racial discrimination often prevented this community's voice from being heard effectively and clearly on a national scale.

The nonprofit American Negro Exposition (also popularly known as the Diamond Jubilee Exposition) opened its doors at the Chicago Coliseum on July 4, 1940, for a two-month run under the slogan "celebrating 75 years of Negro achievement." The project was directed by attorney Truman K. Gibson and managed by a committee of three people, one appointed by Franklin D. Roosevelt and one each from the House of Representatives and the Senate, who worked with the Afra-Merican Emancipation Exposition Commission formed by Illinois governor Henry Horner. On May 25, 1940, President Roosevelt allocated $75,000 to the project, which was matched by the state of Illinois, and $15,000 was contributed by the Julius Rosenwald Fund. Enthusiasm

for the event quickly spread through black America, with cities and states creating local commissions to affiliate with the main exposition authority in Chicago.

The executives of the exposition contacted prominent members of the African American community, inviting them to make appearances as their schedules allowed, among them future Supreme Court justice Thurgood Marshall, at the time legal counsel for the National Association for the Advancement of Colored People (NAACP). The Illinois Writers' Project of the Works Progress Administration produced a companion volume to the exposition, the *Cavalcade of the American Negro*, under the editorship of Arna Bontemps. Illustrated by Adrian Troy of the Illinois Art Project, it provides a general if concise history of American black accomplishments between 1865 and 1940 and includes a description of all the exhibits mounted at the exposition. These included dioramas portraying the achievements of African Americans up to the end of the Civil War based on original drawings by artist William E. Scott, murals (among them the Fisk Jubilee Singers performing for Queen Victoria), and portraits of famous members of the black community, notably Robert Abbott, the recently deceased editor of the black weekly newspaper the *Chicago Defender.* Local history appeared in an exhibit on the black community as builders of Chicago (complete with a topographical map), while topical exhibits on aspects of the national black community ranged from public health, education, and art to eight federal agencies involved with community life. Major figures in the history and role of the black press in national progress were depicted in a mural by Charles White, while the sports exhibit was the personal contribution of boxing great Joe Louis. The exhibits represented the black communities of every American state, several Caribbean islands, and Liberia.

The planned disbanding of Chicago's unit of the federal theater was postponed to allow the troupe members to perform in "Cavalcade of the Negro Theater" and a second show, "Tropics After Dark," written by Bontemps and Langston Hughes. Weekly schedules containing an astonishing number of events were published in the *Defender,* ranging from days devoted to individual states and their black citizens to the work of black organizations as varied as the Urban League, the National Association of Negro Musicians, and the African Methodist Zion churches and Tuskegee Institute. The exposition organizers also originated the idea of a documentary on black schools and colleges, which was produced by the American Film Institute under the title *One Tenth of Our Nation* (1940).

Impact The sheer diversity and national scope of the American Negro Exposition eventually drew a crowd of 250,000, including a significant number of whites, far short of the two million predicted. Although the ongoing war in Europe would nearly erase the exposition from public consciousness, the two-month-long fair galvanized the black community.

Robert Ridinger

Further Reading

Green, Adam Paul. *Selling the Race: Cultural Production and Notions of Community in Black Chicago, 1940-1955.* Ph.D. dissertation, Yale University, 1998.

Rydell, Robert W. *World of Fairs: The Century-of-Progress Expositions.* Chicago: University of Chicago Press, 1993.

Writers' Program of the Work Projects Administration in the State of Illinois. *Cavalcade of the American Negro.* Chicago: Diamond Jubilee Exposition Authority, 1940.

See also African Americans; Negro Leagues; Race riots; Racial discrimination.

American Volunteer Group. *See* **Flying Tigers**

■ *Amos 'n' Andy*

Identification Popular radio series about two black southerners coping with life in a northern city

Creators Charles Correll (1890-1972) and Freeman Gosden (1899-1982)

Date Broadcast 1928-1955

The radio series Amos 'n' Andy, *which starred its white cocreators as two African Americans, was a significant cultural symbol and mass marketing phenomenon in American life during the mid-twentieth century.*

During the 1920's, Charles Correll and Freeman Gosden were a moderately well-known white musical duo who hosted minstrel and vaudeville shows for the Joe Bren performance company in small midwestern communities. Their work captured the attention of Ben McCanna, editor for the *Chicago Tribune*, who set out to create a radio theater replication of Sidney Smith's serial print cartoon "The Gumps." When McCanna approached Correll and Gosden to solicit their help in developing a show, the entertainers rejected his idea and instead proposed building a radio show around "Sam 'n' Henry," a minstrel act they had performed using African American southern dialect. On January 12, 1926, the show was picked up by local Chicago radio station WGN, a subsidiary of the *Tribune*.

The central plot of *Sam 'n' Henry* revolved around two black men from Birmingham Alabama who migrated to Chicago's South Side. Correll and Gosden portrayed Sam and Henry as stereotypically unsophisticated rural "sambos" who were ignorant about the complexities of northern urban milieus. These caricatures were rooted in the minstrel stage "blackface" performance tradition of the nineteenth century. Though genuine and honest, Sam was easily susceptible to Henry's tricks while the latter found comfort in alcohol and was prone to gambling and womanizing. WGN canceled the show after two years, but another Chicago station, WMAQ, took over the show in March, 1928.

Because they were no longer affiliated with WGN, Correll and Gosden were faced with the legal requirement of changing the name of their show. Amos Jones and Andrew H. Brown then replaced Sam and Henry. Correll and Gosden kept their original show's basic storyline intact. Situated in the poor community of Chicago's South Side (later in Harlem), the characters in *Amos 'n' Andy* naively grappled with the challenges of making ends meet while relying on a dilapidated taxi company. Their speech and those of their supporting cast members were presented through a host of mispronunciations and malapropisms. Gosden's portrayal of Amos fit well within the conventional "Tom" motif as an overly trusting dim-witted southerner with a childlike gullibility who repeatedly fell victim to the conniving exploits of Andy's "coon" persona.

The theme song for *Amos 'n' Andy* was borrowed from D. W. Griffith's 1915 film *The Birth of a Nation*, one of the first major films using stereotypical blackface characters to receive national attention. *Amos 'n' Andy*'s success on WMAQ piqued the interest of

Radio stars Charles Correll (left) and Freeman Gosden in blackface for promotional photographs. When Amos 'n' Andy *went on television, African American actors took over the roles.* (Getty Images)

were employed to reinvigorate the show. In 1943, the nightly radio format increased to thirty minutes and encompassed a broader ensemble of entertainment that included an orchestra and recordings before live audiences. More significantly, the show's use of racial stereotyping was even more exaggerated. Ratings rose again, and the show remained in the top ten.

Impact　Although responses to *Amos 'n' Andy* from African Americans varied, most African Americans agreed that the show was not truly reflective of their own lives. This sentiment was strongly voiced during the 1940's, when black soldiers fighting for the Allied forces across the seas also pushed for equality at home. This became known as the "Double V" campaign, as the desire to defeat the Axis Powers abroad matched the hope to knock down the bulwark of racism in their own backyards. Films, radio and print journalism became sites of organized critique. However, *Amos 'n' Andy* was such a success that networks and advertisers were unwilling to seriously consider pulling the plug until the next decade, when the show expanded to television and used an African American cast.

Jermaine Archer

executives of the National Broadcasting Company (NBC), which acquired the programming rights in 1929 just two months before the stock market crashed. During the 1930's, NBC's fifteen-minute show drew more than one-half of the radio audience with as many as forty million listeners six nights a week. It was the top-ranked radio show throughout the Great Depression.

Wartime Changes　When the popularity of *Amos 'n' Andy* began to lose momentum during World War II because of competition from a rising number of vaudeville acts hitting the airwaves, two strategies

Further Reading

Andrews, Bart, and Ahrgus Julliard. *Holy Mackerel: The Amos 'n' Andy Story.* New York: Penguin, 1986.

Bogle, Donald. *Primetime Blues: African Americans on Network Television.* New York: Farrar, Straus and Giroux, 2001.

Ely, Melvin Patrick. *The Adventures of Amos and Andy: A Social History of an American Phenomenon.* Charlottesville: University of Virginia Press, 2001.

See also　Abbott and Costello; African Americans; Benny, Jack; Radio in Canada; Radio in the United States; *Stormy Weather.*

■ Andrews Sisters

Identification   Close-harmony singing trio

LaVerne Sophia Andrews
Born   July 6, 1911; Minneapolis, Minnesota
Died   May 8, 1967; Brentwood, California

Maxene Angelyn Andrews
Born   January 3, 1916; Minneapolis, Minnesota
Died   October 21, 1995; Hyannis, Massachusetts

Patricia "Patty" Marie Andrews
Born   February 16, 1918; Minneapolis, Minnesota

The Andrews Singers were the top-selling popular vocal group in the world before the Beatles; they entertained millions of Americans through their radio broadcasts and live appearances as well as thousands of troops on their frequent United Service Organizations (USO) tours.

The Andrews Sisters—LaVerne, Maxene, and Patty—began their careers in their native Minneapolis but quickly hit the big time in 1937 with their close harmonization of the Yiddish song "Bei Mir Bist Du Schön," which sold one million copies. By the 1940's, they were well known to American audiences. Between 1944 and 1951, they had their own radio shows. The trio toured extensively during World War II to entertain the troops and helped establish the Hollywood Canteen.

The Andrews Sisters specialized in boogie-woogie and swing numbers, but they recorded everything from gospel to polkas, Hawaiian music, and ballads. During their career, they recorded more than six hundred songs, reached the top ten on the *Billboard* charts more often than Elvis or the Beatles, and made seventeen motion pictures.

Impact   The Andrews Sisters revolutionized pop singing in the 1940's and influenced many later artists, including the Supremes, the Pointer Sisters, Bette Midler, and the Manhattan Transfer.

David E. Anderson

Further Reading

Andrews, Maxene. *Over Here, Over There: The Andrews Sisters and the USO Stars in World War II*. New York: Kensington, 2005.

Nimmo, H. Arlo. *The Andrews Sisters: A Biography and Career Record*. Jefferson, N.C.: McFarland, 2004.

Sforza, John. *Swing It! The Andrews Sisters Story*. 2d ed. Lexington: University Press of Kentucky, 2004.

See also   Abbott and Costello; Film in the United States; Music: Popular; Radio in the United States; Recording industry; United Service Organizations; War bonds.

■ Andy Hardy films

Identification   Series of sixteen Hollywood films depicting family life in middle America
Date   Released from 1937 through 1958

This low-budget film series showcased the Hardys, an upper-middle-class midwestern family with two children. The films were sentimental comedies that tackled serious subjects, chronicling the moral education of Andy Hardy, and helped to make their star, Mickey Rooney, one of the most popular American film actors.

The Andy Hardy film series began in 1937 with *A Family Affair*, based on Aurania Rouverol's play *Skidding*. The film's popularity convinced Louis B. Mayer to create a series based on the Hardy family: Judge Hardy, the father; Emily Hardy, the mother; Marian Hardy, Andy's older sister; and Andrew (Andy) Hardy, the teenage son. They lived in Carvel, Idaho, a fictitious town, which Mayer hoped would look like the ideal middle-American hometown.

The first three installments were about the entire family, but by the fourth installment, Andy, played by Mickey Rooney, was the focus of the series. His comic adventures and sweet disposition made him a favorite of the American public. In the fourth film, *Love Finds Andy Hardy* (1938), the series developed its trademark formula. Andy would get into some minor trouble, usually with his friend Beezy. Together, they would try to avoid getting caught and would invariably end up in more trouble. At that point, Andy would seek out Judge Hardy for a man-to-man talk. The Judge, who embodied the American ideals of truth and justice and who believed in equal treatment under the law for all citizens, would gently teach Andy that only by doing the right thing was it possible to become a decent man. Andy would listen to this advice, face the repercussions of his actions, and fix whatever mischief he caused. The crises the family faced were all of a domestic nature and might seem trivial to a modern audience; however, the family values of coming together to solve a problem and turning to loved ones for advice and support were greatly admired in their day and shone a light on the moral values of 1940's America.

The original series ended in 1947, with *Love Laughs at Andy Hardy*. In 1958, the unsuccessful *Andy Hardy Comes Home*, a reunion film aimed at continuing the series, was released. Although it ended with the words "to be continued," no other Andy Hardy film was ever made.

Impact The Andy Hardy films were characterized by a belief in American values and the power of law. Judge Hardy, the moral center of the films, always dispensed advice based on his deep patriotism and love of the law. The character was a practicing judge, often in Washington on special legal business. His devotion to his family and his earnest ways of instilling morality in his children made him a beloved American icon. In *Love Finds Andy Hardy*, the Judge, wanting Andy to understand the value of money, takes him around to see how the less fortunate live and what money could do to help if used for charity rather than personal desires. This film is the most popular of the series and remains insightful into 1940's American values. In 1941, the family was commemorated by setting their hand- and footprints into the cement outside Grauman's Chinese Theatre in Hollywood, in a ceremony calling the Hardys "the first family of Hollywood." In 1943, the series received a special Oscar for depicting American life at its most ideal.

Leslie Neilan

Mickey Rooney (right) driving a jalopy used in the Andy Hardy films, with series regular Ann Rutherford (center), and Judy Garland in August, 1941. The three young actors are arriving at the premiere of a new film, to which all the families in Hollywood named "Hardy" have been invited as special guests. (AP/Wide World Photos)

Further Reading

Ray, Robert B. *The Avant-Garde Films of Andy Hardy.* Cambridge, Mass.: Harvard University Press, 1995.

Zinman, David. *Saturday Afternoon at the Bijou: A Nostalgic Look at Charlie Chan, Andy Hardy, and Other Movie Heroes We Have Known and Loved.* London: Arlington House, 1973.

See also Disney films; Film in the United States; Film serials; Garland, Judy; *It's a Wonderful Life*; Maisie films; *Meet Me in St. Louis*; *National Velvet*; Rooney, Mickey.

■ Animated films

During the 1940's, Walt Disney Productions and animation units located within or associated with Hollywood studios produced a steady stream of audience-pleasing animated films. Cartoons cheered the troops at war and were a beloved part of entertainment that millions of Americans enjoyed at their local film theaters.

Although animated film production began in the earliest days of filmmaking, it was the technical marriage of sound (voice, sound effects, and music) and fast-paced imagery, along with the industrial context of a Hollywood studio system with huge staffs and facilities during the 1930's and 1940's, that provided the environment for the golden age of the American cartoon. Characters that became familiar to and beloved by filmgoers included Mickey Mouse, Donald Duck, and Goofy from Disney; Porky Pig, Daffy Duck, Bugs Bunny, and the Road Runner from the Leon Schlesinger studio associated with Warner Bros.; Tom and Jerry from the Bill Hanna and Joe Barbera unit at Metro-Goldwyn-Mayer (MGM); Popeye and Superman from Max and Dave Fleischer at Paramount; Andy Panda and Woody Woodpecker, created by the Walter Lantz studio, and dozens of others. Cartoons built on the silent film traditions of slapstick comedy, exaggerating the action and comedic violence of live-action films to unprecedented, hilarious extremes.

Feature-Length Films   The great commercial and artistic success of the first full-length studio feature animation—*Snow White and the Seven Dwarfs* (1937)—encouraged the Disney studio to produce thirteen full-length animated features during the 1940's, the most celebrated of which were *Pinocchio* (1940), *Fantasia* (1940), *Dumbo* (1941), and *Bambi* (1942). In contrast to the traditional storytelling of other features, *Fantasia* presented extravagant visual sequences set to classical music, each with a distinctive style and with no unifying narrative line. This groundbreaking feature film was first conceptualized as a short, with Mickey Mouse dramatizing the musical piece "The Sorcerer's Apprentice," in the tradition of Disney's popular Silly Symphonies series (1929-1939). Hugely expensive, at a cost of $2.28 million, and boldly innovative, *Fantasia* was not profitable until its rerelease decades later.

In 1941, animators at the Disney studio, blocked from unionizing by Walt Disney, went on strike. In 1943, some of the strikers founded a studio, United Productions of America (UPA), that would revolutionize the look of American animation. UPA animators advanced a form of limited animation, featuring a flat, stylized, graphic look that contrasted with the three-dimensionality and realism of Disney cartoons. The content of UPA cartoons also shifted from the sentimental stories and anthropomorphized animals that characterized Disney products to a more politically engaged approach. Satire often shaped the escapades of UPA's most popular characters, Mr. Magoo (who first appeared on film in 1949) and Gerald McBoing-Boing (who first appeared on film in 1950).

Cartoons and the War Effort   During World War II, cartoons provided a dynamic and pliable resource for war-related messages to boost morale and provide entertainment both for troops and for those on the home front. Disney and Warner Bros. released their first war-themed short cartoons in January, 1942, shortly after the United States entered the war. Donald Duck won an Oscar for Disney with *Der Fuehrer's Face* (1942), Tom and Jerry picked up a statuette for MGM with *Yankee Doodle Mouse* (1943), and Popeye led the troops at Paramount. The popular Warner Bros. Looney Tunes series first moved to color with *Daffy-The Commando* (1943). A topical war bond short, *Bugs Bunny's Bond Rally* (1942), featured Bugs and his buddies Daffy Duck and Porky Pig urging Americans to buy war bonds. Many animators worked on training films as part of the Eighteenth Air Force Base Unit; a group of them created a foul-up soldier, Private Snafu, whom they featured in a series of cartoons shown exclusively to American soldiers. A home-front live-action feature, *Anchors Aweigh* (1945), showcased the animated characters Tom and Jerry dancing with film star Gene Kelly.

The Demise of Theatrical Cartoon Shorts   Three factors led to the demise of theatrical cartoon shorts, films of around seven minutes in length shown with feature presentations. First, the animation union successfully negotiated a 25 percent pay increase in 1946, adding to production costs. Second, a 1948 U.S. Supreme Court decision prohibited the studio practice of "block booking," by which theater owners had been able to schedule feature films only if they agreed to an exhibition package that included a cartoon, newsreel, or live-action short. After the 1948 ruling, theater owners were willing to pay only small fees for cartoon bookings, amounts that could not sustain profitable cartoon production. The third blow to cartoon shorts was the growth of television, which would become the new showcase for cartoons. Studios sold the rights to broadcast their cartoons to television. Film cartoons entertained all ages of filmgoers, but cartoons developed for television forged an association with children's programming.

An important exception to the television connection between cartoons and children occurred in advertising. During the 1940's, short, clever animated ads and parts of ads began to appear on broadcast television. The Jam Handy Organization, founded by Henry Jamison "Jam" Handy, produced a series of

Walt Disney (left) and singer/actor Nelson Eddy studying the musical score of the 1946 film Make Mine Music, *a compilation of Disney cartoons for which Eddy provided the narration and several character voices.* (Getty Images)

delightful cartoon ads for Chevrolet and AT&T. Probably Handy's most memorable ad, from 1948, featured the inventive stop-motion animation of "dancing cigarettes" for Lucky Strike.

Impact Endearing and enduring cartoon characters created in or showcased during the 1940's became synonymous with American popular culture worldwide. Cartoons projected a vision of America as fast-moving, self-confident, direct, energetic, optimistic, and fun-loving. The Hollywood studios that produced cartoons depended on a large, skilled workforce. Decades later, computer animation techniques came to predominate, taking over many of the formerly labor-intensive tasks involved in producing an animated film.

Carolyn Anderson

Further Reading

Barrier, Michael. *Hollywood Cartoons: American Animation in Its Golden Age.* New York: Oxford University Press, 1999. Expert analysis, built on more than two hundred interviews. "Flip books" within the text demonstrate three animation styles. Extensive notes.

Bendazzi, Gianalberto. *Cartoons: One Hundred Years of Cinema Animation.* Bloomington: Indiana University Press, 1994. Excellent overview of animation from around the world. More than five hundred oversized pages, with thirty-four pages of color plates; hundreds of black-and-white illustrations.

Lenburg, Jeff. *The Encyclopedia of Animated Cartoons.* New York: Facts On File, 1991. A condensed history of the American cartoon is followed by more than four hundred pages of useful, alphabetized entries. Includes many images and a listing of Academy and Emmy Awards relevant to animation.

Maltin, Leonard. *Of Mice and Magic: A History of American Animated Cartoons.* New York: New American Library, 1987. Organized by Hollywood studio, with a concentration on theatrical cartoons. Includes studio filmographies, listings of Academy Award nominees and winners, many illustrations (some in color), and a glossary of animation terms.

Solomon, Charles. *Enchanted Drawings: The History of Animation.* New York: Alfred A. Knopf, 1989. A lavishly illustrated, beautifully designed, oversized book, with considerable attention to the 1940's. Emphasis on American animation.

See also Advertising in the United States; Andy Hardy films; Comic books; Comic strips; Disney films; *Fantasia*; Film in the United States; Films about World War II; Kelly, Gene; Unionism.

■ Antibiotics

Definition Natural or synthetic compounds that kill or inhibit the growth of disease-causing microorganisms

Prior to the discovery of the first antibiotic, penicillin, virtually no treatment existed for bacterial infections. The isolation and mass production of several different antibiotics during the 1940's ushered in a promising age of medical therapy that would save millions of lives.

Infectious diseases are the most common afflictions of humans, but before the 1940's doctors' ability to treat them was limited. Popular folklore advocated the use of molds to treat cuts to prevent infection, and the sulfa drugs had also been discovered, but this was the extent of the medicinal arsenal. The demands of World War II accelerated the search for new battlefield therapies. The subsequent discovery of antibiotics, the rise of clinical science, and the resulting pharmaceutical revolution would redefine medical science during the 1940's, especially in the United States. This decade alone saw the discovery of chemical agents effective against a wide range of bacterial infections, including well-known killers such as pneumonia and tuberculosis (TB). Among these

new wonder drugs were penicillin (1940), streptomycin (1943/1944), chloramphenicol (1947), tetracycline (1948), cephalosporin (1948), and neomycin (1949).

Penicillin In 1929, Alexander Fleming accidentally discovered the toxic properties of penicillin, a soluble chemical produced by the fungus *Penicillium notatum*. Though he made note of penicillin's activity, Fleming took his discovery no further. In 1940, two Oxford scientists, Howard Florey and Ernst Chain, rediscovered Fleming's work, soon proving that penicillin could kill the organisms that caused diphtheria, anthrax, tetanus, syphilis, pneumonia, and bacterial meningitis. By 1941, they had produced enough penicillin to test it on a forty-three-year-old constable, Albert Alexander, who was dying of bacterial sepsis. Alexander's treatment was phenomenally successful, but he died when physicians ran out of penicillin. At the time, British companies were focused on the war effort, and there were fears of a German invasion, so Florey took his penicillin stocks to the United States, where four pharmaceutical companies agreed to begin producing the antibiotic.

By 1943, British companies had joined the effort, and by D Day, 1944, there was enough penicillin available to treat all Allied service personnel across

Selman Abraham Waksman. (©The Nobel Foundation)

The Action of Antibiotics

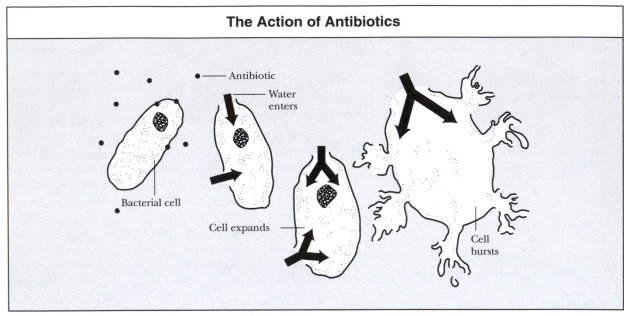

An antibiotic destroys a bacterium by causing its cell walls to deteriorate; water then enters the bacterium unchecked until it bursts.

all theaters of operation. Thousands of soldiers received penicillin, and their treatment helped to define the effective use and dosage requirements of the new drug. Battlefield infections were greatly curtailed, and postoperative infections dropped dramatically. By the end of 1944, penicillin was being made available to civilians, and mortality rates from infections such as pneumonia dropped from pretreatment highs of 30 percent to less than 6 percent. In 1945, Fleming, Florey, and Chain received the Nobel Prize in Physiology or Medicine for their work on penicillin.

Streptomycin and Tuberculosis Microbiologist Selman A. Waksman, working at Rutgers University during the 1920's and 1930's, began a series of comprehensive screening studies on soil microorganisms that, in 1940, resulted in the discovery of actinomycin, a drug effective against bacteria but too toxic for human use. Continued work led to the discovery of streptothricin in 1942, also toxic, and streptomycin in 1943. Streptomycin, isolated from *Streptomyces griseus,* was less toxic and was effective against dysentery, pneumonia, and whooping cough. More important, however, was its effectiveness against *Mycobacterium tuberculosis,* the causative agent of TB.

Merck and Company began rapid manufacture of

streptomycin, and in 1944, William H. Feldman and H. Corwin Hinshaw of the Mayo Clinic began human trials. The first patient treated was a twenty-one-year-old girl with advanced pulmonary TB; she received five courses of streptomycin over the course of 1944-1945 and was released from care in 1947 with an arrested case of the disease. Between 1946 and 1948, the Tuberculosis Trials in Great Britain set the gold standard for randomized, controlled human research trials, establishing the efficacy of streptomycin while at the same time demonstrating the first evidence for the evolution of bacterial drug resistance. Dual therapy with streptomycin and para-amino-salicylic acid (PAS) was soon found to be 80 percent effective in arresting TB, offering hope that tuberculosis might one day be eradicated.

Impact Before the advent of antibiotics, war-related deaths were often due to infections, but World War II saw the end of this phenomenon. Antibiotics not only saved lives but also reduced permanent disability and thus altered the course of the war. On the home front, antibiotics made it easier to survive childhood infections and greatly reduced deaths due to severe infectious diseases such as pneumonia and tuberculosis. American and British medical research during the 1940's paved the way for the discovery of more antibiotics and led to a revolution in medicine. Though antibiotic resistance remains a serious threat to the efficacy of these miracle drugs in the early twenty-first century, the importance of antibiotics cannot be understated. Their discovery revived the perception that science offered much promise to the world.

Elizabeth A. Machunis-Masuoka

Further Reading

Barry, Clifton E., III, and Maija S. Cheung. "New Tactics Against Tuberculosis." *Scientific American* 300, no. 3 (March, 2009): 62-69. Describes the struggle to find new antibiotics to combat drug-resistant tuberculosis. History, current research, and sociological aspects of the disease.

Lax, Eric. *The Mold in Dr. Florey's Coat: The Story of the Penicillin Miracle.* Boston: Little, Brown, 2004. Describes the development of penicillin into the first medically available treatment against bacterial infection. History of discovery, manufacturing, and first uses during World War II.

Porter, Roy. *The Greatest Benefit to Mankind: A Medical History of Humanity.* New York: W. W. Norton, 1997. The definitive history of medicine for a general readership. Covers history from ancient times to the late twentieth century. Extensive bibliography.

Ryan, Frank. *The Forgotten Plague: How the Battle Against Tuberculosis Was Won—and Lost.* Boston: Little, Brown, 1993. Biographical sketches of the scientists involved in the search for a cure for tuberculosis, history of the disease, and documentation of the rise of drug-resistant tuberculosis. Streptomycin features prominently in this account.

Waksman, Selman A. *The Conquest of Tuberculosis.* Berkeley: University of California Press, 1964. Autobiography in which Waksman relates his discovery of streptomycin and its effects on tuberculosis. Photos and bibliography.

See also Casualties of World War II; Health care; Medicine; Nobel Prizes; Tuskegee syphilis study; World Health Organization.

■ Anticommunism

Definition Sentiments against communism and retaliation against U.S. citizens suspected of being communists, amid fears that the Soviet Union was a serious threat to the United States

The late 1940's marked the beginning of the Second Red Scare, with the United States gripped by a wave of hysteria that communists were planning to take over the country. As the Soviet Union sought to gain political, economic, social, and cultural dominance in the world, fear led to purging of communists from U.S. public life.

The fear associated with the First Red Scare abated over time because after World War I, communism did not pose a direct threat to the United States. Even though the Soviet Union was an ally of the United States during World War II, it remained an ideological opponent, and the alliance quickly dissolved as the war neared its end. Key events and movements, such as the Soviet domination of Eastern Europe, the fall of China to communism, and the Soviet testing of an atomic bomb years earlier than U.S. scientists had anticipated convinced many Americans that communism posed a real threat of taking a foothold in the United States, leading to the Second Red Scare.

In March, 1947, President Harry S. Truman created the federal employees Loyalty Program, which established a political loyalty review board. This board had the authority to investigate federal employees and to recommend the firing of those found to be "un-American." The creation of the Loyalty Program has been considered to be a major factor in the development of the anticommunist hysteria during the 1940's because its very existence enhanced and legitimized American anticommunism fears. Some historians believe that the anticommunist attacks of the 1940's actually were politically motivated assaults by the Republican Party on President Franklin D. Roosevelt's New Deal policies because the primary targets of these investigations were liberals, labor unions, and religious organizations.

The military revealed that it had partially broken more than two thousand coded Soviet intelligence messages about an extensive Soviet espionage operation against the United States that included some high-ranking U.S. government officials. As a result, the Federal Bureau of Investigation (FBI) began investigating the Communist Party USA. In 1948, the FBI concluded its investigation that accused the Communist Party USA of violating the Smith Act of 1940, which made it illegal to advocate the overthrow of the government. The subsequent trials resulted in the 1949 convictions of the national leadership of the Communist Party. The House Committee on Un-American Activities (HUAC) conducted its own investigations that included former U.S. State Department official Alger Hiss in 1948, and it held hearings to determine if communists also had infiltrated the film industry. Eventually, more than three hundred actors and directors would be "blacklisted" by the studios because of the HUAC investigations.

Impact Anticommunism was the major issue during the 1948 presidential election, and the Second Red Scare continued to gain momentum well into the next decade, when Senator Joseph McCarthy brandished his list of accused communists. In the late 1990's, classified information was made public concerning Soviet espionage in the United States during the 1940's. Some historians who reexamined the evidence pertaining to both the accused Soviet spies and their accusers concluded that despite denials, some U.S. citizens did spy for the Soviet Union throughout the New Deal and war years, lending some credibility to the fears that had gripped the United States.

Eddith A. Dashiell

Further Reading

Hayes, John Earl. *Red Scare or Red Menace? American Communism and Anticommunism in the Cold War Era.* Chicago: Ivan R. Dee, 1996.

Schmidt, Regin. *Red Scare: FBI and the Origins of Anticommunism in the United States, 1919-1943.* Copenhagen: Museum Tusculanum Press, 2000.

Weinstein, Allen, and Alexander Vassiliev. *The Haunted Wood: Soviet Espionage in America—The Stalin Era.* New York: Random House, 1999.

See also Cold War; Communist Party USA; Federal Bureau of Investigation; Hiss, Alger; Hollywood blacklisting; House Committee on Un-American Activities; Smith Act; Smith Act trials; Socialist Workers Party; Supreme Court, U.S.

■ Appalachian Spring

Identification Pulitzer Prize-winning ballet
Creators Composed by Aaron Copland (1900-1990); choreographed by Martha Graham (1894-1991)
Date Premiered in 1944

Appalachian Spring captures the ideals of the American pioneering spirit through Graham's choreography and Copland's musical scoring. The ballet was an instant success, leading to a Pulitzer Prize in music (the third in the history of the category) and a Music Critics' Circle of New York award.

Commissioned by the Elizabeth Coolidge Foundation, *Appalachian Spring* came to fruition through the collaboration of composer Aaron Copland and dancer-choreographer Martha Graham. The ballet is based on the pioneering spirit of a newlywed couple settling into the frontier lands of Pennsylvania during the early nineteenth century. Copland's score helped establish his reputation as the first composer with a distinctly American style. The most notable element to this style is the use of the Shaker hymn "Simple Gifts." The premiere of the ballet took place in the Coolidge Auditorium at the Library of Congress in Washington, D.C., and featured a small ensemble of thirteen instrumentalists. In addition to her choreography, Graham performed the principal role of the Bride and suggested the title for the ballet (based on the title to a Hart Crane poem). Japanese American artist Isamu Noguchi created a minimalistic and Shaker-inspired set design that reinforced the openness of the frontier and Copland's scoring. A full orchestral suite was arranged by Copland in 1945 and is frequently performed by professional orchestras.

Impact Capturing the excitement of open landscapes and unlimited opportunities, *Appalachian Spring* embodies the spirit of the American experience. Its success in the 1940's was the beginning of widespread and ongoing popularity for Aaron Copland as a distinctly American composer.

L. Keith Lloyd, III

Further Reading

Crist, Elizabeth B. *Music for the Common Man: Aaron Copland During the Depression and War.* New York: Oxford University Press, 2005.

Smith, Julia. *Aaron Copland: His Work and Contribu-*

tion to American Music. New York: E. P. Dutton, 1955.

See also   Art of This Century; Ballet Society; Bernstein, Leonard; Music: Classical; *Rodeo.*

■ Arcadia Conference

The Event   First strategic conference, after the attack on Pearl Harbor, of the president of the United States and prime minister of Great Britain, along with delegations from other countries
Also known as   First Washington Conference
Date   December 22, 1941-January 14, 1942
Place   Washington, D.C.

The Arcadia Conference resulted in the Anglo-American agreement that the defeat of Germany had priority over the war in the Pacific against Japan. It also committed Great Britain and the United States to the establishment of a new international organization, the United Nations, initiated the use of summit meetings for the formulation of allied strategy, and contributed to the development of a working relationship between President Franklin D. Roosevelt and British prime minister Winston S. Churchill.

Winston Churchill arrived in Washington, D.C., during the evening of December 22, 1941, fifteen days after the Japanese attack on Pearl Harbor. With the exception of a trip to Ottawa to address the Canadian Parliament and a five-day vacation in Palm Beach, Florida, Churchill resided in the White House until January 14, 1942. Building on principles advanced in the Atlantic Charter (1941), Roosevelt and Churchill agreed to establish a new international organization, the United Nations. In addition to developing a close working and personal relationship, Roosevelt and Churchill and their staffs established a framework for the Combined Chiefs of Staff Committee (CCOS), which emerged shortly after the conference. Unlike Roosevelt, who deferred to his military experts on military matters, Churchill was actively involved in all aspects of military strategy and tactics—often much to the dismay of British generals. Roosevelt and Churchill agreed to establish Operation Sledgehammer, for the building of an overwhelming offensive force in Britain for operations in Europe. Before the conference concluded, it was agreed that four American divi-

sions would continue their training in Northern Ireland.

Churchill's address to a joint session of the U.S. Congress on December 26, 1941, established his reputation as the leader of a trusted and committed ally. That evening, Churchill suffered a heart attack that was kept secret from everyone except his physician. Undaunted, and with little sleep, Churchill went through the next several days effectively, with his doctor close behind. Churchill's successful speech in Washington was followed by another oratorical triumph when he addressed Canada's Parliament in Ottawa on December 30.

During the conference, the only point of seeming disagreement—it was never raised—emerged when Churchill argued for the restoration of the British Empire after the war. Roosevelt, an anti-imperialist, had no intention of preserving the colonial empires of the past.

On January 14, 1942, the Arcadia Conference concluded, and Churchill departed for London, via Bermuda. To many, the special relationship between the United States and the United Kingdom was sealed irrevocably during these deliberations in Washington.

Impact   The Arcadia Conference, attended by leaders from twenty-six countries, established precedent for the processes and procedures for meetings of the Allied heads of state during World War II. Roosevelt and Churchill, although they differed in their opinions on the future of the British Empire and other colonial empires, agreed on the basic tenets of the United Nations and that they would conduct the war against Germany and Japan until those powers were defeated. They endorsed the Atlantic Charter and agreed not to make a separate peace against the enemies of Germany and Japan, without the agreement of their allies.

William T. Walker

Further Reading
D'este, Carlo. *Warlord: A Life of Winston Churchill at War, 1874-1945.* New York: Harper, 2008.
Keegan, John. *The Second World War.* New York: Penguin, 2005.
Smith, Jean Edward. *FDR.* New York: Random House, 2008.

See also   Cairo Conference; Canada and Great Britain; Canadian participation in World War II; Casablanca Conference; Churchill, Winston; Decolonization of European empires; Marshall, George C.; Paris Peace Conference of 1946; Potsdam Conference; Roosevelt, Franklin D.; United Nations.

■ Arcaro, Eddie

Identification   Jockey
Born   February 19, 1916; Cincinnati, Ohio
Died   November 14, 1997; Miami, Florida

Arcaro was the premier jockey of the 1940's and is arguably the greatest jockey in the history of American thoroughbred horse racing. Known as "The Master," he is the only jockey to win the Triple Crown twice.

After winning his first horse race in 1932, Eddie Arcaro won the Kentucky Derby in 1938. In 1941, he rode Whirlaway to victories in the Kentucky Derby, the Preakness Stakes, and the Belmont Stakes, earning his first Triple Crown title. A very competitive, powerful rider, Arcaro was suspended from horse racing after knocking another rider off his horse during a race in New York in 1942. Through the intervention of Helen Hay Whitney, the powerful owner of the Greentree Stables, Arcaro was later reinstated by the U.S. Jockey Club.

During the early 1940's, Arcaro cofounded the Jockey's Guild, an organization that helps injured riders obtain disability assistance and guards against horse abuse and race fixing. Arcaro won his third Kentucky Derby in 1945. In 1948, he won his second Triple Crown aboard Citation, one of the greatest race horses of all time. He served as the president of the Jockey's Guild from 1949 until 1961.

Impact   Arcaro won more American classic horse races than any other jockey in history. He won 4,779 races and earned more than $30 million. He won the Kentucky Derby five times, the Preakness Stakes six times, and the Belmont Stakes six times. He set the standard, and he was an inspiration and a mentor to many younger jockeys.

Alvin K. Benson

Further Reading

Drager, Marvin. *The Most Glorious Crown: The Story of America's Triple Crown Thoroughbreds from Sir Barton to Affirmed.* Chicago: Triumph Books, 2005.

Hirsch, Joe, and Jim Bolus. *Kentucky Derby: The Chance of a Lifetime.* New York: McGraw-Hill, 1988.

See also   Gambling; Horse racing; Recreation; Sports in Canada; Sports in the United States.

■ Archaeology

Definition   The scientific study of human culture through the analysis of material remains, monuments, and sites

Throughout the 1940's, archaeologists were motivated by the importance of documenting sites threatened by urban development or those of cultural and historic significance. Rescue or salvage archaeology became a necessity for keeping much of the archaeological record from obscurity. The later years of the decade also saw the birth of a new era in archaeological methodology.

Archaeology in the 1940's bore the fruits of Depression-era relief programs designed to encourage archaeological investigation. These programs had been popular because they employed large numbers of people, offered no competition to private industry, and could increase the understanding

Eddie Arcaro riding Citation home to win the Belmont Stakes in 1948—the year in which Citation won the Triple Crown. (AP/Wide World Photos)

of the nation's past. Results, however, were mixed. On one hand, information about many sites increased substantially and fieldwork provided experience for a whole generation of archaeologists; on the other hand, archaeologists were criticized for their lack of professionalism and incomplete postexcavation documentation. These projects came to an end in 1942 after the United States joined the World War II effort, but their impact was not forgotten.

Postwar Administration of Resources The concerns raised over archaeological projects associated with federal work relief programs of the 1930's and early 1940's led to the creation of an advocacy group, the Committee for the Recovery of Archaeological Remains (CRAR), in April of 1945. One of CRAR's first actions was to lobby for rescue archaeology to be included as part of any new development projects. Later that year, the National Park Service (NPS) organized the Interagency Archeological Salvage Program (IASP) in order to implement a program of salvage archaeology and surveys in the river basins throughout the United States that were threatened by flooding from proposed reservoir projects. To improve on the methodology of the prewar years, the IASP also worked to create a network of institutional relationships to manage its efforts: The NPS had legislative responsibilities, while the Smithsonian Institution conducted scientific research alongside capable state and local museums, historical societies, and universities.

Foremost among federal projects was the Missouri Basin Project (MBP), which surveyed about 500,000 square miles over twenty-four years, beginning in 1946. The MBP firmly established the subfield of Plains archaeology, and its archaeological practices shaped the research ideology over the next thirty years.

The often-overlooked archaeological survey of the Lower Mississippi Alluvial Valley (1940-1947) not only documented the Mississippi Valley but also was ahead of its time for its regional research plan, account of settlement forms, and discussions of seriation. For many sites within the region, it remains the only scientific exploration ever done.

Canada Despite the promising interest in archaeology during the early twentieth century, archaeology became a low priority in Canada in the 1930's and 1940's. After World War II, prehistoric archaeologists concentrated on establishing cultural chronologies for all of Canada. Although Kenneth Kidd of the Royal Ontario Museum conducted the first scientific excavations of a historical site (the early Jesuit Mission Sainte-Marie among the Hurons, in southern Canada) between 1941 and 1943, it was not until the years between 1947 and 1951 that excavations were completed and the findings published. The resulting monograph was a milestone for historical archaeology in all of North America.

Theory and Methodology Archaeology in the United States and Canada at the beginning of the 1940's was motivated by a need to establish regional artifact typologies and chronologies in order to define cultural histories. About 1946, University of Chicago chemist Willard F. Libby developed the technique of radiocarbon (carbon-14) dating—a method that uses the radioactive isotope carbon 14 to determine the age of an ancient artifact. He published his findings in 1949. The radiocarbon technique proved to have multiple uses and allowed comparisons locally, regionally, and globally. In the years following its discovery, radiocarbon dating determined that settlement of the Americas occurred 11,000 years ago, and the dating also filled the chronological gaps with later cultural groups. The discovery of radiocarbon dating was the single most important contribution to the field of archaeology during the 1940's and laid the foundation for methodological and theoretical maturation in the field in succeeding decades.

No less innovative was Walter Taylor's appeal for a more rigorous and holistic approach to archaeology, which he laid out in his *A Study of Archaeology* (1948). Taylor criticized North American archaeologists as being too concerned with the classification of artifacts and chronology at the expense of understanding cultural and social changes. Most scholars either became further entrenched in their methodology or dismissed Taylor altogether. Taylor would ultimately be vindicated in the 1960's with the advent of "new archaeology," which was rooted in the scientific and anthropocentric approach he advocated.

Impact The archaeological innovations of the 1940's helped shape the direction of field research in the United States and Canada, while the new scientific methodology for dating became a cornerstone for all areas of archaeology. The need for cooperative efforts between archaeologists and officials at the federal, state, and local levels allowed archaeology to become an integral voice in the shaping of the cultural identity of the United States.

Victor M. Martinez

Further Reading

Dunnell, Robert C. "Archaeological Survey in the Lower Mississippi Alluvial Valley, 1940-1947: A Landmark Study in American Archaeology." *American Antiquity* 50, no. 2 (April, 1985): 297-300. Reassesses the project's importance for American archaeology.

Marlowe, Greg. "Year One: Radiocarbon Dating and American Archaeology, 1947-1948." *American Antiquity* 64, no. 1 (January, 1999): 9-32. Summarizes the initial discovery of radiocarbon dating and the response by archaeologists to the news and its utility.

Taylor, Walter W. *A Study of Archaeology.* Carbondale: Southern Illinois University Press, 1983. Originally published in 1948, this is the seventh reprinting of Taylor's influential and polemical critique of American archaeology. Many of the ideas that Taylor advocated became cornerstones of later archaeological theory.

Thiessen, Thomas D. *Emergency Archeology in the Missouri River Basin: The Role of the Missouri Basin Project and the Midwest Archeological Center in the Interagency Archeological Salvage Program, 1946-1975.* Lincoln, Nebr.: U.S. Deptartment of the Interior, National Park Service, Midwest Archeological Center, 1999. A history of archaeology in the heartland of America derived from archival sources.

Willey, Gordon R., and Jeremy A. Sabloff. *A History of American Archaeology.* 3d ed. New York: W. H. Freeman, 1993. A good overview of the theoretical and methodological developments of American archaeology set within a historical framework.

See also Carbon dating; Education in Canada; Education in the United States; Science and technology.

■ Architecture

Definition The design and building of structures, especially habitable ones

The decade of the 1940's was a crucial transitional period for architecture in the United States and Canada. Revival styles and early attempts at modernism characterized the be-

ginning of the decade. After World War II, a new modernist style of design, called the International Style, was widely embraced. Its influence was pervasive, extending from commercial skyscrapers to modest suburban housing.

Between 1939 and 1941, the United States experienced an active and diverse architectural scene. Some architects worked to develop a modern design vocabulary, while others chose to work in historic architectural styles adapted to the needs and technologies of modern life. In these same years, an increasing interest in architectural heritage sparked the initiation of research into, and preservation of, eighteenth and early nineteenth century architecture. With the founding of the Society of Architectural Historians (SAH) in 1940 and the productive work of several federal agencies, including the Historic American Buildings Survey (HABS) of the National Park Service (NPS), the emphasis on historic preservation increased throughout the decade.

The 1940's also witnessed the rising influence of high modernism. After several prominent European modernist architects assumed leadership roles at major architectural institutions in the United States, it was not long before their aesthetic of stripped-down geometric forms and industrial materials came to be considered the avant-garde of commercial, industrial, and domestic architecture. In the years immediately preceding World War II, and resuming shortly thereafter, the United States experienced a significant increase in urban population, such that the development of suburban communities came to be of paramount importance to the architectural practice of the decade. Some of the most influential architectural work in the final years of the decade linked the modernist aesthetic to the single-family home. The ultimate effect of the decade's architectural progress was the increased acceptance of a simplified, geometric architectural form, whether applied to tall office buildings or to the suburban home.

Revival Styles and American Modernism The opening years of the 1940's found architecture in the United States progressing in multiple directions, with little to unify the differing architectural concerns and preferences. These contrasting architectural vocabularies become clearly evident through the comparison of several high-profile public buildings constructed between 1939 and 1943. Revival styles of architecture, which had characterized much of nineteenth and early twentieth century design, were still in use. John Russell Pope's neoclassical designs for the Jefferson Memorial (completed in 1943) and the West Wing of the National Gallery of Art (1941) show the continued use of Greek and Roman architectural vocabularies in the 1940's. By contrast, the completion of the final buildings of the Rockefeller Center (1940), designed by Reinhard and Hofmeister with Harvey Wiley Corbett and Raymond Hood, offered a triumphant modernism that combined tall, vertical-slab skyscrapers with elegant Art Deco detailing.

American modernism, which had found its roots in the Prairie School architecture of the early twentieth century, was continued by the work of Frank Lloyd Wright. In the late 1930's and early 1940's, Wright sharpened the geometric forms of his architecture and turned to materials such as concrete, glass, and wrought iron in response to global modernist architectural trends. His designs for the campus of Florida Southern College in Lakeland, Florida, are indicative of this progress, with the Annie Pfeiffer Chapel (1941) representing one of the most aggressively modernist buildings of the early 1940's in the United States.

The Rise of Historic Preservation   With the formation of the HABS in 1933, the first nationwide preservation and documentation program for the architecture of the United States was initiated. The work of the HABS led scholars and students of architecture to study the historic buildings of the United States in greater detail. In July, 1940, the American Society of Architectural Historians, later the Society of Architectural Historians (SAH), was formed. During the war, Rexford Newcomb directed the organization to turn its attention to the thorough documentation of architecture and the built environment. After the war, members of the SAH were instrumental in helping to develop a widespread interest in the history of the built environment in the United States.

Education and the International Style   Many of the architectural trends of the 1940's were rooted in developments within architecture schools. During the late 1930's, several prominent European architects immigrated to the United States and became active in architectural education. Two of these architects

German architect Walter Gropius standing next to a drawing of his design for the Chicago Tribune Building. Gropius became chair of the Department of Architecture at the Harvard Graduate School of Design. (AP/Wide World Photos)

were integral in the development of modernism and the International Style in North America: Walter Gropius, who became chair of the Department of Architecture at the Harvard Graduate School of Design, and Ludwig Mies van der Rohe, who became the director of architecture at the Armour Institute (now the Illinois Institute of Technology). The educational work of Wright at Taliesin West in Scottsdale, Arizona, also played a role in disseminating modern architectural ideals.

The 1940's was also a transitional period for the architectural education of women. During the 1930's, the Cambridge School of Architecture and Landscape Architecture had produced a growing community of female architects. The gradual dissolution of the school between 1938 and 1940 was only

Frank Lloyd Wright Buildings Designed or Built in the 1940's

Name	Location
Adelman House	Wisconsin
Administration Building (Child of the Sun)	Florida
Affleck House	Michigan
Alpaugh Studio Residence	Michigan
Alsop House	Iowa
Auldbrass Plantation	South Carolina
Baird Residence	Massachusetts
Brauner Residence	Michigan
Brown Residence	Michigan
Buehler House	California
Bulbulian Residence	Minnesota
Christie House	New Jersey
Community Christian Church	Missouri
Edwards Residence	Michigan
Eppstein Residence	Michigan
Esplanades (Child of the Sun)	Florida
Fountainhead	Mississippi
Arnold Friedman Lodge	New Mexico
Sol Friedman House	New York
Galesburg Country Homes	Michigan
Goetsch-Winckler House	Michigan
Grant House	Iowa
Griggs Residence	Washington
Guggenheim Museum	New York
Howard Residence	Michigan
Industrial Arts Building (Child of the Sun)	Florida
Jacobs House II	Wisconsin
Lamberson House	Iowa
Laurent House	Illinois
Levin House	Michigan

Name	Location
Manson House	Wisconsin
McCartney Residence	Michigan
Meyer Curtis Residence	Michigan
Miller House	Iowa
V. C. Morris Gift Shop	California
Mossberg Residence	Indiana
Neils House	Minnesota
Oboler Complex	California
Parkwyn Village	Michigan
Pfeiffer Chapel	Florida
Pope Residence	Virginia
Pratt Residence	Michigan
Reisley House	New York
Richardson House	New Jersey
Rosenbaum House	Alabama
Roux Library	Florida
Schwartz House	Wisconsin
Seminar Buildings 1-3 (Child of the Sun)	Florida
Serlin House	New York
Smith House	Michigan
Sondern House	Missouri
Unitarian Society Meeting House	Wisconsin
Usonia Homes	New York
Walker Residence	California
Wall House	Michigan
Wall Water Dome (Child of the Sun)	Florida
Walter Residence	Iowa
Weisblat Residence	Michigan
Weltzheimer Residence	Ohio
Winn Residence	Michigan

partially ameliorated by the 1942 decision by the Harvard Graduate School of Design to begin admitting women. Although the female enrollment increased during the war years, it had decreased drastically by the late 1940's. The return of male war veterans to higher education was at least partially the cause of this shift, though the near disappearance of women from the architectural profession in the 1950's suggests a larger cultural shift.

The International Style—a modern architectural aesthetic based on pure geometry, balanced masses, and modern materials, which was first defined and promoted in 1932 by Henry Russell Hitchcock and Philip Johnson—came into its own in the later half of the 1940's. The Harvard University Graduate Center (1950) in Cambridge, Massachusetts, designed by the Architects' Collaborative with Gropius, and the new Illinois Institute of Technology campus plan in Chicago, designed by Mies in 1940 and including the Alumni Memorial Hall (1946), did much to promote the new modernist aesthetic. Also influential were several significant skyscraper projects. The first building in the United States to include a curtain wall (an important structural innovation that allowed a prefabricated "skin" of plate glass and metal to envelope and articulate the exterior of a building) was the Commonwealth Building (1948) in Portland, Oregon, designed by Pietro Belluschi. Two additional buildings brought International Style skyscrapers to the forefront of urban architecture: the United Nations Secretariat Building (1952) in New York City, designed by a collaborative group of architects that included Le Corbusier, Sven Markelius, Oscar Niemeyer, and N. D. Bassov, led by Wallace K. Harrison and Max Abramovitz, and the 860-880 Lake Shore Drive Apartments (1951) in Chicago, designed by Mies.

Modern Houses and Suburbia Modernism spread as rapidly in domestic construction as it did in commercial buildings. The Farnsworth House in Plano, Illinois, designed by Mies in 1945 and built between 1950 and 1951, and the Glass House (1949) in New Canaan, Connecticut, designed by Johnson, offered pure domestic examples of the International Style. Significant contributions to the development of modernist design included work by Marcel Breuer and Richard Nuetra. Other trends in modernist design produced equally significant houses that have little formal similarity to the International Style.

Bruce Goff combined traditional materials with modernist forms and an industrial aesthetic in his Ruth Ford House, designed in 1947 and built in Aurora, Illinois, in 1950. R. Buckminster Fuller developed a postwar modular house that employed industrial materials, exemplified by his prototype, the Wichita House (or Dymaxion House). It was completed in Wichita, Kansas, in 1946. Of paramount significance to the domestic architecture of the period were the twenty-eight Case Study Houses designed and built for the magazine *Arts and Architecture* between 1945 and 1965. These experiments in high-style modernism for the single-family house advertised the modernist aesthetic to a wide audience. Perhaps most notable among these buildings was the Eames House, Case Study House No. 8 (1949), in California's Pacific Palisades, near Los Angeles, designed by husband and wife architects Charles and Ray Eames.

The developments in high-style modern domestic architecture were paralleled by the design of middle-class suburban housing complexes. Wright developed the "Usonian" house type, a term coined by the architect to denote an economical modern house expressive of a domestic type for the United States. Building on the 1930's innovations in suburban housing, suburban developments proliferated in the postwar construction boom of the late 1940's. Most significant among these developments were the Baldwin Hills Village condominium complex (now Village Green) in Los Angeles, completed in 1941 and designed by Reginald D. Johnson and Clarence Stein, among others, and Levittown (built between 1947 and 1950) in New York, developed by Levitt and Sons.

Impact Through the development of innovations in style, form, and materials, the 1940's permanently transformed architecture in the United States and Canada. The modernist movements begun in the 1940's would continue to grow and develop in the prosperous years of the 1950's. Urban architecture in the decades following the 1940's was dependent both on the curtain-wall aesthetic and on the vertical-slab skyscraper, both developed in the International Style. The postwar housing boom that began in the 1940's continued into the 1950's, creating the kernel of the suburban sprawl for which cities in the United States are still known.

Julia A. Sienkewicz

Further Reading

Jackson, Kenneth T. *Crabgrass Frontier: The Suburbanization of the United States.* New York: Oxford University Press, 1985. This history of suburbs in the United States begins with material from the nineteenth century and concludes with a discussion of the 1950's. One of the most complete histories of suburban development in the 1940's.

Jordy, William H. *American Buildings and Their Architects.* Vol. 5, *The Impact of European Modernism in the Mid-twentieth Century.* New York: Oxford University Press, 1972. Organized in a series of case-study chapters, this book offers in-depth studies of key structures in the development of modernism in the United States. Particularly useful are the chapters on Breuer's Ferry Cooperative Dormitory and Mies's Lake Shore Drive Apartments.

Kalman, Harold. *A History of Canadian Architecture.* Vol. 2. Toronto, Canada: Oxford University Press, 1994. Offers a thorough overview of developments in modern Canadian architecture.

Khan, Hasan-Uddin. *International Style: Modernist Architecture from 1925 to 1965.* New York: Taschen, 1998. An overview of the development of the International Style in the United States, conveniently organized in chronological chapters that also address broad concepts. Excellent illustrations, with full captions, allow for detailed study of architecture in the period.

Roth, Leland M. *American Architecture: A History.* Boulder, Colo.: Westview Press, 2001. This survey of American architecture offers a hefty chapter on "The Emergence of Modernism, 1940-1973." Well illustrated and clearly written, Roth's work places 1940's architecture within its historical context.

Smith, Elizabeth A. T. *Blueprints for Modern Living: History and Legacy of the Case Study Houses.* Cambridge, Mass.: MIT Press, 1989. This exhibition catalog offers a thorough and well-illustrated discussion of the twenty-eight Case Study Houses built between 1945 and 1965.

Whiffen, Marcus, and Frederick Koeper. *American Architecture.* Vol. 2, *1860-1976.* Cambridge, Mass.: MIT Press, 1981. With chronological chapters organized into brief topical subheadings, this volume includes a survey of the architectural practices of the 1940's.

See also Housing in Canada; Housing in the United States; Levittown; New Deal programs; White House renovations; Wright, Frank Lloyd.

■ Armistice Day blizzard

The Event Severe winter storm in the central United States

Date November 11-12, 1940

Places Kansas to upper Michigan

One of the deadliest storms the Midwest had ever seen, the blizzard claimed the lives of 154 people nationwide.

The Armistice Day blizzard intensified over the Texas Panhandle on November 10, 1940, then raced north-northeastward through the middle of the United States from Kansas on November 11, Armistice Day, to Wisconsin and upper Michigan, leaving as much as twenty-seven inches of wind-whipped snow in Collegeville, Minnesota (near St. Cloud), before it crossed the Great Lakes into Canada. As is often the case with major midwestern blizzards, the storm was preceded by unusual warmth, with temperatures reaching 60 to 65 degrees Fahrenheit (15.5 to 18 degrees Celsius). The storm began with rain in most areas, followed by a sharp drop in temperatures, then sleet and rising winds, followed by heavy snow. Winds reached eighty miles per hour in some areas, piling snow into drifts as deep as twenty feet.

Impact The combination of wind and heavy snow crippled transportation systems and impeded the rescue of many stranded people, increasing the death toll. Several of the dead were duck hunters who had been lured into the woods by the warmth that preceded the storm. Weather forecasters had not anticipated the severity of the storm, so many of the hunters did not have adequate clothing or supplies. Hunters who took refuge on small islands in the Mississippi River were inundated by five-foot waves driven by the storm's winds and froze to death in the cold snap. On Lake Michigan, sixty-six men died when three freighters, the SS *Anna C. Minch*, the SS *Novadoc*, and the SS *William B. Davock* (and two smaller boats), sank in high seas.

Bruce E. Johansen

Further Reading

Seely, Mark. *Remembering the Armistice Day Blizzard of 1940.* St. Paul: Minnesota Climatology Office, 2000.

Significant Minnesota Weather Events of the Twentieth Century. St. Paul: Minnesota Climatology Office, 1999.

See also Army, U.S.; Great Blizzard of 1949; Natural disasters.

■ Army, U.S.

Identification   Land-based branch of the U.S. armed forces

During a period of only five years in the early 1940's, the U.S. Army changed drastically, rising from a meager, poorly equipped force to one of the largest and most technologically advanced armed forces in the world.

The U.S. Army traces its roots to the establishment of the Continental Army in June, 1775. Since then, it has been a major participant in every armed conflict in which the United States has fought. Throughout much of its history, the United States maintained only a small regular force, as the nation's Founders had bequeathed a fear of the dangers of maintaining large standing armies. Each time, however, that the nation faced a great crisis, the Army underwent rapid and massive expansions. This was especially true during the U.S. Civil War (1861-1865), the brief American involvement in World War I (1917-1918), and World War II (1941-1945).

The Army During the Interwar Period   During World War I, the U.S. Army consisted of several components, the Regular Army, the National Army, which was organized specifically to fight in the conflict, as well as National Guard and Reserve components. After the war, the National Army was disbanded, leaving behind the Guard and Reserves, as well as a small Regular Army.

The 1920's saw a dramatic decline in the size and condition of the Army. The National Defense Act of 1920 created the Army of the United States, which consisted of a Regular force of professional soldiers, and Guard and Reserve components. By 1921, the National Guard had become a major component of the Army, with the Regular Army consisting of about 150,000 officers and men—a level that remained until 1936. As war clouds grew over Europe, the U.S. government began enlarging the authorized strength of the Army, whose active strength increased.

World War II   Germany's invasion of Poland on September 1, 1939 began a period of rapid change for the U.S. Army. In 1940, Congress reinstated the military draft, anticipating a need for rapid expansion of the military. Japan's sudden attack on Pearl Harbor at the end of 1941 thrust the United States into World War II. Entry into the war required a rapid and massive increase in the size of the Army. It also necessitated improved equipment and increased diversity. By the time of Pearl Harbor, the Army had already increased in strength from fewer than 200,000 to 1.6 million troops. This large and sudden expansion created many problems. New soldiers had to train with broomsticks because there were not enough rifles to meet the needs. These issues were soon resolved, however, as American industrial capacity rebounded incredibly from the Great Depression.

As the war progressed, millions more men enlisted and were drafted into the Army, which reached its peak strength of just over 8 million troops at war's end. Before the war, the Army had only a few divisions of ten to thirty thousand soldiers each to more than one hundred divisions by the end of the war. Army soldiers served in both the Pacific and European theaters of the war, but most fought in Europe, in accordance with the Allies' "Europe First" strategy, while U.S. Navy and Marine units did most of the fighting in the Pacific.

In addition to its rapid increase in manpower, the Army also acquired improved equipment. Before the war, American tanks were inadequate for war, but the industrial capabilities of the United States allowed the Army to field better tanks, including the M4 Sherman. Although inferior in some ways to their German counterparts, Sherman tanks were produced in such great quantities that American forces were able to overwhelm the enemy by the sheer force of numbers. American soldiers also benefited from the production of the famed M1 Garand rifle, which was semiautomatic, in contrast to the bolt-action rifled used by German and Japanese troops. These two weapons, along with other advanced technologies, greatly altered the U.S. Army during and after the war.

World War II also changed the composition of the U.S. Army. Members of minority groups gained increased visibility during the war. In 1942, the Women's Army Corps (WAC) was created, giving women the chance to serve and prove their abilities in a male-dominated institution. Approximately 100,000 women served in the WAC, giving rise to increased acceptance of women in the military services that would eventually lead to their full acceptance in the Army. In addition to women, African Americans, Japanese Americans, and members of other racial and ethnic minorities served their country despite facing the restrictions of a segregated mil-

U.S. Army troops marching through Nuremberg during the Allies' advance into Germany in April, 1945. (Getty Images)

itary. Some units made up primarily of minorities distinguished themselves on the battlefield. A prominent example was the Army's 442d Regimental Combat Team, whose Japanese American troops earned twenty-one Medals of Honor. The success of minorities in wartime service paved the way for the eventual full integration of the Army.

The war also propelled several Army officers to prominence during and after the conflict. Douglas MacArthur, Omar N. Bradley, Dwight D. Eisenhower, and George C. Marshall all enjoyed successful post-World War II military and civilian careers, and Eisenhower later served as president of the United States. In addition, many average soldiers became national heroes. For example, young Audie Murphy, who served with the Army's Third Infantry Division, became one of the most decorated soldiers in American history, receiving more than thirty awards, including the Medal of Honor.

Postwar Changes When World War II ended on September 2, 1945, the U.S. Army was one of the largest and most powerful military forces in the world, with more than 8 million troops in uniform. Many of them had served through nearly four years of a war that had left more than 400,000 Americans dead and more than 600,000 seriously wounded. After the fighting ended, the Army began new missions occupying Germany and Japan and preparing for the developing Cold War.

The late 1940's witnessed several important changes to the Army that had been precipitated by the war. Women continued to serve in the Army within the WAC until 1978, when they were permitted to join the regular army. Minorities also gained as a result of the war. Thanks to their distinguished service, the government was forced to reconsider the Army's policy of racial segregation. In July, 1948, President Harry S. Truman signed Executive Order

9981 desegregating the military. While little actual desegregation occurred in the years immediately following this order, it represented a step in a new direction for full opportunities for minorities to serve, as well as recognition of their accomplishments.

The late 1940's also witnessed a far-reaching development in the organization of the U.S. armed forces. In 1947, Congress approved and President Truman signed the National Security Act into law. This act reorganized the armed forces, including the Army, by merging the War and Navy departments into a larger Department of Defense, which was to be headed by a single secretary of defense. In addition, the Army Air Forces were separated from the Army to create the autonomous U.S. Air Force. This change transitioned the military from a World War II structure to a Cold War structure.

A traditional postwar downsizing of the Army occurred after World War II, but it was not as drastic a reduction in size as had occurred after earlier wars. The Army's manpower was reduced to about one-half million men—a much larger number than had been in previous peacetime armies. Meanwhile, the Army participated in such early Cold War operations as the Berlin Airlift and prepared against possible threats from the Soviet Union, while maintaining a large occupation force in Germany.

Impact The U.S. Army underwent dramatic changes during the 1940's. It evolved from a small, ill-equipped peacetime force to one of the largest military forces in the world. As it emerged from war, it slowly became racially integrated and set itself on a course eventually to accept women into its ranks. It also came under the new Department of Defense and, despite being downsized, prepared itself and participated in the early stages of the Cold War.

Daniel Sauerwein

Further Reading

Allison, William T., Jeffrey Grey, and Janet G. Valentine. *American Military History: A Survey from Colonial Times to the Present.* Upper Saddle River, N.J.: Pearson-Prentice Hall, 2007. Comprehensive history of all U.S. armed services through the Iraq and Afghanistan wars of the twenty-first century.

Conn, Stetson, Rose C. Engelman, and Byron Fairchild. *The United States Army in World War II: Guarding the United States and Its Outposts.* Washington, D.C.: Office of the Chief of Military History, Department of the Army, 1964. Official U.S. government history of the Army through the biggest conflict in which it has ever fought.

Dorr, Robert F. *Alpha Bravo Delta Guide to the U.S. Army.* Indianapolis: Alpha, 2003. Popular history of the Army, from its earliest origins, up to the twenty-first century. Part of a series of books on the various branches of the U.S. armed services.

Hogan, David W., Jr. *Two Hundred Twenty-five Years of Service: The U.S. Army, 1775-2000.* Washington, D.C.: U.S. Army, 2000. Commemorative history of the Army since the Revolutionary War commissioned by the Army itself.

Matloff, Maurice, ed. *American Military History.* Vol. 2, *1902-1996.* New York: Da Capo Press, 1996. This second volume of a general history of American military conflicts devotes considerable space to the mobilization, organization, and deployment of the Army in World War II.

Murphy, Audie. *To Hell and Back.* 1949. Reprint. New York: Henry Holt, 2002. Ghostwritten memoir of Murphy's incredible Army experience during World War II. In 1955, Murphy launched an acting career by playing himself in a film adapted from this book.

Van Creveld, Martin. *Fighting Power: German and U.S. Army Performance, 1939-1995.* Westport, Conn.: Greenwood Press, 1982. Fascinating comparative study of the German and American armies during World War II.

Weintraub, Stanley. *Fifteen Stars: Eisenhower, MacArthur, Marshall: Three Generals Who Saved the American Century.* New York: Free Press, 2007. Provocative examination of the intertwined careers of three of the most outstanding U.S. Army generals of the twentieth century.

See also Air Force, U.S.; Bulge, Battle of the; Coast Guard, U.S.; Eisenhower, Dwight D.; Marines, U.S.; Navy, U.S.; World War II; World War II mobilization.

Army Air Forces. *See* **Air Force, U.S.**

■ Army Rangers

Identification   Elite U.S. Army commando unit
Date   Formed in May, 1942

The Army Rangers were an important asset during World War II, conducting effective operations in every theater of operations with impacts that often exceeded the number of troops. The Rangers helped to provide a useful framework for later U.S. Special Operations forces.

The Rangers trace their lineage to Roger's Rangers, who fought for the British in the French and Indian War. Following the successful operations of the British commando units in World War II, the United States moved toward forming a similar unit of commandos. The first Ranger unit was formed in May, 1942, and initial recruits were volunteers drawn largely from two divisions. The volunteers were trained by British commandos, and the dropout rate was relatively high. Many of the volunteers joined because they were enamored with the romantic view of being commandos.

There was initially some debate in the military regarding whether the new unit's members would later be returned to their original units or remain a coherent force. William Darby was assigned to conduct the training of the new Army unit.

The Rangers operated in the European and Pacific theaters of operations. Shortly after the creation of the Rangers, a small number of American Rangers took part in the unsuccessful commando raid on the port of Dieppe in northern France in August, 1942. The unit saw action in North Africa in 1943, conducting a night landing at Arzew, Algeria, that opened up the ports to Allied landings. The Rangers also conducted behind-the-lines raids in Tunisia. During the Italian campaign, Rangers took part in actions at Salerno and Anzio. During fighting at Cisterna, the majority of the Ranger unit was captured or killed when the unit was surrounded.

The most famous Ranger operation during the war was during the D-day invasion in June, 1944. The Second Ranger Battalion was given the task of neutralizing high-caliber cannon emplaced at Pointe du Hoc. When the unit landed on D day, the guns on the cliff could not be located and neutralized, and the Rangers took heavy casualties during the operation. Around five hundred Rangers landed on Omaha Beach as well and helped to break the deadlock during the landing.

In the Pacific theater, the Rangers mounted a number of daring raids. The most famous was a raid by 121 handpicked volunteers to rescue American prisoners of war (POWs) in the Philippines. The POW camp was located thirty miles behind the lines at Cabanatuan. The United States was afraid that the Japanese would execute any remaining prisoners and used the raid to successfully bring out the majority of the POWs with the help of Filipino guerrillas.

Impact   The operations conducted by the Rangers significantly influenced a number of operations, particularly the D-day landings. On the home front, the Rangers were viewed, like the British commandos, as "super soldiers." Following the war, the Ranger units were disbanded, but the successful operations during World War II served as a framework for the later formation of Ranger units in the Korean War.

Michael W. Cheek

Further Reading

DeFelice, James. *Rangers at Dieppe: The First Combat Action of U.S. Army Rangers in World War II.* New York: The Berkley Publishing Group, 2008.

Jeffers, H. Paul. *Onward We Charge: The Heroic Story of Darby's Dangers in World War II.* New York: New American Library, 2007.

Sides, Hampton. *Ghost Soldiers: The Forgotten Epic Story of World War II's Most Dramatic Mission.* New York: Doubleday, 2001.

See also   Army, U.S.; China-Burma-India theater; D Day; Dieppe raid; World War II.

■ Arnold, Henry "Hap"

Identification   Commanding General of the U.S. Army Air Forces, 1941-1946
Born   June 25, 1886; Gladwyne, Pennsylvania
Died   January 15, 1950; Sonoma, California

A pioneer of American military aviation, General Henry "Hap" Arnold commanded the U.S. Army Air Forces during World War II and played a pivotal role in laying the foundations of American air power.

Henry H. Arnold was born into a socially prominent family in Pennsylvania. His father was a physician who had served in the Spanish-American War. He entered the United States Military Academy in 1903.

At West Point, Arnold compiled an undistinguished academic record and earned a reputation among his fellow cadets as a prankster. Upon graduation, he was assigned to an infantry regiment in the Philippines.

Intrigued by the possibilities of aviation, Arnold transferred into the fledgling Aeronautical Division of the U.S. Army Signal Corps in 1911. He became one of the first American military aviators, some of his flights setting early altitude records. Following a series of crashes, he developed a fear of flying. After a break, he returned to aviation and overcame his aversion to flight. When the United States entered World War I, Arnold hoped to get to the front. Instead, he was assigned to Washington and acquired valuable experience working with Congress, manufacturers, and scientists. In the postwar years, Arnold served with Brigadier General William Mitchell, whose strident advocacy of air power led to his court-martial and retirement. Arnold escaped his mentor's fate, rising in rank and winning distinction in 1934 by organizing and leading ten bombers on a flight of more than eight thousand miles from Washington, D.C., to Alaska and back.

In September, 1938, Arnold became chief of the United States Army Air Corps. Arnold was an advocate of research and development in military aviation. He supported the development of the B-17 and B-29 bombers, as well as innovations with radar and bombsights. In 1940, he began the push for jet-propelled aircraft. His close relationship with scientists such as Theodore von Karman of the California Institute of Technology led to the formation of the Scientific Advisory Group in 1944. Arnold initiated Project RAND in 1945, which eventually became the RAND Corporation.

In June, 1941, American military aviation was reorganized, and Arnold became Commanding General of the Army Air Forces. Arnold presided over a rapid expansion of the Army Air Forces that accelerated after the United States entered World War II in December, 1941. His command grew from 21,000 personnel and 2,000 planes in 1939 to 2.3 million personnel and 79,000 planes in 1945. To maintain this force, Arnold supervised the creation of a massive logistical infrastructure.

Arnold was an enthusiastic supporter of strategic bombing. He took an intense interest in the operations of the Eighth Air Force that bombed Germany, and later the Twentieth Air Force that began sending the new B-29's against Japan. Arnold was a demanding superior, and he ruthlessly replaced officers who did not achieve his desired results. When the B-29 offensive against Japan ran into difficulties, he took personal command of the Twentieth Air Force and supported General Curtis LeMay's campaign of fire-bombing Japanese cities.

Arnold suffered four heart attacks during the war years. He retired, after a recurrence of heart problems, in early 1946. Arnold had been promoted to the five-star rank of General of the Army in 1944. On May 7, 1949, he was honorarily appointed General of the Air Force. He is the only person to have held the grade of five-star general in two different military services.

Impact As an organizer and strategist, Henry Arnold made a significant contribution to American victory in World War II. Arnold's farsighted emphasis on research and development ensured the dominance of the American Air Force for decades to come.

Daniel P. Murphy

Further Reading

Arnold, Henry H. *Global Mission*. New York: Harper, 1949.

Coffey, Thomas M. *Hap: The Story of the U.S. Air Force and the Man Who Built It*. New York: Viking Press, 1982.

See also Air Force, U.S.; Aircraft design and development; Army, U.S.; Bombers; Davis, Benjamin O., Jr.; Flying Tigers; Jet engines; Strategic bombing; World War II; World War II mobilization.

■ "Arsenal of Democracy" speech

The Event Address by President Franklin D. Roosevelt on the urgency of providing munitions of war to nations threatened by Axis aggression during World War II

Date Delivered on December 29, 1940

This fireside chat was an important step in securing the support of the American public for the Lend-Lease Act, which supplied much-needed material to Allied nations, in particular Great Britain and the Soviet Union.

The "Arsenal of Democracy" speech was delivered at a time when Nazi Germany had conquered much of

---

"An Unholy Alliance"

Excerpt from Franklin D. Roosevelt's "Arsenal of Democracy" speech, which he delivered to the American public on December 29, 1940.

The history of recent years proves that the shootings and the chains and the concentration camps (of Nazi Germany) are not simply the transient tools but the very altars of modern dictatorships. (The Axis Powers) may talk of a "new order" in the world, but what they have in mind is only a revival of the oldest and the worst tyranny. In that there is no liberty, no religion, no hope. The proposed "new order" is the very opposite of a United States of Europe or a United States of Asia. It is not a government based upon the consent of the governed. It is not a union of ordinary, self-respecting men and women to protect themselves and their freedom and their dignity from oppression. It is an unholy alliance of power and pelf to dominate and to enslave the human race.

Europe. In his radio address, President Franklin D. Roosevelt directly told the American public about the importance of rendering U.S. assistance to those countries threatened by Axis aggression. In a press conference held twelve days before the speech, he had applied a folksy analogy to the international situation, rhetorically asking reporters if they would not lend a garden hose to a neighbor whose house was on fire. In this speech, Roosevelt introduced the more elegant term "arsenal of democracy" to describe the role the United States should play in the war. Looking ahead to the impending legislative battle over the Lend-Lease Act, Roosevelt argued that dramatically increasing U.S. defense production and lending military armaments to the countries threatened by Axis aggression would be a less risky alternative for the United States than either isolation or full-scale belligerency.

Impact In tandem with the "Four Freedoms" speech given a week later, the "Arsenal of Democracy" speech rallied public opinion behind the Lend-Lease Act, which was subsequently passed into law on March 11, 1941. To protect convoys carrying Lend-Lease aid to Britain and the Soviet Union, the United States then embarked on a series of military moves that veered increasingly away from neutrality and toward substantial U.S. involvement in World War II during the months before the Japanese attack on Pearl Harbor in December, 1941.

Larry Haapanen

Further Reading

Davis, Kenneth S. *FDR: The War President, 1940-1943—A History.* New York: Random House, 2000.

Podell, Janet, and Steven Anzovin, eds. *Speeches of the American Presidents.* New York: H. W. Wilson, 1988.

Smith, Jean Edward. *FDR.* New York: Random House, 2007.

See also "Four Freedoms" speech; Isolationism; Lend-Lease; Roosevelt, Franklin D.; World War II.

■ Art movements

Definition Developments in visual arts that were integral to, and the result of, social, political, and cultural changes

During the 1940's, the center of the art world shifted from Europe, notably Paris, to the United States, primarily because of World War II. Unstable physical and political conditions in Europe, especially during the years just previous to the United States' involvement in World War II, brought an influx of European immigrants, including many artists. The visual art styles they brought influenced the work of American artists, who used the new forms to express new American ideals.

The art movements of the 1940's brought a North American focus to creative endeavors that previously had been centered in Europe. Influenced by older genres such as surrealism, the Bauhaus, cubism, and Dadaism, American artists developed what they considered a more necessary, more relevant style of art. By the time the United States entered World War II, the isolationism that had been part of the nation's identity had been replaced by a wider awareness of and interest in the larger world, as well as North America's place in it. Americans soon reacted to their increasing exposure to global schools of expressive arts. American art before World War II was concerned primarily with American scenes, American characters, and, especially during the Great Depression, American problems. Instead of simply replicating real life, American art began to take an abstract turn as a means to draw attention to the deep-rooted emotions of artists and viewers alike.

Abstract Expressionism   Probably the most internationally significant development in visual art during the 1940's was that of abstract expressionism. Also called the New York School because of the principal location of its members, abstract expressionism essentially offered American artists freedom from the overly representational art (painted or drawn to realistically resemble its real-life models) that had come to characterize American works. Abstract expressionism was more concerned with the act of putting color to canvas than with the realistic replication of a subject.

Before 1940, the best-known American artist was arguably Norman Rockwell, who primarily painted halcyon scenes of American life. Using soft lines, soft colors, and easily recognizable figures of boys with dogs, snow-covered small towns, and other evidence of Americana, Rockwell rendered an America that was immediately nostalgic. Conversely, Jackson Pollock's boldly splashed canvases evoke a sort of tension, or even anger; even when they are constrained into discernible human figures, the outlines are blurred and the brush strokes heavy. Representational art demanded that an artist capture both the essence and a near-exact likeness of a subject. Abstract expressionism, on the other hand, relied heavily on subconscious thought, evoked in the form of lines, splatters, and often complicated geometric configurations, to symbolize a variety of negative emotions—and it was irrelevant whether the resulting visual was easily recognizable as something the viewer had previously experienced.

The abstract expressionist movement can be divided into two major groups. One was the action painting group, whose chief members were Jackson Pollock, Philip Guston, and Robert Motherwell. Action painters were concerned with the kinetic energy involved in the physical act of painting.

The other main abstract expressionist group

was known as the color field painting artists. It included Mark Rothko, Kenneth Noland, and Jules Olitski. The goal of the color field approach was to create ambience with color, allowing the mood of the paint to create atmosphere for audiences. Color field artists intended their large paintings to seem as though they were extending beyond the boundaries of the canvas and engulfing viewers. Both types of abstract expressionism met the movement's overall tenet of creating nonrepresentational works, heavy in color and emotional content.

World War II and the European Avant-Garde   By the late 1930's, after Europe's engagement in World War II, several influential leaders of European art movements had immigrated to the United States. The presence of representatives from surrealism and the Bauhaus made European art forms accessi-

Many noted abstract impressionists gathered together for this photograph taken by Nina Leen for Life *magazine. From left to right: Theodoros Stamos, Jimmy Ernst, Barnett Newman, James C. Brooks, Mark Rothko, Richard Pousette-Dart, William Baziotes, Jackson Pollock, Clyfford Still, Robert Motherwell, Bradley Walker Tomlin, Willem De Kooning, Adolph Gottlieb, Ad Reinhardt, and Hedda Sterne.* (Time & Life Pictures/Getty Images)

ble to an increasingly larger number of American artists. Both Bauhaus and surrealism began around 1919 as a reaction against World War I.

Surrealists largely held that "rationalism" was responsible for war, and they sought to break with it. The Bauhaus philosophy was that artists should be utilitarian, or practical, craftspeople. Their drawings often demonstrated various physical science theories in clean lines and rich color.

The avant-garde, or experimental, approach was not limited to visual artists, as writers and others used the principles of surrealism to embrace the absurd and to rid their work of rationalism. Along with the break from rationalism was the idea that the subconscious was a virtual mine of creativity that went untapped in typical everyday life. The spirit or ideology behind both Dadaism and surrealism was that of destruction for the objects created and exhibited, and self-destruction for the artist. The point was that conventionality as a means to art needed to be destroyed. Dadaists were expected to voluntarily give up the traditional mental processes previously thought necessary to create art, and to lose the concern with the audience and the art world, including buyers, sellers, and the media, to focus solely on the creation of art that was true to the spirit of the movement.

Surrealists created a series of games and exercises meant to encourage practitioners to produce art automatically, which was in contrast to the rational process of art taught in early American art schools. An important American artist of this time was painter, photographer, and Surrealist Man Ray, whose arguably absurdist work in multiple media portrayed a willingness to destroy the barriers between those media.

Sociocultural Revolutions   The 1940's began about seventy-five years after the end of slavery and were part of an era of self-realization for African Americans known as the Harlem Renaissance. The Harlem Renaissance began in the 1910's and marked a period that lasted through the 1940's in which the concept of the "New Negro" was developed. Works in visual arts, literature, music, and drama demonstrated the increasingly complex social, economic, political, and artistic realms that defined post-slavery life for African Americans.

During the 1930's, often with the financial support of groups such as the Federal Art Project (FPA) and the Works Progress Administration (WPA), visual art by African Americans told the stories of segregation, poverty, and the need for social change. Such narratives in visual art progressed throughout the 1940's. Instead of breaking with actual reality, like the work of abstract expressionists, Dadaists, and surrealists, many works by African American artists relied on being entrenched in daily negativity to evoke social consciousness, thus making the depiction of reality the means through which art enacted change.

Artists Horace Pippin, Dox Thrash, Archibald J. Motley, and William Johnson depicted themes such as the execution of abolitionist John Brown, new urban nightlife, Christian baptism, and life on a prison chain gang, all of which had an impact, historical or otherwise, on African American life. In some cases, such as Christian baptism, they would prove to be defining factors of African American life for decades to come.

These new scenes were essential for the development of a uniquely African American view of North American life. The paintings reveal bold, sometimes detailed shapes, making the human subjects in them the focus. Backgrounds of skies and nightclub walls highlight the hues and actions of the people in the foreground.

Impact   The art movements of the 1940's were integral to the shaping of America's artistic sensibilities and were indicative of the American quality of reinvention. Art began to move beyond depicting bowdlerized versions of life and to feature emotional representations or responses to a plethora of injustices. The presence of European immigrants helped to establish certain schools of avant-garde art in America and provided the opportunity for more Americans to see the new styles, but the American artists' often groundbreaking approaches to older European styles is what helped to establish modern art in America. The subsequent developments in modern art lasted decades after World War II.

After 1945, abstract expressionism continued to be relevant, with artists such as Pollock producing work that would come to define the movement. The pop art era followed, continuing the spirit of reinvention and rebellion that surfaced among American artists of the 1940's. It retained the ideology of abstract expressionism, with brilliant colors and perspectives that made paintings seem three-dimensional.

It also incorporated collage and found-object sculptures that borrowed from the surrealist practice of juxtaposing disparate objects to create a new reality, as well as the clean lines reminiscent of the Bauhaus. Most pop art functioned to make critical statements about mainstream culture.

Dodie Marie Miller

Further Reading

Anfam, David. *Abstract Expressionism.* New York: Thames and Hudson, 1990. Details the forms' history, practitioners, and complex artistic and social contexts.

Leslie, Richard. *Pop Art: A New Generation of Style.* New York: Todtri Productions, 1997. Offers a historical introduction to the art world before the advent of pop art. Follows the movement from its foreshadowing in the 1930's to its late twentieth century implications. Complete with vivid reproductions of seminal examples of the form.

Sproccati, Sandro, ed. *A Guide to Art.* New York: Harry N. Abrams, 1992. Chronicles the history of visual art. Complete with richly done photographic replicas of masterworks. Provides time lines and contexts for genres and subgenres.

See also   Advertising in the United States; American Negro Exposition; Art of This Century; De Kooning, Willem; Pollock, Jackson; Rockwell, Norman.

■ Art of This Century

Identification   Art gallery of European and American modern art
Date   Opened on October 20, 1942

Art of This Century showcased modern art by both European masters and up-and-coming young American artists, becoming a center for avant-garde art in the United States.

Heiress Peggy Guggenheim founded Art of This Century in New York City to display her collection of modern European art and to exhibit the work of contemporary American artists. Modernist architect Frederick Kiesler created daring and innovative display spaces for the gallery, with abstract paintings suspended on ropes and surrealist works extending from curved wooden walls. Critical opinion of the revolutionary design ranged from "mystifying and delightful" to "vaguely menacing."

During the gallery's brief five-year tenure, Guggenheim gave many talented newcomers their first solo exhibitions, including Jackson Pollock, Robert Motherwell, William Baziotes, Clyfford Still, and Mark Rothko. These artists were part of the burgeoning abstract expressionist movement. Art of This Century's support for these artists, particularly Pollock, was key in providing exposure and acceptance for their work and ideas. After Guggenheim decided to move to Europe, the gallery closed on May 31, 1947.

Impact   Art of This Century championed American avant-garde artists at a time when other galleries were focusing on European artwork. The gallery launched the careers of Jackson Pollock and other remarkable young artists and provided a springboard for the abstract expressionist movement.

Paula C. Doe

Further Reading

Davidson, Susan, and Philip Rylands, eds. *Peggy Guggenheim and Frederick Kiesler: The Story of Art of This Century.* New York: Guggenheim Museum Publications, 2004.

Dearborn, Mary V. *Mistress of Modernism: The Life of Peggy Guggenheim.* Boston: Houghton Mifflin, 2004.

See also   Art movements; De Kooning, Willem; Pollock, Jackson; Rockwell, Norman.

■ Asian Americans

Identification   Diverse ethnic group whose members suffered from stereotyping and discrimination

Asian Americans were generally not viewed by society as fully American. Their contributions to both the war and home fronts during World War II, however, proved them to be valuable Americans, and they eventually won various forms of legal acceptance as part of American society.

Asian Americans are a diverse group who are either naturalized citizens themselves or are descended from immigrants from the nations of East Asia, Southeast Asia, or South Asia. Varied cultural heritages, languages, and religious practices determine which specific ethnic group they belong to, such as Chinese Americans, Korean Americans, Japanese Americans, Cambodian Americans, Philippine Americans, Vietnamese Americans, Asian Indian Americans, and others.

Shared experiences of being excluded and a common interest in being recognized as Americans bonded them together, and World War II created momentum for them to be involved in mainstream activities. Their participation in support of the American war effort helped them to win the repeal of the Chinese Exclusion Laws and other anti-Asian racial discriminatory legislation, setting up a foundation for further reforms in immigration policies.

Service in the U.S. Armed Forces   Asian Americans made up a substantial part of the U.S. armed forces. Approximately 13,000 Chinese Americans—nearly 22 percent of adult Chinese males across the country—were drafted into the armed forces. Joining

with other American soldiers, they were deployed to war zones in all parts of the world, serving as large components of the Third and Fourth Infantry Divisions in the European theater, and in the Sixth, Thirty-second, and Seventy-seventh Divisions in Asia and the Pacific. Twenty-five percent of Chinese American recruits served in the American Air Force, and many served in the Navy. Chinese American women also served as pilots, nurses, and secretaries, both in the Army and in the Air Force.

Despite the injustice of the forced internment of almost 120,000 Japanese Americans by the U.S. government, 9,500 Nisei men (the sons of immigrants) volunteered for military service to demonstrate their American patriotism. Many of them were sent to Camp Shelby, Mississippi, where they became members of the 442d Regimental Combat Team, a segregated unit. Some Japanese Americans served as Japanese language interpreters in the U.S. Army.

More than 200,000 Filipino Americans served with the United States military. They served in multiple combat groups, including the Philippine Scouts and the Philippine Commonwealth Army under the U.S. command in the Japanese-occupied territory of the Philippines. More than 7,000 Filipino Americans served in the First and the Second Filipino infantry regiments.

Korean Americans also became involved in the American war effort. One-fifth of Los Angeles's Korean population joined the California National Guard, preparing to defend the state against an enemy invasion. Those who knew the Japanese language served as translators to decode Japanese secret documents. They also served as teachers in special Army training program classes.

Wartime Industries and Civilian Activities   The increasing demand for labor during the war provided job opportunities for Asian Americans, who found jobs in shipyards, airplane factories, and defense plants. Approximately 1,600 of the 18,000 Chinese Americans living in the San Francisco Bay Area worked in defense industries in 1942. Chinese American workers also joined the shipyard workforces in Delaware, New York, and Mississippi.

Asian Americans engaged actively in such common civilian activities as fund-raising, war

Lieutenant John Ko, a Japanese American member of the U.S. Army's 442d Regimental Combat Team fighting in Italy. (National Archives)

bond purchases, and blood donation. In a one-day fund-raising activity in March, 1942, New York University students collected $6,000 from New York's Chinese residents. By October 9, 1943, New York's Chinese residents had purchased $4,134,075 in war bonds. Korean Americans purchased more than $239,000 worth of defense bonds between 1942 and 1943. On June 5, 1942, more than 1,700 Japanese Americans presented a check to the federal government to support the war against Japanese invasion.

Repeal of the Chinese Exclusion Acts   On November 11, 1943, Congress passed a repeal bill that terminated the Chinese Exclusion Acts, which had barred almost all Chinese immigration since 1882. Historians suggest that the American government's repeal of Chinese exclusion was an emergency war measure to combat Japanese war propaganda. Because China had already been at war against Japan, repeal represented to some a self-interested move to keep China as an ally.

The repeal nevertheless was a major legal achievement for the Chinese in the United States. The wartime repeal efforts of Chinese Americans reflected their growing political consciousness, and their contributions to the American war effort backed up their demands for legal status in the United States.

Asian Americans suffered from racial discrimination and stereotyping, being labeled variously as heathens, cheap laborers, and aliens. Chinese Americans suffered from early institutionalized discrimination through the Chinese Exclusion Acts of 1882, by which Chinese were barred from entering the United States. In 1907, Japanese Americans were restricted by the Gentlemen's Agreement between the United States and Japan. In 1917, Congress created a "barred zone" in South and Southeast Asia, residents of which were declared inadmissible as immigrants. Filipinos were allowed to enter as U.S. nationals, but they could not be naturalized. The quota system of the 1924 immigration legislation barred almost all Asian immigrants from entering the United States.

The 1943 repeal of the Chinese Exclusion Acts marked a historical turning point in U.S. immigration policy. It was a necessary step in undercutting Japanese propaganda accusing the United States of prejudice against Asians. The annual quota of 105 was a token amount of Chinese immigration, but repeal of the Exclusion Acts and the naturalization

prohibition granted legal opportunities for Chinese Americans to build normal lives in America. Moreover, it established the foundation for further changes in immigration policies directed toward Asians.

On July 2, 1946, Congress passed the Luce-Celler Act, which renewed immigration rights from India and the Philippines and gave naturalization rights to immigrants from those countries. Between 1948 and 1964, more than 6,000 Asian Indians came to the United States, another 1,700 became American citizens. Japanese Americans and Korean Americans remained ineligible for naturalization until 1952, with passage of the McCarran-Walter Act. The Immigration and Naturalization Act of 1965 abolished the national origins system.

Impact   The commitment of Asians in the United States to the war effort proved them, as a group, to be patriotic Americans. Their engagement in the military services and employment in wartime industrial production supported the mainstream war effort. Repeal of the Chinese Exclusion Acts and other immigration reforms recognized their right to integrate into American society.

Jingyi Song

Further Reading

Asahina, Robert. *Just Americans: How Japanese Americans Won a War at Home and Abroad: The Story of the 100th Battlion/442d Regimental Combat Team in World War II.* New York: Gotham Books, 2006. The story of the segregated Japanese American 100th Battalion/442d Regimental Combat Team in action on European battlefields during World War II.

Chan, Sucheng. *Asian Americans: An Interpretive History.* Boston: Twayne, 1991. Academic discussions on the experiences of Asian Americans within the context of global and national currents.

Kitano, Harry H. L., and Roger Daniels. *Asian Americans: Emerging Minorities,* 3d ed. Englewood Cliffs, N.J.: Prentice Hall, 2001. Useful overview of the lives and experiences of Asian Americans, including their participation in World War II.

Takaki, Ronald. *Strangers from a Different Shore: A History of Asian Americans.* Boston: Little, Brown, 1989. Comprehensive history of diverse Asian Americans, including their contributions to the American World War II effort.

Wong, K. Scott. *Americans First: Chinese Americans and*

the Second World War. Cambridge, Mass.: Harvard University Press, 2005. Good source on Chinese Americans and their services and sacrifices in the U.S. armed forces.

See also African Americans; Civil rights and liberties; Flying Tigers; Immigration Act of 1943; Immigration to the United States; Japanese American internment; Latinos; Native Americans; Philippines.

■ Astronomy

During the 1940's, astronomy began to reap the rewards of three developments in related fields: atomic physics, nuclear physics, and computer science. The result was a surge of new understanding of the physical nature of the stars and of the cosmic environment and its history.

At the beginning of the decade, the field of astronomy in America was primarily concentrated at a few well-funded institutions on the two coasts. In the West, most active astronomers were in California, at Pasadena's California Institute of Technology, the Mount Wilson and Palomar observatories, and Mount Hamilton. The 200-inch telescope at Palomar was the largest in the world when it saw first light in 1948. The 100-inch telescope on Mount Wilson, for decades the world's largest, continued to dominate the field. In the East, the major centers of astronomical research were private universities, notably Harvard and Princeton, where major breakthroughs in stellar astrophysics occurred.

The Solar System Planetary astronomy was relatively inactive during the war years and continued to develop slowly until the revolutionary developments that would follow the sudden start of the space age after the launch of *Sputnik 1* in 1957. A brief flurry of excitement followed the announcement in 1942 by the Dutch American astronomer Kaj Strand that he had discovered a planet around another star, 61 Cygni. Subsequent observations established that the object was instead a faint star. A true extrasolar planet was not discovered until fifty years later.

The most noteworthy planetary studies of the decade involved the major planets, especially Saturn, Uranus, and Neptune. Using infrared detectors, G. P. Kuiper of the Yerkes Observatory showed that Saturn's rings are made primarily of water ice (snow)

particles. He also observed Pluto, Triton (Neptune's large satellite), and Titania and Oberon (moons of Uranus), finding no evidence of an atmosphere on those cold, barren worlds. In 1949, Kuiper discovered a second satellite of Neptune, named Nereid.

For the inner planets, especially Mars and Venus, emphasis was on their surface markings and atmospheres. Debate continued about whether the faint, straight-line shadings on Mars were "canals," suggesting that intelligent beings exist or existed there and that water may have flowed on the planet's surface. The issue was not completely resolved until years later, when *Mariner 4* flew past Mars in 1965 and showed no artificial canals.

Stellar Astrophysics Despite the fact that many astronomers were diverted from their research programs by the war effort, the early 1940's saw some activity in stellar astronomy. Better understanding of quantum mechanics furthered understanding of the mechanism by which protons could combine to form helium nuclei and provide the energy of stars, an idea promoted twenty years earlier by Sir Arthur Eddington.

Several North American observatories, such as the Dominion Astrophysical Observatory in Canada, were devoted primarily to the analysis of the spectra of stars, which show the amount of light transmitted from stars at each different wavelength, or color. Combining the observed spectra with the physics of light transfer through the stellar medium began to explicate conditions within stars of various types. During the previous decade, stars had been shown to be overwhelmingly made up of hydrogen; new discoveries allowed determination of stars' composition through measurements of the amount of absorption of light by the atoms of the other elements.

The physics of stellar dynamics, which examines stellar motions and the gravitational interactions of stars in groups, made large advances through the mathematically detailed work of Indian American astrophysicist Subrahmanyan Chandrasekhar, who later also pioneered other branches of astrophysics. Stellar positions continued to be a major topic of research, especially at several observatories devoted chiefly to this subject, called astrometry. For example, the Yale Observatory published many volumes of measurements of star positions, largely the work of Ida Barney. The measurements of the orbits of double stars also progressed during the decade.

These data were important to the calibration of fundamental data, such as the masses of stars.

The Milky Way One of the most important astronomical events of the 1940's was the detection of the Milky Way galaxy's spiral arms. It was strongly suspected that the galaxy has spiral structure, because other galaxies of its size are usually spiral in shape. The Sun, however, lies in the midst of a forest of stars, making observations and calculations difficult. Furthermore, the Milky Way is a dusty environment, and most of it is hidden by the obscuring thickness of interstellar dust. During the 1940's, new methods were developed of correcting the brightnesses of stars for the dimming resulting from intervening dust, allowing accurate measurements of the distances of stars.

Photometry (precise measurements of brightness) and spectroscopy (measurements of light spread out into different wavelengths) allowed astronomers to map the positions of stars in different sections of the Milky Way. Spectroscopists W. W. Morgan of the Yerkes Observatory and Philip Keenan of Ohio State University were among the pioneers who developed spectroscopic techniques for accurate distance determinations. In the late 1940's, using these methods, Morgan and two of his students, Donald Osterbrock and S. L. Sharpless, first gleaned the spiral shape of the distribution of stars in the Milky Way. They benefited from the discovery of Walter Baade that in the nearby spiral galaxy M31, a close twin, the spiral arms were defined by the brightest blue, hot stars and the ionized gas clouds. In 1949, the Yerkes Observatory team plotted the positions of those kinds of objects in the Milky Way and saw that they appeared to be arranged in sections of spiral arms. Two years later, the spiral nature of the Milky Way Galaxy was firmly established.

Other major events in 1940's astronomy included the exploration of the sources of radio emissions from the galaxy and the discovery of a galactic magnetic field. A large amount of groundwork data on galactic star clusters was gathered during the decade; these data were elemental in the discovery of the secrets of stellar evolution that occurred during the 1950's.

External Galaxies During the first half of the decade, a large percentage of astronomers in the United States and Canada were involved in war-related activities, and even some of the world's largest observatories were idle part of the time. One of Mount Wilson Observatory's most prominent observers, Walter Baade, was unable to participate in war work, as a German national, so he had unprecedented opportunities to use the 100-inch telescope. Furthermore, Los Angeles, which lies at the foot of Mt. Wilson, was defensively blacked out on many nights, making the observatory's background sky unusually dark and therefore better suited to viewing. These circumstances allowed Baade to make an important discovery: He learned that the Andromeda galaxy is made up of two different kinds of populations of stars. He called them Population I (luminous blue stars) and Population II (low-luminosity red stars). The spiral arms were found to be made up mostly of Population I, and the outer parts of the galaxy, the spherical halo, were made up of Population II. In the following ten years, this important distinction helped astronomers to unravel the amazing puzzle of stellar evolution and to understand for the first time the differences between galaxies.

Impact Although astronomical research activities during the 1940's were interrupted by World War II, several important developments occurred that would lead to major changes in understanding of the cosmos. The source of stars' energy was found to be nuclear fusion of protons into helium nuclei, knowledge of the spiral structure of the Milky Way developed, and the different populations of stars in galaxies were recognized.

Paul W. Hodge

Further Reading

Bok, Bart, and Priscilla F. Bok. *The Milky Way.* Cambridge, Mass.: Harvard University Press, 1981. The engaging book, a classic account of the early days of the modern study of the local galaxy, was written by two astronomers who were leaders of developments in the field during the 1940's.

Couper, Heather, Nigel Henbest, and Arthur C. Clarke. *The History of Astronomy.* Richmond Hill, Ont.: Firefly Books, 2009. Includes several unusual features, such as descriptions of historic telescopes and interviews with famous astronomers. Appropriate for readers new to the subject of astronomy.

Sparke, Linda, and John S. Gallagher. *Galaxies in the Universe.* New York: Cambridge University Press, 2000. The first three chapters of this authoritative text cover basic topics.

Sullivan, Woodruff. *Cosmic Noise: A History of Early Radio Astronomy.* New York: Cambridge University Press, 2009. Tells the fascinating and definitive story of the development of radio astronomy, beginning in the late 1930's and flourishing during the 1940's. Extensive interviews with some of the pioneers of radio astronomy make the text especially interesting.

See also   Big bang theory; Dim-out of 1945; Flying saucers; Gamow, George; Hale telescope; Norton County meteorite; Science and technology; World War II.

■ Atlantic, Battle of the

The Event   Multiyear struggle with U-boats for
   Allied supplies and war materials
Date   1939-1945
Place   Atlantic Ocean

The massive U.S. shipbuilding program and a renewed U.S. naval and merchant marine commitment to the Atlantic after June, 1940, contributed substantially to the elimination of the U-boat threat in that ocean by May, 1943, ensuring that sufficient supplies and troops reached Great Britain in preparation for the invasion of Nazi-controlled Europe.

Describing the struggle of British naval and merchant ships primarily with German U-boats in the Atlantic since September, 1939, British prime minister Winston Churchill coined the term "Battle of the Atlantic" in March, 1941. Five months later, Churchill met U.S. president Franklin D. Roosevelt off the coast of Newfoundland and again emphasized Britain's difficulties in shipping badly needed supplies across the Atlantic. Roosevelt promised all possible assistance short of war. In a radio address to the American people in September, 1941, Roosevelt explained that the U.S. Navy would attack all Axis raiders in U.S. defensive areas. After Adolf Hitler declared war on the United States in December, 1941, U.S. naval forces assisted Britain and Canada in defeating the U-boat threat in the Atlantic by May, 1943. Moreover, during World War II, the U.S. Maritime Commission alone built almost five thousand ships, enabling the transfer of massive amounts of material and troops to Britain. Without this supply and the victory in the Atlantic, the landings in Normandy in June, 1944, would not have been possible.

Operation Drumbeat   Immediately after Hitler's declaration of war, German U-boats targeted the eastern coast of the United States with devastating effect. Along that 1,500-mile coast, Rear Admiral Adolphus Andrews, who was in charge of the area between the Canadian border and North Carolina, initially had only twenty ships available for coastal protection. Even though only two dozen U-boats operated off the North and Central American coast, they sank 485 ships between February and the end of August, 1942. One historian has described this as the greatest American naval defeat in history. Only after the introduction of convoys and air defenses in the summer of 1942 was the U-boat threat eliminated along the U.S. Atlantic coast, although the enemy boats moved south to the Gulf of Mexico and the Caribbean. In response to the U-boat threat to shipping out of Galveston, Texas, a pipeline was built to supply the East Coast with oil.

In early 1942, the U-boats sank more than sixty ships between the Virginia border and Cape Lookout, North Carolina. When a British corvette, the HMS *Bedfordshire*, was sunk off the coast of North Carolina, the sailors were buried on Ocracoke Island; the burial plot, which was decorated by the British flag, was donated to Britain. Given the coastal conflict, rumors about spies and suspicion of Americans of German descent in areas such as Morehead and Salter Path, North Carolina, were rampant. The newspaper, the *Norfolk Virginia-Pilot*, and the journal, *Life*, published specific information about the sinking of American ships off the Atlantic coast that could have benefited the enemy. In addition, Atlantic coastal cities accidentally aided the U-boats by failing to dim their lights at night. Not until midsummer of 1942 did Miami cut its night lights after protests were published in the local newspaper.

The Battle of the North Atlantic   The most crucial battle to control the sea-lanes to Britain and Russia was fought in the North Atlantic, where U-boats were finally defeated in May, 1943, forcing the German naval command to withdraw the boats from the area. The United States fought this battle in two major ways. First came a massive shipbuilding program that eventually produced more tonnage than the U-boats could sink. For example, on September 27, 1941, fourteen Liberty cargo ships were launched in the United States to celebrate "Liberty Fleet Day." This was only the beginning of a program that even-

Battle of the Atlantic

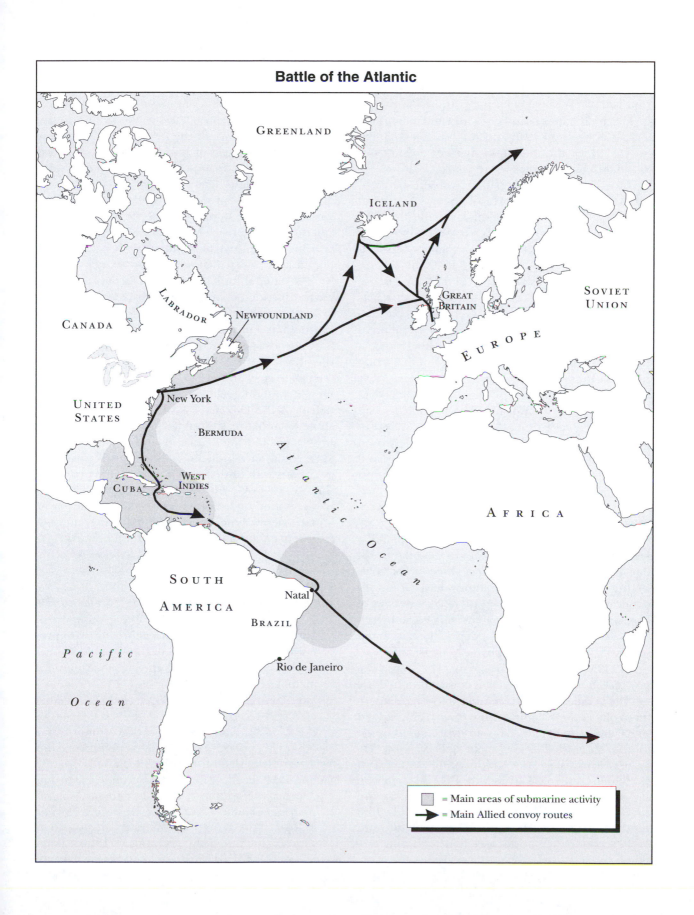

GREENLAND

ICELAND

LABRADOR

NEWFOUNDLAND

CANADA

GREAT BRITAIN

SOVIET UNION

EUROPE

UNITED STATES

New York

BERMUDA

WEST INDIES

CUBA

Atlantic Ocean

AFRICA

SOUTH AMERICA

Natal

BRAZIL

Rio de Janeiro

Pacific Ocean

■ = Main areas of submarine activity

➤ = Main Allied convoy routes

tually produced almost three thousand Liberty ships. Employment in American shipyards increased from 100,000 to 700,000 by 1943. At the same time, the U.S. merchant marine saw a fourfold increase in personnel between 1940 and August, 1945. Unlike the U.S. Navy, the merchant marines did not discriminate against African Americans.

The second major contribution to the Battle of the Atlantic was in the form of convoys and naval protection. The sheer size of this task is illustrated by the fact that 1,462 convoys left New York City during the war. More than three million soldiers departed and returned to that same city. In 1940, the U.S. Atlantic Fleet was reestablished, initially under the command of Admiral Ernest King. Naval conflicts between American ships and German U-boats occurred in the Atlantic long before the declaration of war by Hitler. In 1942, King decided to use his escort ships for troop transports to Britain. Not one troop ship was lost that year. However, U-boats were more successful against merchant ships during that year, particularly since the German navy was able to read British convoy codes in 1941 and 1942. The Allies lost 1,664 ships in 1942, and 80 percent were destroyed by submarines. In January, 1943, Roosevelt and Churchill agreed to give priority to the fight against U-boats. Large antisubmarine groups were formed to hunt U-boats, air support was increased, and technological innovations ranging from short-wave radar to breaking the German Enigma code played a decisive role in the Allied victory in the Atlantic. In May, 1943, the Germans lost forty-three submarines, forcing the German commander Karl Dönitz to withdraw his U-boats to safer waters. New designs of German U-boats never saw active service, although the last U.S. ship sunk by an "older" U-boat occurred on May 5, 1945, near Newport, Rhode Island.

A 1943 Warner Bros. film starring Humphrey Bogart, *Action in the North Atlantic*, commemorated the conflict in the Atlantic. It recounts the heroic experiences of a crew of a convoy ship that was torpedoed on its voyage to Britain. The survivors ended up on another ship, which sailed from Halifax, Nova Scotia, to Murmansk, Soviet Union. At the premiere of the film in New York City in May, 1943, seamen who had survived U-boat attacks and other sailors and merchant mariners honored Jack Warner. The film attracted large audiences in the United States, and the U.S. merchant marines used it in its training program.

Impact One could argue that the challenge faced by the British in the Atlantic in 1939 and 1940 induced the United States to begin significant industrial and military preparations. Most important, however, the control of the Atlantic was absolutely crucial for the defeat of Nazi Germany. Britain was totally dependent on imports in order to survive and continue the fight against Hitler. In addition, one quarter of American supplies received by the Soviet Union had to be shipped across the North Atlantic and the Arctic to reach Murmansk. This not only was crucial for the Russian conduct of the war but also played a key role in maintaining the alliance with the Soviets. When shipping supplies to Russia was temporarily suspended in preparation for Operation Torch in 1942, Soviet leader Joseph Stalin felt betrayed.

Command of the Atlantic sea-lanes was essential for transporting the men and supplies necessary for the invasion of the Continent and to maintain the "Germany first" strategy supported by Roosevelt. Admiral Ernest King had argued at one point, when the defeat of the U-boats was still uncertain, that the strategy should be shifted to "Japan first." A change in strategy and the failure to land in Normandy in 1944 could have induced Stalin to renew peace negotiations with Hitler, which he had first proposed the previous year. Finally, Hitler's massive commitment to building U-boats drained skilled manpower and scarce raw material, which could have been used to produce thousands of tanks and antiaircraft guns.

Johnpeter Horst Grill

Further Reading

Blair, Clay. *Hitler's U-Boat War: The Hunters, 1939-1945.* 2 vols. New York: Random House, 1996. Massively documented, this is the most comprehensive scholarly account of the struggle against German U-boats available in English. Volume 2 includes bibliography and notes.

Bunker, John Gorley. *Liberty Ships: The Ugly Ducklings of World War II.* Annapolis, Md.: Naval Institute Press, 1972. Good coverage of Baltimore and other U.S. port cities. Includes appendix on ship designs but no bibliography. Illustrated.

Gannon, Michael. *Operation Drumbeat: The Dramatic True Story of Germany's First U-Boat Attacks Along the American Coast in World War II.* New York: Harper & Row, 1990. Based on American and German sources, including the accounts of U-boat commander Reinhard Hardegen, it is critical of Admirals Ernest King and Adolphus Andrews for their belated defense of American shipping along the Atlantic coast.

Hoyt, Edwin P. *U-Boat Offshore: When Hitler Struck America.* New York: Stein & Day, 1978. Effective use of local newspaper accounts, ranging from Norfolk to Miami, revealing the impact of Operation Drumbeat on coastal cities. Bibliography and notes.

Milner, Marc. *Battle of the Atlantic.* Strout, England: Tempus, 2005. Helpful for Canadian contributions but very critical of British actions. Map, photos, illustrations, but only a short bibliography and no notes.

Walling, Michael G. *Bloodstained Sea: The U.S. Coast Guard in the Battle of the Atlantic, 1941-1944.* New York: McGraw Hill, 2004. Chronological account of convoys to Britain and Russia by a Coast Guard veteran. Photos, appendixes, list of sources.

Wiggins, Melanie. *Torpedoes in the Gulf: Galveston and the U-Boats, 1942-1943.* College Station: Texas A&M University Press, 1995. Used local newspapers and municipal records to illustrate impact of the U-boat threat to Galveston. Effective use of German naval records deposited in the U.S. National Archives, but weak on maps.

See also   Atlantic Charter; Churchill, Winston; Coast Guard, U.S.; Code breaking; Destroyers-for-bases deal; *Greer* incident; Lend-Lease; Liberty ships; Navy, U.S.

■ Atlantic Charter

The Treaty   Agreement between Franklin D. Roosevelt and Winston Churchill that committed their countries to peace, recognizing the right of self-determination for all nations

Date   Signed on August 14, 1941

Place   Placentia Bay, Newfoundland

This first meeting between Roosevelt and Churchill led to a series of regular meetings throughout World War II, later also involving Soviet leader

The Atlantic Charter

The President of the United States of America and the Prime Minister, Mr. [Winston] Churchill, representing His Majesty's Government in the United Kingdom, being met together, deem it right to make known certain common principles in the national policies of their respective countries on which they base their hopes for a better future for the world.

First, their countries seek no aggrandizement, territorial or other;

Second, they desire to see no territorial changes that do not accord with the freely expressed wishes of the peoples concerned;

Third, they respect the right of all peoples to choose the form of government under which they will live; and they wish to see sovereign rights and self government restored to those who have been forcibly deprived of them;

Fourth, they will endeavor, with due respect for their existing obligations, to further the enjoyment by all States, great or small, victor or vanquished, of access, on equal terms, to the trade and to the raw materials of the world which are needed for their economic prosperity;

Fifth, they desire to bring about the fullest collaboration between all nations in the economic field with the object of securing, for all, improved labor standards, economic advancement and social security;

Sixth, after the final destruction of the Nazi tyranny, they hope to see established a peace which will afford to all nations the means of dwelling in safety within their own boundaries, and which will afford assurance that all the men in all lands may live out their lives in freedom from fear and want;

Seventh, such a peace should enable all men to traverse the high seas and oceans without hindrance;

Eighth, they believe that all of the nations of the world, for realistic as well as spiritual reasons must come to the abandonment of the use of force. Since no future peace can be maintained if land, sea or air armaments continue to be employed by nations which threaten, or may threaten, aggression outside of their frontiers, they believe, pending the establishment of a wider and permanent system of general security, that the disarmament of such nations is essential. They will likewise aid and encourage all other practicable measure which will lighten for peace-loving peoples the crushing burden of armaments.

Joseph Stalin. After the war, the charter became foundational in setting up the United Nations.

At the time of the meeting of the two leaders, the United States was not yet involved in World War II, while Great Britain had been fighting for two years. Although the Americans were beginning to give Britain material help, the antiwar sentiment was still too strong for Franklin D. Roosevelt to commit himself to joining Britain. On the other hand, Winston Churchill realized that without the United States, the war against the Axis forces could not be won.

The first meeting was held in secret. Roosevelt was ostensibly going on a fishing trip and only out at sea transferred to the USS *Augusta*. Churchill sailed from Scapa Flow in the far north of Scotland, also away from public view. He sailed in the premier British warship HMS *Prince of Wales*. Accompanying Roosevelt were his close advisers Harry Hopkins and William Averell Harriman, Sumner Welles from his cabinet, and a number of military officers. With Churchill were Lord Beaverbrook and Alexander Cadogan, a senior Foreign Office official. The military was headed up by Field Marshal Sir John Dill, later to become British representative to Washington.

Military talks ran parallel to the political but were subordinate to them. Churchill and Roosevelt were meeting for the first time, but relations proved to be good between them. Roosevelt could not agree to Churchill's demands to promise to enter the war or even to make a firm stand against the Japanese. They fared better when they discussed what a postwar world could look like.

An initial draft of an agreement drawn up by Cadogan and Welles was presented to the two leaders. The sticking points at first were the British Empire and its system of trade preferences, which cut across policies of free trade. The British cabinet, sitting under Labour leader Clement Attlee, also wanted a clause added to cover welfare and working conditions.

Impact The declaration became known as the Atlantic Charter. It was later approved by the Soviet Union and became the basis for the United Nations. The United States was immediately assured that it had not been committed to war. To the British the charter gave them hope for a future after the war.

David Barratt

Further Reading

Brinkley, Douglas G., and David R. Facey-Crowther. *The Atlantic Charter.* New York: St. Martin's Press, 1994.

Fenby, Jonathan. *Alliance: The Inside Story of How Roosevelt, Stalin, and Churchill Won One War and Began Another.* New York: Simon & Schuster, 2006.

Morton, H. V. *Atlantic Meeting: An Account of Mr Churchill's Voyage in HMS* Prince of Wales *in August, 1941.* London: Methuen, 1943.

See also Atlantic, Battle of the; Churchill, Winston; Decolonization of European empires; Isolationism; Roosevelt, Franklin D.; United Nations; World War II.

■ Atomic bomb

Definition Nuclear fission powered weapon of mass destructive power used against Japan in World War II

Intense scientific study and relentless dedication led to the American development of the atomic bomb during World War II. The success of the United States in producing and deploying the bomb helped hasten the conclusion of the war in the Pacific theater. In the Cold War that followed, rival nations began amassing nuclear arsenals.

Early in the twentieth century, Albert Einstein theorized and John D. Cockcroft and Ernest Walton demonstrated that mass can be converted into energy. In 1939, Otto Hahn and Fritz Strassmann learned that neutrons striking the heavy element uranium made atoms split and caused fission. From the splitting atoms, newly produced neutrons strike other uranium nuclei, and chain reactions ensue. When the fission is maintained at a moderate pace, the chain reactions generates energy. When the fission is allowed to advance rapidly, chain reactions may create explosions. In a famous August 2, 1939, letter to President Franklin D. Roosevelt, Einstein warned that Germany intended to harness this nuclear energy to create an atomic bomb. The president then set in motion a plan for the United States to produce such a weapon first. In 1942, the Manhattan Project began, and by 1945, the United States had workable nuclear weapons that it used against Japan.

Development of the Bomb The Hungarian physicist Leo Szilard recognized the importance of the discovery of nuclear fission and was aware that Germany's seizure of Czechoslovakia in 1938 gave it control over substantial uranium resources. When Germany prohibited the export of Czech uranium, Szilard reasoned that it intended to produce an atomic weapon. Along with other concerned scientists, Szilard prompted Einstein to compose the letter to Roosevelt warning of this danger.

Roosevelt authorized the formation of the Briggs Committee under the direction of Lyman Briggs, and this committee examined the feasibility of using nuclear power to propel submarines or to create powerful bombs. To speed up development, in June, 1940, Roosevelt selected Vannevar Bush to head the National Defense Research Council. The following year, Bush became director of the Office of Scientific Research and Development.

A crucial step in developing the bomb was obtaining sufficient uranium to produce the chain reaction. Two radioactive isotopes, uranium-235 (U-235) and uranium-238 (U-238) occur in nature, but U-235, which is much scarcer than U-238, is the isotope capable of producing fission. Because separating the two isotopes is difficult and expensive, the feasibility of producing enough U-235 had to be ascertained before the project could continue.

In May, 1942, the Office of Scientific Research and Development, undeterred by the potential expense involved in producing fissionable uranium, went forward with five approaches to producing fissionable materials, three for deriving U-235 from U-238, and two for producing plutonium, or Pu-239, another fissionable material identified by chemist Glenn Seaborg. By pursuing five approaches, the United States tried to guarantee a successful outcome within the shortest possible time. In June, Bush advised Roosevelt that the U.S. Army should build facilities to develop the bomb, and the Army Corps of Engineers began constructing the Manhattan Engineering District, which soon became

Photograph of a test explosion of an atomic bomb dropped on the Bikini Atoll on July 1, 1946, taken by a remote-control camera. (AP/ Wide World Photos)

known as the Manhattan Project.

In September, 1942, Colonel Leslie Groves took command of the Manhattan Project. He acquired uranium ore and bought land in eastern Tennessee to build plants to produce U-235 by means of gaseous diffusion and electromagnetic separation. Meanwhile, at the University of Chicago, Enrico Fermi demonstrated the function of a nuclear reactor and thereby established that such reactors could be sources for plutonium through the irradiation of U-238. In January, 1943, the government bought additional land near Hanford, Washington, and constructed reactors to produce plutonium. In Tennessee, production of U-235 was initially insufficient, but by early 1945 production was sufficient for the creation of a nuclear weapon.

Working with physicist Robert Oppenheimer, who with his team of scientists in Berkeley, California, had created a design for an atomic weapon during the summer of 1942, Groves established a central laboratory for the creation of an atomic bomb in April, 1943. This facility, known as the Los Alamos laboratory, was located in New Mexico near Santa Fe, a spot that provided efficient communications for scientists without sacrificing secrecy and security.

Building the Bomb   Using two pieces of U-235, with each piece being too small to generate a sustained chain reaction, scientists at Los Alamos created a gun-type atomic bomb. In a gun barrel, an explosion occurs when the two pieces of U-235 are driven together to create a supercritical mass. Scientists were so sure of this bomb design that they did not test it until the first bomb was dropped on Japan in August, 1945.

Using plutonium, scientists developed a bomb that relied on implosion. Chemical explosives were packed around a noncritical shell, and when the explosives were detonated, they compressed the shell and created a supercritical mass that led to a chain

---

Seeing the Blast Up Close

U.S. brigadier general Thomas F. Farrell provided this description of the first atomic bomb blast to the secretary of war on July 16, 1945. Along with others, Farrell was in a project "control shelter" located merely 10,000 yards from the site of the explosion.

The effects could well be called unprecedented, magnificent, beautiful, stupendous and terrifying. No man-made phenomenon of such tremendous power had ever occurred before. The lighting effects beggared description. The whole country was lighted by a searing light with the intensity many times that of the midday sun. It was golden, purple, violet, gray and blue. It lighted every peak, crevasse and ridge of the nearby mountain range with a clarity and beauty that cannot be described but must be seen to be imagined. It was that beauty the great poets dream about but describe most poorly and inadequately. Thirty seconds after the explosion came first, the air blast pressing hard against the people and things, to be followed almost immediately by the strong, sustained, awesome roar which warned of doomsday and made us feel that we puny things were blasphemous to dare tamper with the forces heretofore reserved to The Almighty. Words are inadequate tools for the job of acquainting those not present with the physical, mental and psychological effects. It had to be witnessed to be realized.

---

reaction and an explosion. Testing of this type of bomb was done at Alamogordo, New Mexico, on July 16, 1945. The "Fat Man" bomb that was dropped on Nagasaki, Japan, on August 9, 1945, relied on the implosion of plutonium.

The Decision to Drop the Bomb   After the United States had a workable atomic bomb, the decision, to deploy had to be made with the consent of the British government, the principal U.S. ally. Implicit in the development of the bomb was the commitment to deploy it if the war was still in progress. By the time the bomb was available, Germany had surrendered, but Japan showed no signs that it was ready to stop fighting.

Alternatives to using an atomic bomb against Japan were considered. A blockade of Japan was possible, and continued conventional bombing by B-29 long-range bombers would be devastating. If the Soviet Union, which had a neutrality treaty with Japan, declared war on Japan, Japan might collapse. Strategists had to decide if dropping the atomic bomb was truly necessary.

On April 12, 1945, President Roosevelt died, and Harry S. Truman became the new president. Amid the distractions of forming a new administration, Truman had to determine whether Japan should be warned about the atomic bomb and whether a demonstration of the bomb's destructive power might prompt a surrender. In July, Truman met with other Allied leaders in Potsdam, Germany, to make plans for the end of the war. The resulting Potsdam declaration called for Japan's unconditional surrender, which the Japanese rejected. On August 6, the first atomic bomb was dropped on Hiroshima. Three days later a second bomb was dropped on Nagasaki. Japan finally surrendered on September 2.

Impact   After the United States used the bomb, an international arms race began that led to the creation of nuclear arsenals and the development of even more powerful thermonuclear weapons. Nuclear proliferation put the world at risk, but strategists hoped that a balance of power might prevent a worldwide nuclear war. The atomic bomb significantly reshaped the culture and psychology of the world.

William T. Lawlor

Further Reading

Boyer, Paul S. *By the Bomb's Early Light*. New York: Pantheon, 1985. Interesting exploration of the influences of the atomic age on culture after World War II.

Joseph, Timothy. *Historic Photos of the Manhattan Project*. Nashville, Tenn.: Turner Publishing, 2009. Eye-catching pictorial history of the making of the atomic bomb.

Rhodes, Richard. *The Making of the Atomic Bomb*. New York: Simon & Schuster, 1986. Award-winning book story of the atom bomb, told from scientific, political, military, and human perspectives.

Rotter, Andrew J. *Hiroshima: The World Bomb*. Oxford, England: Oxford University Press, 2008. Examination of the scientific, technological, military, political, and cultural forces that led to atomic weapons.

Walzer, Michael. *Just and Unjust Wars: A Moral Argument with Historical Illustrations*. New York: Basic Books, 1997. According to Walzer, atomic bombs killed innocent civilians and therefore violated the rules of war.

See also   Cold War; Einstein, Albert; Fermi, Enrico; Groves, Leslie Richard; Hanford Nuclear Reservation; Hiroshima and Nagasaki bombings; Manhattan Project; Nuclear reactors; Oppenheimer, J. Robert; Plutonium discovery.

■ Atomic clock

Definition   A clock that uses resonance frequences of atoms to measure time accurately

Atomic clocks keep time more accurately than any other means of measuring time, including those based on the rotation of the Earth or the movement of the stars. Eventually, innumerable communication, scientific, and navigation systems would rely on the precision of atomic clocks.

In 1945, Isidor Isaac Rabi, a physics professor at Columbia University, proposed making a clock that derived its time scale from resonance frequencies of atoms or molecules. Using Rabi's idea, the National Bureau of Standards (now the National Institute of Standards and Technology) announced the first atomic clock in 1949. It relied on the microwave resonance frequencies of the ammonia molecule.

The core of the first atomic clock was a microwave cavity containing ammonia, a tunable microwave oscillator, and a feedback circuit to adjust the oscillator frequency to the resonance frequency of ammonia. When microwave energy is supplied to the ammonia at its natural vibrating frequency of 23,870 hertz, the ammonia absorbs the energy. A quartz oscillator was used to supply energy to the ammonia gas. When the frequency of the oscillator varied from the resonance value for ammonia, energy was no longer absorbed by the ammonia. A signal was then fed back to the oscillator supply to prevent it from drifting from the resonance frequency, thus maintaining the accuracy of the clock.

Impact   Although different kinds of atomic clocks have been developed, the fundamental operating principle of these devices is the same as that of the ammonia atomic clock. In 1952, an atomic clock using cesium atoms as the vibration source was produced. In 1967, the second was defined as exactly 9,192,631,770 oscillations of the resonance frequency of cesium.

Alvin K. Benson

Further Reading

Audoin, Claude, and Bernard Guinot. *The Measurement of Time: Time, Frequency, and the Atomic Clock.* New York: Cambridge University Press, 2001.

Major, Fouad G. *The Quantum Beat: Principles and Applications of Atomic Clocks.* New York: Springer, 2007.

See also Astronomy; Inventions; Radar; Science and technology.

■ Atomic Energy Commission

Identification Federal government's primary policy-making agency for the development of nuclear energy

Date Established on August 1, 1946; began operating on January 1, 1947

Place Washington, D.C.

The Atomic Energy Commission was created after the end of World War II to serve as the central federal agency overseeing the development of the nuclear power technology developed during the war. The commission was originally intended to promote peaceful uses of nuclear energy, but it soon played a major role in advancing nuclear weapons technology.

On August 1, 1946, the U.S. Congress created the Atomic Energy Commission (AEC) through passage of the Atomic Energy Act (also called the McMahon Act). Its goal for the new federal agency was to promote the growth of the new nuclear power industry while also ensuring the safety of the public from the perils of nuclear radiation. President Harry S. Truman appointed David Eli Lilienthal to be the commission's first chairman.

During the five years immediately before his appointment to the AEC, Lilienthal had served as chairman of the Tennessee Valley Authority (TVA). He had been appointed to that post by President Franklin D. Roosevelt after having served since 1933 as one of the TVA's three directors. His many years as director and head of the TVA had earned him the nickname "Mr. TVA." To assist Lilienthal with providing technical and scientific advice, a general advisory committee of scientists was established, along with the Congressional Joint Committee on Atomic Energy and a Military Liaison Committee.

The general advisory committee was headed by J. Robert Oppenheimer from 1947 to 1952. Oppenheimer had been the chief scientist for the Manhattan Project, which had been created to produce the first atomic bomb. With Oppenheimer lending his technical expertise as head of the advisory committee, the newly created AEC took over the operations of the Manhattan Project on January 1, 1947.

Cold War Priorities Although World War II had ended and the AEC had been created, in part, to promote peacetime nuclear power applications, the Cold War immediately ensued, and the AEC devoted most of its attention over the following twenty years to nuclear weapons development and production. The effect of the atomic bombs dropped on Japan had made the importance of developing nuclear weapons very apparent.

The first activities of the newly created commission included the building of two new plutonium reactors at the Hanford Nuclear Reservation in Washington State and a gaseous diffusion plant to produce uranium 235 at the nuclear production facility at Oak Ridge, Tennessee. To assist with the construction and operation of these facilities, the AEC continued the practice that had existed during World War II of contracting with private companies. Consequently, the first AEC-recommended nuclear testing series took place in April and May of 1948 at Eniwetok Atoll and was called Operation Sandstone. Operation Sandstone also developed and tested a new fission-based weapon system, which was an improvement over the nuclear technology employed during World War II. By the end of 1948, the U.S. government was beginning to stockpile an arsenal of nuclear weapons.

Peaceful Uses of Atomic Power During the AEC's early days, David Lilienthal continued to promote the peaceful applications of nuclear energy research along with weapon development. During World War II, the Clinton Laboratories had been built at Oak Ridge, Tennessee, and in 1948 these research facilities were reorganized as the Oak Ridge National Laboratories, which would become the world's largest supplier of radioisotopes for medical and industrial research. Oak Ridge National Laboratories also became the home for the largest radiation genetics program in the world.

The AEC also approved plans for the Brookhaven National Laboratory to conduct research utilizing high-energy accelerators for research in reactor physics. Argonne National Laboratory in Argonne, Illinois, became the AEC's center for reactor-based research. Meanwhile, the University of California Radiation Laboratory at Berkeley was expanded as another major nuclear research facility. During the late 1940's, the AEC also expanded its funding and sponsorship of numerous nuclear energy research programs at many U.S. universities.

Impact Under Lilienthal's leadership, the AEC made significant progress during the late 1940's with the establishment of research programs for both weapons-based research and peacetime-based research that would continue to have an impact on the national agenda for many decades. However, when President Dwight D. Eisenhower decided it would be in the best interests for the United States to develop a hydrogen bomb, Lilienthal refused to help. In 1950, he resigned and went into private business. Five years later, he founded the Development and Resource Corporation to help the development of public works projects in several underdeveloped nations.

During the early 1950's, Congress enacted several amendments to its original Atomic Energy Act that gave the AEC more control over nuclear power plants. Due to conflict both within and outside the AEC, the AEC was dissolved and replaced by the Nuclear Regulatory Agency and the Energy Research and Development Administration, in 1974.

Jean L. Kuhler

> ## "A Problem More of Ethics than of Physics"
>
> *Before the founding of the Atomic Energy Commission, U.S. president Harry S. Truman asked American financier Bernard Baruch to address the United Nations on how atomic energy—namely its potential to effect both good and bad outcomes—must be controlled by all nations. Baruch spoke before the United Nations on June 14, 1946:*
>
> We are here to make a choice between the quick and the dead. That is our business.
>
> Behind the black portent of the new atomic age lies a hope which, seized upon with faith, can work our salvation. If we fail, then we have damned every man to be a slave of fear. Let us not deceive ourselves, we must elect world peace or world destruction.
>
> Science has torn from nature a secret so vast in its potentialities that our minds cower from the terror it creates. The terror is not enough to inhibit the use of the atomic bomb. The terror created by weapons has never stopped man from employing them. . . .
>
> Science, which gave us this dread power, shows that it can be made a giant help to humanity, but science does not show us how to prevent its baleful use. So we have been appointed to obviate that peril by finding a meeting of the minds and the hearts of our people. Only in the will of mankind lies the answer. . . .
>
> Science has taught us how to put the atom to work. But to make it work for good instead of evil lies in the domain dealing with the principles of human duty. We are now facing a problem more of ethics than of physics.

Further Reading

Duffy, Robert J. *Nuclear Politics in America: A History and Theory of Government Regulation.* Lawrence: University Press of Kansas, 1997. Study of government policies and regulation of the American nuclear power industry.

Hewlett, Richard G., and Oscar E. Anderson, Jr. *The New World, 1939-1946.* Vol. 1 in *A History of the United States Atomic Energy Commission.* University Park: Pennsylvania State University Press, 1962. Reliable study of the wartime development of the Manhattan Project and the congressional maneuvers that resulted in the establishment of the AEC.

Hewlett, Richard G., and Francis Duncan. *Atomic Shield, 1947-1952.* Vol. 2 in *A History of the United States Atomic Energy Commission.* University Park: Pennsylvania State University Press, 1969. This volume begins with the confirmation hearings of the original five appointees to the AEC and carries the story up to 1952.

Lilienthal, David Eli. *Change, Hope, and the Bomb.* Princeton, N.J.: Princeton University Press, 1963. Thoughts of the first chairman of the AEC on issues such as nuclear disarmament, nuclear fuels versus fossil fuels, and peaceful uses of the atom.

Walker, J. Samuel. *A Short History of Nuclear Regulation, 1946-1999.* Washington, D.C.: U.S. Nuclear Regulatory Commission, 2000. Seventy-page history of the Atomic Energy Commission and the Nuclear Regulatory Commission. Can be found on the Nuclear Regulatory Commission's Web site.

See also Atomic bomb; Cold War; Hanford Nuclear Reservation; Manhattan Project; Nuclear reactors; Oppenheimer, J. Robert; Science and technology; Wartime technological advances.

■ Auden, W. H.

Identification English poet
Born February 21, 1907; York, England
Died September 29, 1973; Vienna, Austria

Auden was a major twentieth century poet whose career spanned four decades. During the 1940's, his writing reached a wide audience and influenced many American poets. He also contributed to the intellectual life of mid-century America as a thinker and teacher.

During the 1930's, Wystan Hugh Auden achieved fame in England for his experimental poetry and leftist politics. In 1939, he moved to the United States, making a sharp break with the past and seeking a new direction for his poetry. Shortly after arriving in New York, Auden experienced two life-changing events: He fell in love with a young man, Chester Kallman, who became his lover and then his lifelong companion, and he returned to the Anglican Communion, embracing the Christianity he had abandoned years earlier. These two events strongly influenced his work in the 1940's.

At the start of the decade, Auden was much in demand as a spokesman for left-wing causes, a role he soon rejected. He adopted instead a less public role, and his work became more cerebral and politically detached than that of previous decades. Auden nevertheless became a public figure in America, regularly publishing poetry and prose in such well-known venues as *The New Yorker, The New Republic,* and *The Nation.* The first extended work he wrote in the United States was an opera libretto based on the American legend of Paul Bunyan, suggesting his eagerness to connect with his new country. Later in the decade, Auden and Kallman launched a lifelong collaboration as opera librettists.

Auden's major poetic works of the decade were four long philosophical poems exploring his evolving aesthetic and religious beliefs: "New Year Letter" (1940), "For the Time Being" (1944), "The Sea and the Mirror" (1944), and *The Age of Anxiety: A Baroque Eclogue* (1947). His primary influences during this period include the nineteenth century Danish philosopher Søren Kierkegaard and the contemporary Protestant theologians Reinhold Niebuhr and Paul Tillich. *The Age of Anxiety* won a Pulitzer Prize, and its title became for many an apt catchphrase for a troubled time. The American composer Leonard Bernstein borrowed the title for one of his symphonies.

In 1945, Auden's *Collected Poems* appeared, selling more than fourteen thousand copies in the first year. In 1946, Auden became a U.S. citizen and settled in Greenwich Village, becoming a local celebrity in New York City's famed center of artistic experimentation. Throughout the decade, he was a frequent and much-admired teacher at various colleges. Also in 1946, he gave a series of lectures on Shakespeare at the New School for Social Research, which were reconstructed and published more than half a century later as *Lectures on Shakespeare* (2001).

Impact Auden began his writing career as an unofficial spokesman for the disaffected English intellectuals of his generation. In 1940's America, however, he adopted a new role, exploring the possibilities of living a meaningful life in a flawed world. His literary explorations became part of the intellectual climate of the time. His work also influenced important American poets such as John Berryman, Richard Wilbur, Anthony Hecht, and James Merrill. Auden's poetry remained relevant in the early twenty-first century, even in popular culture. His poem "September 1, 1939," written on the outbreak of World War II shortly after his arrival in America, was widely circulated and publicly read as a response to the calamitous terrorist attacks of September 11, 2001.

Michael Hennessey

Further Reading

Auden, W. H. *Collected Poems.* Edited by Edward Mendelson. New York: Modern Library, 2007.

Mendelson, Edward. *Later Auden.* New York: Farrar, Straus and Giroux, 1999.

Smith, Stan, ed. *The Cambridge Companion to W. H. Auden.* Cambridge, England: Cambridge University Press, 2004.

See also   Eliot, T. S.; Literature in Canada; Literature in the United States; Pound, Ezra.

■ Auto racing

Definition   Competitive, high-speed vehicle racing for cash prizes

At the start of the 1940's, auto racing was a minor American sport that appeared to be on the threshold of extinction when it was essentially shut down during the war years. After the war, however, two seminal events set auto racing on the path to greater popularity than it had ever enjoyed: the reestablishment of the Indianapolis 500 and the birth of NASCAR racing.

The 1940's was an interesting period of auto racing development, even though one major aspect of it was suspended by World War II. At the beginning of the decade, much of the focus of the sport was on open-wheel cars that competed over five hundred miles at the Indianapolis Motor Speedway. Prior to the war, the annual Indianapolis 500 brought as many as 100,000 fans to watch cars that averaged speeds as high as 115 miles per hour. In 1940, fans watched driver Wilbur Shaw win his third Indy 500. The following year featured an unusual circumstance as Floyd Davis and Mauri Rose won the race together; Davis had to leave his car on the seventy-second lap, and then Rose drove the remaining 128 laps.

Indianapolis Transition   After the United States entered World War II at the end of 1941, the federal government suspended auto racing to conserve fuel and help the nation focus on the war effort. During the war years, the Indianapolis Motor Speedway became a makeshift site for repairing airplanes. By the time the war ended in late 1945, the track had become a derelict piece of land. Its wooden grandstands were rotting and weeds covered the track. It seemed that Indy racing was destined to become a part of history, as the track's owner, Eddie Rickenbacker, was looking to sell its land to housing developers.

Tony Hulman, Jr., is the man credited with saving racing at Indy. An Indiana native, Hulman bought the track in 1945, and put a full effort into restoring it to its former condition. By the following year, he had succeeded. When the 1946 Indy 500 was held, George Robson won the race.

The Birth of NASCAR   As Hulman continued to make the Indy 500 one of the premier auto racing events in the world, a new form of racing was emerging in Daytona Beach, Florida. During the 1930's, Daytona Beach was the foremost American location for setting world land-speed records. Drivers from all over the world went there hoping to break records. When the first road course was held at the beach in 1936, promoter Bill France got an idea. He realized the potential of expanding auto racing to include competitions among ordinary passenger cars, "stock cars." In 1947, he established the National Championship Stock Car Circuit (NCSCC). This new organization established fixed rules for sanctioned events, created seasonal points stand-

Cars in the first NASCAR race at Daytona Beach, Florida, on February 15, 1948. (ISC Archives via Getty Images)

ings, and allotted prize money. Red Byron won the inaugural event, which was dubbed the "Battle of the Champions," on Daytona's beach-road course.

France's vision was not one of sticking to one track; his goal was to see stock car drivers race on a variety of tracks, thus providing them with different challenges while offering the sport to more people. In May, 1947, Fonty Flock won the first NCSCC event, at North Wilkesboro Speedway in North Carolina. Flock would go on to win the first overall NCSCC title, while drivers began competing on tracks at High Point, North Carolina; Langhorne, Pennsylvania; Martinsville, Virginia; and Jacksonville, Florida. Almost forty NCSCC events were held during the inaugural year alone, and spectators packed the stands for all of them.

NASCAR Evolves At the end of the 1947 season, France met with a cabal of those working for the NCSCC to examine any changes that needed to be made. The most significant aspect of the meeting was announced in February, 1948, when the NCSCC became NASCAR—the National Association for Stock Car Automobile Racing. Meanwhile, the points system for races and the overall championship were revised.

When it was created, NASCAR was expected to have three different divisions: "modified," "roadster," and "strictly stock." However, the circuit's organizers soon decided to drop the roadster division. No competitions were held in the strictly stock division until 1949, because automobile manufacturers were still having trouble keeping up with the huge postwar demand for passenger cars. The first race for this division was held in Charlotte, North Carolina. Meanwhile, races in the modified division were held predominantly on dirt tracks.

Impact The efforts of Tony Hulman, Jr., and Bill France helped make auto racing an American institution during the 1940's. Hulman rescued a track that had fallen into disrepair during the war and re-established it as one of the foremost speedways in the world. France was able to create an entire racing series, realizing auto racing could succeed as a national touring division. Since the 1940's, both the Indianapolis Motor Speedway and NASCAR have found enormous success, and the two have even become entwined, as NASCAR now holds 400-mile races at the Indy Speedway every August.

P. Huston Ladner

Further Reading

Cardwell, Harold D., Sr. *Daytona Beach: One Hundred Years of Racing.* Charleston, S.C.: Arcadia, 2002. Comprehensive history of automobile racing at Daytona Beach that goes back well before the rise of NASCAR.

Fielden, Greg. *NASCAR: The Complete History.* Lincolnwood, Ill.: Publications International, 2007. Detailed history of the rise of NASCAR during the 1940's and its subsequent development into one of the most popular American spectator sports.

Kenipe, Kenneth E. *Indianapolis 500 Rankings: Records and Rankings of Every Driver Who Ever Competed in the Indianapolis 500 Mile Race.* Bloomington, Ind.: AuthorHouse, 2008. Definitive reference source on Indy racing history.

Lazarus, William P. and J. J. O'Malley. *Sands of Time: A Century of Racing in Daytona Beach.* Champaign, Ill.: Sports Publishing, 2004. Similar to Cardwell's book, this volume examines the full history of automobile racing at Daytona Beach.

Reed, Terry. *Indy: The Race and the Ritual of the Indianapolis 500.* Washington, D.C.: Potomac Books, 2005. Well-illustrated history of Indy racing.

See also Automobiles and auto manufacturing; Ford Motor Company; Freeways; General Motors; Recreation; Sports in the United States.

■ Automobiles and auto manufacturing

During World War II, the automobile industry was one of the chief industries that provided equipment, materials, and supplies to the U.S. military and its allies. The reconversion of this industry from wartime to peacetime pursuits helped usher in a period of great prosperity in the United States.

In 1940, the automobile industry was slowly recovering from the Great Depression and experiencing growth in sales of private and commercial vehicles. The "Big Three"—Ford, General Motors (GM), and Chrysler—dominated the market, but a number of smaller independent companies enjoyed decent sales as the economy recovered from its crisis. Ford and GM had overseas affiliates that generated profits. After September 1, 1939, exports were affected by the war in Europe, limiting sales for some companies. Nevertheless, firms such as Packard and Studebaker introduced new models in 1941 that seemed to satisfy American customers, promising a bright future for these companies. Hence, at the beginning of the decade, auto executives resisted pressure from government officials to convert some automobile manufacturing facilities to assist allies who were fighting the Axis powers in Europe and Asia. Executives were worried that converting factories to produce advanced military machinery during a period of high demand for their automotive products would cause them to lose civilian customers.

Mobilization for War Much of the United States was focused more on domestic recovery than international affairs in 1940, but the Roosevelt administration was already heavily involved in preparing for war. The president and his advisers knew that success against Adolf Hitler, Benito Mussolini, and Japan would require production of war machinery in great quantities, and that the automobile industry was the only one capable of producing tanks, planes, and other items the United States would require. Automobile executives such as Alfred P. Sloan at GM and Henry Ford were deeply distrustful of President Roosevelt's administration and balked at assisting in any way that might be perceived as pushing the United States into the European conflict.

New cars waiting to be transported throughout the United States to help meet the vast postwar demand for automobiles in 1949. The wood-sided DeSoto station wagon at the lower right is an example of what has become known as a "woody." (Time & Life Pictures/Getty Images)

Nevertheless, steps were taken toward mobilizing the automobile industry for wartime production long before America entered the conflict. A 1938 Educational Order Act allowed the government to award contracts to companies to experiment with production of small quantities of military equipment, and some auto manufacturers took advantage of the program to produce items other than cars and trucks. Many in the United States thought that the auto industry could convert from civilian to military production easily and quickly, just as it had done in World War I. Savvy auto executives knew better. Modern military trucks, tanks, and specialized vehicles were nothing like the civilian vehicles being produced in 1940, and retooling plants to make military vehicles and equipment would require months of downtime in production.

In 1940, Roosevelt chose William Knudsen, the president of General Motors and a former executive at Ford Motor Company, to head up the first advisory board on wartime production. With no real authority, however, Knudsen faced difficulties in getting auto executives to speed up conversion. Alfred Sloan was reluctant because he feared that both the original conversion and the reconversion after the war would prove costly. Henry Ford was against any American involvement in support of the war, even that which might help England and France. In 1940, Ford's company was asked to make engines for the Royal Air Force, but Henry Ford refused to accept the contract, as did executives at Chrysler. Eventually, Packard Motors took the contract. Studebaker signed a contract to make trucks for France. At the same time, these firms continued to make cars for the American market.

Factory Sales for Passenger Cars, 1940-1949

In thousands

Year	Value
1940	3,717.3
1941	3,779.6
1942	222.8
1943	0.1
1944	0.6
1945	69.5
1946	2,148.6
1947	3,558.1
1948	3,909.2
1949	5,119.4

Source: Historical Statistics of the United States: Colonial Times to 1970. U.S. Department of Commerce, Bureau of the Census, 1975, p. 392.

One technique used by the government to encourage the auto industry to take on production of war materials was the offer to have the work done in Government Owned Contractor Operated (GOCO) plants. Under this arrangement, the Defense Plant Corporation would construct facilities with government funds for lease to companies that would operate them. This prevented manufacturers from incurring too much debt—and assuming too much risk—by having to make capital investments in plants that might not be needed after the war. Chrysler was one of the first to sign on to this proposal, agreeing in 1941 to make medium-sized tanks in a GOCO plant in Warren, Michigan. Several other firms did the same, and the practice became commonplace after the United States entered World War II in 1941.

Wartime Production Within weeks after the Japanese attacked Pearl Harbor in December, 1941, production of all civilian vehicles ceased. The Automotive Council for War Production, an industry-sponsored and industry-led group, coordinated efforts at production of war material, going so far as to convince manufacturers to share information and resources. Within months, companies such as GM found that 90 percent of their business was coming from the government. Some companies became specialists. For example, Chrysler produced most of the tanks used in the war. Ford partnered with the Willys company to build Jeeps, all-wheel-drive vehicles developed in 1940. By the middle of 1942, manufacturers were turning out trucks, tracked vehicles, tanks, components for aircraft, and a host of other items for the war, including small arms, ammunitions, and even parts for advanced radar systems. Ford ended up building B-24 bombers from start to finish at its new facility in Willow Run, Michigan, where 100,000 workers staffed the assembly line. Chrysler built components for machinery to produce uranium-235, the special isotope of uranium used to build the first atomic bomb. GM estimated that during the war, two-thirds of its work consisted of producing items it had never made before the war.

Despite a general feeling of patriotism and willingness to do whatever was necessary to bring about victory for the Allies, auto manufacturers faced numerous problems in 1942 and 1943. Raw materials were allocated by government agencies created to manage the war effort and keep the civilian economy from collapsing. Shortages often meant delays or even shutdowns of assembly lines. The industry faced serious labor issues as well. Many of the men who worked at auto plants enlisted or were drafted, and companies scrambled to find replacements. Two groups filled the need admirably: women and members of minority groups.

Union issues, a great source of consternation for auto manufacturers during the 1930's, again plagued the industry. Although unions had agreed not to strike during the war, wildcat strikes often shut down facilities, sometimes for weeks. Only strong federal intervention managed to bring management and labor together for the duration of the war.

Although manufacturers had enough government contracts to expand operations during the war, auto dealerships felt the loss of new inventory almost immediately. Within a year, 15 percent were out of business. Americans could not buy new cars, and therefore many held on to their old ones. Additionally, rubber and petroleum products were rationed. Fearing adverse reactions from the American public, automobile manufacturers mounted massive public relations campaigns to let the public know how much they were doing to help the United States win the war.

By the war's end, the automobile industry had fulfilled $29 billion in government contracts. Although the bulk of that work had been in manufacturing trucks, tanks, and aircraft components, the industry had also produced nearly $2 billion in marine equipment, more than $1.5 billion in weapons and ammunition, and $1 billion in other war products. It is no exaggeration to say that the industrial might of the automobile industry was an indispensable component in the Allied victory.

Reconversion to Peacetime Production   Even before the United States entered the war, farsighted executives such as Alfred Sloan at GM were planning for reconverting facilities back to manufacturing civilian automobiles. By 1944, the government was sponsoring reconversion efforts. When the war ended with the signing of surrender documents in September, 1945, the auto industry was as ready as possible to begin producing vehicles for private customers, although retooling from military manufacturing to production of passenger cars took some time. In the remaining months of 1945, only 100,000 new vehicles were produced. By 1949, however, the industry had an annual production output of 5 million passenger cars and 1 million other vehicles.

As they had during the war, automobile manufacturers faced significant problems in the postwar years. Initially, the government was slow to lift price controls. Cars offered for sale in 1946 carried 1942 prices. At the same time, companies were plagued by a series of labor strikes as unions fought to recover what they perceived as losses in earnings and benefits, which had been frozen for nearly four years as a result of the war. As a result, some manufacturers found that they could not charge enough to make a profit on new cars. Most companies had to settle for bringing out "new" cars using the same designs that were in production before the war. Not until 1947 was a truly new vehicle offered for sale.

Problems of reconversion hurt smaller manufacturers even more than the Big Three. Although independents controlled 20 percent of the market in 1949, eventually some brands disappeared, including Studebaker and Packard. Surprisingly, however, after the war both Preston Tucker and shipping magnate Henry Kaiser attempted to enter the automobile manufacturing industry, purchasing plants that had been built for wartime production by other companies. Neither effort was a long-term success in the United States; Tucker's company produced only fifty cars before it was brought down by scandal.

GM emerged as the dominant manufacturer after the war, although Ford made a strong comeback under new president Henry Ford II. Chrysler lagged behind its chief competitors and did not return to prewar sales levels until 1949. Despite initial setbacks, the Big Three firms managed to increase their sales and market share, squeezing out independent manufacturers such as Studebaker and Packard and forcing others such as Hudson and Nash to consolidate in order to compete for customers.

Impact   Unquestionably, the efforts of the automobile industry to supply military vehicles, aircraft, and other items to support the efforts of the United

States and its allies in World War II were crucial, even pivotal, in ensuring victory over the Axis powers. The automobile industry produced one-fifth of everything manufactured for wartime use. Although the scale of production was large, the profit margin was small, and for several years after the war many companies found themselves struggling to regain a solid footing. The labor unrest that plagued many companies in the years immediately following the cessation of hostilities led them to develop more effective strategies in dealing with unions, while union leaders ultimately negotiated better wages, benefits, and working conditions for autoworkers.

Women and minorities saw significant changes in their lifestyles as a result of the war and reconversion. When personnel shortages existed, these groups had filled in admirably on assembly lines and in offices. When white men returned to the workforce and their old jobs, women and minorities often were displaced. The apparent inequality of treatment set the stage for future protests and led to changes in hiring practices involving women and minorities, eventually affecting the entire fabric of American society.

Laurence W. Mazzeno

Further Reading

Critchlow, Donald T. *Studebaker: The Life and Death of an American Corporation*. Bloomington: Indiana University Press, 1996. Surveys the role that Studebaker and other independent auto makers played during World War II. Describes changes in the industry in the years immediately following the war that made survival of companies such as Studebaker virtually impossible.

Farber, David. *Sloan Rules: Alfred P. Sloan and the Triumph of General Motors*. Chicago: University of Chicago Press, 2002. Includes a chapter on General Motors' war production efforts and the work of GM chairman Alfred Sloan to position the company to be profitable after the war.

Hyde, Charles K. *Riding the Roller Coaster: A History of the Chrysler Corporation*. Detroit: Wayne State University Press, 2003. Detailed examination of Chrysler's operations during World War II. Describes the firm's struggle to meet the demand for a variety of military products, including tanks. Discusses problems with reconverting to a postwar economy.

Lichtenstein, Nelson. *The Most Dangerous Man in Detroit: Walter Reuther and the Fate of American Labor*. New York: Basic Books, 1995. Extensive analysis of labor unions' role in supporting American efforts during World War II. Focuses on labor-management relations and the distrust labor leaders had about getting fair treatment of autoworkers from automotive executives and federal officials.

Rae, John B. *The American Automobile Industry*. Boston: Twayne, 1984. Detailed analysis of the automobile industry's efforts during World War II and the struggle to return to normal operations in the years immediately following cessation of hostilities. Includes a chart outlining production of military vehicles and other materials for the war effort.

Watts, Steven. *The People's Tycoon: Henry Ford and the American Century*. New York: Knopf, 2005. Brief account of Ford Motor Company's involvement in wartime production, concentrating on the company's involvement in constructing the B-24 Liberator bomber.

See also   Auto racing; Credit and debt; Ford Motor Company; Freeways; General Motors; Kaiser, Henry J.; Labor strikes; Unionism.

■ Baby boom

Definition The period between 1946 and 1964 during which birthrates rose dramatically, resulting in an exceptionally large generation

Though America experienced a sharp increase in births beginning in 1946, most demographers dismissed it as a temporary phenomenon due to the return of soldiers from World War II. Instead, it was just the beginning of an enormous wave of births that would continue for almost twenty years and change America completely.

When American birth numbers began to slide during the 1920's, then plummeted through the 1930's, demographers predicted that the nation's population would decline well into the future. Then suddenly in 1946, birth numbers shot up dramatically and went even higher the following year. By the end of the decade, America had experienced 33 percent more births in the 1940's than in the 1930's. Even more important, having children became both fashionable and patriotic. Americans married in greater numbers and at younger ages than at any time in the twentieth century, and babies soon followed. By the end of the 1940's, childbearing had become one of the most cherished American values.

Impact The birthrate continued to skyrocket through the 1950's and into the 1960's, creating a generation so large that it dramatically altered the

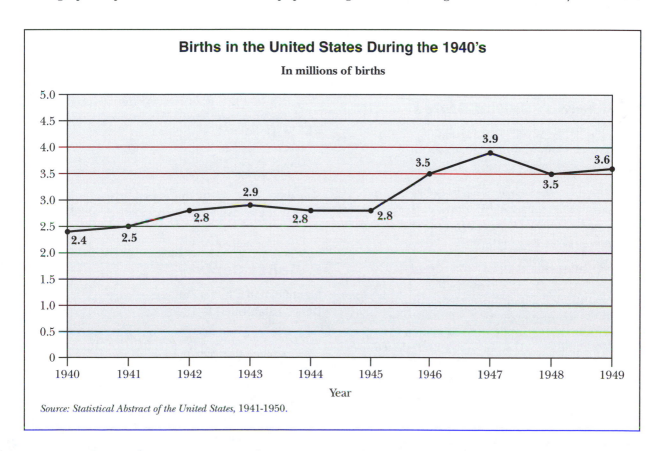

Births in the United States During the 1940's

In millions of births

Source: Statistical Abstract of the United States, 1941-1950.

American character at every stage of its lifespan. During the 1960's, new schools were built by the thousands; by the 1970's, colleges were expanding their faculties and course offerings; by 1980, the economy had grown sluggish and prices soared as baby boomers joined the workforce and became consumers. Eventually, the birthrate rose again as boomers had children themselves. As they reached retirement age in the early twenty-first century, their impact continued to be felt as questions arose about whether Social Security would be able to support their numbers.

Devon Boan

Further Reading

Jones, Landon. *Great Expectations: America and the Baby Boom Generation.* New York: Coward, McCann & Geoghegan, 1980.

Steinhorn, Leonard. *The Greater Generation: In Defense of the Baby Book Legacy.* New York: St. Martins Griffin, 2007.

See also Birth control; *The Common Sense Book of Baby and Child Care*; Demographics of the United States; Fads; "Greatest Generation"; Sex and sex education; Women's roles and rights in the United States.

■ *Ballard v. United States*

The Case U.S. Supreme Court ruling on sex discrimination in federal jury service
Date Decided on December 9, 1946

In this decision, the Supreme Court ruled for the first time that federal law prohibited the intentional exclusion of women from serving on federal juries in states that allowed women to serve on state court juries.

Despite the major social changes experienced by women during the 1940's, most state and federal courts continued a longstanding practice of excluding women from jury service. The prevailing social attitude was that the obligation of women to look after their families and home took precedence over civic obligations. In 1911, California began admitting women to jury service. In practice, however, few women were called to serve, even as late as the 1940's.

Ballard v. United States originated in the case of a woman named Edna Ballard who was tried for mail fraud in a federal court in California. After being convicted, she challenged the verdict on the grounds that the jury in her trial was assembled in violation of federal law. At that time, federal law required federal courts to maintain the same jury requirements as those of the local state courts, which in California were supposed to include women jurors. California courts rarely summoned women to serve, and the local federal courts followed their example. Ballard therefore charged that California's federal courts systematically and illegally excluded women from juries.

By a 5-4 vote, the Supreme Court reversed Ballard's conviction. Speaking for the majority, Justice William O. Douglas reasoned that the various federal statutes on the topic demonstrated that Congress desired juries to represent a cross section of the community. Because women were eligible for jury service under California law, they must be included in the federal trial juries. Although the Ballard decision was an interpretation of congressional statutes, its reasoning would later be used to arrive at basically the same requirement under the Sixth Amendment in the Court's 1975 *Taylor v. Louisiana* ruling

Philip R. Zampini

Further Reading

Goldstein, Leslie Friedman. *The Constitutional Rights of Women: Cases in Law and Social Change.* Rev. ed. Madison: University of Wisconsin Press, 1988.

Rhode, Deborah L. *Justice and Gender: Sex Discrimination and the Law.* Cambridge, Mass.: Harvard University Press, 1989.

See also Civil rights and liberties; Supreme Court, U.S.; Women's roles and rights in the United States.

■ Ballet Society

Identification Ballet company
Date Established in 1946

The forerunner of the New York City Ballet, the Ballet Society was responsible for the establishment of ballet in the United States. As a showcase for George Balanchine's choreography, it also created an American style of ballet.

The Ballet Society was founded in 1946 by Lincoln Kirstein, a patron of the arts, and George Balanchine, a Russian choreographer who had been chief choreographer with Sergei Diaghilev's Ballets Russes de Monte Carlo. Kirstein had for some time hoped to form an American ballet company composed of American dancers. In 1929, he attended a Ballets Russes performance of Balanchine's *Prodigal Son* and was fascinated by the innovative choreography. In 1933, both he and Balanchine were in London. With the help of Romola Nijinsky, Kirstein arranged a meeting with Balanchine and asked him to come to the United States to form a ballet company. Balanchine was eager to join him, but, following the advice of Vladimir Dmitriev, who had brought him out of Russia and uncompromisingly insisted upon accompanying him, he accepted Kirstein's offer only with the provision that

George Balanchine dancing as Don Quixote to Suzanne Farrell's Dulcinea in 1965. (Library of Congress)

first they would establish a school. Thus, on January 2, 1934, the School of American Ballet opened in New York; Balanchine had thirty-two pupils. In 1935, he created a professional ballet company, the American Ballet.

Some eleven years later in November, 1946, Kirstein and Balanchine established the Ballet Society, a nonprofit organization devoted to promoting ballet and its performance in the United States. Kirstein served as the secretary and Balanchine as the artistic director. The Ballet Society was a private society, and its performances were for members only. A subscription audience of about eight hundred attended the company's first performance on November 20, 1946, at the Central High School of Needle Trades in New York City. The Ballet Society company included students from the School of American Ballet and dancers who had previously worked with Balanchine in other companies. The program consisted of two ballets choreographed by Balanchine, *The Spellbound Child* (*L'Enfant et les sortilèges*) and *The Four Temperaments*. On November 12, 1947, the company presented *Symphonie concertante* at the New York City Center. The ballet did not tell a story but rather used dance to reflect the musical qualities and properties of Mozart's Sinfonia Concertante in E-flat Major for Violin and Viola. In 1948, the Ballet Society performed *Symphony in C* in March and *Orpheus* in April at the New York City Center. In October, 1948, the Ballet Society became the New York City Ballet and the resident company at the City Center.

Impact With the founding of the Ballet Society, Lincoln Kirstein and George Balanchine laid the foundation for establishing ballet as an American art form. The Ballet Society enabled Balanchine to develop a truly American ballet with dancers trained in the United States and a repertoire of innovative ballets in which he presented a choreography different from, yet still based on, traditional ballet. The Ballet Society's evolution into the New York City Ballet assured American dancers and choreography a permanent role in ballet, both nationally and internationally.

Shawncey Webb

Further Reading

Duberman, Martin. *The Worlds of Lincoln Kirstein.* Evanston, Ill.: Northwestern University Press, 2008.

Gottlieb, Robert. *George Balanchine: The Ballet Maker.* New York: HarperCollins, 2004.

Walczak, Barbara, and Una Kai. *Balanchine the Teacher: Fundamentals That Shaped the First Generation of New York City Ballet Dancers.* Gainesville: University Press of Florida, 2008.

See also *Appalachian Spring*; Broadway musicals; Dance; Music: Classical; Robbins, Jerome; *Rodeo.*

■ Balloon bombs, Japanese

The Event Japan attacked western North America with bomb-carrying balloons launched into the jet stream above the Pacific Ocean

Also known as Japanese fire balloons; Fu-Go weapons

Date November 3, 1944-April, 1945

Place Pacific coast

Although the Japanese attempted to start fires and weaken morale in the United States and Canada using bomb-carrying balloons, the weapons were relatively unsuccessful, and their effect on morale was negligible.

The Japanese had experimented with a short-range bomb-carrying balloon as early as 1933, but the Doolittle raid of April 18, 1942, the first air raid on a Japanese home island (Honshu) in which American planes bombed Japan, spurred the country to develop the weapon as a means of long-range retaliation. A program of intensive research resulted in a prototype about thirty-three feet in diameter made of layers of tissue paper glued together. The unmanned hydrogen balloon carried sand for ballast, a mechanism for releasing the sand as necessary, a simple radio apparatus for monitoring the balloon's progress, an antipersonnel bomb, and an array of incendiary bombs. Released into the jet stream during winter, such a balloon was capable of crossing the North Pacific Ocean, a distance of some 6,200 miles, in two to three days.

Between November 3, 1944, and early April, 1945, the Japanese launched about nine thousand balloons, or Fu-Go weapons, as they were known. An American naval patrol ship discovered one of the first of these on the afternoon of November 4, floating in the waters off San Pedro, California. (The apparent discrepancy in time is the result of the balloon crossing the international date line.) Parts of a second balloon were found at sea on November 14, off the coast of Hawaii, and more fragments were recovered in Wyoming, Montana, Alaska, and Oregon the following month.

Only a few of the Fu-Go weapons reached their intended targets or resulted in any damage. The incendiary devices set off a number of small forest fires, but these were put out quickly. In a mission called Operation Firefly, members of the 555th Parachute Infantry Battalion (the first African American parachute unit, also known as the Triple Nickels) stationed in Oregon and California participated in the fire fighting. The only American casualties from the balloons occurred on May 5, 1945, when Sunday school teacher Mrs. Archie Mitchell and five children died after accidentally detonating a bomb near Lakeview, Oregon. Ironically, the Japanese had suspended the program a month earlier.

By August of 1945, about three hundred incidents involving balloons or balloon fragments had taken place on American soil, including two as far

Balloon bomb photographed over New York State after crossing both the Pacific Ocean and most of North America in mid-1945. (AP/Wide World Photos)

east as Michigan. In addition to balloons found in Hawaii and Alaska, several had been identified in Canada and Mexico. A number of others had been recovered far out at sea or shot down by American fighter planes.

Impact Operation Firefly was classified, and the Office of Censorship secured the cooperation of American newspapers in suppressing almost all news of the balloons. Because of these steps, the Japanese concluded that their Fu-Go weapons were a failure. Occasional discoveries of debris from the balloons continued throughout the western United States and Canada for decades after the war, and members of the public were warned that any bombs they might discover remained dangerous.

Grove Koger

Further Reading

McPhee, John. "Balloons of War." *The New Yorker* 71, no. 46 (January 29, 1996): 52-60.

Mikesh, Robert C. *Japan's World War II Balloon Bomb Attacks on North America.* Washington, D.C.: Smithsonian Institution Press, 1973.

Webber, Bert. *Silent Siege III: Japanese Attacks on North America in World War II: Ships Sunk, Air Raids, Bombs Dropped, Civilians Killed: Documentary.* Medford, Oreg.: Webb Research Group, 1997.

See also Doolittle bombing raid; Midway, Battle of; Oregon bombing; Wartime technological advances; World War II.

■ Ballpoint pens

Definition Writing pens containing long-lasting supplies of ink that is transferred to surfaces by rotating metal balls at the tips of the pens

The basic concept of the ballpoint pen was known as early as the late nineteenth century, but pen manufacturers did not devise a practical method to mass-produce the identically sized balls needed by the pens until the mid-1940's. After ballpoint pens reached the market, they revolutionized the pen industry.

The introduction of ballpoint pens to the market after 1944 created a race among manufacturers to produce and sell their products to consumers. During World War II, the U.S. War Department sent Biros, a pen patented by Laszlo Biro, to Sheaffer Pen Com-

pany asking that the company model a prototype for use by the military. They were unsuccessful, but Milton Reynolds launched a commercial model of their pen at Gimbel's department store in New York City October 29, 1945,

Sales of ballpoint pen soon outstripped those of fountain pens and proved lucrative. Reynolds's deployment of the International pen was premature, however, as scores of them proved defective and were returned to the company. Nevertheless, by the time that Reynolds left the industry in 1948, he had earned $5 million.

Impact Competition among more than 150 small pen manufacturers, along with such well-established companies as Parker, Sheaffer, and Paper Mate, flooded the market with imperfect ballpoint pens. By the late 1940's, prices plummeted from a high of as much as twelve dollars to less than one dollar per unit. Consumer confidence in the product was markedly dismal as problems with ink—both leakage and permanence—as well as design flaws, plagued production and failed to meet advertised claims. However, these problems would be solved, and ballpoints would become commonplace during the 1950's.

Rebecca Tolley-Stokes

Further Reading

Gostony, Henry, and Stuart Schneider. *The Incredible Ball Point Pen: A Comprehensive History and Price Guide.* Altgen, Pa.: Schiffer, 1998.

Martini, Regina. *Pens and Pencils: A Collector's Handbook.* 3d ed. Altgen, Pa.: Schiffer, 2001.

See also Education in Canada; Education in the United States; Inventions.

■ Barkley, Alben William

Identification U.S. senator, 1927-1949, and vice president of the United States, 1949-1953

Born November 24, 1877; Lowes, Kentucky

Died April 30, 1956; Lexington, Virginia

A member of Congress for nearly forty years, Barkley helped shape the New Deal and was an active vice president under Harry S. Truman.

Alben William Barkley was born in a log cabin in western Kentucky. He began his professional life as a

Senate majority leader Alben W. Barkley (left) with Senator Prentiss Brown of Michigan (standing), Senator James Byrnes of South Carolina (right), and Vice President John Nance Garner (seated) in 1938. (Library of Congress)

lawyer and judge before his election to the House of Representatives in 1912 as a Democrat. From 1927 to 1949, Barkley served as a federal senator. He became Senate majority leader in 1937 and, when the Democrats lost their majority in the elections of 1946, served as Senate minority leader from 1947 to 1949.

Barkley's ability to compromise and his affable personality made him an excellent political partner with Joseph T. Robinson, the Democratic Senate majority leader from 1933 to 1937. Barkley's oratorical skills enabled him and Robinson to gain passage of Franklin D. Roosevelt's New Deal economic programs during the president's first term. Robinson's death in 1937 and Roosevelt's insistence on the passage of his "Court-packing plan" to reorganize the Supreme Court defined battle lines in the Senate between Barkley and Senator Pat Harrison for the post of Senate majority leader. Barkley won the majority leadership by one vote. His election was interpreted as a win for the White House, but Barkley could not dominate the overwhelming Senate majority of seventy-six Democratic senators to sixteen Republicans. As a result, his reputation suffered. The division of the Democratic Party into liberal and conservative wings was not breached until U.S. entry into World War II in 1941.

During World War II, Barkley met regularly with Roosevelt, Vice President Henry A. Wallace, and House Speaker Sam Rayburn to develop domestic and foreign policy strategies. Barkley's national reputation improved, and he was consistently recognized for his hard work and positive approach during a time of national and international crises. Although perceived as Roosevelt's front man in the Senate, Barkley and Roosevelt split politically over the president's veto of a 1944 revenue bill that would have increased taxes during wartime. Barkley successfully won a Senate override of Roosevelt's veto and immediately resigned his office. The next day, he was unanimously reelected to the majority leader position. Senator Barkley lost the chance to replace the unpopular Wallace at the 1944 Democratic Convention because he had opposed the president on a major spending bill. Harry S. Truman replaced Wallace as Roosevelt's running mate.

Disguising any bitterness over Vice President Truman's sudden elevation to the presidency in 1945 following Roosevelt's death, Barkley worked closely with President Truman as both Senate majority leader and later as minority leader when the Republicans won control of Congress in the 1946 elections. Barkley liked Truman from their first meeting, stating that Truman voted the right way. Many at the dispirited 1948 Democratic Convention feared a Republican presidential landslide. In spite of Truman's misgivings about Barkley, the Democratic Convention elected him their vice presidential nominee based on his long political career, his oratorical skills, and his general affability. Barkley was seventy. Truman's political upset over Thomas E. Dewey made Barkley vice president. Truman regularly briefed Barkley, remembering his own isolation from policy discussions under Roosevelt. Barkley used his political influence to gain support for Truman's Fair Deal legislation for housing, inner-city urban renewal projects, desegregation of the military, and increases in the minimum wage and Social Security. He failed to gain support for a national health insurance program.

Barkley was the first vice president to marry while in office. In 1948, at the age of seventy-one, the widower Barkley married thirty-eight-year-old Jane Hadley.

Truman's decision not to run for reelection in 1952 allowed Barkley to consider a run for the presidency, but he lost to Adlai Stevenson in the Democratic nomination process. Barkley returned to the Senate in 1955. He died while delivering a speech at Washington and Lee University in Lexington, Virginia, in 1956, only sixteen months into his last term of office.

Impact Alben William Barkley worked to bring much of the New Deal legislation into law. His distinguished career was rewarded with his election to the vice presidency. President Truman made Barkley the first working vice president, assigning him duties in addition to presiding over the Senate.

William A. Paquette

Further Reading

Barkley, Jane Rucker. *I Married the Veep.* New York: Vanguard Press, 1958.

Davis, Polly Ann. *Alben W. Barkley: Senate Majority Leader and Vice President.* New York: Garland, 1979.

McCullough, David. *Truman.* New York: Simon & Schuster, 1992.

See also Dewey, Thomas E.; MacArthur, Douglas; New Deal programs; Roosevelt, Franklin D.; Truman, Harry S.; Wallace, Henry A.

■ Baseball

Baseball was one of the most popular forms of American entertainment during the 1940's, though its continued existence was threatened during World War II, when many of the top players served in the military. During the war, baseball served a dual purpose, providing entertainment for those back home while also boosting the morale of troops abroad. After the conclusion of the war, baseball was racially integrated in 1947, one of the first prominent American cultural institutions to do so.

The 1940's were a decade of major change and innovation in American baseball. Prosperous throughout the 1920's, Major League Baseball was greatly affected by the Great Depression during the 1930's. Attendance numbers finally returned to their 1929 levels during the 1940 and 1941 seasons, only to be reduced again by the Unites States' entry into World War II. During the war, Major League Baseball barely managed to survive, as many of the top baseball players either enlisted or were drafted into the military. After the players returned from the war, baseball underwent another substantial change when it was racially integrated with the signing of Jackie Robinson with the Brooklyn Dodgers for the 1947 season. Soon, increasing numbers of African American players were added to the rosters of major- and minor-league teams.

Major League Baseball during the 1940's was dominated by a number of prominent franchises. The New York Yankees continued their successes of the 1920's and 1930's by winning five American League pennants and four World Series titles. Similarly, the National League was dominated by the St. Louis Cardinals during the war years, winning the National League pennant from 1942 to 1944 and again in 1946, though the Brooklyn Dodgers emerged during the later portion of the 1940's to capture National League pennants in 1947 and 1949. Before Major League Baseball became integrated, the top African American players played in the Negro leagues.

The 1941 Season The 1941 baseball season, the last full season before the American entrance into World War II, featured a number of notable milestones. Joe DiMaggio of the New York Yankees amassed baseball's longest hitting streak by collecting at least one hit in fifty-six consecutive games from May 15 to July 16. His streak, which surpassed William Keeler's hitting streak of forty-five games with the Baltimore Orioles in 1896 and 1897, was reported closely by mainstream news outlets and contributed to a resurgence by the New York Yankees. The Yankees, who went 41-15 during the streak, went on to win the World Series, and DiMaggio received the American League's most valuable player award that year. Ted Williams, an outfielder for the Boston Red Sox, accomplished another notable benchmark by ending the 1941 season with a .406 batting average. Through the first decade of the twenty-first cen-

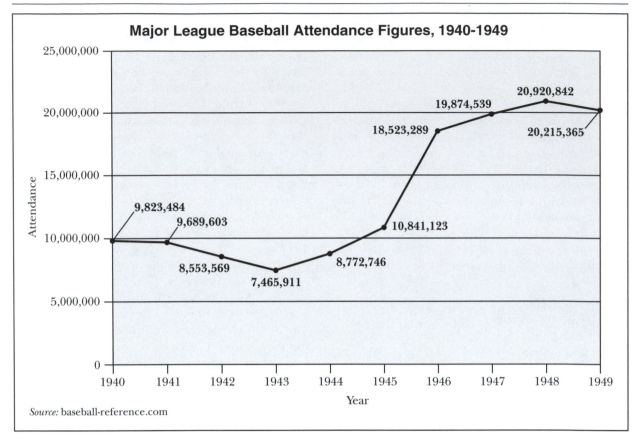

Major League Baseball Attendance Figures, 1940-1949

Source: baseball-reference.com

tury, no major league player since Williams finished a season with a batting average of .400 or better.

In addition to the milestones that occurred on the field, 1941 also marks the first time that an organ was utilized at a baseball stadium, when it appeared for a one-day event at Wrigley Field, home of the Chicago Cubs, on April 26. The following season, the first permanent organ was installed at Ebbets Field, home of the Brooklyn Dodgers.

The War Years After the bombing of Pearl Harbor resulted in the United States entering World War II in December, 1941, the commissioner of Major League Baseball, Kenesaw Mountain Landis, wrote to President Franklin D. Roosevelt on January 14, 1942, asking for his input regarding whether baseball should continue or cease operations for the duration of the war. Roosevelt stated in his response, referred to as the "green light" letter, that baseball should continue because of to its ability to provide entertainment, but that players of military age should serve in the armed services. Hundreds of

major-league players and thousands of minor-league players served in the military during World War II, including top players such as DiMaggio, Williams, and Stan Musial. Most major-league players in the armed services either played on military baseball teams in an effort to raise funds and boost morale or were given preferential noncombat assignments. Some ballplayers received, and in some cases requested, combat duty, although not a single major-league ballplayer was killed in combat. Bob Feller served on the USS *Alabama,* and Harry Walker saw action during the Battle of the Bulge. Others, such as DiMaggio and Hank Greenberg, requested combat duty but were denied.

Because of the large number of major-league ballplayers who either enlisted or were drafted during the war, major-league teams were filled with old players, very young players, and those who had 4F draft classification and thus were exempt from the draft. With most of the top players abroad, the quality of the game declined during the war years, as did attendance at games. Many minor-league teams either folded or suspended play because of the lack of available talent, though Major League Baseball continued throughout the duration of the war. Additionally, the All-American Girls Professional Baseball League was created by Philip K. Wrigley, owner of the Chicago Cubs, to maintain interest in baseball during the war years. The league consisted of women from throughout the United States and Canada and utilized a mixture of elements drawn from both baseball and softball. The league initially was successful but declined in popularity after the conclusion of World War II. Many of the top Negro League players also served in the military, but unlike the major leagues, the Negro Leagues prospered during the war years as a result of migration of African Americans to northern cities.

Major League Baseball supported the war effort in various ways. During the off-season, groups of players went overseas on United Service Organizations (USO) tours, and team owners demonstrated their patriotism by having "The Star-Spangled Banner" played before every game and providing free tickets to wounded veterans. The limit on the number of night games was also increased in 1942, from seven to fourteen, to allow more workers to attend games. In support of those serving abroad, Major League Baseball also donated baseball equipment to be used at military bases. Baseball was played by American soldiers everywhere they were stationed and helped boost morale during breaks in combat.

The Postwar Years   In 1946, Major League Baseball began a return to its prewar state as players returned from serving in the military. Attendance reached record levels. The game was about to undergo a major change, becoming racially integrated. Commissioner Landis had blocked any early efforts at integration, including Bill Veeck's attempt in 1943 to purchase the Philadelphia Phillies and field the team with several Negro League players. After Landis's death in 1944, he was replaced as commissioner by Senator Albert Benjamin "Happy" Chandler. Chandler, who resigned his Senate seat to take the commissioner's post, was more receptive than Landis to the prospect of African American ballplayers in the major leagues, though the majority of baseball team owners still opposed integration.

Branch Rickey, the general manager and part-owner of the Brooklyn Dodgers, started scouting black players in 1945 in order to find the ideal player to break baseball's color barrier. Jackie Robinson, a former Negro League player and war veteran, was signed by Rickey and appeared with the Montreal Royals, the Dodgers' AAA affiliate, in 1946. The next year, Robinson broke the Major League Baseball color barrier when he appeared with the Brooklyn Dodgers on opening day, April 15, 1947, amid much controversy and opposition. Robinson won the inaugural rookie of the year award that year and later received the National League's most valuable player award in 1949. Following Robinson's first appearance with the Dodgers in 1947, other major-league teams gradually added African American players to their rosters. By 1959, when the Boston Red Sox integrated their team, all the teams were racially integrated.

After Jackie Robinson broke the color line in Major League Baseball in 1947, other Negro League players began joining major league clubs. In 1948, one of the greatest of them, pitcher Satchel Paige, signed with the Cleveland Indians. At forty-two, his best years were already behind him, but he still had a productive rookie season. (Getty Images)

Baseball saw a number of other changes after World War II. Its games first appeared on television in 1939, but they were not regularly broadcast until after the war, when much larger numbers of American homes had television sets. The World Series was first televised in 1947. That same year, fan voting was instituted to determine the starting line-ups for the All-Star Game, with the exception of pitchers. Managers had selected the rosters for All-Star Games played since 1935. The game of baseball also became more globalized after World War II, as a number of Latin American and European countries established their own professional leagues.

Impact As late as the second decade of the twenty-first century, the milestones set by DiMaggio and Williams during the 1941 season had yet to be matched. The longest hitting streak since DiMaggio's was Pete Rose's hitting streak of forty-four games during the 1978 season. The only two players to approach a batting average of .400 were George Brett of the Kansas City Royals, who batted .390 during the 1980 season, and Tony Gwynn of the San Diego Padres, who batted .394 during the strike-shortened 1994 season.

Organ music at baseball games would eventually become the signature sound of major league baseball games. Baseball would also see a significant increase in the number of night games; eventually, every major-league team except the Chicago Cubs, would play the vast majority of its games at night. Additionally, virtually every major-league game would eventually be televised, and television revenues would constitute significant portions of team incomes.

The integration of baseball allowed players from different minority groups and, eventually, foreign players to play baseball in the United States. Only a small number of African Americans played in the major leagues during the 1940's, but increasing numbers of African Americans were featured on the rosters of teams in the major and minor leagues in subsequent years. In 1959, the Boston Red Sox would become the last major-league team to integrate. Racial integration of baseball would also signal the end of the Negro Leagues, as the top players migrated to the major and minor leagues. The Negro National League played its last season in 1948, while the Negro American League lasted until 1960. Baseball was one of the first prominent American cultural institutions to become desegregated, and as such it contributed to the burgeoning Civil Rights movement.

Matthew Mihalka

Further Reading

Bullock, Steven G. *Playing for Their Nation: Baseball and the American Military During World War II.* Lincoln: University of Nebraska Press, 2004. Explores how baseball was played at American military installations throughout World War II to boost morale.

Dorinson, Joseph, and Joram Warmund, eds. *Jackie Robinson: Race, Sports, and the American Dream.* London: M. E. Sharpe, 1998. Essays address Jackie Robinson's role in integrating baseball and the impact that the integration of Major League Baseball had on society.

Heaphy, Leslie A. *The Negro Leagues: 1869-1960.* London: McFarland & Company, 2003. Follows the rise and fall of the Negro Leagues.

James, Bill. *The New Bill James Historical Baseball Abstract.* New York: Free Press, 2001. Dedicates a chapter to the game of baseball during each decade, from the 1870's to the 1990's, with an emphasis on statistics. Also provides statistical ratings of players, both past and present, at each position.

Marshall, William. *Baseball's Pivotal Era, 1945-1951.* Lexington: University Press of Kentucky, 1999. Explores the various changes to baseball, as both a business and a sport, in the postwar years under new commissioner Albert Benjamin Chandler.

Rader, Benjamin G. *Baseball: A History of America's Games.* Chicago: University of Illinois Press, 2008. Traces the development of baseball from before the Civil War to the present.

Ward, Geoffrey C., and Ken Burns. *Baseball: An Illustrated History.* New York: Alfred A. Knopf, 1994. Based on a documentary by the authors, this book follows the history of baseball. Numerous photographs.

See also All-American Girls Professional Baseball League; Basketball; DiMaggio, Joe; Football; Gehrig, Lou; Gray, Pete; Paige, Satchel; Robinson, Jackie; Sports in the United States; Williams, Ted.

■ Basketball

Although basketball enjoyed a steadily growing popularity in North America from the time James Naismith invented it during the early 1890's, it was not until the late 1940's that the game would grow professional roots and begin the growth spurt that would eventually make it one of the most popular team sports in the world.

The 1940's was not a fertile time for the development of basketball or almost any other team sport. North America was still recovering from the economic devastation of the Great Depression of the previous decade, and the huge need for manpower to fight in World War II cut deeply into professional sports. More than 30 percent of the players in the National Football League ranks enlisted in the armed services, and so many baseball players went into the military that Major League Baseball nearly shut down during the war. Organized sports, in general, went into a decline until the war ended in 1945. When the players returned after the war, professional baseball and football experienced a renaissance.

Up to this time, basketball was much more of a participant sport than a spectator sport. It was widely played in schools and colleges and had its amateur leagues, but it was often regarded as slow-paced and cumbersome and had never caught on as a professional sport.

College Basketball   Until the late 1930's, basketball games were handicapped by the requirement of having a fresh jump ball at center court after every basket was scored. In 1938, college basketball dropped that requirement by awarding automatic possession of the ball to the defending team after scores. This single rule change opened up much faster-paced offenses, allowing for more action and fewer stoppages. The increased tempo of play appealed to spectators, and college basketball made another change that would eventually develop into one of the most popular sports events in the United States.

In 1938, New York City's Madison Square Garden responded to the increasing popularity of college basketball by starting the end-of-season National Invitational Tournament, better known simply as the NIT. Over the next two decades this invitational event would become one of the popular tournaments in American team sports. Meanwhile, in 1939, the National Collegiate Athletic Association (NCAA) started its own tournament in direct competition with the NIT. Until the NCAA tournament finally pulled ahead in popularity and prestige during the late 1950's, it and the NIT competed to attract college basketball's best teams each year, and the fans were major beneficiaries. Another development enhancing basketball's popularity was television broadcasting of games, which began in 1940, when a game between the University of Pittsburgh and Fordham was televised from Madison Square Garden. Meanwhile, the University of Oregon won the first NCAA tournament in 1939. In 1940, Indiana won the title, followed by Wisconsin in 1941, Stanford (1942), Wyoming (1943), Utah (1944), Oklahoma A&M (1945 and 1946), Holy Cross (1947), and Kentucky (1948 and 1949).

The birth of the two tournaments proved to be the cornerstone for basketball's future popularity. As collegiate stars such as George Mikan of DePaul and Bob Kurland of Oklahoma, and the University of Kentucky coach Adolf Rupp became popular, so did the new fast-paced, big-play, professional league, which welcomed the college stars into its ranks. Fans were particularly glad to see former college stars, such as Mikan and Kurland, finally play against one another.

Organized Basketball   Before professional basketball gained a solid footing during the late 1940's, the best basketball played outside colleges was organized by the Amateur Athletic Union, which had been created primarily for former college athletes to hone their skills for Olympic competition without compromising their amateur status by playing professionally. However, many AAU players were on teams sponsored by corporations with which they hoped later to find jobs. Throughout the 1940's, one team dominated AAU competition: The Phillips 66ers (named after a petroleum company) of Bartlesville, Oklahoma. It won seven championships between 1940 and 1949, including a run of six in a row between 1943 and 1948.

AAU basketball had gained popularity after basketball was reinstated as an official Olympic sport in the 1936 Games in Berlin. However, the sport experienced a temporary setback during the war years, when both the 1940 and 1944 Olympic Games were cancelled. When the Olympics resumed in 1948, the

George Mikan rebounding for the Minneapolis Lakers in a January, 1949, game in which he set a Basketball Association of America record of 48 points. (AP/Wide World Photos)

United States men's team beat France for the gold medal.

Women also competed in AAU basketball. For several seasons, Hazel Walker was a player/coach in women's traveling leagues and often played men's squads in pick-up games. During the 1940's, she led her teams to four AAU national championships. A pioneer in women's basketball, she would be instrumental in the development of women's professional basketball.

Professional Basketball   Before the late 1940's, the most successful attempt to professionalize the sport had been the American Basketball League, which had lasted fewer than six years before folding during the early 1930's. In 1937, another attempt to professionalize the sport was made with the formation of the National Basketball League (NBL). Made up mostly of rural midwestern teams, this league foundered during the war years and was on the verge of extinction by the time the war ended.

In 1946, a rival league called Basketball Association of America (BAA) was formed. In contrast to the cruder style that characterized the NBL, the BAA stressed sound basketball fundamentals and sportsmanship, enabling the best players to showcase what they could do. In 1949, the NBL and BAA merged to form the National Basketball Association (NBA). The Philadelphia Warriors won the first NBA title in 1946, followed by the Baltimore Bullets in 1947. Led by former college star center George Mikan, the Minneapolis (later Los Angeles) Lakers won championships in 1948 and 1949.

Professional basketball was still a long way from rivaling the popularity of the college game, and in some regions it could not even challenge the popularity of AAU teams, but it was gaining. During the 1950's, its growth would be aided by the movement of popular college stars into the league.

Impact   The future popularity of both college and professional basketball could scarcely have been imagined at the end of the 1940's. By the early twenty-first century, the NBA would grow from a rickety league of eight teams to a prosperous thirty-team league. Thanks to the growth of television revenue, particularly of the annual NCAA tournaments, the college game would become a multibillion-dollar business, too. As the college and professional game grew in popularity, the AAU leagues disbanded during the 1960's. However, the amateur game would later experience a resurgence, particularly in high schools and in girls and women's basketball, and the game would also grow in worldwide popularity.

Keith J. Bell

Further Reading

Grundman, A. *The Golden Age of Amateur Basketball: The AAU Tournament, 1921-1968.* Lincoln, Nebr.: Bison Books, 2004. Interesting history of AAU basketball in the United States, with attention to what the game contributed to creating sports stars and developing sportsmanship.

Havlicek, John. *NBA's Greatest.* New York: DK, 2003. A look at the NBA's greatest players and moments, including upsets and famous rivalries.

Hubbard, Jan. *The Official NBA Encyclopedia.* 3d ed. New York: Doubleday, 2000. This volume of more than nine hundred pages includes a complete history of the NBA, with full statistics for every player who ever played in the league, and information on referees and coaches. Also includes statistics for the predecessor leagues.

Naismith, James, and W. Baker. *Basketball: Its Origin and Development.* Lincoln, Nebr.: Bison Books, 1996. The history of James Naismith, inventor of basketball, and the development of the modern game.

Peterson, Robert W. *Cages to Jump Shots: Pro Basketball's Early Years.* Lincoln: University of Nebraska Press, 2002. History of the first decades of the NBA, beginning with basketball's origins in 1891 to 1954, the year the league instituted the 24-second shot clock.

See also   Baseball; Football; National Basketball Association; Olympic Games of 1948; Recreation; Sports in Canada; Sports in the United States.

■ Bataan Death March

The Event   Japanese forced march of American and Filipino prisoners of war in the Philippines that resulted in thousands of deaths and charges of war crimes against Japanese officers

Date   April 10-17, 1942

The abuse of American and Filipino prisoners of war further enflamed American public opinion against Japan in the wake of the Pearl Harbor attack and eventually led to a rescue of Bataan survivors from a prisoner-of-war camp by United States Army Rangers and Filipino guerrilla forces.

The Bataan Peninsula on Luzon Island in the Philippines was the site of a humiliating defeat of 12,500 American and 67,500 Filipino troops at the hands of Japan's Lieutenant-General Masaharu Homma, whose forces had invaded the Philippines in December, 1941. President Franklin D. Roosevelt had ordered American commander General Douglas MacArthur to evacuate to Australia, which he did on March 11, 1942. American forces, which were short on food, ammunition, and basic supplies, surrendered on April 9, 1942. Several thousand American troops had retreated to the island of Corregidor, but they surrendered on May 6, 1942.

American and Filipino defenders in Bataan were marched more than sixty miles, under brutal conditions, from the southern tip of the peninsula at Mariveles to San Fernando. Thirst, starvation, beatings, bayonetings, and cold-blooded shootings took thousands of lives. Japanese troops showed almost no regard for human life because they regarded the prisoners' surrender as a shameful act and because the prisoners were more numerous and in worse physical condition than the Japanese thought. The Japanese believed that the march to Camp O'Donnell and Camp Cabanatuan had gone well. The deplorable conditions in the camps, however, resulted in the deaths of thousands of detainees from disease, starvation, and abuse by guards. A few prisoners escaped to join Filipino guerrillas, others were sent as slave laborers to Japan, and a few escapees returned to America, bringing information about the death march and conditions in the camps.

In January, 1944, the Departments of War and the Navy released information obtained from escapees. Newspaper and magazine coverage produced outrage in the American public, still angry from the attack on Pearl Harbor. On December 14, 1944, Japa-

American prisoners of war carrying their disabled comrades on the Bataan Death March in May, 1942. (National Archives)

Bataan Death March

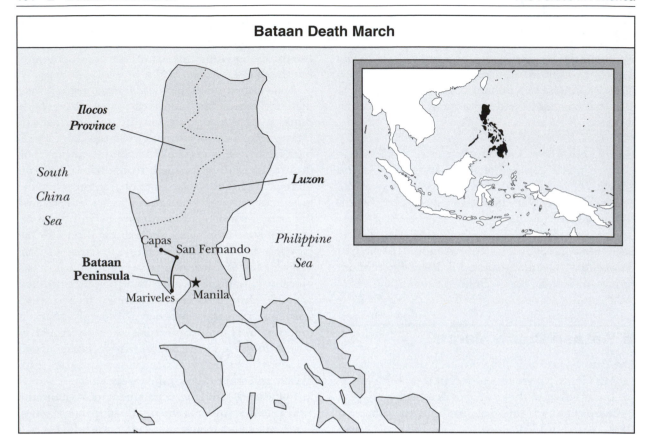

nese forces massacred approximately 150 prisoners at the Palawan camp in the Philippines by burning them alive in ditches. Fearful that this might presage similar action against prisoners in other camps, the United States authorized a raid of the Cabanatuan camp on January 30, 1945, by Army Rangers working with Filipino guerrillas and civilians. The raiders freed all 513 prisoners, who embarked for the United States one week after their liberation.

Impact The Bataan Death March, along with other Japanese atrocities and the attack on Pearl Harbor, left a legacy of bitterness on the part of Americans toward the Japanese. General Homma was convicted of war crimes because of the march and executed on April 3, 1946. In May, 2009, the Japanese ambassador to the United States, Ichiro Fujisaki, apologized on behalf of the Japanese government at a meeting of the American Defenders of Bataan and Cor-

regidor. The Japanese government in August, 2009, invited a number of former American prisoners of war, including survivors of the Bataan Death March, to Japan to promote friendship.

Mark C. Herman

Further Reading

Dyess, William E. *Bataan Death March: A Survivor's Account.* 1944. Reprint. Lincoln: University of Nebraska Press, 2002.

Tenney, Lester I. *My Hitch in Hell: The Bataan Death March.* Washington, D.C.: Brassey's, 1995.

See also Army, U.S.; Army Rangers; MacArthur, Douglas; Marines, U.S.; Pearl Harbor attack; Philippine independence; Philippines; Prisoners of war, North American; Prisoners of war in North America; War crimes and atrocities; War heroes; World War II.

■ Baugh, Sammy

Identification   American football player
Born   March 17, 1914; Temple, Texas
Died   December 17, 2008; Rotan, Texas

Baugh was one of the greatest professional quarterbacks of all time. He holds the record for the most seasons with the lowest interception percentage in the National Football League (five) and is tied with Steve Young for the most seasons leading the league in passing (six).

After a brilliant career at Texas Christian University, Sammy Baugh was drafted into the National Football League (NFL) by the Washington Redskins in 1937. Playing quarterback, defensive back, and punter, Baugh established the record for the best NFL punting average (51.4 yards) for a season in 1940. Behind his leadership and play at quarterback, the Redskins advanced to the NFL championship game in 1940, 1942, 1943, and 1945, winning the 1942 contest over the Chicago Bears. Baugh led the NFL in punting four consecutive seasons from 1940 until 1943.

In 1943, Baugh led the NFL in passing, punting, and interceptions. During the 1945 season, he completed 70.33 percent of his passes, ranking second only to Ken Anderson's record of 70.55. Baugh was the first NFL player to intercept four passes in a game. On "Sammy Baugh Day," November 23, 1947, he passed for a phenomenal 355 yards and six touchdowns against the Chicago Cardinals.

Impact   When Baugh retired from professional football in 1952, he had set thirteen NFL records, while playing at three different positions. He established the way that the quarterback position is played by making the forward pass an effective offensive weapon from the T-formation. In 1999, he was named by the Associated Press as the third-greatest NFL player of the twentieth century.

Alvin K. Benson

Further Reading

Canning, Whit. *Sam Baugh: Best There Ever Was.* Dallas, Tex.: Masters Press, 1997.

Rand, Jonathan. *Riddell Presents The Gridiron's Greatest Quarterbacks.* Champaign, Ill.: Sports Publishing, 2004.

See also   Davis, Glenn; Football; Recreation; Sports in Canada; Sports in the United States.

■ Benét, Stephen Vincent

Identification   American writer
Born   July 22, 1898; Bethlehem, Pennsylvania
Died   March 13, 1943; New York, New York

During the early 1940's, as one of the best-known American poets and fiction writers, Benét spearheaded the home-front embrace of American involvement in World War II by publishing a series of passionately idealistic patriotic works in a wide variety of genres.

Stephen Vincent Benét was the son of a distinguished Army colonel and was educated at prestigious military academies. Only poor health (a childhood bout with scarlet fever left him with a weakened heart and he suffered from poor eyesight) prevented him from serving in the military in World War I. During the war, he worked as a cipher-clerk in Washington. That unquestioning love of country led Benét, after graduating from Yale University in 1919, to turn his considerable writing talents to pursuing what he saw as the noblest ambition of any writer: to hymn the history of one's own country and thus raise the spirits of its citizens. Such a conservative (and implicitly optimistic) agenda put Benét at odds with the Lost Generation of famously disenchanted expatriates, but it made him an immensely popular writer at home.

Benét's 15,000-line epic poem *John Brown's Body,* a recitation of the history of the Civil War from the perspective of a child caught up in events, was awarded the 1929 Pulitzer Prize in poetry and, remarkably for a long work of poetry, was a national best seller. Indeed, on the strength of that work, Benét was awarded the 1933 Theodore Roosevelt Distinguished Service Medal, cited for his selfless service and patriotic idealism, an award most often given to politicians, military strategists, and social activists. Coupled with his remarkable success as a magazine fiction writer, largely for *The Saturday Evening Post* (most notably the 1937 classic "The Devil and Daniel Webster"), and his work as an editor of landmark poetry anthologies and as the screenwriter for a number of successful films, Benét was uniquely positioned to become a most effective civilian proponent of the war effort when the United States entered World War II.

Impact   Benét suffered from arthritis and the effects of a series of strokes as well as a weak heart, but even as his own health deteriorated he wrote a flurry of uplifting articles and inspirational radio scripts geared to encourage the country to commit its emotional support to the immense task of defeating totalitarianism. In early 1942, during the darkest period of the war effort, Benét conceived of a monumental epic poem, *Western Star,* that would celebrate the four-hundred-year history of the European settlement of the American continent (he planned nine volumes). He saw the work as tonic for a home front growing uncertain over victory: The poem would celebrate the resiliency of the American spirit and its irrepressible optimism despite forbidding circumstances. He devoted immense effort to the project—and the effort took its toll. Before the first volume was published in 1943, Benét, just forty-four, died of a massive heart attack. With the country now caught up in the momentum toward victory, the book sold well and garnered significant critical plaudits. It was awarded the 1944 Pulitzer Prize in poetry.

Benét's literary reputation suffered enormously (and declined precipitously) in the years immediately after the war. His epic-style poetry appeared dated and propagandistic, and his parable-fictions centered on American folklore and historic figures unadventurous and formulaic.

Joseph Dewey

Further Reading

Erenberg, Lewis A., and Susan E. Hirsch. *The War in American Culture: Society and Consciousness During World War II.* Chicago: University of Chicago Press, 1996.

Fenton, Charles. *Stephen Vincent Benét: The Life and Times of an American Man of Letters, 1898-1943.* New Haven, Conn.: Princeton University Press, 1965.

Konkle, Lincoln, and David Garrett Izzo, eds. *Stephen Vincent Benét: Essays on His Life and Work.* Jefferson City, N.C.: McFarland, 2002.

See also Great Books Foundation; Literature in the United States; Magazines; *Saturday Evening Post.*

■ Benny, Jack

Identification American comedian, actor, and radio personality
Born February 14, 1894; Chicago, Illinois
Died December 26, 1974; Hollywood, California

One of the most popular, most recognizable, and most adept radio personalities of the 1940's, Benny had a genius for creating visual images from sound alone.

The older of two children born to Meyer and Emma Kubelsky, Benjamin Kubelsky, Jack Benny, showed an early interest in music and was presented with a violin on his sixth birthday. An indifferent student in public school, he dropped out in the ninth grade but continued his violin lessons and joined the pit orchestra in a local theater before teaming up with a series of piano players to form a vaudeville act. A stint in the U.S. Navy during World War I offered Benny opportunities to perform for fellow servicemen, and he began to mold the comic delivery and musical presentations for which he would later become famous. In 1921, he legally changed his name to Jack Benny.

Refining his comedy act throughout the 1920's, Benny became one of the highest-paid vaudeville players. He eventually moved to an MGM contract and a starring role in *Earl Carroll's "Vanities"* on Broadway. In March, 1932, he appeared as a guest on a radio program hosted by *New York Daily News* columnist Ed Sullivan. His first line was "This is Jack Benny talking. There will be a short pause while everyone says, who cares?" He then got his own regularly scheduled radio show on the National Broadcasting Company (NBC).

Throughout the 1930's, Benny perfected his performance, creating a professional persona as a stingy, vain, perpetually thirty-nine-year-old man and built a regular cast of characters around himself. Don Wilson became his announcer, and Eddie Anderson became Rochester, his African American butler and companion. Sayde Marks, whom he married in 1927, became Mary Livingstone, his secretary and companion. By 1939, he had added Phil Harris as his band director; Mel Blanc, who provided voices of several characters; and Dennis Day, his silly, naive boy singer. By 1940, his weekly program was at the top of the national radio ratings and would remain there throughout the 1940's.

Benny's radio program centered around Jack,

who put on a weekly radio show, and the action usually involved rehearsals for the various acts to be presented, including a sketch parodying a recent feature film. Regular routines involved Jack in an ever-increasing series of confrontations with fellow cast members and with a series of grotesquely offbeat comical characters. In these exchanges, Jack himself usually played straight man. The other characters included abusive clerks, messengers, telephone operators, floorwalkers, ticket agents, dentists, and waitresses. Mel Blanc played many characters, most notably Professor LeBlanc, Jack's long suffering violin teacher. Sheldon Leonard was Jack's racetrack tout, Frank Nelson, whose "ye-e-e-s-s-s-s-s?" was a constant lead-in to a confrontation with Jack, and Artie Auerbach was Mr. Kitzel, a friend who simply showed up to tell funny stories.

Jack Benny playing the violin on his television show in 1949. (Time & Life Pictures/ Getty Images)

Jack Benny also starred in several profitable films during the 1940's, always playing opposite big-name stars. They included *Buck Benny Rides Again* (1940), *Charley's Aunt* (1941), *To Be or Not to Be* (1942)— which has become a major classic—and the infamous *The Horn Blows at Midnight* (1945)

In 1948, Benny's radio program jumped from NBC to the Columbia Broadcasting System (CBS) in a deal that gave him more control of its content and a significantly higher income. On May 8, 1949, he made a test appearance on the Columbia Broadcasting System (CBS) that led to the first televised broadcast of *The Jack Benny Program* on October 28, 1950. From that time, he gradually increased his television appearances.

Impact Although Jack Benny enjoyed his greatest popularity during the 1940's, his popularity endured through the remainder of his life. His radio series had its final broadcast on May 22, 1955. When CBS-TV cancelled his television series in 1965,

Benny was seventy-one, but until his death, he remained a popular guest on many other shows. He also performed benefit concerts playing his violin with symphony orchestras around the world, and he appeared in television commercials.

Benny's deadpan style of self-deprecating humor, delivered with a studied, precise sense of timing, often using silence and an exasperated stare at the audience, was copied by many comedians, most notably Johnny Carson.

James R. Belpedio

Further Reading

Benny, Jack, and Joan Benny, *Sunday Nights at Seven: The Jack Benny Story.* New York: Random House, 1992.

Fein, Irving. *Jack Benny, An Intimate Biography.* New York: Putnam, 1976.

Schaden, Chuck. *Speaking of Radio.* Morton Grove, Ill.: Nostalgia Digest Press, 2003.

See also Abbott and Costello; Berle, Milton; Film in the United States; Radio in the United States; Television.

■ Bentley, Elizabeth

Identification American anticommunist activist
Born January 1, 1908; New Milford, Connecticut
Died December 3, 1963; New Haven,
  Connecticut

Elizabeth Bentley helped fuel anticommunist hysteria by revealing that she had passed secrets from U.S. government officials to Soviet agents in the United States. Although the Federal Bureau of Investigation could not corroborate any of Bentley's investigations, she helped to destroy the career of Harry Dexter White of the Treasury Department.

Elizabeth Bentley initially pursued a conventional path as a scholar. Upon graduating from Vassar College in 1930 with a degree in English, she taught languages briefly before earning a master's degree in Italian from Columbia University in 1935. While completing her degree, Bentley spent the 1933-1934 academic year at the University of Florence in Italy. She returned to the United States to become active in the American League Against War and Fascism. Through friends in the organization and at Columbia University, Bentley became familiar with communists. She joined the Communist Party in March, 1935, a common choice during the Great Depression when many people had become disillusioned with capitalism. In June, 1938, Bentley became a secretary and research assistant for the Italian Library of Information, an arm of the Italian Propaganda Ministry. She began secretly passing information garnered at her job to communist leaders. To become a more effective agent, Bentley dropped her Communist Party membership.

Under the guidance of her lover, Jacob Golos, a member of the Control Commission of the Communist Party USA and a leading Soviet agent, Bentley gained a cover as vice president of the U.S. Service and Shipping Corporation. The company had been created with Communist Party funds to handle passenger and freight traffic between the United States and the Soviet Union. From 1940 to 1943, Bentley routinely traveled between New York City and Washington, D.C., collecting information from government employees in numerous agencies, including the Treasury Department, Commerce Department, Board of Economic Warfare, Farm Security Administration, War Production Board, War Department, Office of the Coordinator of Inter-American Affairs, and Office of Strategic Services. The latter was the predecessor to the Central Intelligence Agency, or CIA. Upon Golos's death in November, 1943, Bentley reported to a series of Soviet officials that she knew only by code names. She stopped spying in December, 1944, frightened that the Federal Bureau of Investigation (FBI) would discover her or that the Russians would try to kill her because she knew too much about clandestine Soviet activities in the United States.

Overwhelmed by her fears, Bentley began visiting FBI offices in New Haven, Connecticut, and New York City in August, 1945, to discover whether the agents knew her about her spying. New York City FBI officials regarded Bentley as a bit of a lunatic but still asked her to return in November, 1945, for an interview. At this time, Bentley provided the FBI with the names of more than 150 individuals of suspect loyalty, including Harry Dexter White, a Treasury Department official. The FBI concentrated on fifty-one people, including twenty-seven still employed by the federal government, but could not find corroborating evidence. On July 31, 1948, Bentley became a national figure when she testified before the House Committee on Un-American Activities. For the next few years, the "Blond Spy Queen" regularly appeared before congressional committees holding hearings on communist influence. Bentley then returned to teaching until her death.

Impact Bentley helped fuel the Second Red Scare by providing the FBI, Department of Justice, and numerous congressional committees with the information that they needed to launch an anticommunist crusade.

Caryn E. Neumann

Further Reading

Bentley, Elizabeth. *Out of Bondage: The Story of Elizabeth Bentley.* New York: Devin-Adair, 1951.

Kessler, Lauren. *Clever Girl: Elizabeth Bentley, the Spy Who Ushered in the McCarthy Era.* New York: HarperCollins, 2003.

See also Anticommunism; Cold War; Communist Party USA; Federal Bureau of Investigation; House Committee on Un-American Activities; White, Harry Dexter.

■ Berle, Milton

Identification   American television actor and
comedian
Born   July 12, 1908; New York, New York
Died   March 27, 2002; Beverly Hills, California

*Berle became the nation's first television superstar during
the advent of television in the 1940's. His weekly comedy
show not only entranced the nation but also helped popularize television.*

Born Milton Berlinger, the comedian and actor officially changed his professional name to Milton Berle
in 1924 at the age of sixteen. By the 1930's, Berle had
become a successful stand-up comedian and radio
personality. Throughout the 1940's, he hosted numerous radio shows, including *Stop Me If You've
Heard This One* (1939), *Let Yourself Go* (1944), *Kiss
and Make Up* (1945), and the *Milton Berle Show*
(1947). In 1948, Berle hosted the *Texaco Star Theater*
radio show. That same year, the National Broadcasting Company (NBC) transformed the popular radio
show into a television show. On the air from 1948 to
1956, the one-hour comedy variety show aired on
Tuesday nights at 8:00 P.M. Berle quickly became
America's first television star and was affectionately
nicknamed "Mr. Television" and "Uncle Miltie" by
television audiences. For many Americans, watching
the program on Tuesday nights became a national
pastime. Berle's show has also been credited with increasing television sales during the 1940's.

Impact   The popularity of Berle's weekly comedy
show had an enormous influence on how quickly
the television became integrated into mainstream
America.

Bernadette Zbicki Heiney

Further Reading
Berle, Milton, and Haskel Frankel. *Milton Berle: An
Autobiography.* New York: Applause Theatre and
Cinema Books, 2002.
Berle, William, and Bradley Lewis. *My Father, Uncle
Miltie.* New York: Barricade Books, 1999.

See also   Benny, Jack; Jews in the United States; Radio in the United States; Television.

■ Berlin blockade and airlift

The Event   International crisis in which the Soviet
Union attempted to cut off West Berlin from
the Allied occupation zone in Germany,
resulting in an Allied airlift
Also known as   Berlin blockade; Operation
Vittles
Date   June 24, 1948-May 12, 1949
Place   Berlin, Germany

*The Berlin airlift operation was the first confrontation be-
tween the Soviet Union and the three Western powers, notably the United States, over ideological and political issues.
However, the confrontation never escalated into an armed
combat.*

The Berlin airlift operation in response to the Berlin
blockade by the Soviet Union was the culmination of
the breakdown of political and diplomatic relations
with the Soviet Union's wartime allies—England,
France, and the United States—over the future of
the city of Berlin. Following World War II, Germany
was divided into five parts, four Allied occupation
zones (American, British, French, and Soviet) and
the city of Berlin (surrounded by the Soviet zone)
subdivided into four sectors.

Beginning of East-West Misunderstanding   The Soviet Union wanted to establish friendly nations
on Russia's western border as a protective buffer
against the resurgence of a strong, unified Germany.
Its long-range goal was to expel the Western powers
from Germany and establish a communist government in the region. During the winter of 1945-1946,
the Soviets imposed a communist dictatorship in
their occupation zone in eastern Germany. The
Western Allies responded by merging their respective zones under a Supreme Economic Council by
the summer of 1947. In early 1948, the British foreign secretary Ernest Bevin scheduled a two-phase
meeting of Western officials in London to decide
the next steps for Germany and Europe. During the
first half of the conference (February 23-March 6), it
was agreed that German recovery was the key to European recovery.

April Crisis: "Baby Blockade"   The Soviets de-
nounced the London meeting at the Allied Control
Council (ACC), which formed on July 30, 1945, in
Berlin as a violation of the ACC mandate and the

Potsdam Agreement, and on April 1, 1948, they blocked military trains running between the Western zones and Berlin. When the American military governor of Germany, General Lucius Clay, dispatched a train to go through the Soviet zone, it was shunted to a siding by the Soviet authorities. Thereupon, Clay directed Lieutenant General Curtis LeMay, commander of the Army Air Forces in Europe, to deliver supplies to the military garrisons (numbering sixty-five hundred troops, half of whom were Americans) in Berlin by airplane. The British Air Forces of Occupation followed suit by airlifting supplies for the British garrison in Berlin. The crisis eventually petered out by April 10, when the Soviets relaxed restrictions. However, during June 10-15, the Russians attempted to blockade West Berlin again.

The April crisis, nicknamed "baby blockade," provided the backdrop of the second phase of the London Conference (April 20-June 17, 1948), which decided to create a West German state. On June 20, the West German *Kommandatura* introduced a new deutsche mark in the Western zone (and extended to West Berlin on June 23), replacing the reichsmark with a view to putting an end to inflation, the black market, and the existing restrictions and anomalies in the economy.

Planes unloading airlift cargo at Berlin's Tempelhof Airport. (Smithsonian Institution)

Blockade and Airlift Responding to this Western challenge, the Soviets also introduced on June 23 the East German mark in the Soviet zone and in East Berlin. On June 24, they closed the railroads and autobahns linking West Berlin to the Western occupation zones and cut off power, the main plant being situated in East Berlin. The next day, the Soviet Union called a meeting of East European states and issued the Warsaw Declaration in response to the London Declaration. This blockade was meant to force the West to withdraw its plan for a separate West German state. General Clay tried an airlift operation to rescue the Berliners from starvation as he had done in April, though initially he was not supported by the U.S. government. Thus, the airlift, dubbed Operation Vittles, began on June 26. On the same day, the British government requested that the United States dispatch two squadrons of B-29 bombers to England. By the end of September, a plane was landing every three minutes at the Tempelhof Airport in West Berlin. By April, 1949, a plane was landing every minute. The blockade was called off on May 12, 1949.

During the airlift, the Americans used 441 planes and the British 147. The Allied airplanes flew a total of 124,420,813 miles, equaling 133 round trips to the Moon or four thousand times around the world. About 2.3 million tons of food and supplies was flown to Berlin. Approximately 75,000 people were involved in the operation on the Continent. The airlift cost the United States approximately $500,000 per day and Britain between $50,000 and $100,000 per day.

Impact The Berlin airlift led to significant developments: the division of Germany into West (Federal Republic of Germany, proclaimed on May 23, 1949) and East (German Democratic Republic, formed on October 7, 1949), and the emergence of two superpowers—the United States and the Soviet Union. The democratic West united under the North Atlantic Treaty Organization (NATO), established on

April 4, 1949, and the communist East under the Warsaw Pact, signed on May 14, 1955. This great divide signaled the onset of the ideological rivalry between the two superpowers known as the Cold War, which lasted for more than four decades.

Narasingha P. Sil

Further Reading

Collier, Richard. *Bridge Across the Sky: The Berlin Airlift: 1948-1949.* New York: McGraw-Hill, 1978. A reliable source on logistics and chronology not readily available in other accounts.

Laqueur, Walter. *Europe in Our Time: A History, 1945-1992.* New York: Viking Press, 1992. Mandatory reading for an understanding of the blockade in the wider background of diplomatic and ideological rivalries in postwar Europe.

Miller, Roger G. *To Save a City: The Berlin Airlift 1948-1949.* Washington, D.C.: Air Force History and Museums Program, 1998. A mine of factual information on the blockade and airlift.

Shlaim, Avi. *The United States and the Berlin Blockade, 1948-1949.* Berkeley: University of California Press, 1983. Arguably the best critical account of the blockade and airlift.

Smyser, W. R. *From Yalta to Berlin: The Cold War Struggle over Germany.* New York: St. Martin's Press, 1999. Includes a clear, concise, and competent analysis of the blockade and airlift.

Urwin, Derek W. *A Political History of Western Europe Since 1945.* 5th ed. New York: Longman, 1997. A shrewd analysis of American foreign policy, postwar treaties, the Truman Doctrine, and the significance of the Berlin blockade.

See also Anticommunism; Germany, occupation of; Historiography; "Iron Curtain" speech; Marshall, George C.; Marshall Plan; Potsdam Conference; Roosevelt, Franklin D.; Truman, Harry S.; Truman Doctrine.

■ Bernstein, Leonard

Identification American composer, conductor, pianist, educator, and author
Born August 25, 1918; Lawrence, Massachusetts
Died October 14, 1990; New York, New York

Rising to prominence in the 1940's, Bernstein embarked upon one of the most versatile musical careers of the century. As a composer, he helped to revolutionize the fully integrated Broadway musical and tackled relevant political and religious subject matter in his concert music. The first American-born conductor to hold a major orchestral post, he led the New York Philharmonic for over a decade (1958-1969) and made art music more accessible to the masses through his prime-time television broadcasts.

Leonard Bernstein graduated from Harvard in 1939, after which time he enrolled in the Curtis Institute of Music to continue studies in piano, conducting, and composing. In 1940, he met the conductor of the Boston Symphony and the man who would become his mentor, Serge Koussevitsky. Koussevitsky immediately appointed Bernstein to be his assistant at the Tanglewood Music Center, a summer academy with which Bernstein would remain actively involved throughout his life. In 1943, Bernstein was appointed assistant conductor of the New York Philharmonic, gaining international celebrity overnight when, on November 14, 1943, he made his conducting debut at Carnegie Hall in a nationally broadcast concert, originally slated to be led by the ailing Bruno Walter. Suddenly, the previously unknown Bernstein found himself in high demand, soon serving as music director of the New York City Symphony (1945-1947). In 1947, he traveled to Israel for the first time to conduct its orchestra, beginning a profound relationship with the country that would prove lifelong.

During this same period, Bernstein became acquainted with playwrights Betty Comden and Adolph Green and choreographer Jerome Robbins, all of whom would prove important longtime collaborators. In 1944, he and Robbins premiered their ballet *Fancy Free*, which subsequently inspired the Broadway musical *On the Town* that very same year. This youthful effort on the part of Bernstein, Robbins, Comden, and Green showed great promise and sophistication, and it paved the way for Bernstein's future Broadway endeavors. Bernstein also composed a number of formative concert works in the 1940's, including his Symphony No. 1, "Jeremiah" (1942), and Symphony No. 2, "The Age of Anxiety" (1949). Both works—infused with metric variety, energetic rhythms, and the language of jazz—offer a glimpse into the salient features of his highly eclectic compositional language.

Bernstein was an outspoken champion for liberal political causes throughout his life, and, not surprisingly, he fell under great scrutiny during the reign of McCarthyism. Unlike his close friend and teacher Aaron Copland, Bernstein was never summoned to testify before a congressional subcommittee.

Impact Bernstein utilized mass media to educate audiences all over the world, and his popular lectures are still widely disseminated today. Through his own success as a conductor, he paved the way for an entire generation of American-born conductors to achieve worldwide success, also mentoring many now-famous students such as Michael Tilson Thomas and John Mauceri. Bernstein and his collaborators likewise set a new artistic precedent for the Broadway musical with *West Side Story* (1957), creating a musical play that masterfully unified music, dance, and libretto. Bernstein's flair for musical theater led him to compose a number of dramatic concert works that are now staples of the orchestral repertoire, most notably *Chichester Psalms* (1965) and the overture to his operetta, *Candide* (1956). In addition to leaving behind a mammoth discography as a conductor, Bernstein contributed a number of widely regarded recordings as a pianist; most notable are his renditions of George Gershwin's *Rhapsody in Blue* (1924) and *An American in Paris* (1928).

Erica K. Argyropoulos

Further Reading

Burton, Humphrey. *Leonard Bernstein.* New York: Doubleday, 1994.

Secrest, Meryle. *Leonard Bernstein: A Life.* New York: Alfred A. Knopf, 1994.

See also Broadway musicals; Jews in the United States; Music: Classical; Music: Jazz; Robbins, Jerome; Theater in the United States.

■ The Best Years of Our Lives

Identification Feature film about three World War II veterans returning home to the same town and adjusting to civilian life after the war

Director William Wyler (1902-1981)

Date Released on November 21, 1946

During the mid-1940's, when 16 million Americans were readjusting to civilian life following service in World War II, The Best Years of Our Lives *was the quintessential Hollywood film on the topic. It was a major box-office* success and won seven Academy Awards, including best picture and best director.

The Best Years of Our Lives brought together some of Hollywood's greatest talents from the 1940's. Producer Samuel Goldwyn was known for quality productions that were also profitable. Director William Wyler was a perfectionist who elicited award-winning performances. Cinematographer Gregg Toland was known for his innovative deep-focus camerawork in *Citizen Kane* (1941). Screenwriter Robert E. Sherwood was a celebrated playwright and former speechwriter for President Franklin D. Roosevelt.

The film begins with three veterans returning to their hometown, Boone City, somewhere in the Midwest. The eldest is Al Stephenson (played by Fredric March), an Army sergeant who quickly resumes his position in banking but is troubled by the bank's reluctance to grant loans to veterans. Fred Derry (Dana Andrews), the highest ranking of the three, served as an Army Air Forces captain but cannot find a job better than soda jerk in a drugstore. Homer Parrish (Harold Russell) is a Navy veteran who lost both forearms in a shipboard explosion and now uses prosthetic metal hooks for hands. In the end, each overcomes his problems. Al stands up to his superiors at the bank; Fred finds a job converting wartime scrap into construction material for new houses; and Homer discovers that his girlfriend, Wilma (Cathy O'Donnell), still genuinely loves him.

Impact Although American popular culture typically regards World War II as the "good war," from which victorious veterans readjusted painlessly into postwar affluence, *The Best Years of Our Lives* presents a different pattern, albeit one with a Hollywood happy ending. Readjustment for veterans of any war—good or otherwise—is difficult, and the film succeeds in presenting this subject.

James I. Deutsch

Further Reading

Beidler, Philip D. "Remembering *The Best Years of Our Lives.*" *Virginia Quarterly Review* 72, no. 4 (1996): 589-604.

Gerber, David A. "Heroes and Misfits: The Troubled Social Reintegration of Disabled Veterans in *The Best Years of Our Lives.*" *American Quarterly* 46, no. 4 (1994): 545-574.

Hoppenstand, Gary, Floyd Barrows, and Erik Lunde.

"Bringing the War Home: William Wyler and World War II." *Film and History* 27, nos. 1-4 (1997): 108-118.

See also   Academy Awards; *Citizen Kane*; Films about World War II; G.I. Bill; "Greatest Generation"; War heroes.

■ Biddle, Francis

Identification   Attorney general of the United States, 1941-1945, and chief American judge at the Nuremberg Trials

Born   May 9, 1886; Paris, France

Died   October 4, 1968; Hyannis, Massachusetts

As attorney general during World War II, Biddle had to deal with the issue of civil rights and civil liberties during a great national emergency, which included such concerns as Japanese relocation and the trial of Nazi saboteurs. As chief American judge at Nuremberg, he was a force in the conduct of these trials.

Francis Biddle was born to a prominent Philadelphia family. He was also a direct descendant of Edmund Randolph, the first attorney general of the United States. As a youth, Biddle attended Groton School in Connecticut, the same institution from which Franklin D. Roosevelt graduated. Biddle graduated from Harvard College in 1909 and Harvard Law School in 1911 and served as law clerk to the eminent Supreme Court justice Oliver Wendell Holmes, Jr.

After practicing law in Philadelphia for a number of years, Biddle was called to serve in a number of New Deal agencies during the 1930's. He was appointed attorney general in September, 1940. As attorney general during World War II, Biddle tried to avoid some of the excesses against civil liberties that took place during World War I. For instance, soon after the United States entered World War II following the Japanese attack on Pearl Harbor on December 7, 1941, Biddle worked to avoid the wholesale internment of citizens of enemy countries living in the United States, and he was partially successful in doing so. He initially opposed attempts to remove individuals of Japanese ancestry (both citizens and noncitizens) from the West Coast and their internment in camps in the interior of the country. However, when it became clear that others in the Roosevelt administration thought otherwise, he acquiesced in the decision.

In 1942, when a small number of Nazi saboteurs were caught trying to enter the United States, Biddle recommended that they be tried by a military tribunal rather than in civilian courts. He served as coprosecutor in the proceedings against the saboteurs, which took place in secret. The men were convicted, and most were sentenced to death. As attorney general, Biddle argued before the Supreme Court against any meaningful civilian review of the conviction. The Court essentially agreed with his position, and the executions proceeded.

Soon after Roosevelt's death in 1945, Biddle was asked by President Harry S. Truman to step down from the position of attorney general. Shortly thereafter, Truman requested that Biddle serve as the senior American judge at the International Military Tribunal at Nuremberg. There he worked with representatives from the other victorious nations (Soviet Union, Great Britain, and France) to conduct the trial of a number of prominent officials of Nazi

U.S. attorney general Francis Biddle (right) with FBI director J. Edgar Hoover leaving a White House meeting with President Franklin D. Roosevelt on April 7, 1942. (AP/Wide World Photos)

Germany. In this capacity, he sought to influence the proceedings in ways that provided a modicum of rights, and some of those charged were given relatively light sentences or acquitted.

After Biddle returned to the United States, he involved himself in a number of liberal causes and wrote his memoirs. He died of a heart attack in 1968.

Impact In his positions of authority during the 1940's, Biddle sought to protect civil liberties in various ways. However, he worked under the trying conditions of a major war, during a time when many in the United States and other countries sought revenge against the defeated Germans. His actions mitigated some of the more extreme attacks on civil liberties.

David M. Jones

Further Reading

Biddle, Francis. *In Brief Authority*. Garden City, N.Y.: Doubleday, 1962.

Fisher, Louis. *Nazi Saboteurs on Trial: A Military Tribunal and American Law*. 2d ed. Lawrence: University Press of Kansas, 2005.

See also Censorship in the United States; Civil rights and liberties; Federal Bureau of Investigation; Hoover, J. Edgar; Nuremberg Trials; Presidential powers; Roosevelt, Franklin D.; Stone, Harlan Fiske; Truman, Harry S.; Wartime sabotage.

■ Big bang theory

Definition Astronomical theory holding that the universe originated some 15 billion years ago as an extremely hot, dense mass that has reached its current state through continued expansion

This theory addressed the creation and evolution of the universe as a scientific question, describing the universe as finite rather than infinite in space and time, and offering the first explanation of the origin of the chemical elements. The theory was conceived in Europe during the years 1915 through 1930, but the focus of this research moved to North America during the 1940's as a result of the exodus of scientific talent from Nazi Germany and the Stalinist Soviet Union prior to World War II.

In 1915, Albert Einstein published his general theory of relativity, which implied that the universe must either expand or contract in response to gravity—a notion contrary to the then widely held view that the universe was infinite and static. Astronomical observations during the 1920's directed by Edwin Hubble at the Mount Wilson Observatory in Southern California revealed that objects then known as spiral nebulae were actually distant collections of stars called galaxies and that the Milky Way, which contains the solar system, is just one such galaxy. Hubble also discovered that virtually all galaxies are receding from the Milky Way with a speed of recession proportional to the distance from Earth. Extrapolating the galactic recession into the past implies that 15 to 18 billion years ago, the entire universe was an extremely compact, hot mass. At some point very early in the youth of the universe, the temperature and pressure were so great that ordinary matter in the form of atoms and molecules could not exist. The universe must then have been a mixture of free electrons, protons, and neutrons dominated by intense electromagnetic radiation.

During the late 1930's, uranium fission was discovered. The possibility that this process might used to develop a weapon by Germany led the U.S. government to initiate the Manhattan Project in 1942. The voluminous research on neutron production and capture necessary to make nuclear weapons was partially declassified and published during the late 1940's. Russian-born American physicist George Gamow recognized in 1946 that the extreme temperatures and pressures existing early in the universe would have driven nuclear reactions that partially determine the chemical composition of the present-day universe. Using the recently released neutron data, Gamow, in collaboration with Hans Bethe and Ralph Alpher, published a comprehensive theory of the formation of atomic nuclei heavier than hydrogen in 1948.

Impact The paper's conclusions on the chemical composition of the universe as a result of the big bang have been superseded by later research, but the authors also recognized that as the universe cooled during expansion, it would eventually reach a temperature where neutral atoms could exist. From that point onward, the universe would be transparent to the thermal radiation then in existence. They predicted that this thermal radiation would cool as the universe expanded and would still exist with a current temperature a few degrees above absolute zero.

In 1948, Fred Hoyle, Hermann Bondi, and Thomas Gold offered a theory of continuous creation called the steady state theory as an alternative to the big bang theory. Their theory has no mechanism for uniform background radiation as predicted by the big bang theory. In 1964, Arno Penzias and Robert Wilson discovered a faint diffuse microwave radiation of celestial origin with a temperature of 6 degrees absolute, identified as the relict radiation predicted by Alpher, Bethe, and Gamow. It is regarded as definitive refutation of the steady state theory.

Billy R. Smith, Jr.

Further Reading

Bartusiak, Marcia. *The Day We Found the Universe.* New York: Pantheon Books, 2009.

Weinberg, Steven. *The First Three Minutes: A Modern View of the Origin of the Universe.* New York: Bantam Books, 1977.

See also Astronomy; Atomic bomb; Einstein, Albert; Manhattan Project; Science and technology.

■ Bikini bathing suits

Definition Revealing two-piece women's bathing suits

Although Americans in the 1940's were slow to accept the bikini as suitable public attire, the two-piece garment represented a major step forward in easing the traditional restrictiveness of women's bathing suits.

While women's two-piece garments for bathing and athletics have existed since ancient Greece, the term "bikini" was not introduced until the summer of 1946, when two French designers independently unveiled designs for daring two-piece suits that revealed far more skin than the American public was accustomed to seeing. Jacques Heim first introduced the "Atome," which he dubbed the world's smallest bathing suit, but only a few weeks later, Louis Réard showed his "bikini," boasting that it was even smaller. Réard's suit was so skimpy that he had to hire striptease artist Micheline Bernardini to model it, as no professional fashion models were willing to do so. Réard had named his creation for Bikini Atoll, a tiny Pacific island that had been destroyed by American nuclear testing earlier

that summer, thus indicating that he expected his bathing suit to have as much impact as a nuclear bomb.

Impact Although the bikini became a worldwide sensation when it debuted in 1946, American newspapers disapprovingly insinuated that the scandalous garment was inappropriate for the American people. Indeed, throughout the 1940's, bikinis were discouraged and often banned at many public beaches and private resorts in the United States. Nonetheless, sales of the tiny swimsuits increased steadily over several years, indicating that American women were buying and wearing them privately. The bikini finally gained a large degree of public acceptance in the 1960's.

Amy Sisson

Further Reading

Alac, Patrik. *The Bikini: A Cultural History.* New York: Parkstone Press, 2002.

Lenček, Lena, and Gideon Bosker. *Making Waves: Swimsuits and the Undressing of America.* San Francisco: Chronicle Books, 1989.

See also Fashions and clothing; Inventions; Pinup girls; Women's roles and rights in Canada; Women's roles and rights in the United States.

■ Binary automatic computer

Identification First general-purpose electronic digital computer
Also known as BINAC
Date Introduced in August, 1949

The development of this early digital computer led directly to modern methods of computation. Although the binary automatic computer was primitive by later standards, even its limitations fueled future advances, as they made clear the initial steps necessary in order to realize the potential of digital computers.

The 1940's saw the birth of one of the most transformative innovations for future society: the stored-program concept developed by Hungarian American mathematician John von Neumann. Until the late 1940's, the most advanced electronic computational device was the ENIAC (electronic numeric integrator and calculator), which had originally been built for military calculations. It was used primarily

John William Mauchly at the BINAC central control unit in 1948. (Hagley Museum and Library)

von Neumann architecture and contains five parts—an arithmetic-logic unit, a control unit, a memory, a tool for input and output, and a bus that provides the path for data to be transmitted among these parts.

The stored-program concept designed by John von Neumann allows instructions that control a computer to be stored in the same memory as the data being manipulated by the instructions. This architecture, sometimes also called the von Neumann machine, was designed to store programs electronically in binary format. Two of the engineers who contributed the most to this digital computer were John W. Mauchly and J. Presper Eckert.

Binary Logic   Due to its dependence on binary logic, the computer that first implemented this stored-program concept as it was envisioned by von Neumann was called the binary automatic computer, or BINAC. Lacking alpha characters, it was totally numeric. It was a bit serial binary computer with a 512-word acoustic mercury delay line memory divided into 16 channels, each of which held 32 words of 31 bits with an additional 11-bit space between words to allow for circuit delays in switching.

for routine computations, but it had the drawback of operating essentially like an old-fashioned telephone switchboard, with electronic wiring that needed to be reconfigured for each new task.

With the concept of stored programming, which von Neumann published in 1945, it became possible to store separate, simple instructions for one task in a computer's memory and then combine these instructions with other simple instructions to allow a computer to solve complex problems. For example, one set of instructions could be put in a computer's memory to tell it to complete long division, and then another set of instructions could be input to complete square-root calculations. These sets of instructions to the computer are called programs and are stored on a physical type of storage medium, such as magnetic tape or a hard disk. The overall type of computer architecture is often called von Neumann architecture. The binary automatic computer uses

Each of these words could hold two instructions, and each of these instructions had a 5-bit operating code and a 3-octal digital address. Pairs of digits were used to match algebraic expressions. Subroutines were stored in memory, and the symbolic code was then used to reference these subroutines. The subroutines were stored in memory, and data was later entered for these subroutines to act upon—a characteristic of the serial access memory used in the BINAC. One difficulty was to make sure that data for the instructions were entered with a sufficient time delay to ensure that the instructions would already be in memory, ready to act on data being entered. Therefore, the engineers converted an IBM 010 keypunch, which had keys for the digits of 0 through 9 and a key for spaces, into an 8-key, octal digit keypad to enter new programs and data. Because there was not enough room in memory for a conversion subroutine to convert between octal and decimal, all of the data entered had to be converted from decimal to octal and then back to decimal, thus producing a time delay.

Developing the BINAC   Mauchly and Eckert began work on this BINAC in 1946 in response to specifications supplied by Northrop Aircraft, which was developing a long-range guided missile system for the U.S. Air Force. Although Mauchly and Eckert had already completed a government contract to build the first digital computer—the electronic numerical integrator and computer (ENIAC)—to complete mathematical computations, ENIAC had relied upon a series of approximately 18,000 vacuum tubes, which required 18,000 valves, measured 24 meters in length, and used punched cards to store data. The BINAC, which used circuits instead of vacuum tubes and magnetic tape instead of punched cards to store data, was a major improvement.

Impact   Upon its completion in 1949, the BINAC could complete several differential equations within fifteen minutes that had previously required two operators using electric calculators a total of six months to complete. The operational speeds for the BINAC were measured in millionths of a second, and this binary logic together with the stored-program concept, which was first implemented in the BINAC, became the foundations of all the computer hardware and software ubiquitous in modern gadgets ranging from cell phones to supercomputers.

Jean L. Kuhler

Further Reading

Davis, Martin. *The Universal Computer: The Road from Leibniz to Turing.* New York: W. W. Norton, 2000.

Goldstein, Herman H. *The Computer from Pascal to Von Neumann.* Princeton, N.J.: Princeton University Press, 1972.

Hally, Mike. *Electronic Brains: Stories from the Dawn of the Computer Age.* Washington, D.C.: Joseph Henry Press, 2005.

Norberg, Arthur L. *Computers and Commerce: A Study of Technology and Management at Eckert-Mauchly Computer Company, Engineering Research Associates, and Remington Rand, 1946-1957.* Cambridge, Mass.: MIT Press, 2005.

See also   Computers; ENIAC; Science and technology; Transistors.

■ Birth control

Definition   Methods to prevent conception

As the United States left the Depression and entered World War II, the federal government began a concerted effort to control population. The political and cultural climate in the United States underwent significant changes, and increased access to information about birth control connected with other changing elements in society, such as women's rights and economic dependence of women.

The federal government began suppressing information about birth control during the 1870's, when Anthony Comstock pushed a bill through Congress that defined contraceptive information as obscene. This suppression lasted until the 1940's, when, largely as the result of efforts by Margaret Sanger, the federal ban on birth control was lifted.

Birth Control Strategies   Before the process of reproduction was truly understood, infanticide was considered a solution to overpopulation in pre-industrial societies. Abortion has also been used since ancient times. Studies during the 1920's and 1930's indicated that coitus interruptus was the most common form of birth control, followed by the condom. Other birth control methods that have been used over time include suppositories that form an impenetrable coating over the cervix; diaphragms, caps, and other devices that are inserted into the vagina over the cervix and withdrawn after intercourse; intrauterine devices; douches; and rhythm methods.

Although people have been attempting to control reproduction since the beginning of recorded history, prior to the 1940's, legislation in the United States had prohibited the distribution of birth control and any advertisements or information related to it. The Comstock Act of 1873 had made it illegal to send obscene materials through the mail, and in its definition of "obscene," it included contraceptive devices and information about them, as well as about abortion. Margaret Sanger, who coined the term birth control, fought to remove the negative connotations associated with birth control as she worked to provide women with contraceptive education, counseling, and services. The ban on contraceptives was declared unconstitutional in 1936, but elements of Comstock laws remained on the books, and public attitudes regarding contraception were slow to change.

Proponents of birth control had three essential strategies available to them: They could support research, organize public health campaigns tied to increasing the number of birth control clinics and improving sex education, and develop programs to provide simple, inexpensive, practical methods of birth control. Additionally, during World War II, the Birth Control Federation, which changed its name to Planned Parenthood in 1942, connected population control to patriotism, national strength, and military victory in some of its informational pamphlets.

After World War II, public acceptance of birth control increased rapidly. The widespread use of the condom to prevent venereal diseases (as sexually transmitted diseases were called then) following World War I contributed to the acceptance of contraception, even though it was still considered "immoral" to distribute condoms to American G.I.'s. This argument was connected to biblical directives about being fruitful and multiplying. Nevertheless, during World War II the Army concluded that the health benefits of condoms outweighed the risks.

Canadian Birth Control Movement A parallel movement, with the same arguments on both sides of the birth control debate, occurred in Canada as Elizabeth Bagshaw and A. R. Kaufman worked to bring birth control to the masses. Bagshaw was the medical director of Canada's first birth control clinic, which provided information, pessaries, jellies, and condoms. Although for many years the clinic remained illegal under an 1870's Canadian law, the realities of poverty brought by the Depression overwhelmed legal concerns. Bagshaw observed that because the lack of jobs, welfare programs, and unemployment benefits meant that people were starving, for them to go on having children was a detriment to society. Simply put, people could not afford children if they could not afford even to feed themselves. Families came to the clinic and received information despite resistance from many in the medical community and local clergy, who believed birth control tended to corrupt morals.

Corresponding with Bagshaw's effort, A. R. Kaufman's Parents' Information Bureau (PIB) provided a birth control program for low-income women throughout the 1930's and 1940's that distributed contraceptives by mail order and gave referrals for diaphragms and sterilization. The PIB assisted 25,000 clients a year.

Impact The sea change in birth control politics led to improved maternal and infant mortality rates, autonomy for women, and greater family stability. Those changes did not come without cost. Sex and gender roles changed and have continued to evolve as women acquired reproductive choice and freedom, which led to a measure of economic independence, as women no longer faced a firm expectation of having children and therefore being dependent on men. Many women experienced personal conflict as the cultural mandate to reproduce, which remained in place, collided with the desire to control individual reproductive rights.

Paul Finnicum

Further Reading

Critchlow, Donald T. *Intended Consequences: Birth Control, Abortion, and the Federal Government in Modern America.* New York: Oxford University Press, 1999. Chronicles how the federal government found its way into the private bedrooms of American families. Critchlow describes how, after World War II, policy experts thought that population growth threatened global disaster and therefore initiated federally funded family planning.

Johnston, Carolyn. *Sexual Power: Feminism and the Family in America.* Tuscaloosa: University of Alabama Press, 1992. Offers insight into issues surrounding birth control during the 1940's and women's conflicting experiences of empowerment and entrapment.

Kennedy, David M. *Birth Control in America: The Career of Margaret Sanger.* New Haven, Conn.: Yale University Press, 1970. A thorough examination of the role of Margaret Sanger. Kennedy provides insight into the issues of feminism, sexuality, and morality that emerged alongside the birth control movement.

McCann, Carole R. *Birth Control Politics in the United States, 1916-1945.* Ithaca, N.Y.: Cornell University Press, 1994. A look at the political nature of the birth control issue. Interesting description of the use of language, such as the shift from the term "birth control" to "family planning," which McCann suggests also helped to expand the movement beyond its liberal and feminist roots. Shows the careful consideration given to the class and racial issues that were woven into the politics of birth control.

Reed, James. *The Birth Control Movement and American*

Society Since 1830. New York: Basic Books, 1978. A description of how a small group of Americans spread the practice of contraception. This book focuses on a few key contributors to the birth control movement and shows how the movement became a metaphor for individual responsibility and a step in the effort to achieve self-direction.

See also Baby boom; Health care; Sex and sex education; Sexually transmitted diseases; Women's roles and rights in Canada; Women's roles and rights in the United States; World War II.

■ Black Dahlia murder

The Event Unsolved torture and murder of
  Elizabeth Short
Date January 15, 1947
Place Los Angeles, California

Elizabeth Short's murder became notorious through newspaper articles highlighting its sensational aspects. The media portrayed Short as a beautiful aspiring actor whose Hollywood dreams ended in horrible suffering. Public interest in Short's murder continued when detectives failed to identify her killer, and the crime lent itself to a variety of possible solutions.

The story of the "Black Dahlia" was a gripping and cautionary tale for young women in the postwar era. On the morning of January 15, 1947, a woman walking on Norton Avenue in southwest Los Angeles found the nude body of twenty-two-year-old Elizabeth Short lying in a vacant lot. Short's body had been drained of blood, cut in half at the waist, and arranged in a sexually suggestive pose just feet from the sidewalk. An autopsy showed that Short had been tortured and died from blows to the head and face. Her body had been further mutilated, possibly after her death, then bisected by someone with medical knowledge and skill. Newspapers reported that Short was called the "Black Dahlia" (a nickname playing on the title of the 1946 movie *The Blue Dahlia*) for her black hair and preference for black clothing. Friends and family called her Betty or Beth.

Robert "Red" Manley, a married salesman whom Short had dated briefly, and the last known person to see her alive, was arrested on January 19 but released

a day later. On January 24, postal inspectors intercepted an envelope addressed to Los Angeles newspapers that contained Short's address book, other personal papers, and a note composed of cutout newspaper headlines saying, "Here is Dahlia's belongings. Letter to follow." More letters were received but none could be conclusively connected to the case. On January 28, Army veteran Daniel Voorhees gave police the first demonstrably false confession in the case.

Short was a challenge to investigators. Having traveled to California from Massachusetts to become an actor or model, she was rarely employed, moved frequently, and lied often about her travels and jobs she had never held. Short also dated widely and had known at least fifty men at the time of her death. Detectives never learned where Short had been during the week before her body was found.

Impact In October, 1949, the Los Angeles grand jury asked the district attorney's office to examine police handling of the Short case. The grand jury noted that 192 suspects had been investigated and dismissed, and it found the murder remained unsolved through a lack of evidence and not because of police misconduct. In the following years, independent researchers continued to publish conflicting theories, suggest possible suspects, and argue over the facts of the case. Two novels inspired by Short's life and murder, John Gregory Dunne's *True Confessions* (1977) and James Ellroy's *The Black Dahlia* (1987), were adapted as major motion pictures.

Maureen Puffer-Rothenberg

Further Reading

Douglas, John, and Mark Olshaker. "American Dreams/American Nightmares." In *The Cases That Haunt Us: From Jack the Ripper to JonBenet Ramsey, the FBI's Legendary Mindhunter Sheds Light on the Mysteries That Won't Go Away.* New York: Scribner, 2000.
Hodel, Steve. *Black Dahlia Avenger: A Genius for Murder.* Rev. ed. New York: Harper Paperbacks, 2006.
Wolfe, Donald H. *The Black Dahlia Files: The Mob, the Mogul, and the Murder That Transfixed Los Angeles.* New York: ReganBooks, 2005.

See also Crimes and scandals; Federal Bureau of Investigation; Newspapers.

■ Black market

Definition   Illegal wartime buying and selling of goods subjected to government restrictions

During World War II, black markets were the flip side of government-imposed rationing of consumer goods in both the United States and Canada. Although the full extent of black market activity in North America during the war may never be determined, it is clear that many millions of Americans participated in it.

A major problem facing the U.S. government and its citizens during World War II was a scarcity of consumer goods. This was due to the fact that fighting a war necessitated a priority for allocating goods to the war effort. In addition, the war limited imports and exports. Hence, the federal government enacted a policy of rationing certain goods. This meant that citizens were limited in the amounts and types of goods they could purchase throughout the years of the war. Meats, canned goods, sugar, coffee, and gas-

Sign appealing to New Yorkers not to buy on the black market in late 1942. (Getty Images)

oline were among the rationed commodities.

The U.S. government also began its own rationing program in 1942. Enforcement of the program to the newly created Office of Price Administration. Rationing was justified primarily as a means of ensuring that the national war effort received sufficient quantities of needed materials, but it was also justified by concerns that no hoarding of goods should take place, as well as a fear of a wartime inflation in prices.

The United States was not alone in legislating a strict rationing program during the war. Canada initiated a similar program in January of 1942. Its rationing program even included beer. The Royal Canadian Mounted Police were given the additional responsibility of investigating black market activity.

Rationing and the Black Markets   An almost inevitable result of the U.S. rationing program was an increase in the criminal activity known as black marketing—a term was applied to the buying and selling of scarce consumer commodities illegal to sell outside the government rationing program. Black market buyers obtained items they wanted but could not easily get through legal channels. Sellers received higher profits than they would receive through legal sales. Both sides thus gained but did so by breaking a federal law. Black markets tend to arise wherever governments impose restrictions on sales of certain goods, including times when governments place restrictions on when goods can be sold. This is exactly what occurred during World War II.

Black markets cannot exist without buyers willing to flout the law. Reasons that Americans violated the rationing rules during World War II ranged from their inability to get along with the quantities of goods that the system permitted them, to their belief that certain items were not sufficiently scarce to justify being rationed. Another possible excuse was the belief that black market transactions would not really hurt the war effort. Persons who sold goods through the black market, on the other hand, were motivated mostly by a simple desire to make money.

A more interesting question about the black market, perhaps, is what motivated Americans who could have taken advantage of the black market not to do so. In many cases, it was undoubtedly patriotism and a desire to support the war cause. For others, it may have been a sense of morality and a desire not to violate any laws. For still others, it may have been a resentment against paying inflated black market prices. In any case, the federal government instituted a public relations program to encourage compliance with the rationing program and to counter black market activities.

The Black Market in Operation The extent of black market activity varied across the United States and had much to do with local economic conditions and consumer needs. For example, black markets in foodstuffs could not flourish in agricultural regions, where residents could easily grow their own food without regard to rationing restrictions. In fact, Americans were encouraged by the federal government to save money (and avoid the black market) by growing food in their own personal "Victory Gardens."

Participants in black market activity who were caught faced possible civil and criminal punishments. However, enforcement of anti-black market laws was not easy. Dissatisfied black market customers were unlikely to reveal their participation in the illegal activity by complaining to the government. A technical problem in prosecuting sellers arose when the goods were found to have been purchased with counterfeit ration coupons. Government-issued coupons were used to purchase rationed items. The coupon system naturally gave rise to a market in counterfeit ration coupons.

The Size of the Black Market The exact amount of black market activity that occurred during World War II is not easy to determine because most participants in the black market kept no records, and those who did kept them secret. However, it can be confidently estimated that the amount of black market activity was substantial. In 1944, *The New York Times* published an article estimating the annual size of the black market in foodstuffs at $1.2 billion. Another *Times* article published the same year estimated that 70 percent of the residents of New York City had used the black market, and about one-third of them used it regularly.

Impact One of the more interesting questions that still remains to be answered is what the effect of the black market was on the American war effort. Because the United States emerged from the war victorious and apparently had enough goods to conduct the war successfully, it seems reasonable to assume that the impact of the black market on the war was negligible. However, there is little doubt that the black market itself played a role in raising public awareness of the war effort by bringing the effects of the war so close to home that ordinary people could feel them.

William E. Kelly

Further Reading

Chandler, Lester V. *Inflation in the United States, 1940-1948.* New York: Harper & Brothers, 1951. Analysis of the forces responsible for inflation during and following World War II. Emphasizes the role of government fiscal and monetary policies.

Chandler, Lester V., and Donald H. Wallace, eds. *Economic Mobilization and Stabilization: Selected Materials on the Economics of War and Defense.* New York: Henry Holt, 1951. Collection of materials treating problems of economic mobilization and stabilization during wartime,

Harris, Seymour. *Price and Related Controls in the United States.* New York: McGraw-Hill, 1945. Sympathetic and detailed account of the Office of Price Administration price and rent controls by an economist who served with the agency.

Hoopes, Roy. *Americans Remember the Home Front.* New York: Berkley Books, 2002. An oral history that focuses on the transformations of families, industries, and American society as a whole during World War II.

Lingeman, Richard R. *Don't You Know There's a War On? The American Home Front, 1941-1945.* Rev. ed. New York: Nation Books, 2003. Details all aspects of the American domestic experience during World War II, from the black market to rationing.

See also Crimes and scandals; Gross national product of the United States; Office of Price Administration; War Production Board; Wartime rationing; Wartime salvage drives.

■ Bobby-soxers

Identification   Teenage girls who wore heavy white socks with the tops rolled over, and were identified as the screaming fans of crooners such as Frank Sinatra

Although bobby socks had been around since the mid-1930's, they became identified with high school girls who screamed and swooned over stars, especially Frank Sinatra, but also including others such Mickey Rooney and Van Johnson. Socks had slowly replaced stockings by the late 1930's for college and high school women, but by the 1940's they were adopted mostly by high schoolers.

Prior to the 1940's, teens were identified as an age group but were not considered a distinct social group. Bobby-soxers initially were portrayed as fe-male juvenile delinquents by *Newsweek* in 1944, but the term as used by newspapers and magazines such as *The New York Times* and *Time* magazine came to refer to teenage girls who swooned over their idols (Frank Sinatra in particular). The epithet referred to the bobby socks (or bobby sox) worn by many teenage girls. These thick, ankle-high white cotton socks were worn with the tops rolled over, with cuffed denim pants or skirts (often embroidered with poodles), and with saddle shoes. The socks became popular because at many school dances, students were required to remove their shoes to protect the floor, and bobby socks stood up well to dancing.

Teenagers did not often refer to themselves as bobby-soxers, but Shirley Temple played such a girl, infatuated with an older man, in the 1947 film *The Bachelor and the Bobby-Soxer.* The look of bobby socks

Bobby-soxer fans of Frank Sinatra eagerly read about him in Modern Screen *magazine while waiting for him to appear at a New York nightclub.* (Getty Images)

began a trend toward more casual dress, with teens as leaders in the trend. The launch of *Seventeen* magazine in 1944 recognized teenage culture as a profitable market.

Impact   The term "bobby-soxer" came to epitomize teenage girls in popular culture. Bobby-soxers were part of an emerging teenage lifestyle that would develop into a consumer demographic of fashion, music, magazines, and cosmetics.

Jane Brodsky Fitzpatrick

Further Reading

Palladino, Grace. *Teenagers: An American History.* New York: Basic Books, 1996.

Schrum, Kelly. "Teenagers." In *Encyclopedia of Children and Childhood: In History and Society,* edited by Paula S. Fass. New York: Macmillan Reference USA, 2004.

Sickels, Robert C. *The 1940s.* Westport, Conn.: Greenwood Press, 2004.

See also   Fads; Fashions and clothing; Music: Popular; Nylon stockings; Rooney, Mickey; Sinatra, Frank.

■ Bogart, Humphrey

Identification   American film star
Born   December 25, 1899; New York, New York
Died   January 14, 1957; Hollywood, California

A bit player on stage during the 1920's who became typecast as a B-picture gangster during the 1930's, Bogart rose to prominence during the 1940's, when he became the highest-paid actor in the world and one of the most recognized and respected icons of the silver screen.

The son of a wealthy surgeon, Humphrey Bogart served in the U.S. Navy in World War I before drifting into acting, playing walk-on roles on stage in romantic comedies throughout the 1920's. In 1930, he went to Hollywood, earning a reputation during the decade as a hardworking, reliable second lead capable of playing a variety of roles.

Having served his apprenticeship, Bogart dominated the 1940's like no other male actor of his era. A series of meaty roles showcased his unique talent for portraying tough guys of substance. His expressive eyes, his intensity, and his no-nonsense delivery—accented with a slight lisp as the result of a scarred lip—combined to make his characters believable. Bogart's incredible run began with *High Sierra* (1941), headlining as a former convict masterminding one last crime. In the same year, he was private eye Sam Spade in the noir-flavored mystery *The Maltese Falcon.* He followed up in 1942 as nightclub owner Rick Blaine in the Oscar-winning wartime drama *Casablanca,* considered one of the greatest movies of all time, for which he was nominated for an Academy Award for best actor. Other patriotic combat dramas featuring Bogart included *Across the Pacific* (1942), *All Through the Night* (1942), *Action in the North Atlantic* (1943), *Sahara* (1943), *Passage to Marseille* (1944), and *To Have and Have Not* (1944). After World War II, Bogart continued his winning ways in a wide range of starring vehicles—as detective, ex-soldier, sympathetic escaped convict, conscience-stricken prospector, or crusading attorney—in such compelling films as *The Big Sleep* (1946), *Dead Reckoning* (1947), *Dark Passage* (1947), *The Treasure of the Sierra Madre* (1948), *Key Largo* (1948), and *Knock on Any Door* (1949).

The 1940's were meaningful to Bogart in other ways. In 1943 and 1944, he joined United Service Organizations (USO) and war bond tours to Europe and North Africa. He married his fourth wife, youthful actor Lauren Bacall, in 1945, and fathered his only son, Stephen Humphrey Bogart, in 1949. In 1948, he became one of the first actors to establish his own production company, Santana Productions.

Impact   Bogart's superior work during the 1940's (of seventy-two films in which he appeared, twenty-seven were released between 1940 and 1949) made him a box-office star, earning $10,000 per week by 1946. His work also earned him first shot at choice roles throughout the remainder of a career terminated by throat cancer. In 1951, he won his only best actor Oscar, for the *The African Queen.* He was nominated again for his performance in *The Caine Mutiny* (1954), and his last three films—*The Left Hand of God* (1955), *The Desperate Hours* (1955), and *The Harder They Fall* (1956)—are all considered classics of their type.

More than a half century since his death, the image of Bogart in fedora and trench coat, squinting through cigarette smoke, is universally recognized. It is no wonder that in 1999 he was named the American Film Institute's greatest male star of all time.

Jack Ewing

Further Reading

Bacall, Lauren. *By Myself and Then Some.* New York: HarperEntertainment, 2005.

Schickel, Richard, and George Perry. *Bogie: A Celebration of the Life and Films of Humphrey Bogart.* Foreword by Stephen Bogart. New York: Thomas Dunne Books, 2006.

Ursini, James, and Paul Duncan, eds. *Humphrey Bogart.* Cologne, Germany: Taschen, 2007.

See also Academy Awards; *Casablanca*; Chandler, Raymond; Film noir; *The Maltese Falcon*; *The Treasure of the Sierra Madre*; United Service Organizations; Wartime propaganda in the United States.

■ Bombers

Identification American planes of various classifications that delivered payloads to tactical and strategic targets

American bombers played a crucial role in World War II in both the European and Pacific theaters. Bombers established America's air superiority, solidifying the United States as the premier global military and industrial power for decades to come.

American bombers were generally classified as light, medium, and heavy, typically differentiated by engine power, aircraft size, and payload. The bombers, operated by the U.S. Army Air Forces (USAAF), were further classified as tactical and strategic bombers, depending on their missions. Tactical bombers were used primarily against forward troops and equipment, whereas strategic bombers attacked cities, factories, and infrastructure.

Light bombers typically were single-engine, short-range aircraft carrying a bomb load of 1,100-2,200 pounds. They were tactical bombers stationed at forward bases and on aircraft carriers seeing action in both the European and Pacific theaters. Dive and torpedo bombers were both classified as light bombers.

The A-20/DB-7 Havoc was a light bomber and night fighter, built primarily by an American manufacturer, Douglas. The Havoc was a dual-engine craft yet still classified as a light bomber, mostly because of its range and payload. Nearly 7,500 Havocs were manufactured between 1937 and 1944. As the B-26 Marauder medium bomber entered the fray, Havocs were relegated to use as trainers. The aircraft was used not only by the United States Army Air Forces but also by the Soviet, British, and French air forces.

Medium bombers covered approximately 1,500-2,000 miles and carried payloads of about 4,000 pounds. The B-25 Mitchell was an American twin-engine medium bomber used mostly in the European theater during the war. North American Aviation built nearly 10,000 Mitchells. This aircraft, named after military aviation pioneer General Billy Mitchell, was the only American military aircraft named after a specific person.

Heavy bombers were the most famous and, in the end, most widely credited for ending the war. These large, multiengine aircraft could carry payloads exceeding 8,000 pounds and covered nearly 3,600 miles, allowing for maximum protection away from the theater of battle. Some of the best-known bombers of World War II were heavy strategic bombers.

Boeing went from design to test flight of the B-17 Flying Fortress in less than twelve months, with the British Royal Air Force taking deliveries in 1941. The aircraft was the first built by Boeing with a flight deck instead of the open cockpit design. Boeing, Douglas, and Lockheed built nearly 12,000 B-17's. The planes, carrying a crew of ten, were extremely durable, heavily armed, and able to reach high altitudes. They performed in both of the main theaters of battle during the war.

The most famous B-17 Flying Fortress was the *Memphis Belle*, the first heavy bomber to complete twenty-five combat missions; it was the subject of a 1944 documentary (*The Memphis Belle: A Story of a Flying Fortress*) and a 1990 Hollywood film (*Memphis Belle*). The crew of the *Memphis Belle* toured the United States to inspire Americans and help sell war bonds.

The Boeing B-29 Superfortress was the descendant of the B-17 Flying Fortress. The Superfortress was a long-range, four-engine, heavily armed bomber that carried a crew of ten and was used mostly in the Pacific theater during the war. Nearly 4,000 B-29s were built between 1940 and 1946, primarily by Boeing but also by the Bell and Martin aircraft companies.

The *Enola Gay*, a B-29 Superfortress bomber, dropped the first atomic bomb, named "Little Boy," on Hiroshima, Japan on August 6, 1945. The airplane was named by pilot Colonel Paul W. Tibbets, Jr., for his mother, Enola Gay Tibbets. A lesser known B-29, named *Bockscar*, dropped the second atomic

Eighty-eight journalists stand atop the wings of a Convair B-36 Peacemaker in late 1949. The strategic bomber's 270-foot wingspan was the widest of any combat airplane ever made, and the plane was unusual in having its propellers facing the rear. (Time & Life Pictures/ Getty Images)

bomb, named "Fat Man," on Nagasaki, Japan, three days later. Japan surrendered shortly thereafter.

After World War II, bomber classification blurred as fighters and light bombers became bigger, faster, and able to carry more weight, thus eliminating the medium class bomber. The heavy bomber classification remained.

Impact   The American bombers of the 1940's were instrumental in stopping the surge of Nazi Germany, the empire of Japan, and other belligerents during World War II. The nearly nonstop strategic bombing throughout Europe paved the way to Berlin, and the direct bombing of Japan ended the war in the Pacific, establishing the United States as the world's major military power.

Jonathan E. Dinneen

Further Reading

Astor, Gerald. *The Mighty Eighth: The Air War in Europe as Told by the Men Who Fought It.* New York: Random House, 1997.

Miller, Donald L. *Masters of the Air: America's Bomber Boys Who Fought the Air War Against Nazi Germany.* New York: Simon & Schuster, 2006.

See also   Air Force, U.S.; Aircraft carriers; Aircraft design and development; Army, U.S.; Atomic bomb; Doolittle bombing raid; *Enola Gay*; Hiroshima and Nagasaki bombings; Strategic bombing; World War II.

■ **Book publishing**

Definition   Business of printing bound volumes of literature and information that changed during the 1940's as the number and variety of book sellers increased and as changes in the industry led to increased sales

Publication of books in quantity has long been an important way to disseminate human knowledge, as well as entertaining stories, to masses of people. During the 1940's, even with wartime restrictions on materials, book ownership and readership increased, with the introduction of cheaper, faster printing technologies and the paperback format.

The 1940's were dominated by World War II and the nationwide effort to defeat the coalition of Japan, Germany, and Italy. From 1941 to 1945, war measures severely limited the normal commercial activity of American businesses, but the book publishing business never languished during those years. It continued producing books that reflected the varying interests and moods of the American public while remaining profitable and relevant.

The War Years In 1940, the United States was not yet an active combatant in the war against Nazi Germany and Japan, but it had sided with and was supporting Great Britain and China in their struggles. Still, many of the writers of books published and circulated that year seemed more concerned about America's past and the issues of American society than with war. Thomas Wolfe's *You Can't Go Home Again* (1940) and Christopher Morley's *Kitty Foyle* (1939) were popular works that chronicled, respectively, a writer's return to his hometown and the affairs of an independent businesswoman.

American history and culture, real and imagined, were the subjects of Van Wyck Brooks's *New England:*

John Steinbeck with his wife, writer Elaine Andersen, in Italy in early 1947. (Time & Life Pictures/Getty Images)

Indian Summer, 1865-1915 (1940) and Walter Van Tilburg Clark's *The Ox-Bow Incident* (1940). Circumstances of race and poverty were delineated in Richard Wright's *Native Son* (1940) and John Steinbeck's *The Grapes of Wrath* (1939). *For Whom the Bell Tolls* (1940) was Ernest Hemingway's story about an American fighting idealistically against fascism in the Spanish Civil War.

After Germany invaded France in June, 1940, many writers fled the Vichy government for Canada, adding to the ranks of first-rate Canadian writers. Between 1940 and 1946 in Montreal alone, more than 20 million books were published. Among them, Hugh MacLennon's novel *Barometer Rising* (1941) critiqued contemporary Canadian life and, like American novels of the time, seemed less interested in the war than in local issues.

After the Pearl Harbor attack of December, 1941, and America's entrance into the war, even with paper shortages, book sales continued. Bible sales went up 25 percent, and books with religious themes increased in popularity. *The Keys of the Kingdom* (1941) by A. J. Cronin, *The Song of Bernadette* (1942; translated from *Das Lied von Bernadette*, 1941) by Franz Werfel, and *The Robe* (1942) by Lloyd C. Douglas all appeared in the early years of the decade. Their themes of hardship and the awakening of religious faith appealed to American readers, and all three were made into films. War stories began to appear as well; for example, Pearl S. Buck's *Dragon Seed* (1942) showed Chinese peasants' reaction to the Japanese occupation, war correspondent John Hersey wrote about the Pacific conflict in *Men on Bataan* (1942), and the resistance movement against the Nazi occupation of Norway was allegorized by John Steinbeck in *The Moon Is Down* (1942).

The war was not going well for the United States and its allies in 1942, so perhaps a somewhat lighthearted view of the American military, *See Here, Private Hargrove* (1942) by Marion Hargrove, was just what American readers needed. The book stayed on *The New York Times* bestseller list for fifteen weeks and in 1944 was made into a successful movie. The year 1942 also saw the publication of Canadian writer Thomas Raddall's *His Majesty's Yankees*; its war theme related, however, to the American Revolution and depicted customs and idioms of the people of Nova Scotia.

Between 1943 and 1947, the subjects and themes of America's most popular books included war stories of heroism and horror, tales of nostalgia for "the good old days" before the war, and decades-old societal issues. Books about the war included Ted Lawson's *Thirty Seconds over Tokyo* (1943), *Guadacanal Diary* (1943) by Richard Tregaskis, the fictional *A Bell for Adano* (1944) and nonfiction *Hiroshima* (1946) by John Hersey, *Here Is Your War* (1944) by Ernie Pyle, *Up Front* (1945) by Bill Mauldin, and *Mister Roberts* (1946) by Thomas Heggen.

Small towns and close-knit neighborhoods untouched by war or the Depression were recollected in both fictional and nonfictional works, including the popular *A Tree Grows in Brooklyn* (1943) by Betty Smith, *The Human Comedy* (1943) by William Saroyan, Cornelia Otis Skinner's *Our Hearts Were Young and Gay* (1942), John Steinbeck's *Cannery Row* (1945), *The Egg and I* (1945) by Betty MacDonald, and *The Member of the Wedding* (1946) by Carson McCullers. These books recalled times when families were concerned with making a living and upholding traditional values and ways of life.

Canadian writers also dealt with social issues, especially those relating to families' struggles against poverty. Gabrielle Roy's *Bonheur d'occasion* (1945) and Germaine Guèvremont's *Le Survenant* (1945) were French-language novels depicting, respectively, poor working-class urban dwellers and peasant family life. *Le Survenant* was so popular that its stories became the basis for a television series; the book was later translated and published in the United States as *The Outlander* (1950).

Race and poverty were explored in Erskine Caldwell's *Georgia Boy* (1943), *Strange Fruit* (1944) by Lillian Smith, *An American Dilemma: The Negro Problem and Modern Democracy* (1944) by Gunnar Myrdal, *If He Hollers Let Him Go* (1945) by Chester Himes, and Richard Wright's *Black Boy* (1945). Although many books about the war and the years closely preceding it were turned into films within a year or two of publication, few books about race or poverty were filmed.

The Postwar Years   When the war ended, America turned to other concerns, such as the perceived communist threat, the need to assimilate four million returning soldiers back into the home society, and the need to help war-ravaged countries to rebuild. Writers helped the reading public understand aspects of the recent conflict that may have been overlooked or never known. Both fictional and nonfictional works giving insight into wartime situations include Anne Frank's *Het Achterhuis* (1947; English translation, *The Diary of a Young Girl*, 1952), *The Naked and the Dead* (1948) by Norman Mailer, *The Young Lions* (1948) by Irwin Shaw, and *The Gathering Storm* (1948) by Winston Churchill.

Canadian publishers reverted to their prewar custom of publishing mostly educational works. Relative prosperity had returned to Canada, and people of all levels were returning to school. Publishers were quick to provide the textbooks and other works for these new customers.

Young men and women, many returning from foreign settings, had to adjust their ingrained preconceptions and prejudices as racial issues became more prominent, particularly after integration of the military became a reality. Writers rushed to incorporate themes of race and discrimination into their works. Those that dealt with African Americans' situations included Sinclair Lewis's *Kingsblood Royal* (1947), William Faulkner's *Intruder in the Dust* (1948), E. Franklin Frazier's textbook *The Negro in the United States* (1949), and *Killers of the Dream* (1949) by Lillian Smith. Discrimination against Jews was explored in *Gentleman's Agreement* (1947) by Laura Hobson. Even apartheid in South Africa was treated, in Alan Paton's novel *Cry, the Beloved Country* (1948), which was made into both a musical drama, *Lost in the Stars* (1949), and a 1951 film.

Other social concerns served as themes for books during the latter half of the decade, including drug addiction, sexual practices, existentialistic approaches to living, the specter of loss of personal privacy, and civil rights. The public's fascination with such issues led writers to produce fiction and nonfiction addressing, explaining, and exploring them. Jean-Paul Sartre's work *L'Existenialisme est un Humanisme* (1946) was translated and published in the United States as *Existentialism* in 1947, introducing Americans to a philosophical system centered in the individual and his or her relationship to God and/or the universe. Drug addiction, as delineated in Nelson Algren's *The Man with the Golden Arm* (1949), was an early description of a "dope" addict that, when made into a film in 1955, was disparaged as an unrealistic distortion of the real thing. *Inside U.S.A.* (1947), by John Gunther, gave an overview of the spirit of a nation that had fought and won a difficult war.

Realistic, contemporary characters and plots and greater freedom to incorporate blunt language and graphic violence found their way into books published after the war. Mickey Spillane's *I, the Jury* (1947) had a style, a plot, and characters unlike what most readers of mysteries and detective stories were used to. (In 1946, Joseph T. Shaw had published his edited work *The Hard-Boiled Omnibus*, containing crime stories earlier published in the popular *Black Mask* magazine. Spillane might have been influenced by that book.) *The Harder They Fall* (1947), by Budd Schulberg, and *Knock on Any Door* (1947), by Willard Motley, portrayed the hard lives of young men of low socioeconomic levels, whereas *A Rage to Live* (1949), by John O'Hara, and *Point of No Return* (1949), by John P. Marquand, told of life among a more privileged class. Going back to earlier times, Ross Lockridge recaptured the Civil War era in his *Raintree County* (1948), and *Cheaper by the Dozen* (1948), by Frank B. Gilbreth, Jr., and Ernestine Gilbreth Carey, takes the reader back to the early days of the twentieth century. John Steinbeck wrote the picaresque *The Wayward Bus* (1947), and Truman Capote offered the surreal *Other Voices, Other Rooms* (1948).

Publishing Trends The availability of improved mass-production methods such as high-speed presses, stereotyping, and mechanical typesetting and typecasting made it possible for book publishers to churn out millions of books at relatively low cost, covering a bewildering variety of topics in fiction and nonfiction, to satisfy every reader. They were sold in about 2,500 bookstores as well as in department stores. In addition, members of mail-order book clubs in America purchased millions of books each year. The clubs were opposed at first by publishers and booksellers, who resented the competition and also disliked the emphasis the clubs put on bestsellers. The clubs soon demonstrated their value: They encouraged the purchase of books and lessened the enormous proportion of library borrowing.

During the late 1930's, a British firm, Penguin Books, began printing paperback books, a cheaper format than the hardcover volumes to which readers were accustomed. American publishers soon followed suit. One company, Simon & Schuster, in 1939 published a twenty-five cent Pocket Book that was immediately successful. Many hardcover books at the time cost two or three dollars, quite a bit of money to people just coming out of the Great Depression. The pocket-size, softcover, inexpensive paperback could be purchased at a wide variety of outlets, including variety stores, drugstores, and even railroad and bus stations, for the enjoyment of travelers. Within a few years, nearly fifty million were bought annually. They were treated much like magazines: read and then discarded. During the war, 119 million free, special edition paperbacks were distributed to members of the American military services.

Because books have the power to introduce new ideas and values to a culture, some have always faced opponents who would censor and/or ban them to halt the spread of what were considered unseemly ideas. During the 1940's, books were banned by a variety of groups, including a Boston censor, school board censors, church groups, and even parent groups. Some of the banned books became popular, both at the time and later, partly as a result of this notoriety. John Steinbeck's *The Grapes of Wrath*, Shirley Jackson's short story "The Lottery" (banned in the Union of South Africa), Anne Frank's *The Diary of a Young Girl*, and Richard Wright's *Native Son* were among the literature banned in certain states and/or countries other than the United States.

Impact The continual proliferation of books demonstrates the importance of the book publishing industry. The paperback phenomenon that created wider readership, along with the creation of more and different venues where books could be bought, made book publishing an increasingly profitable business. Film, theatrical, and (ultimately) television adaptations of popular books further encouraged book writing and reading. Since the 1940's, the pocket-size, inexpensive paperback book has morphed into more costly, larger-sized volumes, but these still sell for much less than hardback copies, whose prices have risen to double-digit dollars.

Jane L. Ball

Further Reading

Barker, Nicholas, ed. *A Potencie of Life: Books in Society.* New Castle, Del.: Oak Knoll Press, 2001. Lectures on many aspects of book history, including the creation and distribution of books from author to reader, and the social, political, religious, and commercial influences on book publication. Suitable for undergraduate and graduate students.

Epstein, Jason. *Book Business: Publishing Past, Present*

and Future. New York: W. W. Norton, 2002. Based on lectures by a publisher instrumental in starting the "paperback revolution." Examines how the book business changed from a kind of "calling" to the source of large profits. Discusses trends, authors, business considerations, and other topics.

Kaledin, Eugenia. *Daily Life in the United States, 1940-1950: Shifting Worlds.* Westport, Conn.: Greenwood Press, 2000. Part 1 is devoted to the 1940's and discusses writers and books influencing American culture.

Macskimming, Roy. *The Perilous Trade: Book Publishing in Canada, 1946-2006.* Toronto: McClelland & Stewart, 2007. Chronicles the history of English-language publishing in Canada over a span of sixty years, discussing generations of book publishers who brought books by Canadians to Canadian readers.

Schiffrin, Andre. *The Business of Books.* New York: Verso, 2000. Discusses the founding of Pantheon Books in the early 1940's, along with other paperback publishers, and discusses the success of the paperback format.

See also Curious George books; Faulkner, William; *For Whom the Bell Tolls*; Great Books Foundation; *Hiroshima*; *The Human Comedy*; Literature in Canada; Literature in the United States; *The Naked and the Dead*; Wright, Richard.

Margaret Bourke-White photographing Manhattan's skyline from atop one of the gargoyles on the sixty-first floor of New York City's Chrysler Building. (Time & Life Pictures/Getty Images)

■ Bourke-White, Margaret

Identification American photojournalist
Born June 14, 1904; New York, New York
Died August 27, 1971; Stamford, Connecticut

Bourke-White was a prominent photographer whose work captured some of the most significant social and political events of the 1940's.

Margaret Bourke-White was daring and aggressive in her efforts to get important pictures. She covered sharecroppers, war, the Dust Bowl, and apartheid for *Fortune* magazine and later for *Life* magazine. Her 1936 photograph of the massive Fort Peck Dam in Montana graced the cover of *Life*'s first issue. Her feats included taking pictures of New York's Chrysler Building from an 880-foot tower while it was under construction and descending deep into a South African gold mine to document black miners.

Bourke-White was the first woman to be accredited as a correspondent during World War II, working for the U.S. Army Air Forces while freelancing for *Life*. In 1941, she and her husband, Erskine Caldwell, were the only foreign journalists in the Soviet Union when the Germans invaded Moscow. Bourke-White survived a torpedo attack on a ship en route to North Africa and was with troops during a bombing mission that destroyed a German airfield near Tunis.

Bourke-White's famous subjects included Franklin D. Roosevelt, Winston Churchill, and Joseph Stalin. In 1946, she took one of her most enduring photographs—India's Mohandas K. Gandhi at a spinning wheel. During the Korean War, she worked as a war correspondent embedded with South Korean troops. In the early 1950's, she was diagnosed with Parkinson's disease, and she had to give up photography as a career later that decade.

Impact Bourke-White wrote or coauthored eleven books featuring her photographs. She will be remembered as one of the world's first photojournalists and as a woman who succeeded in a "man's profession."

Sherri Ward Massey

Further Reading

Bourke-White, Margaret. *Portrait of Myself.* New York: Simon & Schuster, 1963.

Caldwell, Erskine, and Margaret Bourke-White. *You Have Seen Their Faces.* 3d ed. Athens: University of Georgia Press, 1995.

Goldberg, Vicki. *Margaret Bourke-White: A Biography.* Reading, Mass.: Addison-Wesley, 1987.

See also *Life; Look*; Magazines; Photography.

■ Boxing

Often called the "golden age" of boxing, the 1940's saw many changes in the sport. The decade began with many of its champions entering the armed forces, effectively freezing their world titles. After the war, however, professional boxing blossomed as African Americans and Italian Americans began dominating the sport.

The 1940's produced many great fighters and rivalries. From the lower weight divisions to the heaviest divisions, outstanding boxers won world championships during the decade. Willie Pep and Sandy Saddler became featherweight champions; Sugar Ray Robinson became welterweight champion, Tony Zale, Rocky Graziano, Marcel Cerdan, and Jake LaMotta became middleweight champions; and Joe Louis remained heavyweight champion. The decade also saw major rivalries developed between pairs of boxers such as Pep and Saddler, Robinson and LaMotta, Louis and Billy Conn, and Graziano and Zale. By the end of the decade, these fighters were becoming stars because of their boxing skills, their growing television exposure, and—most particularly for Joe Louis—the public's gratitude for their military service during World War II.

Three Great 1940's Boxers On June 21, 1937, Joe Louis beat James Braddock to become the youngest heavyweight champion in history. Before that moment, many people had doubted Louis's ability to win the championship because he had lost to the German boxer Max Schmeling in June, 1936. After beating Braddock and defending his title three times, Louis again fought Schmeling in New York City in 1938 and knocked him out in the first round. In 1941, *Ring Magazine* and the Boxing Writers Association of America named him fighter of the year. At the end of that year, Japan launched its surprise attack on Pearl Harbor. Shortly afterward, Louis voluntarily joined the U.S. Army, which used him as a recruiting tool and morale booster throughout the war. After the war, he resumed his boxing career. By the time he finally retired in 1949, he had defended his title a record twenty-five times, a record that has remained unbroken through the first decade of the twenty-first century. He made a comeback in 1950 but lost a decision to then-champion Ezzard Charles. He was also later knocked out by future champion Rocky Marciano.

Many boxing fans regard Sugar Ray Robinson as the greatest boxer ever. He had speed, power, great footwork, exceptional boxing ability, and a strong chin. During his long amateur career, he won eighty-five bouts without a single loss and then turned professional in October 1940. During the ensuing decade, his lone loss was to Jake LaMotta in 1943. By the time he won the world welterweight championship, he had defeated many name fighters including Fritzie Zivic, Henry Armstrong, LaMotta, and future welterweight champion Kid Galivan. On December 20, 1946, he beat Tommy Bell for the vacant welterweight title. He defended that title four times before taking the middleweight championship from LaMotta on February 14, 1951. During the 1950's, he would lose and regain that title four times and also challenge Joey Maxim for the light-heavyweight title in 1952. Meanwhile, during the 1940's, he compiled a record of 101 wins, 1 loss, and 2 draws, despite taking out time to serve in the Army after *Ring Magazine* named him fighter of the year.

In contrast to Louis and Robinson, Willie Pep was a master boxer with limited punching power who had to use defense and counterpunching to best his opponents. Pep ended the 1940's with a record of 142 wins, 2 losses, and 1 draw. He won the world featherweight title from Chalky Wright on November 25, 1942, in New York City. Like Louis and Robinson, he served in the military. He was in the Navy in 1943 and in the Army in 1944. His greatest rival was Sandy Saddler, whom he fought four times between

1948 and 1951, winning one bout and losing three. Pep was *Ring Magazine*'s fighter of the year in 1945, and the magazine designated his defeat of Saddler in 1949 to regain his featherweight title the fight of the year.

World War II   In addition to Louis, Robinson, and Pep, many American boxers served in the military during World War II, including Billy Conn, Lew Jenkins, and Tony Zale. Indeed, so many boxers saw military service that the Boxing Writers Association of America named them all "fighter of the year" in 1943. Thanks to the war, few title fights were held between 1942 and 1945. Joe Louis defended his heavyweight title twice, and Freddie Mills defended his light heavyweight title once, but middleweight Tony Zale and welterweight Freddy Cochrane had no title defenses during those

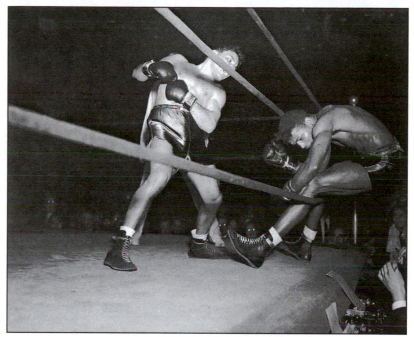

Jake LaMotta knocking Sugar Ray Robinson through the ropes while on his way to give Robinson his first defeat in 130 bouts, in February, 1943. LaMotta and Robinson had one of the most intense rivalries in boxing during the 1940's, but Robinson would eventually prevail. (AP/Wide World Photos)

years. Consequently, boxing found most of its championship bouts in the lightweight, featherweight, bantamweight, and flyweight divisions.

Impact   For every African American boxer such as Joe Louis and Sugar Ray Robinson who overcame racial prejudice to win a shot at a world title during the 1940's, many more were never given a chance. Instead they were forced to fight one another numerous times. Fighters such as Archie Moore, Ezzard Charles, Jersey Joe Walcott, and Charley Burley were refused title shots. However, Charles, a light heavyweight boxer who had been kept from his division's title, won the vacant heavyweight title in 1949. Walcott would win the same title in 1951, Moore would win the light heavyweight title in 1952, but Burley, whom some consider the best of the group, was never able to challenge for any title.

Brett Conway

Further Reading

Astor, Gerald. *". . . And a Credit to His Race": The Hard Life and Times of Joseph Louis Barrow, a.k.a. Joe Louis.* New York: E. P. Dutton-Saturday Review Press, 1974. Well-written biography of one of boxing's greatest heavyweight champions.

Louis, Joe, with Edna Rust and Art Rust, Jr. *Joe Louis: My Life.* New York: Harcourt Brace Jovanovich, 1978. Written in the first person, this book is especially useful for its abundant photographs and supplement listing each bout in Louis's professional boxing career.

Marciano, Rocky, with Charley Goldman. *Rocky Marciano's Book of Boxing and Bodybuilding.* Englewood Cliffs, N.J.: Prentice-Hall, 1957. Includes photographs of Marciano training.

Mead, Chris. *Champion: Joe Louis, Black Hero in White America.* New York: Charles Scribner's Sons, 1985. One of the best biographies of Louis, this book sees him within the framework of American popular culture and places much emphasis on Louis as symbol.

Rosenfeld, Allen S. *Charley Burley: The Life and Hard Times of an Uncrowned Champion.* Bloomington, Ind.: First Books, 2003. Sympathetic biography of one of boxing's least appreciated great fighters.

Sammons, Jeffrey T. *Beyond the Ring: The Role of Boxing in American Society.* Urbana: University of Illinois

Press, 1990. Scholarly analysis of boxing within the larger context of American social history.

Skehan, Everett. *Undefeated Rocky Marciano: The Fighter Who Refused to Lose.* Cambridge, Mass.: Rounder Books, 2005. Assisted by two of Marciano's brothers and his daughter, Skehan produced a definitive account of the boxer's life and career. Lavishly illustrated.

Sullivan, Russell. *Rocky Marciano: The Rock of His Times.* Urbana: University of Illinois Press, 2002. Solid biography, recounting the events of Marciano's life and career and providing detailed descriptions of his fights.

See also African Americans; Louis, Joe; Robinson, Sugar Ray; Sports in Canada; Sports in the United States.

■ Bracero program

Identification Program that provided for the importation of temporary contract laborers from Mexico into the United States

Also known as Mexican Farm Labor Supply Program; Mexican Labor Agreement

Date 1942-1964

This program was conceived as a short-term emergency effort to provide workers for the U.S. agricultural industry during World War II, when there was a significant shortage of manual labor. It would become the largest guest-worker program in U.S. history.

The Bracero program, which provided for the recruitment of Mexican contract workers, was the result of an executive agreement signed by Presidents Franklin D. Roosevelt and Manuel Ávila Camacho on August 4, 1942. The length of the bracero contracts varied but typically lasted about one year. Many laborers made repeated trips to the United States under multiple contracts.

Specific provisions insisted on by the Mexican government to protect braceros included humane treatment of the workers, while ethnic and racial discrimination was forbidden. Recruitment, transportation, housing, food, and wages of the braceros were strictly regulated by the agreement. Specifically, laborers were initially paid thirty cents per hour, with 10 percent of their wages withheld and paid to the workers upon their return to Mexico.

Even if the braceros were unable to work because of inclement weather or other problems, they were guaranteed wages for three-quarters of the contract period.

Most of the Mexican contract workers during the 1940's found employment on California farms, most on large agribusiness operations that raised fruits, vegetables, and other produce. Much of the labor was devoted to harvesting crops, although workers were involved in all facets of the farming operations. Although California was the destination for most braceros, immigrant farm laborers were dispersed to twenty-six states. While only 4,203 workers were recruited during 1942, about 107,000 were contracted in 1949. Between 1942 and 1949, an average of 45,243 Mexican laborers entered the United States annually.

Almost from the program's inception, mistreatment of some workers was reported. Most mistreatment resulted from growers being unprepared, and in some cases unwilling, to provide adequate shelter, food, sanitation, and health care to the laborers. Mexican workers were ill-prepared to deal with the growers. Few had even a rudimentary understanding of English. For most, the details of their contracts and their contractual rights remained obscure or bewildering. Many of the impoverished immigrants came from rural, isolated areas and were naïve when dealing with unscrupulous growers. Reports of worker abuses overshadowed the positive aspects of the program.

The program provided a reliable supply of low-cost labor to the nation in a time of war. The braceros benefited from a wage rate far exceeding that in Mexico. Many accumulated substantial savings before returning home, and most sent periodic payments to family in Mexico. Thousands of unskilled workers gained experience in modern farm methods that they utilized upon their return to Mexico.

Impact The Bracero program created a number of migratory labor patterns and relationships between Mexico and the United States. Specifically, the program resulting in a sharp and lasting increase in illegal immigration and focused attention on immigration as a national issue. The program continued until 1964, when it was officially terminated because of alleged negative influences on the employment of domestic workers.

Robert R. McKay

Bracero Program Agreement

The Bracero program was developed as a labor agreement between the governments of Mexico and the United States. General provisions of the "Agreement for the Temporary Migration of Mexican Agricultural Workers to the United States" include the following:

General Provisions

1. It is understood that Mexicans contracting to work in the United States shall not be engaged in any military service.
2. Mexicans entering the United States as result of this understanding shall not suffer discriminatory acts of any kind in accordance with the Executive Order No. 8802 issued at the White House June 25, 1941.
3. Mexicans entering the United States under this understanding shall enjoy the guarantees of transportation, living expenses and repatriation established in Article 29 of the Mexican Federal Labor Law as follows:

Article 29—All contracts entered into by Mexican workers for lending their services outside their country shall be made in writing, legalized by the municipal authorities of the locality where entered into and vised by the Consul of the country where their services are being used. Furthermore, such contract shall contain, as a requisite of validity of same, the following stipulations, without which the contract is invalid.

I. Transportation and subsistence expenses for the worker, and his family, if such is the case, and all other expenses which originate from point of origin to border points and compliance of immigration requirements, or for any other similar concept, shall be paid exclusively by the employer or the contractual parties.

II. The worker shall be paid in full the salary agreed upon, from which no deduction shall be made in any amount for any of the concepts mentioned in the above subparagraph.

III. The employer or contractor shall issue a bond or constitute a deposit in cash in the Bank of Workers, or in the absence of same, in the Bank of Mexico, to the entire satisfaction of the respective labor authorities, for a sum equal to repatriation costs of the worker and his family, and those originated by transportation to point of origin.

IV. Once the employer has established proof of having covered such expenses or the refusal of the worker to return to his country, and that he does not owe the worker any sum covering salary or indemnization to which he might have a right, the labor authorities shall authorize the return of the deposit or the cancellation of the bond issued.

4. Mexicans entering the United States under this understanding shall not be employed to displace other workers, or for the purpose of reducing rates of pay previously established.

Further Reading

Driscoll, Barbara A. *The Tracks North: The Railroad Bracero Program of World War II*. Austin: CMAS Books, Center for Mexican American Studies, University of Texas at Austin, 1998.

Gamboa, Erasmo. *Mexican Labor and World War II: Braceros in the Pacific Northwest, 1942-1947*. Seattle: University of Washington Press, 2000.

Garcia y Griego, Manuel. "The Importation of Mexican Contract Laborers to the United States, 1942-1964." In *Between Two Worlds: Mexican Immigrants in the United States*, edited by David G. Gutiérrez. Wilmington, Del.: Scholarly Resources, 1996.

Gonzalez, Gilbert G. *Guest Workers or Colonized Labor? Mexican Labor Migration to the United States*. Boulder, Colo.: Paradigm, 2006.

See also   Agriculture in the United States; Immigration Act of 1943; Immigration to the United States; Latin America; Latinos; Mexico; Racial discrimination.

■ Bradley, Omar N.

Identification American military commander
Born February 12, 1893; Clark, Missouri
Died April 8, 1981; New York, New York

Bradley was one of the foremost American military leaders of World War II. His Twelfth Army Group in Europe was the largest field command in American history. He was the fifth, and last, man to hold the rank of five-star General of the Army.

Omar Nelson Bradley was born in a log cabin to a family of humble means. After graduating from high school, he was persuaded to apply to the United States Military Academy at West Point, New York. Bradley scored first in his competitive exam. At West Point, he was a solid student and an enthusiastic athlete. He graduated in 1915 with a class that became famous for the number of its members who became generals.

Becoming the "Soldier's General" Bradley served along the Mexican border in 1916 but saw no action. When the United States entered World War I in

General Omar N. Bradley. (Library of Congress)

1917, he yearned for a posting to the front lines in France, but instead he spent the war in the United States. In the postwar years, Bradley threw himself into the study of his profession. Missing the fighting on the western front may have been professionally beneficial for Bradley in the long run, as he did not internalize the increasingly antiquated tactics of trench warfare. Instead, he studied and admired the campaigns of Civil War general William Tecumseh Sherman. He prepared himself intellectually for a war of maneuver. During these years, first as an instructor at Fort Benning, Georgia, and then working in the War Department, Bradley favorably impressed George C. Marshall, who in 1938 became Army chief of staff. With the outbreak of war in Europe in 1939, the Army began expanding rapidly. In 1941, Bradley, marked for advancement by Marshall, was promoted directly from lieutenant colonel to brigadier general and sent to command the Infantry School at Fort Benning. Here Bradley promoted the development of airborne forces in the Army. He also created an officer candidate school (OCS) that became the model for the OCS program during the war.

Following the Japanese attack on Pearl Harbor on December 7, 1941, Bradley commanded first the Eighty-second and then the Twenty-eighth Infantry Divisions. He proved to be an exceptional trainer, working to keep morale high with his citizen soldiers even as he honed their physical fitness and military skills. Early in 1943, Bradley was ordered overseas. His job was to be the eyes and ears for General Dwight D. Eisenhower at the front line in North Africa. American troops had just suffered a humiliating defeat at the Kasserine Pass. Bradley recommended that the commander of the II Corps be relieved. General George S. Patton took over the II Corps with Bradley as his deputy. Bradley succeeded Patton on April 15 and led the II Corps to a series of victories in the final battles of the North African campaign.

Bradley and his II Corps fought in Sicily as part of Patton's Seventh Army. Here the war correspondent Ernie Pyle termed Bradley the "soldier's general." Bradley's concern for his troops, his military skills, and his calm and collected manner all stood him in good stead in contrast to the grandiloquent Patton, who disgraced himself in a soldier-slapping incident near the end of the Sicilian campaign. The always reliable Bradley was chosen to command the American component of Operation Overlord, the invasion of Normandy.

General of the Army   On D Day, June 6, 1944, Bradley watched the American landings from the bridge of an American cruiser, unable to do much to affect the course of the battle. He went ashore with the staff of the First Army on June 9. Efforts at an early breakout were frustrated by the rough Norman hedgerow country and determined German resistance. Bradley designed Operation Cobra, which relied on an intense aerial bombardment to blast a hole in the German defensive lines near Saint-Lô. Launched on July 25, Cobra was a success, and American armor raced toward the German rear. As American troops poured through this breach into France, Bradley moved up to the command of the Twelfth Army Group, composed initially of the First Army under General Courtney Hodges and the Third Army under Patton. Adolf Hitler ordered his commanders to attack in the face of the Allied advance. Bradley defeated this thrust at Mortain. He tried to trap the remaining Germans in the Falaise Pocket. He failed to close the pocket, and though thousands of Germans were killed or captured, a crucial remnant escaped.

The Allies pursued the retreating Germans across France. Logistical problems, especially shortages of gas, slowed the Allied armies as they neared the German frontier. Bradley supported Eisenhower's broad-front strategy and resented British field marshal Bernard Montgomery's attempts to get logistical priority. Bradley's First Army was hit by the German Ardennes offensive on December 16. He coordinated operations on the southern flank of the Battle of the Bulge. After restoring the American front by the end of January, 1945, Bradley struck back. In a series of offensives, Bradley's forces broke into Germany. This was facilitated in March by the capture of an intact bridge over the Rhine at Remagen. In the last weeks of the war, Bradley's troops took 300,000 Germans prisoner. By this point, the Twelfth Army Group comprised four armies: the First, Third, General William Simpson's Ninth, and General Leonard Gerow's Fifteenth—in all, 1.3 million men.

Following the war, Bradley reformed the Veterans Administration. He then served as Army chief of staff from 1948 to 1949 and as chairman of the Joint Chiefs of Staff from 1949 to 1953. He helped frame military policy during the early years of the Cold War, played an important role in the formation of the North Atlantic Treaty Organization (NATO),

and served as an adviser to President Harry S. Truman during the Korean War.

Impact   No American has directly commanded as many Americans in battle as did Bradley. He was one of the most important and successful American generals of World War II. His service was recognized with the rank of General of the Army in 1950.

Daniel P. Murphy

Further Reading

Axelrod, Alan. *Bradley.* New York: Palgrave Macmillan, 2007. A brief, sympathetic biography.

Bradley, Omar N. *A General's Life.* New York: Simon & Schuster, 1983. A posthumous autobiography, written with historian Clay Blair.

_____. *A Soldier's Story.* New York: Modern Library, 1999. A reprint of Bradley's classic 1951 memoir.

Weigley, Russell. *Eisenhower's Lieutenants.* Bloomington: Indiana University Press, 1990. A scholarly study of Eisenhower's commanders, including Bradley.

See also   Army, U.S.; Bulge, Battle of the; Department of Defense, U.S.; Eisenhower, Dwight D.; Italian campaign; Korea; Marshall, George C.; North African campaign; Patton, George S.; Pyle, Ernie; World War II.

■ Braun, Wernher von

Identification   German rocket scientist who immigrated to the United States after World War II

Born   March 23, 1912; Wirsitz, Germany (now Wyrzysk, Poland)

Died   June 16, 1977; Alexandria, Virginia

Von Braun is widely considered to be the preeminent rocket scientist of the twentieth century. He was responsible for the design of the German V-2 rocket used during World War II and for several American rockets after the war, including the Saturn V rocket that transported the Apollo astronauts to the Moon.

As a child, Wernher von Braun became fascinated with rocketry. This fascination led him to pursue studies in physics. However, his Ph.D. in physics came during the Great Depression, which had affected Europe as it did the United States. Having had great difficulty securing funding for his rocket

Wernher von Braun with a model of a V-2 rocket. (NASA)

of the war, Hitler renamed the A-4 rocket the Vergeltungswaffe 2 (V-2), for "vengeance weapon." More than three thousand V-2 missiles were constructed and fired at Allied targets, causing considerable damage and killing more than seventy-two hundred people. The V-2 rocket followed a ballistic trajectory to the edge of space after the propellant was expended, making it the first rocket to leave the atmosphere.

As Germany neared defeat in World War II, von Braun arranged for himself and his rocket scientists to surrender to American forces. The German rocket scientists were taken to Fort Bliss in Texas, where they began work building missiles for the U.S. Army. In 1956, von Braun became the technical director of the Army's newly created Army Ballistic Missile Agency (ABMA) in Huntsville, Alabama.

In 1955, von Braun became a U.S. citizen. Later, he worked to put the first American satellite, Explorer 1, into orbit in January, 1958. Soon afterward, von Braun and the ABMA were transferred to the newly created National Aeronautics and Space Administration (NASA). Working for NASA, von Braun helped design and build the Saturn V rocket, which carried the Apollo missions to the Moon.

research, he persuaded the German army in 1932 to fund his work with a goal of developing rockets for use as ultralong-range artillery weapons. The army established a rocketry center near Peenemünde, Germany.

By 1940, von Braun had been forced to join both the Nazi Party and the Schutzstaffel (SS) for political reasons in order to remain director of the research program at Peenemünde; however, he never wore his uniform or his swastika armband, and he remained critical of Adolf Hitler's policies. The criticisms resulted in his arrest and imprisonment by the Gestapo for a while. However, his work on rocket artillery could not be continued in his absence, so he was released at the insistence of the army.

During World War II, von Braun developed an alcohol-water- and liquid-oxygen-fueled rocket designated the Aggregat 4 (A-4). The A-4 was capable of carrying a 2,000-pound warhead about 200 miles (320 kilometers). In 1944, during the waning years

Impact While a powerful weapon, von Braun's V-2 rocket came far too late in the war to play a decisive role in World War II. However, his work in developing the V-2 was used in many other rocketry programs that followed. Von Braun's crowning achievement is generally regarded as the massive Saturn V rocket, the largest operational rocket that has ever been constructed.

Though von Braun spent much of his career building weapons of war, he never let go of his true dream of building rockets for manned spaceflight. His persistence paid off, and he ultimately became one of the pivotal figures of space exploration, though he died of cancer before he could realize his personal dream of traveling into space.

Raymond D. Benge, Jr.

Further Reading
Bergaust, Erik. *Wernher von Braun.* Washington, D.C.: National Space Institute, 1976.

Neufeld, Michael J. *Von Braun: Dreamer of Space, Engineer of War.* New York: Alfred A. Knopf, 2007.

Ward, Bob. *Dr. Space: The Life of Wernher von Braun.* Annapolis, Md.: Naval Institute Press, 2005.

See also Army, U.S.; Education in the United States; Inventions; Rocketry; Science and technology; Wartime technological advances; World War II.

■ Brenda Starr

Identification Comic strip about a woman newspaper reporter

Creator Dale Messick (1906-2005)

Date Debuted on June 30, 1940

Brenda Starr modeled a glamorous version of wartime professional women that mirrored both unconventional and traditional perceptions of American women's domestic and professional lives, while also reinforcing formulaic depictions of women as preoccupied with romance.

The outspoken heroine Brenda Starr evolved from female Roaring Twenties comic-strip characters by illustrators such as Nell Brinkley and Gladys Parker. Her creator, Dale Messick, fought the prevailing bias against female cartoonists to launch the series in the Sunday supplement of the *New York Daily News* on June 30, 1940, moving to the daily edition in 1945.

Messick drew on Hollywood star Rita Hayworth and the extravagant socialite Brenda Frazier for her news reporter's prominent red hair and name, but Brenda Starr also reflected contemporary journalists such as Clare Boothe Luce and war photographers Margaret Bourke-White and Toni Frissell. Her tumultuous adventures for her newspaper, *The Flash,* magnified the broader work roles for American women during the war period, but her appeal also derived from soap-opera plots featuring a woman's quest for romance. Always contemporary, Brenda pursued her exotic lover, Basil St. John, for decades; she married, divorced, and went on to further romances and further extraordinary adventures.

The heroine endures today for the Tribune Media Syndicate, with writer Mary Schmich and illustrator June Brigman. She appeared in a film serial, *Brenda Starr, Reporter,* in 1945; a television movie in 1976; and a film in 1992. A commemorative stamp featuring the adventurous reporter was released in 1995.

Impact *Brenda Starr* lifted the dreariness of wartime for female readers with a champion adventurer. This icon of a transformed workplace served to recognize the advance of women into professional careers. More important, her creator, Dale Messick, launched the genre of female action heroines in the male-dominated world of comic art.

M. Sheila McAvey

Further Reading

Hartmann, Susan M. *The Home Front and Beyond: American Women in the 1940's.* Boston: Twayne, 1982.

Robbins, Trina. *A Century of Women Cartoonists.* Northampton, Mass.: Kitchen Sink Press, 1993.

See also Bourke-White, Margaret; Comic books; Comic strips; Newspapers; Wonder Woman.

■ Bretton Woods Conference

The Event Meeting of financial leaders of Allied governments designed to create a monetary arrangement for the postwar world

Date July 1-21, 1944

Place Bretton Woods, New Hampshire

The goal of this international meeting was to devise a postwar system that would ensure vibrant world trade and healthy economies. The agreement resulting from the meeting provided the basis for the postwar fixed exchange-rate system and the establishment of the International Monetary Fund and the World Bank.

As World War II progressed, it became increasingly evident that the Allies would win, and the governments of the two primary Western allies, the United States and Great Britain, were anxious to create a postwar economic system that would not fall back into the Great Depression that had engulfed the 1930's. Economists in particular believed that a major factor in the economic climate that had led to the Depression was the failure of sustained world trade. High levels of trade required institutions that could act to maintain stable monetary exchange rates to defuse economic dislocations. To achieve this goal, Britain and the United States arranged for the meeting at Bretton Woods, New Hampshire, that would lead to the creation of the International

Monetary Fund (IMF) and the World Bank (which would later evolve from a body designed to rebuild the war-shattered economies of the West to a body designed to promote economic development in underdeveloped economies). The Bretton Woods Agreement was essentially the brainchild of two economists: the world-renowned John Maynard Keynes, who represented the British government at

the negotiations, and Harry Dexter White, a little-known American economist employed by the U.S. Treasury.

Keynes was concerned to preserve what he believed was the mechanism that would enable Britain to rebuild its economy after the war, particularly its close economic ties to the countries that had constituted its empire, bound together by preferential tariffs called "imperial preference." White believed that the world needed a system with low tariffs and free-flowing funds from one country to another, anchored in relatively fixed exchange rates.

The Conference Keynes, who had been representing the British government in negotiating a system of payments for the war materials that Britain needed to continue fighting in World War II, was very familiar with the various positions of the U.S. government on international trade. He held doggedly to British arguments on future trade relations between an economically battered Britain and a triumphant United States. White, who was thoroughly familiar with American politics, held out for positions that would not require congressional approval, in particular one giving the president the authority to negotiate trade agreements.

The negotiations were divided into two parts called Commissions. "Commission I" dealt with the creation of the International Monetary Fund, which would monitor, and occasionally intervene, to ensure that international currencies remained stable. "Commission II" dealt with the conditions needed for future economic development, which would be the responsibility of the new World Bank. White chaired Commission I and guided negotiations leading to the creation of the International Monetary Fund. Keynes chaired Commission II, which looked at the needs for a healthy postwar international economy in which there was still room for imperial preference tariffs.

The International Monetary Fund

The Bretton Woods Conference outlined guidelines for economic relations within the international community. One provision included in the accord was the establishment of the International Monetary Fund (IMF), as outlined below in an excerpt from the agreement.

Since foreign trade affects the standard of life of every people, all countries have a vital interest in the system of exchange of national currencies and the regulations and conditions which govern its working. Because these monetary transactions are international exchanges, the nations must agree on the basic rules which govern the exchanges if the system is to work smoothly. When they do not agree, and when single nations and small groups of nations attempt by special and different regulations of the foreign exchanges to gain trade advantages, the result is instability, a reduced volume of foreign trade, and damage to national economies. This course of action is likely to lead to economic warfare and to endanger the world's peace.

The Conference has therefore agreed that broad international action is necessary to maintain an international monetary system which will promote foreign trade. The nations should consult and agree on international monetary changes which affect each other. They should outlaw practices which are agreed to be harmful to world prosperity, and they should assist each other to overcome short-term exchange difficulties.

The Conference has agreed that the nations here represented should establish for these purposes a permanent international body, the International Monetary Fund, with powers and resources adequate to perform the tasks assigned to it. Agreement has been reached concerning these powers and resources and the additional obligations which the member countries should undertake.

The Quota Issue   One of the most contentious issues at Bretton Woods was the question of quotas—the sums that participants would have to provide to finance the IMF (and, subsequently, the World Bank). The largest quota was that assigned to the United States. Great Britain and its colonies were assigned half the U.S. quota. The U.S. quota of about $2.5 billion secured leadership in the IMF for the United States. The quotas were supposedly based on the relative national incomes of the participant countries. To ensure some flexibility, IMF members that had used currency devaluation to solve their economic problems during the 1930's were permitted to adjust their foreign exchange rates by 10 percent, provided they notified the IMF of their intent. Greater rate changes would disqualify countries from further participation in the IMF.

The dominant role of the United States in funding the IMF effectively ensured that the IMF's administrators would be based in the United States, despite Keynes's attempts to have them based in London. He believed that basing the IMF or World Bank in London would assist in the recovery of Britain's position as a leader in world trade.

Impact   The Bretton Woods Agreement created the institutions that were to persist for more than half a century dealing with international monetary relations and international development. They presupposed the dominance of the dollar in international trade, a situation that persisted for about twenty-five years. As other currencies—such as the revived British pound and the German mark—achieved important positions in international trade, adjustments would be made.

The United States took on the role of supplying additional liquidity to the world by running balance of payment deficits on a continuous basis. The U.S. dollar rapidly became the world's major vehicle for payment and reserve currency, or currency used to support the value of the domestic currency. Through these continuous balance of payments deficits, U.S. dollars sent abroad to buy goods and services and for investment purposes did not return. The rest of the world used additional U.S. dollar holdings for monetary reserves and to supplement world liquidity.

As deficits in the United States balance of payments became chronic, this would lead to a weakening of the U.S. dollar. Monetary crises would follow, and confidence in the dollar would wane. Eventually, the ability of the U.S. Treasury to convert U.S. dollars into gold would become difficult and the Bretton Woods system would collapse.

Nancy M. Gordon

Further Reading

Acheson, A. L. Keith, John F. Chant, and Martin F. J. Prachowny, eds. *Bretton Woods Revisited.* Toronto: University of Toronto Press, 1972. Primarily addresses the problems that arose when the dollar no longer dominated foreign exchange rates.

Bakker, A. F. P. *International Financial Institutions.* London and New York: Longman, 1996. Provides a good summary of the roles of the various institutions, especially the IMF, governing foreign trade and monetary exchange.

Best, Jacqueline. *The Limits of Transparency: Ambiguity and the History of International Finance.* Ithaca, N.Y.: Cornell University Press, 2005. Analysis of international finance revolving around the Bretton Woods Agreements, which are the subject of three of the book's seven chapters.

Kirschner, Otto, ed. *The Bretton Woods-GATT System: Retrospect and Prospect After Fifty Years.* Armonk, N.Y.: M. E. Sharpe, 1996. Includes contributions by individuals who have had experience with world trade.

Scammell, W. M. *International Monetary Policy: Bretton Woods and After.* New York: John Wiley & Sons, 1975. This easy-to-understand work examines the development of the system, the changes in the environment, and the role the International Monetary Fund played up to 1973. Contains a good discussion of the merits and shortcomings of both the Bretton Woods system and the International Monetary Fund.

Sidelsky, Robert. *John Maynard Keynes: Fighting for Britain, 1937-1946.* London: Macmillan, 2000. This third volume of a lengthy biography of Keynes contains far and away the best detailed description of the negotiations that took place at Bretton Woods.

See also   Business and the economy in Canada; Business and the economy in the United States; Canada and Great Britain; General Agreement on Tariffs and Trade; International trade; Keynesian economics; Marshall Plan; War debt; White, Harry Dexter.

■ Broadway musicals

Definition   Musical theater productions opening
on Broadway

During the 1940's, the Broadway musical was reborn after
the economic and artistic slump of the 1930's. The decade
was dominated by the presence of Rodgers and Ham-
merstein, whose first collaboration, Oklahoma! *(1943),*
signaled a new era for the Broadway musical. The decade
also netted more hits for Cole Porter and Irving Berlin, and
Alan Jay Lerner and Frederick Loewe and Leonard
Bernstein made their Broadway debuts. The "concept" mu-
sical was invented, and many shows reflected wartime
themes.

In the first years of the 1940's, Broadway musicals
continued to reflect the aesthetics of the previous
decade. Irving Berlin and Cole Porter were still contributing successful shows to Broadway, and Richard
Rodgers and Lorenz Hart wrote their final two shows
(as a collaborative team) in 1940 and 1942. Although the revue was not as popular as it had been in
previous decades, musicals still were, in general,
light comedies, and the regular appearance of the

"book" musical (in which the songs are intertwined
with a dramatic plot) had not yet emerged. Rodgers
teamed with Oscar Hammerstein II in 1943, and
their works set new standards for the musical as a significant art form. Rodgers and Hammerstein almost
single-handedly reinvented the Broadway musical
over the course of the decade.

The most significant shows of the decade in-
cluded the following: Berlin's *Louisiana Purchase*
(1940); Vernon Duke and John La Touche's *Cabin*
in the Sky (1940); Porter's *Panama Hattie* (1940);
Rodgers and Hart's *Pal Joey* (1940); Kurt Weill and
Ira Gershwin's *Lady in the Dark* (1941); Rodgers and
Hart's *By Jupiter* (1942); Berlin's *This Is the Army*
(1942); Porter's *Something for the Boys* (1943);
Rodgers and Hammerstein's *Oklahoma!* (1943);
Weill and Ogden Nash's *One Touch of Venus* (1943);
Frederick Loewe and Alan Jay Lerner's *What's Up?*
(1943); Georges Bizet and Hammerstein's *Carmen*
Jones (1943); Robert Wright and George Forrest's
Song of Norway (1944); Harold Arlen and E. Y.
Harburg's *Bloomer Girl* (1944); Bernstein, Betty
Comden, and Adolph Green's *On the Town* (1944);
Sigmund Romberg and Dorothy Fields's *Up in Cen-*
tral Park (1945); Rodgers and Hammerstein's *Carou-*
sel (1945); Harold Arlen and Johnny Mer-
cer's *St. Louis Woman* (1946); Harold
Rome's *Call Me Mister* (1946); Berlin's *An-*
nie Get Your Gun (1946); Weill and Langston
Hughes's *Street Scene* (1947); Burton Lane
and Harburg's *Finian's Rainbow* (1947);
Loewe and Lerner's *Brigadoon* (1947); Jule
Styne and Sammy Cahn's *High Button Shoes*
(1947); Rodgers and Hammerstein's *Alle-*
gro (1947); Weill and Lerner's *Love Life*
(1948); Frank Loesser's *Where's Charley?*
(1948); Porter's *Kiss Me, Kate* (1948);
Rodgers and Hammerstein's *South Pacific*
(1949); Weill and Maxwell Anderson's *Lost*
in the Stars (1949); and Styne and Leo
Robin's *Gentlemen Prefer Blondes* (1949).

The Rodgers and Hammerstein Revolu-
tion   Rodgers and Hammerstein's first
collaboration was *Oklahoma!*, which was an
integrated book musical in the tradition of
Show Boat (1927) that closely integrated
plot, music, and dance into a seamless work
of art. *Oklahoma!* abandoned old traditions
and invented new ones: The show began

Longest-Running Broadway Plays and Musicals of the 1940's

Opening dates of plays or musicals between
January, 1940, and December, 1949.

Name	Opening Date	Number of performances
Oklahoma!	March 31, 1943	2,212
South Pacific	April 7, 1949	1,925
Harvey	November 1, 1944	1,775
Born Yesterday	February 4, 1946	1,642
The Voice of the Turtle	December 8, 1943	1,557
Arsenic and Old Lace	January 1, 1941	1,444
Angel Street	December 5, 1941	1,295
Annie Get Your Gun	May 18, 1946	1,147
Kiss Me, Kate	December 30, 1948	1,077
Anna Lucasta	August 30, 1944	957
Kiss and Tell	March 17, 1943	956

with an empty stage instead of the formulaic opening chorus number, songs furthered the plot, characters died, and a dramatic "dream ballet" concluded act 1. The show had an unprecedented run of 2,212 performances and was awarded a special Pulitzer Prize. *Carousel* was equally radical, containing a tragic plot with flawed characters and dealing with the then-taboo subject of domestic violence. The less successful *Allegro* is often considered to be the first "concept" musical, covering a half century and using minimal sets and a Greek chorus to segue from one tableau to the next. *South Pacific* wove together several stories against a World War II military backdrop and tackled issues of racial prejudice and miscegenation. *South Pacific* won eight Tony Awards and the Pulitzer Prize in drama.

Cole Porter continued to write important works for Broadway, including the war-themed *Panama Hattie* and *Something for the Boys*, but *Kiss Me, Kate* became one of the most successful and important shows of the decade. Irving Berlin also continued his success with *Louisiana Purchase* and *This Is the Army*, but his best musical of

New York City's Times Square, looking north on Broadway Avenue into the theater district in early 1946. (AP/Wide World Photos)

the decade (and perhaps his career) was *Annie Get Your Gun*, an Ethel Merman vehicle about the life of famed sharpshooter Annie Oakley. Kurt Weill contributed five edgy shows, each with a different lyricist: *Lady in the Dark, One Touch of Venus, Street Scene, Love Life*, and *Lost in the Stars*. *Love Life* is considered to be one of the first concept musicals. New names also entered the scene during the 1940's: *On the Town* marked the Broadway debuts of Leonard Bernstein and lyricists Betty Comden and Adolph Green. Alan Jay Lerner and Frederick Loewe also made their Broadway debut with *What's Up?*, followed by *Brigadoon*.

Many stars from the 1930's continued their careers as major performers during the 1940's. Mer-

man performed leading roles in *Panama Hattie*, *Something for the Boys*, and *Annie Get Your Gun*; Ray Bolger took starring roles in *By Jupiter* and *Where's Charley?*; and Fred Astaire made his last great Broadway appearance in the title role of *Pal Joey*. The careers of other performers flourished, including Mary Martin in *One Touch of Venus* and *South Pacific*, and Alfred Drake in *Oklahoma!* and *Kiss Me, Kate*. Agnes de Mille emerged as the most important choreographer of the decade; she leapt to fame by choreographing the dream ballet sequence in *Oklahoma!* and continued to choreograph many more shows over the next seven years. Jerome Robbins also made his debut as choreographer with *On the Town*. Joshua Logan was perhaps the most significant musical director of the decade, increasing the importance of the directing with such shows as *Annie Get Your Gun* and *South Pacific.*

Recorded Legacy and Awards *Oklahoma!* was not the first original cast album, but it was the first such album to receive mass distribution and to directly influence the continued success of a Broadway production. The recording industry and Broadway have remained intertwined ever since. Decca was the most important recording label of the 1940's, with Victor, Columbia, and Capitol also producing and distributing many important original cast recordings. Cast recordings made throughout the decade allowed Broadway musicals to be archived in a way that had not been done before.

In 1947, the annual Antoinette Perry "Tony" Awards were established by the American Theatre Wing to recognize outstanding theater productions, particularly Broadway shows, of the past season. A category for best musical was inaugurated in 1949, with Porter's *Kiss Me, Kate* winning in that category as well as in four others.

Impact The 1940's is perhaps the most significant decade in the history of Broadway. It was during this decade that the modern form of the book musical was established and a plethora of classic musicals were produced that are still in the repertoire today. *Oklahoma!* was such a turning point in the history of the musical that it can be argued that all musicals composed before 1943 were simply forerunners to the Broadway musical as it is known today.

Matthew Hoch

Further Reading

Block, Geoffrey. *Enchanted Evenings: The Broadway Musical from Show Boat to Sondheim.* New York: Oxford University Press, 2004. Concerns the creative process behind fourteen of the most significant shows in Broadway history, including examinations of *Pal Joey, Lady in the Dark, One Touch of Venus, Carousel,* and *Kiss Me, Kate.*

Bloom, Ken. *The Routledge Guide to Broadway.* New York: Routledge, 2007. Designed to be a student resource for Broadway theater in general, Bloom's guide focuses on major performers, writers, directors, plays, and musicals.

Everett, William A., and Paul R. Laird. *Historical Dictionary of the Broadway Musicals.* Lanham, Md.: Scarecrow Press, 2008. A valuable source not only for its entries devoted to composers, lyricists, performers, and terminology but also for its detailed historical time line, bibliography, and plot summaries of important shows.

Green, Stanley, and Kay Green. *Broadway Musicals: Show by Show.* 5th ed. Milwaukee, Wis.: Hal Leonard, 1999. A chronological reference work of virtually every significant show in Broadway history. Excerpts from opening-night reviews are included. A seven-volume companion collection of sheet music—one of which is devoted exclusively to musicals of the 1940's—is sold separately.

Kantor, Michael, and Laurence Maslon. *Broadway: The American Musical.* New York: Bulfinch Press, 2004. The companion volume to Maslon's six-hour PBS documentary on the history of Broadway. The 470-page tome is packed with photographs and essays from every era of Broadway.

McLamore, Alyson. *Musical Theater: An Appreciation.* Upper Saddle River, N.J.: Pearson Prentice Hall, 2004. A survey of the musical as an art form from its European roots to the early twenty-first century. The history is presented within a social-political context, and each chapter is complete with listening examples and analyses of specific song lyrics.

Mordden, Ethan. *Beautiful Mornin': The Broadway Musical in the 1940's.* New York: Oxford University Press, 1999. This 278-page history of the Broadway musical is perhaps the best work on the subject. Mordden is erudite while remaining accessible and humorous.

See also Bernstein, Leonard; Coles, Honi; *Oklahoma!*; Rodgers, Richard, and Oscar Hammerstein II; *South Pacific*; Theater in Canada; Theater in the United States.

■ Bulge, Battle of the

The Event Last major German offensive on the western front during World War II
Date December 16, 1944-January 25, 1945
Place Ardennes region of Belgium, France, and Luxembourg

The German offensive in the Ardennes in December, 1944, was a bold attempt by Adolf Hitler to turn the tide of the war in the west. The attack drove a bulge in the American line sixty-five miles deep and forty-five miles wide before being repulsed with heavy losses. The Allied victory, won largely by American troops, destroyed the remaining reserves of the German army. The battle was the bloodiest engagement fought by the U.S. Army in World War II.

By December, 1944, the rapid Allied progress across France to the German border had come to an end. Supply difficulties and stiffening German resistance slowed the Allied advance. The German supreme commander in the west, Field Marshal Gerd von Rundstedt, and the commander of Army Group B, Field Marshal Walther Model, managed to rebuild and reinforce the forces routed out of France. As the year ended, the Germans had created formidable defenses along their frontier.

Surprise Offensive   Partial military recovery in the west encouraged Adolf Hitler to plan a counterattack. Consumed by apocalyptic fantasies in his last months, Hitler conceived the idea of an offensive in the Ardennes, the scene of his great success in 1940. He envisioned his panzers piercing the Allied line, crossing the Meuse River, and pressing on to the Allied logistical depot at Antwerp. Hitler believed that this would cut off the British armies in the north from the Americans in the south, and might even lead to the collapse of the western alliance. Rundstedt and Model opposed the offensive, believing Hitler's goals wildly optimistic. They recommended an attack with more limited objectives but were overruled.

Hitler marshaled much of the remaining strength of the *Wehrmacht* (German armed forces) for his offensive, drawing units from the eastern front and creating *Volksgrenadier* units that mixed veterans with under- and overaged conscripts. He gathered a force of twenty-four divisions, including ten panzer divisions. These formations suffered from shortages of manpower and supplies, especially fuel. The Germans masked their buildup by maintaining radio silence.

In one of the great intelligence failures of the war, the Allies failed to anticipate the German onslaught. The supreme commander of the Allied forces, General Dwight D. Eisenhower, and his chief subordinates believed that the Germans were incapable of launching a major offensive. Allied intelligence did detect signs that the enemy was massing troops, but this was misinterpreted as a defensive measure. Allied manpower was stretched to the limit at the end

of 1944. The only Allied reserves were the American 82d and 101st Airborne Divisions. American troops were spread especially thin in the Ardennes, which was regarded as a quiet area.

Defensive Victory   The Germans struck on the morning of December 16. An artillery barrage was followed by German armor and infantry streaming into the American lines. Assisting the German breakthrough was overcast weather that kept Allied airpower from intervening in the battle. German commandos dressed as U.S. soldiers slipped into the American rear areas, sowing confusion until they were rounded up or dispersed. Some American units were overwhelmed. Most fiercely resisted the German advance. On the northern and southern shoulders of the offensive, American defenders held firm. In the center, the Germans scattered the American troops in front of them and began to drive rapidly toward the Meuse. Members of the First SS Panzer Division exhibited characteristic brutality, murdering civilians encountered on their way and eighty-six American prisoners of war at Malmédy.

When Eisenhower recognized the magnitude of the German offensive, he took decisive steps to contain it. He instructed his commanders to regard this attack as an opportunity to inflict a crushing reverse on the enemy. He placed British field marshal Bernard Montgomery in command of Allied troops

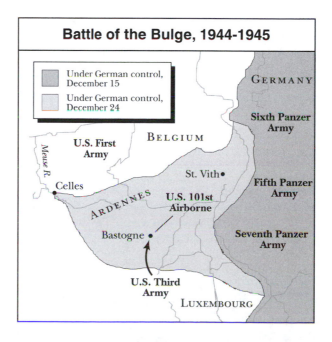

Battle of the Bulge, 1944-1945

north of the bulge created by the Germans. American general Omar Nelson Bradley commanded the American forces to the south. Eisenhower ordered the 101st Airborne Division to the crucial crossroads town of Bastogne. General George S. Patton's Third Army to the south shifted the direction of its advance and began to attack the exposed German flank.

The Germans were already experiencing difficulties. American resistance at strategic roadway junctions disrupted German progress in the heavily wooded Ardennes. Americans at St. Vith held out for six days before falling back. At Bastogne, American armor kept the Germans at bay until the 101st Airborne reinforced the defenders. The Screaming Eagles kept on fighting after being surrounded. When called upon to surrender, the American commander, General Anthony McAuliffe, refused with a one-word reply: "Nuts!" The skies cleared on December 23, and Allied aircraft began to inflict devastating losses on German armored columns. The next day, leading German units were within three miles of the Meuse, sixty-five miles from their starting point. They would advance no farther. Gas shortages became endemic, and Allied pressure was increasing. On December 26, Patton's troops relieved Bastogne. The German field commanders urged a retreat, but Hitler refused permission. On January 3, Montgomery's forces joined in the attack on the German salient. By January 25, the last of the German gains had been erased.

Impact Despite initial tactical successes, Hitler's Ardennes offensive was a military disaster for the failing Third Reich. The Bulge used up the last reserves of German manpower and armor. A renewed Allied advance would be irresistible. The United States suffered 81,000 casualties, including 19,000 dead. British casualties included 1,200 wounded and 200 killed. Germany lost nearly 100,000 men, killed, wounded, or captured.

Daniel P. Murphy

Further Reading

Eisenhower, John S. D. *The Bitter Woods: The Battle of the Bulge.* New York: Da Capo Press, 1995. Informed, authoritative account of the battle by the son of General Eisenhower.

MacDonald, Charles B. *A Time for Trumpets: The Untold Story of the Battle of the Bulge.* New York: William Morrow, 1985. Classic narrative by a veteran of the Bulge.

Parker, Danny. *Battle of the Bulge.* 1991. Reprint. New York: Da Capo Press, 2001. A highly regarded history of the battle.

Sears, Stephen. *The Battle of the Bulge.* New York: IBooks, 2005. A solid history for younger readers.

Toland, John. *Battle: The Story of the Bulge.* 1959. Reprint. Lincoln: University of Nebraska Press, 1999. The classic account of the Bulge, based on extensive interviews with participants.

See also Army, U.S.; Bradley, Omar N.; Eisenhower, Dwight D.; Hitler, Adolf; Patton, George S.; World War II.

■ Bunche, Ralph

Identification American diplomat and Nobel Peace Prize recipient
Born August 7, 1903; Detroit, Michigan
Died December 9, 1971; New York, New York

Bunche's intellectual acuity, empathic nature, and negotiating prowess helped him to mediate peace during the Arab-Israeli War of 1948-1949. Bunche received the 1950 Nobel Peace Prize for his efforts, becoming the first African American to receive the prestigious award.

At the start of World War II, Ralph Bunche was a political science professor at Howard University and was working on the Carnegie Corporation's Survey of the Negro in America project. His contributions to this project were later published in *An American Dilemma: The Negro Problem and Modern Democracy* (1944), authored by Swedish sociologist Gunnar Myrdal. Unable to join the military because of an old football injury, in 1941 Bunche joined the Office of the Coordinator of Information (later the Office of Strategic Services, the precursor to the Central Intelligence Agency). Working as a senior social analyst on Africa and the Far East, he distinguished himself with his vast experience in international affairs and was rapidly promoted.

In 1944, Bunche joined the State Department, and in 1945 he became the first African American to head a division in the State Department. While there, he contributed to the formation of the United Nations in 1945 and the creation and adoption of the U.N. Declaration of Human Rights. In 1946, he was asked to take a leave from the State Department to become director of the newly created U.N. Division of Trust-

Ralph Bunche. (Library of Congress)

eeship. In 1947, the United Nations formed the Special Commission on Palestine (UNSCOP), which voted to divide Palestine into a Jewish state and an Arab state. Bunche was appointed as special assistant to the representative of the U.N. secretary-general. The state of Israel was established on May 14, 1948, but disagreements between Israel and its Arab neighbors resulted in a violent conflict. The United Nations appointed a mediator, Count Folke Bernadotte, to negotiate for peace.

Together Bunche and Bernadotte labored tirelessly through the summer to draw up a satisfactory peace treaty after a cease-fire in June, 1948, was negotiated. On September 17, 1948, Bernadotte traveled to Jerusalem to meet with Israeli and Arab leaders. Bunche, who was to join him, was detained as a result of travel delays and red tape. Bernadotte preceded Bunche to the meeting but was assassinated along the way. Bunche would later say that he believed that he would have been assassinated, too, if he had been with Bernadotte as planned. On September 20, Bunche was appointed acting U.N. mediator and embarked on difficult and lengthy negotiations to resolve the conflict. His unique ability to be trusted and accepted by both Israelis and Arabs allowed him to negotiate armistice agreements, signed by Israel and four of its Arab neighbors—Egypt, Jordan, Lebanon, and Syria—on February 24, 1949, on the Greek island of Rhodes. The Rhodes armistice talks ended the Arab-Israeli War and achieved long-standing peace in the region. Bunche won the Nobel Peace Prize in 1950 for his contribution to peace in the Middle East, and the Spingarn Medal in 1949, awarded by the National Association for the Advancement of Colored People (NAACP) for the highest or noblest achievement by an African American.

Impact   Ralph Bunche became one of the first African Americans to attain an influential position on the international front. An ardent civil rights activist, he worked diligently to achieve equal rights for African Americans. He distinguished himself as an experienced and skillful peacemaker on the international scene, and his accomplishments were vital for peace in the Middle East.

Alice C. Richer

Further Reading

McKissack, Pat, and Fredrick McKissack. *Ralph J. Bunche: Peacemaker.* Berkeley Heights, N.J.: Enslow, 2002.

Urquhart, Brian. *Ralph Bunche: An American Life.* New York: W. W. Norton, 1993.

See also   African Americans; Foreign policy of the United States; Israel, creation of; National Association for the Advancement of Colored People; United Nations.

■ Bureau of Land Management

Identification   Federal agency overseeing a
    portion of federal lands
Date   Established in July, 1946

The Bureau of Land Management was created during the mid-1940's by combining the General Land Office and U.S. Grazing Service. The agency's formation coincided with growing interest in conservation and the introduction of scientific principles to guide range management.

The origin of the U.S. Bureau of Land Management (BLM) dates back to land ceded to the federal government after American independence. The Land Ordinance of 1785 and Northwest Ordinance of 1789 specified federal oversight of public lands along with properties transferred from Indian tribes and lands acquired from France, Spain, and other countries. In 1812, Congress created the General Land Office (GLO) within the Treasury Department to survey, record, and sell federal land-holdings. The GLO, which became part of the Department of the Interior in 1849, played an important role in facilitating westward expansion following passage of the Homestead Act of 1862 and other laws.

The later half of the nineteenth century saw a shift in federal policy concerning the stewardship of public lands. Public interest in conservation led to the transfer of GLO land for use in the creation of national parks, forests, and wildlife refuges. Overgrazing of publicly held grasslands resulted in passage of the Taylor Grazing Act in 1934 and the creation of the Division of Grazing under the GLO. Renamed the U.S. Grazing Service in 1939 and separated from the GLO, the agency soon became the focus of disagreements over public land management.

Elected officials from eastern states complained that western ranchers benefited from below-market prices for grazing permits, while their counterparts from western states pushed for lower grazing fees and the privatization of rangeland. Overlapping jurisdictions between the GLO and Grazing Service contributed to problems. At the same time that the Grazing Service was under pressure to reform fees, the GLO was understaffed and poorly structured for evaluating the validity of land claims. In 1945, the headquarters of the Grazing Service was moved from Washington, D.C., to Salt Lake City, and in 1946 Congress voted to reduce its budget by half.

Formation of the BLM   In May, 1946, President Harry S. Truman proposed creation of the BLM as a unit within the Department of the Interior by combining the GLO and U.S. Grazing Service. In the absence of an objection from Congress, the BLM became an agency in July, 1946. As stated in Executive Reorganization No. 3, the new agency combined the GLO's responsibilities for overseeing homestead claims and managing unassigned public lands with the Grazing Service's mission of supervising public lands used for ranching. At the time the BLM was created, more than two thousand unrelated and sometimes conflicting laws addressed the management of public lands. The BLM received no legislative mandate from Congress, contributing to a perception among western ranchers and others that the agency existed only to distribute remaining public lands.

Appointed as the new agency's first director, economist Marion Clawson had the task of bridging diverse functions from two agencies. Along with administrative restructuring, an important objective in the agency's early years was to reduce livestock impacts. Using scientific studies of soil and vegetation, the BLM was able to set the number of livestock permits according to the carrying capacity of individual land units. Clawson further extended his advocacy for scientific principles by applying a policy of multiple use that had previously been implemented within the Forest Service. For example, he required grazing advisory boards to include wildlife experts.

In 1947, the Acquired Minerals Leasing Act added responsibility for leasing mineral estates acquired by the federal government to the BLM's management portfolio. Facing growing pressure for access to its lands, the BLM's mission was expanded in 1964 to include recreation. In addition to minimally developed camping areas, BLM lands include recreational trails, scenic rivers, and federally designated wilderness areas.

Impact   By the early twenty-first century, the BLM managed 256 million acres of land, mostly in western states. The acreage comprises 13 percent of the land area of the United States and roughly 40 percent of land managed by the federal government.

BLM landholdings are almost as large as the combined acreage of U.S. Forest Service and National Park Service lands.

In 1976, Congress passed the Federal Land Policy and Management Act (FLPMA), sometimes called BLM's "Organic Act." Among its provisions, FLPMA formally ended BLM's responsibility for transferring public land into private hands. It also mandated that 50 percent of grazing fees collected must be used for range improvement. Despite its conservation efforts, BLM is not without controversy. An alliance between BLM officials and western landowners led environmental writer Edward Abbey to dub the agency the "bureau of livestock and mines."

The BLM is known for managing "leftover" lands not wanted by homesteaders or by other federal agencies. Under its first director, the BLM utilized scientific research in making decisions about grazing capacities and adopted a multiple-use principle for managing lands under its control. Despite its major role in managing public land, most Americans know little about the BLM.

Thomas A. Wikle

Further Reading

Clawson, Marion. "Reminiscences of the Bureau of Land Management, 1947-1948." In *The Public Lands,* edited by Vernon Carstensen. Madison: University of Wisconsin Press, 1963. Focusing on the administration of the new agency, Clawson reviews the inefficiency of the GLO and Grazing Service operations.

Foss, Phillip O. *Politics and Grass.* Seattle: University of Washington Press, 1960. A detailed analysis of the influence of grazing advisory boards and the capture of the Grazing Service and BLM by the livestock industry.

Muhn, James, and Hanson R. Stuart. *Opportunity and Challenge: The Story of the BLM.* Washington, D.C.: Bureau of Land Management, 1988. A detailed, uncritical chronology of the BLM and its predecessor organizations.

U.S. Department of the Interior. Bureau of Land Management. *Rangeland Reform '94.* Washington, D.C.: Government Printing Office, 1993. The secretary's proposals for reform of the BLM's rangeland programs.

Vincent, Carol Hardy. "Bureau of Land Management." In *Federal Land Management Agencies,* edited by Pamela D. Baldwin. New York: Novinka Books, 2005. Profile of the bureau, placing it in the context of other U.S. land management agencies. Bibliographic references and index.

See also   Agriculture in the United States; National parks; Truman, Harry S.

■ Business and the economy in Canada

Determined to avoid a repeat of the rampant unemployment and economic distress that their country had suffered following World War I, Canada's business and government leaders began preparations for a post-World War II economy long before the hostilities in Europe and the Pacific had even concluded. Public policies were enacted that maintained high levels of income and stable employment while protecting the domestic manufacturers but encouraging outside economic investment.

Historians of Canadian economic policies have identified the 1940's as a turning point in national attitudes toward urbanization, business expansion, and the economy. Prior to the beginning of World War II, Canada's national policy had mirrored the early expansionism of the United States. During the late nineteenth and early twentieth centuries, tariffs were put in place to protect the developing manufacturing base while government revenues financed the construction of railroads that eventually connected the East and West coasts. Those same railroads carried immigrants to the midwestern sections of the country, where they became farmers and produced agricultural products for export, primarily to Europe. Great Britain was a major trading partner during the early history of Canada. The advent of the Great Depression and World War II forced previously conservative political and business leaders to enact sweeping economic and social reforms, including regional economic development strategies, manufacturing and construction initiatives, as well as provincially sponsored hospital insurance programs that would become the precursor of Canada's publicly funded national health system.

Canada's War Economy   At the beginning of the 1940's, Canada's business and agricultural sectors had not yet fully recovered from the devastation caused by the Great Depression. The war proved to

Valentine tanks coming out of a Montreal factory in late 1941. Canada was mass-producing military equipment well before the United States even entered the war. (Getty Images)

be a boost for the sagging economy as orders for manufacture of war machines and materials increased employment and industrial output. Canada's war effort dramatically changed how business was conducted in the country. Mining and steel production were greatly expanded. Iron mining and oil exploration during the war set the stage for a postwar oil boom in Western Canada. During the wartime boom—in contrast to the situation that had occurred during World War I—the government enacted controls and rationing that managed to keep inflation under control.

Economic Growth and Interdependence In the national government's White Paper on Employment and Income, issued in April of 1945, proposals presented to the Dominion-Provincial Conference on Reconstruction called for renewed efforts with respect to federal initiatives on housing, vocational training, and economic development. The goal of the government was for Canada to play a critical role in the new economic world order, alongside the United States, its neighbor to the south. The key to national prosperity, it was believed, lay in the export markets of the new global economy that was being fostered by American growth and foreign investment, as well as Europe's postwar recovery. High tariff policies, aimed at building and strengthening domestic production, encouraged foreign investment in the form of loans as well as the construction of branch plants of American manufacturers.

The influx of American capital brought with it widespread criticism of the government because many Canadians were uncomfortable with the increasingly cozy relationship Canada's Liberal government had with U.S. business interests. During the 1940's, billions of dollars in U.S. capital poured across the border. So much so, that by the mid-1950's Americans owned, or had a controlling interest in, almost 40 percent of Canadian manufacturing, nearly 60 percent of the nation's petroleum and natural gas industries, and almost 50 percent of mining operations. The flow of goods and services between the two countries was so interconnected that during the postwar period the proportion of Canada's total exports that went to the United States soared to 60 percent, while at the same time 70 percent of imports were coming from the United States.

Impact During the 1940's, the economic and business climate of Canada was transformed by the wartime and postwar global economy. Canadian agricultural producers and manufacturers benefitted from global shortages during World War II and were quick to join the United States as an emerging economic power during the postwar recovery. By the 1950's, the country had been transformed from one highly dependent on employment in agriculture into a highly industrialized urban nation. The result was stronger ties to and a greater dependence on the United States.

Donald C. Simmons, Jr.

Further Reading

Careless, J. M. S. *Canada: A Story of Challenge.* Toronto: Macmillan, 1970. Revised edition of book first published in the early 1950's. The final chapters specifically address economic issues of importance to Canadians during the 1940's and 1950's.

Eden, Lorraine, and Maureen Appel Molot. "Canada's National Policies: Reflections on 125 Years." *Canadian Public Policy/ Analyse de Politiques* 19, no. 3 (1993): 232-251. Broad review of Canadian government policies through the first century and a quarter of the country's history as a nation, with close attention to government economic policies.

Grant, Harry M., and M. H. Watkins, eds. *Canadian Economic History: Classic and Contemporary Approaches.* Ottawa: Carleton University Press, 1999. This collection provides a thorough survey of issues in Canadian economic history by sixteen scholars.

Kohn, Robert, and Susan Radius. "Two Roads to Health Care: U.S. and Canadian Policies 1945-1975." *Medical Care* 12, no. 3 (1974): 189-201. Comparative study of national health policies in the United States and Canada through the first three decades following World War II.

Mackintosh, W. A. "Canadian War Financing." *Journal of Political Economy* 50, no. 4 (1942): 481-500. Useful examination of how the Canadians financed their participation in World War II.

See also Advertising in Canada; Agriculture in Canada; Business and the economy in the United States; Canada and Great Britain; Canadian nationalism; Canadian participation in World War II; Foreign policy of Canada; Gross national product of Canada.

■ Business and the economy in the United States

World War II and its aftermath transformed the American economy radically, from the persistent Depression of the 1930's to a period of full employment, consumer abundance, and optimism. The role of government continued to enlarge, particularly in the use of monetary and fiscal policies to maintain full employment. The United States became the world leader in promoting trade, finance, and economic development.

The economic history of the 1940's can be divided into three distinct periods:

- 1940-1941, before the United States officially entered World War II
- 1942-1945, when the United States was actively at war
- 1946-1949, the postwar years

Despite this periodization, the period from 1940 to 1944 saw a continuous upsurge of spending, output, and employment, during which the unemployment rate declined from 15 percent to 1 percent, with employment rising from 48 million to 54 million, despite the induction of 11 million potential workers into the armed forces. The nation's real gross national product, as measured in constant prices, rose by almost 60 percent. The increase was recognized as nearly miraculous and contributed immensely to the Allied victory.

In its way, the period of postwar economic growth was also near miraculous. Widespread fear that the American economy would lapse back into serious depression proved misplaced. Instead, private consumption spending and especially business investment spending rose to fill the gap. The number of persons in military service dropped by 10 million between 1945 an 1947, but the number of unemployed remained below 3 million until the recession of 1948-1949.

Prewar Preparations, 1940-1941 After the outbreak of World War II in Europe in 1939, many officials in the U.S. government expected that the United States would be drawn into the fighting. Preparations for a military draft began with the Selective Service Act of September, 1940. In January, 1941, President Franklin D. Roosevelt established the Office of Production Management (OPM), the beginning of a long series of agencies to manage military production and procurement. April, 1941, saw creation of the Office of Price Administration (OPA), anticipating the need for price controls. The Lend-Lease Act of March, 1941, committed the United States to providing economic aid to the Allies. The armed forces expanded by a million persons in 1941 over 1940.

Government spending for national defense rose from $2 billion in 1940 to $14 billion in 1941. As these and other expenditure increases added to household incomes, consumption rose by $10 billion (14 percent). Tax rates were raised significantly in June and September of 1940, including an excess-profits tax.

The Economy in Wartime, 1942-1945 By December of 1941, defense spending had hit an annual rate of $20 billion, and it continued to rise rapidly. Officials recognized that they could not simply buy the things they needed; rather, they had to arrange for them to be produced, which often involved arranging for expansion of plants and equipment. The government provided as much as five-sixths of the financing for such capital expenditures. Business incentives were met by the widespread use of "cost-plus" contracts, which guaranteed profits to suppliers regardless of their efficiency. The government's Defense Plant Corporation built nine aluminum smelters and a number of fabricating facilities to aid war production. These facilities were operated by The Aluminum Company of America (Alcoa) under lease.

The government was heavily involved in technological research and innovation related to the war effort, most notably, perhaps in the Manhattan Project, which produced the atom bomb and paved the way for nuclear energy. Others fields of technological research included radar, jet propulsion, and computers.

Production expanded at a furious rate. The West Coast shipbuilding enterprise of Henry J. Kaiser became noted for rapid production of Liberty ships—their Vancouver, Washington, shipyard built a 10,500-ton ship in four and a half days. Despite the loss of manpower into military service, civilian employment grew from 48 million in 1940 to 54 million in 1944 and 1945. "Rosie the Riveter" symbolized the entry of many women into industrial jobs. The civilian labor force increased from 55 percent of the population in 1940 to 58 percent in 1943.

By 1945, total output was one-third larger than in 1941. Of course, the composition of the output was far different, with a large share of war production. In 1942 the government had ordered a halt to production of civilian motor vehicles. Shortages of materials led to curtailment of many other items of civilian use, notably construction of houses. Civilian use of rubber decreased by 80 percent. Gasoline and fuel oil were in scarce supply, despite the creation of an extensive pipeline network connecting Texas sources with northeastern markets.

The military draft moved into high gear, drawing heavily on the formerly unemployed and on students. By 1944 there were eleven million persons in military service. Between the draft and the expansion of defense employment, the number of unemployed workers dropped from eight million in 1940 to three million in 1942 and less than one million in 1944.

An extensive network of government economic controls quickly developed. In January, 1942, the War Production Board (WPB) replaced OPM. Priorities and allocation orders were applied to many products related to war production. After the consumer price index rose by 1 percent a month in 1941, Congress passed the Emergency Price Control Act in January, 1942. In April, 1942, the Office of Price Administration issued the General Maximum Price Regulation (nicknamed "General Max"), which provided for government control of most prices and wages. During that same month, the president established the National War Labor Board, which was intended to maintain wage guidelines and prevent labor disputes from interfering with production. Rationing was instituted for products in scarce supply, notably gasoline, sugar, meat, and food products generally. Each household received ration coupons that were required before the products could be purchased.

Wartime Financial Policies Military spending, which had been less than $2 billion in 1940, reached $81 billion in 1945, driving total federal spending to nearly $100 billion. Through the six years beginning in June, 1940, federal tax collections covered about half of expenditures—far more than in previous major American wars. Beginning in 1943, federal income tax was withheld from employees' pay by employers. For the first time, the income tax became a mass levy, reaching most families. Marginal tax rates on high incomes were pushed to very high levels, exceeding 90 percent in 1944-1945 on personal incomes over $200,000.

The other half of federal spending was covered by borrowing. In 1940-1941, interest rates on U.S. government securities remained at the very low levels they had reached during the Depression. Long-term government bonds yielded 2 percent or less, and three-month Treasury bills paid only about 0.33 percent. The U.S. Treasury feared that large issues of new bonds would drive up interest rates. Powerful advertising campaigns promoted the sales of U.S. savings bonds to households. These were issued in denominations as low as twenty-five dollars and redeemable on demand at predetermined values. They yielded 2.9 percent interest when held the full ten years to maturity, but much less when redeemed sooner. About $40 billion in savings bonds was sold between 1941 and 1945.

Most of the remaining federal deficit was financed by issuing marketable securities. These could be bought and sold among investors, with yields that varied with their prices. The Federal Reserve bought about $20 billion of marketable issues. These purchases created bank reserves, which enabled commercial banks to create new deposits and buy bonds with them. The Federal Reserve agreed to buy government bonds at prices that would prevent the interest rates from rising above 2.5 percent (for long-term bonds) and 0.375 percent (for short-term bills.) The interest cost of war finance averaged only about 2 percent.

As a result of Federal Reserve policies, the money supply, measured as currency plus bank deposits, doubled between the end of 1941 and mid-1945. However, the price level of the gross national product increased only 29 percent from 1941 to 1945. The velocity of money declined, as households cut their proportional consumption spending from 88 percent of disposable income in 1941 to 75 percent in 1943-1944. Because the unemployment rate was initially so high, the rise in spending could be met by higher production rather than higher prices. Finally, the price controls, rationing, and withdrawal from the market of products such as automobiles encouraged people to accumulate cash, bonds, and other liquid assets for the postwar period.

The increase in employment during the war was particularly strong in the manufacturing sector. Ac-

Detroit Chrysler plant applying assembly-line techniques developed to manufacture automobiles to mass-produce twenty-eight-ton tanks in 1942. The speed with which plants such as this one converted to wartime production reflected the strength and resiliency of U.S. industry. After the war, automobile plants would return to manufacturing passenger cars just as quickly. (Time & Life Pictures/Getty Images)

cording to WPB head Donald Nelson this produced 300,000 war planes, 124,000 ships, 41 billion rounds of ammunition, 100,000 tanks and armored cars, 2.4 million military trucks, 434 million tons of steel, and 36 billion yards of cotton textiles. From 11 million workers in 1940, the manufacturing sector expanded to more than 17 million in 1943-1944.

This sector was strongly affected by the extension in labor union membership arising from the Wagner (National Labor Relations) Act of 1935. Union membership increased from about 9 million in 1940 to nearly 15 million in 1945. Unionization was prominent but new to mass-production industries such as steel and motor vehicles, which were busy with war production. Union leaders were determined to flex their muscles to impress their new members and potential recruits. National union leaders pledged support for a no-strike policy, but this commitment was sometimes ignored, particularly in the heat of campaigns to organize firms and persuade them to engage in collective bargaining in good faith. Imposition of wage controls was a source of friction. The coal industry experienced a major strike when more than 500,000 workers left their jobs in May, 1943, prompting the government to seize the coal mines.

A similar action was taken in December, 1943, against a threatened railroad strike. In March, 1945, a major strike hit Chrysler Motor Company and important suppliers. However, during 1942-1945, the impact of work stoppages was relatively low compared with previous and subsequent time periods. In general, labor did well during the war. The economy returned to full employment, wage rates increased, and workers earned great amounts of overtime pay. Real average annual earnings per employed worker rose about 40 percent from 1940 to 1945, after removing the effect of inflation.

Some major policy innovations introduced during the war had important postwar implications. For example, the Serviceman's Readjustment Act of 1944—better known as the G.I. Bill—offered several major benefits to veterans. These included financial support for schooling, preferential credit for housing, and unemployment compensation. Also in 1944, the United States became the major sponsor of a variety of international economic agencies, including the International Monetary Fund, the International Bank for Reconstruction and Development (World Bank), and the General Agreement of Tariffs and Trade. These international ties signalled the federal government's commitment to lead the world toward reduction of trade barriers and expansion of international credit facilities.

Postwar Boom When the war in Europe ended in May, 1945, many feared the fighting against Japan in the Pacific theater of the war would be prolonged. Many military personnel in Europe were shipped to the Pacific. All this changed, however, after atomic bombs were dropped on Hiroshima and Nagasaki in August, prompting the unconditional Japanese surrender. A rapid demobilization of the U.S. armed services then began, but it was not instantaneous. Some draftees had to wait nearly a year to get home from overseas because of transport shortages. Between mid-1945 and mid-1946, the number of personnel in military service decreased by 9 million. Vast amounts of American military supplies were left in Europe and Asia as part of postwar relief efforts, particularly programs administered by the United National Relief and Rehabilitation Agency.

In the fiscal year ending June 30, 1945, the federal government spent slightly less than $100 billion. Expenditures declined by nearly $40 billion in the next year and an additional $21 billion the following year. Although major reductions in federal tax rates occurred in 1945 and 1948, the numbers of taxpayers and the general levels of rates on large incomes remained much higher than they had been before the war. By 1947, drastic cuts in federal spending eliminated the budget deficit and shifted the budget into a surplus. Congress was eager to cut tax rates further, but President Harry S. Truman vetoed tax-cut bills in 1947. In 1948, Congress passed a tax bill over his veto.

Total spending for current output by all private and public spenders levelled off around $210 billion per year from 1944-1946. Since prices were rising rapidly, real output declined from $355 billion (in 1958 prices) to $310 billion in 1947. However, this reduction in output did not make people worse off. Rather, it reflected the cutback of production of "means of destruction" and reduction of the involuntary employment of millions of young men. The government also "demobilized" its vast control network. Wage and price controls were phased out during 1946.

After a minor dip in 1946, spending for gross national product resumed its upward trend, reaching $258 billion in 1948. Consumer spending alone surged upward from $120 billion in 1945 to $174 billion in 1948. Some of this was absorbed in price increases, but the real value of consumption rose 15 percent over that same period. A centerpiece of the consumption boom for many veterans was the automobile. During the 1930's, many American families could not afford to buy cars. During the war, they were not produced. Mass production resumed in 1946, with 2 million cars, rising to 5 million in 1949. They came in many sizes and shapes, including the fantasy models of Preston Tucker and the valiant economy models of Henry J. Kaiser.

Much the same pattern developed for housing. During the 1930's, many people could not afford new homes; during the war, production was very limited. The number of private housing starts jumped from 325,000 in 1945 to 1 million in 1946 and 1.4 million in 1949. These starts drew extensively on home-finance innovations of the 1930's, notably the home-mortgage insurance program of the Federal Housing Administration, and on the G.I. Bill.

The housing boom was simply one manifestation of the national return to domesticity, as young men returned from the military to marry, raise children, and develop family lives. The beginnings of the ensuing baby boom appeared in the steady increase in the number of children under five years of age. In 1940, there were 10.6 million. By 1949, there were 15.6 million. Many of the new houses were in suburban developments. Much publicity was given to Levittowns produced by Abraham Levitt and his sons, beginning on Long Island. The developments included parks, shops, and schools. And the new houses were sold fully equipped with modern appliances. New products, most notably television sets, which had been developed during the 1930's, rapidly penetrated the household market after 1948. Three million sets were sold in 1949 alone. AM radio continued to be very popular, increasingly supplemented by FM broadcasting. Long-playing records, widely sold after 1948, enabled listeners to listen to as much as a half hour of music without interruption.

For many types of business, production facilities had not been kept up because of either the Depression or the war. The postwar boom of consumption brought a postwar boom of investment as well—spending for machinery and buildings. Business spending for fixed assets rose from $10 billion in 1945 to $27 billion in 1948, then dipped slightly in the recession of 1949. A drastic readjustment of the aluminum industry occurred when the government sold its wartime facilities to Reynolds Aluminum and Kaiser Aluminum, undermining the former monopoly position of Alcoa.

Spending for housing and investing in business capital were spurred by the continuing low level of interest rates, sustained by Federal Reserve policy and by Treasury surpluses used for reducing the national debt. Rates on high-grade corporate bonds and on business loans remained below 3 percent through 1949.

The rise of GNP expenditures was also spurred by export sales. These had reached record levels during the war. They dipped at the war's end, and there was concern that the countries that had been involved in the war had no means to pay for products they desperately needed. This problem was addressed by the Marshall Plan in 1947 and generous United States financial contributions to the World Bank and International Monetary Fund. Particularly noteworthy was American aid for the economic reconstruction of Germany and Japan—a contrast to the vindictive measures following World War I.

An important symbolic gesture was the passage of the Employment Act of 1946. This committed the federal government to promoting "maximum employment, production, and purchasing power," and implicitly pledged that fiscal and monetary policies would be directed to these goals. The law directed the president to submit an annual report to Congress on the condition of the economy, and created a three-person Council of Economic Advisers to prepare it.

Inflation reached painful levels after wartime controls were removed and private spending surged. By 1948 consumer prices were about one-third above 1945. During the war, the Federal Reserve had enforced controls over consumer credit, but Congress abolished these in 1947. In 1948 President Harry S. Truman called a special session of Congress to deal with inflation. This resulted in temporary authority to impose consumer credit controls again, as well as increase bank reserve requirements.

Labor unions and labor relations were important elements in the inflation process. Unions were still striving to expand membership, and added at least two million workers between 1945 and 1948. With wage controls abolished, unions were free to bargain vigorously for higher pay and other job improvements, such as cost-of-living adjustments. There were major coal strikes in October, 1945, and April, 1946, to the detriment of business and household users. General Motors was shut down by a strike in November, 1945. A steel strike in Pittsburgh involved 800,000 workers in January-February, 1946. A railroad strike in May, 1946, led to government seizure of the facilities. Maritime unions shut down much of the shipping industry in the summer of 1946. That year was one of the worst on record for work stoppages, with a loss of 116 million person-days.

In response, Congress adopted the Taft-Hartley Act in January, 1947, passing it over President Truman's veto. The law imposed a number of restrictions on union leaders and union actions—outlawing secondary boycotts, for example. It also created a procedure for dealing with strikes that posed a threat to national welfare. An important provision authorized individual state governments to adopt "right-to-work" laws that forbade requiring union membership as a condition of employment. By the early 1990's, twenty-one states had adopted such laws. Union membership continued to increase, but strikes ceased to be a major national problem.

By the end of 1948, the rise of prices had stopped and the economy was moving into a recession. However, the tax-rate reduction that had overridden the president's veto proved an appropriate remedy. The recession was mild and brief.

Impact   Despite the many negative effects of World War II, during the late 1940's, the American economy was in vastly better shape than it had been ten years earlier. Home ownership, which had declined during the Depression to 44 percent of households, shot up to 55 percent by 1950. The number of automobile registrations increased from 27 million in 1940 to 36 million in 1949. Enrollment in colleges and universities went from 1.5 million in 1940 to 2.4 million in 1948, spurred by the G.I. Bill. Millions of young people had their horizons broadened by their war experience, which drew them into far-flung travel and unfamiliar but well-paid and challenging work in many sectors.

Paul B. Trescott

Further Reading

Chandler, Lester V. *Inflation in the United States, 1940-1948*. New York: Harper & Brothers, 1951. Clear, simple review of the entire American macroeconomic situation during the 1940's.

Chandler, Lester V., and Donald H. Wallace. *Economic Mobilization and Stabilization*. New York: Henry Holt, 1951. Detailed examination of the entire range of government policies related to the wartime economy during the 1940's.

Fishback, Price, et al. *Government and the American Economy: A New History*. Chicago: University of Chicago Press, 2007. The 1940's figure prominently in several chapters of this book, but the most relevant is Robert Higgs's chapter on the effects of the two world wars on the American economy.

Lichtenstein, Nelson. *Labor's War at Home: The CIO in World War II*. New York: Cambridge University Press, 1982. There are chapters on labor conditions both before and after the war.

Nelson, Donald. *Arsenal of Democracy: The Story of American War Production*. New York: Harcourt Brace, 1946. This autobiographical memoir by the head of the War Production Board captures the spirit as well as the detail of wartime production controls.

Robertson, Ross M. *History of the American Economy*, 2d ed. New York: Harcourt, Brace & World, 1964. Part 4 of this excellent college text deals extensively with the 1940's as part of the long-term evolution of the American economy.

Wilson, Richard L., ed. *Historical Encyclopedia of American Business*. 3 vols. Pasadena, Calif.: Salem Press, 2009. Comprehensive reference work on American business history that contains substantial essays on almost every conceivable aspect of U.S. economic history.

See also   Credit and debt; Demographics of the United States; Economic wartime regulations; Gross national product of the United States; Housing in the United States; Income and wages; Inflation; International trade; Unionism.

■ Byrd, Richard E.

Identification   American polar explorer
Born   October 25, 1888; Winchester, Virginia
Died   March 11, 1957; Boston, Massachusetts

A central figure in the history of naval aviation, Byrd was also a major figure in Arctic and Antarctic exploration. During the 1940's, he led the biggest and most productive of his five major research expeditions to Antarctica. That expedition did pioneering work in aerial photography and mapping that has contributed greatly to modern polar research.

Richard Evelyn Byrd graduated from the U.S. Naval Academy in 1912 after growing up in a prominent Virginia family, whose ancestors included John Rolfe, the Jamestown pioneer who married Pocahontas. At the age of eleven, Byrd traveled to the Philippines by himself to visit a relative, and his dispatches during that journey were published in several newspapers. As a naval aviator in World War I, Byrd showed impressive abilities that led to his becoming supervisor of two U.S. Navy air bases in Nova Scotia. Also instrumental in establishing the navy's Bureau of Aeronautics, he was promoted to lieutenant commander in 1922.

In 1925, Byrd was made commander of the aviation unit accompanying MacMillan polar expedition to northwest Greenland that was sponsored by the National Geographic Society. He had begun developing an interest in polar exploration as a child and made the first-ever flight over the North Pole in 1926. This feat made Byrd a national hero and the winner of the Medal of Honor. The Navy also awarded him its Distinguished Flying Cross after he and three companions flew from Long Island, New York, to France in 1927, demonstrating that flight across the Atlantic was practical.

In 1929, Byrd increased his fame by flying over the South Pole—a feat that enhanced his ability to raise money for Antarctic exploration and research. During his first major Antarctic expedition in 1928-1930, he help map about 150,000 square miles of territory, and he was promoted to rear admiral. During his second expedition, in 1933-1935, he nearly died while collecting weather data in temperatures ranging as low as −78° Fahrenheit. Despite that harrowing experience, which he described his 1938 book *Alone*, Byrd returned to Antarctica several more times, always making use of new technologies to make his research safer and more efficient. During his 1940's expeditions, for example, he used helicopters, not only for the transportation of his crews and equipment but also to help him complete the first aerial photography of the region.

Byrd led his third expedition to Antarctica in 1939-1941, after President Franklin D. Roosevelt placed him in command of the U.S. Antarctic service. This was his first expedition to receive official financial backing of the U.S. government. During this expedition Byrd discovered Thurston Island, and two bases were established in order to gather scientific data which ultimately provided information for more than twenty branches of science.

After returning to active naval service during World War II, Byrd was placed in charge of the U.S. Navy Antarctic Developments Project for 1946-1947—a project more commonly known as Operation High Jump. Byrd's fourth and largest Antarctic expedition, this one used thirteen ships, twenty-five airplanes, and 4,700 men and mapped approximately 537,000 square miles of the continent.

Impact   Byrd's contributions to twentieth century Antarctic research are unparalleled in the history of polar exploration, and the pinnacle of his exploration came during this 1946-1947 expedition. In 1955-1956, he would make his final research expedition to the southern continent in Operation Deep Freeze. During that expedition, he established permanent bases at McMurdo Sound, the Bay of Whales, and the South Pole itself that have continued to serve as research stations into the twenty-first century.

Jean L. Kuhler

Further Reading

Bertrand, Kenneth J. *Americans in Antarctica, 1775-1948.* New York: American Geographical Society, 1971.

Byrd, Richard E. *Alone.* New York: G. P. Putnam's Sons, 1938. Reprint. Los Angeles: Jeremy P. Tarcher, 1986.

Hoyt, Edwin P. *The Last Explorer.* New York: John Day, 1968.

Rose, Lisle A. *Assault on Eternity: Richard E. Byrd and the Exploration of Antarctica, 1946-47.* Annapolis, Md.: Naval Institute Press, 1980.

See also   Aircraft design and development; Alaska Highway; Navy, U.S.; Science and technology.

■ Byrnes, James

Identification   U.S. secretary of state, 1945-1947
Born   May 2, 1879; Charleston, South Carolina
Died   April 9, 1972; Columbia, South Carolina

Because of the authority he exercised as director of the Office of Economic Stabilization and the Office of War Mobilization, Byrnes was known as the "assistant president for domestic affairs." As secretary of state, he accepted the transition from the conciliatory policy of Franklin D. Roosevelt toward the Soviets to the doctrine of containment espoused by Harry S. Truman.

James Byrnes served in county and state government as well as in all three branches of the federal government. After entering politics as a solicitor for the Second Circuit of South Carolina (1908-1910), he served seven consecutive terms in the U.S. House of Representatives (1911-1925) and nearly two full terms as a U.S. senator (1931-1941). In the Senate, Byrnes emerged as one of the most influential Democrats who supported Franklin D. Roosevelt's policies. Roosevelt rewarded Byrnes for his loyalty by appointing him an associate justice of the U.S. Supreme Court (1941-1942).

Dissatisfied with his duties on the Court, Byrnes resigned to become director of the Office of Economic Stabilization (1942-1943), and director of the Office of War Mobilization (1943-1945). As head of economic stabilization, Byrnes regulated prices, wages, and rents and also supervised the rationing of food and fuel. As director of war mobilization, he managed programs that coordinated all war agencies and federal departments involved in war production.

Following his failure to gain the Democratic Party's vice presidential nomination in 1944 and thus succeed Roosevelt in the White House, Byrnes accompanied Roosevelt to the Yalta Conference in February, 1945, serving as a personal adviser to the president. He sold the Yalta Agreement to senators and the press by expressing hope that U.S.-Soviet cooperation would continue after the war. His knowledge of the conference "secrets" played a key role in his appointment as secretary of state under President Harry S. Truman.

Byrnes accompanied Truman to the Potsdam Conference in the summer of 1945, advising the president to make quick use of the atomic bomb against Japan without prior warning, that the devel-opment of the weapon should be kept secret from the Soviets, and that the United States should not insist that Japan accept "unconditional surrender" because it would only prolong the war. He later pushed for the continuation of Japan's imperial dynasty under Allied jurisdiction to hasten Japan's acceptance of Allied peace terms.

Throughout the remainder of 1945, Byrnes copied Roosevelt's style of diplomacy through compromise at the Council of Foreign Ministers at London and at Moscow in an attempt to maintain U.S.-Soviet friendship. However, by early 1946 Truman and the American public favored a "get-tough" policy toward the Soviets, mostly due to Soviet control over Eastern Europe and the Iran crisis. Byrnes was criticized for appeasing the Soviets in Eastern Europe and for his independent handling of American foreign policy. Byrnes lost control over American diplomacy, but he remained loyal to the Truman administration by accepting the Cold War doctrine of containment. At the London and Paris conferences of 1946, Byrnes assumed a tougher stance toward the Soviets during the negotiation of peace treaties with Italy, Romania, Bulgaria, Hungary, and Finland. He later

James Byrnes in 1940. (Library of Congress)

publicized the Soviet military presence in Iran before the U.N. Security Council, which contributed to the removal of Soviet troops from that country in late 1946. He also demanded the resignation of Secretary of Commerce Henry A. Wallace after Wallace questioned the policy of containment in a public address.

After leaving the State Department, Byrnes practiced law in Washington, D.C. (1947-1950) and published *Speaking Frankly* (1947), the first of his two memoirs. In 1948, he broke with the Truman administration over civil rights. After serving one term as governor of South Carolina (1951-1955), he retired from public office.

Impact   Byrnes became an important figure in the Democratic Party in the 1930's and 1940's because of his keen sense of political pragmatism and party loyalty. Such factors, however, undercut his efforts to sustain U.S.-Soviet cooperation after 1945. Unable to exercise the same authority in foreign affairs under Truman as he had wielded over domestic affairs under Roosevelt, Byrnes offered no alternative to the developing Cold War consensus. Thus, he accepted containment as the most practical means to check Soviet expansion and avoid war.

Dean Fafoutis

Further Reading

Byrnes, James F. *Speaking Frankly.* New York: Harper & Brothers, 1947.

Messer, Robert L. *The End of an Alliance: James F. Byrnes, Roosevelt, Truman, and the Origins of the Cold War.* Chapel Hill: University of North Carolina Press, 1982.

Robertson, David. *Sly and Able: A Political Biography of James F. Byrnes.* New York: W. W. Norton, 1994.

See also   Acheson, Dean; Atomic bomb; Foreign policy of the United States; Lend-Lease; Marshall, George C.; Office of War Mobilization; Paris Peace Conference of 1946; Potsdam Conference; Roosevelt, Franklin D.; Truman, Harry S.; Yalta Conference.

C

■ Cabrini canonization

The Event   First conferment of sainthood on an American citizen
Date   July 7, 1946

The canonization of Mother Frances Xavier Cabrini, coming soon after the end of World War II, served to direct Americans' attention on the international community, with a focus on relieving the perilous conditions of those orphaned and displaced by the war.

Mother Frances Xavier Cabrini (1850-1917), founder of the Missionaries of the Sacred Heart of Jesus in 1880, was the first American citizen to be canonized. Cabrini established her order of nuns to honor Saint Frances Xavier, whose missionary work in the Far East inspired her own zeal to aid orphans in her native Italy. The wretched conditions of Italian immigrants in America prompted Pope Leo XIII to convince Cabrini that her vocation lay in America. From her arrival in 1889, Cabrini worked and traveled relentlessly in the United States and abroad to establish orphanages, schools, convents, and hospitals to serve Italian immigrants and children. In her lifetime, she founded sixty-seven institutions in the United States, South America, and Europe.

The canonization was an astute decision by Pope Pius XII. His refusal to publicly condemn Nazi persecution of the Jews during World War II for fear of reprisals to those under Nazi regimes was controversial, despite his multiple personal efforts to aid the Jews. Immediately following the war, the pope called for international attention to the plight of all displaced persons, particularly children, in his encyclical *Quemadmodum* (pleading for the care of the world's destitute children), issued in January, 1946. In 1950, Pius XII declared Cabrini the patron saint of immigrants.

Impact   Given that Cabrini had dedicated her life to charitable work for children and the impoverished, her canonization in July, 1946, was an appro-priate and signal measure of the papal efforts to emphasize rebuilding the world with attention to the most needy.

M. Sheila McAvey

Further Reading

Gerard, Noel. *Pius XII: The Hound of Hitler.* New York: Continuum, 2008.

Sullivan, Mary Louise. *Mother Cabrini: Italian Immigrant of the Century.* New York: Center for Migration Studies, 1992.

See also   CARE; Immigration to the United States; Refugees in North America; Religion in the United States; UNICEF.

■ Cairo Conference

The Event   World War II summit of Allied leaders that resulted in a declaration imposing peace terms on Japan
Date   November 22-26, 1943
Place   Cairo, Egypt

The summit was attended by U.S. president Franklin D. Roosevelt, British prime minister Winston Churchill, and Chinese Nationalist leader Chiang Kai-shek. Roosevelt used the meeting to bolster Chiang's standing as an important ally and to discuss Far Eastern military strategy and postwar planning. The conference produced the Cairo Declaration, an agreement signed by the three Allied leaders in attendance regarding peace terms to be imposed on Japan.

At Cairo, Franklin D. Roosevelt, much to Winston Churchill's annoyance, was preoccupied with shaping the postwar world in Asia. In an effort to end British colonial rule over India, Burma, Malaysia, and Hong Kong, Roosevelt looked to China to act as a counterweight against European colonialism in Asia. This, he hoped, would not only secure permanent decolonization in the region but also offer protection against a resurgent Japan, as well as check possible Soviet expansion in Asia. Roosevelt thus envisioned China as one of the "Four Policemen" that would maintain peace and order after the war.

Roosevelt faced several problems in pursuing his vision of China as a great power. Chiang Kai-shek's political weakness, recognized by Churchill and all American diplomatic and military officers assigned to China, especially General Joseph Warren Stilwell, complicated matters. They all viewed Chiang as corrupt, ineffective, and tyrannical, and they believed that he would lose a power struggle with the Chinese communists after the war. Moreover, Roosevelt could not fulfill his promise of increasing Allied assistance to China due to commitments to the ongoing Italian campaign and Operation Overlord.

Roosevelt, nonetheless, tried to bolster China's confidence and offer political encouragement to Chiang. To keep China in the war, Roosevelt promised to arm ninety Chinese divisions. He also discussed plans for an offensive in northern Burma, accompanied by an Allied amphibious assault on the Andaman Islands in the Bay of Bengal, to open a supply route to China. Such promises, however, quickly fell victim to the realities of the war. By 1943, the China-Burma-India theater had lost much of its significance in the Allied war effort. The United States had recently captured Tarawa, which put it within striking distance of the Mariana Islands. The capture of those islands would reduce the need for Allied air bases in southern China to attack Japan. Nor could Roosevelt overcome Churchill's opposition to the proposed Burma operation. Furthermore, at the Tehran Conference (which succeeded the Cairo Conference), Roosevelt secured a pledge from Joseph Stalin that the Soviets would enter the war against Japan. Consequently, Roosevelt reneged on his promises to Chiang, claiming that limited resources had forced the postponement of the Burma operation.

To console Chiang, Roosevelt announced the Cairo Declaration on December 1, 1943. According to the agreement, Japan would be stripped of all the islands in the Pacific that it had seized or occupied since 1914 as well as all territories stolen from China. Manchuria, Formosa (Taiwan), and the Pescadores would thus be restored to China. Japan would also be expelled from all other territories—that is, the Philippines, Indochina, Malaya, and the Netherlands East Indies—that it had acquired through "violence and greed." Korea, part of the Japanese

---

The Cairo Declaration

Adopted at the Cairo Conference of 1943, this declaration underscores the alliance among the United States, Great Britain, and China against Japan.

The Three Great Allies are fighting this war to restrain and punish the aggression of Japan. They covet no gain for themselves and have no thought of territorial expansion. It is their purpose that Japan shall be stripped of all the islands in the Pacific which she has seized or occupied since the beginning of the first World War in 1914, and that all the territories Japan has stolen from the Chinese, such as Manchuria, Formosa, and The Pescadores, shall be restored to the Republic of China. Japan will also be expelled from all other territories which she has taken by violence and greed. The aforesaid three great powers, mindful of the enslavement of the people of Korea, are determined that in due course Korea shall become free and independent.

Empire since 1905, would become free and independent "in due course."

Impact The Cairo Declaration probably intensified the Japanese war effort, but it kept China in the war and assured the Soviets that the United States would not seek a separate peace with Japan. More important, political and military realities undercut Roosevelt's hope of China becoming a great power. American and British complaints regarding Chiang's weaknesses proved to be accurate when the Chinese communists defeated the Chinese Nationalists in 1949 and took control of China.

Dean Fafoutis

Further Reading
Sainsbury, Keith. *The Turning Point: Roosevelt, Churchill, Stalin, and Chiang Kai-shek, 1943, The Moscow, Cairo, and Teheran Conferences.* Oxford: Oxford University Press, 1986.
Stone, David. *War Summits: The Meetings That Shaped World War II and the Postwar World.* Washington, D.C.: Potomac Books, 2005.

See also Casablanca Conference; China-Burma-India theater; Churchill, Winston; Decolonization of European empires; Philippine independence; Potsdam Conference; Roosevelt, Franklin D.; Stilwell, Joseph Warren; Tehran Conference; Unconditional surrender policy.

■ Canada and Great Britain

Canada, the oldest dominion in the British Empire, played a vital role during World War II in supplying the British war effort, and military forces fought alongside those of Britain. After the war, Canada helped frame the development of the British Empire into the modern world.

Through the 1940's, Canada's relationship with Great Britain was defined by its status as a dominion within the British Empire, or Commonwealth, as it became known. This meant that it was bound by the 1931 Statute of Westminster that created the Commonwealth, with the British monarch as head of state for each country. The Privy Council, sitting in London, was the highest law court for Canada. Canada's trading was bound by the 1932 Ottawa Imperial Conference, which gave preferences to trade within the Commonwealth.

In terms of foreign policy, each dominion was independent. At the Dominion Conference of 1937, Canada and South Africa both showed their reluctance to be drawn again into any European war, and they backed British prime minister Neville Chamberlain's appeasement policy with Adolf Hitler. In fact, so isolationist was Canada's foreign policy during the late 1930's that Britain thought that Canada might opt out of any war against Germany. When Britain declared war at the beginning of September, 1939, all the Commonwealth countries followed suit. This involved fifty territories and more than one-fourth of the world's population.

Entry into World War II During the first half of the 1940's, Canada and Great Britain were bound to each other as allies in World War II, rather than Canada being subordinate. Canada supplied manpower, money, and munitions for the British war effort, and its army fought alongside British armies, as did its air force, the Royal Canadian Air Force (RCAF), and its navy, the Royal Canadian Navy (RCN).

British naval power had been decreased during the 1930's as part of the Lausanne Agreement, whereby all naval powers were urged, in the interests of peace, to reduce their navies. The war brought Canada and Britain closer in general, but it also showed Canadians that they no longer could rely on British naval power to defend them. This led Canada to develop the third largest navy in the world by the end of the war, as well as to enter into joint defense treaties with the United States, most notably through the Ogdensburg Declaration of August, 1940.

Canada declared war on Germany one week after the British, on September 10, 1939. At the time, its military consisted of fewer than ten thousand active members, a low point in its forces, so that it was not immediately able to render manpower. The Canadian government, under Prime Minister William Lyon Mackenzie King, promised no conscription, though this promise was revoked in 1944. So strong was the volunteer system that by the end of the war, out of a total population of 12 million, some 1.5 million Canadians had served in the military.

Canada could offer Britain several forms of assistance immediately. One was sanctuary for children whose parents wished them evacuated from Britain. This continued until September, 1940, when the sinking by Germany of a ship carrying children put an end to such transatlantic crossings.

Canada also set up the British Commonwealth Air Training Plan, whereby pilots went to Canada to be trained. Some 120,000 personnel eventually passed through this facility.

Units of the Canadian Army and RCAF began arriving in Britain by Christmas, 1939, but a full buildup of the Canadian First Army took several years to achieve. Not until the spring of 1943 was it at the full strength of two corps of five divisions each and a further two independent tank brigades. The Canadian Second Division was in place by the summer of 1940, and after the Dunkirk debacle, Canadians represented one of the most organized fighting forces ready to defend Britain from invasion.

At first, individual Canadian crews and planes served with the British Royal Air Force (RAF), but soon an autonomous Canadian Air Group was flying with Bomber Command. Individual Canadians, however, continued to fly with the RAF until the end of the war.

Battle of the Atlantic The greatest Canadian military assistance during the first several years of the

Troops in the first Canadian army division to go to France to join the British Expedition Force wave farewell as their ship leaves an English port. (Popperfoto/Getty Images)

British war effort was performed by the RCN the Battle of the Atlantic. Both the United States and Canada began supplying vast quantities of ammunitions, food, oil, and personnel across the Atlantic in merchant ships. These ships were under constant threat from German raiders and submarines. By 1942, losses had become so great that the very survival of Britain was threatened.

The RCN and the United States Navy began working with the British Royal Navy (RN) to protect supply ships and to sink the German attack boats. A convoy system was introduced and defense techniques became refined, until by May, 1943, German submarines were ordered out of the Atlantic. The Canadian port of Halifax was crucial, especially when sunk vessels hindered the St. Lawrence passage. Many convoys began there, being escorted by RCN vessels first to Newfoundland, then across to Iceland, where the RN assumed their defense. RCAF planes, based primarily at Gander, Newfoundland, flew defensive sorties over the western Atlantic, while the RAF covered the eastern half. By 1944, the RCN was doing much of the convoy work in the mid-Atlantic.

Canada also contributed by increasing its ship-building capacity enormously. It produced merchant ships to replace those sunk, as well as corvettes and other naval ships to help patrol the convoys. Canada provided the RN with more than twenty corvettes and destroyers, more than sixty minesweepers, and many smaller craft.

Supplies and Financial Assistance Before the United States began its lend-lease program to supply military hardware to the British and other Allied forces, Canadian supplies played an especially crucial role. In fact, by the end of the war, Canada had supplied one-seventh of the total Commonwealth war production. Its financial contribution to Great Britain was second only to that of the United States, totaling some $4 billion. By the fall of 1941, Canada's bank balance in London had grown so large, for payments from Britain for war materials and services, that the Canadian government under Prime Minister King converted most of it into a $700 million interest-free loan, to be used to purchase further Canadian goods and supplies. In January, 1942, Canada gave munitions and supplies valued at about $1 billion to Great Britain. When British credit finally ran out in 1943, Canada donated its surplus production to the Allies through the Canadian Mutual Aid Board; some $1.25 billion worth went to Britain.

By the end of the war, Britain owed Canada huge amounts of money. In 1946, Canada forgave Britain its war debt. This was on top of a loan of $1.25 billion made at the end of the war.

Military Action   As the Canadian military built up to full strength in Great Britain, its members became impatient to see action, an impatience shared by the Canadian government. This led to two early ill-fated ventures. First, a unit was sent to Britain's Hong Kong garrison to defend it against the Japanese. The garrison fell within a matter of weeks, with many Canadian casualties. The second involved substitution of Canadian units for British ones in the Dieppe raid of August, 1942. This raid, intended to test out German defenses on the coast of northern France, was ill-planned and the German defenses underestimated, again resulting in heavy losses of Canadian troops.

A better experience occurred when the Canadian Third Division was substituted for British forces in the invasion of Sicily. The Canadian units were always under Canadian leadership, sometimes creating difficulties with the Allied command. The Third Division continued with the British Eighth Army into Italy and was withdrawn only when the Normandy D-day landings became imminent.

During these landings, in June, 1944, the Canadian army under General H. D. G. Crerar was able to fight at full force. One of the five landing beaches, Juno, was under Canadian control. Canadian units were mainly responsible for capturing Caen, and then moving along the northern French coast to take the ports of le Havre, Boulogne, and Dieppe. The RCAF mustered some sixteen squadrons for the invasion.

The First Canadian Army continued fighting along the Belgian coast in November to the Scheldt estuary between the Belgian and Dutch borders. In the spring of 1945, it took part in the crossing of the Rhine, continuing to fight under the overall leadership of British field marshal Bernard Montgomery, then returning to Holland to clear the rest of that country from German forces.

The Postwar Period   Canada's rapid economic growth during the war resulted in a changed status for it in the emerging new world order. As an independent nation, it became a founding member of the United Nations and the North Atlantic Treaty Organization. Its ties with Britain became more those of equals, rather than of subordinate to superior. Canada's own Supreme Court became the country's highest law court, rather than Britain's Privy Council.

Canadian troops returned home, along with tens of thousands of war brides from Britain. Other migrants from Britain followed, including many with specific skills who perceived diminished employment prospects and a limited future in Britain's shattered economy.

As a member of the British Commonwealth, Canada attended the meetings of Commonwealth prime ministers. Only one, in May, 1944, was held during the war years, to discuss postwar prospects and the future of the Commonwealth. The April, 1945, meeting of Commonwealth statesmen discussed the peace terms. Further meetings in 1948 and 1949 decided to allow republics into the Commonwealth, even those that did not acknowledge the British monarch as head of state, such as India.

Some Commonwealth institutions took longer to reestablish. For example, the British Empire Games, which had been inaugurated in Canada in 1930, were not reconvened until 1950, when they were held at Auckland, New Zealand.

Newfoundland   The Dominion of Newfoundland and Labrador, established in 1907, was not originally a part of Canada, instead being a dominion of the British Empire. In 1935, it reverted to being a British colony. In 1949, when its status came up for review, a referendum was held to choose between continuing as a British dependency, becoming part of the Dominion of Canada, or joining the United States. Labour Party leader Joey Smallwood campaigned vigorously for the Canadian connection. After his successful campaign, he became the first leader of the province of Newfoundland as it was transferred from British to Canadian sovereignty. The province was renamed in 2001 as Newfoundland and Labrador.

Impact   The 1940's were a period of tremendous transition for Canada as a world power. Nowhere was this more clearly seen than in its relationship with its former mother country, Britain. By the end of the war, Canada was much more prosperous and no longer needed British tutelage. Its economic development derived primarily from capital and trade with the United States rather than from British ties. The British relationship nevertheless continued to be important in defining a Canadian identity separate from its relationship with the United States.

David Barratt

Further Reading

Buckner, Phillip. *Canada and the British Empire.* New York: Oxford University Press, 2008. Part of the Oxford History of the British Empire Companion Series. Chapter 6 is titled "Canada and the End of Empire, 1939-1982." Other chapters deal with immigration patterns from Britain and the relationship between the Canadian and British legal systems.

Douglas, W. A. B., and Brereton Greenhous. *Out of the Shadows: Canada in the Second World War.* New York: Oxford University Press, 1977. Full account of Canada's development during the war, including its relationship with Britain.

Granatstein, J. L., and Desmond Morton. *A Nation Forged in Fire: Canadians and the Second World War, 1939-1945.* Toronto: Lester and Orpen Dennys, 1989. A detailed account of Canada's emergence as a powerful nation and the impact on its citizens. Granatstein is a leading Canadian modern historian.

Jackson, Ashley. *The British Empire and the Second World War.* New York: Hambledon Continuum, 2006. Chapter 5 deals fully with Canada's war effort, especially in and after the Battle of the Atlantic, and Canada's relationship with the British war effort.

See, Scott W. *The History of Canada.* Westport, Conn.: Greenwood Press, 2001. Part of the Greenwood Histories of the Modern Nations. Chapters 7 and 8 deal with the 1940's and include extensive coverage of relationships with Britain.

See also   Atlantic, Battle of the; Business and the economy in Canada; Canadian participation in World War II; Churchill, Winston; Foreign policy of Canada; Immigration to Canada; King, William Lyon Mackenzie; Military conscription in Canada.

■ Canadian Citizenship Act of 1946

The Law   First Canadian legislation that provided a legal basis for citizenship

Date   Enacted on June 27, 1946; came into effect on January 1, 1947

The passage of Canada's first citizenship act marked Canada's move away from British common law, since it recognized Canadian citizenship as separate from British subjecthood. The act was intended to create a sense of national unity and political participation among the ethnically diverse peoples of Canada.

Paul Joseph James Martin, secretary of state under Prime Minister William Lyon Mackenzie King, introduced his Canadian Citizenship bill in the House of Commons on March 20, 1946, arguing that it would lead all Canadians to share an interest in the future of the country at home and abroad. This notion was particularly important, as Canada was emerging from World War II as a middle power trying to create an identity beyond its membership in the British Empire. The new act replaced earlier legislation regarding immigration and naturalization—namely, the Immigration Act of 1910, the Naturalization Act of 1914, and the Canadian Nationals Act of 1921. Martin initially argued that Canadian citizenship should replace British subjecthood, but the cabinet refused such a radical move; instead, the Citizenship Act held that all Canadian citizens would automatically be considered British subjects as well.

Legal Changes   Prior to 1947, the concept of Canadian citizenship existed only under the realm of immigration law, and it was used primarily to distinguish Canadian residents from aliens. For purposes of census, people identified themselves using hyphenation (for example, English-Canadian, Chinese-Canadian, and so on). The Immigration Act of 1910 defined three categories of citizens: those born in Canada who had not become aliens; British subjects who lived in Canada; and naturalized Canadians.

The Citizenship Act of 1946 bestowed citizenship upon these three groups and also allowed non-British subjects to apply for citizenship. Applicants had to meet four basic criteria: be at least twenty-one years of age; have at least five years of residency in Canada; have an understanding of Canadian citizenship; and have an adequate knowledge of English or French. This last criterion was softened from previous legislation so that those who did not meet the language requirement but had twenty years residency in Canada could also become citizens. The act also allowed British subjects two additional privileges: They could vote in Canadian elections after only one year of residency, and after five years of residency they could become citizens without seeing a citizenship judge. In addition, the act addressed gender bias in previous laws relating to immigration and naturalization status in Canada by treating women as independent from their husbands.

Social Changes The first week of 1947 was declared National Citizenship Week, and citizenship ceremonies were held in major cities across Canada during January. Speakers at these ceremonies emphasized the unifying potential of citizenship, which would draw together people of differing ethnic backgrounds under the umbrella of "Canadian." The most famous speech from these ceremonies, known as the Gray Lecture, occurred in Toronto on January 13, 1947, when Louis St. Laurent, then secretary of state for international affairs, eloquently explained that national unity within Canada would allow its people to better participate in world affairs, leaving partisan affiliations aside to present a united front.

Many of the ceremonies introducing the new legislation were deliberately orchestrated to highlight the diversity of Canada's new citizenry. For example, the national ceremony in Ottawa gave the first certificate of citizenship to Prime Minister King and the second to Wasyl Eleniak, a Ukranian farmer. As for ceremonies in smaller cities, transcripts from the Winnipeg celebration show certificates being presented to three groups: people not born in Canada and not previously British subjects, who were encouraged to retain their cultural traditions to make Canada stronger; naturalized Canadians or British subjects; and Canadian-born people.

Impact The passage of the Citizenship Act of 1946 led other countries in the British Commonwealth to follow Canada and adopt their own laws of citizenship, including the United Kingdom's British Nationality Act of 1948. The Citizenship Act was also an important intermediate step for Canada to move beyond its historically racist practices in which American, British, and Western European immigrants were highly preferred, while those of Asian descent often faced discrimination. The year 1947 also saw the repeal of the Chinese Immigration Act, which had prohibited entry to some, charged a head tax on others, and denied even longtime Chinese residents of Canada the right to vote. In 1951, Canada allowed the immigration of dependents of nonwhite Canadian citizens, and in 1962 it removed discrimination based on national and ethnic origin, although many argue that such bias continued to occur. It was not until passage of the Citizenship Act of 1977 that all biases based on gender and country of origin were removed from Canada's citizenship law.

Pamela Bedore

Further Reading

Brown, Robert Craig. "Full Partnership in the Fortunes and in the Future of the Nation." In *Ethnicity and Citizenship: The Canadian Case*, edited by Jean Laponce and William Safran. London: Frank Cass, 1996. Informative essay traces the legislative history of immigration, citizenship, and voting rights for different ethnic groups within Canada.

Chapnick, Adam. "The Gray Lecture and Canadian Citizenship in History." *American Review of Canadian Studies* 37, no. 4 (2007): 443-457. Highly readable article summarizes Louis St. Laurent's famous speech on the Citizenship Act and traces resulting media and scholarly responses to the speech.

Kaplan, William, ed. *Belonging: The Meaning and Future of Canadian Citizenship*. Montreal: McGill-Queen's University Press, 1993. Excellent collection of essays about historical, regional, legal, and social issues surrounding Canadian citizenship, including an essay by Paul Joseph James Martin, who initially introduced the Canadian Citizenship bill in 1946.

Korneski, Kurt. "Citizenship Ceremony, 10 January 1947." *Manitoba History* 51 (February, 2006): 34-39. Transcript of a citizenship ceremony in Winnipeg, with useful introductory notes. Speakers reference the political and social impacts of the Citizenship Act.

Saufert, Stacey A. "*Taylor v. Canada* (Minister of Citizenship and Immigration): Discrimination, Due Process, and the Origins of Citizenship in Canada." *Alberta Law Review* 45, no. 2 (2007): 521-536. A legal analysis of a specific citizenship case that provides an applied history of Canadian legislation regarding immigration and citizenship.

See also   Canadian nationalism; Demographics of Canada; Foreign policy of Canada; Immigration Act of 1943; Immigration to Canada; King, William Lyon Mackenzie; St. Laurent, Louis.

■ Canadian minority communities

Multicultural Canada is often characterized as a nation of immigrants, with the stipulation that First Nations (Canadian Indians) and Inuit peoples were the earliest residents of the area. By 1941, the proportion of non-British and non-French immigrants had reached almost 19 percent, demonstrating the multigenerational histories of many contemporary Canadian minority groups.

At the start of the 1940's, Canada was already enmeshed in World War II; Prime Minister William Lyon Mackenzie King had declared war on Germany on September 10, 1939. Because of the war, immigration to the nation slowed significantly relative to previous decades, although immigration also had been low in the 1930's because of the Great Depression (1929-1939 in Canada). By 1941, the people of Canada were mainly native English speakers (50 percent classified themselves as European of British origin) or French speakers (30 percent of French origin). At the time, the population (numbering 11.5 million) was 98 percent derived from Europe, as a result of racially restrictive immigration policies.

Canadian immigration guidelines were laid out in the Immigration Act of 1910, which was revised in 1919, at the end of World War I, to keep enemy nationals out of Canada. By 1923, increased preference for selected source nations was declared by the federal Order in Council P.C. 183, specifically Britain, the United States, the Irish Free State, the Dominion of Newfoundland and Labrador (which became the Canadian province of Newfoundland on March 31, 1949), Australia, New Zealand, and South Africa. Some private initiatives continued to recruit non-preferred nationals, as long as they were farmers or domestic workers. All immigration to Canada, with the exception of British and American citizens, was abruptly halted with the passage of Order in Council P.C. 695 in 1931. This legislation prevailed until 1947.

Given these restrictive policies and the challenges of wartime travel, few immigrants disembarked in Canada. From 1940 to 1944, a meager 21,800 new settlers arrived, mostly women and children of British or Irish ancestry. Few Jews were provided with sanctuary during this time period, and a mere 1,900 Jews immigrated to Canada, although there was a sizable Jewish community already in the country, located mainly in Montreal and Toronto.

The largest minority group was German (464,682 people recorded in the 1941 Canadian census), followed by Ukrainians (303,929), Dutch (212,863), Jews (170,241), Poles (167,485), Italians (112,625), and Norwegians (100,718). Other ethnic communities numbered less than 90,000 each. First Nations and Inuit populations were enumerated at 125,521 people, only 1.2 percent of Canadian residents.

First Nations, Inuit, and Metis   Canadian aboriginal communities were governed by the Indian Act of 1876, which defined their status, ensuing rights, and the goals of federal policy—basically to assimilate them into mainstream Canadian society, with scant recognition of the value of their practices or beliefs. Numerous amendments to the act occurred over the years, with the final revision prior to the 1940's taking place in 1930. All of these amendments were designed to promote assimilation.

The Inuit were not mentioned in the Indian Act, and federal interest in the Canadian Arctic developed only during World War II and later, during the Cold War. National legislation involving the Inuit was a product of post-1950's events. Another group excluded from the Indian Act was the Metis, the descendants of Canadian Indian women and European settler men. They lived primarily in the southern Prairie Provinces, although many also were found along many of the principal fur-trading rivers in western Canada and in the northern United States. In 1938, the provincial government of Alberta passed the Métis Population Betterment Act, which formally established twelve regions of Metis settlement and provided a template for community self-government. Within three years, the province had assumed governing control of these settlements, including resource extraction, meaning that the Metis were treated much like the Indians through the 1940's.

Despite disheartening national and provincial legislation governing their lives, many aboriginal people volunteered to fight for Canada in World War II. By the war's end, more than two hundred First Nations soldiers had died, of the more than three thousand who enlisted. They fought in all the major battles and received high military honors, but this did not translate into better treatment once back home in Canada.

The provincial and federal decrees, or lack thereof in the case of the Inuit, did little to alleviate the grinding poverty of most aboriginal communities. Prejudice against First Nations people was rampant, most chillingly demonstrated by the residential schools, established under the auspices of the Indian Act but founded and run by various Christian denominations. Children were forcibly removed from their families and enrolled in the schools, where they were required to speak English or French (resulting in loss of their traditional language), cut their hair (which often had ritual significance), and abandon their cultural beliefs and prac-

tices. Some more modern thinking considers these boarding schools to be tools of cultural genocide.

In addition to treating First Nations people harshly, the Canadian government also has a poor human rights record regarding its dealings with Asian immigrants in general during the pre-1950's period, and with Japanese Canadians in particular during the 1940's.

Internment of Japanese Canadians   Canada has a long history of denying Asian peoples immigration opportunities, and several early twentieth century policies continued this trend. In 1907, Japanese immigration to Canada was limited to 450 people annually (usually women moving to live with their resident husbands), and even that maximum was not achieved most years. In 1928, the quota was decreased to only 150 Japanese immigrants per year.

At a slightly earlier date, the Chinese Immigration Act of 1923 was passed, remaining in force until 1947. This meant that only fifteen Chinese people are reported as immigrating legally to Canada between 1923 and 1947, although Chinese immigrants had been instrumental in constructing the Canadian Pacific Railway four decades earlier. Anti-Asian sentiment was widespread along the western seacoast in both the United States and Canada, and both nations experienced anti-Asian riots in the early part of the twentieth century.

Despite these high levels of discrimination, by 1941, there were 34,627 Chinese community members living in Canada, along with 23,149 Japanese. In the spring of that same year, the government reacted to wartime uncertainties by ordering the Royal Canadian Mounted Police (RCMP) to register all Japanese Canadians age sixteen and older.

The Canadian Japanese situation became dramatically worse when the Japanese attacked Pearl Harbor, Hawaii, on December 7, 1941. By evening of that day, Prime Minister King (who governed Canada from 1935 to 1948) had declared war on Japan. The

Eskimos living on Baffin Island greeting a U.S. Navy patrol plane that has landed in the water. (AP/Wide World Photos)

passage of the War Measures Act, Order in Council P.C. 9591, required that Japanese nationals and Japanese Canadians of less than twenty years Canadian (technically, British subject) citizenship enroll with the Registrar of Enemy Aliens. Almost immediately, the government impounded 1,200 Japanese fishing boats, closed schools, and shut down newspapers. By December 16, 1941, all Japanese with Canadian citizenship had to register themselves.

Most Japanese Canadians lived in western British Columbia. Within a few weeks of the federal declaration of war, the government removed them from the western coastal regions and assigned families to camps located in interior British Columbia or the western Prairie Provinces. By February, 1942, approximately 22,000 Japanese Canadians and Japanese nationals were residing in Canadian detention camps. Three-fourths of these people were either naturalized citizens or born in Canada. All of them had their home, land, and possessions sold by the government to pay for their internment.

Victory in Europe (or V-E Day) was May 8, 1945, and V-J Day (Victory in Japan Day, of greater significance to Japanese Canadians) occurred on August 15, 1945. By the end of the war, Japan was in shambles and its people impoverished. The Canadian government legislated that Japanese Canadians were to be released from the camps but forced to choose between either residing in Canada east of the Rocky Mountains or departing for Japan. A year later, the federal government tried to forcibly deport 10,000 Japanese Canadians, but massive protests prevented this step. It was not until April 1, 1949, that Japanese Canadians managed to regain their lost citizenship rights.

Postwar Legislation and Immigration Canada became more prosperous after World War II, and unemployment gradually decreased from the prewar years, resulting in government debate about immigration needs. Discussion also increased on an international level about how to assist the massive population of displaced persons, many of them living in displaced persons camps in Europe under horrendous conditions.

The federal government issued Order in Council P.C. 3112 on July 23, 1946, designed to allow the immigration of displaced persons. From 1947 to 1948, Canada admitted only 14,250 displaced persons, but the following year this figure rose to 50,610. Among

these immigrants were few Jews; lower numbers immigrated to Canada than to the United States or to Australia. It seems likely that anti-Semitism played some role, despite the fact that returning servicemen had brought stories about the European atrocities back to Canada and Canada had signed the United Nations' Universal Declaration of Human Rights.

Many returning servicemen also brought home wives, and approximately 48,000 war brides immigrated to Canada. These higher levels of immigration and increased Canadian diversity failed to translate into national legislation to diminish discrimination against minority community members. The provincial level saw progress, however, with passage of the Saskatchewan Bill of Rights Act in 1947, which opposed discrimination based on race and religion. Earlier legislation in other provinces had lacked enforcement, and the Saskatchewan legislation was also problematic in this regard, because few prosecutions resulted.

On January 1, 1947, the Canadian Citizenship Act of the previous year changed the legal definition of Canadians from "British subjects" to "Canadian citizens." This change in terminology did not dramatically alter the reality of citizenship for most Canadians but instead merely increased nationalist sentiments.

Later in the year, Prime Minister King publicly announced that renewed immigration was important and that government immigration policy would continue to support the ethnic mixture already present in Canada. This initiative continued the emphasis on immigration from English-speaking Europe, and it was not until Order in Council P.C. 4186 passed in 1948 that French moneyed immigrants could also move to Canada. Certainly, the strength of King's statement, and the ensuing legislation, is borne out by the 1951 census, which documented that the most sizable ethnic group in Canada was now German (with a population of 619,995 people), followed by Ukrainians (395,043), Dutch (264,267), and Poles (219,845), with communities of Jews, Italians, and Norwegians each numbering more than 100,000. These minority communities all predated World War II.

Impact The 1940's were characterized by national policies encouraging English-speaking immigrants, with lower levels of French speakers, and some admixture from selected European nations. The First

Nations, Inuit, and Metis communities remained small, with their cultural influence largely unrecognized or downplayed. True multiculturalism did not occur in Canada until more recently.

Susan J. Wurtzburg

Further Reading

Bothwell, Robert, Ian Drummond, and John English. *Canada, 1900-1945*. Toronto: University of Toronto Press, 2003. Social, economic, and political history of Canada covering events up to and including World War II.

_____. *Canada Since 1945*. Rev. ed. Toronto: University of Toronto Press, 2006. Social, economic, and political history of Canada covering the period after the end of World War II.

Howe, R. Brian. "The Evolution of Human Rights Policy in Ontario." *Canadian Journal of Political Science* 24, no. 4 (1991): 783-802. History of human rights in Ontario, with relevant details on the 1940's.

Iacovetta, Franca, with Paula Draper and Robert Ventresca, eds. *A Nation of Immigrants: Readings in Canadian History, 1840s-1960s*. Toronto: University of Toronto Press, 2006. Compilation of relevant works for understanding Canadian minority communities.

Minister of Supplies and Services Canada. *The Canadian Family Tree: Canada's Peoples*. Don Mills, Ontario: Corpus Information Services, 1979. Written in a simple manner, but a wonderful resource for the different minority communities and their populations in the 1940's.

Shewell, Hugh E. Q. *"Enough to Keep Them Alive": Indian Social Welfare in Canada, 1873-1965*. Toronto: University of Toronto Press, 2004. Archival data and interviews applied to an interpretation of federal government policy directed toward American Indian communities.

Sugiman, Pamela. "Memories of Internment: Narrating Japanese Canadian Women's Life Stories." *The Canadian Journal of Sociology* 29, no. 3 (2004): 359-388. Personal experiences combined with historical documents about the 1940's internment of Japanese Canadian families.

See also Canadian Citizenship Act of 1946; Demographics of Canada; Immigration to Canada; Japanese Canadian internment; Jews in Canada; Native Americans; Racial discrimination; Refugees in North America; Universal Declaration of Human Rights.

■ Canadian nationalism

Definition Canadian popular sentiment about the country as an independent entity developed during the decade from a previously widely held colonial mentality

During the 1940's, Canadian nationalism moved beyond simply seeking distinction as a strong and meaningful part of the British Empire, and as a North American entity not to be overshadowed by the United States.

Canadian nationalism during the 1940's embraced the landscape of Canada and tried to fashion an independent cultural tradition. Paradoxically, it also expressed itself through internationalism, by participation in the United Nations and its peacekeeping mission. The two extant strains of Canadian nationalism morphed in such a way as to make them viable for the remainder of the twentieth century.

One part of traditional nationalism emphasized differentiation from the United States. That perspective was wary of the liberalism and free market individualism of the United States, and during the 1940's it also sought to distance Canada from what some saw as the United States' overbearing sense of purpose as the new leader of the Western world. Another element of nationalism was directed toward federative imperialism. It moved from an emphasis on cooperation among the English-speaking peoples to a worldwide outreach, often expressing itself in sympathy for newly independent nations, such as those that emerged in the late 1940's in Asia, and in its mediatory role in the Commonwealth of Nations that replaced the British Empire in 1947.

The 1940's saw Canada establish large-scale diplomatic representation abroad. Canadians no longer had to go through Britain to make a difference in the world. This was expressed in the career of Charles Ritchie, a young Canadian diplomat whose diaries of his time in London during the 1940's are among the important literary documents of the era. Ritchie could have had a career in Britain, where he had many contacts in the cultural and political establishments, but he returned to Canada after the war.

World War II saw an upsurge in a sense of Canadian national identity. Military efforts in which Canadian troops were heavily involved, such as the failed 1942 amphibious assault on the Belgian town of Dieppe and the deployment of Canadian troops on Juno beach on D Day, gave Canada a sense of pride and accomplishment distinct from that of the general Anglo-American war effort. Nationalism, though, also had its problematic side, as evidenced by the internment of Japanese Canadians on the west coast out of a fear that they would engage in sabotage on behalf of Japan.

Another manifestation of growing nationalism was the change of the Dominion of Newfoundland to a Canadian province in 1949. The change provided a sense that Canada was at last complete. The accession of Newfoundland meant Canada now had more direct access to the Atlantic and thereby was truly qualified to belong to the North Atlantic Treaty Organization (NATO), the anticommunist alliance formed in 1949. Another reason that Canadian possession of Newfoundland was seen as important was that the United States had established wartime military bases there.

Impact   Wartime cooperation meant new closeness to the United States. Rhetoric of nationalism helped mask that closer interdependence yet also enabled Canada to more confidently participate in it. Nationalism also enabled Canada to feel a growing sense of coherence and overall identity that assisted it in forging a distinct identity in the postwar years.

Nicholas Birns

Further Reading

Blake, Raymond B. *Canadians at Last: Canada Integrates Newfoundland as a Province.* Toronto: University of Toronto Press, 1994.

Cook, Ramsay. *Canada, Quebec, and the Uses of Nationalism.* Toronto: McClelland & Stewart, 1995.

Granatstein, J. L. *Yankee Go Home? Canadians and Anti-Americanism.* Toronto: HarperCollins, 1996.

Morton, Desmond, and J. L. Granatstein. *Victory 1945: The Birth of Modern Canada.* Toronto: HarperCollins, 1995.

Ritchie, Charles. *Undiplomatic Diaries, 1937-1971.* Toronto: Emblem, 2008.

See also   Canada and Great Britain; Canadian Citizenship Act of 1946; Canadian participation in World War II; Canadian regionalism; Dieppe raid; Education in Canada; Foreign policy of Canada; Literature in Canada; Quebec nationalism.

■ Canadian participation in World War II

As a long-standing dominion of the British Commonwealth, Canada joined England in declaring war against Germany in September, 1939. Canada's contributions helped turn the tide in major military campaigns.

Until the actual onset of World War II, the Canadian government was reluctant to commit funds to reequip and modernize its army, particularly costly armored tank units. The air force was also ill equipped to meet the needs that arose once war was declared against the Axis. Beginning with very few ships capable of meeting the demands of transoceanic deployment, the Canadian navy grew to more than four hundred vessels by the end of World War II.

Prewar Military Strength and Buildup   Canada's state of military preparedness held little promise for early major participation in the Allied war effort. Canada's only standing military force in 1939 (the Permanent Active Militia) contained slightly more than 4,000 men, including officers. Although a force of about 51,000 reservists (the Non-Permanent Active Militia) existed prior to the war, it lacked significant equipment and advanced training for combat.

For several years after the beginning of the war, Canada was able to field only a single division (usually numbering between 15,000 and 30,000 soldiers) for service in Europe. These numbers reached the strength of the corps level (combined forces of two or more divisions) by 1943, when First Corps (I Canadian Corps) forces were deployed for the first time in a major European campaign during the Allied invasion of Italy. Mobilization efforts through 1944 eventually brought enlistments to about 1.1 million, nearly three-quarters of whom joined the army. The air force reached 260,000 members, and 115,000 joined the Canadian navy.

During the early years of the war, most of the Canadian forces remained on home soil; they joined major campaigns in 1943 and 1944 with the aim of dislodging Nazi Germany from Western Europe. Canadians joined the buildup of Allied forces needed to meet that task, amassing a total of five divisions stationed in England just prior to the D-day invasion of France in 1944.

Early Battle Participation   The first involvement of Canadian forces in the European theater of war

Pilots training in radio communication at the elementary flying school in Ontario in October, 1941. (AP/Wide World Photos)

ended unsuccessfully. Operation Jubilee (better known as the ill-fated Dieppe raid) in August of 1942 involved landing several thousand soldiers from the Second Canadian Division, together with 1,000 British commando forces, on the coast of France near the key port city of Dieppe. Even though the landing troops had substantial support from both the air and the sea, German defenses were able to repel the raid, killing more than 1,000 soldiers and capturing more than 2,300.

The Dieppe raid, however, provided important intelligence information regarding the nature of German coastal defenses, information that was later used to plan the 1944 D-day invasion. The initial setback at Dieppe stood out in contrast to the impressive accomplishments of Canadian forces in two later stages of the European conflict, first during the Allied invasion of Sicily (Operation Husky) in July,

1943, followed by operations on the Italian mainland, and then during and following the D-day landings in France in 1944.

The troops that fought in Italy included forces from the First Canadian Division, tanks from the Fifth Canadian Armored Division, and an additional armored brigade. Canadians fought alongside other Allied forces in several key battles during the Italian campaign, notably in the Moro River campaign, the battle to take the coastal zone around Ortona (Chieti Province) and, in May, 1944, the important advance that broke the so-called "Hitler Line" of defense in central Italy between the coast and the Aurunci Mountains. This campaign, which was a joint operation involving the British Eighth Army, the First Canadian Infantry Division, the Fifth Canadian Armored Division, and Polish forces, played a key role in the advance toward the liberation of Rome in June, 1944.

D-day Operations The Third Canadian Division, technically still under the command of the British First Army Corps, participated in the June 6, 1944, Allied invasion of Normandy on D Day. The Canadians landed on Juno Beach, situated between the main British landing points at Sword Beach and Gold Beach (all code names assigned by the Allies). In the first stages of combat, the Canadians suffered important casualties, about 1,000 killed or injured.

Once their assigned beachhead was secured, the Canadian forces moved inland with the goal of linking up with British forces advancing from the Sword Beach landing site. Their progress inland on D Day outpaced all other Allied forces, bringing them to the main road connecting Bayeux to the provincial capital of Caen. That city had been identified by British field marshal Bernard Law Montgomery as key to the overall success of the Normandy invasion. Even though the Canadian push was reinforced by other troops (notably by American forces that had landed at Omaha and Utah Beaches), fierce German resistance meant that the city would not fall for another month.

Operations After D Day Once Allied forces succeeded in liberating most of France, an enormous task still lay ahead: pushing the Germans back past the Rhine River and defeating Adolf Hitler on his own ground. Canadian responsibilities during these later stages of the war were critical and were carried out mostly independently, without the joint command structure that had characterized earlier operations.

A key example of this was the famous Battle of the Scheldt, which was part of the drive to liberate Belgium and the Netherlands in the last months of 1944. Although British forces captured the major Belgian port of Antwerp on the Rhine, the strategic river delta separating Antwerp from the North Sea (the Scheldt) remained in German hands. The job of occupying the Scheldt fell to the First Canadian Army, whose forces attacked several key German strongholds, particularly at the Leopold Canal on the Scheldt's southern zone, and in the zone of the Beveland Canal. By the time German forces lost control of the Scheldt (on November 8, 1944), it was clear that one key to the success of Canadian troops was the work of engineers, especially those who built bridges that enabled infantry forces (principally the Sixth Canadian Infantry Brigade) to advance where

amphibious attacks had tried, but failed, to break German defense lines. The cost of this offensive was great: By the time the ports were cleared on November 8, after five weeks of fighting, nearly thirteen thousand Allied forces were killed, wounded, or missing, about half of them Canadian.

During what would be called the Rhineland campaign in the first months of 1945, Canadian forces were responsible for a battle line of about 360 kilometers (about 220 miles) running from the Maas River (called the Meuse in France, where it has its origins before joining the Rhine) to Dunkirk near the French-Belgian Flemish border. In an initial stage of the Rhineland campaign (starting February 8), Allied forces, including nine British divisions (plus Belgian, Polish, Dutch, and U.S. units) were under the command of General H. D. G. Crerar of the First Canadian Army. Moving toward the strategic German defense zone of the Reichswald forest (much of which had been flooded when the Germans destroyed an entire network of dikes), these forces had to rely heavily on amphibious operations headed by the Canadian Third Division (known as the Water Rats).

The Rhineland campaign depended on the capture of major fortifications in the Hochwald forest, an operation (dubbed Blockbuster) that was carried out by the Second Canadian Corps between February 27 and March 3. The Canadians captured Xanten (just east of the Hochwald forest) on March 10, opening the way for the American Ninth Army to move into the area from the south. As the Germans retreated across the Rhine, the two main Allied forces, including major Canadian units, joined and were able to cross the Rhine. Germany's defeat in Western Europe became imminent.

Impact Canadian military forces expanded quickly from prewar levels to participate as a major part of the Allied war effort. By the D-day offensive of June, 1944, they were able to make significant contributions, and they continued to play large roles in major campaigns that brought down the German war effort.

Byron Cannon

Further Reading

Bryce, Robert B., and Matthew Bellamy. *Canada and the Cost of World War II: The International Operations of Canada's Department of Finance, 1939-1947.* Montreal: McGill-Queen's University Press, 2005. A detailed study of the use of eight years of appropriations earmarked for expanding Canada's military capacities, which initially were quite limited.

Halford, Robert G. *The Unknown Navy.* Saint Catharines, Ont.: Vanwell, 1994. The story of Canada's merchant marine fleet and its role in shipping vital wartime supplies across the Atlantic to Europe.

Nicholson, G. W. L. *The Canadians in Italy, 1943-1945.* Vol. 2 in *Official History of the Canadian Army in the Second World War.* Ottawa: Edmond Cloutier, Queen's Press, 1956. Detailed documentation of Canadian participation in the Italian campaign.

Stacey, C. P. *Arms, Men, and Governments: The War Policies of Canada, 1939-1945.* Ottawa: Queen's Printers, 1970. Concise overview of Canadian defense policy through World War II.

_____. *Official History of the Canadian Army in the Second World War.* 3 vols. Ottawa: Edmond Cloutier, Queen's Printer, 1955-1960. Definitive work on the Canadian army's operations through World War II.

Wilmot, Laurence F. *Through the Hitler Line.* Waterloo, Ont.: Wilfred Laurier University Press, 2003. Memoir of a Canadian participant in the important Italian campaign in May and June, 1944, that helped open the way to the liberation of Rome.

See also Canada and Great Britain; Canadian nationalism; Casualties of World War II; Foreign policy of Canada; Japanese Canadian internment; Military conscription in Canada; Wartime propaganda in Canada; World War II.

■ Canadian regionalism

Definition Sentiments and related actions concerning regional identity in various Canadian provinces and regions, particularly Quebec, Atlantic Canada, the prairies, and British Columbia

Canadian regionalism during the 1940's helped Canada became more of a nation, as the association of various regions and their identities reflected growing internal confidence and increasing commerce with the world.

Although in other eras of Canadian history, Canadian regionalism showed the potential to draw the country apart, the war effort and the rapid changes of the 1940's led to regional sentiments bolstering Canada's sense of itself as a coherent nation with a shared collective purpose. The most immediate manifestation of Canadian regionalism during the 1940's was the political posture of French-speaking Quebec.

The province was overwhelmingly dominated by English-speaking economic interests, but it was ruled politically by the Union Nationale, a conservative, French-speaking party aligned closely in sociocultural terms with rural farmers and with the Roman Catholic Church. The Union Nationale was neither separatist nor socialist; it challenged neither the unity of Canada nor the right of wealthy English-speakers in exclusive Montreal neighborhoods such as Westmont to dominate the province. What the Union Nationale insisted upon was preservation of the French cultural fabric of Quebec. It also had no strong sentiments concerning the British Empire and felt no urgency in defending and aiding Britain in World War II.

As during World War I, both the religious hierarchy and major labor and business groups in Quebec were opposed to conscription, even though France was a British ally and had been occupied by the Germans. Quebecers did not wish to fight for France, both because of France's original abandonment of Quebec in the 1763 Treaty of Paris and the republican and liberal character of prewar France, alien to the religious and generally conservative character of Quebec. Many Québécois sympathized with the agricultural and corporatist sympathies of the Vichy regime in France, although Quebec's political ideology contained little that came close to genuine fascism.

The Prairies and the Cooperative Commonwealth Federation The situation in Quebec was typical of that across Canada, with regional sentiment often expressed through the prism of a locally dominant political party or figure. In the Prairie Provinces (Alberta, Saskatchewan, and Manitoba), that force was most often the Cooperative Commonwealth Federation (CCF). The CCF was a consortium of small farmers who had banded together to oppose the large business combines and railroads, and had become a political party when existing liberal forces were insufficiently opposed to business interests. In the 1944 Saskatchewan elections, the CCF swept to power in the province under the leadership of the charismatic Tommy Douglas. His provincial government was the farthest left of center in Canadian history. The success of the CCF was an index of how internationalism and regional fostered each other, as the party was influenced by such American movements as Minnesota's Farmer-Labor Party and North Dakota's Nonpartisan League. Without the interaction across the U.S.-Canada border initiated by the wartime alliance, this influence would not have been so strongly felt.

Alberta and British Columbia   Saskatchewan's western neighbor, Alberta, produced a different kind of radical movement: the Social Credit Party. This operated out of a populist ideology that, unlike the ideology of the CCF, was not so much about mass mobilization of the disempowered but more about giving everyone a stake in the society, in this case by granting everyone a government payment of twenty-five dollars per year. Like the CCF, the Social Credit Party was a product of the Depression economy, but its ideology reflected Alberta's more individualistic and free market tendencies, as the money was given to everyone, to spend as they wanted. Regional political parties expressed already existing provincial ideologies but also served to establish a distinct provincial profile on the national scene.

Although the Social Credit Party later gained power in British Columbia as well, that province's most distinctive premier during the 1940's was Thomas Dufferin "Duff" Pattullo, who served from 1933 until 1941. The Scottish-descended Pattullo remained within the Canadian Liberal Party politically but advocated redistributionist and social-welfare measures not far from the ideology of the CCF. Under Pattullo and his successor, John Hart, a distinctly British Columbian version of liberalism was established. The province had already established a distinct identity, partially attributable to the strong indigenous presence and the visibility of native arts, which influenced such Anglo-Canadian painters as Emily Carr. Internationalization also contributed to regional sentiments, as the war—and specifically the Japanese attack on the Aleutians—led to the building of the ALCAN (Alaska) Highway, which brought British Columbians into far closer contact with their neighbors in both the continental United States and Alaska.

Impact   Even the so-called Laurentian heartland of Ontario and English-speaking Québec—long considered, along with Atlantic Canada, the Canadian

mainstream—sought regional expression during the 1940's. This is seen in Canadian literature, in the work of the rural Ontarian Mazo de la Roche, the Anglo-Quebecer John Glassco, and the Nova Scotians Thomas Raddall and Hugh McLennan. When Newfoundland joined Canada as a province in 1949, the nation genuinely achieved its ideal of confederation—regional diversity bolstering a national unity oriented toward internationalism, particularly the achievement of world peace, sorely desired after Canada's second grueling war of the century.

Nicholas Birns

Further Reading

Bell, David V. J. *The Roots of Disunity: A Study of Canadian Political Culture.* Toronto: Oxford University Press, 1992. Penetrating study of the divergent separatist forces within modern Canada.

Bothwell, Robert, Ian Drummond, and John English. *Canada, 1900-1945.* Toronto: University of Toronto Press, 2003. Social, economic, and political history of Canada covering events up to and including World War II.

_____. *Canada Since 1945: Power, Politics, and Provincialism.* Rev. ed. Toronto: University of Toronto Press, 1989. An informative account of Canadian political, economic, and cultural developments during the post-World War II years.

Bumsted, John, *A History of the Canadian Peoples.* New York: Oxford University Press, 2004. Useful and up-to-survey of the full sweep of Canadian history.

Fisher, Robin. *Duff Pattullo of British Columbia.* Toronto: University of Toronto Press, 1991. Biography of British Columbia's premier from 1933 to 1941.

Kaplan, William, ed. *Belonging: The Meaning and Future of Canadian Citizenship.* Montreal: McGill-Queen's University Press, 1993. Excellent collection of essays about historical, regional, legal, and social issues surrounding Canadian citizenship, including an essay by Paul Joseph James Martin, who initially introduced the Canadian Citizenship bill in 1946.

McCann, L. D., ed. *Heartland and Hinterland: A Geography of Canada.* Scarborough, Ont.: Prentice Hall, 1987. Discusses economic conditions, regional disparities, and underdevelopment in post-World War II period.

Quinn, Herbert Furlong, *The Union Nationale: Québec Nationalism from Duplessis to Lévesque.* Toronto:

University of Toronto Press, 1979. Examination of the half century of Quebec nationalism, from Maurice Le Noblet Duplessis's first term as provincial premier in the late 1930's up to the beginning of the era of René Lévesque, who was premier from 1976 to 1985.

Resnick, Philip. *The Politics of Resentment: British Columbia Regionalism and Canadian Unity.* Vancouver: University of British Columbia Press, 2000. Scholarly analysis of British Columbia's sometimes troubled relationship with the rest of Canada.

See, Scott W. *The History of Canada.* Westport, Conn.: Greenwood Press, 2001. Part of the Greenwood Histories of the Modern Nations. Chapters 7 and 8 deal with the 1940's and include extensive coverage of Canada's relationship with Great Britain.

See also Alaska Highway; Canada and Great Britain; Canadian minority communities; Canadian nationalism; Demographics of Canada; Elections in Canada; Foreign policy of Canada; Immigration to Canada; Newfoundland; Quebec nationalism; Religion in Canada.

■ Cancer

Definition Often fatal disease caused by abnormal cell growth that can invade and destroy normal healthy tissue

During the early twentieth century, cancer treatments were so few that five-year survival rates were virtually nonexistent. However, the 1940's saw a significant advancement in cancer research and treatment options. Five-year survival rates improved to approximately 25 percent during the 1940's, and significant discoveries using chemotherapies resulted in a new era of cancer treatments.

During the early twentieth century, cancer diagnoses were often equivalent to death sentences. Folk remedies, surgery, and radiation treatments were the only available medical options in the cancer treatment. However, the 1940's ushered in a new era of cancer research and treatment options, and chemotherapy emerged as a promising and effective cancer treatment. The German scientist Paul Ehrlich was the first to discover that some altered chemical compounds could cure disease during the early twentieth century. The medicines colchicine, arsenic, and urethane exhibited mild antitumor effects, but the connection between chemical compounds and future cancer treatments was not apparent. Advancement in the use of chemical compounds as a treatment option for cancer became clear during World War II.

Mustard Gas Research During World War I (1914-1918), the Germans had introduced the poisonous compounds chlorine gas and mustard gas as weapons of warfare. By the end of World War I, casualties attributed to these gases would account for approximately 1.3 million deaths. In 1919, the research scientist Edward Kumbhaar studied the effects of mustard gas. Autopsies on soldiers exposed to that gas showed toxic effects on bone marrow, in which human blood cells are formed, causing initial increases in white blood cell counts followed by rapid declines. Exposure to mustard gas caused bone marrow cells to be completely destroyed, severely compromising the victims' immunity to infections. Those who survived mustard gas attacks developed cancer over time.

While the effects of World War I's poisonous gases were devastating, there was also a silver lining. As World War II became imminent during the late 1930's, the Office of Scientific Research and Development of the U.S. government contracted with Yale University to investigate chemical warfare agents. In 1942, Louis S. Goodman, Fred Philips, and Alfred Gilman began research to develop antidotes for gas attacks. Since mustard gas was difficult to study safely, they purified it into nitrogen mustard gas, a closely related and safer compound with which to work in laboratory settings. Their study results showed that poisonous gases had their most devastating effects on bone marrow and lymphoid tissues, as well as to skin and gastrointestinal lining.

Birth of Chemotherapy During this same time period another Yale researcher, Thomas Dougherty, was studying the effects of estrogens on leukemia in mice. Upon learning about the effect nitrogen mustard had on lymph tissues, Dougherty administered nitrogen mustard to a lymphoma tumor transplanted to a mouse. The size of the tumor decreased and softened significantly, although it returned after treatment was stopped. A second treatment produced the same results. Although the mouse died, the experiment marked the first time life had been successfully extended for any significant amount of time from a cancer treatment. Further multicenter studies would later produce the same positive results and these findings were published in the *Journal of the American Medical Association* in May 1946.

Using chemical compounds as a cancer treatment would get unfortunate validation from an accidental large-scale exposure to mustard gas during World War II. On December 2, 1943, Allied naval ships were docked in the port of Bari, Italy. With no warning, the harbor was bombed by the Germans. Along with the resulting naval devastation, large amounts of mustard and other gases were released into the air and the water when the SS *John Harvey* was hit. Before they could protect themselves, more than six hundred Allied soldiers were exposed to the dangerous gases. The soldiers experienced severe chemical burns, blindness, and internal burns from swallowing contaminated water. In the days that followed, the soldiers still alive began to show significant decreases in their white blood cell counts. Called upon to investigate the effects of nitrogen gas at the time, Colonel Steward F. Alexander reported

that the soldiers' lymph tissues were melting away and their blood cells were disappearing. Although these results were horrifying, they called attention to a potentially valuable theory. Cornelius Rhoads, the head of the U.S. Army Chemical Warfare Division, theorized that if the chemical nature of mustard gas reduced white blood cell counts, it might also be effective against some forms of leukemia—a cancer of the bone marrow that produces too many white blood cells. He forwarded Alexander's findings to Gilman and Goodman.

Using nitrogen mustard as a cancer treatment turned out to be unpredictable. Treatments did not reduce all tumors and had no effect on leukemia. Nevertheless, nitrogen mustard therapy was tried on a patient with late stage non-Hodgkin's lymphosarcoma after radiation therapy was no longer effective. Within ten days Gilman and Goodman noted that all signs and symptoms of the tumors had disappeared. However, the patient suffered damage to his bone marrow and died from the side effects of the

Comedian Milton Berle (seated behind table) hosting a telethon to raise money for the Damon Runyon Cancer Memorial Fund in New York City on April 9, 1949. Telephoners at the back are taking calls from television viewers making donations. (AP/Wide World Photos)

nitrogen gas. Eventually, thirteen patients with non-Hodgkin's lymphoma and twenty-seven with Hodgkin's disease would undergo nitrogen mustard therapy. Not all patients would experience benefits, but most experienced dramatic improvements in their condition. Trials with nitrogen mustard therapy paved the way for the development of alkylating therapeutic agents, which damage the deoxyribonucleic acid (DNA) structure of cells, specifically designed to kill rapidly proliferating cancer cells.

Nutritional and Hormone Therapies During this same time period, nutritional and hormone therapies for cancer treatment were also being studied. Other studies during World War II had proven that anemia, pernicious anemia, and tropical anemia were easily cured with large doses of the vitamin folic acid. This led Sidney Farber, a pathologist at Children's Hospital in Boston, Massachusetts, to theorize that leukemia might also be cured with drug therapies. Noticing that folic acid increased white blood cell count dramatically, Farber concluded that folic acid might stimulate growth and maturation of bone marrow cells. However, the use of folic acid actually made leukemia patients worse. Therefore, an antifolate drug was tried in an attempt to treat leukemia. The pharmaceutical company Lederle synthesized a compound, aminopterin, that was similar in structure to folic acid but caused cancer cells to die. Farber treated sixteen children with aminopterin and ten went into remission, but not all the results from Farber's studies were positive. Some patients actually experienced toxic effects to healthy tissues because aminopterin destroyed normal cells along with cancer cells.

Remissions also proved to be temporary. Two years later, Farber altered the chemical composition of aminopterin and developed the successful antifolate drug methotrexate, which would be a common cancer treatment drug during the early twenty-first century. This would later lead to the development of antimetabolite drugs that treat leukemia. Farber would help establish the Jimmy Fund to raise funds for pediatric cancer research and the first state-of-the-art clinic for cancer research and treatment for children and adults was built in Boston—the Dana-Farber Cancer Institute.

Purines Around the same time that Farber was conducting his research, George Hitchings and Gertrude Elison, two researchers at the Wellcome labs in New York, were studying purines. These key components in the DNA of cells and their research produced a new drug called diaminopurine in 1949. This drug altered the pathway by which nucleic acids were synthesized and Joseph Burchenal tested it with four leukemia patients at Memorial Sloan-Kettering Institute. Two patients went into remission, but the side effects were intolerable. Although initial clinical results of diaminopurine were disappointing, this early research showed that altered purine compounds could kill cancer cells. This paved the way for the emergence of purine-related drugs that were very effective against leukemia without severe side effects. In 1945, Alfred P. Sloan, Jr., and Charles F. Kettering donated money to build the Sloan-Kettering Institute for Cancer Research, a private, nonprofit establishment devoted to prevention, treatment, and cure of cancers.

Impact During the 1940's, research into the effects of poison gases used during World War I led to a medical breakthrough that would eventually produce new and effective chemotherapies for the treatment of cancers. Five-year survival rates for cancer patients were improved from nearly zero during the early twentieth century to more than 60 percent by the twenty-first century. Since the 1940's, more than four hundred chemotherapy drugs have been developed to combat the devastating effects of cancer.

Alice C. Richer

Further Reading

Bardhan-Quallen, Sudipta. *General Medical Discoveries: Chemotherapy.* Farmington Hills, Mich.: Lucent Books, 2004. Accessible volume on the historical development of chemotherapy techniques.

Greaves, M. F. *Cancer: The Evolutionary Legacy.* New York: Oxford University Press, 2002. Survey of what is known of cancer's causes and the obstacles to research. Author's almost chatty style helps nontechnical readers through some of the complicated immunological and genetic issues and humanizes a topic that can easily overwhelm readers.

Lee, H. S. J., ed. *Dates in Oncology: A Chronological Record of Progress in Oncology over the Last Millennium.* New York: Parthenon, 2000. Summary of the study and treatment of cancer throughout recorded history, from ancient times through the twentieth century.

Morange, Michel. *History of Cancer Research.* Westport, Conn.: John Wiley & Sons, 2003. Comprehensive history of the progress made in the long and complex question to understand cancer and find cures.

See also   DNA discovery; Health care; Medicine.

■ *Cantwell v. Connecticut*

The Case   U.S. Supreme Court ruling on religious freedom
Date   Decided on May 20, 1940

This ruling on the free exercise of religion was one of several Supreme Court rulings in the 1940's involving members of the Jehovah's Witness religion that resulted in expanded civil liberties for all Americans.

Newton Cantwell, a Jehovah's Witness, actively promoted his religious beliefs on the streets of New Haven, Connecticut. He was arrested for violating a state law that prohibited anyone from soliciting money for a religious or charitable cause in public without a license granted by a state official, and for breach of peace. In *Cantwell v. Connecticut,* the Supreme Court struck down the state law, and the licensing provision in particular, for imposing an unconstitutional burden on Cantwell's right to free exercise of religion, as protected in the First and the Fourteenth Amendments to the Constitution. The Court also dismissed the charge of breach of peace, saying that Cantwell's religious expression, though offensive to many, did not incite violence.

Impact   During the 1940's, Jehovah's Witnesses became targets of harassment by state and local officials for their unorthodox religious views and aggressive proselytizing. Up to 1940, the religious protections in the First Amendment only applied against the federal government. However, in the *Cantwell* decision, the Court announced for the first time that the free exercise clause of the First Amendment would apply to state and local government officials through the Fourteenth Amendment. *Cantwell* became the basis for several Court rulings in the 1940's involving Jehovah's Witnesses that struck down government rules aimed at discouraging public expression of unpopular religious views.

Philip R. Zampini

Further Reading

Nussbaum, Martha. *Liberty of Conscience: In Defense of America's Tradition of Religious Equality.* New York: Basic Books, 2008.

Peters, Shawn Francis. *Judging Jehovah's Witnesses: Religious Persecution and the Dawn of the Rights Revolution.* Lawrence: University of Kansas Press, 2000.

See also   Civil rights and liberties; *Murdock v. Pennsylvania*; Religion in the United States; Wartime propaganda in the United States.

■ Capra, Frank

Identification   American film director
Born   May 18, 1897; near Palermo, Italy
Died   September 3, 1991; La Quinta, California

Capra's career underwent unexpected changes during the 1940's. His departure from Columbia Pictures to become an independent director-producer did not produce the successful results he had anticipated. After World War II interrupted his career for more than three years, changes in the postwar entertainment industry left little room for his filmmaking approach.

By 1940, Frank Capra was at the height of his career with two Oscars for best picture and three for best director. After working under Harry Cohn at Colum-

Frank Capra Films of the 1940's

- *Meet John Doe* (1941)
- *The Battle of Britain* (1943)
- *The Battle of Russia* (1943)
- *Divide and Conquer* (1943)
- *The Nazis Strike* (1943)
- *Prelude to War* (1943)
- *Arsenic and Old Lace* (1944)
- *The Battle of China* (1944)
- *Tunisian Victory* (1944)
- *Know Your Enemy: Japan* (1945)
- *Two down and One to Go* (1945)
- *War Comes to America* (1945)
- *Your Job in Germany* (1945)
- *It's a Wonderful Life* (1946)
- *State of the Union* (1948)

bia Pictures for more than a decade, he formed Frank Capra Productions in 1939. Capra produced *Meet John Doe* (1941), the company's only film, a social commentary on the political and journalistic manipulation of the public. A departure from his lighthearted comedies with likeable heroes, the movie was not a hit at the box office, so he dissolved the company. Doing a one-picture contract for Warner Bros. in 1941, Capra directed an adaptation of the Broadway hit *Arsenic and Old Lace*. This wacky comedy about two likeable elderly women who are serial murderers was released in 1944 after the play ended its run.

When Pearl Harbor was attacked on December 7, 1941, Capra enlisted in the Army and was quickly assigned by General George C. Marshall to produce training films. Capra's *Why We Fight* series—seven documentaries, the first of which won an Oscar for best documentary—explained the war's causes and the enemy's ideology. His most significant other documentary was *The Negro Soldier* (1944). Concerned about discrimination and morale among black troops, the Army wanted to educate soldiers about the contribution of African Americans to the nation. The film was a mandatory part of training for all the troops and was influential in the desegregation of the Army in 1948. Promoted to major, Capra was awarded the Distinguished Service Medal in 1945.

In 1946, Capra formed Liberty Films with three other directors. Capra's first postwar film, *It's a Wonderful Life* (1946), which affirms that every person's life has a purpose, would become his most famous. His next film, *State of the Union* (1948), a satire on politics with a flawed hero, was his last attempt at social commentary. When neither film did well at the box office, Capra and his partners sold their company.

Capra made only five more feature films after the 1940's, each focused on light entertainment. With declining numbers in movie audiences, the rise of television entertainment, the lack of funding for directors by major studios, and the increasing influence of actors on directorial film decisions, Capra's famous "one man, one film" approach could not thrive in the postwar Hollywood environment. His career shifted to making educational films and documentaries and lecturing in a variety of venues.

Impact Although Capra's Hollywood career declined from the 1940's on, many of his films, includ-ing those from the 1940's, became classics. He received the Lifetime Achievement Award from the Directors Guild of America in 1959 and the National Medal of Arts in 1986. Reflecting his Italian American Roman Catholic heritage, his films affirm the democratic ideals and shared values of the middle class in small-town America: optimism, courage, honesty, hard work, the dignity of each individual, and the triumph of good over evil. Capra's artistic and technical skills in communicating his uplifting themes earned him recognition as one of Hollywood's greatest directors.

Marsha Daigle-Williamson

Further Reading

Bohn, Thomas William. *An Historical and Descriptive Analysis of the "Why We Fight" Series.* New York: Arno Press, 1977.

Poague, Leland, ed. *Frank Capra: Interviews.* Jackson: University Press of Mississippi, 2004.

See also Academy Awards; Desegregation of the U.S. military; Film in the United States; Ford, John; *It's a Wonderful Life*; Marshall, George C.; Stewart, James; Wartime propaganda in the United States.

■ Carbon dating

Definition Technique for dating ancient organic materials by measuring their carbon-14 content

Also known as Carbon-14 dating; radiocarbon dating

Date Discovery published on March 4, 1949

Also known as carbon-14 dating and radiocarbon dating, this technique has revolutionized archaeological research by making it possible to assign highly accurate dates to artifacts for which no other precise form of dating is possible.

During the late 1940's, Professor Willard F. Libby developed carbon dating at the University of Chicago. After Libby had received his bachelor and doctoral degrees from the University of California at Berkeley, he became a lecturer and then an assistant professor spent his research time during the early 1930's developing the Geiger counter—a device still use to detect and measure weak natural and artificial radioactivity.

During the early 1940's Libby was awarded a Guggenheim Fellowship and went to Princeton University to continue his research in radiochemistry. That work was interrupted by World War II, during which he worked on the Manhattan Project at Columbia University. There he developed a technique for gaseous diffusion separation and enrichment of Uranium-235 that was used in the atomic bomb that was dropped on Hiroshima. After the war ended, Libby accepted a position as professor of chemistry at the University of Chicago, where he continued his research in radiochemistry, which included applications involving isotope tracers, tritium for uses in hydrology and geophysics, and radiocarbon. His research involving radiocarbon led to the application of carbon-14 dating to determine the age of carbon-containing materials up to about 50,000 years old. It would become an important dating tool for archaeology.

How Carbon Dating Works   The stable and most abundant form of carbon is carbon-12, which contains six protons and six neutrons, giving it a total of twelve subatomic particles. Carbon-12 atoms are ubiquitous in all living organisms. However, another, less abundant, form of carbon, carbon-14, also contains six protons. However, it has eight neutrons, instead of six, causing it to be radioactive when it is also present in biological organisms. Carbon-14 atoms produced when energetic cosmic rays collide with nitrogen-14 atoms which are present in the nitrogen gas that constitutes 78 percent of Earth's atmosphere. Carbon-14 atoms then react with oxygen in the air to form carbon dioxide. During photosynthesis plants take up this carbon dioxide and incorporate it into their plant fibers, which are eventually eaten by animals and humans. Thus, *all* biological organisms contain small amounts of carbon-14.

After a biological organism dies, it stops taking up carbon dioxide, and the carbon-14 it already has is not replaced. Its carbon-14 continues to decay by giving off energy in the form of electrons that can be measured by radiation counters. The counters thus measure the amount of carbon-14, which is usually expressed as a ratio against the amount of carbon-12. A ratio in a sample from an old biological artifact, such as a piece of word or a bone, can be compared to the ratio in a living organism to determine the age of the artifact that used to be alive

Half-life is the time required for half of the number of radioactive atoms in a given sample to decay.

The half-life for carbon-14 has been determined to be 5,730 years. These means that half of the carbon-14 in a given sample decays every 5,730 years. Therefore, the age of an organism that died many years ago can be calculated by determining how much of its carbon-14 has been lost over time. For example, an object that has lost one-half its carbon-14 would be about 5,730 years old. One that has lost three-quarters of its carbon-14 would be about twice that old.

Impact   In 1960, Willard Libby won the Nobel Prize for his development of the carbon-14 dating technique. Since his time, his technique has been used to determine the age of a wide variety of materials, ranging from bones and antlers to charcoal, wood, and various marine and freshwater shells. However, the technique has received some criticism for being a less than perfect method. For example, the presence of nuclear reactors and open-air testing of nuclear bombs may influence any organisms that die after the 1940's. In addition, Libby built the technique on an exchange reservoir hypothesis based on the assumption that the exchange of carbon-14 for

Willard F. Libby. (©The Nobel Foundation)

carbon-12 would continue to be constant all over the world. There has been disagreement regarding the validity of this premise.

Jean L. Kuhler

Further Reading

Deevey, Edward S. "Radiocarbon Dating." *Scientific American* 186 (February, 1952): 24-28.

Hedges, Robert E., and John A. J. Gowlett. "Radiocarbon Dating by Accelerator Mass Spectrometry." *Scientific American* 254 (January, 1986): 100-107.

Libby, Willard F. *Radiocarbon Dating*. 2d ed. Chicago: University of Chicago Press, 1965.

_____. "Radiocarbon Dating." In *The Frontiers of Knowledge*. Garden City, N.Y.: Doubleday, 1975.

Maschner, Herbert D. G., and Christopher Chippindale, eds. *Handbook of Archaeological Methods*. 2 vols. Lanham, Md.: AltaMira Press, 2005.

Taylor, Royal E. *Radiocarbon Dating: An Archaeological Perspective*. New York: Academic Press, 1987.

See also   Archaeology; Historiography; Manhattan Project; Science and technology.

■ CARE

Identification   Relief organization established to deliver food packages to European civilians after World War II

Also known as   Cooperative for American Remittances to Europe; Cooperative for Assistance and Relief Everywhere

Date   Established in 1945

CARE and its CARE food packages helped stave off widespread starvation and disease throughout much of Europe for several years after World War II. CARE constructed the only guaranteed delivery distribution network in war-destroyed Europe that allowed American civilians to send food packages to civilians in Europe.

Starvation, disease, and massive social disturbances were widespread threats immediately after the war. CARE, founded in 1945 as the Cooperative for American Remittances to Europe, originated as an umbrella organization of two dozen humanitarian relief organizations, all of which were involved in delivering food aid to Europe after World War II. Arthur Ringland was the primary source of the organization's concept and was a major figure in securing financial backing. Cofounder Lincoln Clark focused on practical administration, and cofounder Wallace Campbell helped maintain CARE's focus on voluntary agencies. CARE bought surplus military rations in huge quantities, chartered cargo ships that had been released from military duties, and transported food to distribution points throughout Europe.

CARE Packages   The most common CARE package was the U.S Army "10-in-1" food package, originally intended to feed soldiers during the invasion of Japan. One package was intended to feed ten soldiers for one day, hence its name. The package contained approximately twenty-two pounds of food, about 40,000 calories of protein and carbohydrates. Designed to be air dropped to soldiers in the field, each food package was encased in heavy waxed cardboard wrapped with metal bands. Inside the large package were four tightly wrapped smaller packages containing complete individual meals.

Each CARE food package cost an American donor ten dollars. Delivery to the intended recipient was guaranteed within four months, or the donor's money would be refunded. Recipients in Europe received notification at their last known address that a CARE package was being held in their name. They were instructed to pick up their CARE package at the nearest distribution depot. Upon receiving the CARE package, the recipient signed a delivery receipt that was returned to the donor as proof of delivery. Americans of all income levels, including President Harry S. Truman, donated money to buy "10-in-1" CARE packages. Each CARE package included pictures of the contents as well as a translation of the contents into the recipient's language.

The first CARE packages, 22,000 in total, arrived at the port of Le Havre, France, in May, 1946. Packages were shipped throughout Europe to regional and local distribution centers. Although CARE packages could be addressed to specific individuals, many donors instructed that their donated package be sent to a schoolteacher, or an elderly person, or simply to a hungry family in Europe. CARE improved its distribution network rapidly as roads throughout Europe were repaired sufficiently to be reopened. CARE agreed to set up a distribution network in any country that agreed to exempt CARE packages from customs duties and allowed CARE workers to supervise delivery procedures. By early 1947, CARE was delivering 10,000 packages per week to recipients throughout Germany. By the end of 1947, CARE had bought, shipped, and delivered almost 45 million pounds of U.S. Army surplus "10-in-1" food packages. In Germany alone, CARE delivered more than one million food packages.

Personal accounts from CARE package recipients indicate that notification to pick up a CARE package caused widespread curiosity among neighbors, all of whom were equally hungry and equally intrigued to see what food from another country looked like. The process of unpacking a CARE package was complicated and required tools to cut the metal wrapping bands and a slicer to cut through the heavy cardboard. Recipients often displayed each item to groups that attended the unwrapping. As important as the food was to people who had been hungry for so long, equally as important was the fact that someone from beyond the area destroyed by war remembered them and cared enough to help.

After exhausting U.S. Army surplus food stores, CARE developed its own food packages to include those foods most nutritionally necessary and in shortest supply in Europe. CARE bought in huge quantities and shipped in uniform-sized containers in order to keep prices low. CARE also developed a "blanket" package consisting of two U.S. Army wool blankets, a sewing kit, a shoe repair kit, and patterns from New York design firms showing how to turn the blankets into winter clothing. CARE shipped more than 25,000 of these "blanket" packages, each costing an American donor the same ten dollars as a food package. CARE also developed a "woolen" package using military surplus woolen fabric. This package also included a sewing kit and instructions on how to sew different types of clothing for children and adults.

CARE remained active in Germany through the 1940's. When the Soviet Union military blockaded its sector of Berlin from June, 1948, until May, 1949, CARE packages were airlifted into the city as part of what was termed the Berlin airlift. When the blockade was lifted months later, a CARE relief truck loaded with critical food supplies was one of the first vehicles to reenter the Soviet-occupied zone.

Celebrities in America participated in public relations campaigns to remind Americans to continue to donate funds for CARE packages even after the initial crisis passed. These efforts allowed CARE to ex-

tend its humanitarian relief efforts into the Philippines in 1949. From there, CARE expanded into Korea as the Korean War intensified, leaving tens of thousands of civilians homeless and hungry. CARE was asked to extend its mission to India and China but was forced to decline because the lack of functioning road systems in much of the rural territories made delivery of CARE packages impossible.

Impact   From its origins as a food distribution organization after World War II, CARE, renamed Cooperative for Assistance and Relief Everywhere, expanded operations throughout the developing world. By the beginning of the twenty-first century, it directed more than fourteen thousand workers worldwide from its secretariat in Geneva, Switzerland. As one of the largest international relief organizations, CARE supports a variety of self-help projects leading to economic self-sufficiency, respect for human rights (particularly the rights of women), and an end to poverty.

Victoria Erhart

Further Reading

Milward, Alan S. *The Reconstruction of Western Europe, 1945-1951.* Berkeley: University of California Press, 1984. Study of all aspects of Europe's postwar economic recovery, with numerous tables documenting progress of the recovery in detail.

Rieff, David. *A Bed for the Night: Humanitarianism in Crisis.* New York: Simon & Schuster, 2002. Examination of how humanitarian organizations have lost sight of their original principle of neutrality by encouraging international communities.

Smyser, W. R. *Humanitarian Conscience: Caring for Others.* New York: Palgrave Macmillan, 2003. Comprehensive study of global humanitarianism that includes recommendations on how to respond to twenty-first century challenges.

Stanneck Gross, Inge Erika. *Memories of World War II and Its Aftermath: By a Little Girl Growing Up in Berlin.* Eastsound, Wash.: Island in the Sky Publishing, 2004. A young German girl in Berlin when World War II began, the author recalls the joy and gratitude her family felt when they received their first CARE package from America after the war.

See also   Marshall Plan; Refugees in North America; UNICEF.

■ *Casablanca*

Identification   Romantic drama set in North Africa during World War II
Director   Michael Curtiz (1888-1962)
Date   Premiered on November 26, 1942

Combining romance, an exotic locale, idealism, a stellar case, and clever dialogue in a critique of American isolationism in the face of expanding Nazism conquests in Europe and Africa, Casablanca *quickly became one of the best known and most successful of war-related films of its time.*

Set in the Vichy-controlled Moroccan city of Casablanca during the early years of World War II, *Casablanca* revolves around the American nightclub owner Rick Blaine (Humphrey Bogart), who has letters of transit that allow their bearers to travel leave Morocco freely. Although he has an opportunity to leave safely with his former lover, who suddenly arrives with her husband, Blaine ultimately chooses fighting against Nazism over his love for Ilsa.

The film opens with Casablanca swarming with refugees in December of 1941, as the Nazis are tightening their grip on Europe. Ugarte, a petty crook (Peter Lorre) has murdered two German couriers and stolen two letters of transit that would be of immense value to any refugee desperate for an exit visa. After Ugarte asks Blaine to hide the letters for him,

he is killed trying to flee when French police captain Renault (Claude Rains) comes to arrest him. Blaine is unmoved by Ugarte's death but is badly shaken by the unexpected arrival of Victor Laszlo (Paul Henreid) and his beautiful wife, Ilsa Lund (Ingrid Bergman), who had been his lover in Paris.

A black marketeer named Ferrari (Sydney Greenstreet) tells Laszlo that Blaine probably has the letters of transit. When Blaine refuses to give them to Laszlo, Ilsa begs him for help. She admits she has loved him all along and had thought her husband, Laszlo—a European underground leader—was dead when she planned to go off with him during their affair in Paris. When she had learned that Laszlo was actually still alive, she could not abandon him. After hearing this, Blaine promises to help Ilsa but secretly arranges with Renault to arrest Laszlo. However, when they all reach the airport, Blaine gives the letters to Laszlo and puts him and Ilsa on the departing plane. He then shoots the German officer attempting to stop Laszlo from leaving. Instead of arresting Blaine, Renault decides to leave Casablanca with him to join a Free French force.

The film premiered on the same day that the Allied Expeditionary Forces invaded North Africa, the region in which Casablanca lies, to begin driving Nazi German occupation forces out. The film's general release date on January 23, 1943, coincided with the Ally's Casablanca Conference. The film touched on the personal sacrifices that were being made during the war and served to further anti-Axis sentiments.

Impact   Now considered one of the greatest films ever made, *Casablanca* won three Academy Awards, including one for best picture. Decades after its release, the film consistently ranked near the top of industry lists of the best films of all time. The film was later selected for preservation in the United States National Film Registry. It also helped the war effort by providing characters who—even though they were not all necessarily ethical—chose to make correct moral choices.

James J. Heiney

Humphrey Bogart and Ingrid Bergman in Casablanca. *(Getty Images)*

Further Reading

Francisco, Charles. *You Must Remember This: The Filming of "Casablanca."* Englewood Cliffs, N.J.: Prentice Hall, 1980.

Harmetz, Aljean. *Round Up the Usual Suspects: The Making of Casablanca: Bogart, Bergman, and World War II.* New York: Hyperion, 1992.

Rosenzweig, Sidney. "'A Hill of Beans': *Casablanca.*" In *Casablanca and Other Major Films of Michael Curtiz.* Ann Arbor, Mich.: UMI Research Press, 1982.

See also   Academy Awards; Bogart, Humphrey; Casablanca Conference; Film in the United States; Films about World War II; North African campaign; Wartime propaganda in the United States; World War II.

■ Casablanca Conference

The Event   Summit meeting at which British and American leaders drew up a plan that would direct the course of Allied operations through the next two years of World War II

Date   January 14-24, 1943

Place   Casablanca, Morocco

Held at a major turning point in World War II, the Casablanca Conference involved the United States directly in planning the invasion of Europe. The policy of a final unconditional surrender fixed the nature of the end of the war.

The Casablanca Conference between President Franklin D. Roosevelt and British prime minister Winston S. Churchill was one of a series of conferences held by the Allied leaders during the war. This was the first conference to which the Soviet leader Joseph Stalin had been invited as one of the Allied team. In the end, Stalin declined the invitation, as the crucial battle of Stalingrad was still being fought at that time. The choice of Casablanca was symbolic. It was the site of the first major American intervention in the European war. American troops had landed there November 7, 1942, and took Morocco from the French Vichy regime. They then met up with British forces and swept through Algeria.

The conference was code-named Symbol. Accompanying Roosevelt were senior military staff including Generals George C. Marshall and Dwight D. Eisenhower. Averell Harriman, and Harry Hopkins, the chief presidential adviser, were the most important political representatives. With Churchill came General Sir Alan Francis Brooke, chief of the British General Staff; General Harold Alexander, British commander in chief of Middle Eastern forces (later first Earl Alexander of Tunis); Rear Admiral Lord Louis Mountbatten; and Air Chief Marshall Portal. The British political representatives included future prime minister Anthony Eden and Sir John Dill, the British representative in Washington.

First Negotiations   The conference's initial discussions were among the military representatives. From the beginning, it was obvious that the British were better prepared than the Americans. The British were keen to keep the Americans firm on the Eu-

U.S. president Franklin D. Roosevelt and British prime minister Winston Churchill (both seated at left) announcing their decision on unconditional surrender at the Casablanca Conference. (Library of Congress)

Conference at Casablanca, 1943

Lisbon

PORTUGAL

SPAIN

Atlantic

Ocean

Gibraltar

Tangier

Mediterranean Sea

Rift Mountains

Casablanca

★ Rabat

Fez

M O R O C C O

Mountains

Marrakech

Atlas

Agadir

ALGERIA

- complete the invasion of North Africa and then push into Sicily
- step up bombing of Germany through nighttime raids by the British and daytime raids by the American air forces
- continue building up American forces in Great Britain in preparation for a major invasion of northern France in 1944
- complete the Battle of the Atlantic to ensure safety of transoceanic shipping
- help the Chinese forces against Japan with an Allied landing in Burma

When Roosevelt held a press conference to announce these policies, he added a further one: to demand from the Axis powers an unconditional surrender. Churchill appeared surprised, as did Roosevelt's own chiefs of staff. Their reactions have led to some controversy as to whether Roosevelt's pronouncement was a last-minute addition of his own. Unconditional surrender was rare in major conflicts. The U.S. Civil War had been ended by the South's unconditional surrender, but World War I had notoriously been fought to a conditional surrender involving U.S. president Woodrow Wilson. It could be argued the dissatisfaction with Germany's conditional surrender in that war had led to World War II, and that therefore history suggested unconditional surrenders ended wars better.

rope theater-first policy previously agreed. Brooke's style, however, was sharp and abrasive, and the Americans became rather defensive. The British had had much greater experience at fighting the Germans, and this showed in the lack of American expertise and detailed plans.

The biggest disagreement was whether the advance into Europe and the opening of the second front should be through Sicily and Italy in the south, as Churchill wanted, or through an invasion of the northern coast of France, as the Americans preferred. However, Sir John Dill, who until recently had been a British army chief, used his considerable diplomatic skills to suggest that position papers be prepared to present to the two leaders. This helped focus the minds of the conference attendees and brought about more cooperation. Then, when the two principal national leaders came into the discussions, they were quickly able to agree on the priorities that had emerged from these papers.

Roosevelt and Churchill eventually agreed on these principal objectives:

The French The other set of negotiations conducted at Casablanca was with the two leaders of the Free French forces. The Vichy collaborationist government had been brought to an end by the Germans on November 11, 1942. The Americans were, it appeared, content to work with former Vichy regime military who then came over to the Allied forces in North Africa, including Admiral François Darlan. The Free French forces were divided in their loyalty between Charles de Gaulle, based in London and supported by the British, and General Giraud, who had escaped from a German prison.

In the end, Darlan was assassinated and Giraud and de Gaulle were persuaded to attend the Casablanca Conference in a show of unity, thus giving

France a place in the Allied forces. De Gaulle was the natural leader, but intensely uncompromising, and his part in the conference proved to be the most difficult.

Impact   The decisions made at the conference coincided with decisive victories in North Africa and at Stalingrad. However, stubborn German resistance in Tunisia and the continuing Battle of the Atlantic meant many of the policies took much more time to implement than had been expected. The Burma landings were abandoned altogether and events took a different turn in the Far East. The British got their way with the invasion of Italy, but the Normandy landings did still take place in 1944, though somewhat delayed.

The policy of seeking unconditional surrender, it has been argued, prolonged the war, and ensured that the United States, with its superior resources, would emerge from the war the strongest nation. Roosevelt made it clear at Casablanca he was not interested in saving the British Empire, and a weakened Britain would indeed lose its empire in the decades after the war. However, in hindsight, the unconditional surrender policy ultimately did seem the right course in that Nazism and fascism were eventually destroyed in Germany and Italy, which eventually emerged from the war as fully democratic nations.

David Barratt

Further Reading

Churchill, Winston S. *The Second World War.* Vol. 4: *The Hinge of Fate.* Boston: Houghton Mifflin, 1950. This volume includes Churchill's memoirs of the Casablanca Conference.

Fenby, Jonathan. *Alliance: The Inside Story of how Roosevelt, Stalin and Churchill Won One War and Began Another.* New York: Simon & Schuster, 2006. Sets the Casablanca conference within the wider context of all the meetings of the Allied leaders throughout the war.

Harriman, Averell. *Special Envoy.* New York: Random House, 1975. Includes a firsthand account of the conference from the senior American diplomat who was in attendance.

Haycock, D. J. *Eisenhower and the Art of Warfare: A Critical Appraisal.* Jefferson, N.C.: McFarland, 2004. Discussion of Eisenhower's military career includes chapters on the Casablanca Conference, the operations arising from it, and Eisenhower's relationship with General Marshall.

Kimball, Warren F. *The Juggler: Franklin Roosevelt as Wartime Statesman.* Princeton, N.J.: Princeton University Press, 1991. Kimball places emphasis on Roosevelt's personal diplomacy and sees Casablanca and unconditional surrender as a commitment of Russia to the Allied effort and a sense that the Anglo-Americans would run the show after the war.

Sherwood, Robert E. *Roosevelt and Hopkins.* New York: Harper & Row, 1948. This work gives a thorough treatment of the Roosevelt polices from the perspective of a close adviser.

Wilt, Alan F. "The Significance of the Casablanca Decisions, January, 1943." *Journal of Military History* 55 (October, 1991): 517-529. Concludes that this meeting provided a realistic agenda for the Anglo-American conduct of the war.

See also   Atlantic Charter; Cairo Conference; Churchill, Winston; Italian campaign; Paris Peace Conference of 1946; Potsdam Conference; Roosevelt, Franklin D.; Strategic bombing; Tehran Conference; Yalta Conference.

■ Casualties of World War II

History's deadliest war resulted in tens of millions of casualties, including military personnel, civilians, and the victims of the first nuclear bombs.

World War II left a wake of destruction and East-West tensions. The conflict was history's deadliest, with nearly 70 million people killed, including 40 million civilians. The statistics are numbing. Among the ultimately successful Allies, the casualty totals include 8.8-10.7 million soldiers and 10.4-13.3 million civilians from the Soviet Union, 382,700 soldiers and 67,100 civilians from the United Kingdom; 416,800 soldiers and 1,700 civilians from the United States, 2-4 million soldiers and 8-16 million civilians from China, and 217,600 soldiers and 267 civilians from France. The figures for the defeated Axis nations also are sobering: 5,333,000 soldiers and 840,000-2,800,000 civilians from Germany, 301,400 soldiers and 145,100 civilians from Italy, and 2,120,000 soldiers and 580,000 civilians from Japan.

The casualties spared few European and Asian countries and extended into Africa. Casualties began to mount after the commencement of Japan's aggression in China in 1931, when it invaded Manchuria. Although that invasion is not generally considered to be part of the world war, it was an important precursor.

By 1940, Adolf Hitler's Germany had annexed several countries in Western Europe. Although Germany bombed Great Britain extensively, ground forces did not invade. Joseph Stalin's Soviet Union had agreed to divide the Baltic States and Poland with Hitler in 1939, but in June, 1941, the Nazis turned on Stalin and invaded Russia. The siege of Leningrad lasted from 1941 to 1944. Civilians resisted the advance, aided by winter weather and improvised barricades. About 1 million noncombatants succumbed in the siege, which lasted from September, 1941, to January, 1944.

Japan's surprise attack on the United States at Pearl Harbor in December, 1941, resulted in 2,403 killed and 1,178 wounded. After launching an invasion of the Philippine Islands, the Japanese in 1942 herded 78,000 captured Allied troops across sixty-five miles of the Luzon Peninsula in the Bataan Death March, resulting in many casualties and deaths among the prisoners. Allied casualties in battles against Italy also were enormous, totaling more than 300,000. The Axis forces suffered 434,000 casualties.

Initially, Hitler's approach to minority peoples under his control was emigration. By 1940, however, he had launched the so-called Final Solution of internment and extermination. Approximately 6 million Jews were murdered in the Nazis' death camps, 3 million in Poland alone. Ethnic hatred was not reserved solely for Jews; Hitler also annihilated Roma (Gypsies) and Czechs.

Operation Overlord used 7,000 ships to ferry Allied troops and supplies to Nazi-held France in June, 1944. The landing at Normandy resulted in 4,300 British and Canadian military personnel suffering casualties on Normandy's beaches, as well as 6,000 American servicemen. Hitler's counteroffensive began in December, 1944, and continued into early 1945. Allied casualties numbered 100,000, with a similar number for Germany.

In addition to ground battles, both Allied and Axis forces used bombing against civilian targets, often centers of military production but often, or coincidentally, centers of population. Dresden, Germany, suffered a particularly devastating air attack from the Royal Air Force and United States Army Air Force on February 13-15, 1945. Estimates of the number of German civilians killed during the bombing and subsequent burning of the city range from the tens of thousands to more than 100,000.

An American invasion in 1945 at Iwo Jima demonstrated the turning tide in the Pacific theater, but the cost was enormous: 5,931 American and 17,372 Japanese casualties. The war's seminal moment occurred on August 6, 1945. A nuclear device detonated at Hiroshima, Japan, killed an estimated 80,000 people initially; radiation poisoning and other injuries brought the total number of casualties to an estimated 90,000 to 140,000. A second atomic bomb dropped on Nagasaki three days later inflicted about 40,000 deaths.

Allied troops pouring ashore on the Normandy coast of France during the D-day invasion of June, 1944. Facing heavy German resistance, the first troops to land suffered exceptionally heavy casualties. (U.S. Coast Guard)

Impact World War II was the deadliest war in history, with millions of lives lost on each side, along with tens of millions of combatants and civilians injured. Final victory for the Allies came only after the detonation of two atomic bombs that introduced new horrors to the casualties of war.

Joseph Edward Lee

Further Reading

Dower, John W. *War Without Mercy.* New York: Pantheon Books, 1986.

Ellis, John. *World War II: A Statistical Survey.* New York: Facts On File, 1993.

Ishikawa, Eisei, and David L. Swain, trans. *Hiroshima and Nagasaki.* New York: Basic Books, 1981.

Keegan, John. *The Second World War.* New York: Viking Penguin, 1990.

See also Bataan Death March; Bulge, Battle of the; D Day; Health care; Hiroshima and Nagasaki bombings; Pearl Harbor attack; Prisoners of war, North American; Prisoners of war in North America.

■ Censorship in Canada

Definition Restrictions on the content of printed and film materials, determined on a province-by-province basis

During World War II, various Canadian provinces defined censorship in accordance with policies that restricted the public expression of ideas believed to have the potential to undermine the moral order.

Some theorists have contended that a heightened concern with shielding adolescents from corrupting influences during the 1940's led to activism against books and publications regarded as salacious and indecent literature. Various community groups (teachers, parent-teacher groups, religious associations, women's groups, and other civic organizations) campaigned against a variety of publications. In addition, censors targeted media portrayals that promoted communist ideas.

In 1942, Canada's chief postal censor conferred with the Royal Canadian Mounted Police (RCMP) and the three branches of the military to help define and itemize the kinds of information to be censored. In 1943, postal censorship in Canada was transferred from the jurisdiction of the postmaster general to the minister of national war services. As a result, the private correspondence of many homosexual servicemen was censored as obscene.

Among the primary manifestations of censorship in Canada during the 1940's was prohibition of importation of certain books and periodicals. Statistics compiled by one researcher show that the list of prohibited publications determined by Canada's customs department grew from 43 books and 24 periodicals in 1933, to 370 books and 262 periodicals in 1946. In 1948, Canada Customs banned the entry of 126 publications, including 29 considered "seditious," that is, subversive or treasonous.

American writer James T. Farrell's novel *Bernard Clare* (1946) was banned in 1946; another of his books, *Gas-House McGinty* (1933), had been banned in 1945 without his knowledge. Leon Trotsky's *Chapters from My Diary* (1918) also was banned, presumably because of Trotsky's identification as a communist. Ironically, some titles banned from importation were freely available in Canadian-printed versions, including versions of Erskine Caldwell's *God's Little Acre* (1933). In 1949, Norman Mailer's *The Naked and the Dead* (1948) was banned in Canada by personal order of the minister of national revenue. The book had been a best seller in Canada for ten months prior to the ban.

Some five hundred books remain banned during the 1940's under Article 1201 of the Customs Tariff, including short stories by Guy de Maupassant, William Faulkner's *Sanctuary* (1931), Erskine Caldwell's *Tobacco Road* (1932), Ben Hecht's *A Jew in Love* (1931), Radclyffe Hall's *The Well of Loneliness* (1928), and Sir Richard Francis Burton's sixteen-volume translation of the anonymously written epic *The Book of the Thousand Nights and a Night* (1885).

During this period, censorship was closely associated with propaganda. Publications such as *Radio Broadcasting Censorship: Handbook Consolidation of Directives* (1941) specified guidelines that regulated radio transmissions and content. The National Film Board of Canada (NFB) itself was investigated in 1949, following an investigation of its founder, John Grierson, because of his suspected communist sympathies. A number of animators were fired as suspected communist sympathizers.

Even cartoons were subject to censorship. Amendment of the obscenity provision of the Criminal Code in 1949 resulted in a prohibition on particular printed comics. Filmed cartoons also were subject to censorship. The Warner Bros. cartoon *Thugs With Dirty Mugs* (1939), for example, was banned in Winnipeg, Manitoba, because censors believed that it glorified criminality.

Impact In 1949, *Maclean's* magazine, under managing editor W. Arthur Irwin, called on the federal government to abandon censorship and repeal Article 1201 of the Customs Tariff. Irwin became the head of the NFB in 1950. Canada lifted some of its bans after further consideration. The ruling that James Joyce's *Ulysses* (1922) was obscene, for example, was reversed in 1949. This ruling pointed out the subjective nature of censorship guidelines that prohibited and censored material as obscene, seditious, or morally corrupting.

Nicole Anae

Further Reading

Cohen, Karl F. *Forbidden Animation: Censored Cartoons and Blacklisted Animators in America.* Jefferson, N.C.: McFarland, 2004.

Cohen, Mark. *Censorship in Canadian Literature.* Montreal: McGill-Queen's University Press, 2001.

Jackson, Paul. *One of the Boys: Homosexuality in the Military During World War II.* Montreal: McGill-Queen's University Press, 2004.

Petersen, Klaus, and Allan C. Hutchinson, eds. *Interpreting Censorship in Canada.* Toronto: University of Toronto Press, 1999.

See also Advertising in Canada; Book publishing; Canadian participation in World War II; Censorship in the United States; Literature in Canada; *Maclean's*; Pornography; Radio in Canada; Theater in Canada; Wartime propaganda in Canada.

■ Censorship in the United States

Definition Official and unofficial restrictions on the content of films, newspapers, and even— during World War II—private communications

The government of the United States, at the urging of various pressure groups, has tried on numerous occasions to suppress information on a variety of topics. Countervailing groups of citizens have opposed these efforts at suppression in the courts, with varying degrees of success. Censorship during the 1940's retained its focus on "moral" issues as well as concentrating on military information and "undesirable" political activity and communications.

The first federal efforts at censorship in the United States came after the passage of the Alien and Sedition Acts of 1798. Among other things, these acts made it a federal crime to publish "false, scandalous, and malicious writings" concerning the U.S. government or its officials (specifically excluding the vice president, who was not a member of the majority party in the U.S. Congress). The acts also gave the president the power to arrest and deport resident aliens if their country of origin was at war with the United States. This provision remains in effect.

During the nineteenth century, agencies of the U.S. government made a number of efforts at censorship, often concerning what some officials considered obscenity. The first national law of this kind came with the Tariff Act of 1842, which among other things prohibited the "importation of all indecent and obscene prints, paintings, lithographs, engravings and transparencies." In the same year, a grand jury in New York State handed down the first indictments against publishers of obscene books. In 1864, the U.S. postmaster general reported to Congress that many "dirty" pictures and books were being mailed to the troops fighting in the U.S. Civil War. Congress quickly passed a law making it a crime to send any "obscene book, pamphlet, picture, print, or other publication of vulgar and indecent character" through the U.S. mail. These laws remain in effect, though the courts and censors have varied in their interpretations of what constitutes obscenity and indecency.

One of the major pieces of legislative censorship affecting the United States during the 1940's dates from 1873. The so-called Comstock Act, named for Anthony Comstock (1844-1915), the leader of the New York Society for the Suppression of Vice, made it a federal crime to "offer to sell, or to lend, or to give away, or in any manner to exhibit . . ." any written material "for the prevention of conception, or for causing unlawful abortion. . . ." Anyone convicted of such a crime might be imprisoned for not less than six months nor more than five years. Additional related legislation passed by the federal and state governments became known as Comstock Laws. In 1938, a decision by the Supreme Court effectively ended the federal ban on birth control information, but not the ban on information concerning abortions, which remained in effect throughout the 1940's.

Motion Picture Censorship Another major factor in censorship in the United States during the 1940's also originated before the beginning of the decade. The Hays Code, as it was called, dated from 1930 and was developed, in part, by William H. Hays, Sr., the president of the Motion Picture Producers and Distributors of America and a former postmaster general. Motion picture producers created this self-regulation, properly known as the Motion Picture Production Code, to avoid government imposing its own regulations. The industry-appointed Production Code Administration, headed by Joseph I. Breen from 1934 until his retirement in 1954, enforced the code from 1934 to 1968, when the industry developed a system of rating films according to the suitability of their content for various audiences. Deriving its substance largely from religious organizations, the code sought to protect the American public from what Breen and Hays deemed obscenity. It also prohibited portrayals of interracial or homosexual sexual relationships and any content regarded as anti-Christian or anti-religious.

Two of the most famous cases of censorship of motion pictures during the 1940's involved the films *Kings Row* (1942) and *The Outlaw* (1943). The former was based on Henry Bellamann's controversial 1940 novel of the same name, which contained considerable sexual content including references to incest, homosexuality, and euthanasia. Censorship resulted in a screenplay nearly unrecognizable as a derivative of the original novel. The Hays Code kept *The Outlaw* out of theaters for years because the film's advertising focused on the breasts of its female star, Jane Russell.

Print and Broadcast Media Censorship　Freedom of the press is guaranteed by the First Amendment to the U.S. Constitution; nevertheless, at various times during American history the government has censored the press, especially during wartime. The press also frequently censors itself in the national interest, as it often did during the 1940's. One notable example concerns President Franklin D. Roosevelt. The polio he contracted in 1921 left him unable to stand unassisted, but the press refrained from publishing photographs or releasing film footage of his being assisted or using a wheelchair so that he would not appear to be handicapped.

War correspondents often accompanied U.S. military forces during overseas activities during World War II. Military authorities usually censored their reports prior to release, so as to preserve military secrets. The Office of Censorship (an emergency wartime agency created by Roosevelt on December 19, 1941) released a Voluntary Censorship Code that went through four major revisions during the war. Director of Censorship Byron Price had the power to censor international communications at "his absolute discretion," but he placed responsibility for censorship on journalists themselves.

Price gave the power to release information to those directly involved. Military commanders and

Louis J. Crouteau (right), secretary of the New England Watch and Ward Society—the self-styled "watchdog of New England's morals"—examining Esquire *magazine's provocative "Varga girl," painted by Alberto Vargas, as an attorney for the magazine looks on. At an October, 1943, hearing of the U.S. Post Office, Crouteau testified that the magazine was not dangerous to the nation's morals. In the course of his search for indecency, Crouteau attended five or six burlesque shows a week and perused sixty to seventy suspect magazines a month.* (AP/Wide World Photos)

government department heads made decisions about what information concerning their activities would be released to the public. Price was able to maintain the independence of his office and keep it separate from the Office of War Information and the Military Intelligence Division of the War Department, both of which attempted to appropriate the duties of his agency.

The approximately fifteen thousand employees of the Office of Censorship occupied themselves primarily with monitoring overseas cables, telephone messages, and letters to keep sensitive information from falling into enemy hands. They left the monitoring of the U.S. press to the editors of the various newspapers, who voluntarily restricted themselves from printing information could be useful to the enemy. The most serious challenge to this self-censorship policy came in June, 1942, when the *Chicago Tribune* published a story concerning the U.S. Navy's ability to read secret Japanese naval codes prior to the Battle of Midway. The Department of Justice prepared to prosecute the newspaper for violating the Espionage Act of 1918 but ultimately dropped the case for fear that a public trial would reveal more information to the Japanese than had the newspaper story itself.

Price's agency then revised and reissued the Voluntary Censorship Code, placing more restrictions on editors. The revised code seemed to make editors more cooperative in censoring their own news stories. Thus, when in 1944 reporters began to pick up bits of information about something called the Manhattan Project, they made no effort to publish stories about the United States' efforts to develop an atomic bomb, largely because of an appeal by the Office of Censorship to refrain from publishing such information. Also in 1944, newspapers voluntarily refrained from publishing stories about the extent of the success of the German Ardennes Offensive.

On May 15, 1945, the Office of Censorship requested continued restraint on the part of newspapers regarding secret military weapons having anything to do with atomic energy. Only the *Cleveland Press* breached this restraint, in a story about a "forbidden city" in New Mexico whose inhabitants were engaged in developing secret military weapons.

Wartime Censorship of the Mails   During World War II, the U.S. military censored the letters written and received by service personnel. Officers of the armed forces carried out these censorship activities, a duty that many regarded as undesirable. Consequently, commanding officers often assigned censorship duty to junior officers such as dentists and chaplains.

Officially, the censors looked for two things: anything that could be of value to the enemy and anything relating to the morale of the troops. In practice, the censors often restricted explicit sexual language as well. Any mention of the location of the letter writer was deleted; a letter's recipient could not even tell if the writer was in the Pacific or European theater of war. Censors often confiscated letters written in languages other than English because they couldn't read them. The Office of Censorship also censored letters going to or coming from overseas during World War II. This agency also often confiscated letters in languages other than English.

Postwar Censorship   In 1940, the Alien Registration Act, or Smith Act, made it a criminal offense for anyone to

> knowingly or willfully advocate, abet, advise or teach the . . . desirability or propriety of overthrowing the Government of the United States or of any State by force or violence, or for anyone to organize any association which teaches, advises or encourages such an overthrow, or for anyone to become a member of or to affiliate with any such organization.

Between 1941 and 1957, hundreds of alleged communists were prosecuted under this law. In 1949, eleven leaders of the Communist Party were charged and convicted under the Smith Act. The court sentenced ten of the defendants to five years of imprisonment, while the eleventh received a three-year sentence.

Beginning in 1947, the House Committee on Un-American Activities (informally known as the House Un-American Activities Committee, or HUAC) became a force in the unofficial censorship of Hollywood films. Members of HUAC seemed determined to prove that the Screen Writers Guild had communist members who inserted subversive propaganda into Hollywood films and that President Roosevelt had encouraged pro-Soviet films during World War II. HUAC eventually called eleven men to testify before it, one of whom testified and then returned to East Germany. The other ten (known as the "Hollywood Ten," one director and nine screenwriters) took the Fifth Amendment and refused to testify.

Code of Wartime Practices for the American Press and Radio, 1945

All media of publication and radio are asked not to publish or broadcast information in the following classes except when such information is made available for publication or broadcast by appropriate authority or is specifically cleared by the Office of Censorship:

War Plans

Secret war plans, or diplomatic negotiations or conversations which concern military operations.

Enemy Attacks

Information about actual or impending enemy attacks on continental United States.

Armed Forces

Identify movement, or prospective movement of Allied Army, Navy, or Marine Corps units which are in, have been alerted for, or are on their way to, the Pacific-Asiatic area from American territory anywhere; those moving or about to move directly from Europe to the Pacific-Asiatic area . . .

Ships

Identity, location, character, description, movements, and prospective movements of naval vessels, transports, and convoys . . .

Planes

Disposition, composition, movements, missions, or strength of Allied military air units within or proceeding to or from the Pacific-Asiatic area; military activities of commercial airlines in the Pacific-Asiatic area . . .

Fortification and Installations

Location and description of fortifications, coast defense emplacement, antiaircraft guns, and other air defense installations, including defense installation details of public airports used for military purposes, location or description of camouflaged objects.

Production

New or secret weapons, identity and location of plants making them; secret designs, formulas, processes or experiments connected with the war . . .

Military Intelligence

Information concerning war intelligence or counterintelligence, operations, methods, or equipment of the United States, its allies, or the enemy . . .

War Prisoners

Information as to arrival, movements, confinement, or identity or military prisoners from the Pacific-Asiatic area.

Travel

Advance information on routes, times, and methods of travel by the President.

Movements of ranking Army, Navy, and Marine officers to, from, within the Pacific-Asiatic area.

Photographs and Maps

Photographs or maps conveying any of the information specified in other sections of this code; aerial photographs of harbors, war plants, military or vital defense installations.

Source: "Code of Wartime Practices for the American Press and Radio." United States Government Office of Censorship. Washington, D.C.: United States Government Printing Office, 1945.

Hollywood executives effectively blacklisted these men and anyone else suspected of communist sympathies.

In 1946, the Supreme Court handed down an important decision regarding de facto censorship by the U.S. Post Office. It held that the Post Office could not cancel the second-class mailing privilege of a periodical on the grounds that the magazine was not considered to be for the "public good," while concededly not obscene. The court rejected the argument that the use of the mails is a privilege that the government may regulate at will, and therefore ruled that the government could not refuse to allow *Esquire* magazine mailing privileges.

Impact Attempts at censorship usually succeeded in the short term during the 1940's. Motion pictures and popular literature usually remained bland and lacking in controversial themes. The American public remained for the most part supportive of the war effort and of the U.S. military and government during World War II, and it largely supported censorship intended to protect military secrets. Marxism and communism never gained widespread acceptance in the United States, and censorship of information supporting these movements was widely supported. As the decade closed, most Americans seemed content to acquiesce to the various forms of censorship, both official and self-imposed, that remained.

Paul Madden

Further Reading

Beisel, Nicola. *Weeder in the Garden of the Lord: Anthony Comstock's Life and Career.* Lanham, Md.: University Press of America, 1995. An account of the life and career of the man responsible for the so-called Comstock Laws, which illegalized the distribution and sale of contraceptives and information about contraceptives or abortion in the United States.

Black, Gregory D. *Hollywood Censored: Morality Codes, Catholics, and the Movies.* New York: Cambridge University Press, 1994. Concentrates primarily on the Hays Code and its implementation during the period 1934-1954. Emphasizes the influence of Catholic morality on the decisions of Joseph Breen in implementing the Production Code laid down by William H. Hays, Sr., in 1934.

Doherty, Thomas. *Hollywood's Censor: Joseph I. Breen and the Production Code Administration.* New York: Columbia University Press, 2007. An account of the life and career of the man who enforced the Production Code on the motion picture industry during the period 1934-1954. The Production Code represented an attempt by Breen to protect American citizens from the temptations of motion-picture images of sex, immorality, and sin.

Roeder, George, Jr. *The Censored War: American Visual Experience During World War II.* New Haven, Conn.: Yale University Press, 1993. Shows that the control exercised by the Office of Censorship over the release of visual representations of the war significantly affected perceptions by the public of the nature and effects of war.

Sweeney. Michael S. *Secrets of Victory: The Office of Censorship and the American Press and Radio in World War II.* Chapel Hill: University of North Carolina Press, 2001. An account of the founding of the Office of Censorship and its activities during the period 1941-1945. According to Sweeney, the organization was successful in informing the American people about the course of the war without giving any secrets to the enemy.

See also Book publishing; Comic books; Communist Party USA; Film in the United States; Homosexuality and gay rights; Manhattan Project; Newspapers; Roosevelt, Franklin D.; Smith Act; Smith Act trials; Wartime propaganda in the United States.

■ Central Intelligence Agency

Identification Agency within the executive branch of the federal government charged with coordinating intelligence activities on a governmentwide basis, including the correlation, analysis, and dissemination of foreign intelligence relating to national security

Date Established by the National Security Act of 1947

The Central Intelligence Agency was an important Cold War tool for the United States during the late 1940's. The agency gathered intelligence and carried out covert and clandestine national security operations.

The Central Intelligence Agency (CIA) was formed from the remnants of the Office of Strategic Services (OSS), which had been disbanded after World War II, its functions scattered among the Interim Research and Intelligence Service of the State Department and the Psychological Warfare Division and the Strategic Services Unit of the War Department. Quickly recognizing a need for permanent coordination of intelligence gathering, analysis, and dissemination, President Harry S. Truman, by executive order, brought those units together again in the Central Intelligence Group. Despite heavy opposition from the State Department, the military, and the Federal Bureau of Investigation (FBI)—all of which had intelligence and counterespionage roles they wanted to preserve—Congress took up the reorganization of the entire national security apparatus. Truman signed the National Security Act on July 26, 1947. The act restructured the nation's military, foreign policy, and intelligence operations at the outset of the Cold War. It set up the National Security Council (NSC) in the White House, created the Department of the Air Force, merged the Departments of War and the Navy into the National Military Establishment (later renamed the Department of Defense), and established the CIA as the nation's first peacetime intelligence agency.

In 1948, the president, through the NSC, gave the CIA the authority to conduct covert operations, and in 1949 Congress exempted it from the usual fiscal and administrative procedures and allowed it to keep its personnel and organizational functions secret. Covert operations soon began, and the CIA was instrumental in defeating communist insurgents in Greece and communist candidates at the polls in Italy. In 1949, after the Soviets detonated their first atomic bomb, the CIA began parachuting agents into the Soviet Union and other Soviet bloc countries.

The CIA and its first director, Rear Admiral Roscoe H. Hillenkoetter, soon came under severe criticism. Two reports in 1949—the Eberstadt Report of the First Hoover Commission and the Dulles-Jackson-Correa Report by the NSC—both recommended further centralizing the intelligence functions and consolidating covert and clandestine operations within a single directorate in the CIA. Implementation of the suggested reforms began in the 1950's.

Impact With the CIA, the United States became the last of the post-World War II major powers to establish a national intelligence agency. The CIA was analogous in some respects to the British Secret Intelligence Service (MI6) and the Soviet NKVD and MVD (later the KGB), though unlike the Soviet agencies, the CIA had no domestic police powers. Despite its role in coordinating military intelligence activities, the CIA was by law a civilian agency, and Congress specified that it would have no police, subpoena, or law-enforcement powers or internal-security functions.

The CIA was created as an intelligence agency in response to fears of Soviet expansion after World War II. With its subsequent authority to conduct co-vert and clandestine operations while maintaining budgetary and administrative secrecy, it soon became the U.S. government's primary tool in carrying out the Truman Doctrine of Soviet containment during the Cold War that followed. These operations laid the groundwork for the controversies that would swirl around the CIA for decades afterward.

William V. Dunlap

Further Reading

Leary, William Matthew. *The Central Intelligence Agency, History and Documents.* Tuscaloosa: University of Alabama Press, 1984.

Parry-Giles, Shawn J. *The Rhetorical Presidency, Propaganda, and the Cold War, 1945-1955.* Westport, Conn.: Praeger, 2002.

Smith, W. Thomas. *Encyclopedia of the Central Intelligence Agency.* New York: Facts On File, 2003.

Weiner, Tim. *Legacy of Ashes: The History of the CIA.* New York: Doubleday, 2007.

See also Cold War; Department of Defense, U.S.; Federal Bureau of Investigation; Foreign policy of the United States; Hoover Commission; National Security Act of 1947; Office of Strategic Services; Truman, Harry S.; Truman Doctrine; Voice of America; Wartime espionage in North America.

■ Chandler, Raymond

Identification American novelist and screenwriter
Born July 23, 1888; Chicago, Illinois
Died March 26, 1959; La Jolla, California

Chandler wrote hard-boiled detective fiction that had an enduring significance in American letters and culture.

With his first novel, *The Big Sleep* (1939), Chandler established himself as a premier practitioner of the uniquely American style of hard-boiled fiction. He eschewed violence as a principal plot device, focusing on the troubled consciousness of his private detective, Philip Marlowe, and his chivalric code of ethics. Marlowe stands in sharp contrast to the modern wasteland that is Chandler's Southern California of the 1940's.

In his four novels from the 1940's, Chandler anatomizes American society, presenting characters from the highest and lowest walks of life and revealing a world of greed and venality through which the lone-wolf detective must wander and exact some slim measure of justice. While *Farewell, My Lovely* (1940) is arguably his best novel, *The Little Sister* (1949) offers the most revealing, and dyspeptic, view of the film industry, criminality, and police corruption in the wonderland of Hollywood. During this time, Chandler also became one of the most successful American screenwriters. His novels and screenplays represent the acme of noir fictions.

Impact Although he gives scant attention to World War II, Chandler is unmistakably a writer of the 1940's. He clearly understood the moral vacancy and cultural confusions of mid-twentieth century America. With the call of the West long vanished, Chandler understood that the American search for the wilderness now resided in its urban centers, where the possibilities for personal renewal and heroism still prevailed.

David W. Madden

Further Reading

MacShane, Frank. *The Life of Raymond Chandler.* New York: E. P. Dutton, 1976.

Speir, Jerry. *Raymond Chandler.* New York: Ungar, 1981.

See also Black Dahlia murder; Bogart, Humphrey; Book publishing; *Double Indemnity*; Faulkner, William; Film in the United States; Film noir; Literature in the United States; Pulp magazines.

■ Chaplains in World War II

Clergy from all major American religious groups participated in the armed forces during World War II, serving both in battlefront positions and in more permanent installations. Through their presence and willingness to help whenever needed, chaplains proved themselves invaluable to the war effort.

Since General George Washington's time, chaplains have been part of U.S. military life. Their presence, however, sometimes has been small. Just before the Pearl Harbor attack, the number of regular army chaplains was 140; in the buildup of armed forces that followed, the number grew to 9,111 within a year. For the rapid expansion, the army drew on reserve and National Guard chaplains and on volunteers from among civilian clergy.

Candidates had to be clergy in good standing with their own denomination. After completing a five-week "chaplain school" in army protocol and regulations, new chaplains received orders assigning them to a duty station. This could be a combat unit, a larger base, or a stateside location. Those assigned to smaller units found themselves responsible for the spiritual welfare of soldiers with religious traditions other than their own. Because of this, chaplains usually learned the basic prayers and rituals of other faiths and would use them in emergency situations.

Besides performing religious rites, chaplains' pastoral duties included large amounts of listening, counseling, and trying to resolve servicemen's problems. The many young men newly away from home and facing unknown dangers needed moral and practical support. The civilian population backed the chaplaincy because they saw chaplains as meeting this need of "the boys" as well as providing spiritual guidance.

The Geneva Convention forbade chaplains from carrying arms, but many did face situations of ex-

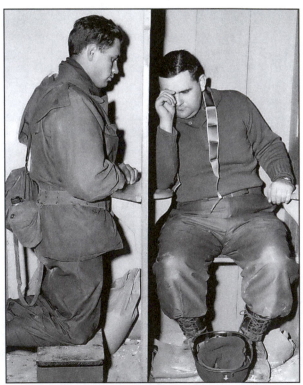

Roman Catholic chaplain (right) hearing the confession of a young American soldier in Germany in early 1945. (AP/Wide World Photos)

treme danger. Chaplains with frontline assignment came under fire as they helped evacuate wounded, and as they brought them water and other aid on the battlefield. Perhaps the best known case of chaplains' heroism occurred during the sinking of the troopship *Dorchester*, which was torpedoed in icy waters off Greenland's coast in February, 1943. In the twenty-seven minutes before the ship sank, the four army chaplains aboard passed out life jackets, guided terrified young men into life rafts, gave up their own life jackets to men who needed them, and finally linked arms and prayed as the cold waves closed in. Their example, reported by men who were rescued, inspired others as the war went on.

Impact Within the services, chaplains' work proved so essential to the war effort that the Chaplains' Corps became firmly established as part of the American military. Ordinary combat veterans often remembered their chaplain as "our guy" to whom they turned for moral support.

Within the larger society, chaplains' experiences helped bolster the incipient interfaith movement and sentiments in American life. Just as the war brought together young men from disparate backgrounds, chaplains also served with other clergy and servicemen from many different faiths. Working together, often using unfamiliar prayers and rituals, made it impossible to maintain rigid attitudes about religion. Clergy carried this wider understanding of religious beliefs back to civilian pulpits; it helped fuel a growing belief in the value of a multifaith America.

Emily Alward

Further Reading

Carpenter, Alton E. *Chappie: World War II Diary of a Combat Chaplain*. Mesa, Ariz.: Mead, 2007.

Gushwa, Robert L. *The Best and Worst of Times: The United States Army Chaplaincy, 1920-1945*. Honolulu: University Press of the Pacific, 2004.

Kurzman, Dan. *No Greater Glory: The Four Immortal Chaplains and the Sinking of the Dorchester in World War II*. New York: Random House, 2004.

See also Army, U.S.; Casualties of World War II; Conscientious objectors; Navy, U.S.; Religion in Canada; Religion in the United States; Theology and theologians; World War II; World War II mobilization.

■ Chaplinsky v. New Hampshire

The Case Supreme Court decision upholding a man's conviction for derisive speech on the grounds that "fighting words" are not constitutionally protected

Date Decided on March 9, 1942

This ruling established that freedom of speech is not absolute and that "fighting words" can be restricted without violating First and Fourteenth Amendment protections.

On a Saturday afternoon in November of 1941, a man named Walter Chaplinsky distributed literature promoting the Jehovah's Witnesses on a busy public street in Rochester, New Hampshire. A crowd around him grew restless, and the city marshal told Chaplinsky to leave before a disturbance ensued. Chaplinsky replied, "You are a Goddamned racketeer" and "a damned Fascist and the whole government of Rochester are Fascists." Chaplinsky was arrested for disturbing the peace and for violating a public statute that prohibited use of "offensive, derisive or annoying word[s]." Chaplinsky maintained that the statute was invalid under the Fourteenth Amendment as an unreasonable restraint on free speech.

Justice Frank Murphy delivered the opinion for the unanimous Court. He observed that freedom of speech is protected by the First Amendment from infringement by Congress and is also among the fundamental personal rights and liberties that are protected by the Fourteenth Amendment from state encroachment. The right of free speech, however, is not absolute at all times and under all circumstances. Certain well-defined and narrowly limited classes of speech can be restricted, including, obscene, profane, libelous, and insulting speech as well as "fighting words"—which inflict injury or incite an immediate breach of the peace. Such utterances are not the essential part of any exposition of ideas, and any benefit from them is outweighed by social interests in order and morality.

The statute's purpose was to preserve the public peace, and that peace might be threatened by "fighting words." Such words plainly tend to excite the addressee, or those observing a speech act, to a breach of the peace and can be restricted by statute.

Impact The thrust of this decision was considerably narrowed over time, though it has not been overturned. The definition of "fighting words" has been tested in various contexts, including business advertising, public swearing, and pornography, with wider free speech protection being granted. *New York Times Co. v. Sullivan* (1964) gave wider latitude to print publications concerning libel, and verbal challenges to police officers enjoy constitutional protection.

Joseph A. Melusky

Further Reading

Abraham, Henry Julian, and Barbara A. Perry. *Freedom and the Court: Civil Rights and Liberties in the United States.* 8th ed. Lawrence: University Press of Kansas, 2003.

Blanchard, Margaret A. *Revolutionary Sparks: Freedom of Expression in Modern America.* New York: Oxford University Press, 1992.

Shiffrin, Steven H., and Jesse H. Choper. *The First Amendment: Cases, Comments, Questions.* St. Paul, Minn.: West, 1996.

See also   Censorship in the United States; Central Intelligence Agency; Civil rights and liberties; Supreme Court, U.S.

■ China and North America

During the 1940's, U.S.–Chinese relations were determined largely by the struggle for domination between the Chinese Communist Party and the Nationalist (Kuomintang) Party. The rivalries among American military commanders and their strategic preferences also influenced the course of the relationship. Although Canada was not involved in the Asian theater of operations, it participated in the postwar search for an advantageous relationship with China.

When Japan invaded China in 1937 during the Second Sino-Japanese War, Chiang Kai-shek's Nationalist forces were already engaged in fighting the Chinese Communist Party (CCP), led by Mao Zedong, among others. The two factions declared a truce (although their cooperation was always minimal). Even before entering the war, the United States was intent on supporting the British defense of India and Burma and was anxious to keep China engaged against Japan. President Franklin D. Roosevelt was able to send aid to China as long as the war was undeclared, as the U.S. Neutrality Act of 1939 prevented direct aid to countries at war. American public opinion was sympathetic to China, based on missionaries' accounts of Japanese brutality and on the inspirational novels of Pearl S. Buck. In 1942, Roosevelt dispatched General Joseph Warren Stilwell to China, with responsibility for Lend-Lease materials and for supervising the China-Burma-India theater of war.

Stilwell, known as "Vinegar Joe" for his caustic personality, had served in China between the wars and was fluent in Chinese. He thought Chiang weak and unreliable. Chiang was equally mistrustful of Stilwell; although he named Stilwell chief of staff, he undercut Stilwell's authority by indicating to the Chinese generals that the American was an adviser, not their commander. Chiang was determined to keep American supplies coming, and he thought that giving Americans "commands on paper" would guarantee their cooperation. Yet he hoped to save his own troops for the conflict with the communists.

Stilwell's challenge was to deliver war materials over the formidable obstacle of the Himalayas on China's southwest border. Flights over "the Hump" were extremely dangerous, although the volunteer Flying Tigers had been delivering supplies since 1941. After surveying land routes through northern Burma, Stilwell determined to build a road that could accommodate truck convoys. The Ledo Road (renamed the Stilwell Road in 1945) was plagued by heat, insects, disease, battle, and monsoons. Built and washed out repeatedly, the road never became a particularly effective supply route. The project was also undercut by air route advocates such as Colonel Claire Chennault, who breezily assured his superiors from 1942 on that aircraft could deliver the goods to China. Chiang took advantage of every wedge to keep his allies involved on China's behalf and to gain advantage over the CCP. At his urging, Stilwell was recalled in October, 1944.

Canada established informal relations with China in 1942 and contributed some $52 million (Canadian dollars) in combat supplies (subject, as always, to the geographical difficulties of delivery). Although the Americans were not necessarily in favor of this assistance, Canada had an eye toward its future trade relationship with China and benefited from reducing its surplus of war materials.

Postwar Developments As World War II drew to a close, the KMT moved to consolidate its power. The Americans decreed that Japanese forces should surrender only to the KMT, and American and other foreign aid was steered to KMT-held areas. Although few Chinese seemed to think communism would be the inevitable or better government for China, the KMT alienated many segments of the population with clumsy policies. They failed to move against local leaders who had collaborated with the hated Japanese, and they were widely perceived to be corrupt. When protests broke out, the KMT was heavy-handed in putting them down.

The Americans were dismayed by the continuing conflict in China. Although they strongly preferred a KMT victory, it became clear that prolonged chaos would be destabilizing. In late 1945, President Harry S. Truman dispatched General George C. Marshall to mediate between the KMT and CCP. American policy was modified to support Marshall's mission, with a partial ban on shipments of combat materials in late 1946, and Truman promised no direct involvement in the conflict. Yet the Americans had guaranteed their unpopularity by prolonging the conflict with their earlier support of the Nationalists and by their postwar support for rehabilitating the Japanese economy. Marshall returned home in failure in early 1947. In China, food riots and student protests broke out, and military clashes continued. The KMT was in constant retreat as it lost popular support. Mao proclaimed the establishment of the People's Republic of China in October, 1949, and in December the KMT loyalists finally fled to Formosa (Taiwan).

Impact The emergence of a huge, communist-led country with a certain amount of anti-American feeling complicated the Cold War for the West. Arguably, the United States backed the wrong side in China, because it never fully understood the political situation or Chinese public opinion.

Jan Hall

Further Reading

Daugherty, Leo J., III. *The Allied Resupply Effort in the China-Burma-India Theater During World War II.* Jefferson, N.C.: McFarland, 2008. A military historian's detailed take on the competing policies of rival commanders and the heroic efforts to carry out orders.

Chiang Kai-shek. (Library of Congress)

Granatstein, J. L. *The Last Good War: An Illustrated History of Canada in the Second World War, 1939-1945.* Vancouver/Toronto: Douglas & McIntyre, 2005. A rare glimpse of Canadian life at home and at war.

Koerner, Brendan. *Now the Hell Will Start.* New York: Penguin Press, 2008. Principally about a black G.I. who fled into the Burmese jungle from the Ledo Road, the book offers great insight into the virulent racism of the U.S. military and the impact of policy disputes in the China-Burma-India theater.

Pepper, Suzanne. *Civil War in China: The Political Struggle, 1945–1949.* 2d ed. Lanham, Md.: Rowman & Littlefield, 1999. Detailed account of how the Kuomintang-communist struggle affected both ordinary Chinese and international relations.

Tuchman, Barbara. *Stilwell and the American Experience in China, 1911–1945.* New York: Grove Press, 2001. Well-written biography and account of how the United States failed to understand its inability to influence China.

■ China-Burma-India theater

The Event Japanese invasion and occupation of China and Southeast Asia and the Allied response

Date 1939-1945

Places China, India, and Burma

The China-Burma-India theater of World War II evolved in response to the Japanese invasion of China in 1937 and the bombing of Pearl Harbor in 1941. This theater was organized to coordinate the protection of Burma and India and to support the Chinese. A particularly brutal theater, which involved many atrocities, it was often ignored by the press and public.

The China-Burma-India (CBI) theater of World War II has often been called the "forgotten theater." Operations in this theater were designed to defend India and to keep the Chinese actively involved in the war. Part of China's significance lay as a staging area for the future invasion of Japan. The Allied emphasis on defeating Adolf Hitler relegated the CBI to a secondary theater, resulting in the commitment of fewer forces and less material to the theater. The

success of the campaign in the Pacific further diminished the importance of China for the invasion of Japan.

The Second Sino-Japanese War actually began with the Japanese attack on July 7, 1937. Responding to an incident at the Marco Polo Bridge, the Japanese Kwantung army advanced against Chiang Kai-shek's Nationalist army. Japanese forces quickly captured Beiping (Beijing) and all the major coastal cities, effectively isolating China.

With the Japanese conquest of the coastal cities, China was forced to rely on the Burma Road from Kunming to Lashio, a railhead in Burma, which connected to the port of Rangoon (Yangon). At best, this road was inadequate to meet China's needs. With the Japanese bombing of Pearl Harbor on December 7, 1941, the United States became more directly involved with the resupply effort, granting $26,000,000 in relief supplies. This amount had grown to $1,107,000,000 by 1945. Even with this massive increase in support, U.S. forces in the theater accounted for less than 2 percent of the total U.S. forces involved in the war.

In 1941, Captain Claire Chennault became a special adviser to Chiang. Chennault formed the American Volunteer Group, which came to be known as the Flying Tigers. He recruited pilots and crews and obtained Air Corps P-40 fighter aircraft. The Flying Tigers were to defend Chinese cities and the Burma Road from Japanese aircraft. By January, 1942, the unit had destroyed more than seventy-five Japanese aircraft. In spite of the success of the Flying Tigers, by April, 1942, the Japanese had conquered Burma, cutting off the Burma Road and the lifeline to China. The Allied forces under General Joseph Warren Stilwell retreated into India.

In an effort to continue supplying China with critical equipment and supplies, the India-China Ferry Command was established, which flew supplies from bases in India over the Himalayan Mountains to Kunming. This was known as flying "the Hump" and was very dangerous. Operating at altitudes in excess of 20,000 feet, aircraft were lost to accidents as well as to

Convoy of trucks carrying supplies along the Burma Road. (National Archives)

China-Burma-India Theater

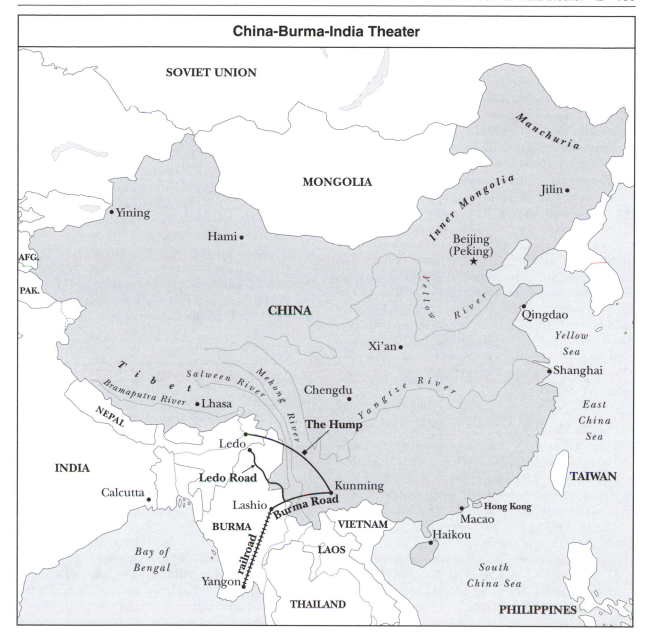

Japanese fighter attacks. Nevertheless, planes continued to depart twenty-four hours a day in the supply effort. By war's end, 650,000 tons of supplies were flown over the Hump at the cost of six hundred aircraft and numerous crews.

While General Stilwell was reorganizing in India, he ordered the construction of a road from Ledo, India, to Mong Yu, China. At Mong Yu, the Ledo Road (later renamed Stilwell Road) joined the existing Burma Road. This construction effort included a fuel pipeline with pumping stations along the entire route. Eventually, 35,000 tons of material traveled this road into China. Construction of this road was an integral part of Stilwell's plan for the reconquest of Burma.

In spite of strained relations with Chiang and Chiang's distrust of the British, Stilwell commanded five divisions of Chinese forces; in concert with the British attacking from the south, he reconquered Burma and reopened the supply lines to China.

Conflict between Stilwell and Chiang over command of Chinese troops and the need for offensive operations led to Stilwell's recall in October, 1944.

Impact Japan surrendered on August 15, 1945, after two devastating atomic bomb attacks—the first on Hiroshima on August 6 and the second on Nagasaki on August 9. The CBI theater had prevented hundreds of thousands of Japanese troops from being deployed elsewhere. However, the defeat of Japan did not signal an end to fighting in China. At the conclusion of hostilities, the United States assisted the Nationalists, moving troops to areas abandoned by the Japanese. Nevertheless, the communist armies of Mao Zedong controlled a large a portion of the country, and the long-simmering conflict between these groups reignited. In 1949, Mao's forces drove Chiang and the Nationalist army from mainland China to Formosa (Taiwan), and the People's Republic of China became the official government. American support of Chiang and the Nationalists contributed to strained relations between the People's Republic and the United States that continued for decades.

Ronald J. Ferrara

Further Reading

Daugherty, Leo J., III. *The Allied Resupply Effort in the China-Burma-India Theater During World War II.* Jefferson, N.C.: McFarland, 2008. A military historian's detailed take on the competing policies of rival commanders in the CBI theater and the heroic efforts to carry out orders.

Davies, John Paton, Jr. *Dragon by the Tail: American, British, Japanese, and Russian Encounters with China and One Another.* New York: W. W. Norton, 1972. An American foreign service officer stationed in China, Davies presents a unique perspective on Sino-Japanese relations as well as profiles of the major characters in the China-Burma-India theater.

Peers, William R., and Dean Brelis. *Behind the Burma Road: The Story of America's Most Successful Guerrilla Force.* Boston: Little, Brown, 1963. The authors recount the experience of organizing and leading OSS Detachment 101 and the ensuing guerrilla operations that contributed to the capture of the Japanese-held city and airbase at Myitkyina and the reconquest of Burma.

Stilwell, Joseph Warren. *The Stilwell Papers.* Edited by Theodore H. White. New York: Sloane, 1948. An intimate look at the China-Burma-India theater by the commander of the American forces in the CBI theater.

Thorne, Bliss K. *The Hump: The Great Military Airlift of World War II.* New York: J. B. Lippincott, 1965. A pilot's personal reminiscences of flying the Hump and the incredible challenges that existed in supplying the Chinese with vital material.

Webster, Donavan. *The Burma Road: The Epic Story of the China-Burma-India Theater in World War II.* New York: Farrar, Straus and Giroux, 2003. An well-researched work that examines the entire China-Burma-India theater of operations beginning with the retreat from Burma and concluding with the completion of the Burma Road.

See also China and North America; Cold War; Flying Tigers; Foreign policy of the United States; Marshall, George C.; Stilwell, Joseph Warren.

■ Chips the War Dog

Identification Dog that served with American combat troops in Europe during World War II
Born 1940; Pleasantville, New York
Died April 12, 1946; Pleasantville, New York

One of the most decorated dogs in history and the first to be sent overseas in World War II, Chips demonstrated that dogs can offer services crucial to war troops.

Chips was a pet of the Edward Wren family, who volunteered Chips to the U.S. Army after he showed his combat potential by biting at least one garbage collector. Although trained as a sentry dog, Chips excelled at flushing out enemy troops. With the Third Infantry Division under General George S. Patton in 1942, he served in North Africa, Sicily, and Naples-Amo, as well as in the French, Rhineland, and central European theaters. While under fire from machine gunners in Sicily in 1943, Chips charged an enemy bunker and viciously seized an Italian soldier by the throat. Four others who unsuccessfully shot at him then surrendered. Later, Chips alerted his company to ten escaping prisoners. He was also a sentry for the 1943 Casablanca Conference. It is thought that he may have sired nine pups with a female dog named Mena belonging to the canine Women's Army Corps.

Impact   Chips was the subject of two congressional speeches, and General Dwight D. Eisenhower personally thanked him, though Chips did nip him once. The courageous canine received the Distinguished Service Cross, the Silver Star, and the Purple Heart. Unofficially, he earned a theater ribbon for an assault landing and a battle star (service star).

Chips returned home, accompanied by six photographers and reporters, and was discharged on December 10, 1945. He died later from complications of his combat wounds. Chips's medals were later revoked because he was a dog. Disney made a television film about him, *Chips, the War Dog*, that aired in 1990 and was released for sale in 1993.

Jan Hall

Further Reading

Derr, Mark. *A Dog's History of America: How Our Best Friend Explored, Conquered, and Settled a Continent*. New York: North Point Press, 2004.

Lemish, Michael G. *War Dogs: A History of Loyalty and Heroism*. Washington, D.C.: Brassey's, 1999.

West, Nancy. *Chips: A Hometown Hero*. Thornwood, N.Y.: Off Lead Publications, 2004.

See also   Casablanca Conference; Eisenhower, Dwight D.; War heroes; Wartime propaganda in the United States; World War II.

■ Chuck and Chuckles

Identification   American comedy dance team made up of Charles "Chuck" Green and James Walker

Charles "Chuck" Green

Born   November 6, 1919; Fitzgerald, Georgia
Died   March 7, 1997; Oakland, California

James Walker

Born   c. 1919; Georgia?
Died   1968; Frankfurt, Germany

Chuck and Chuckles made up one of the most popular comedy dance groups of the early 1940's. Green became a leading figure in dance and a later inspiration to several generations of young dancers.

Childhood friends from Georgia, Charles "Chuck" Green and James Walker were teamed up by New York agent Nat Nazzaro to capitalize on the success of the comedy dance duo Buck and Bubbles. John Bubbles, the original Sportin' Life in the musical *Porgy and Bess*, made Green his protégé. In their act, Walker ("Chuckles"), tall and thin and a very leggy dancer, would play a broken-down vibraphone and engage Green ("Chuck") in rapid rhythmic banter to sell the act, while the diminutive Green dazzled the audience with his rhythm tap dancing. The duo toured the United States, Europe, and Australia with big bands, playing up to five shows a day.

The stress took its toll on Green, who had a breakdown in 1944 and was committed to a mental institution for fifteen years. Walker later teamed up with LeRoy Myers. Green reemerged as a dancer during the 1960's and became a revered figure in the field.

Impact   Green and Walker transmitted the style and technique of early jazz tap artists such as John Bubbles to young dancers for several decades after the duo's heyday. Green continued to perform into the 1980's and was inducted into the Tap Dance Hall of Fame in 2003.

David E. Anderson

Further Reading

Frank, Rusty E. *Tap! The Greatest Tap Dance Stars and Their Stories, 1900-1955*. Rev. ed. New York: Da Capo Press, 1994.

Stearns, Marshall, and Jean Stearns. *Jazz Dance: The Story of American Vernacular Dance*. 2d ed. New York: Da Capo Press, 1994.

See also   African Americans; Coles, Honi; Dance; Kelly, Gene; Music: Jazz; Music: Popular.

■ Churchill, Winston

Identification   Prime minister of Great Britain, 1940-1945
Born   November 30, 1874; Blenheim, Oxfordshire, England
Died   January 24, 1965; London, England

As British prime minister through most of World War II, Churchill emerged, along with U.S. president Franklin D. Roosevelt and Soviet premier Joseph Stalin, as a primary opponent to the forces of fascism and totalitarianism—Germany, Italy, and Japan. Through perseverance, conviction, rhetoric, and wit, Churchill rallied the British and influenced the Americans during the World War II. During the years immediately following the World War II, he in-fluenced American foreign policy and public opinion in his condemnation of expanding Soviet control in Eastern Europe.

During the 1940's, Winston Churchill played an important role in American history through his close partnerships with Franklin D. Roosevelt and as a friendly confidant of Harry S. Truman, even though he was out of power. Churchill left his mark on American affairs and policies as no other foreigner did during this turbulent decade.

World War II Before the attack on Pearl Harbor on December 7, 1941, which resulted in American entry into World War II, Churchill and Roosevelt had begun to work together to save the West and develop common values that would prevail after the war. Churchill, who became prime minister of Great Britain on May 10, 1940—the same day as the German invasion of France—cultivated a relationship with Roosevelt during 1940 and 1941. In March, 1941, Lend-Lease was enacted and resulted in providing the British, along with other Allied nations, with much-needed supplies. On August 14, 1941, Churchill and Roosevelt met on naval ships off of the coast of Newfoundland; they agreed to peace aims that were espoused in the Atlantic Charter. After the Japanese attack on Hawaii and the Philippines and the subsequent American declaration of war against Japan, the United States joined in the larger struggle against Germany and Italy.

The Churchill-Roosevelt relationship during 1941-1943 developed into a friendship. Churchill visited the United States several times and met with Roosevelt at summit meetings such as Casablanca (January 14-24, 1943). By late 1943, Churchill realized that Roosevelt's antipathy to "imperialism" (he was a Wilsonian anti-imperialist) was shifting Britain into a secondary position; Roosevelt looked to Joseph Stalin's Soviet Union as the major American partner during the postwar era. At the Yalta Conference (February 7-12, 1945), Churchill experienced isolation when he was not invited to several important meetings between Roosevelt and Stalin. Roosevelt died on April 12, 1945, and the new and inexperienced U.S. president Harry S. Truman came into power. Churchill was defeated in the postwar general election in July, 1945; the Labour leader Clement Attlee became Britain's prime minister (1945-1951).

British prime minister Winston Churchill walking the deck of the battleship HMS Prince of Wales during his August, 1941, voyage to North America to meet with President Franklin D. Roosevelt. (AP/Wide World Photos)

Origins of the Cold War Between 1945 and 1951, Churchill occupied himself with writing his *Memoirs of the Second World War* (1959) and completing *A History of the English-Speaking Peoples* (1957). As leader of Britain's Conservative Party, he maintained a keen interest in foreign affairs and became convinced that the Soviet Union posed a grave threat to the West and its values. In response to an invitation to speak at Westminster College in Fulton, Missouri—which was endorsed by President Truman—Churchill visited the campus on March 5, 1946, and delivered his famous "Iron Curtain" speech, in which he argued that Soviet aggression in Eastern Europe denied liberty to the subject peoples and posed a threat to Western Europe. Churchill called for a mutual defense alliance directed to limit Soviet expansion; he argued that central to this new alliance would be the "special relationship" between the United States and the United Kingdom.

Within a year of the speech, Churchill's influence was evident in the Truman Doctrine, which was focused on preventing the Soviets from expanding their sphere to include Greece and Turkey, and in the Marshall Plan (European Economic Recovery Act), launched to accelerate the economic recovery of the Western European states. In 1949, Churchill's call for a defensive alliance was realized when the United States, the United Kingdom, and most of the Western European states joined to form the North Atlantic Treaty Organization (NATO).

Impact   Churchill's war leadership and his relationships with Roosevelt and Truman resulted in a close alliance between the United States and the United Kingdom that has survived for more than six decades after the conclusion of World War II. Churchill's historical insights on the ambitions of the Soviet Union helped shape American foreign policy during the second half of the twentieth century.

William T. Walker

Further Reading

Gilbert, Martin. *Churchill and America.* New York: Free Press, 2005. An outstanding scholarly account on Churchill's visits, impressions, and experiences in the United States, with emphasis on the 1940's.

Harbutt, Fraser J. *The Iron Curtain: Churchill, America and the Origins of the Cold War.* New York: Oxford University Press, 1986. A reliable and useful history of Churchill's influence on American policy in the emergence of the Cold War.

Kimball, Warren F. *Forged in War: Roosevelt, Churchill, and the Second World War.* Chicago: Ivan R. Dee, 2003. An excellent scholarly examination of the evolution of the Roosevelt-Churchill relationship and its impact on the prosecution of World War II.

Meacham, Jon. *Franklin and Winston: An Intimate Portrait of their Epic Friendship.* New York: Random House, 2003. A well-written and reliable study of the Roosevelt-Churchill relationship and its impact on Anglo-American relations.

Muller, James W., ed.. *Churchill's "Iron Curtain" Speech Fifty Years Later.* Columbia: University of Missouri Press, 1999. An important analysis of Churchill's speech in Fulton, Missouri, in which he warned of the Soviet threat to the West and its values.

Pilpel, Robert H. *Churchill in America, 1895-1961: An Affectionate Portrait.* New York: Harcourt Brace Jovanovich, 1976. A sympathetic description of Churchill's experiences and relationships in the United States.

Reynolds, David. *From World War to Cold War: Churchill, Roosevelt, and the International History of the 1940's.* New York: Oxford University Press, 2006. The best source for an understanding of Churchill's role in the diplomacy of the 1940's and the outbreak of the Cold War.

See also   Atlantic Charter; Cairo Conference; Canada and Great Britain; Cold War; Decolonization of European empires; "Iron Curtain" speech; Quebec Conferences; Roosevelt, Franklin D.; Tehran Conference; World War II; Yalta Conference.

■ Cisco Kid

Identification   Fictional character in film, radio, television, and comic-book series

Appearing in a variety of media, the Cisco Kid was one of the earliest characters to provide major roles for Latino actors, even though some ethnic stereotypes remained. He first appeared in a short story in 1907 and became a staple of films during the 1930's, but he rose to much greater fame during the 1940's when he found his way into radio and a syndicated comic strip.

The Cisco Kid originated in 1907 in "The Caballero's Way," a story in the famous American short-story writer O. Henry's book *Heart of the West.* In 1929, the character reappeared in the first of what would become many films. During the 1940's, he began appearing in radio programs and a comic strip, and he would later add a television series. Through all these years, his character continuously evolved, as he was variously portrayed as a ruthless outlaw and a Latino Robin Hood. In 1929, he appeared in the first major Western talkie film, *In Old Arizona* (1929). That film was nominated for several Academy Awards, including best actor, which Warner Baxter—a non-Latino actor—won for portraying the Cisco Kid as a happy-go-lucky bandit. In later years, the character would provide important roles for Latino actors.

Duncan Renaldo as the Cisco Kid. (Getty Images)

Among the leading Latino actors who played the Cisco Kid during the 1940's were César Romero, Duncan Renaldo, and Gilbert Roland. Renaldo also reprised his role as the Cisco Kid in *The Cisco Kid* television series during the 1950's. Jimmy Smits would played him in a television film broadcast in 1994. Among the actors who played Cisco's sidekick were Chris-Pin Martin, first as "Gordito" and later as "Pancho"; Martin Garralaga as Pancho; Frank Yaconelli as Baby; and Leo Carrillo as the best-known Pancho. The Cisco Kid and Pancho became positive role models for children as they dispensed justice with a sense of humor and nonviolence.

Impact A dashing and romantic figure, the Cisco Kid and his jovial companion Pancho, engaged in quick-witted repartee as they roamed the Southwest fighting injustice and helping the needy. Cisco Kid items such as lunch boxes, toy guns, and coloring books contributed to licensed-product merchandising.

Sharon K. Wilson and Raymond Wilson

Further Reading

Nevins, Francis M., and Gary D. Keller. *The Cisco Kid: American Hero, Hispanic Roots.* Tucson: Arizona State University: Bilingual Review Press, 2008.

Rodríguez, Clara E. *Heroes, Lovers, and Others: The Story of Latinos in Hollywood.* New York: Oxford University Press, 2008.

See also Comic books; Cowboy films; Film in the United States; Film serials; Mexico; Radio in the United States; Renaldo, Duncan; Roland, Gilbert; Romero, César; Television.

■ *Citizen Kane*

Identification Film about the rise and fall of a rich newspaper tycoon, told in a newsreel documentary and then nonchronologically to an inquiring reporter in flashbacks from five people who knew the man

Director Orson Welles (1915-1985)

Date Released on May 1, 1941

Citizen Kane is undoubtedly one of the most important and influential films in filmmaking history. Consistently ranked as the greatest film of all time by the American Film Institute and Sight and Sound polls, it fostered the dark chiaroscuro look and flashbacks of the emerging film noir crime thrillers of the 1940's and 1950's and helped establish the idea of the director as auteur of the film.

At the age of twenty-five, Orson Welles signed an unprecedented contract at RKO Pictures giving him "final cut," or complete control, over making his first feature film. Though he had much stage and radio experience, he had no knowledge about making motion pictures. That this novice auteur could harness and inspire the talents of his crew in this project—including famed cinematographer Gregg Toland, screenwriter Herman J. Mankiewicz, composer Bernard Herrmann, editor Robert Wise, RKO special effects and makeup artists, and the Mercury Theatre Players, with whom Welles had acted on stage—makes the achievement of *Kane* all the more remarkable.

While few of the film techniques in the unconventional *Kane* are new, they are refined and perfected to an incredible degree: deep-focus photography, low-key lighting, unusual low camera angles, overlapping dialogue, startling and abrupt edits and montage sequences, fluid and suprising camera movements, asymmetrical compositions, special effects (estimated in more than 50 percent of the film) not detected until recently, flashforwards and linked flashbacks, and a "mock" newsreel about Kane's life. The film is replete with justifiably famous symbols: Xanadu (Kane's palatial mansion), the "Rosebud" sled, the glass snow-scene paperweight, second wife Susan's puzzles, Kane's statues, Kane's reflections in mirrors, and so on.

Rather than answer what happens next, the non-linear story departs from Hollywood tradition by asking, who is this newspaper tycoon Charles Foster Kane, a man who rises in power and influence but loses love and innocence? The search for the mystery of "Rosebud," Kane's last word before he died and the most famous opening word of dialogue in cinema, ends ambiguously like a puzzle with missing pieces or a cubist portrait of an infinity of Kanes reflected in mirrors.

Though Welles denied it, Kane bore an uncomfortable resemblance to newspaper magnate William Randolph Hearst, and Kane's second wife, Susan, to Hearst's mistress, actor Marion Davies. In response to the extremely unflattering portraits, Hearst and his minions in radio stations and Hearst newspapers at first completely banned all references to the movie, and so it lacked advertising. Afraid of a backlash from the Hearst news empire, major Hollywood moguls offered RKO more than $800,000 (the film's budget) to burn the negative. When the film was released, studio boycotts prevented it from being shown in large key theaters. It is no wonder, then, that the film was not a box-office success and that it won only a single Academy Award for the screenplay by Mankiewicz and Welles, despite the immediate critical acclaim upon release.

Impact   The fiftieth anniversary DVD edition of *Citizen Kane* demonstrated the film's sustained interest and significance, its influence on the film noir style and the later French New Wave, and the audacious creative vision of the novice auteur Welles that still inspires filmmakers today.

Joseph Francavilla

Further Reading

Carringer, Robert L. *The Making of "Citizen Kane."* Berkeley: University of California Press, 1985.

_____, ed. *Focus on "Citizen Kane."* Film Focus Series. Englewood Cliffs, N.J.: Prentice-Hall, 1971.

Naremore, James, ed. *Orson Welles's "Citizen Kane": A Casebook.* Casebooks in Criticism. New York: Oxford University Press, 2004.

See also   Academy Awards; Film in the United States; Film noir; Newspapers; Theater in the United States; Welles, Orson.

Citizenship Act of 1946. *See* **Canadian Citizenship Act of 1946**

■ Civil defense programs

Definition   Programs to defend civilians and their property from military attack and, more generally, from disasters

World War II involved widespread civilian participation in civil defense programs in both the United States and Canada. These programs stimulated strong patriotic identification with the war effort and helped maintain morale, as well as providing experiences that facilitated implementation of civil defense during the Cold War.

The fall of France to German forces in June, 1940, brought the issue of civil defense to the forefront in North America. At the time, although concerns about the war in Europe were widespread, the United States was following a strict "America first" policy of isolation and was preoccupied with recovering from the Great Depression. Although Canada entered the war six days after Great Britain declared war on Germany in 1939, the war was an ocean away. It was expected that, as in World War I, France would be the main battlefield of the war. It was predicted, however, that France's seemingly impenetrable Maginot Line would halt the German attack and bring a rapid end to the war. The capitulation of France after German forces circumvented the Maginot Line, along with the beginning of the bombing of London shortly afterward, brought more immediacy to the conflict.

World War II   In Canada, as in World War I, the St. John Ambulance Association played a major role in first aid training for civil defense workers. It prepared air raid wardens for possible emergencies, lobbied to install civilian warning systems, and trained citizen groups in survival techniques. In addition, Women's Voluntary Services in larger Canadian cities ran day care centers for women working in war industries work, aided the Red Cross in emergency blood donor clinics, and assisted the staff of the Ministry of War Services. Specially trained civilian groups served as auxiliary fire fighters and as auxiliary police to guard against sabotage. They served as plane spotters to supplement the early warning radar system, inspectors to enforce blackouts, and rescue and emergency relief workers. Auxiliary services were placed under the direction of the Ministry of War Services and financed by the government.

On May 20, 1941, ten days after the German invasion of France, President Franklin D. Roosevelt issued an executive order establishing the Office of Civilian Defense (OCD), which would be under the president's Office of Emergency Planning. The OCD was responsible for promoting protective measures and identifying ways that local citizen groups could participate in national defense. Fiorello La Guardia, the popular mayor of New York City, was appointed to head the OCD, and he appointed the president's wife, Eleanor Roosevelt, to act as assistant director of voluntary participation.

By the summer of 1941, American industries were being encouraged to develop security to ward off spies and saboteurs, and an Air Raid Service was developed. The duties of an air raid warden were defined as directing traffic and directing people to shelters, controlling lights in blackouts, going to disaster areas and reporting damage, assisting in controlling fires, and rendering first aid and other assistance. An air spotter system was established, and the army set up a system of air spotter posts. In October, 1940, La Guardia sent a committee a fire fighters to London to gain insights into the protection of civilians during aerial bombings.

In December, 1941, one week before the attack on Pearl Harbor, La Guardia capitulated to the wishes of Gill Wilson, a New Jersey aviation advocate, and created the Civil Air Patrol (CAP) to act as a coastal patrol. Following the attack on Pearl Harbor, civil defense became a national obsession. Air observation posts were ordered to be on constant alert, and anti-aircraft batteries were constructed in a large number of strategic places. The OCD was replaced with the Civil Defense Administration. Each community was placed under the direction of a civil defense director. Voting districts were assigned wardens, who were assisted by deputy wardens, plane spotters, auxiliary fire fighters, and messengers. Each sector was supposed to have its own shelter, equipped with telephone and radio communication. To fine-tune the system, numerous unannounced air raid drills were held. During the course of the war, it is estimated that more than ten million civilians volunteered to serve in civil defense. Duties increased to include bomb squads, decontamination squads, emergency food and housing corps, medical corps, and demolition and road clearance crews.

Volunteers posted atop the Empire State Building to watch for incoming enemy planes in a prewar civil defense test in early 1941. (The Chrysler Building can be seen on the right.) (AP/Wide World Photos)

Preparations for Attack　The devastation caused by German bombing of European cities and the destruction at Pearl Harbor caused a major preoccupation with air attacks. Important national documents were moved by the Library of Congress to remote and secure locations. Through most of the war, the Declaration of Independence was housed at Fort Knox. Major museums relocated their most important pieces or built special reinforced vaults to provide added protection. Across the United States, libraries became war information centers for disseminating government-prepared pamphlets related to civil defense and places for holding civil defense training sessions. Many libraries were structured to serve as local civil defense headquarters or bomb shelters in the event of an attack.

In industrial and coastal cities, local police were used to patrol important bridges, water supply sources, and war manufacturing plants, as well as to keep tabs on the activities of potentially subversive groups and individuals. They carried out Selective Service investigations and helped supervise prisoners of war who were on work details. The effectiveness of such monitoring was increased exponentially with the widespread use of the two-way radio beginning in 1942. Police were also used to create evacuation plans and other emergency and disaster plans. Because many police departments were stretched thin by war-related duties, auxiliary or reserve police units were created to help relieve the shortage. Women filled many of these roles.

The CAP played an important role in monitoring conditions from the air, particularly on America's lengthy dual coasts. Early in 1942, an initial ninety-day trial period began off the East Coast to search for enemy submarines or U.S. ships in distress. At first, CAP pilots were used as spotters to direct attacks on submarines and to coordinate rescue operations. Later in the war, aircraft were armed with bombs and depth charges to initiate attacks. CAP pilots logged in one-half million hours during World War II, flew 24 million miles, and found 173 subs, attacking 10 and sinking 2. Inland, CAP pilots transported strategic cargo between defense plants and between military bases. CAP pilots had to supply their own planes, though donations and government remuneration of eight dollars a day helped defray some of the costs. Women served in CAP and by the end of the war constituted 20 percent of the pilots.

The Cold War　During World War II, more than ten million volunteers served in the Civil Defense Corps. The mass involvement was excellent for morale, but some have questioned whether the effort and expense were worthwhile in terms of actual accomplishments, given that the Japanese staged only a few minor attacks on North American soil after Pearl Harbor. On June 4, 1945, as the war against Germany ended and the war against Japan was winding down, the Office of Civilian Defense was ended by President Harry S. Truman's Executive Order 8757.

After the conclusion of World War II, consciousness of an ongoing threat to the security of the United States was slow to emerge. Civil defense remained an important issue mostly within the War Department, which worried about what the world would be like when the Soviet Union also became a nuclear power. On November 25, 1946, the War Department established a small Civil Defense Board staffed solely by the military, with the purpose of studying the issue of resurrecting civil defense. In March, 1947, it issued a report, *A Study of Civil Defense*, which recognized the importance of civil preparedness and proposed the creation of a federal civil defense agency, subordinate to the secretary of war but independent of the armed forces. The proposal also advocated state and local governments playing important roles in civil defense. In July, 1947, however, there was no mention of civil defense when the National Security Act was passed, creating the Air Force as an equal branch of the military and creating the Central Intelligence Agency.

As diplomatic crises with the Soviet Union mounted, the military issued a new Civil Defense Plan in October, 1948, entitled *Civil Defense for National Security*, more commonly referred to as the *Hopley Report*. The new plan, put forth in three hundred pages by Russell J. Hopley, the first director of the Office of Civil Defense Planning, proposed a state-run civil defense program, directed by the governor of each state with only minimal federal involvement. This plan was not put into effect. President Truman insisted that civil defense remain in the planning stage.

In Canada, the first peacetime civil defense coordinator was appointed in October, 1948. His job was to supervise planning for public air raid shelters, providing emergency food and medical supplies, and mass evacuation of likely targets. The first major action in civil defense preparedness came in 1955 in Operation Lifesaver, an unusual affair in which the city of Calgary was evacuated in a practice drill.

On September 23, 1949, it was announced to the American public what the military had known for a month: The Soviet Union had successfully tested its first atomic bomb. The United States no longer had the security of a nuclear monopoly. One week later, it was announced that China and its 500 million people were now under communist rule. Almost immediately, congressmen expressed shock that civil defense was only in its planning stage. On their own, state governments began to enact plans to deal with the potential medical dangers of radiation and the massive structural damage caused by nuclear bombs.

Impact On June 25, 1950, communist North Korea invaded South Korea. The United States intervened militarily, although the activity was termed a police action under United Nations mandate, rather than a war. Popular hysteria about the menace of communism accelerated. On January 12, 1951, President Truman signed the Civil Defense Act of 1950 (Public Law 920), putting into effect most of the proposals in the Hopley Report regarding state supervision but also creating the Federal Civil Defense Administration as an umbrella organization.

Experience with civil defense during World War II eased the way into civil defense in the nuclear age of the Cold War. The federal civil defense program was repealed by Public Law 93-337 in 1994. Various activities of civil defense were reallocated to different agencies, and overall the focus shifted from emergencies related to natural disasters rather than war.

Irwin Halfond

Further Reading

Becker, Patti C. *Books and Libraries in American Society During World War II: Weapons in the War of Ideas.* New York: Routledge, 2004. A study of the transformation of libraries in World War II to meet new societal demands. Based on a wealth of primary and secondary sources.

Davis, Tracy C. *Stages of Emergency: Cold War Nuclear Civil Defense.* Raleigh, N.C.: Duke University Press, 2007. A study of civil defense exercises in the United States, Canada, and Great Britain during the early years of the Cold War.

Garrison, Dee. *Bracing for Armageddon: Why Civil Defense Never Worked.* New York: Oxford University Press, 2006. A critical analysis, based on a wealth of primary source materials, of the U.S. government's civil defense plans from World War II through the end of the Cold War.

Hogan, Michael J. *A Cross of Iron: Harry S. Truman and the Origins of the National Security State.* Cambridge, England: Cambridge University Press, 2000. A study of the debate concerning national security policy emerging from World War II by a noted scholar in twentieth century U.S. foreign policy.

Kennedy, David M. *Freedom from Fear: The American People in Depression and War, 1929-1945.* New York: Oxford University Press, 2001. A massive and highly readable study of American life during a major period of crisis. Extensive sources and copious footnotes.

See also Anticommunism; Atomic bomb; Balloon bombs, Japanese; Canadian participation in World War II; Cold War; Dim-out of 1945; Isolationism; Los Angeles, Battle of; Oregon bombing; Truman, Harry S.

■ Civil rights and liberties

Civil rights and liberties came under pressure during the decade, first because of World War II and later because of the Cold War. During the 1940's, the government interned American citizens because of their race, declared martial law in Hawaii, imposed price controls and rationing throughout the nation, and began to conduct witch-hunts for suspected communists that culminated in the McCarthyism of the 1950's.

On December 7, 1941, the Imperial Japanese Navy carried out a devastating surprise attack on the U.S. naval base at Pearl Harbor, Hawaii, laying waste to much of the U.S. Pacific battleship fleet. Fears of sabotage or outright invasion by the Japanese empire led to overreaction and hysterical efforts to contain those suspected of being enemies within the nation's borders. After the end of World War II, the United States shifted attention to its former ally, the Soviet Union, as the Cold War commenced. This also led to repression, with suspected communists becoming the subject of government attention.

Japanese American Exclusion and Internment   After the devastating sneak attack on Pearl Harbor, President Franklin D. Roosevelt issued Executive Order 9066, which authorized military commanders to declare certain areas of the United States off-limits, in an effort to protect against sabotage. Pursuant to this executive order, General John L. DeWitt issued a series of orders directed against all persons of Japanese descent, of whom approximately seventy thousand were American citizens. (Although exclusion laws in effect at the time prohibited Asians from acquiring U.S. citizenship through naturalization, those born within the United States were granted birthright citizenship under the Fourteenth Amendment.)

Support for General DeWitt's military orders was widespread. Even California Attorney General Earl Warren, who would later, as chief justice of the United States, champion the rights of minorities and the underprivileged, publicly called for the removal of Japanese Americans from California.

Near the end of March, 1942, General DeWitt established a curfew applicable to all persons of Japanese ancestry, requiring them to remain within their residences between 8 P.M. and 6 A.M. Soon thereafter, he began excluding all persons of Japanese descent from large parts of the West Coast and eventually called for relocation to other areas. Relocation typically occurred in two stages, with Japanese aliens and Japanese Americans initially reporting to civilian assembly centers, mostly in California but with several in other western states. Subsequently, the detainees were moved to internment camps in California, Arizona, Colorado, Wyoming, Arkansas, Idaho, and Utah.

In *Hirabayashi v. United States* (1943) and *Korematsu v. United States* (1944), the Supreme Court upheld the curfew and exclusion orders as legitimate exercises of government authority, given the military necessity of the time and the perceived threat of sabotage by Japanese agents. In *Ex parte Endo* (1944), however, the Court concluded that the internment

President Franklin D. Roosevelt signing a proclamation declaring December 15, 1941, Bill of Rights Day, in observance of the 150th anniversary of ratification of the first ten amendments to the U.S. Constitution. New York mayor Fiorello La Guardia, whose civilian defense organization is to sponsor the celebration, looks on. (AP/Wide World Photos)

order had deprived American citizens of their due process by not requiring proof of disloyalty before internment.

More than forty years after the end of World War II, the federal government paid each surviving detainee $20,000; President Ronald Reagan—and subsequently, President George H. W. Bush—also officially apologized for the internment.

Martial Law in Hawaii   Although the government never attempted to implement curfew, exclusion, or internment orders in Hawaii, the territorial governor did declare martial law immediately after the Pearl Harbor attack, with President Roosevelt giving his approval of this declaration two days later. Martial law remained in effect until October, 1944. As a result of the declaration of martial law, the military commander in Hawaii assumed governance of the territory as military governor. He displaced the civilian courts with military tribunals for the prosecution of civilian criminals; these military courts were bound neither by the usual rules of evidence or procedure nor by the statutory maximum penalties prescribed by statute. There was no appeal of decisions by the military tribunals. In addition, the military governor issued a number of military orders that governed the day-to-day activities of civilians, including one that broadly forbade civilians from interfering with military personnel.

One civilian was prosecuted in a military court in 1942 for embezzling stock from another Hawaii resident. Civilian courts had been opened to a limited extent by this time but had not had their criminal jurisdiction restored. By 1944, the civilian courts had largely been reopened, but military courts retained jurisdiction to try cases involving violations of military order; one civilian was prosecuted in a military court for engaging in a bar fight with off-duty soldiers.

In *Duncan v. Kahanamoku* (1946), the Supreme Court concluded that the territorial governor's authorization to declare martial law did not empower the military governor to replace civilian courts with military courts. The Court concluded that martial law allowed the governor to ensure that the military could carry its mandated duties of defending the territory and ensuring civil order, but in this case involving the arrest of a citizen for public intoxication, trial by military tribunal was ruled unconstitutional.

Price Controls and Rationing   With World War II demanding incredible industrial production directed toward the war effort, even before official U.S. entry into the war, the federal government instituted severe price controls to fight inflation and restricted use of various goods. President Roosevelt created the Office of Price Administration through Executive Order 8875 on August 28, 1941. Congress created various regulations and created a price administrator who was charged with establishing maximum prices and rents. Any challenges to the price administrator's price determinations had to be made to the price administrator first, then to the Emergency Court of Appeals, a federal court consisting of at least three federal judges. Appeals from that court's decisions went to the Supreme Court.

If, however, a person violated the price controls without challenging them before the price administrator and the Emergency Court of Appeals, he or she was subject to injunctive relief, treble damages, or even criminal punishment. Significantly, it was not a valid defense in this prosecution to argue that the price administrator's price determinations were unreasonable. Failing to take advantage of the

Emergency Court of Appeal's forum for challenging the price controls, therefore, acted as a waiver of rights. In *Yakus v. United States* (1944), the Supreme Court upheld this divided procedure, despite a dissenting opinion arguing that it violated "the constitutional integrity of the judicial process."

The federal government also rationed various goods under local War Price and Rationing Boards, also under the Office of Price Administration. These boards were responsible for issuing ration coupons to individuals for such scarce and/or war-related goods as gasoline, rubber, sugar, coffee, and meat.

Free Speech During World War II   Free speech fared better during World War II than during the Civil War and World War I, when war protesters were subject to being charged with sedition or other such crimes simply for speaking out against the government. The emergence of the Cold War led to a variety of direct or indirect restrictions on free speech, many aimed at cracking down on communism within the United States.

One symbol of the greater respect for free speech during World War II than existed during World War I was President Roosevelt's appointment in 1941 of Francis Biddle as U.S. attorney general. A noted civil libertarian, Biddle had previously criticized the World War I sedition prosecutions as hysterical. Although the government managed not to repeat the excesses of the past, at least to as great a degree, free speech nevertheless was more constrained than it is today.

In the late 1930's, Congress had convened the House Committee on Un-American Activities (also known as the House Un-American Activities Committee, or HUAC) to investigate anti-U.S. propaganda. Its chair, Representative Martin Dies, Jr., of Texas, attacked organizations such as the American Civil Liberties Union as "un-American" and controlled by communists. Other organizations accused of communist ties included the Boy Scouts, the Camp Fire Girls, and much of Hollywood. Dies and HUAC opened the door to the even more intrusive and abusive investigations by Senator Joseph McCarthy of Wisconsin in the 1950's.

The Alien Registration Act of 1940, also known as the Smith Act, prohibited anyone from advocating the violent or forceful overthrow of the U.S. government. President Roosevelt signed the bill into law, but his attorneys general largely refused to prosecute anyone under it during World War II. During the Cold War, however, the Smith Act emerged as a potent weapon, and the Supreme Court ultimately upheld its validity in *Dennis v. United States* (1951).

Impact Restrictions on civil rights and liberties during the 1940's resulted largely from the perceived necessities of war. People of Japanese ancestry as a group suffered the most severe curtailments of rights through forced relocation to internment camps. All Americans shared the material cost of engaging in war by being subject to price controls and rationing that restricted their abilities to buy and sell goods and services.

Tung Yin

Further Reading

Fisher, Louis. *Nazi Saboteurs on Trial: A Military Tribunal and American Law.* Lawrence: University Press of Kansas, 2003. A trade publication that covers the events leading up to and including *Ex parte Quirin* in 1942 (the case of the German saboteurs).

Rehnquist, William H. *All the Laws but One: Civil Liberties in Wartime.* New York: Vintage, 2000. A historical overview of the clash between civil liberties and the demands of war, focusing primarily on the Civil War and World War II.

Schwartz, Bernard. *A History of the Supreme Court.* New York: Oxford University Press, 1993. A readable summary of major Supreme Court decisions, organized chronologically.

Stone, Geoffrey R. *Perilous Times: Free Speech in Wartime, from the Sedition Act of 1798 to the War on Terrorism.* New York: W. W. Norton, 2004. A comprehensive historical account of infringements of free speech and other civil liberties in the United States during wartime.

See also *An American Dilemma: The Negro Problem and American Democracy*; Asian Americans; Censorship in the United States; Hollywood blacklisting; House Committee on Un-American Activities; Racial discrimination; Smith Act; Supreme Court, U.S.; Universal Declaration of Human Rights; Voting rights.

■ Clifford, Clark

Identification Special counsel to the president, 1946-1950
Born December 25, 1906; Fort Scott, Kansas
Died October 10, 1998; Bethesda, Maryland

Clifford served as speechwriter and trusted counsel to Democratic president Harry S. Truman. He played a major role in orchestrating Truman's successful 1948 reelection bid and in formulating American foreign policy at the start of the Cold War.

Before World War II, Clark Clifford prospered as a St. Louis trial lawyer. In 1943, he volunteered for the Navy, where he attracted the attention of President Harry S. Truman, who soon came to rely on his counsel on matters of foreign affairs. As Truman's adviser, Clifford championed the Truman Doctrine, the Marshall Plan, American involvement in the North Atlantic Treaty Organization (NATO), and the 1947 National Security Act, which created the Central Intelligence Agency (CIA) and unified the armed forces. He also served as one of the first and most vocal supporters of immediate American recognition of the nation of Israel, founded in 1948.

In 1948, Clifford orchestrated Truman's seemingly doomed reelection bid against the heavily favored Republican candidate Thomas E. Dewey, urging the president to embrace the cause of civil rights and to embark on a whistle-stop tour of the nation. Following Clifford's guidelines, Truman prevailed in one of the greatest election upsets in American political history.

Impact After leaving his government post in 1950, Clifford opened a lucrative law practice in Washington, D.C. He continued serving Democratic presidents, including John F. Kennedy; Lyndon B. Johnson, whom he also served as secretary of defense from 1968 to 1969; and Jimmy Carter. Allegations of financial impropriety plagued his later years and damaged his reputation. Nevertheless, he had played a key role in postwar plans to rebuild Europe and to protect American interests.

Keith M. Finley

Further Reading

Acacia, John. *Clark Clifford: The Wise Man of Washington.* Lexington: University Press of Kentucky, 2009.

Clifford, Clark. *Counsel to the President: A Memoir.* New York: Random House, 1991.

Frantz, Douglas, and David McKean. *Friends in High Places: The Rise and Fall of Clark Clifford.* Boston: Little, Brown, 1995.

See also   Central Intelligence Agency; Civil rights and liberties; Dewey, Thomas E.; Elections in the United States: 1948; Israel, creation of; Marshall Plan; National Security Act of 1947; North Atlantic Treaty Organization; Truman, Harry S.; Truman Doctrine.

■ Cloud seeding

The Event   An airplane pilot made a flight over western Massachusetts's Berkshire Mountains to perform the first scientific seeding of a supercooled cloud with dry ice

Date   November 13, 1946

Place   Berkshire Mountains of western Massachusetts

Cloud seeding, as the first example of weather modification, offered the possibility of artificially creating rain, thereby helping farmers avoid the ravages of droughts. The ability to change the weather also offered the hope that humans would someday be able to control hurricanes, tornadoes, and other weather disasters.

On November 13, 1946, Vincent J. Schaefer dropped about three pounds (1.5 kilograms) of dry ice pellets (solid carbon dioxide) from a light aircraft into a supercooled lenticular stratocumulus cloud near the Berkshire Mountains of western Massachusetts. Within about five minutes, the cloud generated snowflakes. With his actions, Schaefer culminated nearly half a century of research into the physics of clouds and precipitation.

Scientists learned during the early years of the twentieth century that atmospheric processes, including precipitation of rain and snow, sometimes occur because of the abundance of ice-forming nuclei in the atmosphere. They realized that rain could be triggered by artificially supplying ice-forming nuclei. During World War II, Irving Langmuir headed a group of scientists at the General Electric Research Laboratories in Schenectady, New York. The group focused on the generation of smoke screens and ways to halt aircraft icing. After the end of the war, the group continued to focus on manipulating the weather.

In 1946, Schaefer, a member of Langmuir's group, conducted experiments on supercooled clouds in a cold box. (A cloud is a collection of minute water or ice particles that are sufficient in number and density to be seen.) In a rush to make the box cold enough for his experiments, Schaefer dropped a pellet of dry ice into the box. Immediately, a trail of tiny ice crystals appeared along the path of the piece of ice. Schaefer quickly recognized that the extremely low temperature near the surface of the dry ice had caused the droplets along its path to freeze. He immediately made plans to test his discovery in a natural atmosphere, resulting in the cloud seeding experiment on November 13, 1946.

Impact   After Schaefer's experiment proved successful, a few meteorologists began seriously to contemplate changing the weather. Most had been content to observe, explain, and forecast weather events, but Schaefer opened the door to weather modification that had the potential to increase rainfall, suppress damaging hail, and alter the course of severe storms. In later years, critics of cloud seeding argued that it led to the formation of more but smaller raindrops, hence to increased evaporation between the cloud and the ground, with a resulting loss of total rainfall. They also blamed cloud seeding for droughts. Other critics have linked cloud seeding to plant and animal diseases, albeit with little evidence. Largely as a result of the criticism, cloud seeding has lost much governmental support since the 1970's and is not commonly used. Cloud seeding has spread around the world since 1946, but it remains controversial, in part because it has failed to prevent droughts.

Caryn E. Neumann

Further Reading

Battan, Louis J. *Cloud Physics and Cloud Seeding.* Westport, Conn.: Greenwood Press, 1962.

Dennis, Arnett S. *Weather Modification by Cloud Seeding.* New York: Academic Press, 1980.

Keyes, Conrad G., Jr., et al., eds. *Guidelines for Cloud Seeding to Augment Precipitation.* 2d ed. Reston, Va.: American Society of Civil Engineers, 2006.

See also   Aircraft design and development; Natural resources; Science and technology.

■ Coast Guard, U.S.

Identification   U.S. maritime military and civilian
service

Also known as   USCG

*The U.S. Coast Guard is a unique multimission, maritime
agency categorized as one of the five branches of the U.S.
armed forces. Its primary function is to protect the nation's
ports and waterways or any maritime region, including international waters, as required or requested to support national security. Responsible for many missions throughout
World War II, the Guard played a major role in the successful outcome of the war.*

The United States Coast Guard (USCG) is tasked
with enforcement of maritime law, mariner assistance including search and rescue, and national security of all major waterways (such as coasts and
ports) and bodies of water (such as lakes, streams,
and rivers) in the United States and sometimes in international waters. The history of the USCG can be
traced back to August 4, 1790, when the First Congress, under the encouragement of Secretary of the
Treasury Alexander Hamilton, authorized the construction of ten vessels to enforce tariff and trade
laws while attempting to prevent
smuggling, thus predating the nation's first official Navy by eight
years.

Through the early twentieth
century, the Coast Guard was
known as the Revenue Marine
and Cutter Service, until it received its present name in 1915
under an act of Congress combining its maritime service with the
new mandate of life-saving operations. This new single maritime
armed service would now dedi-
cate its efforts to saving lives at sea
and enforcing the nation's maritime laws. As the country's population grew, more responsibilities
were given to the USCG, including operation of the nation's
lighthouses and former tasks of
the Bureau of Marine Inspection
and Navigation, including merchant marine licensing and merchant vessel safety.

One of the most important roles that the Coast
Guard would be assigned would be to assist the Navy
during World War II. World War II saw the Coast
Guard spring into action against the Japanese Empire and Adolf Hitler's notorious submarine fleet,
nicknamed "hearses" by American servicemen. During the war, the Navy credited Coast Guard forces
with sinking or assisting in the sinking of nearly a
dozen of Nazi Germany's U-boats. The USCG was
also the first U.S. armed service to capture Nazi prisoners of war. It also seized the only two German surface vessels to be captured by U.S. forces during the
war. In the Pacific, the Navy credited USCG warships
with sinking two Japanese submarines. Toward the
end of the war, Coast Guard-manned Navy warships
joined the battle and continued escorting convoys
and sailing in hunter-killer groups until the Allies
had won the war.

Impact   The Coast Guard entered World War II as
novices in antisubmarine warfare, but the Guardsmen learned quickly and adapted to combat on the
seas, becoming a integral part of the Allied victory at
sea. During the campaign across the open waters of
the Atlantic, battling weather as well as the highly

*Marines landing equipment on the island of Iwo Jima in February, 1945. As in most am-
phibious landings during World War II, the bulk of the landing craft were operated by
Coast Guardsmen, who suffered the highest rate of casualties of any U.S. service during
the war.* (AP/Wide World Photos)

trained German U-boat fleet, the famous Treasury-class Coast Guard cutters along with other ships earned the respect of their allies and enemies alike.

Paul M. Klenowski

Further Reading

Beard, Tom, ed. *The Coast Guard.* Seattle: Foundation for Coast Guard History, 2004.

Ostrom, Thomas P. *The United States Coast: 1790 to the Present.* Rev. ed. Oakland, Oreg.: Red Anvil Press, 2006.

Willoughby, Malcolm. *U.S. Coast Guard in World War II.* Annapolis, Md.: Naval Institute Press, 1989.

See also Air Force, U.S.; Army, U.S.; Atlantic, Battle of the; Casualties of World War II; *The Good War: An Oral History of World War II; History of the United States Naval Operations in World War II;* Navy, U.S.

■ Cochran, Jacqueline

Identification American pilot and entrepreneur
Born May 11, 1906 or 1910; Pensacola, Florida
Died August 9, 1980; Indio, California

Cochran played a pioneering role in female aviation and military service by organizing and directing the Women's Air Force Service Pilots during World War II. She was also a leading figure in the development of the American cosmetics industry.

Jacqueline Cochran was an orphan of obscure origins raised in rural poverty. She dropped out of school at an early age to begin working. In 1932, she met her future husband, Floyd Odlum, who convinced her to obtain her pilot's license, which she received in under three weeks. She soon began winning air races and breaking female flight records. She also founded her own successful business, Jacqueline Cochran Cosmetics. During World War II, Cochran traveled to Great Britain to ferry planes, becoming the first woman to take off from an aircraft carrier and to pilot a bomber across the Atlantic.

Cochran returned to the United States to organize and serve as director of the Army Air Force's Women's Air Force Service Pilots (WASPs). After the war, she continued flying, setting altitude, speed, and distance records, most notably becoming the

first woman to break the sound barrier. She won numerous honors, including the Distinguished Service Medal and fifteen Harmon Trophies as the top female pilot of the year. Her cosmetics business flourished, and she was twice named woman of the year in business by the Associated Press. She retired from flying in 1970 and was inducted into the National Aviation Hall of Fame in 1971.

Impact Cochran's efforts to train female pilots in the British and U.S. military to ferry planes and supplies freed male pilots for active combat missions. Significantly, her work helped break opposition to women in the military and commercial aviation.

Marcella Bush Trevino

Further Reading

Cochran, Jacqueline, and Maryann Bucknum Brinley. *Jackie Cochran: An Autobiography.* New York: Bantam Books, 1987.

Rich, Doris L. *Jackie Cochran: Pilot in the Fastest Lane.* Gainesville: University Press of Florida, 2007.

See also Air Force, U.S.; Arnold, Henry "Hap"; Jet engines; Women in the U.S. military; Women's roles and rights in the United States; World War II.

■ Cocoanut Grove nightclub fire

The Event A devastating fire that resulted in the destruction of a popular nightclub and nearly five hundred deaths
Date November 28, 1942
Place Boston, Massachusetts

The fire at Cocoanut Grove took 492 lives and injured hundreds. The response to the victims' injuries included application of new medical treatments and innovative psychological practices that aided the survivors. Stricter adherence to existing safety laws and more stringent fire and building codes followed soon after.

In 1942, on the Saturday following Thanksgiving, the newly renovated Cocoanut Grove was a choice nightclub for celebrating in Boston. The club, located near the theater district on Piedmont Street, was packed with nearly 1,000 people (approved occupancy was for 460) who were enjoying an evening of gaiety and frolic and a respite from the realities of World War II. At 10:15 P.M., the revelry ended.

A fire started in the downstairs' Melody Lounge of

the nightclub. The flame ignited the tropical decorations, stole across the ceiling, surrounded the occupants with smoke and fumes, and exploded up into the lobby. As the flame advanced, many of those in the lounge raced to the Shawmut Street exit, only to find themselves trapped behind a locked door. A few guests successfully exited the single main door, but soon the revolving door stuck, and many customers were trapped inside. Customers in the newly opened cocktail lounge section of the club found their exit obstructed, too, but this time the problem was that the door opened inward. The flame and smoke also trapped people in the dining room area.

Firefighters helping victims escape from the Cocoanut Grove fire in Boston's Back Bay section. (AP/Wide World Photos)

As the Cocoanut Grove occupants shouted and screamed, firemen, responding to a local car fire, heard their pleas and quickly reacted. While the timeliness was fortunate, their services were impeded by smoke and clogged entrances. Nearly all people in the vicinity—citizens, servicemen, and professional rescuers, including members of the Red Cross and the Salvation Army—were mobilized to assist. Luckily, a Boston disaster emergency exercise that had occurred six days earlier, on November 22, provided some of these same rescuers with practice in handling triage.

Victims were initially transported to Boston City Hospital, but Massachusetts General Hospital and other hospitals were also used. Since it was a time of war, the hospitals' medical supplies were well stocked, and civil defense authorities agreed to lend additional resources. Patients were prioritized and treated for burns, smoke and toxic fume inhalation, and injuries sustained from being trampled. When possible, the latest burn therapy techniques—including new drugs for pain management and infection and better respiratory surveillance—were used.

Impact The Cocoanut Grove fire brought chaos that led authorities to declare martial law later that night. The disaster became the major news story for several days after. Contributing factors in the catastrophe included a building filled well over capacity; easily combustible interior materials; blocked egresses; and a lack of emergency lighting, sprinkler systems, and signage. In addition, the club's owner, Barney Welansky, had not obtained final occupancy permits for the cocktail lounge.

The most devastating nightclub fire in history provided a test for new medical treatments and therapies and resulted in more rigorous fire-safety standards. The verdict in the legal case that resulted from the fire, *Commonwealth v. Welansky* (1944), has been used as precedent in other law cases.

Cynthia J. W. Svoboda

Further Reading

Esposito, John. *Fire in the Grove: The Cocoanut Grove and Its Aftermath.* Cambridge, Mass.: Da Capo Press, 2005.

Keyes, Edward. *Cocoanut Grove.* New York: Atheneum, 1984.

Schorow, Stephanie. *The Cocoanut Grove Fire.* Beverly, Mass.: Commonwealth Editions, 2005.

See also Recreation; Rhythm nightclub fire; Smoking and tobacco.

■ Code breaking

The Event   The Allies achieved dramatic successes during World War II by breaking both the Japanese diplomatic Purple code and the German Enigma ciphers. The information gained from Purple became known as Magic and that from Enigma as Ultra

Date   1940 for Magic; 1940-1941 for Ultra

Places   Washington, D.C., for Magic; Warsaw, Poland, and Bletchley Park, England, for Ultra

By breaking the Purple code a year before the Pearl Harbor attack, Leo Rosen and Genevieve Grotjan gave the United States a great advantage unknown to the Japanese. The brilliant work of Marian Rejewski, Henryk Zygalski, and other Polish mathematicians in the 1930's enabled the successes of Alan Mathison Turing and the other British code breakers working at Bletchley Park during World War II.

The attack on the Japanese Purple code was led by William F. Friedman of the Army Signal Intelligence Service and the crew of talented cryptanalysts he assembled at Arlington Hall Junior College across the Potomac from Washington, D.C. The difficult technical problem Friedman's team faced was figuring out the Purple machine scrambling patterns. Leo Rosen, an electrical engineer at the Massachusetts Institute of Technology (MIT), discovered the way the six most common letters were rotated through twenty-five contacts—a major advance, but of no help with the other twenty letters. Then, one year later, on September 20, 1940, Genevieve Grotjan had the crucial insight into the manner by which the many thousands of patterns were linked in their own pattern of cycles. Whereas a single scrambler mixed up the six common letters, three scramblers interconnected by hundreds of wires transmitted the other twenty letters. Finally, after three weeks, Rosen and Frank Rowlett soldered the last of thousands of connections, flipped a switch, typed in a Purple cipher text, and watched the deciphered message roll out of the printer.

The first Enigma machine was exhibited in Bern, Switzerland, in 1923, and over the next two decades several versions of increasing complexity, both commercial and military, were developed. The first breakthrough in solving Enigma codes came in 1932 when Marian Rejewski discovered the patterns of encipherment programmed into the machine's three rotors, an accomplishment that stunned the French and British code breakers when they learned of it in 1939.

The Germans created separate Enigma codes for its army, air force, and navy and added more rotors to complicate the work at Bletchley Park. However, the British benefited from several advances of their own. First, they invented what they called a Bombe, an arrangement of multiple Enigma machines connected for use with IBM cards. Another great help was the capture of Enigma materials from several trawlers and from the submarines *U 110* and *U 559*. Finally, in the most dazzling intellectual feat of the war, Alan Mathison Turing perceived that matching strings of plain and cipher text revealed a geometrical relationship, and he intuited that introducing a contradiction into an interconnected loop of Enigma machines would bypass the Germans' built-in safeguards. Historian Stephen Budiansky has said that this idea was really the crux of Turing's invention, an idea that went beyond ordinary brilliance.

A four-rotor Enigma machine. (SSPL/Getty Images)

Impact Deciphering the Japanese Purple code played an important role in the U.S. defeat of Japan, but it was the decipherment of a crucial Japanese naval code that enabled the stunning U.S. naval victory at Midway Island in early June, 1942, and the ambush and death of Admiral Isoroku Yamamoto on April 18, 1943. Breaking the German Enigma ciphers was extremely helpful in thwarting General Erwin Rommel in Africa in 1942 and in forcing Admiral Karl Dönitz to withdraw his U-boats from the North Atlantic in May, 1943.

Frank Day

Further Reading

Budiansky, Stephen. *Battle of Wits. The Complete Story of Codebreaking in World War II.* New York: Free Press, 2000.

Kahn, David. *The Codebreakers: The Comprehensive History of Secret Communication from Ancient Times to the Internet.* Rev. ed. New York: Scribner, 1996.

See also Aircraft carriers; Code talkers; Liberty ships; Midway, Battle of; Navy, U.S.; North African campaign; Pearl Harbor attack; Submarine warfare; World War II.

■ Code talkers

Definition Native American military personnel who relayed messages in codes based on their native languages

During World War II, Comanche and Navajo combat communication specialists created and implemented an unbreakable code based on their native languages, saving the lives of untold numbers of American sailors and troops.

During World War II, the U.S. military needed to send reliable, rapid, and secure coded messages concerning supplies of ammunition, food, and medicine as well as messages concerning the numbers of dead, among other sensitive military topics. Information about the enemy and instructions for Allied forces were communicated from division to division, and from ship to shore. Many German, Italian, and Japanese personnel of the Axis forces intercepted Allied communications. Existing methods for securing information, including cryptograph machines and Morse code, were slow and could be broken by the enemy.

Several Native American groups used noncoded forms of their native languages to send messages. For example, Hopi soldiers relayed battle messages in their native language at Guadalcanal. In 1941, the U.S. Army recruited Comanche to create a specialized code. Because the Comanche language did not contain words for many specialized military terms, such as ".30 caliber machine gun," code talkers created new words or used existing Comanche words to mean different things. For other terms and words precise transmission, such as place names, the code talkers used a Comanche word to represent each letter of the English word. For example, to spell a place name that began with *S*, the code talker would take a word in Comanche that translated into an English word beginning with the letter *s*, such as the Comanche word for "sheep," to represent the first letter. The rest of the word or term would be spelled out similarly.

In 1944, thirteen Comanche infantrymen of the Fourth Signal Company became the first organized native code-talking unit in the European campaign. A man at one end would translate an English message into Comanche code, and a man at the other end would receive the message in code and translate it back into English. The method was fast, accurate, and secure. The military kept secret the formation and use, but not the existence, of the code.

In the Pacific theater of the war, U.S. Marines needed a quick and reliable code that was secure from the Japanese. In 1942, twenty-nine Navajo Marines became the "First 29." These men created a Navajo code to coordinate movement of men and artillery. Similar to Comanche code talkers, the Navajo used short, easily memorized words in their native language that were descriptive of military terms. For example, the Navajo word for buzzard was used for "bomber." The code also consisted of Navajo words with literal translations in English that, when combined, formed the actual English word. For example, the code for the word "been" was a combination of the Navajo words for "bee" and "nut."

A compilation of 211 Navajo code words for the most common military terms grew to more than 600 by the end of the war. Multiple Navajo words represented each letter of the English alphabet (such as Navajo words for "ant," "ax," and "apple" representing the letter *a*). A code talker could transmit three lines of English in twenty seconds, compared to thirty minutes using a cryptograph machine.

Group of Comanche members of the Fourth Signal Company at the Army Signal Center at Fort Gordon, Georgia. (U.S. Army)

An estimated 350 to 400 Navajo communication specialists transmitted messages in a code that was never broken. The existence of the code remained a secret until declassified in 1968.

Impact   In 1982, President Ronald Reagan issued a Certificate of Recognition to the Navajo code talkers, and code talkers have received various other military and civilian honors and forms of recognition. The experiences of the code talkers led to a revitalization of the Comanche and Navajo languages and traditions. The experiences of code talkers were fictionalized in the 2002 film *Windtalkers*.

Elizabeth Marie McGhee Nelson

Further Reading

Aaseng, Nathan. *Navajo Code Talkers: America's Secret Weapon in World War II*. New York: Walker & Company, 1992.

McClain, Sally. *Navajo Weapon: The Navajo Code Talkers*. Tuscon, Ariz.: Rio Nuevo, 1981.

Meadows, William C. *The Comanche Code Talkers of World War II*. Austin: University of Texas Press, 2002.

See also   Code breaking; Department of Defense, U.S.; Guadalcanal, Battle of; Marines, U.S.; Native Americans; War heroes; World War II.

■ Coinage

Definition Government-minted metal tokens that serve as money, a circulating medium of exchange used for commercial transactions

During the 1940's, effects of global warfare brought alloy and design changes to United States coins. New designs on the coins reflected national pride and respect for important historical figures, and many of the coins themselves became collectors' items.

During the 1940's, U.S. coinage retained the denominations of the penny, nickel, dime, quarter, and half-dollar. No other coinage denominations were produced. It had been illegal to own gold since 1933, so no gold coins were minted, and the silver dollar coin had last been minted in 1935. Wartime conditions prompted several changes in coinage, including temporary alterations in the metallic composition of coins and continuation of the shift from emblematic to biographical subjects in coin design.

Wartime demand occasioned revised alloys for coinage in order to conserve vital war supplies and control mint costs in an uncertain market for base metals. Silver coins—the dime, quarter, and half-dollar—retained their traditional 90 percent silver composition, but the nickel and cent underwent several changes. The first to be affected was the Jefferson nickel. Nickels had, since their introduction in 1766, been composed of an alloy of 75 percent copper and 25 percent nickel. "Silver" nickels began to be minted during 1942 to conserve on nickel, which had become a scarce commodity because of wartime use. These coins consisted of an alloy of 35 percent silver, 56 percent copper, and 9 percent manganese. Minting of these nickels continued through 1945. To indicate the changed composition, the "silver" nickels had their mint marks—including, for the first time, a "P" for Philadelphia—enlarged and placed above the dome of Monticello on the reverse of the coin.

In 1943, the mints at Philadelphia, Denver, and San Francisco produced zinc-coated, silvery-white steel pennies because copper, like nickel, had become a coveted wartime commodity. A few copper cents were struck in error in 1943. From 1944 to 1946, Lincoln cents were made of salvaged cartridge cases, again to preserve valuable copper for wartime uses.

By the 1940's, presidential content graced the Lincoln cent, Washington quarter, and Jefferson nickel. Several coins began the 1940's with figures emblematic of liberty and ended the decade with biographical designs. The death of Franklin D. Roosevelt in office in 1945 hastened conversion in 1946 from the Liberty Head or "Mercury" dime to the Roosevelt dime, which was designed by John R. Sinnock. In 1948, the image of Benjamin Franklin, also designed by Sinnock, replaced the Walking Liberty half-dollar. Franklin was the first nonpresident to grace a United States regular issue coin. His coin featured a Liberty Bell and a small, legally mandatory eagle on its reverse.

The government recognized the concerns of coin collectors by issuing government-packaged mint sets and proof sets. Mint sets, which then consisted of two uncirculated coins of each denomination and each mint mark, were first issued in 1947. Proof sets, consisting of coins struck from heavily polished dies to create a mirror or frosty appearance, had been revived in 1936. They were issued from 1940 to 1942 but then not struck again until 1950.

Issuance of commemorative coins subsided during the 1940's. Commemorative coins struck by the U.S. government after the war included the Iowa Centennial commemorative of 1946 and the Booker T. Washington Memorial, issued beginning in 1946. Mint errors during the 1940's included the very rare 1942 "2" over "1" dime, which was struck at both the Philadelphia and Denver mints. In 1944 and 1945, government mints struck coins for the Philippines, as it existed under the sovereignty of the United States.

Impact Mintage figures at the three mints in Philadelphia, Denver, and San Francisco indicated a burgeoning and slightly inflationary economy, particularly after the end of the war. Coinage, like so much else in the country, reflected a maturing sense of the perils and opportunities of American power.

Myron C. Noonkester

Further Reading

Bowers, Q. David, with foreword by Eric P. Newman and valuations by Lawrence Stack. *A Guide Book of United States Type Coins: A Complete History and Price Guide for the Collector and Investor: Copper, Nickel, Silver, Gold.* 2d ed. Atlanta, Ga.: Whitman Publishing, 2008.

Lange, David W., with Mary Jo Mead. *History of the U.S. Mint and Its Coinage.* Atlanta, Ga.: Whitman Publishing, 2006.

Yeoman, R. S. *A Guide Book of United States Coins: The Official Redbook, 2010.* Edited by Kenneth Bressett. 63d ed. Racine, Wis.: Western Publishing, 2009.

See also Business and the economy in the United States; Hobbies; Recreation; Roosevelt, Franklin D.

■ Cold War

The Event Period of sustained animosity, fear, and suspicion as well as ideological and geopolitical conflict between the United States and the Soviet Union

Date 1945-1991

After World War II, much of American foreign policy attention became committed to winning what was termed the Cold War. The conflict became an ideological clash involving propaganda weapons that effectively divided the world into two blocs, one headed by the capitalist-oriented United States and the other dominated by the socialist-dominated Soviet Union.

World War II ended with the United States as the world's only economic and nuclear superpower, but the Soviet Union remained a significant military power in terms of conventional weapons. Americans were eager for a return to peace and prosperity, and few expected a war-devastated Europe to become a main theater of conflict anytime in the near future.

Wartime cooperation among nations had not been perfect. Rivalries had surfaced in the race to Berlin and in the effort to recruit and capture German scientists involved in the new jet propulsion and V-2 rocket technology. Disagreements occurred at the Yalta Conference (February, 1945) and the Potsdam Conference (July, 1945) about what constituted free and democratic elections in Soviet-occupied Eastern Europe and the delineation of occupation zones in postwar Germany and the city of Berlin. Suspicion grew as Russian troop occupation of Eastern Europe turned into establishment of entrenched communist regimes.

In a speech delivered at Westminster College in Fulton, Missouri, on March 5, 1946, British prime minister Winston Churchill spotlighted to Americans that an "Iron Curtain" had descended across Europe. Most Americans thought the former British prime minister was being overly alarmist. One year later, Bernard Baruch, an adviser to President Harry S. Truman, used the term "Cold War" to describe the increasingly frigid relations between the United States and the Soviet Union. By the end of 1947, noted political columnist Walter Lippmann had published a book titled *The Cold War.* Within a few years, the term had become part of political terminology, used to describe the postwar clash of policies, ideologies, and actions taking place between the United States and its followers, on one side, and the Soviet Union and its followers, on the other.

Containment and Confrontation Baruch himself had witnessed, in June of 1946, Soviet refusal to cooperate with a nuclear disarmament plan bearing his name, proposed in cooperation with the U.N. Atomic Energy Commission. Soviet leader Joseph Stalin would not permit regulatory inspection of war-ravaged Russia or give up his right to develop an atomic bomb, even if the United States destroyed its stockpile of nuclear weapons. Because the United States had nuclear technology, he reasoned, it could replenish its supply at will. Upset by the exclusion of the Soviet Union from the occupation of Japan, by the immediate ending of the lend-lease program at the end of the war with Germany, as well as by exclusion from the World Bank and International Monetary Fund organized by the United States after the war, Stalin turned up the propaganda war.

The United States became the center of an anticommunist drive to cripple the Soviet Union, and Stalin came under increasing attack as another Hitler seeking world domination. As early as September, 1945, Igor Gouzenko, a young Russian defector interviewed by the *Ottawa Citizen,* made allegations of a large Soviet spy ring operating in Canada that caused a strong reaction in both the United States and Canada. Gouzenko's defection has been viewed as one of the precipitating events in the Cold War.

The Truman Doctrine and the Marshall Plan By 1947, Soviet policies were being criticized openly in the United States and particularly incensed Americans of East European origins with relatives who lived under Soviet rule. A civil war in Greece and demands for a joint Russian-Turkish supervision of the Dardanelles provided the opportunity for the Truman administration to define an interventionist foreign policy. The Truman Doctrine, declared in a speech to Congress on March 12, 1947, established that the United States would provide political, military, and economic assistance to democratic nations threatened by communist expansion. In addition, the United States promised Turkey support in resisting Russian demands. Secretary of State Dean Acheson explained that if Soviet ambitions were not stopped in Greece and Turkey, communist objectives would expand to the Middle East and Western Europe.

The Truman Doctrine was soon followed, in June of 1947, by the announcement of the Marshall Plan. The United States committed $13 billion to speed up economic recovery in Western Europe and to create jobs and a stable middle class as a bulwark against communism, even though U.S. taxpayers were unused to the concept of foreign aid. Several weeks later, in a famous article published in *Foreign Affairs* (July, 1947), presidential adviser George Kennan (writing under the pseudonym X) proposed a long-term U.S. foreign policy of "containment" of communism through use of strategic counterforce. The containment policy soon would become a fundamental doctrine of U.S. foreign policy during the Cold War. To make U.S. military capacity more efficient, Truman signed the National Security Act of 1947, creating the Central Intelligence Agency (CIA), the National Security Council, and the U.S. Air Force. The Department of War and Department of the Navy were also merged into one organization.

Berlin Blockade and Airlift　As part of European recovery, the United States sought German recovery. It gradually merged its zone of influence economically with those of France and Great Britain. In February, 1948, plans were made for the political merging of the zones to create an independent West German Federal Republic. To stop this, in June of 1948 the Soviet Union cut off

Seeds of the Cold War

On February 9, 1946, Soviet premier Joseph Stalin delivered a speech in Moscow arguing that the world wars were the result of capitalism and that communism, especially as it played out in Eastern Europe, was a superior system that would eventually prevail. The speech, which alarmed Western leaders, was part of the newly emerging Cold War propaganda:

Marxists have more than once stated that the capitalist system of world economy contains the elements of a general crisis and military conflicts, that, in view of that, the development of world capitalism in our times does not proceed smoothly and evenly, but through crises and catastrophic wars. The point is that the uneven development of capitalist countries usually leads, in the course of time, to a sharp disturbance of the equilibrium within the world system of capitalism, and that group of capitalist countries which regards itself as being less securely provided with raw materials and markets usually attempts to change the situation and to redistribute "spheres of influence" in its own favor—by employing armed force. As a result of this, the capitalist world is split into two hostile camps, and war breaks out between them. . . .

The issue now is not whether the Soviet social system is viable or not, because after the object lessons of the war, no skeptic now dares to express doubt concerning the viability of the Soviet social system. Now the issue is that the Soviet social system has proved to be more viable and stable than the non-Soviet social system, that the Soviet social system is a better form of organization of society than any non-Soviet social system.

One of the leaders alarmed by Stalin's speech was British prime minister Winston Churchill, who warned in a speech of his own that Stalin's plan was expansion for Russia. Angered, Stalin struck back, and the Cold War was under way:

In substance, Mr. Churchill now stands in the position of a firebrand of war. And Mr. Churchill is not alone here. He has friends not only in England but also in the United States of America.

In this respect, one is reminded remarkably of Hitler and his friends. . . . Mr. Churchill begins to set war loose, also by a racial theory, maintaining that only nations speaking the English language are fully valuable nations, called upon to decide the destinies of the entire world.

Sources: Joseph Stalin, *Speeches Delivered at Meetings of Voters of the Stalin Electoral District* (Moscow: Foreign Language Publishing, 1950). "Stalin's Reply to Churchill." *The New York Times*, March 14, 1946, p. 4.

all road access routes to West Berlin, which lay deep in the Soviet zone of Germany. The Soviets knew that West Berlin had food and water supplies to last only about a week. The ensuing crisis threatened to turn the Cold War into a hot war involving military action.

The Soviet Union's huge conventional army was well positioned to assert its will in Germany. Forces in the Berlin area alone totaled 1.5 million men, compared to U.S. and allied forces in Berlin of slightly more than 22,000. After contemplating risking war by sending tanks and trucks through the blockade, Truman instead chose the novel plan of keeping West Berlin supplied from the air. Berlin was kept supplied by drops of material from aircraft over the course of the next eleven months. To show U.S. resolve, Truman instituted the second peacetime draft in U.S. history. The Soviet Union suffered a major humiliation while the West showcased its techno-organizational superiority. The lifting of the Soviet blockade in May, 1949, seemed to support Kennan's theory of the viability of containment and counterforce.

In April, 1949, during the final weeks of the Berlin Blockade, Canada and the United States were able to organize Britain, France, Italy, Denmark, Norway, the Netherlands, Luxembourg, and Belgium with them into the North Atlantic Treaty Organization (NATO), the nations of which pledged mutual assistance in the event that any signatory nation was attacked. On August 29, 1949, the Soviet Union successfully tested its first atomic bomb. It was nicknamed Joe-1 and gave new dimensions to any scenario of armed conflict.

Developments in Asia   Although the Cold War was born in relation to events in Europe, by the end of the 1940's the focus was rapidly turning to Asia. In 1946, civil war broke out in China between Chiang Kai-shek's Nationalist government and the People's Liberation Army (PLA) headed by Mao Zedong. Well aware of the corruption ingrained in Chiang's regime and its inability to motivate popular support, the Truman administration gave only limited support to the Nationalists. When Mao seized power in 1949, forcing Chiang's forces to seek refuge in a new base in Taiwan, the Truman administration issued a white paper placing the blame for the disaster on the inherent weaknesses of Chiang's regime. A swell of public opinion began to percolate blaming the fall of China on the "soft on communism" policies of the Roosevelt and Truman administrations, a backlash that culminated in the Red Scare hysteria of the Joseph McCarthy era. Extending containment policies to Asia, Truman positioned the U.S. Seventh Fleet in the Straits of Formosa to protect Taiwan and also recognized Chiang's as the only legitimate government. The myth was fostered that Chiang would soon return to power.

The containment policy was also manifest in U.S. financial support for the French (and the sending of a token U.S. force of 123 noncombat troops) in their efforts to maintain Vietnam as a colony and battle a national liberation force headed by communists. Asia became the main theater of the Cold War in June, 1950, when communist North Korea invaded South Korea. For the next three years, the Cold War was in reality a hot war.

U.S. ambassador to the United Nations Warren Austin angrily reading a newspaper headline reporting that the Soviet Union has successfully exploded an atomic bomb. Soviet acquisition of nuclear weapon capability dramatically changed the dynamics of the Cold War. (Getty Images)

Impact   During the five-year period following World War II, two wartime allies, the United States and the Soviet Union, became the nuclei of two opposing armed camps, each with its own set of assumptions about how the world should be organized. The years 1947 to 1949, in particular, set the stage for continuing conflict that would last over the next two generations, until the end of the Cold War in 1989, and threaten the world with nuclear extinction. Each side viewed the other's intentions in the worst terms and came to believe its own propaganda about the "battle between good and evil."

Mainstream historians came to view President Truman as a feisty, plain-talking American hero who stood up to the communist threat. In his postwar world, there would be no American isolationism or appeasement of aggression. Truman's lack of foreign policy expertise was more than compensated for by the use of some of America's best foreign policy minds to craft farsighted policies.

Following the end of the Cold War with the rapid fall of communism in Europe and quick evaporation of public concern about communism, revisionist historians became intrigued with the causes of the Cold War. They saw contributing factors in Truman's limited grasp of foreign affairs and Wilsonian view of the battle of the forces of good against the forces of evil, which steered American foreign policy away from Roosevelt's policies of cooperation toward a conflict-laden policy of containment. Also stressed was Truman's early involvement with secret intelligence operations to destabilize communist regimes by using propaganda, subversion, and paramilitary confrontation. The policy of open containment and secret rollback, they argued, was initiated by Truman and augmented during the administration of Dwight D. Eisenhower. Experts also have defined a concerted propaganda effort, for both foreign and domestic consumption, launched by intelligence agencies working in cooperation with private agencies. This propaganda generated a syndrome of fear and anger that further encouraged Cold War antagonisms and policy.

Irwin Halfond

Further Reading

Gaddis, John L. *Strategies of Containment: A Critical Appraisal of American National Security Policy During the Cold War.* New York: Oxford University Press, 2005. A standard scholarly study of Cold War policy from the end of World War II to the aftermath of the fall of communism in Europe.

Leffler, Melvin P. *For the Soul of Mankind: The United States, the Soviet Union, and the Cold War.* New York: Hill & Wang, 2008. An extensively researched study of the policies involved in the Cold War, written by a winner of the Bancroft Prize.

Lucas, Scott. *Freedom's War: The American Crusade Against the Soviet Union.* New York: New York University Press, 1999. A study of how propaganda, psychological warfare, and covert activity, involving a wide variety of governmental and cooperating nongovernmental agencies, were used to fixate the Soviet threat in the minds of the American public.

Miscamble, Wilson D. *From Roosevelt to Truman: Potsdam, Hiroshima, and the Cold War.* Cambridge, England: Cambridge University Press, 2007. A study of Truman's slow evolution from Roosevelt's friendly and conciliatory policies to policies of confrontation, resulting from increasing mistrust of Stalin and the Soviet Union.

Mitrovich, Gregory. *Undermining the Kremlin: American Strategy to Subvert the Soviet Bloc, 1947-1956.* Ithaca, N.Y.: Cornell University Press, 2000. Using recently declassified intelligence documents, the author reveals U.S. attempts to destabilize communist regimes during the 1940's and 1950's through the use of covert action and psychological warfare.

Offner, Arnold. *Another Such Victory: President Truman and the Cold War, 1945-1953.* Palo Alto, Calif.: Stanford University Press, 2002. A major revisionist study of Truman as a narrow-minded nationalist who led his nation into confrontational positions that set the tone for future U.S. Cold War policies.

Spalding, Elizabeth E. *The First Cold Warrior: Harry Truman, Containment, and the Remaking of Liberal Internationalism.* Lexington: University Press of Kentucky, 2006. A detailed political analysis that attempts to portray Truman (and not George Kennan) as the driving force behind the policy of containment.

See also   Anticommunism; Berlin blockade and airlift; Foreign policy of the United States; "Iron Curtain" speech; Kennan, George F.; Marshall, George C.; Marshall Plan; Potsdam Conference; Roosevelt, Franklin D.; Truman Doctrine; Yalta Conference.

■ Coles, Honi

Identification   African American tap dancer
Born   April 2, 1911; Philadelphia, Pennsylvania
Died   November, 12, 1992; New York, New York

Coles created a fast, rhythmically intricate variety of tap dancing that mirrored the music of big-band soloists and bebop jazz during the 1940's. Together with his partner Charles Atkins he elevated the artistry of tap in the post-World War II American musical theater.

Philadelphia-born Charles "Honi" Coles was a self-taught dancer who began his performing life on the streets of his home city. At the age of twenty he joined New York-based vaudeville dance act called the Miller Brothers. Recognized for the complexity of his footwork, Coles performed for the opening of Harlem's Apollo Theater in 1934. By 1936, he was touring with swing bands led by Count Basie and Duke Ellington.

In 1940, Coles met Charles "Cholly" Atkins, with whom he later formed the tap duo Atkins and Coles. Their career plans were interrupted by the World War II, which the United States entered at the end of 1941. Shortly after marrying dancer Marion Edwards in 1944, Coles was drafted into the U.S. Army and deployed to India. Following the war in 1946, Atkins and Coles crafted an act that featured a quick-paced song-and-tap segment followed by a swing dance and soft shoe routine. The latter, danced to "Taking a Chance on Love," was remarkable for its difficulty and slow tempo. Atkins and Coles ended the number with a tap challenge in which each featured his most advanced steps.

Throughout the 1940's, Atkins and Coles gained popularity in short television segments and appearances with bands led by Count Basie, Louis Armstrong, and Lionel Hampton. In 1949, the duo appeared in the Broadway musical *Gentlemen Prefer Blondes*. During that same year, Coles cofounded the Copasetics, a tapping fraternity named in honor of dancer Bill "Bojangles" Robinson, whose favorite catchphrase was "Everything is copasetic." As tap's popularity faded during the 1950's, Coles became production manager of the Apollo Theater and later served as president of the Negro Actors Guild.

Impact   Honi Coles worked as a teacher and advocate for tap dance throughout his life; his artistry influenced generations of American theater performers. In 1978 his appearance with the Joffrey Ballet's Conversations in Dance, which was choreographed by Agnes de Mille, secured a position for tap in the realm of concert dance. In 1983, he received Tony, Drama Desk, and Fred Astaire awards for his work in the Broadway show, *My One and Only*. Coles died of cancer in New York in 1992.

Margaret R. Jackson

Further Reading

Atkins, Cholly, and Jacqui Malone. *Class Act: The Jazz Life of Cholly Atkins.* New York: Columbia University Press, 2003.

Fox, Ted. *Showtime at the Apollo: The Story of Harlem's World Famous Theater.* Rhinebeck, N.Y.: Mill Road Enterprises, 2003.

Frank, Rusty E. *Tap! The Greatest Tap Dancers and Their Stories.* New York: Da Capo Press, 1994.

Stearns, Jean, and Marshall Winslow Stearns. *Jazz Dance: The Story of American Vernacular Dance.* New York: Da Capo Press, 1994.

See also   Broadway musicals; Dance; Ellington, Duke; Kelly, Gene; Music: Jazz; Music: Popular; *Oklahoma!*; Theater in the United States.

■ Comic books

Definition   Illustrated stories printed in magazine format, with glossy four-color covers and flat four-color interiors

The 1940's fostered a Golden Age of comic books. Although the standard comic-book format was developed in the late 1930's, the 1940's brought a creative and commercial boom to this medium. Some of the great superheroes that persisted into the twenty-first century were created in the 1940's, and many other later comic heroes derived from the characters developed during this Golden Age.

To understand the origins of the comic-book boom of the 1940's, one must know the origins of the comic book itself. Max Gaines, a salesman and brother of William Gaines (who later co-created *Mad* magazine in 1952 with Harvey Kurtzman), is credited with inventing the comic book. In 1933, he decided to collect his favorite newspaper "funnies" and publish them in a sequential order. He called this first comic book *Funnies on Parade.* Although his boss at Eastern Color Printing doubted that any-one would pay for something they had already read, Gaines's first publication sold well.

Eastern eventually excluded Gaines from its comic book profits, so Gaines partnered with McClure Syndicate to publish comics of his own. His success there caught the attention of pulp magazine publishers. The most successful "pulps" of the time featured stories about gritty real-life crime fighters and heroes who often were forced into vigilantism to accomplish their goals during the Prohibition era. Pulp publisher Major Malcolm Wheeler-Nicholson (founder of Detective Comics, later DC Comics) began pub-lishing comic books with original characters and story lines as early as 1935. Pulp publishers such as Martin Goodman (founder of Marvel Comics) and pulp printers such as Harry Donenfeld and Jack Liebowitz (co-founders of DC Comics) began to develop comic books fea-turing characters who would become some of the most influential fictional personages of the twentieth century.

Creating a New American Mythology   Of the hundreds of superheroes who appeared in the 1940's, along with dozens of comic-book heroes from the jungle and Western genres, approxi-mately fourteen stand out as great comic-book heroes. Those fourteen have been deemed great superheroes because of their long-lasting impact on American popular culture, the fact that they never seem to fade away from production for long, and the enormous influence their artists and creators had on the later dominant Marvel and DC artists. All of these superheroes, sometimes in significantly al-tered forms, remaained part of either the DC or the Marvel universe into the twenty-first century.

By 1941, more than thirty comic-book publishers were selling more than 150 different titles. An im-mense number of comic-book artists, often working in cramped apartments under serious time con-straints and strict competition, struggled to get is-sues to the printer on time. Prominent among these artists and characters are Joe Shuster and Jerry Siegel, creators of Superman, who first appeared on June 30, 1938. Siegel also created, with Bernard Baily, the Spectre, who first appeared in February, 1940. Other artists include Bob Kane, the co-creator of Batman, who first appeared in May, 1939; Bill

Young New York City boy studying the latest comic book issues in 1946. (Time & Life Pictures/Getty Images)

Everett, creator of Sub-Mariner (also known as Namor the Sub-Mariner), who appeared in October, 1939; Carl Burgos, creator of Human Torch, who first appeared in October, 1939; C. C. Beck and Bill Parker, creators of Captain Marvel, released in Feb-ruary, 1940; Will Eisner, creator of the Spirit, appear-ing in June, 1940; Mart Dellon and Bill Finger, cre-ators of Green Lantern, appearing in July, 1940 (Finger was also the co-creator of Batman and the creator of Robin); Mort Weisinger and Paul Norris, creators of Aquaman, released in November, 1941; Charles Moulton, creator of Wonder Woman, first appearing in December, 1941; Joe Simon and Jack Kirby, creators of Captain America, who appeared in March, 1941; and Jack Cole, creator of Plastic Man, released in August, 1941.

Jack Kirby and Gardner Fox were among the most commercially successful artists of this Golden Age. King and Harry Lampert created the Flash, who first appeared in January, 1940. Just as important, Fox created the DC comics universe and co-created the Justice Society of America (1940), the first team of superheroes in comic-book history, with Sheldon Mayer, the man who saved Shuster and Siegel's Superman from the trash bin. In addition, Fox created Hawkman (1940) with Dennis Neville.

DC, Marvel, and Silver Pictures (with Warner Bros.) continue to produce, or have reintroduced, all of the above-mentioned superheroes. Captain Marvel reemerged afte a disappearance of more than a decade that resulted from legal action by Superman's company, National Periodical Publishers. National's lawyers consistently brought cases against Fawcett Comics, citing the fact that Captain Marvel's artists virtually copied Superman, from his visage to his build to certain poses. Comic-book artists of the time have admitted to training themselves to draw like the masters of the genre, so it is no surprise that superheroes were derivative of another. Even Superman's appearance was based strongly on the comic-strip hero Flash Gordon. The distinction between Captain Marvel and all the other Superman copies is that Captain Marvel outsold Superman during the 1940's. Captain America also outsold both Superman and Batman during World War II, however, without being the subject of any lawsuits.

Origins of the Superheroes To call the above-mentioned characters the pantheon of comic-book superheroes is appropriate because the publication boom was more than financial or artistic; it also was cultural. In the 1940's, the superhero began to replace the Minuteman, the frontiersman, and the Western gunslinger in the American popular mythology. The superhero subgenre is based on the true crime stories of the pulp/Prohibition era, but the human vigilantes were not the same stuff of mythology. Comic-book stories do share narrative elements with stories of American Revolutionaries, the frontier people who are said to have pulled themselves up by their own bootstraps, and Wild West gunslingers, but the superhero genre takes these elements to extremes. World War II provided clear moral issues and enemies that fueled the adventures of the superheroes.

Furthermore, those in the comic-book industry sought to establish a mythological system based on their superheroes, as evidenced by the monikers "DC universe" and "Marvel universe" that developed to refer to the common settings and characters of two major streams of comic books. It is no mistake that the creators of Timely/Atlas Comics, which be-

came Marvel, named their company after one of the iconic Titans in Greek mythology; they had a vision for their place in American culture.

Direct references to Greek and Roman mythology occurred from the beginning of the Golden Age: The Flash is the reincarnation of the Roman god Mercury, and Captain Marvel is famous among baby boomers and Gen Xers for saying "Shazam!," a word calling forth various attributes and combining the first letters of their holders:

Solomon (wisdom)
Hercules (strength)
Atlas (stamina)
Zeus (power)
Achilles (courage)
Mercury (speed)

Two minor characters during the Golden Age were Vulcan (1940), descendant of the Roman smith god, and Diana the Huntress (1944). The superhero Diana was sent to Earth by Zeus, who wanted to intervene directly in World War II on behalf of the Allies. Wonder Woman, though an Amazon by birth, is also named Diana, and much like Diana/Artemis of the Greeks, she is the one female in the comic pantheon who can strike down a brigade of mortal men without suffering so much as a hangnail. As further examples of references to heroes of previous ages, Aquaman and Namor are from Atlantis.

Blending Science and Superpowers A strong culture needs a strong mythology. In the 1940's, strength meant technological dominance. Notwithstanding the numerous references to ancient mythologies, where superhero comics formed a truly American mythology was in the genre's reverence toward science, technology, and invention. The American public knew technology was important in defeating the Nazis, and many people knew that America would need to remain technologically dominant throughout the twentieth century if it was to remain a dominant power.

Part of being technologically dominant is being able to control many aspects of the physical world through the application of science. Most of the superheroes listed above, along with dozens of minor heroes during the Golden Age, either displayed this ability (in a grandly exaggerated way) or were the personification of applied science. For example, the most likely precursor to Iron Man is Target (1940), or Niles Reed, a metallurgist who created an indestructible suit of armor for himself to help the U.S. Army. A possible precursor to Hulk is Doc Strange (1940), who harnessed the atoms of the Sun into an elixir called Alosun. This atomic energy gives him superhuman strength and the ability to leap great distances. Captain America himself is a super soldier created through genetic manipulation by Professor Reinstein. Reinstein's ethics might be considered questionable, but they can be viewed in the context that many Americans of the time believed that the Nazis were trying to create a whole race of super soldiers. As another example, Aquaman's father was an engineer who had the ability to create an amphibian boy, and Professor Harton created an android, named Human Torch, capable of harnessing and controlling fire.

Many of the superheroes are scientists themselves. Batman's alter ego, Bruce Wayne, has a vast knowledge of chemistry and becomes a great inventor. He was the genius of all superheroes until Iron Man and Tony Stark were created years later. Green Lantern is engineer Alan Scott, who seems to be the only human ethically worthy of wearing a ring that gives him the ability to control the physical world. The new American mythology born out of this Golden Age thus combined heroes from the lineage of classic mythology with those who used scientific progress to help them protect the innocent.

This new mythology was decidedly monocultural, with all the major superheroes being of white, European origin and only Wonder Woman being female. That cultural bias persisted into the twenty-first century and seemed likely to continue, given that only a few companies controlled comic-book mythology and had no strong reason to tamper with the formula that had yielded so much success.

Intertextuality   Many of the characters produced during the Golden Age showed literary influences. For example, many believe that Shuster and Siegel based Superman partly on the Jewish legend of Golem, who was created to protect innocent people from injustice. Batman and Green Lantern, among many others, were based on the Scarlet Pimpernel, created by Baroness Emmuska Orczy in a 1944 book of the same name, and on Johnston McCulley's Zorro. Edgar Rice Burroughs's Tarzan was adapted prolifically during the 1940's; in fact, Tarzan and

Sheena, Queen of the Jungle, were almost as popular in comic books as the major superheroes of their time. The popularity of Tarzan and Sheena inspired a jungle subgenre during the golden age. Versions of Frankenstein's monster, the original vision of Mary Shelley, also became extremely popular. They sparked a horror genre that, combined with a new science fiction subgenre led by the art of Frank Frazetta, rivaled the sales of superhero comics. A teen romance genre, derived from 1940's Archie comics, also became popular.

Impact   The Golden Age of comic books was one of the great movements in American popular culture. Its major characters have been valued by at least three generations of readers, and even some of the minor characters and villains created during this era recur in contemporary productions. The boom in comic-book sales created the basis for the multimillion-dollar Marvel and DC companies, and it has inspired screenwriters and film producers, with the Batman film franchise standing as a strong example. In addition to being financially remunerative, the Golden Age of comics helped bring together elements of recurrent American fictional themes to form a coherent and distinctive American system of secular mythology.

Troy Place

Further Reading

Fieffer, Jules. *The Great Comic Book Heroes.* New York: Bonanza Books, 1965. A former comic-book artist provides an insightful look at thirteen of the most important and enduring superheroes of the Golden Age.

Goulart, Ron. *Comic Book Encyclopedia: The Ultimate Guide to Characters, Graphic Novels, Writers, and Artists in the Comic Book Universe.* New York: Harper, 2004. A visually engaging reference work that ambitiously covers a broad spectrum of this art form.

Rhoades, Shirrel. *A Complete History of American Comic Books.* New York: Peter Lang, 2008. A former publisher of Marvel Comics shares little-known facts and insider vignettes about many facets of the comic-book industry.

Thomson, Don, and Dick Lupoff, eds. *The Comic Book Book.* New Rochelle, N.Y.: Arlington House, 1973. A collection of academically sound articles on topics ranging from Mickey Mouse comic books to the popularity of Tarzan and Frankenstein's monster during the Golden Age.

See also Animated films; Book publishing; Censorship in the United States; Comic strips; Cowboy films; Disney films; Magazines; Mauldin, Bill; Pulp magazines; Superman.

■ Comic strips

Definition Sequential narrative cartoon drawings published in newspapers and magazines

The newspapers of the 1940's ran a variety of comic strips, from humor and adventure to soap opera. Comic strips reflected a changing society, from American involvement in World War II to the experience of postwar prosperity and the early Cold War. Newspaper comics were widely read, and many of their characters appeared in other media such as radio or movie serials.

Newspaper comics in the 1940's were near the height of their popularity. Top strips such as Al Capp's hillbilly comedy *Li'l Abner* and Milton Caniff's Asia-based adventure *Terry and the Pirates* were carried in hundreds of newspapers, and their characters appeared in radio and the movies as well as in the "funny papers."

Comics and the War The comics were immediately affected by the Pearl Harbor attack of December 7, 1941. The heroes of adventure comics joined up with the armed services or undertook war-related missions. Even Crockett Johnson's *Barnaby*, a whimsical fantasy strip that first appeared in 1942 and revolved around the titular child and his relationship with his disreputable fairy godfather, Mr. O'Malley, introduced a plot about a scrap-metal drive. *Terry and the Pirates* had relatively little adjustment to make, as in many ways it was already a war comic, with many story lines revolving around the Japanese war against China.

The war interrupted the careers of several cartoonists. Alex Raymond abandoned the strip with which he was identified, the science-fiction epic *Flash Gordon*, in 1944, when he entered the Marines. Gus Arriola, whose *Gordo* was one of the few comics to deal with Latino characters in a nonstereotypical way, was forced to put his strip on hiatus shortly after its debut in 1941, bringing it back after the war.

The war also created niches for new comics about military life. The newspapers that sprang up around military bases were a new market crying out for comics like the ones American soldiers had read as civilians. Caniff's *Male Call*, a gag strip featuring the sexy but unobtainable Miss Lace (based on Burma, a character in *Terry and the Pirates*) in a variety of service-related settings, appeared in about three thousand service newspapers, making it the most widely distributed comic strip in the world. It ran from January 24, 1943, to March 3, 1946. Caniff drew *Male Call* for free as his contribution to the war effort. An-

George Baker (center), creator of the Sad Sack *comic strip, with fellow* Stars and Stripes *staff members.* (Time & Life Pictures/Getty Images)

other service newspaper hit, which crossed over to the civilian world, was Bill Mauldin's one-panel *Willie and Joe*, which ran in *Stars and Stripes*. The Disney films veteran George Baker's *Sad Sack* first appeared in *Life* magazine in 1941 and eventually moved to newspaper and comic-book publication. Many of these comics, aimed at an audience often thought to be composed entirely of men, could be sexier than mainstream newspaper comics.

The Postwar Period　After the war, comics "demobilized" as comics creators returned to start new projects. Caniff relinquished *Terry and the Pirates* in 1946. Like most strips, it was the property of the syndicate that distributed it, the *Chicago Tribune* Syndicate. Caniff wanted to develop a new property for which he would retain ownership and control. (*Terry and the Pirates* passed into the hands of George Wunder.) Caniff's new strip, *Steve Canyon*, was bought by newspapers even before they saw samples, purely on the strength of Caniff's reputation. Caniff also won the first Billy DeBeck Award from the newly founded National Cartoonists Society in 1946. (The award is better known by its later name, the Reuben Award, and remains the premier individual award in American newspaper comics.) Canyon was another adventurer, and over time *Steve Canyon* would be influenced by America's Cold War struggles. Raymond also created a new strip after the war, *Rip Kirby*, starring an ex-Marine turned private eye. The strip, of which Raymond had partial ownership, debuted in 1946. Raymond would earn a Billy DeBeck Award for *Rip Kirby* in 1949. Ray Gotto's *Ozark Ike*, a strip about a "dumb hillbilly" baseball player that was heavily influenced by *Li'l Abner*, first appeared in 1945. Other postwar strips included Ed Dodd's *Mark Trail*, which combined a weekday strip about the adventures of a pipe-smoking outdoorsman with a Sunday panel devoted to exploring nature, and it first appeared in 1946.

Nicholas P. Dallis's *Rex Morgan, M.D.,* first appearing in 1948, was one of the earliest in a wave of soap opera strips that would continue into the next decade. The continuing vitality of the "funny animal" genre was demonstrated by Walt Kelly's *Pogo*, which brought characters and settings Kelly had first developed for comic books into the funny pages. *Pogo* first appeared in the *New York Star* in 1948.

Impact　Several of the comic strips of the 1940's survived for decades, some to the present day. However, the type of continuity-heavy adventure strip with detailed drawing that dominated the 1940's gave way to strips with simpler art and less complicated stories.

William E. Burns

Further Reading

Blackbeard, Bill, and Martin Williams, eds. *The Smithsonian Collection of Newspaper Comics*. Washington, D.C.: Smithsonian Institution Press, 1977. Generally considered the finest anthology of newspaper comics, with reproductions of comics from favorites to obscure gems.

Harvey, R. C. *Meanwhile . . . : A Biography of Milton Caniff, Creator of "Terry and the Pirates" and "Steve Canyon."* Seattle: Fantagraphics Books, 2007. The standard biography of the most admired and influential comics creator of the 1940's.

_____, with contributions by Brian Walker and Richard V. West. *Children of the Yellow Kid: The Evolution of the American Comic Strip*. Seattle: Frye Art Museum in association with the University of Washington Press, 1998. A scholarly history of the comic strip, with an emphasis on its artistic development.

Roberts, Tom. *Alex Raymond: His Life and Art*. Silver Spring, Md.: Adventure House, 2008. Biography of a leading creator of the 1940's, including a discussion of Raymond's wartime experience and much of his art.

Walker, Brian. *The Comics: The Complete Collection*. New York: Harry N. Abrams, 2008. Combines two of Walker's earlier books, *The Comics Since 1945* (2002) and *The Comics Before 1945* (2004), to form a complete history of the comic strip in twentieth century America. Strong on the business aspects.

See also　*Brenda Starr*; Mauldin, Bill; Newspapers; Sad Sack; Superman.

■ The Common Sense Book of Baby and Child Care

Identification　Child-care manual
Author　Benjamin Spock (1903-1998)
Date　First published in 1946

Spock's reassuring child-care manual found an eager audience among a post-Depression and post-World War II generation of parents at the beginning of the baby boom. He advised mothers and fathers to trust their own instincts, and he advocated a warm, loving style of parenting—a departure from the authoritarian approach recommended in other child-care manuals of the time.

Benjamin Spock begins *The Common Sense Book of Baby and Child Care* with these heartening words: "Trust yourself. You know more than you think you do." He addresses readers directly in a plain writing style and cautions, "Don't be overawed by what the experts say." The book urges parents to trust their common sense instead.

Spock had been practicing pediatrics for at least ten years in New York when, in the early 1940's, the paperback publisher Pocket Books asked him to write a child-care manual. By then, he had become known among colleagues and clients as a forward-thinking pediatrician who combined his interest in Freudian psychology with pediatrics. Spock agreed to write a manual because he saw a need for a book that united pediatrics and psychology. However, his most important aim, he says in Lynn Bloom's 1972 biography, "was to write a book that increased parents' comfort and independence; I wanted the book to avoid as much as possible telling parents what to do. I wanted to tell them how children develop and feel and then to leave it to the parents to decide on their own course of action."

Spock said that he wrote the book from his own experience. He dictated the manuscript to his first wife, Jane Cheney Spock, who typed it and provided other help over the years it took to produce. He wanted the book to be complete, and he organized the topics by age, from birth through puberty. In 1946, the guide was published simultaneously in paperback by Pocket Books as *The Pocket Book of Baby and Child Care* and in a 527-page hardcover edition by Duell, Sloan and Pearce as *The Common Sense Book of Baby and Child Care*. The lower-priced paperback version sold hundreds of thousands of copies in the first year of publication. Spock received dozens of letters from grateful parents.

Spock set out to write with a gentle voice in contrast to the severe style of other child-care books of the time. "Most books for parents—pediatric and psychological—appeared to me to be condescending, scolding, or intimidating in tone," Spock says in Bloom's biography. One section of *Baby and Child Care* is headed "Enjoy your baby" and begins, "He isn't a schemer. He needs loving." (Spock refers to babies as "he" to avoid confusion when referring to

the mother as "her.") In addition to encouraging affection toward children, *Baby and Child Care* advocates flexibility with schedules: "You may hear people say that you have to get your baby strictly regulated in his feeding, sleeping, bowel movements, and other habits—but don't believe this either." Spock emphasizes that children will develop patterns according to their needs.

At a time when breast-feeding was declining and bottle-feeding was popular, Spock promoted the advantages of nursing. In an era when hospitals banned fathers from delivery rooms, Spock encouraged fathers to help care for their babies from the start. Spock had studied Sigmund Freud's theories about psychoanalysis, and that influence is reflected in the book's advice about weaning, toilet training, and sexual development.

Impact   *Baby and Child Care* became a best seller among parents of the baby-boom generation. Updated editions were published in later decades, and Spock's now classic guide has sold millions in the United States and around the world.

Lisa Kernek

Further Reading

Bloom, Lynn Z. *Doctor Spock: Biography of a Conservative Radical.* Indianapolis: Bobbs-Merrill, 1972.

Maier, Thomas. *Dr. Spock: An American Life.* New York: Harcourt Brace, 1998.

Spock, Benjamin. *The Common Sense Book of Baby and Child Care.* New York: Duell, Sloan and Pearce, 1946.

See also   Baby boom; Demographics of the United States; Psychiatry and psychology; Women's roles and rights in the United States.

■ Communist Party USA

Identification   Political party
Date   Established on August 30, 1919; reconstituted as the Communist Political Association, May 22, 1944

The Communist Party had some influence on events during World War II because of the U.S. alliance with the Soviet Union. It attracted a number of intellectuals, but after the war its numbers and adherents dwindled as the Cold War began.

The Communist Party of the United States (CPUSA) rode a rollercoaster of highs and lows through the 1940's. In 1940, the general secretary of the party was Earl Browder, who had replaced William Z. Foster after the latter suffered a heart attack in 1932. The party had grown to about 70,000 members during the Great Depression but lost many members after the Nazi-Soviet Pact of August, 1939. Following the position of the Comintern—the Moscow-based Communist International—during the first two years of the war, the party stopped the antifascist propaganda it had been promulgating since 1930, advocated American neutrality, and printed many pamphlets and conducted rallies and marches to that effect. In fact, the party's *Daily Worker* attacked the Allies more than Germany.

In the election of 1940, Browder ran for president of the United States from prison, where he was serving a sentence for passport violations. He received only 46,000 votes, a little more than half the votes he had received in 1936.

On June 22, 1941, when Germany suddenly attacked the Soviet Union, the American party reversed itself immediately. Picketers in front of the White House, who the day before held placards demanding that the United States stay out of the war, brought new ones calling for Washington to join in the antifascist struggle.

By the end of the year, the United States was in the war as an ally of the Soviet Union. Anticommunist propaganda in America lessened considerably but did not disappear. Joseph Stalin was the *Time* magazine man of the year twice during the war, even though the magazine's publisher, Henry R. Luce, had been notorious in the past for his anti-Soviet and anticommunist views. The CPUSA supported the war wholeheartedly. Previous pamphlets advocating world peace were shelved. Browder tried to distance the party from the Soviet Union and dissolved the party in 1944; it was reconstituted on May 22 as the Communist Political Association to work in concert with the Democratic Party. Almost immediately after the war, tensions developed between the Soviet Union and the West. Leading Stalinists abroad criticized Browder's wartime attitudes, retiring him in 1945 and putting Foster back in place as general secretary. The party also purged its membership of extremists on both the left and the right.

The party's greatest problem was the wave of anticommunism that swept through America. Even persons marginally associated with the party were ostracized and harassed. Members were arrested and jailed under old and new sedition laws. The labor unions that had used party members' organizing talents in the 1930's and early 1940's now expelled them. The party membership dropped from a peak of about 75,000 during the war to a few thousand.

Impact During World War II, the CPUSA reached its peak membership and attracted a number of intellectuals, artists from all fields, and labor unionists. Its members found positions in government and important areas of society. After the war, the anticommunist harassment that had characterized the 1920's and 1930's returned. Ambitious politicians such as Joseph McCarthy and Richard Nixon used anticommunism as a vehicle to further their careers, and the party lost its importance in American politics and society.

Frederick B. Chary

Further Reading

Isserman, Maurice. *Which Side Were You On? The American Communist Party During the Second World War.* Urbana: University of Illinois Press, 1993.

Ryan, James Gilbert. *Earl Browder: The Failure of American Communism.* 2d ed. Tuscaloosa: University of Alabama Press, 2005.

See also Anticommunism; Cold War; Guthrie, Woody; Hiss, Alger; House Committee on Un-American Activities; "Iron Curtain" speech; Oppenheimer, J. Robert; Seeger, Pete; Smith Act; Smith Act trials; Socialist Workers Party.

■ Computers

Definition Electronic devices that input, process, store, and output data efficiently and quickly, using programmed instructions

During the 1940's, the stored-program digital computer was conceived, developed, and commercialized. Computers progressed from operating using relays or vacuum tubes to those using transistors, and processor and memory discoveries of the 1940's provided the technology for the introduction of many commercial computers during the 1950's.

The ENIAC (Electronic Numerical Integrator and Computer), the first reprogrammable digital electronic computer built in the United States, was designed and built between 1943 and 1946 by a team led by John W. Mauchly and J. Presper Eckert. Mauchly and Eckert were employed at the Moore School of the University of Pennsylvania during World War II, and their work on computing ballistic tables led them to consider several designs for programmable electronic calculators and computers. The ENIAC was a decimal machine, rather than binary, and its programs contained loops, branches, and subroutines. It was delivered to the U.S. Army's Ballistic Research Laboratory in Maryland in 1946 and was used by the government for nine years.

In 1944, Mauchly and Eckert began work on a more advanced computer, the EDVAC (Electronic Discrete Variable Automatic Computer), which operated on binary principles. In 1945, John von Neumann, a professor at Princeton University who was serving as a consultant on the EDVAC project, introduced the concept of storing a program and data for the program in the memory of a computer in his famous "First Draft of a Report on the EDVAC." In addition to introducing the concept of a stored-program computer, von Neumann also defined the standard architecture for single-processor computers, the "von Neumann architecture," in this report. Using von Neumann's stored-program concept and many other new ideas, Mauchly and Eckert delivered the first EDVAC to the Ballistic Research Laboratory in August, 1949. Mauchly and Eckert disagreed with the University of Pennsylvania as to who had the rights to the patents associated with the EDVAC. As a result of this disagreement, Eckert and Mauchly founded the first computer company in the United States, the Eckert-Mauchly Computer Corporation (EMCC), in 1946.

The first computer produced by EMCC was the BINAC (BINary Automatic Computer), developed for Northrop Aircraft Company in 1949. In 1951, Remington Rand (which had acquired EMCC) developed the UNIVAC I (UNIVersal Automatic Computer I), the first American computer intended for commercial use. The UNIVAC was a stored-program digital computer with most of the features seen on modern computers.

Other Electronic Calculators and Computers During the 1940's, a large number of general- and special-purpose electronic calculators were developed in addition to the ENIAC. Many of these supported a high degree of programmability, ultimately leading

to the first real stored-program computer in the United States, the EDVAC, and the world's first commercial digital computer, the UNIVAC I.

The first special-purpose electromagnetic calculator to be developed was the ABC (Atanasoff-Berry Computer), developed at Iowa State University by John Atanasoff and Clifford Berry between 1937 and 1942. It supported performing multiple computer operations on a single data set but was not programmable. In 1939, George Stibitz built the Complex Number Calculator (CNC), which was capable of adding, subtracting, multiplying, and dividing complex numbers. This showed that calculators are capable of doing more than simple arithmetic.

International Business Machines (IBM), founded in 1896 as the Tabulating Machine Company, developed a number of tabulating devices during the twentieth century, including several electronic calculators. In 1944, Howard Aiken, a Harvard professor, designed an automated electromechanical calculator, the Mark I, to help solve some differential equations. He also persuaded IBM to build the Mark I (and II, III, and IV) at Harvard.

Grace Hooper, who would later create the COBOL (COmmon Business-Oriented Language) computer language, helped with the programming for the Mark I and II and also developed the first compiler for the Mark II. IBM called the Mark I the ASCC (Automatic Sequence Controlled Calculator). IBM developed an improved version of the Mark I, called the SSEC (Selective Sequence Electronic Calculator), which was installed at the IBM Computer Center in Manhattan in 1948. It was an electromechanical computer that used a stored program for control and set the stage for the development of the IBM mainframes built during the 1950's.

Computer Memory Developments A number of important developments occurred in computer memory during the 1940's that shaped evolution of the computer industry during the second half of the twentieth century. Early computers used a variety of electromechanical devices for memory (used to store data). The mechanical systems often stored numbers in decimal format (base 10), whereas electronic memory systems stored numbers in both decimal and binary (base 2, zeroes and ones) format. The ENIAC and SSEC used vacuum tubes that could store hundreds of bits of information per tube.

In 1946, Fred Williams developed a better vacuum tube storage technology, increasing the storage capacity of each tube to thousands of bits per tube. IBM's first commercial computer, the IBM 701, used Williams's vacuum tubes for primary memory and a spinning magnetic drum for secondary memory. Magnetic drum memory was discovered during the 1930's and improved by Andrew Booth in 1949. Mauchly and Eckert developed a primary memory system used in the EDVAC and the UNIVAC I, based on Mercury delay lines. This type of memory was considered more reliable but slightly slower than the vacuum tube memory. The vacuum tube and delay line memory systems of the 1940's were used extensively in the mainframe computers of the 1950's.

The most important hardware discovery of the 1940's was the transistor. William Shockley, Walter Brattain, and John Bardeen successfully developed a rudimentary transistor in 1947 at Bell Laboratories. Improved models of the transistor were developed at Bell Laboratories over the next few years, and during the 1960's the transistor replaced vacuum tube and delay line memory.

European Computer Development During the 1940's, several European countries developed computers and theories of computers that had substantial influence on the development of computers in the United States. In 1941, Konrad Zuse built the Z3, the first program-controlled computer. It was made from telephone relays, and it supported 64-bit floating-point arithmetic and a stored program coded on a paper tape. Zuse also founded one of the first computer companies, in 1946, and designed

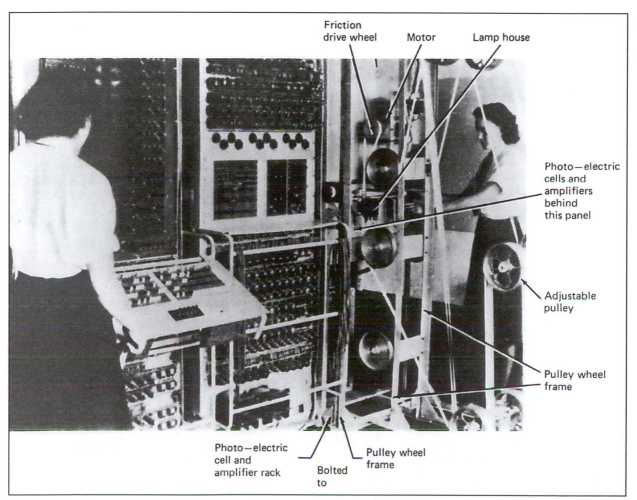

A Colossus computer in 1943. (Smithsonian Institution)

the first theoretical high-level programming language in 1948.

Alan Turing was a British computer scientist who earned his Ph.D. from Princeton in 1938. He published his theory of computability in 1936 and led development of both the first British electronic calculating machine, Colossus, in 1943 and the Mark I in 1949. Turing's importance to computing is reflected by the fact that the most prestigious award in computer science in the United States is the Turing Award.

The electronic delay storage automatic calculator (EDSAC) was developed by Maurice Wilkes at the University of Cambridge in 1949. This computer, considered by some to be the first stored-program electronic computer, was based on von Neumann's EDVAC report and contributed to the development of the UNIVAC I.

Impact At the beginning of the 1940's, scientists were just beginning to develop electronic calculators that could perform multiple operations on a single set of input data. World War II provided a stimulus for developing more sophisticated programmable calculators, and in 1945 John von Neumann provided the breakthrough needed to make the leap from electronic calculators to computers with his introduction of the stored-program computer. The 1940's provided the basic architecture and hardware that led to the rapid deployment of mainframe computers during the 1950's.

George M. Whitson III

Further Reading

Aspray, William. *John von Neumann and the Origins of Modern Computing.* Cambridge, Mass.: MIT Press, 1990. Interesting book about the founder of modern computing.

Campbell-Kelly, Martin, and William Aspray. *Computer: A History of the Information Machine.* New York: Basic Books, 1996. Short but engrossing history of computers.

Goldstine, Herman H. *The Computer: From Pascal to von Neumann.* Princeton, N.J.: Princeton University Press, 1972. Absorbing history of the development of the stored-program computer at the University of Pennsylvania by one of the scientists who was part of the development team.

Ralston, Anthony. *Encyclopedia of Computer Science.* New York: John Wiley & Sons, 2003. One of the standard reference works in its field. The fourth edition has accurate articles covering a wide variety of topics related to computers, including many articles on computers of the 1970's.

Rojas, Raúl, ed. *Encyclopedia of Computers and Computer History.* Chicago: Fitzroy Dearborn, 2001. More than 600 articles about computers, written by scholars in computer science and the history of science.

Rojas, Raúl, and Ulf Hashagen, eds. *The First Computers: History and Architectures.* Cambridge, Mass.: MIT Press, 2002. Includes articles about the architecture of the computers of the 1940's.

Wurster, Christian. *The Computer: An Illustrated History.* Los Angeles: Taschen America, 2002. History of computers, interfaces, and computer design. Numerous photos of computers.

See also Binary automatic computer; Code breaking; ENIAC; Inventions; Science and technology; Telephone technology and service; Transistors.

■ Congress, U.S.

Identification Legislative branch of the federal government comprising the U.S. House of Representatives and the U.S. Senate

The U.S. Congress of the 1940's was concerned mainly with legislative activities pertaining to World War II and its lasting effects, both domestic and international. Congress adapted to changing circumstances by coordinating legislative activity with the executive branch, particularly during the presidency of Franklin D. Roosevelt.

The U.S. Congress of the 1940's was heavily influenced by the prior commitment of the United States to official neutrality in the developing war in Western Europe that was initiated by German military advances beginning in the late 1930's. Under the direction of President Franklin D. Roosevelt, the U.S. Congress slowly began to alter this official stance of neutrality. The history of legislation enacted by the U.S. Congress throughout the 1940's shows an increasing American commitment to World War II and attention to the problems brought by the war, both domestic and international, and both during the war and afterward.

Congressional Legislation, 1939-1945 Of particular importance in the Seventy-sixth Congress (1939-

1941) was the passage of the Neutrality Act of 1939, which repealed the restrictions on selling arms to nations involved in World War II, with the caveat that those wishing to purchase arms had to pay in cash and use their own mode of transportation to move the arms. This legislative action was seen as necessary to allow the United States to respond to those nations with whom American national security interests were closely aligned.

In another move toward ending an official stance of neutrality, Congress also passed the Selective Training and Service Act of 1940, which required all males between the ages of twenty-one and thirty-five to register for one year of active duty and to serve for ten years in the reserves. In subsequent Congresses, this legislation was changed incrementally, lowering the age limits for registration and increasing the time commitment for active duty. By passing this legislation (and subsequent versions), Congress created a mechanism to fill manpower needs should the United States become involved in war.

By the Seventy-seventh Congress (1941-1943), events had changed dramatically. Congress passed the Lend-Lease Act on March 11, 1941; it allowed the president to sell defense materials to any nation deemed vital for the protection of American security interests. The defining event that pushed the United States to enter World War II occurred on December 7, 1941, when the Japanese caught the United States off guard by attacking Pearl Harbor in Hawaii. Subsequently, Congress declared war on Japan, passing the declaration on December 8, 1941. In addition, Congress declared war on Germany and Italy, passing these declarations on December 11, 1941. The United States was now officially engaged in World War II. To allow for effective war preparations, two War Powers Acts were passed, allowing the president to use the executive branch as a means to mobilize the United States for war in both Western Europe and the Pacific.

With the dawning of the Seventy-eighth Congress (1943-1945), the United States was heavily involved in World War II, requiring the mobilization of male service members and, for the first time, women. Such pieces of legislation as the Army and Navy Female Physicians and Surgeons Act and the creation of the Women's Army Corps allowed women to have a direct impact on the U.S. war effort. As the United States became more deeply involved, a need for tax revenue to finance American efforts in World War II created a revolution in the American tax system with the passage of the Current Tax Payment Act of 1943. This legislation changed the way the U.S. government collected taxes by reintroducing the "pay-as-you-go" system of withholding taxes from individual paychecks that had been used from 1913 to 1916, and it further required employers to engage in withholding of worker wages. Congress also passed the Smith-Connally Act (War Labor Disputes Act) on June 25, 1943, over President Roosevelt's veto. It restricted organized labor from striking in industries important to the war effort.

The Smith-Connally Act served as a prelude to other antistrike legislation such as the Labor-Management Relations Act (Taft-Hartley Act), passed in the Eightieth Congress on June 23, 1947. In response to the anticipated return of soldiers from war, Congress passed the Servicemen's Readjustment Act of 1944 (G.I. Bill), which provided educational benefits, help in acquiring home loans, and the opportunity for employers to give preference to former soldiers in hiring for some jobs. The G.I. Bill

President Franklin D. Roosevelt signing the declaration of war against Japan on December 8, 1941. (National Archives)

was seen as a way to reward soldiers for service to their country.

Congressional Legislation, 1946-1949 The use of nuclear weapons by the United States on the Japanese cities of Hiroshima and Nagasaki prompted Congress to pass the Atomic Energy Act of 1946, which created a five-person civilian Atomic Energy Commission (AEC) to oversee atomic research and development. The members of the AEC were appointed by the president. Congress then created the Joint Committee on Atomic Energy (JCAE) to oversee this civilian commission appointed by the president.

As World War II came to a close, nations had recognized the need for international cooperation to achieve the rebuilding of nations devastated by war (and to avoid such a cataclysmic war in the future). This perspective facilitated creation of the United Nations in 1945, with the United States as a founding member. In addition, Congress committed to helping rebuild international financial stability by passing legislation to abide by agreements reached at the Bretton Woods Conference (United Nations Monetary and Financial Conference) of July, 1944. The United States became a member of the International Monetary Fund (IMF) and the International Bank for Reconstruction and Development (IBRD), later known as the World Bank. Congress also engaged in sweeping reforms of Congress itself by passing the Legislative Reorganization Act of 1946, which helped to streamline Congress's committee system and provided for professional staffing to committees.

By the Eightieth Congress (1947-1949), the end of World War II had created a set of new international tensions between the United States and the Soviet Union. Much of the legislative activity of Congress during this session centered on finding ways to constrain communism's spread internationally and to maintain military dominance over the Soviet Union in the Cold War. To combat Soviet influence in war-ravaged nations, the United States gave unprecedented levels of international aid both to countries within Soviet influence, such as Greece and Turkey, and to Western European nations through the Marshall Plan. The official title of the legislation, the Economic Cooperation Act of 1948, allocated almost $6 billion for international reconstruction projects.

To consolidate the American military, Congress passed the National Security Act on July 26, 1947. It centralized military control under the secretary of defense and created the National Security Council and the Central Intelligence Agency (CIA). Congress also sent the Twenty-second Amendment to the U.S. Constitution to the states. This amendment limited individuals to serving only two terms as president of the United States. It was ratified by the states on February 27, 1951. This amendment has been termed the Roosevelt Amendment because only Franklin D. Roosevelt had gone against tradition and served more than two terms as president of the United States.

Partisan Composition of Congress Throughout most of the 1940's, the Democratic Party enjoyed majorities in the U.S. House and Senate, as well as in the executive branch. In the 1946 congressional elections, however, the Republican Party won a majority of the seats in the U.S. House (245 of 435) and in the Senate (51 of 96). This change in the partisan composition of the Congress made the work of President Harry S. Truman, a Democrat, more difficult. Even after the 1948 congressional elections, in which Democrats regained majorities in both the House and the Senate, Truman still encountered difficulties. Despite partisan problems in Congress, Truman was able to pursue his policy agenda of containing communism and reconstructing Western Europe. He did so through international aid, U.S. membership in the United Nations, and U.S. participation in the agreements reached at Bretton Woods.

Impact Overall, the U.S. Congress of the 1940's was heavily engaged in dealing with the domestic and international implications of World War II and its aftermath. From an initial policy of neutrality during the 1930's to full-scale involvement of the United States in World War II by the end of 1941, Congress continually needed to adapt to changing circumstances. It passed legislation that dealt with a host of issues ranging from taxation to national security and foreign policy. The Selective Service system remained in place, so that a military draft could be imposed. Payroll tax withholding also remained in place. The United Nations and the World Bank increased their roles in world events. Marshall Plan funding contributed to the rebuilding of Europe into the early 1950's. Probably of most importance was the development of the Cold War mentality, which characterized relations with the Soviet Union to greater or lesser degrees until declaration of the end of the Cold War in 1991.

William K. Delehanty

Further Reading

Bacon, Donald C., Roger H. Davidson, and Morton Keller, eds. *Encyclopedia of the United States Congress.* 4 vols. New York: Simon & Schuster, 1995. Excellent source for understanding the basics of the U.S. Congress, including its development over time, how Congress is organized, and how Congress adapts to changing historical circumstances.

Christianson, Stephen G. *Facts About the Congress.* New York: H. W. Wilson, 1996. Detailed accounting of every Congress through 1995, including legislation passed, partisan composition of each Congress, and brief historical background discussions to place each Congress in its historical context.

Dodd, Lawrence C., and Bruce I. Oppenheimer, eds. *Congress Reconsidered.* 8th ed. Washington, D.C.: CQ Press, 2005. Good overview of how scholars study the U.S. Congress and how Congress has developed over time.

Josephy, Alvin M., Jr. *On the Hill: A History of the American Congress.* New York: Simon & Schuster, 1980. Useful overview of the U.S. Congress throughout history, with a good description of congressional politics during the 1940's.

Schickler, Eric. *Disjointed Pluralism.* Princeton, N.J.: Princeton University Press, 2001. Overview of how the U.S. Congress has developed over time, with an excellent discussion of congressional politics from 1937 to 1952.

Stathis, Stephen W. *Landmark Legislation: 1774-2002.* Washington, D.C.: CQ Press, 2003. Provides a detailed accounting of all major legislation passed by the U.S. Congress through the early years of the twenty-first century.

Stewart, Charles, III. *Analyzing Congress.* New York: W. W. Norton, 2001. Good overview of Congress. Provides a detailed historical account of how the U.S. Congress developed during the 1940's.

See also   Cold War; Elections in the United States: 1940; Elections in the United States: 1942 and 1946; Elections in the United States: 1944; Elections in the United States: 1948; National Security Act of 1947; Roosevelt, Franklin D.; Taft-Hartley Act; Truman, Harry S.

■ Congress of Industrial Organizations

Identification   American labor federation
Also known as   CIO
Date   Founded on November 9, 1935

The Congress of Industrial Organizations, a New Deal-era rival to the American Federation of Labor, set out to change the idea of labor organizing. In particular, it promoted the idea of organizing workers by industry rather than by craft and went on to organize the major American industries of the period. In the process, the labor federation created a more democratic, socially conscious form of unionism, whose political inclusiveness would be increasingly challenged during the 1940's.

The Congress of Industrial Organizations (CIO), which rose to prominence during the New Deal era, reached its peak of power and influence by the mid-1940's. Its principal constituent unions included the United Auto Workers (UAW), the United Electrical, Radio, and Machine Workers of America (UE), the Amalgamated Clothing Workers of America (ACWA), the United Steelworkers (USW), and the United Mine Workers (UMW). The federation also included a number of unions that were unabashedly leftist. Principal leaders in the CIO hierarchy included Walter Reuther of the UAW, Sidney Hillman of the ACWA, Philip Murray of the USW, and John L. Lewis of the UMW. Rather than organizing by specific skills, they organized on the basis of numbers.

By the mid-1940's, the CIO had organized most of the major American industries in the American industrial Northeast and Midwest. The CIO also took the lead in promoting more racially equitable organizing, including African American workers, which the American Federation of Labor (AFL) never had up to that time. Enforcing the ideal of equality, however, would prove difficult at times, and the CIO's willingness to accept segregation would affect the otherwise bold 1946 southern organizing effort known as Operation Dixie. Nonetheless, the CIO's willingness to organize African Americans on a more equitable basis than the AFL, as well as its tolerance for political leftism, made the CIO and its political arm, the CIO Political Action Committee (PAC), seem increasingly suspect politically, resulting in the investigations of the CIO PAC as well as its founder, Sidney Hillman. As a result, as the CIO grew and its bureaucracy became increasingly entrenched, its leaders became more politically cautious and willing to cooperate with the U.S. government, as a way of ensuring that labor's interests were heard and recognized.

Impact During World War II, the CIO and its constituent unions observed a "no-strike pledge" and supported the Allied war effort as a matter of policy, in spite of periodic opposition from the Left over foreign policy and Lewis's highly public opposition to a closer alliance with the federal government. Nevertheless, the CIO made sure that labor had a voice in the formation of wartime and industrial labor policy, largely through Hillman's leadership of the National War Labor Board and cochairmanship of the War Production Board. During the war years, as employment shot up, the CIO unions organized most major American heavy industries, and the union's numbers increased to four million members by 1945.

In 1946, however, the participation of the CIO unions in a massive postwar strike wave contributed to a governmental and public turn against organized labor. In 1947, Congress passed the Labor-Management Relations Act, popularly known as the Taft-Hartley Act, which put strict new limits on the activities of unions and required unions and their members to sign anticommunism affidavits. During this period, the CIO maintained a difficult balance between promoting a voice for labor in international affairs and distancing itself from international efforts such as the World Federation of Trade Unions that appeared to be too communist-dominated. Meanwhile, at home, the CIO leadership initially resisted this push toward a purge, even while trying to discourage endorsements of the left-leaning Progressive presidential candidate Henry A. Wallace. By 1949, however, political conditions had shifted so that most of the constituent unions saw the necessity of cooperation with the anticommunist provisions. The holdouts were purged, and from the late 1940's until the early 1950's the CIO dedicated itself to destroying and replacing the so-called communist unions in each of the constituent industries. As a result, the CIO lost its militant edge and by 1955 was politically and organizationally similar enough to the AFL for the two federations to merge and form the AFL-CIO.

Susan Roth Breitzer

Further Reading

Levenstein, Harvey A. *Communism, Anticommunism, and the CIO*. Westport, Conn.: Greenwood Press, 1981.

Tucker, Spencer, and Priscilla Mary Roberts, eds. *Encyclopedia of World War II: A Political, Social, and Military History*. Santa Barbara, Calif.: ABC-Clio, 2004.

Zieger, Robert H. *The CIO: 1935-1955*. Chapel Hill: University of North Carolina Press, 1997.

See also American Federation of Labor; Communist Party USA; Hillman, Sidney; Income and wages; Labor strikes; National War Labor Board; Taft-Hartley Act; Unemployment in the United States; Unionism; War Production Board; Wartime industries.

■ Congress of Racial Equality

Identification Organization committed to civil rights and racial integration
Also known as CORE; Committee of Racial Equality
Date Established April, 1942

The Congress of Racial Equality (CORE) is an interracial organization dedicated to achieving racial equality in the United States through nonviolent direct action. Although it grew slowly during the 1940's and 1950's, CORE became a major contributor to the civil rights movement during the 1960's.

In Chicago in October, 1941, a group of young people met to discuss the problem of racism in the United States. Most were members of the United States Fellowship of Reconciliation (FOR USA), a pacifist organization formed during World War I. They were heeding the call of the new executive director of FOR USA, A. J. Muste, who upon taking office in 1940 had encouraged pacifists to address all forms of social injustice. Some in the group decided to go beyond discussing racism and take action against it.

By April, 1942, six people had assumed leadership roles in forming the Chicago Committee of Racial Equality (renamed the Congress of Racial Equality, or CORE, in 1943). Four were University of Chicago students and dedicated pacifists. Joe Guinn was black, and Bernice Fisher, Homer Jack, and

James R. Robinson were white. Two staff members of the Chicago FOR office joined the students as CORE's cofounders. James Farmer, who was black, and George Houser, who was white, were strong pacifists trained in the progressive youth movement of the Methodist church.

These founders envisioned CORE as a clear alternative to the groups then dominating national struggles against racism, the National Association for the Advancement of Colored People (NAACP) and the National Urban League. The NAACP and the National Urban League used strategies such as lobbying and lawsuits to whittle away at racial discrimination. Both generally avoided confrontational interventions with racist businesses and institutions. In contrast, CORE's founders believed that direct nonviolent protests could overturn oppression, and they drew inspiration from two powerful examples of nonviolent mass action from the 1920's and 1930's: India's independence movement under Mohandas Gandhi and sit-down industrial strikes in the United States.

Slow Expansion   Initially, CORE developed primarily in Chicago, and members established the mission and character of what they envisioned as a national movement. After much deliberation, they framed a "Statement of Purpose" and "Action Discipline," guidelines that defined membership in CORE as highly participatory. Members should plan and undertake specific projects aimed at ending segregation. Decisions should be made collectively through dialogue. CORE would model the ideals it wished to achieve, such that black and white members alike would never practice segregation.

The founders realized that for CORE to succeed, it needed more members, but especially during wartime there were few pacifists to be found. At the first national CORE conference in June, 1943, after vigorous debate, participants agreed that members need not be pacifists but must use nonviolent tactics. CORE should expand, but it needed to emphasize public actions against racism; paying dues to the national office was far less important. The disregard for fund-raising meant that CORE had little money and often relied on FOR's resources. For example, most of the growth outside Chicago during the 1940's came from the efforts of FOR's youth director, Bayard Rustin.

Modest experiments with direct action in north-ern and western cities achieved occasional victories, such as having segregated restaurants serve interracial groups. The effort that was necessary to integrate a few restaurants reinforced the fact that CORE needed to expand to make real gains. Despite the group's efforts, growth remained slow. The leaders acknowledged that too few Americans were ready during the 1940's to take public actions against racism.

From 1942 to 1947, CORE remained almost invisible in comparison to the NAACP and the National Urban League. Thirteen groups were linked to the tiny national office by 1947, with only hundreds of total members instead of the thousands CORE hoped to attract. Only one joint project with FOR, the Journey of Reconciliation in 1947, drew significant publicity to CORE. Journey participants tried to put into action the Supreme Court ruling in *Morgan v. Virginia* that banned segregation on interstate buses. The Journey of Reconciliation had great symbolic power and demonstrated that white and black people could act together against racism. After the project ended, however, bus companies still ignored the Supreme Court ruling and CORE still struggled for support.

Impact   During the 1940's, CORE's small but dedicated membership proved that with enough volunteers, a mass movement using nonviolent tactics might make significant progress against segregation. During the 1950's, CORE managed to add southern affiliates. By the beginning of the 1960's, the organization was poised to play a leadership role when thousands of students, most of them black, launched widespread nonviolent protests against Jim Crow segregation.

Between 1961 and 1965, CORE, the Student Non-Violent Coordinating Committee, and the Southern Christian Leadership Conference were the three most significant organizations using nonviolent protest to end Jim Crow. James Farmer became national director of CORE in 1961 and helped coordinate the Freedom Rides, a major effort to challenge bus segregation throughout the South. CORE also co-sponsored the interracial March on Washington in 1963.

After 1966, the organization shifted away from its nonviolent and interracial roots. From a peak membership of around eighty thousand during the mid-1960's, CORE's support base plummeted. The organization in the twenty-first century bears little resemblance to its 1942-1966 form.

Beth Kraig

Further Reading

Chatfield, Charles. "Peace as a Reform Movement." *OAH Magazine of History* 8, no. 3 (1994): 10-14. Summary of pacifist-led movements based in the United States, including CORE and the Fellowship of Reconciliation.

D'Emilio, John. *Lost Prophet: The Life and Times of Bayard Rustin.* New York: Free Press, 2003. Chapters 3-6 address Rustin's contributions to the development of CORE during the 1940's.

Farmer, James. *Freedom, When?* New York: Random House, 1965. Farmer, a CORE cofounder and eventual national director, discusses the importance of nonviolent direct action in his work against racism from the 1940's to 1965.

Meier, August, and Elliott Rudwick. *CORE: A Study in the Civil Rights Movement, 1942-1968.* New York: Oxford University Press, 1973. The best objective source on CORE's history, including its development during the 1940's.

Robinson, Jo Ann Ooiman. *Abraham Went Out: A Biography of A. J. Muste.* Philadelphia: Temple University Press, 1981. Chronicles Muste's leadership of FOR and discusses his influence on CORE's creation and his relationships with pivotal CORE members such as James Farmer and Bayard Rustin.

See also African Americans; Desegregation of the U.S. military; Jim Crow laws; Journey of Reconciliation; *Morgan v. Virginia*; National Association for the Advancement of Colored People; Racial discrimination; Randolph, A. Philip.

■ Conscientious objectors

Definition Persons who refused to participate as combatants in war on moral or ethical grounds

In contrast to governments of the Axis Powers, the governments of the United States and its allies generally provided for the possibility of refusing military service on religious grounds. Despite the public opprobrium they endured, many war resisters performed public service as wartime medics, conservation workers, and caretakers of helpless patients that made valuable contributions to American life.

In 1940, the U.S. Congress passed the first peacetime conscription law, more than a full year before the United States entered World War II in the wake of the Japanese attack on Pearl Harbor on December 7, 1941. The Selective Training and Service Act of 1940 defined legal options and classifications for those opposed to military service. The law excused men who by reason of religious training or belief were conscientiously opposed to participating in war in any form. Moral, ethical, or political opposition by themselves were not acceptable. Men who would not carry weapons but were willing to serve in the medical corps were given a special classification. Those who were opposed to all forms of military service but were willing to perform civilian work deemed of national importance were given another special classification. Men who refused to register for the draft or who refused induction after being denied conscientious objector (CO) status were prosecuted for felony draft evasion and were sent to prison when convicted.

Certain Christian denominations, such as the Quakers (Friends), Mennonites, and Brethren, were recognized as having been historically pacifist. However, many mainstream Protestant denominations formed antiwar groups between 1939 and 1942. Although pacifism and isolationism had been regarded as strong and respectable reactions to World War I, public attitudes changed sharply during World War II. The brutality of Nazi Germany and Japan's surprise attack on Pearl Harbor turned American public opinion against pacifism and isolationism. Conscientious objectors who considered applying for exemptions from service faced a difficult moral decision that went against the tide of public opinion. They were often accused of being cowards and draft dodgers.

Civilian service usually meant Civilian Public Service Camps, in which resisters worked on conservation projects and fought forest fires. The camps were typically located in remote rural areas, where the COs were less likely either to influence other citizens or to encounter public hostility. Although the camps were nominally civilian, they were often run under military rules that chafed on war resisters. Another type of CO assignment was in mental hospitals. COs working as orderlies were shocked by the conditions and treatments they witnessed in mental hospitals, which some characterized as "snake pits." By bringing these conditions to public attention, they were responsible for the earliest reforms benefiting psychiatric patients.

More than 70,000 American men claimed CO exemptions based on the 1940 law. The Selective Service System accepted about half their applications. About 25,000 men were assigned to noncombat military duty and some 12,000 to alternative service in public service camps. More than 5,500 men were sent to prison for refusing to register or serve in World War II. About one-third of these were Jehovah's Witnesses, whose applications for exemption were refused because their objection was to the current war, not to all warfare. Others were black nationalists who refused to serve in a "white men's war" while they faced segregation and discrimination at home. Still others were imprisoned for walking away from their civilian service camps because of their military regimentation or who had been denied CO status despite their strong convictions.

Impact   Some World War II resisters went on to fame in later life. They include David Dellinger, who would become a celebrated Vietnam War protester and Chicago Seven defendant; Bayard Rustin, a future civil rights leader; actor Lew Ayres; and poet Robert Lowell.

Jan Hall

Further Reading

Eller, Cynthia. *Conscientious Objectors and the Second World War: Moral and Religious Arguments in Support of Pacifism.* New York: Praeger, 1991.

Gara, Larry, and Lenna Mae Gara. *A Few Small Candles: War Resisters of World War II Tell Their Stories.* Kent, Ohio: Kent State University Press, 1999.

Matthews, Mark. *Smoke Jumping on the Western Fire Line: Conscientious Objectors During World War II.* Norman: University of Oklahoma Press, 2006.

See also   Anticommunism; Bureau of Land Management; Civil rights and liberties; Military conscription in the United States; Religion in Canada; Religion in the United States; World War II mobilization.

American mothers gathered in front of the U.S. Supreme Court Building in Washington, D.C., in August, 1940, to protest against the Selective Training and Service bill then being considered by Congress. (AP/Wide World Photos)

■ Conservatism in U.S. politics

The conservative resurgence in the late 1930's marked the end of largely unchallenged government experimentation that typified the early New Deal. Following World War II, conservative forces figured prominently in curtailing government expansion and in leading the nation into a hard-line stance against Soviet expansionism abroad and domestic subversion at home.

Until the 1937 attempt to pack the Supreme Court with liberal justices, President Franklin D. Roosevelt faced little conservative opposition. Roosevelt's effort to alter the balance of governmental power, however, elicited immediate criticism from conservative southern Democrats, who soon found themselves in an unofficial alliance with the Republican minority. Adding to conservative solidarity was Roosevelt's 1938 drive to unseat conservative Democrats. Together, southern Democrats and Republicans created a powerful "conservative coalition" that influenced the American legislative agenda for decades.

As World War II began in 1939, conservative leaders remained faithful to the isolationist tenets that had long marked their "America First" brand of diplomacy. For a period, they believed that the United States should not get embroiled in another of what appeared as a seemingly endless array of European conflicts. France's rapid fall at the hands of the Nazi war machine in 1940 raised questions regarding the prudence of isolationism. The bombing of Pearl Harbor in December, 1941, erased any remaining doubts about American intervention. Liberals and conservatives united to fund and then to fight the war.

Postwar peace brought new challenges and a return to the partisanship that was briefly and unevenly put on hold during the war. Postwar inflation and labor unrest undermined the ability of the new president, Harry S. Truman, to maintain the wartime consensus forged by Roosevelt. Adding to Truman's difficulties were growing Republican charges that so-called communists had infiltrated the government. The 1946 off-year elections brought the Republican Party back to power in both houses of Congress for the first time since 1928. Adding to the Republicans' strength were fiscally conservative southern Democrats who looked to the Republican Party for support against an increasingly pro-civil rights Truman administration. Congressional sparring with the president over the antilabor Taft-Hartley Act and reductions in taxes obscured the national uniformity that did exist in the field of foreign affairs.

Senate approval of the United Nations Charter occurred with only two dissenting votes. The National Security Act of 1947 passed with bipartisan support. Congressional approval for efforts to thwart the spread of global communism found widespread support from both liberals and conservatives alike.

By 1948, the embattled Truman administration appeared on the verge of defeat. The Republican Party, confident in its chances to secure the White House, drafted New York governor Thomas E. Dewey as its presidential nominee. Southern defections from the Democratic fold and the emergence of the ultraliberal Progressive Party also augured ill for Truman's reelection bid. Much to the surprise of political pundits, Truman pulled off a shocking electoral victory, but his next four years in office would be marked by bitter disappointment and renewed conflict with congressional conservatives.

Impact Conservatism in American politics rebounded in the late 1930's and became a viable force in the 1940's. Conservative American leaders made their peace with the New Deal legislation already in place but vowed that they would resist any further expansion of federal authority either in the form of profligate government spending or in attempts to alter the power of the federal government at the expense of private citizens or individual states. In the field of foreign policy, conservatives joined with all but the most extreme liberals in a crusade to fight communist expansion.

Keith M. Finley

Further Reading

Patterson, James T. *Congressional Conservatism and the New Deal: The Growth of the Conservative Coalition in Congress, 1933-1939.* Lexington: University of Kentucky Press, 1967.

Rosenof, Theodore. *Patterns of Political Economy in America: The Failure to Develop a Democratic Left Synthesis, 1933-1950.* New York: Garland, 1983.

See also Civil rights and liberties; Congress of Industrial Organizations; Dewey, Thomas E.; Elections in the United States: 1948; Fair Deal; National Security Act of 1947; New Deal programs; Taft-Hartley Act; Truman, Harry S.

Continental Shelf Proclamation and Coastal Fisheries Proclamation. *See* **Truman proclamations**

■ Convention on the Prevention and Punishment of the Crime of Genocide

The Treaty International convention designed to prevent genocide

Date Approved by U.N. General Assembly on December 9, 1948

Also known as Genocide Convention

A landmark in international law, the Genocide Convention declared genocide, regardless of the circumstances in which it was committed, an international crime that signatories were obliged to prevent or punish.

Passed by a unanimous 55-0 vote by the U.N. General Assembly in 1948, the Convention on the Prevention and Punishment of the Crime of Genocide defined genocide as an act aiming at the destruction, but not exclusively murder, of an ethnic, national, racial, or religious group in whole or in part, regardless of circumstances. The convention committed contracting nations to prevent and punish this crime. The convention, building upon the U.N. Resolution of December 11, 1946, which declared genocide an international crime, owed much to Raphael Lemkin, a Polish Jewish lawyer who proposed an international law against mass atrocities before World War II and who, in 1944, coined the term "genocide" to describe crimes against humanity, with particular focus on the murder of Europe's Jews that had been perpetrated by Adolf Hitler's Germany since 1933.

International revulsion at the extent of Nazi crimes, graphically revealed during the Nuremberg Trials in 1945-1946, facilitated Lemkin's efforts to criminalize genocide and created the context for the convention's adoption. Although U.S. President Harry S. Truman publicly supported the convention, the Senate, concerned about the potential impact on American sovereignty, refused to ratify it.

Impact In February, 1986, the U.S. Senate finally ratified the Genocide Convention. By then, events in Bangladesh, Burundi, and Cambodia had demonstrated that the convention was not fulfilling its advocates' expectations. American adherence made no appreciable difference, as evidenced by developments in Rwanda, Bosnia, and Kosovo during the 1990's.

Bruce J. DeHart

Further Reading

LeBlanc, Lawrence J. *The United States and the Genocide Convention.* Durham, N.C.: Duke University, 1991.

Power, Samantha. *"A Problem from Hell": America and the Age of Genocide.* New York: Harper Perennial, 2007.

See also International Court of Justice; Nuremberg Trials; Truman, Harry S.; United Nations; Universal Declaration of Human Rights; War crimes and atrocities; World War II.

■ Cowboy films

Definition Films based on themes unique to the mythology of the American West

Cowboy films instilled values emphasizing fair play, the importance of socialization, and a sense of rugged independence tempered by human decency. Action-packed, entertaining, and carrying a consistent moral message, cowboy films shaped behavior and attitudes by presenting a code of conduct reinforced weekly on theater screens in thousands of America's cities and small towns; during the 1940's, such films emphasized themes of honor and sacrifice.

In 1940, the three top Hollywood money-making film stars in America were Mickey Rooney, Spencer Tracy, and Clark Gable. In fourth place was a B-movie star who received fifty thousand fan letters every month: Gene Autry. For thirty-five cents, a young girl or boy could go to the movies on Saturdays, see a Gene Autry Western, a Boston Blackie or Charlie Chan detective film, a serial featuring Captain Marvel or Zorro, and the previews for next week's attractions, and still have money left over for popcorn and a soda. During the early 1940's, Autry, "the Singing Cowboy," was box office gold for Republic Pictures, making six or seven features every year.

The Singing Cowboys There were other cowboy film stars, even other singing cowboys, but none ever achieved the combination of Autry's popularity and earning potential. Autry's films, which ran sixty to seventy-five minutes, were shown primarily in the Midwest, the South, and the southwestern United States. In large cities, Autry's pictures rarely played in first-run theaters; Autry, his horse Champion, and his sidekick Smiley Burnette were genuine grassroots sensations. Despite his success, Autry left his stardom behind to serve his country in World War II and did not make a single picture from 1943 until 1946.

Autry's departure for the war helped to advance the career of a cowboy actor named Dick Weston (born Leonard Slye), who appeared with the musical group the Sons of the Pioneers. He was born near Cincinnati, Ohio. Although he had appeared in a small role in an Autry film under his real name, film fans got to know him best by a third name: Roy Rogers. Herbert Yates, the founder and president of Republic Pictures, who once had Autry, Rogers, and John Wayne all under contract, helped choose the cowboy actor's new name, based on that of newspaper columnist and entertainer Will Rogers.

By 1940, Roy Rogers had already starred in thirteen pictures for Republic, many with sidekick George "Gabby" Hayes. In 1944, Dale Evans starred with Rogers in *The Cowboy and the Senorita*, marking the first of twenty consecutive films together. Rogers and Evans married and continued to star in Republic's films throughout the decade. As the "King of the Cowboys" and the "Queen of the West," and with Roy's horse Trigger, the "Smartest Horse in Show Business," the couple continued to make contemporary Westerns (complete with telephones, radios, and automobiles). Other singing cowboys of the

1940's included Tex Ritter, Eddie Dean, Monte Hale, Dick Foran, and Jimmy Wakely. Their popularity would finally wane by the middle of the next decade.

Transformation of the Cowboy Hero As the war years ensued, the nonsinging, "Old West" cowboy hero was transformed from a solitary, independent, strong-willed town-tamer to a gentler do-gooder with a greater connection to his community, a man who would settle down and raise a family and attend church. The heroes became government agents, good guys sent from Washington to help townspeople fight corruption or a land-grabbing, claim-jumping dictator threatening the future of the town and the territory, standing in the way of civilization and statehood. Cowboy films during the war years stressed team effort, with all the townspeople pulling together against a common enemy. Meanwhile, the leader and hero in the film was often still the drifter, the man of conscience, the weathered moral voice of authority who stood up for what was right and, by doing so, won the girl and the undying admiration and respect of all upstanding citizens.

No actor appeared in more A-list Westerns than Randolph Scott—more than fifty of them. Scott personified the quiet, self-assured, trail-hardened cowboy in such films as *Western Union* (1941), *Abilene Town* (1946), and *Albuquerque* (1947). The decade's other film stars appearing in the genre's better films included Errol Flynn, remembered best for such roles as Robin Hood and Captain Blood; he made four high-quality Westerns during the decade: *Virginia City* (1940), *Santa Fe Trail* (1940), *They Died with Their Boots On* (1941), and *San Antonio* (1945).

More typical Western film stars included Joel McCrea in *The Virginian* (1946) and *Ramrod* (1947)

Cowboy singing star Roy Rogers (right) and his wife, Dale Evans (left) at Grauman's Chinese Theater in Hollywood in early 1949. They have just signed their names in a cement slab, and Rogers is helping his horse Trigger add his hoofprint. (Getty Images)

and Glenn Ford in *The Man from Colorado* (1949). Westerns produced for larger studios employing the best directors and top stars included *The Ox-Bow Incident* (1943), directed by William Wellman and starring Henry Fonda; *My Darling Clementine* (1946), directed by John Ford and also starring Fonda; *The Westerner* (1940), directed by William Wyler and starring Gary Cooper; and the first psychological Western, *Pursued* (1947), directed by Raoul Walsh and starring Robert Mitchum. John Wayne starred in Howard Hawks's *Red River* (1948), a film some critics believe to be the decade's most outstanding Western.

Wayne's and Ford's names became synonymous with Western films. Including B-list projects, Wayne made more than twenty films with Ford. Ford's own career began with silent films, and his work in Westerns during the 1940's included two of his "cavalry trio" films, *Fort Apache* (1948) and *She Wore a Yellow Ribbon* (1949). The third film of the trio, *Rio Grande*, was released in 1950. All three films starred Wayne and typical stables of Ford supporting actors such as Ward Bond, Victor McLaglen, and Ben Johnson. Another 1948 Ford film starring Wayne, *The Three Godfathers*, was a remake of an earlier 1936 Ford film of the same name.

Often shot on location in Utah's Monument Valley, Ford's Westerns were grand, sweeping films. Filmed either in black and white (*My Darling Clementine*, *Fort Apache*) or in Technicolor (*She Wore a Yellow Ribbon*), these pictures captured the hardscrabble existence of pioneers or of the U.S. cavalry making their way across unforgiving landscapes in the shadows of daunting buttes and other towering rock formations. The scenery was an impressive costar in any Ford Western.

Three films foreshadowed the genre's future and paved the way for later directors to take more risks with the Western formula. Jennifer Jones, who was nominated for best actress for her performance, Gregory Peck, and Joseph Cotten starred in the sultry *Duel in the Sun* (1946), a pet project of David O. Selznick that was supposed to recapture the magic of Selznick's *Gone with the Wind* (1939). To complicate matters, Jones and Selznick had been married and recently divorced. King Vidor received credit for direction after six other directors, including the great Josef Von Sternberg and Selznick himself, had bowed out.

Another Western that was literally a trailblazer and, like *Duel in the Sun*, suffered at the hands of its creator, was Howard Hughes's *The Outlaw* (1943), starring Jane Russell in her film debut. This film was built on the myth of Billy the Kid, but Hughes's efforts to push the boundaries of decency in displaying Russell's breasts on screen made *The Outlaw* the most salacious Western of its day.

A film that is often not thought of as a Western, *The Treasure of the Sierra Madre* (1948), starred Humphrey Bogart, veteran cowboy actor Tim Holt, and Walter Huston as three obsessed men searching for gold in Mexico. Huston and his son John, the film's director, both won Oscars for this film classic.

Parodies   Parody is an important indicator in measuring the success of any genre. Cowboy films were spoofed by some of the decade's best comedians. Groucho, Harpo, and Chico Marx starred in Metro-Goldwyn-Mayer's *Go West* (1940), one of the brothers' last films together. Bud Abbott and Lou Costello sent up the Old West in two features during the 1940's, *Ride 'em Cowboy* (1942), considered one of the best of the Western parody films, and *The Wistful Widow of Wagon Gap* (1947), costarring comedic actor Marjorie Main. One of the best-known Western parodies partnered Bob Hope with Jane Russell in *The Paleface* (1948). Even the Three Stooges delved into Western parodies with their film shorts *Rockin' Thru the Rockies* (1940), *Cactus Makes Perfect* (1942), *Phony Express* (1943), and *Out West* (1947). In 1945, the Stooges made a B-list film, *Rockin' in the Rockies*, one of the few feature-length films to feature Curly Howard along with his brother Moe and partner Larry Fine.

Impact   The Western had made several seamless leaps, from dime novels to Western classics by authors such as Zane Grey and Max Brand, to films and radio, and finally to television. It has been argued by some critics that Westerns had little influence on the lives of those generations who embraced them and their stars. The Western, it is argued, was pure escapism, harmless entertainment for a Saturday afternoon's leisure time. Other critics, however, point to the messages, the examples, and the lessons reinforced on the big screen by such stars as Gene Autry, Roy Rogers, and Randolph Scott. The values, it is argued, remained constant in most cowboy films, and the socialization and sense of community that resulted was a lasting benefit.

Randy L. Abbott

Further Reading

Fenin, George N., and William K. Everson. *The Western: From Silents to the Seventies.* New York: Grossman, 1973. Illustrated survey of the complete history of Western films through the early 1970's.

Garfield, Brian. *Western Films: A Complete Guide.* New York: Rawson Associates, 1982. Encyclopedic reference source on individual film titles.

Loy, R. Philip. *Westerns and American Culture, 1930-1955.* Jefferson, N.C.: McFarland, 2001. Thoughtful study of the role that Western films played in wider American culture during the mid-twentieth century.

Place, J. A. *The Western Films of John Ford.* Secaucus, N.J.: Citadel Press, 1974. Lavishly illustrated history of Ford's Western films, with synopses and complete credits for each film.

Rothel, David. *The Singing Cowboys.* South Brunswick: A. S. Barnes, 1978. Appreciative tribute to the era of musical Westerns, when stars such as Gene Autry and Roy Rogers ruled the screen.

Tuska, Jon. *The American West in Film: Critical Approaches to the Western.* Westport, Conn.: Greenwood Press, 1985. Scholarly examination of the themes underlying Western films and critical studies of the genre.

See also Bogart, Humphrey; Film in the United States; Film noir; Film serials; Films about World War II; Flynn, Errol; Ford, John; Hope, Bob; Hughes, Howard; *The Treasure of the Sierra Madre.*

■ Credit and debt

Definition Loaning or borrowing money or its equivalent at the national (federal), state, municipal, corporate, and individual consumer levels

The 1940's was a transitional period in the American credit economy, marked by very rapid escalation of the national debt during World War II, followed by an explosion of consumer debt during the postwar period. This set the stage for later structural changes that prolonged the exponential growth phase, generating instability that led to collapse during the early part of the next century.

Modern economies depend on extending credit and incurring debt. The terms and structure of credit markets have a profound effect on economic well-being and exert a strong influence on public policy. World War II dominated all aspects of life in America between 1940 and 1950, and the economics of borrowing and lending were no exception. At the beginning of the decade, the country was just emerging from the Great Depression. Total public and private indebtedness, which declined during the 1930's, had recovered to its 1929 level but included a higher proportion of federal debt. Between 1940 and 1945, total indebtedness doubled, due entirely to federal borrowing to support the war effort. Individual and corporate debt actually declined slightly. Between 1946 and 1951, corporate and individual borrowing increased total indebtedness by another 30 percent. The lack of any attempt at war debt paydown after 1945 represented a departure from established public policy.

Credit and Debt in 1940 By 1940, most of the New Deal legislation aimed at stabilizing American finances had been in place long enough for its effects to be apparent. Banks had money to lend, and individual confidence both in the security of savings and the prudence of borrowing had recovered from the traumas of the early 1930's. Gross aggregate public, corporate, and individual debt stood at $242 billion, up slightly from its 1929 level of $214 billion and much exceeding a low of $150 billion in 1934. Between 1929 and 1941, federal debt increased from $35 to $89 billion, while individual debt declined from $72 to $56 billion.

The steady rise in public debt between 1932 and 1941 departed from a long-standing policy of paying down war debts during peacetime. In incurring this indebtedness, the U.S. government counted on pump priming to revive the economy sufficiently to pay off the debt. By 1940, direct government expenditures for infrastructure and employment had declined, but public spending to underwrite the wartime budgets of American allies became a major contributor to economic recovery, and the national debt continued to grow.

Home mortgages represent the largest slice of individual consumer debt. The National Housing Act of 1934 revived a moribund housing industry. By 1940, the rate of new housing construction and the percentage of Americans living in owner-occupied homes had regained its 1929 level. A net drop in mortgage indebtedness (from $31.6 to $27.6 billion between 1929 and 1940) was the result of declining housing prices. Other consumer debt, mainly appliances and automobiles, dipped sharply in 1933-1934 and then rose to its previous level.

The War Years   U.S. entry into World War II altered the credit picture drastically. Between 1941 and 1945, total indebtedness rose from $242 to $463 billion, all from federal borrowing. During the same period, corporate debt remained steady, with a modest shift toward shorter-term loans, while individual, state, and municipal indebtedness all declined slightly.

The American public became, in essence, its government's creditor. Wartime wages and corporate profits, which in peacetime would have gone toward increasing the American material standard of living, were instead invested in the war. For nearly four years, few homes were built or exchanged hands. New cars and appliances were virtually unavailable. While the war created a tremendous backlog of consumer demand and a correspondingly large body of consumer savings, those savings were tied up in long-term bonds, most of which did not reach maturity until the early 1970's.

In 1956, individuals owned 50.7 percent of the American national debt, American corporations 21 percent, and foreign investors 2.9 percent. These percentages were relatively stable between 1945 and 1965 but are in sharp contrast to the situation in the early twenty-first century.

Interest rates remained low throughout the 1940's. The Federal Reserve prime rate was 1.8 percent between 1933 and 1946, increasing to 2 percent by 1950. Wartime price controls under the Office of Price Administration encouraged individual investment in government bonds at low interest rates by allaying fears of inflation. Following the war, the low cost of borrowing money made incurring long-term debt a sustainable proposition for consumers.

Total debt per capita was $1,437 in 1940, $2,904 in 1945, and $3,235 in 1950. The ratio of debt to gross domestic product (GDP) remained nearly constant at about 2.0 between 1941 and 1975. It was higher during the Depression because of low productivity, and it has increased steadily since 1970.

The Postwar Years   Historically, the end of a major war produces a serious, though short-lived, economic downturn as demobilized soldiers flood the workforce and war-dependent industries struggle to adjust. This did not occur in America after World War II for a number of reasons, most prominent among which were continuing high military spending due to the Cold War and a tremendous expansion of the consumer economy built on credit.

Between 1945 and 1951, gross debt in America rose from $463 to $608 billion. Public debt actually declined, from $309 to $297 billion, while corporate and consumer debt increased from $154 to $311 billion. The most dramatic increases were in state and municipal debt ($17 to $27 billion) and nonfarm consumer debt ($47 to $107 billion). The federal government was able to balance its budget and retire short-term debt obligations as they came due, but it allowed the long-term war debt to remain on the books, where, due to low interest rates and a steadily expanding economy, the costs of servicing the debt did not figure highly in budgeting decisions.

The Servicemen's Readjustment Act, also known as the G.I. Bill, became law on June 22, 1944. Of the bill's three main provisions—tuition subsidies for higher education, low-cost home loans, and unemployment benefits—the home-loan program most affected credit and indebtedness. Through the G.I. Bill, the federal government guaranteed zero-down, low-interest home loans made by banks to returning war veterans. Between 1945 and 1952, 2.4 million families took advantage of this program.

Most of the growth in indebtedness between 1945 and 1951 was tied, directly or indirectly, to the explosive growth of suburbia the G.I. Bill spawned. In addition to the home mortgage, the family needed a car, furniture, and appliances. Communities borrowed money to construct roads and schools. States also incurred indebtedness to build up the larger infrastructure, and to expand colleges and universities to accommodate veterans taking advantage of the educational provisions of the G.I. Bill.

The mechanisms of borrowing and lending remained similar to those in place after the reforms of the 1930's. Local financial institutions originated and serviced home loans with standards for loan-to-value and debt-to-income ratios that ensured affordable loans with a low default rate, but they discriminated against racial minorities and favored new suburban construction over existing inner-city real estate. Auto dealers and banks provided automobile loans, and stores extended credit for big-ticket items such as appliances through time-payment plans.

Revolving credit and general-purpose credit cards were nonexistent before 1958. Individual retailers offered arrangements whereby regular customers could charge multiple purchases, paying them off in a lump sum at the end of the month. Sears and other national retailers extended such charge accounts to multiple outlets. In 1950, a consortium of New York City restaurants established the Diners Club, which allowed business customers to charge meals at any participating establishment.

With very few exceptions, incurring individual and corporate debt during the 1940's proved to be a sound economic choice. Most of the 2.4 million veterans who bought homes paid off their mortgages in the standard fifteen years. Many sold their cramped Levittown-style tract homes at a modest profit and moved their baby-boomer children, now in their teens, to more spacious quarters in a second wave of suburban expansion. That first car was long paid for by the time it started to show its age.

In 1945, most Americans still clung to a cautious and conservative attitude toward debt, a legacy of the Depression. Overcoming that and replacing it with unqualified acceptance of a "buy now, pay later" mentality was a gradual process. It began with housing. Accustomed as people were to making do and going without until they could pay up front, a couple with a baby on the way, in a market where rental housing was nonexistent, willingly signed a mortgage agreement in preference to living in a travel trailer without plumbing. A car, a washing machine, and a television soon followed. The television, purchased on time payments since it cost nearly a month's wages in 1950, brought the "buy now, pay later" message into the living room as an incessant refrain.

As long as interest rates remained low, the cost of most goods and services increased at a steady rate, and wage growth outpaced overall inflation. Both borrowing and lending were reinforced, and borrower, lender, and the overall economy benefited. With minor perturbations, all these conditions persisted in America until about 1965. Economists who doubted that they would persist indefinitely were in the minority.

Impact In order to win World War II, the United States borrowed heavily from its own citizens, in effect exacting present sacrifices in exchange for the promise of future cash payment. Rather than gradually retiring that debt after the war, the government then made it easy for individual borrowers to attain

the deferred good life. That postwar borrowing stimulated the economy, initiating a prolonged period of growth during which prevailing economic thinking and policy decisions based upon it shifted from a cyclical model to an unlimited growth model. Debt and credit financed the American Dream during the late 1940's and early 1950's, simultaneously shaping its expansionist exuberance and shaky foundations.

The unlimited growth model began to break down during the late 1960's, as the nation became embroiled in a major and costly war in Vietnam at the same time that long-term bonds from World War II finally became due and payable. Unable to appeal to patriotism to borrow from its citizens, the government had to pay higher interest rates to refinance the old debt and pay increasing costs at a time when real, inflation-adjusted growth was slowing. A large birth cohort entering adulthood had the same needs for housing and durable goods that their veteran parents experienced a quarter century earlier. They ended up borrowing more, on less favorable terms, and needed two full-time incomes to sustain a modest lifestyle. The prime interest rate, 2 percent in 1950 and 4.5 percent in 1960, rose sharply to 8.5 percent in 1970, 12 percent in 1974, and a peak of 20 percent in 1981. The ratio of federal debt to GDP—which declined from 120 percent in 1946 to 55 percent in 1950 and 40 percent in 1970—began rising, to 69 percent in 2005. The ratio of total indebtedness—federal, local, corporate, and personal—to GDP remained very close to 2.0 from 1941 to 1975, then rose exponentially to 3.0 in 1990, 3.5 in 2000, and 5.5 in 2008. Most of the visible signs of the impending early twenty-first century debt and credit crisis appeared long after the 1940's, but at least some of the seeds were sown in the aftermath of World War II.

Martha A. Sherwood

Further Reading

Chamber of Commerce of the United States. Committee on Economic Policy. *Debt, Public and Private.* Washington, D.C.: Author, 1957. Useful statistics on different classes of debt in 1929, 1941, 1945, and 1951. A good snapshot of consumer debt before credit cards.

Kelley, Robert E. *The National Debt of the United States, 1941-2008.* 2d ed. Jefferson, N.C.: McFarland, 2008. Analyzes the American fiscal policies and their relationship to contemporary events by administration. Pages 29-68 cover the Roosevelt and Truman years.

Skeel, David A., Jr. *Debt's Dominion: A History of Bankruptcy Law in America.* Princeton, N.J.: Princeton University Press, 2001. Thorough and scholarly, with coverage from the colonial period through the end of the twentieth century.

Sullivan, Theresa, Elizabeth Warren, and Jay Westbrook. *As We Forgive Our Debtors: Bankruptcy and Consumer Credit in America.* New York: Oxford University Press, 1989. Based on a large study of consumer bankruptcies, focuses on economic trends. A good treatment of women's issues.

U.S. Department of Commerce. *Indebtedness in the United States, 1929-41.* Washington, D.C.: Government Printing Office, 1942. Comprehensive source on public and private debt on the eve of World War II, with projections for policy.

Wilson, Richard L., ed. *Historical Encyclopedia of American Business.* 3 vols. Pasadena, Calif.: Salem Press, 2009. Comprehensive reference work on American business history that contains substantial essays on almost every conceivable aspect of U.S. economic history.

See also   Business and the economy in the United States; Diners Club; G.I. Bill; Gross national product of the United States; Housing in the United States; Inflation; Levittown; National debt; War bonds; War debt.

■ Crimes and scandals

Definition   Violations of laws and public standards of morality

The 1940's marked the beginning of the end for the Great Depression but remained an era of sensationalism in news reporting of crime and scandal. Memories of the infamous bank robbers, gangsters, and gang wars of the 1930's were still fresh in the minds of the public. Although news of the war dominated the media, sensational crimes and scandals managed to find a place in the press.

The 1940's was a turbulent era. As the decade began, the United States and most of the rest of the Western world were struggling to come back from the Great Depression. World War II had already begun in Europe, and the United States was struggling to avoid getting involved. Domestically, the United States was still combating racist groups such as the Ku Klux Klan, increasingly frequent race riots, and the continued growth of organized crime. At the same time, medical experimentation rivaling that of Nazi Germany was being conducted. It included such practices as the involuntary sterilization of career criminals. In Canada's Quebec province, the provincial government, officials of the Roman Catholic Church, and psychiatrists such as Pierre Lamontagne conspired to have orphans declared mentally ill so medical experiments could be conducted on them. This so-called Duplessis orphan affair was regarded as one of the most infamous scandals of the decade.

Sensational Crimes   As in virtually any decade, both Canada and the United States had their share of sensational, headline-grabbing crimes during the 1940's. In January, 1945, for example, the Royal Canadian Mounted Police reported that a Mrs Nelson of Calgary, Alberta, had poisoned her twenty-two-year-old mentally ill son and herself. She apparently poisoned her son, who had been scheduled to be interned in a mental hospital, because he had been judged a danger to himself and the public. In a 1947 crime that horrified the citizens of Ontario, a man named Sidney Chambers admitted to abducting, strangling, and burning the body of a nine-year-old girl two days before Christmas. After killing the girl, he made five suicide attempts. Another sensational Canadian crime occurred in Quebec in 1949, when a man named Joseph Albert Guay murdered his wife and twenty-two other people by placing a bomb in his wife's luggage on an airline flight. The plane crashed into the mountains shortly after take-off.

In October, 1941, a Washington State bus driver named Monty Illingworth was charged with having strangled his wife three years earlier. He had tied weights to her body and thrown it into Washington's very deep and cold Crescent Lake. The well-preserved body remained submerged until July 1940, when it suddenly surfaced and was found by fishermen. The well-known criminologist Hollis Fultz investigated the crime, whose unusual circumstances caused many people to regard it as the "crime of the decade." However, an even more sensational crime occurred on July 6, 1944, when a teenage roustabout named Robert Segee started a fire in a crowded Ringling Brothers circus tent in Hartford, Connecticut, causing the deaths of about 169 people. Segee himself escaped detection until six years later, when he was questioned about two other, similar arson fires. Segee confessed to having started the circus fire but was never tried for the crime and later recanted his confession.

Another grisly murder occurred in Chicago, Illinois, where a six-year-old girl named Suzanne Degnan was killed and mutilated in January, 1946. A sixty-five-year-old janitor named Hector Yerbaugh was questioned after police found human blood and pieces of flesh and internal organs in basement wash basins that he used. Another suspect in the case was a former mental patient and former dentist who had worked at a nursing home that previously owned the ladder used to enter Degnan's bedroom. In July, as public interest in the case was still mounting, a college student named William George Heirens confessed to killing Suzanne Degnan. He also admitted to having killed a WAVE named Frances Brown and a housewife named Josephine Ross. He was sentenced to three life sentences in Joliet Prison.

The 1940's crime that has probably been the most remembered of the decade was the brutal unsolved murder of twenty-two-year-old Elizabeth Short, an aspiring actor, in Los Angeles on January 15, 1947. Although nearly two hundred suspects in the crime were investigated, the case was never solved.

In 1948, members of California attorney general Fred Howser's staff were investigated in a plot involving organized gambling, bribery, and protection in California. In July of the following year, the Los Angeles Police Department was alleged to have been involved in the shotgun slaying of mob boss Mickey Cohen. Cohen was apparently scheduled to testify before a grand jury hearing on police corruption. A second scandal rocked Los Angeles police in late 1949, when members of the city's vice squad were charged with accepting protection money from a prostitution ring.

Another well-published crime story of the late 1940's was that of the so-called "lonely hearts" killers, Raymond Fernandez and Martha Beck. They were convicted of murdering at least three people they "met" through the mail. The details of these murders were particularly lurid, as the culprits killed their victims by beating them with a hammer and strangling them with a scarf. Fernandez and Beck apparently met each other through the mail and entered into a bizarre relationship during which Fernandez met women through the mail, courted them, and even married more than one of them, before he and Beck killed them.

Political Scandals In 1940, Assistant U.S. Attorney General John Rogge, who had made a name for himself fighting the corruption of Louisiana governor Huey P. Long's regime during the 1930's, began investigating corruption in other states. He considered setting up special investigators in Louisiana, Arkansas, Oklahoma, Michigan, Georgia, New Jersey, Pennsylvania, and Florida to deal with corruption scandals in those states. For example, New Orleans mayor Robert Maestri was investigated because of his involvement in the local oil industry. Former Louisiana governor Richard Leche was tried for mail fraud in connection with a scheme involving the overcharging of the state for the purchase of trucks.

Political corruption and homicide converged on January 11, 1945, when Michigan state senator Warren G. Hooper was assassinated a few days before he was scheduled to testify before a grand jury investigating corruption in his state's legislature. His murder case was never solved.

In 1947, Illinois governor Dwight H. Green was investigated for his administration's possible involvement in a scheme that paid mine inspectors to ignore safety violations. An explosion in a mine in Centralia, Illinois had resulted in 111 deaths.

Suspected Subversion The end of World War II saw the breakdown of the alliance between the United States and the Soviet Union and the beginning of the long Cold War, which gave rise to public fear of communist subversion in the American government. By 1948, paranoia about possible subversion had become a major issue on the American political front. That year, the federal government indicted twelve leaders of the Communist Party USA under the provisions of the 1940 Smith Act, which made it a crime to teach or preach overthrowing the government. Whittaker Chambers, who quit the Communist Party in 1937, testified at the House Committee on Un-American Activities (HUAC) hearings. He named three former members of Franklin D. Roosevelt's New Deal Administration as members of the Communist Party: Alger Hiss, a former head of the U.S. State Department's office of special affairs; Lee Pressman, a former general counsel of the Works Progress Administration; and Nathan Witt, a former executive on the National Labor Relations Board. Chambers claimed that the Communist Party was intent on overthrowing the government of the United States, by any means necessary.

Other Scandals The point-shaving scandal that would rock college basketball during the early 1950's began in Brooklyn, New York, in 1945, when agents of the Federal Bureau of Investigation arrested thirty-nine bookies in an investigation of gambling on college games. Two men were charged with bribing five Brooklyn College players to throw a game. At the time, the offense was merely a misdemeanor in New York State, but a state assemblyman introduced a bill to classify bribing amateur players as a felony.

Gambling was also beginning to infect other sports, as well. In 1946, the National Hockey League suspended hockey player Babe Pratt of the Toronto Maple Leafs for sixteen days for betting on games not involving his own team. Two years later, Billy Taylor of the New York Rangers and Don Gallinger of the Boston Bruins were banned for life for betting on their own games and for associating with a known gambler with criminal ties, James Tamer of Detroit. Meanwhile, in 1947, boxer Rocky Graziano was offered protection if he would identify the mobsters who had allegedly tried to bribe him to throw a fight. Racketeers had also earlier attempted to fix a football game between the Chicago Bears and the New York Giants.

Public attitudes toward morality were so conservative during the 1940's that any hint of sexual impropriety among celebrities and other public figures could quickly flame into a major public scandal. One of the most sensational Hollywood scandals of the decade erupted in late 1942, when film idol Errol Flynn was accused of statutory rape by two different teenage girls. Flynn was brought to trial on these charges but was acquitted to resume his acting

Mob boss Mickey Cohen reading about himself in a Los Angeles newspaper in August, 1949. (Time & Life Pictures/Getty Images)

career with an enhanced reputation as a dashing rake.

Next, it was the turn of legendary film comedian and director Charles Chaplin. In 1943, he became the focus of another big Hollywood scandal when an aspiring female actor filed a paternity suit against him, charging that he was the father of her unborn child. She demanded expenses for care and for child support. The following year, Chaplin was arrested for violation of the 1910 Mann Act, which made it a federal crime to transport a woman across state lines for "immoral purposes." Chaplin's accuser claimed that he had paid for her transportation from New York to Los Angeles so that he could have sexual relations with her. FBI director J. Edgar Hoover was behind the charge because he considered Chaplin to be a communist and therefore an enemy of the state. Although acquitted of the charges brought against him, Chaplin left the country to live in Europe.

Impact Every decade has had its share of sensational crimes and scandals, and the 1940's were no different than any other period in this respect. What most set the decade apart was the growth of organized crime, which reached into politics, sports, and entertainment, and rising fears of communist subversion during the early years of the Cold War after World War II.

Gerald P. Fisher

Further Reading

Fox, Stephen. *Blood and Power: Organized Crime in Twentieth-Century America.* New York, N.Y.: Penguin Books, 1989. Comprehensive history of organized crime in the United States from the 1920's through the 1980's.

Friedman, Lawrence. *Crime and Punishment in American History.* New York: Basic Books, 1993. Interesting perspective on deviance in America and society's response from the colonial era through the twentieth century.

Nelli, Humbert S. "A Brief History of American Syndicate Crime." In *Organized Crime in America: Concepts and Controversies*, edited by Timothy S. Bynum. Monsey, N.Y.: Criminal Justice Press, 1987. This chapter describes the growth and development of organized crime from bootlegging, gambling, and the development of Las Vegas to the efforts of crime organizations to appear legitimate.

Parish, James R. *The Hollywood Book of Scandals: The Shocking, Often Disgraceful Deeds and Affairs of More than One Hundred American Movie and TV Idols.* Columbus, Ohio: McGraw-Hill Professional, 2004. Encyclopedia reference work on major scandals in the entertainment industry.

Rosen, Fred. *The Historical Atlas of American Crime.* New York, N.Y.: Facts On File, 2005. Provides information on the locations and dates of infamous crimes in America.

Walker, Samuel. *Popular Justice: A History of American Criminal Justice,* New York: Oxford University Press, 1998. Comprehensive coverage of the background, birth, and growth of our criminal justice system in the United States.

See also Black Dahlia murder; Farmer, Frances; Federal Bureau of Investigation; Gambling; Hobbs Act; Hoover, J. Edgar; Race riots; Siegel, Bugsy; Tokyo Rose.

■ Crosby, Bing

Identification American singer and actor
Born May 3, 1903; Tacoma, Washington
Died October 14, 1977; near Madrid, Spain

Crosby was a pivotal figure in American culture, not only as a singer of jazz and popular music but also as an actor and popular icon. His greatest performance of the 1940's was his rendition of Irving Berlin's "White Christmas."

Bing Crosby marked the start of the 1940's with the beginnings of a partnership that would bring him much success throughout the decade and into the 1960's: the series of "Road" movies costarring Bob Hope. Beginning with *The Road to Singapore* (1940), the pair went on to produce six more films of slapstick, irreverent humor over the next twenty-two years.

Although the "Road" films were quite successful,

Bing Crosby and Ingrid Bergman in The Bells of St. Mary's. (Getty Images)

becoming number one at the box office, even more significant in the development of Crosby's popular persona was his portrayal of Father O'Malley in the films *Going My Way* and *The Bells of St. Mary's*. In these films, he subverted the stereotype of the stern Roman Catholic priest, playing the role as an approachable young man possessing a human past and real connections to those around him. *Going My Way* was released in 1944, which was the first year that Crosby was the number-one-ranking star at the box office, a position that he would maintain through 1948. The film is also notable for being the vehicle in which Crosby premiered the classic song "Swinging on a Star." It was written especially for the movie by the songwriting team of Johnny Burke and Jimmy Van Heusen, who were asked to write a catchy song with strong moral overtones for a scene in which Bing, as Father O'Malley, sings to a group of children. It spent nine weeks on top of the *Billboard* charts and won the Academy Award for best song in 1944.

However, the most iconic moment of Crosby's career during the 1940's, and possibly in his entire career, was his performance of Irving Berlin's classic seasonal ballad "White Christmas" in the 1942 film *Holiday Inn*, which costarred Fred Astaire. Crosby had actually premiered the song on his Kraft Music Hall NBC radio show on Christmas Day, 1941.

Crosby's recording of "White Christmas" is the best-selling single in music history, having sold more than 50 million copies. The song was so successful that it inspired a 1954 film of the same name starring Crosby, Danny Kaye, and Rosemary Clooney, which is essentially a Christmas-themed remake of *Holiday Inn*.

Impact   In an era when the economic turmoil of the 1930's was still strongly in the memories of many Americans, and in the midst of World War II, Crosby provided a persona in his music and films that combined simple American values and outlooks with a laid-back and quirky façade that belied a thoroughly modern sense of humor. Also, his interpretations of many Tin Pan Alley standards, both in recordings and in his films, helped to mold and influence the American musical tradition.

Daniel McDonough

Further Reading

Giddins, Gary. *Bing Crosby: A Pocketful of Dreams—The Early Years, 1903-1940*. Boston: Little, Brown, 2001.

Grudens, Richard. *Bing Crosby: Crooner of the Century*. Stony Brook, N.Y.: Celebrity Profiles Publishing, 2003.

See also   Bogart, Humphrey; Garland, Judy; Hope, Bob; Music: Popular; Sinatra, Frank; Stewart, James.

■ Curious George books

Identification   Children's book series about a mischievous monkey
Authors   H. A. Rey (1898-1977) and Margret Rey (1906-1996)
Date   First published in 1941

The first Curious George books set a standard for children's books written purely for enjoyment. The series' success can be measured in part by its long-standing popularity.

The Curious George series began in 1939, when Hans Augusto and Margret Rey were working from their home in Brazil to publish *Cecily G. and the Nine Monkeys* (also published as *Raffy and the Nine Monkeys*). Although the Reys' experiences in Brazil were influential in their use of a tropical monkey as the main character in the series that would make them famous, their life in France also marked important progress in the series. The early part of 1940 found the couple living near Dordogne, France. There they formed George into a main character for his own line of books. During the early years of World War II, as Nazi Germany conquered large parts of Europe, the Jewish Reys were forced to flee the country as a German army was occupying France in 1940. Among the few possessions they took with them was a manuscript with illustrations for a Curious George book. Their flight took them to New York, where they established ties with Houghton Mifflin and signed a contract for four books.

Curious George was published in 1941, under H. A. Rey's name only. In April, 1946, both Reys became naturalized American citizens. In later years, they wrote and illustrated five additional Curious George books: *Curious George Takes a Job* (1947), *Curious George Rides a Bike* (1952), *Curious George Gets a Medal* (1957), *Curious George Flies a Kite* (1958), *Curious George Learns the Alphabet* (1963), and *Curious George Goes to the Hospital* (1966). The series focuses on the well-meaning but irrepressible monkey and the unnamed "Man with the Yellow Hat." In each installment, George gets into trouble from which the Man with the Yellow Hat must rescue him.

Impact The Curious George series fostered the idea that children's books could be fun in such a powerful way that it continued even after the Reys' deaths and has carried on through new stories, television programs, and film versions starring George and the Man with the Yellow Hat.

Theresa L. Stowell

Further Reading

Borden, Louise, and Allan Drummond. *The Journey That Saved Curious George: The True Wartime Escape of Margret and H. A. Rey.* Boston: Houghton Mifflin, 2005.

Rey, H. A., and Margret Rey. *The Complete Adventures of Curious George.* Boston: Houghton Mifflin, 2001.

See also Book publishing; Immigration to the United States; Jews in the United States; Literature in the United States; Refugees in North America.

D

■ D Day

The Event   Date on which the landing of Allied forces in Normandy opened the Allied campaign to liberate France and conquer Germany

Date   June 6, 1944

Place   France's Normandy coast, near the cities of Caen and Bayeux

Also known as   Operation Overlord, Operation Neptune

The Normandy landings constituted history's largest amphibious assault and served as an expression of the successful and intimate Allied collaboration between the United States and Great Britain. The landings were the culmination of America's strategic plan that came to dominate Anglo-American strategy. Finally, the landings were the "tipping point" of the war; once the Allies were ashore, Germany's defeat appeared inevitable.

America's strategic vision for the European theater of World War II was that the fastest route to victory was a landing in France followed by the destruction of German forces and the invasion of Germany to compel unconditional surrender. This direct approach was antithetical to British strategy because heavy casualties were likely to result. British leaders, especially Winston Churchill, feared such a direct drive; instead, they preferred to wear Germany down through a peripheral strategy.

America's first plan, proposed by General George C. Marshall, was for Operation Sledgehammer, a landing in France in 1942. This was postponed for logistical reasons. In 1943, a similar plan was also stymied by the British. By 1944, America's might in manpower, aircraft, shipping, and industrial capacity made it the dominant Anglo-Allied partner, and U.S. strategic plans slowly came to direct the Anglo-American strategy.

Planning the Assault   Shortly after France fell to the Germans in 1940, the British began planning for a landing on the German-occupied shore. Once the United States entered the war, joint planning for an invasion was the responsibility of the Chief of Staff of Supreme Allied Command (COSSAC). COSSAC's initial plans were shaped by the failure of a large-scale commando landing near the port of Dieppe in August, 1942. British planners realized that although ports offered facilities for unloading ships, seizing a port would invariably result in damage to such facilities and heavy casualties. COSSAC determined instead to land on open beaches and chose Normandy because it was within striking distance

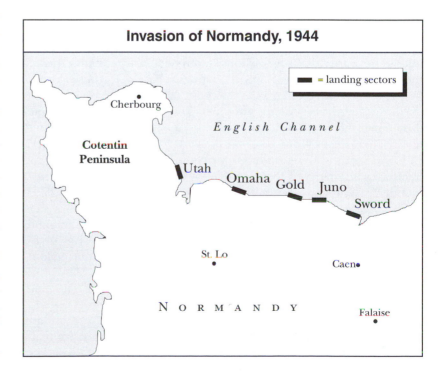

Invasion of Normandy, 1944

= landing sectors

English Channel

Cherbourg

Cotentin Peninsula

Utah Omaha Gold Juno Sword

St. Lo

Caen

NORMANDY

Falaise

Landing forces massing on Omaha Beach shortly after D Day. (Naval Historical Center/USCG Collection)

but did not appear to be an obvious landing site, like the narrowest part of the English Channel at Pas de Calais.

When American general Dwight D. Eisenhower was named the commander of Supreme Headquarters Allied Expeditionary Forces (SHAEF), the COSSAC plans were upgraded to expand the lodgment area and landing forces. Eisenhower also demanded a redirection of the strategic bombing campaign to attack road and railroad nets throughout France. To improve inter-Allied cooperation and trust, Eisenhower interleaved the nationalities of officers at different command levels. Thus, Eisenhower, an American, commanded SHAEF, but the ground and naval forces were commanded by British officers, and national commanders controlled field armies. This intermixing of responsibilities fostered close cooperation and understanding.

Allied planners harnessed technology to en-

hance the landing force's capabilities and to sustain those forces. Because getting large numbers of troops and supplies to the beaches would be difficult from regular ships, the Allies cooperated in designing and building a spectrum of specialized landing craft such as LSTs (landing ship tanks). The time required for the construction of such vessels was a major factor in delaying the landing from 1943 to 1944. To provide enough gasoline to support an advance inland, a secret pipe-line under the ocean (PLUTO) was designed, as were artificial harbors called Mulberries that could facilitate off-loading of supplies after the landings.

SHAEF planned to isolate the landing area by dropping airborne troops near bridges and important crossroads, with the drops occurring at night to avoid antiaircraft fire. The landings would be at low tide so that beach obstacles could be seen and avoided. The proper conditions of full moon and early low tide occurred during only a few periods in the summer, which the Germans were likely to anticipate. Bad weather in June of 1944 made landings then seem improbable, so that Germany was unlikely to expect a landing. In addition, complex Allied efforts at disinformation had convinced German intelligence analysts that the landings would be in the Pas de Calais area.

The Landings   The landings surprised the Germans. Allied troops landed on five beaches, codenamed (from west to east) Utah, Omaha, Gold, Juno, and Sword. Americans landed at Utah and Omaha, the British at Gold and Sword, and the Canadians at Juno and Sword. German opposition varied in intensity, with the strongest resistance encountered at Omaha and Juno. Although many Germans were second-rate "garrison troops," those at Omaha were led by veteran officers and noncommissioned officers with experience from combat in Russia. This combination of veteran leadership and well-sited guns created heavy casualties among the first Americans ashore, but courage and inspirational leadership at all levels carried the assault forward. Smaller warships called destroyers came as close to shore as possible and provided direct artillery support. By afternoon, troops were pushing inland.

Impact   Although troops landed successfully on June 6, they did not reach all of their objectives. It took nearly two months of fierce fighting in Normandy's restricted terrain before the Allied forces broke out and advanced into France's interior. The close combat of June and July inflicted heavy losses on all sides, yet it was the Americans who had the manpower to break through the German defenses near Saint-Lô. In the end, the overall size of the U.S. war effort allowed American troops to maintain assaults despite heavy casualties and ensured that America would continue to direct the Anglo-Allied strategy.

Kevin B. Reid

Further Reading

Balkoski, Joseph. *Omaha Beach: D-day, June 6, 1944.* Mechanicsburg, Pa.: Stackpole Books, 2006. A detailed look at the challenges faced at Omaha Beach and how American soldiers overcame the surprisingly stark defenses.

Hastings, Max. *Overlord: D-day and the Battle for Normandy.* New York: Simon & Schuster, 1984. An in-depth look at the fighting required to break out from Normandy and drive into France.

Penrose, Jane. *The D-day Companion.* Oxford, England: Osprey, 2004. Individual chapters provide analyses of the plans of both sides and the fighting on D Day and beyond.

Ryan, Cornelius. *The Longest Day.* New York: Simon & Schuster, 1994. This blockbuster narrative provides an intimate look at the soldiers' D-day experiences.

Zaloga, Steven. *D-day Fortifications in Normandy.* Oxford, England: Osprey, 2005. A detailed look at the German defenses that explains why the landings proved so difficult on some, though not all, of the beaches.

See also   Army, U.S.; Canada and Great Britain; Canadian participation in World War II; Churchill, Winston; Eisenhower, Dwight D.; Landing craft, amphibious; Marshall, George C.; Navy, U.S.; Strategic bombing; Unconditional surrender policy.

■ Dance

Definition   Form of entertainment and self-expression that can be either participatory or oriented toward performance with an audience; it may follow an established criteria of steps and movements or be totally free for individual creation

During the 1940's, dance played a significant role in the development of a national artistic identity in the United States and Canada as dance companies and specific types of dance were created. In the United States, dance also made an important contribution to maintaining morale during World War II.

From the early twentieth century, dancers and choreographers had been attempting to create new forms of dance in a reaction against the formal technique of ballet, which permitted only certain types of movement and dance steps. The 1920's and 1930's were decades of experimentation and innovation. By 1940, various types of dance had begun to be accepted as alternative genres of dance. During the 1940's, these forms of dance borrowed from each other, and even ballet choreographers incorporated new movements and steps into their ballets. Dance was no longer a set form but rather an ever-changing fluid expression of the individual and of the society in which he or she lived. In the United States and Canada, dancers and choreographers viewed dance as a reflection of national identity and a means for bringing about social change.

Ballet   During the early twentieth century, ballet in Canada and the United States was limited primarily to performances by touring European companies. Dancers wanting to pursue a professional career had to go to Europe to do so. In 1934, Lincoln Kirstein, a patron of the arts, brought the Russian dancer and choreographer George Balanchine to the United States in the hope of making his dream of an American ballet a reality. The following year, they established the American School of Ballet. Eleven years later, in 1946, they created the Ballet Society to promote both the teaching and the performance of ballet. In 1948, the Ballet Society became the New York City Ballet. This was the beginning of American ballet, with a ballet company of American-trained dancers performing ballets choreographed in the United States.

Canada's national ballet companies also had their beginnings during the 1930's. Gweneth Lloyd, Betty Farrally, and Celia Franca had immigrated from England, and Ludmilla Chireaeff from Latvia. During the 1940's, these ballerina/choreographers were responsible for establishing ballet as a national art form in Canada. By the 1950's, Canada had three ballet companies: the Royal Winnipeg Ballet, the National Ballet of Canada, and Les Grands Ballets de Montréal. By the 1950's, the companies were performing a regular season in Canada and also touring.

Modern Dance   Modern dance responded to the mind-set of the 1940's with its emphasis upon uninhibited movement, self-expression by the dancer, and involvement with contemporary social issues. In the United States, modern dance became a recognized and appreciated form of dance. Continuing the work of Martha Graham, Ruth St. Denis, Helen Taminis, and Charles Wiedman, dancer/choreographers such as Katherine Dunham, Merce Cunningham, José Limon, Pearl Primus, and Hanya Holm created dances based on new themes and concepts. They abandoned myths and legends drawn from ancient history in favor of subjects dealing with contemporary social issues. They used elements of African and Caribbean dance in their choreography.

Marion Chace, a dancer/choreographer/teacher and former student of Ruth St. Denis, took dance off the stage and into schools and hospitals, where she used it as a tool for therapy and rehabilitation.

In Canada, Jeanne Renaud and her sisters Thérèse and Louise were creating a form of modern dance that relied on spontaneity and improvisation and sought to express the subconscious of the performer. The Renauds became involved with the Automatiste movement, which rejected conformity both in society and in art. Françoise Sullivan, also an Automatiste, was another pioneer of modern dance in Montreal. She viewed dance as both an art form and a force for social change. In 1948, she published "La Danse et l'espoir" (dance and hope) in the manifesto of the Automatiste. Jeanne Renaud and Sullivan organized modern dance concerts in Montreal from 1946 to 1948. Two works choreographed by Sullivan in 1947, *Dédale* and *Dualité*, are regarded as Canadian classics of modern dance.

Dance in Broadway Musicals and Hollywood Films   The 1940's witnessed a comeback of the Broadway musical and the development of the Hollywood musical. The use of dance in these performances underwent a dramatic change. Dance was no longer relegated to the position of an entr'acte or diversion; it became an essential part of the depiction of the story line. Musicals relied on a combination of spoken dialogue, song, and dance to unfold their plots. Agnes de Mille set the standard for innovative choreography that combined elements of ballet, jazz, tap, and modern dance in musicals such as *Oklahoma!* (which opened on Broadway in March, 1943, and was turned into a film in 1955). The dance sequences were filled with exuberant leaps and kicks.

Hollywood produced films that showcased dancers and entertained the American public. Jack Cole was the resident choreographer for Columbia Pictures from 1944 to 1948. His choreography established standards for the modern or jazz dancing performed by dancers such as Gwen Verdon and Carol Haney. Throughout the 1940's, Hollywood entertained the American public with exceptional dancers. Ann Miller set a record for fast tap dancing, Gene Kelly delighted audiences with his dancing, and Fred Astaire and Ginger Rogers embodied elegance and sophistication in partnered dancing.

Swing Dance Partnered or ballroom dancing has played an important role in American social life since the earliest days of the United States. During the 1920's and 1930's, swing, Lindy Hop, and jitterbug had become popular in the black community. During the 1940's, ballroom was a major form of entertainment. The dance was well suited to the popular jazz and swing music played by the big bands during the 1940's. By 1942, swing was recognized as an accepted form of dance. The Arthur Murray Dance Studios and others began teaching a simplified version of it. Mail-order dance lessons became popular, and swing dancing swept the United States. It had become an American dance and provided a common and uniting element in American life.

Dancers at Harlem's legendary Savoy Ballroom in 1947. (Getty Images)

Dance and the War Effort Dancing, especially swing dance, was the main feature of the Stage Door Canteens. The first Stage Door Canteen opened in March, 1942, at the Schubert Theatre in New York City. Operated by the American Theater War Service, it offered free dancing and food to all military personnel as well as an opportunity to meet stars of the theater and other entertainers. In 1943, Bette Davis and John Garfield opened the Hollywood Canteen, modeled on the Stage Door Canteens. These canteens reflected the support of the American artistic community for the soldiers and served to help the morale of the soldiers and the United States during the war. Dance became a uniting influence in the United States war effort.

Impact Dance played an important role in the creation of an American culture and became an American phenomenon. Balanchine created not only an American ballet company but also American choreography and technique; Agnes de Mille choreographed *Rodeo* (1942) and Aaron Copland created *Appalachian Spring* (1944), both ballets with Ameri-

can themes. Dance was being performed and enjoyed throughout the United States both on stage and on the dance floor. Dance made an important contribution to American morale during World War II and united Americans as it crossed social and racial barriers.

In Canada during the 1940's, dance played a significant role in creating a national Canadian consciousness. Dance assumed a major place in Canadian artistic culture and proved itself as a medium capable of depicting the social issues facing the nation. Thus, dance in the 1940's developed to give both the United States and Canada important places in the world of dance, and both countries continue to enjoy prominent positions in dance choreography and performance throughout the world.

Shawncey Webb

Further Reading

Giordano, Ralph. *Lindy Hop to Hip Hop, 1901-2000.* Vol. 2 in *Social Dancing in America: A History and*

Reference. Westport, Conn.: Greenwood Press, 2006. Discusses social dance in relation to economics, politics, and social mores. Emphasizes dance as a force for change and a social and cultural phenomenon.

Odom, Selma Landen, and Mary Jane Warner, eds. *Canadian Dance: Visions and Stories.* Toronto: Dance Collection Danse Press/es, 2004. Contains Françoise Sullivan's "Dance and Hope" and information on major Canadian choreographers and dancers.

Reynolds, Nancy, and Malcolm McCormick. *No Fixed Points: Dance in the Twentieth Century.* New Haven, Conn.: Yale University Press, 2003. Detailed history of dance in the twentieth century placing 1940's dance in North America in a historical context revealing its roots, its accomplishments, and how its developments later changed dance of the late twentieth century. Excellent coverage of dance in Broadway musicals and Hollywood films.

Smith, Kathleen E. R. *God Bless America: Tin Pan Alley Goes to War.* Lexington: University of Kentucky Press, 2003. Although primarily focused on music, provides good insights into how the canteens for military personnel boosted morale with music and dance.

Thomas, Helen. *Dance, Modernity and Culture: Explorations in the Sociology of Dance.* New York: Routledge, 1995. Excellent for understanding developments in dance that made possible the establishment of dance forms and companies during the 1940's. Good discussion of the role of women in making dance an accepted art form.

Walzak, Barbara, and Una Kai. *Balanchine the Teacher: Fundamentals That Shaped the First Generation of New York City Ballet Dancers.* Gainesville: University Press of Florida, 2008. Excellent for understanding Balanchine's influence on American ballet—how he created it and the New York City Ballet. Discusses his contribution to making ballet an innovative, ever-evolving art.

See also *Appalachian Spring;* Ballet Society; Broadway musicals; Coles, Honi; Jitterbug; Kelly, Gene; Music: Classical; Music: Jazz; Music: Popular; Robbins, Jerome; *Rodeo.*

■ Davis, Benjamin O., Jr.

Identification   Commander of the Tuskegee Airmen during World War II
Born   December 18, 1912; Washington, D.C.
Died   July 4, 2002; Washington, D.C.

The first African American general in the U.S. Air Force, Davis commanded the elite, all-black 332d Fighter Group, known as the Tuskegee Airmen. Like his father, Davis broke racial barriers in the military, and he helped pave the way for desegregation of the Air Force.

Benjamin Oliver Davis, Jr., had a distinguished military career that included serving as commander of the famed Tuskegee Airmen. In 1932, he enrolled at the United States Military Academy at West Point, New York. Four years later, he became the first African American in the twentieth century to graduate from the prestigious academy. Davis wanted to enter aviation, but African Americans were not permitted to join the Army Air Forces (later the Air Force). In

Lieutenant Colonel Benjamin O. Davis, Jr. (right) with his father, Brigadier General Benjamin O. Davis, Sr., at a War Department conference in Washington, D.C., in September, 1943. (AP/Wide World Photos)

1941, Franklin D. Roosevelt created the all-African American 99th Pursuit Squadron, of which Davis was given command. The squadron later became part of the 332d Fighter Group, which Davis also commanded. He gained prominence during World War II, as his Tuskegee Airmen had the distinction of never having lost a bomber to enemy fire. In 1970, he retired as a lieutenant general and as the senior black officer in the military.

In 1998, President Bill Clinton promoted Davis to full general. Davis passed away from complications from Alzheimer's disease at Walter Reed Army Medical Center on July 4, 2002, at the age of eighty-nine.

Impact   Davis was a pioneer in the racial integration of the Air Force as well as the acceptance of African Americans as military aviators. His units' exploits during World War II shattered preconceived notions of African Americans. In 2006, the Civil Air Patrol honored Davis by naming an award after him.

Daniel Sauerwein

Further Reading

Applegate, Katherine, *The Story of Two American Generals Benjamin O. Davis, Jr. and Colin L. Powell*. Milwaukee, Wis.: Gareth Stevens, 1995.

Davis, Benjamin O., Jr. *Benjamin O. Davis, Jr., American: An Autobiography*. Washington, D.C.: Smithsonian Institution Scholarly Press, 2000.

Francis, Charles E., and Adolph Caso. *The Tuskegee Airmen: The Men Who Changed a Nation*. Boston: Branden, 1997.

See also   African Americans; Air Force, U.S.; Tuskegee Airmen; World War II.

■ Davis, Bette

Identification   American film star

Born   April 5, 1908; Lowell, Massachusetts

Died   October 6, 1989; Neuilly-sur-Seine, France

Davis was one of the most popular and influential female actors of the 1940's. By choosing a wide range of characters

to portray, she broadened the range of roles offered to other female actors. In 1941, she became the first female president of the Academy of Motion Picture Arts and Sciences.

During the 1940's, Ruth Elizabeth "Bette" Davis became one of the most sought-after actors in Hollywood. Popular at the box office, Davis had previously won two Academy Awards for her roles in the movies *Dangerous* (1936) and *Jezebel* (1938). Under contract with Warner Bros., Davis became the studio's most profitable movie star during the 1940's, starring in numerous films and earning several Academy Award nominations. Some of her more popular movies included *All This and Heaven Too* (1940), *The Letter* (1940), *Watch on the Rhine* (1943), *Thank Your Lucky Stars* (1943), *Mr. Skeffington* (1944), *Deception* (1946), and *June Bride* (1948). Davis's popularity was in part attributed to her willingness to take on various film genres and roles, including unsympathetic characters. She was also famous for her strong, independent personality and her captivating eyes.

Impact   A prolific and versatile actor, Davis appeared in some twenty films during the 1940's. In 1949, she ended her eighteen-year stint with Warner Bros. after a series of unsuccessful films. She soon staged a comeback, however, starring in the Acad-

Actor Bette Davis presenting a cake to servicemen celebrating their birthdays at the USO's Stage Door Canteen in New York City in July, 1943. (AP/Wide World Photos)

emy Award-winning *All About Eve* (1950). Davis continued to win acclaim in subsequent decades.

Bernadette Zbicki Heiney

Further Reading

Chandler, Charlotte. *The Girl Who Walked Home Alone: Bette Davis—A Personal Biography.* New York: Simon & Schuster, 2006.

Sikov, Ed. *Dark Victory: The Life of Bette Davis.* New York: Henry Holt, 2007.

See also Academy Awards; Bogart, Humphrey; Film in the United States; Garson, Greer; Hitchcock, Alfred.

■ Davis, Glenn

Identification American football player
Born December 26, 1924; Claremont, California
Died March 9, 2005; La Quinta, California

One of the most heralded college running backs of all time, Davis helped lead Army to national championships in 1944 and 1945 and won the Heisman Trophy as the nation's best player in 1946.

Glenn Davis was arguably the most acclaimed college football star of the 1940's. Combining with Doc Blanchard, called "Mr. Inside" by the press, Davis, known as "Mr. Outside," made the United States Military Academy team the most powerful in its long history.

Davis ran for 2,957 yards during his Army career, scoring fifty-nine touchdowns, and also passed for 855 yards during the single-wing era. His average of 8.26 yards per rushing attempt remains a National Collegiate Athletic Association record. His 354 points scored is still an Army record, as are his fourteen career interceptions. Davis also set school records in track and earned varsity letters in basketball and baseball.

Davis and Blanchard played themselves in the 1947 film *The Spirit of West Point.* Davis seriously injured his right knee during filming, limiting his effectiveness during his subsequent professional career with the Los Angeles Rams from 1950 to 1951.

Impact A scoreless tie with Notre Dame in 1946 was the only blemish on Army's record in the Davis-Blanchard era. One of the last of the great all-around college athletes, Davis was an all-American

in football three times and was elected to the College Football Hall of Fame in 1961.

Michael Adams

Further Reading

Devaney, John. *Winners of the Heisman Trophy.* New York: Walker, 1986.

Mattox, Henry E. *Army Football in 1945: Anatomy of a Championship Season.* Jefferson, N.C.: McFarland, 1990.

Wilner, Barry, and Ken Rappoport. *Gridiron Glory: The Story of the Army-Navy Rivalry.* Lanham, Md.: Taylor, 2005.

See also Army, U.S.; Film in the United States; Football; Sports in the United States.

■ Davis, Miles

Identification Jazz trumpeter and composer
Born May 26, 1926; Alton, Illinois
Died September 28, 1991; Santa Monica, California

With his 1949 Birth of the Cool *recording sessions, Davis broke from his bebop past and expanded jazz to include a softer sound, focusing on arrangement and ensemble dynamics. "Cool jazz," or the West Coast jazz school, took the* Birth of the Cool *as its biggest influence. The eventual success of the recordings furthered Davis's capabilities as a bandleader and propelled him to the forefront of jazz.*

Composer-arrangers Gil Evans and Gerry Mulligan started discussing a break from the breakneck speed of bebop in the winter of 1948. Miles Davis was drawn into the discussions because of his desire to respectfully break from his bebop saxophonist Charlie Parker and move into a controlled, softer sound focused on arranging and composition rather than lengthy improvised solos around skeletal musical compositions. Davis had come of age in New York City playing with the bebop mainstays of Parker and trumpeter Dizzy Gillespie, but he felt the need to move into his own musical territory separate from bebop.

In early 1949, discussions turned into composed music charts, and, by late summer, rehearsals spawned a nonet to perform the arranged compositions of Davis, Mulligan, Evans, and John L. Lewis. Coming from the traditions of Duke Ellington via Claude

Thornhill, Davis included trumpet, baritone saxophone, piano, trombone, French horn, tuba, drums, bass, and alto saxophone. Davis booked a two-week stay in September of 1949 at Manhattan's Royal Roost jazz club, opposite the Count Basie Orchestra, and another two weeks that same month at Manhattan's Clique Club. The audience response to the live performances was tepid, and only a few critics and musicians responded positively to the nonet that produced a soft, fluid, and lyrical sound that drastically departed from bebop.

The nonet existed primarily as a recording studio ensemble, unlike most other jazz ensembles of the time. The group recorded in January and April of 1949 and March of 1950. Over the first half of the 1950's, singles were released from the recording sessions and were met with mild critical acclaim.

Birth of the Cool Recordings   The *Birth of the Cool* recordings, when finally issued collectively in 1957 (except for the track "Darn that Dream"), established Davis as a talented and well-practiced bandleader and a musician with a drive for new sounds. The released singles influenced the formation of "cool jazz," or the West Coast jazz school, during the mid-1950's, which embodied a soft sound and small-group instrumentation. Several of the *Birth of the Cool* musicians, including Lewis, Mulligan, and Lee Konitz, would become central figures of West Coast jazz.

Davis created controversy by employing white artists in the recordings, much to the consternation of unemployed African American musicians. Davis looked beyond race when considering the lineup of his ensemble, employing the best in the industry regardless of color. While playing at the Royal Roost, Davis was the first bandleader to credit the arrangers on the club's marquee, drawing attention to the importance of the compositions and arrangements.

The *Birth of the Cool* also questioned the relationship of the soloist to the ensemble, breaking away from traditional jazz and bebop where soloists were put out in front of the ensemble as the rest of the musicians served as accompaniment. On the *Birth of the Cool*, the soloist played shorter solos only slightly apart from and still in conjunction with the ensem-

Miles Davis in 1948. (Getty Images)

ble. Davis continued his career into the 1980's, continually fueled by a desire to create new sounds.

Jasmine LaRue Hagans

Further Reading

Carr, Ian. *Miles Davis: The Definitive Biography.* New York: Thunder's Mouth Press, 1998.

Davis, Miles with Quincy Troupe. *Miles: The Autobiography.* New York: Simon & Schuster, 1989.

See also   African Americans; Ellington, Duke; Goodman, Benny; Holiday, Billie; Music: Jazz; Music: Popular; Parker, Charlie; Recording industry.

■ Daylight saving time

The Event   Federally imposed system shifting the clock to provide an extra hour of daylight in the evening to help the war effort

Date   February 9, 1942-September 30, 1945

The system of daylight saving time instituted in the United States during World War II was modeled on a World War I

law that had been designed to conserve coal by turning clocks forward during the spring months. With the extra hour of daylight in the evenings, citizens conserved power, enjoyed greater safety during blackouts, and experienced greater morale because of the longer opportunity to enjoy outdoor activities.

Benjamin Franklin conceived the idea of daylight saving time (DST) in 1784 as a means of conserving candles by guaranteeing extra sunshine at the end of the day, when more people would be able to use it. The idea proved controversial and did not find many supporters until the twentieth century. With the advent of World War I, pressure rose to impose daylight saving time. Before World War II, Germany and Great Britain had already instituted it. Many places throughout the United States already observed local daylight saving time, including New England, Florida, Kentucky, Tennessee, and parts of Michigan.

On July 15, 1941, President Franklin D. Roosevelt proposed a bill to establish daylight saving throughout the United States to conserve electricity. In response to his request, North Carolina, Mississippi, and parts of Virginia, Kentucky, and Tennessee instituted local daylight saving time. Congress subsequently passed daylight saving time legislation and stipulated that it would end six months after the close of World War II hostilities. It became effective on February 9, 1942. Congress repealed the bill three weeks after the war's end and terminated federal daylight saving time on September 30, 1945.

Impact   Daylight saving time proved so successful at conserving fuel sources that it again became national law during the 1970's in response to the oil crisis. The United States continued to use a schedule of setting clocks ahead one hour in March or April, then setting them back the hour sometime in September through November.

Caryn E. Neumann

Further Reading

Bauer, Steven. *Daylight Savings.* Salt Lake City, Utah: Peregrine Smith Books, 1989.

Prerau, David. *Seize the Daylight: The Curious and Contentious Story of Daylight Saving Time.* New York: Thunder's Mouth Press, 2005.

See also   Atomic clock; Economic wartime regulations; Roosevelt, Franklin D.; World War II; World War II mobilization.

■ Death of a Salesman

Identification   Play about a family in crisis as the father, a suicidal unsuccessful salesman, struggles with his professional and personal failures
Author   Arthur Miller (1915-2005)
Date   First staged in 1949

One of the masterpieces of world literature, this play portrays the modern tragedy of an ordinary man named Willy Loman, his wife, and his two adult sons as they try to cope with the failure of their dreams and as they struggle with conflicts that threaten to destroy the family.

When *Death of a Salesman* was first performed on Broadway in February, 1949, it was an enormous critical and popular success and won a number of awards, including a Pulitzer Prize. While the play explored universal themes, part of the reason for its popularity was that it reflected and questioned some of the realities of the time period in which it was created, including the patriarchal family structure with the assumption of family loyalty to the father as head of a household even when he was living a life of illusions that was destructive for the family. The play was controversial during this Cold War period, and conservatives harshly criticized it as an attack on capitalism and the American Dream.

Impact   *Death of a Salesman* challenged and undermined the sentimental idealization of the American family and the widely held but narrow interpretation of the American Dream as merely material prosperity and social status. Its powerful exploration of the conflict between fathers and sons, the battle to differentiate between illusions and reality, and the problems of a dysfunctional family in crisis have contributed to the popularity of this drama throughout the world ever since it was first performed.

Allan Chavkin

Further Reading

Gottfried, Martin. *Arthur Miller: His Life and Work.* Cambridge, Mass.: Da Capo Press, 2003.

Murphy, Brenda. *Miller: Death of a Salesman.* New York: Cambridge University Press, 1995.

See also   *A Streetcar Named Desire;* Theater in Canada; Theater in the United States; *Where's Charley?.*

■ Decolonization of European empires

Definition   Process by which colonies attained autonomy or independence, whether gradually, under the auspices of the colonizer, or through revolution

In 1940, Europeans occupied most of Africa and South Asia. World War II disrupted already shaky relationships between colony and parent country. Between 1945 and 1975, all but a few small colonies achieved independence. Attempts by the United States and the Soviet Union to influence independence movements and establish hegemony fed major wars in Korea and Vietnam, as well as numerous local conflicts. The results of American policy in Indochina and Palestine in the immediate postwar period had many negative long-term consequences.

In 1940, large sections of Asia and Africa belonged to European nations. At the end of World War I, the Treaty of Versailles parceled out Germany's African colonies among the victors and established a system of mandates under the League of Nations to administer former territories of the Ottoman Empire, including Palestine. This colonial system was already beginning to break down during the 1930's. Depression reduced the need for raw materials, and, especially in the British Empire, an educated and prosperous native elite mounted effective campaigns for increased autonomy.

World War II   World War II disrupted colonial relations in a number of ways. French colonies fell under the jurisdiction of Vichy France, a Fascist puppet regime controlled by Nazi Germany. Taxation and exploitation increased, and administration became more racist and authoritarian. The French government in exile encouraged native resistance movements. These continued to operate even after the Allies liberated France from the Germans and the French attempted to resume control.

Japan occupied the British colonies of Burma and Malaysia. In India (including present-day Pakistan and Bangladesh), Ceylon (now Sri Lanka), and Ghana, where movement toward autonomy was already well under way, the outbreak of war stalled progress, and local economies were strained to support the war effort. Raising troops in all parts of the British Empire produced, in some instances, trained officers and fighters who later contributed to the violent overthrow of colonial regimes. The period 1937-1941 saw a large influx of Jewish refugees into the British Mandate of Palestine. Pressure from the United States and the British public induced the British colonial administration to admit far more settlers than they thought prudent given their mandate to govern the country in the best interests of the indigenous population.

The Dutch East Indies, present-day Indonesia, fell under Japanese domination while Germany occupied the Netherlands itself. Other foreign-dominated territories whose independence was established or put into motion during the 1940's were Lebanon (from France, 1941); Korea (from Japan,

U.S. president Harry S. Truman (center) greeting a delegation from newly independent India that includes G. S. Bajpai (left) of the Indian Foreign Office; Prime Minister Jawaharlal Nehru (second from right); Vijaya Pandit (second from left), Indian ambassador to the United States; and Nehru's daughter, Indira Gandhi (right)—a future prime minister of India. (AP/Wide World Photos)

1945, partitioned between the United States and Soviet Union); Formosa, now known as Taiwan (originally Portuguese, then Japanese, and independent under a Chinese government after 1945); the Philippines (from the United States, 1946); and Libya (from Italy, 1951).

The Postwar Period   Europe emerged from World War II physically and financially exhausted, unable to reassert control over colonial possessions without substantial material aid from the United States. In principle, the United States opposed colonialism, but this philosophy was strongly tempered by growing recognition of the influence the Soviet Union exercised over a number of nationalist movements.

The U.S. government supported independence movements when the likely outcome was a government more open to American business development, continued colonial occupation if it was a leftist regime allied to the Soviet Union and hostile to American business development, and neutrality in the case of former British colonies where the independent state remained firmly within an ally's economic sphere. This produced mixed results.

In Indonesia, American policy contributed to the success of a native independence movement. During the war, the Japanese occupation forces encouraged nationalism in Java. Sukarno, a nationalist leader cultivated by the Japanese, proclaimed a republic on August 17, 1945. A United Nations commission, headed by an American, attempted to resolve competing Dutch and native claims. America elected to withhold military aid to the Dutch in the civil war that raged among the Dutch, Sukarno's nationalists, and Indonesian communists between 1945 and 1948. Indonesia became fully independent, with Sukarno as its first president, in 1949. Its commercial policies during the 1950's led it to closer ties with China rather than the United States or the Soviet Union.

The United States played a minor role in Indian independence. U.S. involvement in French Indochina, in contrast, eventually drew Americans into a major war. The war years saw the growth of a well-organized and frankly communist resistance movement against the Fascist French colonial administration. The Potsdam Conference in 1945 partitioned Vietnam, with the North under Chinese and the South under temporary British administration. The

North immediately asserted its independence under Ho Chi Minh, while the South reverted to French colonial status.

Impact   In terms of its impact on the United States, decolonization during the 1940's had its greatest effect in French Indochina and Palestine. By adopting a policy that assigned the highest priority to containing communism rather than working with the nationalist movement that appeared to have the broadest popular support and promised the greatest stability, the United States committed itself to escalating involvement in Vietnam, beginning with general material aid to France, progressing through providing arms and advisers, and finally committing itself to massive troop deployment in a full-scale war.

Whether the events leading up to Israel's establishment as a nation in 1948 constitute decolonization is debatable, since the effect was to displace a large proportion of the native population and subject the remainder to rule by recent European immigrants. However justifiable on moral and historical grounds, this action, which American capital and global political influence facilitated, created a continuing source of tension that fed several minor wars during the later twentieth century.

Martha A. Sherwood

Further Reading

Betts, Raymond F. *Decolonization.* 2d ed. New York: Routledge, 2004. Chronological history, subdivided by geographical region and colonial power; traces roots of later twentieth century conflicts.

Duara, Prasenjit, ed. *Decolonization: Perspectives from Now and Then.* New York: Routledge, 2004. Collection of papers dealing with specific topics; includes reprints of works by Sun Yat-sen, Ho Chi Minh, and Jawaharlal Nehru.

Rothermund, Dietmar. *The Routledge Companion to Decolonization.* New York: Routledge, 2006. Chronological and historical, this work stresses economic factors influencing decolonization.

Springhall, John. *Decolonization Since 1945: The Collapse of European Overseas Empires.* New York: Palgrave, 2001. Presents a British anticolonial perspective.

See also   Anticommunism; China-Burma-India theater; Cold War; Foreign policy of the United States; Philippine independence; United Nations.

■ De Kooning, Willem

Identification Dutch-born American abstract expressionist painter

Born April 24, 1904; Rotterdam, the Netherlands

Died March 19, 1997; East Hampton, New York

De Kooning earned recognition as a leader of the burgeoning abstract expressionist movement in America with his first solo exhibition in 1948.

Willem de Kooning immigrated to the United States in 1926, working as a commercial artist in New York City before devoting himself to painting fulltime in 1936. Classically trained in drawing as a teenager in the Netherlands, de Kooning combined his interest in the figure with painterly gestures and abstracted forms.

In 1938, de Kooning began his first series of abstract paintings based on women, inspired in part by his relationship with artist Elaine Fried, whom he met in 1938 and married in 1943. Continuing through the mid-1940's, these vividly colored canvases featured ambiguous geometric backgrounds and increasingly fragmented figures. De Kooning's first one-man show took place at the Charles Egan Gallery in New York in 1948 and featured a series of large black-and-white abstractions, densely packed with biomorphic forms and calligraphic lines. The show earned critical acclaim, establishing de Kooning as a leader in the new abstract expressionist movement.

Impact Unlike his fellow abstract expressionists, de Kooning never abandoned the figurative element, creating a unique style that defied categorization. His "Women" paintings of the 1940's laid the foundation for his seminal women series during the 1950's, which would shock the public and critics alike. As a primary figure in the abstract expressionist movement, de Kooning heavily influenced the shape of post-World War II art in America.

Paula C. Doe

Further Reading

Stevens, Mark, and Annalyn Swan. *De Kooning: An American Master.* New York: Alfred A. Knopf, 2004.

Willem de Kooning at a Modern Art in Advertising exhibition in Chicago in late 1944. (Time & Life Pictures/Getty Images)

Yard, Sally. *Willem de Kooning: Works, Writings, and Interviews.* Barcelona, Spain: Ediciones Polígrafa, 2007.

See also Art movements; Art of This Century; Pollock, Jackson.

■ Demographics of Canada

Definition Changing characteristics of the composition of Canada's population

As in the United States, significant changes in Canada's demographics occurred during the 1940's. The most significant of these include a sharp increase in immigration after the conclusion of World War II and a resumption of the growth rates of the country's native peoples.

In 1940, Canada's total population was slightly more than 11 million persons—a figure equivalent to less than 10 percent of the U.S. population at that time. By 1949, the country's population had grown by 16 percent, to 13,549,000, but it still remained less than 10 percent of the U.S. total. Most of Canada's residents were concentrated in the regions within two hundred miles of the U.S. border, but a growing portion of the people were living in cities rather than in rural areas as had been true in the past.

Canada's fertility rate, which had fallen during the Depression era of the 1930's, rose after World War II until it reached a level close to that prevailing during the 1920's. A major factor was the introduction of Canada's Medicare, available to all citizens and supported by tax payments, though the management of Medicare remained with the provinces, subsidized in part by the national government.

In 1941, there were more male than female residents in Canada. At that time, the ethnic origin of 50 percent of Canada's residents was the British Isles (including Ireland). Another 31 percent had originated in France, though mostly in the seventeenth and eighteenth centuries. Added to these were significant numbers of people whose families had come from Germany, Russia (chiefly from Ukraine), Scandinavia, the Netherlands, and Poland. Even as early as 1941, however, a small but clearly identifiable group of Canadians had come from India. The largest number of Canadians adhered to Protestant faiths, but the number of Roman Catholics was only slightly smaller. In addition, there were small groups of Jews and of Greek Orthodox.

Canada's population was profoundly changed by the large number of immigrants who came to Canada after World War II. Even in the last year of the war Canada had offered a refuge to displaced persons, and this continued in the immediate postwar period. Between 1945 and 1950, more than 250,000 new immigrants landed in Canada, mostly from Europe, as the country went out of its way to facilitate the immigration of those whose lives had been disrupted by the war. As a result the proportion of the population descended from persons from the British Isles as well as those from France fell.

Meanwhile, Canada's aboriginal population, which had been declining steadily during the first half of the twentieth century, began at last to rise. Special efforts were made to assist the aboriginal peoples, including several thousand Eskimos, almost all of whom lived in the northernmost parts of Canada.

Requirements for Canadian citizenship changed significantly on January 1, 1947, when the Canadian Citizenship Act went into effect. Before passage of this law, Canadians had been classified as British subjects resident in Canada. After the law went into effect, all persons born in Canada were classified as Canadian citizens.

Impact At the start of World War II, Canada's demographics differed from those of the United States in two marked respects. Despite Canada's much larger geographical size, its population was only about one-tenth that of the United States. It was also more ethnically homogeneous, with the bulk of its residents having come from the British Isles and France or being descended from immigrants from those countries. By the late 1940's, however, new immigration from other parts of Europe and a resurgence of the growth of the Native Canadian population set the country on a path toward greater ethnic diversity

Nancy M. Gordon

Further Reading

Driedger, Leo, ed. *Multi-Ethnic Canada: Identities and Inequalities.* Toronto: Oxford University Press, 1996.

Hawkins, Freda. *Canada and Immigration.* 2d ed. Montreal: McGill-Queen's University Press, 1988.

Iacovetta, Franca, with Paula Draper and Robert Ventresca, eds. *A Nation of Immigrants: Readings in Canadian History, 1840s-1960s.* Toronto: University of Toronto Press, 2006.

Kalbach, W. E., and W. McVey. *The Demographic Basis of Canadian Society.* 2d ed. Toronto: McGraw-Hill Ryerson, 1979.

See also Canadian Citizenship Act of 1946; Canadian minority communities; Health care; Housing in Canada; Immigration to Canada; Jews in Canada; Refugees in North America; Urbanization in Canada.

■ Demographics of the United States

Definition Selective characteristics of the population that are important in social science research, marketing, and government planning

Significant changes in the nation's demographics took place during the 1940's, and these changes promoted a number of trends that would have a profound impact on subsequent history.

The 1940's was marked by two major demographic trends: a growth in family income and a growth in population. Government spending during World

War II ended the Great Depression and created large numbers of good-paying jobs. At the same time, severe restraints on the availability of consumer goods encouraged people to save money; when peace returned, the combination of pent-up demand and savings resulted in a buying spree that further stimulated employment. This economic expansion helped to bring about an unexpected surge in the U.S. population. In 1940, the U.S. Bureau of the Census reported that the population was 132,164,569, and ten years later the bureau reported that the number had expanded to 151,325,798. Even though the increase of 14.5 percent was twice the rate of the previous decade, it was considerably less than the growth rate of the 1950's, and it was less than half the average rate of increase that had occurred in the nineteenth century.

Characteristics of Population Growth　The main reason for population growth was the increase in the crude birth rate (CBR), as measured in the number of births per 1,000 persons. The Great Depression of the 1930's had driven fertility rates below what most people would have preferred for family size. The improvement in the economy at the eve of the war encouraged people to have larger families. In 1940, according to the National Center for Health Statistics, the CBR was 19.4 births per 1,000, which was slightly higher than the average rate for the previous decade. The upward trend was temporarily repressed because so many men of marriageable age entered the armed services, but their return to civilian life after the war resulted in the beginning of the so-called baby-boom generation. Whereas the CBR of 1945 stood at 20.4, it grew to 24.5 by 1949. The CBR for whites was significantly lower than the CBR for other racial groups. For whites, it was 18.6 in 1940, while it was 26.7 for all others. In 1949, the rate grew to 23.6 for whites, while it increased to 33.0 for the other categories. Separate CBR statistics for African Americans and Hispanics are not available for the 1940's.

The reduction in the crude death rate (CDR) also contributed to the growing population. The National Center for Health Statistics reported that the CDR of 1940 was 10.8 per 1,000 persons, and by 1950 the rate had declined to 9.6. It might be noted that the 292,131 battle deaths of the war had only a slight impact on the CDR. The decline of the CDR during the decade was a small portion of a long-term trend for the twentieth century (from 17.2 in 1900 to 8.8 in

1975). As in other decades, the racial differences in the CDR of the 1940's were significant. In 1945, for instance, the CDR was 10.4 for whites, while it was 11.9 for African Americans. The sexual differences were even more significant. For 1945, the CDR for men was 12.6, while it was 8.8 for women. One of the most important components of the CDR was the infant mortality rate (IMR), which refers to the deaths of infants under one year old. In 1940, the IMR was 47.0 per 1,000 live births, compared to 29.2 in 1950. For perspective, it might be noted that the IMR in 1920 was 85.8, whereas it was only 9.2 in 1990.

The average life expectancy of Americans at birth increased from 62.9 years in 1940 to 68.2 in 1950. The expectancy was significantly higher for whites and for women. For men, the average life expectancy in 1945 was 63.6 years, compared to 67.9 for women. The differences between African Americans and whites were of similar magnitude. For whites, the average life expectancy in 1945 was 66.8 years, compared with 57.7 for African Americans. The change in the average life expectancy during the 1940's was part of the gradual increase for the century. Whereas the average expectancy was only 47.3 years in 1900, it would grow to 74.5 by 1982. The increase in life expectancy meant that the average age of the population was becoming older. In 1940, 6.8 percent of the population was sixty-five or older, compared with 8.1 percent in 1950.

Marriage and Family　Beginning in the early 1940's, according to demographer Donald Bogue, a "marriage boom" predated the more publicized baby boom. During the three decades from the 1940's to the late 1960's, marriage became significantly more common than it had been during the Great Depression, and the number of single persons shrank dramatically. In 1940, 59.7 percent of men fifteen years and older were married, compared with 68.2 percent in 1950. For women at least fifteen years old, 59.5 percent were married in 1940, while 66.1 percent were married in 1950. The median age for first marriages in 1940 was 24.3 years for men and 21.5 years for women. These averages were similar to those of the previous twenty years. By 1950, in contrast, the median age for first marriages had declined to 22.8 years for males and to 20.3 years for women.

Significant differences in marital status existed among various racial groups. The percentage of marriages for whites was larger than that for African Americans. In 1940, 56.9 percent of female African Americans older than fifteen were married, while the marriage rate for white female Americans of the same age was 59.8 percent. Ten years later, 62.0 percent of black women were married, compared with 66.2 percent of white women. The rate of married black males over the age of fifteen grew dramatically, going from 33.4 percent in 1940 to 58.2 percent in 1950. During these years, the rate of married white males increased from 59.9 percent to 67.9 percent. For the 1940's, unfortunately, the marriage rates for Hispanics are not available.

In 1940, the divorce rate was 2.0 per 1,000 people, which was only 0.4 more than the rate in 1920. Although the rate more than doubled to 4.3 during the war years, it temporarily declined after 1945, falling to 2.7 in 1949. From the perspective of the twentieth century, the changing divorce rate was part of an upward trend, going from only 0.5 in 1900 to over 9.0 by the end of the century. In 1940, 1.4 percent of the population was classified as divorced, whereas the percentage had increased to 2.2 percent by 1950. It might be noted that the percentage at midcentury was about four times the percentage in 1900 but less than one-fourth of that of the 1990's.

Crime Changes in the crime rate for the 1940's varied greatly according to the crime under consideration. The number of reported robberies during the decade grew at about the same rate as the increase in population. Aggravated assaults, in contrast, increased from 20,312 in 1940 to 32,144 in 1944. Surprisingly, however, the 1940's also saw a significant decline in the homicide rate, which was part of a downward trend from the 1920's until the late 1950's. In 1935, the rate was 10.1 homicides per 100,000 people, compared with 6.1 in 1940, 5.0 in 1944, 6.4 in 1946, and 5.5 in 1949. The rate for homicide victimization varied dramatically by race. For whites, the rate in 1940 was 2 victims per 100,000, whereas it was 26 for African Americans. As in other decades, known offenders in a large majority of all crimes belonged to the same racial category as the race of the victims.

The decline in the homicide rate correlated fairly closely with the decline in the execution rate of prisoners. In 1940, a total of 124 persons were executed. By 1950, the number of executions had declined to 82. Compared with the first decade of the twenty-first century, the prison population of the 1940's was relatively low. For the decade, the average number of incarcerated people in federal and state prisons was approximately 160,000 inmates, or a rate of slightly more than 0.1 percent of the general population. Forty years later, the prison population would begin to grow dramatically, reaching a rate of over 0.7 percent in 2005.

In contrast to the previous six decades, lynchings were becoming uncommon and socially unacceptable by the 1940's. Whereas the archives of the Tuskegee Institute recorded a total of 886 lynchings during the first decade of the twentieth century, the institute reported a total of 32 for the 1940's. The numbers per year varied from one to six. Only two of these victims were white, whereas the other thirty were African American. In addition to declining in number, the lynchings of the 1940's were different from earlier incidents in that they rarely at-

Three generations of a California family during the late 1940's. (R. Kent Rasmussen)

tracted large crowds of cheering spectators. The era of widespread lynchings was effectively coming to an end, even though there continued to be victims, including a few veterans who had participated in the war effort.

Employment and Social Welfare During the war years, much of the population enjoyed relative prosperity, particularly in comparison with the previous decade. Despite wage controls, the average wage of workers in manufacturing almost doubled. In 1940, the average gross weekly wage in manufacturing was $25.29, compared with $46.08 in 1944. Less than half of this increase resulted from inflation. Per capita expenditures grew by about 30 percent from 1940 until 1945. Personal savings for 1944 reached an all-time high of $37 billion, which was more than ten times the amount for 1940. This accumulation of savings would be one of the major stimulants of economic growth after 1945.

The number of people participating in the total labor force from 1940 to 1945 increased from 55.6 million to 65.3 million. Much of the increase was due to the growth in the number of military and government employees. The size of the civilian labor force did not change significantly: There were 55.6 million civilian workers in 1940, 55.5 million in 1942, and 54.6 in 1944. In August, 1945, some 2.5 million workers in war industries were discharged, but the impact on the civilian labor force was temporary and minor. In 1947, there were 57.8 million civilian workers in the country, and three years later the number had increased to 59.7 million.

The unemployment rate varied dramatically during the decade. For 1940, the year before the United States entered the war, the rate stood at 14.6 percent (or 8.1 million persons). In 1941, the rate decreased to 9.9 percent (5.6 million persons), and by 1944 it had further declined to only 1.2 percent (0.7 million persons). For 1945, the last year of the war, the unemployment rate was 1.9 percent, and during the next year it grew to 3.9 percent. By 1949, the rate had grown to 5.9 percent, which was still relatively small by historical standards.

Programs under the Social Security Act had a profound impact during the 1940's. For 1941, the year that payments began, the total number of beneficiaries was only 222,000, of which 112,000 received old-age pensions. By 1945, a total of 1.3 million persons were receiving benefits, including 518,000 old-age pensions. By the end of the decade, the number of beneficiaries had grown to almost 3.5 million, with almost 1.8 million retirees receiving pensions. Because of these pensions, the number of elderly persons receiving public assistance increased only slightly, going from 2.07 million in 1940 to 2.8 million in 1950. The number of families receiving Aid to Dependent Children (later renamed Aid to Families with Dependent Children), in contrast, grew significantly, increasing from 370,000 families in 1940 to 652,000 ten years later.

Armed Forces During the war, a total of more than 16 million men and women served in the armed forces. By the end of 1943, 7.5 million men were serving in the Army and 2.8 million were in the Navy and Marines. More than 18 percent of the nation's families contributed at least one person to the military. Although the Selective Service Act of 1940 prohibited racial discrimination, the Selective Service System tended to minimize recruitment from African American communities. As a result, whereas African Americans made up 10.6 percent of the population, they constituted less than 7 percent of the military personnel in 1943. Following the war, the military services rapidly demobilized, and there was little need for additional conscription. Only 20,348 men were drafted in 1948, and the number decreased to 9,781 in 1949.

The Selective Service Act allowed deferments for conscientious objectors based on religious beliefs and practices. More than seventy thousand men claimed exemption based on this provision. The Selective Service System accepted about half of these claims. Authorities consigned about twenty-five thousand to noncombat military duty and some twelve thousand to alternative service in Civilian Public Service Camps. About six thousand men, mostly Jehovah's Witnesses, were imprisoned because of their opposition to the particular war, not violence in general.

Women World War II had a profound impact on the number of women working outside the home, particularly in the manufacturing sector, where female workers were dubbed "Rosie the Riveter." More than 19 million women were participating in the labor force by the war's end, more than at any other time in American history. During the war, women constituted one-fourth of automobile workers, but in 1946 they made up only one in twelve. Although women left manufacturing jobs in droves following the war, their participation rate in the labor force still increased from 25.4 percent in 1940 to 33.9 percent in 1950. Whereas male participation in the labor force increased by 10.1 percent during the decade, the number of women increased by 42.6 percent. This increase was part of a long-term trend for female employment, reaching 57.4 percent by 1989.

From 1945 to 1947, women's employment declined by more than two million. Although some women gave up their wartime jobs voluntarily, surveys reported that most of them wanted to keep working. The majority of those wanting to work were able to find employment, and by 1950 the number of women in the workforce equaled that of the wartime peak. A large number of women, however, lost the opportunity to participate in the traditionally male jobs that paid higher wages. Their share of jobs in the automobile industry, for instance, fell from 25 percent in 1944 to 10 percent in 1950, and their proportion in the Los Angeles aircraft industry fell from 40 percent in 1944 to only 12 percent in 1945.

Education By the 1940's, a clear majority of school-age children (ages five to nineteen) were attending school. In 1940, slightly more than 70 percent of children were in attendance, and in 1950 the rate grew to 75 percent. At the beginning of the twentieth century, in contrast, only about half of school-age children had been enrolled, whereas the rate would increase to about 85 percent in 1980. Despite the growth in school attendance, only 24.5 percent of Americans were high school graduates in 1940. The rate increased to 34.3 percent in 1950 and would reach 75.2 percent in 1990. During the 1940's, the racial gap in education was striking. Only 7.7 percent of African Americans were graduates in 1940, and the rate increased only to 13.0 percent in 1950. The comparable rate for white Americans was 26.1 percent in 1940, and it stood at 36.4 percent in 1950.

Before and during World War II, only a small minority of Americans attended college, but following the war, enrollment in higher education began to increase at an unprecedented rate. During the 1920's, institutions of higher education had conferred an average of about 50,000 degrees per year. By 1940, the total number of degrees conferred had quadrupled to 214,521. In 1944, the number of degrees ac-

tually declined to 141,582, but in large part due to the G.I. Bill, the number ballooned to 421,282 in 1949. Most of this growth was made up by white male students. In 1949, college degrees were awarded to 303,347 men, compared to 117,935 women. That year, some 6 percent of the general population graduated from college, including only 2.1 percent of African Americans. Although regional differences existed, they were not nearly as great as racial differences. The West, with 7.7 percent in 1950, had the highest rate of college graduates, whereas the South, with 5.3 percent, had the lowest rate. The growth in college graduates would continue into subsequent decades—doubling by the 1970's and then doubling again by the 1990's.

Impact For the decade of the 1940's, important demographic changes are seen in the statistics relating to a variety of topics, including military conscription, wartime employment, educational expansion, postwar prosperity, and increasing rates in both marriage and divorce. The decade's most consequential development for the future was the postwar expansion of the birth rate, initiating a baby boom that would continue into the next two decades. As in the case of the birth rate, a large percentage of the demographics of the 1940's represented long-term trends.

Thomas Tandy Lewis

Further Reading

Bogue, Donald J., Douglas Anderton, and Richard Barrett. *The Population of the United States.* 3d ed. New York: Free Press, 1997. An updated version of Bogue's pioneering reference work, with clearly written introductions and many helpful tables.

Carter, Susan B., et al., eds. *Historical Statistics of the United States: Millennial Edition.* 5 vols. New York: Cambridge University Press, 2007. A monumental product of eighty scholars, these large volumes provide comprehensive statistical information about all fields of American history. Available in an online edition.

Kennedy, David M. *The American People in World War II.* New York: Oxford University Press, 1999. Winner of the Pulitzer Prize in history, Kennedy's well-written book includes a great deal of demographic information about American society during the war.

Klein, Herbert S. *A Population History of the United States.* New York: Cambridge University Press,

2004. Chapter 5 provides a useful summary of several major trends from 1914 to 1945.

Stouffer, Samuel, et al. *Studies in Social Psychology in World War II: The American Soldier.* 4 vols. Princeton, N.J.: Princeton University Press, 1949-1950. A classic in sociological research, these volumes provide abundant information about the characteristics and attitudes of the personnel in the armed forces.

U.S. Bureau of the Census. *The Statistical History of the United States: Colonial Times to the Present.* New York: Basic Books, 1976. A useful volume with statistical charts related to changes in population, economics, and government.

Wright, Russell. *A Twentieth-Century History of the United States Population.* Lanham, Md.: Scarecrow Press, 1996. A good analysis of census data from 1900 until 1990, providing insight into the social, economic, and political factors that have shaped the United States.

See also African Americans; Asian Americans; Baby boom; Demographics of Canada; Housing in the United States; Immigration to the United States; Jews in the United States; Latinos; Native Americans; Refugees in North America; Urbanization in the United States.

Deoxyribonucleic acid. *See* **DNA discovery**

■ Department of Defense, U.S.

Identification Federal cabinet-level department responsible for issues of national security
Also known as DOD
Date Established on September 18, 1947

The U.S. Department of Defense is the federal department tasked with overseeing numerous federal agencies responsible for matters related to national defense. In particular, the department coordinates and supervises the major branches of the United States military.

The Department of Defense was created in 1947 as a military department with a single secretary to preside over the entire national defense system. The department combined the former Department of War, Department of the Navy, and Department of the Air

Force. The major goal of the department was to create a more centralized command structure by uniting all the various agencies responsible for the nation's security. In particular, President Harry S. Truman, along with various World War II commanders, believed that the fragmentation and rivalry between military branches during World War II may have reduced the overall military effectiveness of U.S. forces.

From December, 1945, to the spring of 1947, Truman drafted several versions of the new department. On July 26, 1947, he gained enough congressional support and signed the National Security Act of 1947, creating the National Military Establishment (NME), which began official operations on September 18, 1947. Eventually the new department changed its name from NME to the Department of Defense in 1949, partly because the pronunciation of the acronym NME sounded like "enemy."

Impact Creation of the Department of Defense in the aftermath of World War II was the first major step toward integrating various national defense agencies, specifically the major branches of the United States military. This important initiative established a unified command structure in which various federal agencies could coordinate, monitor, and determine when the safety of the United States was threatened by a foreign power. In the early twenty-first century, this federal department remained the cornerstone of the American national defense system. The Department of Homeland Security, formed in 2003, coordinates in some projects but is concerned primarily with threats to the United States within its borders, while the Department of Defense is concerned with external threats.

Paul M. Klenowski

Further Reading
Marcum, Cheryl Y., et al. *Department of Defense Political Appointments: Positions and Process.* Santa Monica, Calif.: National Defense Research Institute/RAND Corporation, 2001.
Trask, Roger, and Alfred Goldberg. *Department of Defense 1947-1997: Organization and Leaders.* Washington, D.C.: Historical Office, Office of the Secretary of Defense, 1997.

See also Air Force, U.S.; Army, U.S.; Coast Guard, U.S.; Desegregation of the U.S. military; Marines, U.S.; Military conscription in the United States; Navy, U.S.; Women in the U.S. military.

■ Desegregation of the U.S. military

The Event An executive order signed by President Harry S. Truman mandated the desegregation of the armed services and established an advisory committee to explore ways to implement the order

Also known as Executive Order 9981

Date July 26, 1948

Place Washington, D.C.

Requiring the armed forces to desegregate was a direct challenge to prevailing Jim Crow laws and segregationist attitudes. Desegregation of the military acted as a precedent for other societal institutions, and as a result, civil rights began gaining prominence as a national issue during the late 1940's.

Following on the heels of Executive Order 9980, which sought to establish fair employment practices in the federal workforce, Truman issued Executive Order 9981 on July 26, 1948. He called for "equality of treatment and opportunity for all persons in the armed services without regard to race, color, religion or national origin." He authorized an advisory committee, the President's Committee on Equality of Treatment and Opportunity in the Armed Forces (later, the last word was changed to "Services"), to outline ways to achieve this goal. Without specifying a definitive time frame for enactment, he was able to assuage his critics, both politicians and military leaders alike. Despite mixed sentiments about this military policy, a confluence of factors contributed to the fruition of Executive Order 9981, namely the military performance of black soldiers in World War II, the political pragmatism of President Truman in his bid for reelection, a social climate within the United States that was challenging the existing racial stratification system, and the global context of the Cold War.

Military Issues Race relations during the 1940's were rooted in segregationist attitudes supported by Jim Crow laws and institutionalized racism. The armed forces reflected the larger societal context and maintained segregated units, despite the facts that African Americans had served in the military since the Revolutionary War. Their participation was characterized by segregation, quotas, and unequal access to top commissions. For example, in 1946 only one black soldier in seventy was a commissioned officer, while the rate for whites was one for every seven men.

The military service of African Americans was controversial. The justification for requesting slaves and former slaves to defend America was morally suspect. In addition, some claimed that black soldiers did not perform well. The military nevertheless utilized black soldiers and even integrated small units when confronted with manpower shortages.

By the end of World War II, the military was still segregated; however, some black units partnered with white units to carry out select missions. Although there was not uniform agreement about the success of the units' combat performance or morale issues, their efforts demonstrated that camaraderie between African Americans and whites in the military was possible. For example, when the black 99th Fighter Squadron was prevented from attending an Air Force celebration, the white 79th defied their superior officers to insist on the inclusion of the black unit. The heroic efforts of the all-black 332d Fighter Group—the Tuskegee Airmen—of which the 99th Fighter Squadron became a part, won a Presidential Unit Citation, adding momentum to the call for military desegregation. The Tuskegee symbol of the "Double V" became a rallying point in the campaign against two enemies: fascism abroad and racism at home.

Political, Social, and Global Context The issue of race was a salient factor in Truman's 1948 presidential reelection campaign. The timing of Executive Order 9981 led Truman's critics to conclude that his mandate was fueled more by political pragmatism than by humanitarian goals. Politically, Truman needed to garner the African American vote to win the Democratic nomination and the presidency. Desiring to support Franklin D. Roosevelt's New Deal, black voters in the North became Democrats. This created contentiousness within the Democratic Party between northern liberals and conservative southern Dixiecrats. The balance tilted toward the northern liberals in 1948, when the party platform of the Democratic National Convention included a strong civil rights plank.

A southern contingent led by South Carolina governor Strom Thurmond left the convention in protest. Their behavior actually solidified support among black voters, who, already benefiting from a strong economy, came to believe that Truman was sincere in supporting civil rights. In fact, a survey by the National Association for the Advancement of Colored People (NAACP) confirmed that 69 percent of all black voters in twenty-seven major American cities and communities did indeed vote for Truman. The black vote played a significant role in Truman's presidential victory.

Truman also had to avoid looming social protests. A new draft law was to go into effect on August 16, 1948. A. Philip Randolph and fellow civil rights activist Grant Reynolds organized the League for Non-Violent Civil Disobedience Against Military Segregation and vowed resistance by African American youths if the armed forces remained segregated. About 71 percent of black youths polled at the time supported civil disobedience activities to promote desegregation. Fear of societal unrest was fueled by Randolph's efforts in organizing protests, in addition to the work of the Congress of Racial Equality and the NAACP, led by its executive secretary, Walter White.

The NAACP and others highlighted the incongruity between behavior toward African Americans in America and the global post-World War II environment. The international climate in the late 1940's was conducive to egalitarianism. The ideologies of Nazism and fascism were overcome by the United States and its allies, and scientific racism was no longer in vogue. The United Nations was created in 1945, followed by a Commission on Human Rights in 1946 to provide a global forum to voice human rights concerns. Despite these efforts, African Americans in America were still denied equal footing with whites. In fact, in 1946, black veteran Isaac Woodward was blinded by South Carolina policemen, and two black veterans and their wives were shot to death by a white mob in Georgia. This disturbed Truman, who instructed Attorney General Tom C. Clark to investigate and prosecute racially motivated crimes.

The dilemma Truman faced was reconciling America's position in the world as a superpower fighting communism with the fact that the country maintained a segregationist culture at home. The United States had to bring societal reality in the United States more in line with its professed democratic foreign policy values. One step in that direction was Executive Order 9981 and the creation of the Fahy Committee (President's Committee on Equality of Treatment and Opportunity in the Armed Forces), under former solicitor general Charles Fahy.

Desegregating the U.S. Armed Forces

U.S. president Harry S. Truman issued Executive Order 9981 in 1948 to desegregate the U.S. armed forces:

Whereas it is essential that there be maintained in the armed services of the United States the highest standards of democracy, with equality of treatment and opportunity for all those who serve in our country's defense:

Now therefore, by virtue of the authority vested in me as President of the United States, by the Constitution and the statutes of the United States, and as Commander in Chief of the armed services, it is hereby ordered as follows:

1. It is hereby declared to be the policy of the President that there shall be equality of treatment and opportunity for all persons in the armed services without regard to race, color, religion or national origin. This policy shall be put into effect as rapidly as possible, having due regard to the time required to effectuate any necessary changes without impairing efficiency or morale.

2. There shall be created in the National Military Establishment an advisory committee to be known as the President's Committee on Equality of Treatment and Opportunity in the Armed Services, which shall be composed of seven members to be designated by the President.

3. The Committee is authorized on behalf of the President to examine into the rules, procedures and practices of the Armed Services in order to determine in what respect such rules, procedures and practices may be altered or improved with a view to carrying out the policy of this order. . . .

Findings of the Fahy Committee *Freedom to Serve*, the final report of the Fahy Committee, was submitted on May 22, 1950. The report indicated that the Navy still limited the proportion of black soldiers on each ship to 10 percent. The Marine Corps integrated basic training but not its units. The Air Force was progressive in integrating units, eliminating quotas, and basing placement solely on ability. Within the Army, African Americans did not have access to about 40 percent of job classifications and 80 percent of its schools. The Fahy Committee recognized the need for military efficiency. Among its key recommendations was for the armed services to focus on ability, not race, in determining quotas and placement. All military branches officially accepted the committee's report. The outbreak of the Korean War accelerated the process of desegregation. By the Vietnam War era, the military was fully integrated.

Impact Regardless of his motivation, Truman ensured that the 1940's would be pivotal in the history of race relations in the United States when he issued Executive Order 9981. From that moment, civil rights equality was pursued as a legitimate national concern. Advocates of racial equality became empowered, and the foundation was set for challenging the existing social order. The military became a model for the integration of other societal institutions. In particular, school desegregation followed in 1954 with the landmark *Brown v. Board of Education* decision. Military desegregation set a precedent for incorporating women into the military, which began in 1973. Executive Order 9981 also created an economic opportunity structure within the military institution for African Americans, as exemplified by the career of General Colin Powell. Executive Order 9981 was, in spirit, a call for tolerance.

Rosann Bar

Further Reading

Berman, William C. *The Politics of Civil Rights in the Truman Administration*. Columbus: Ohio State University Press, 1970. Documents Truman's role in bringing civil rights issues onto the national stage.

Borstelmann, Thomas. "Jim Crow's Coming Out: Race Relations and American Foreign Policy in the Truman Years." *Presidential Studies Quarterly* 29, no. 3 (1999): 549-569. Sheds light on the international context of Truman's initiatives on race.

Gardner, Michael R. *Harry Truman and Civil Rights: Moral Courage and Political Risks*. Carbondale: Southern Illinois University Press, 2002. Provides a detailed history of the Turnip Day Session of Congress on July 26, 1948, at which Truman issued Executive Orders 9980 and 9981.

Geselbracht, Raymond H., ed. *The Civil Rights Legacy of Harry Truman*. Kirksville, Mo.: Truman State University Press, 2007. A fine array of essays from multiple perspectives, including descendants of slaves, that evaluates Truman's civil rights agenda.

Percy, William Alexander. "Jim Crow and Uncle Sam: The Tuskegee Flying Units and the U.S. Army Air Forces in Europe in World War II." *The Journal of Military History* 67, no. 3 (2003): 773-810. A good history of the Tuskegee Airmen and their impact on military desegregation.

President's Committee on Equality of Treatment and Opportunity in the Armed Services. *Freedom to Serve*. Washington, D.C.: Government Printing Office, 1950. Report of the Fahy Committee on implementing Executive Order 9981.

Segal, David R. *Recruiting for Uncle Sam: Citizenship and Military Manpower Policy*. Lawrence: University Press of Kansas, 1989. Looks at parallelisms between racial and gender integration in the military.

See also African Americans; Army, U.S.; Civil rights and liberties; Executive orders; Jim Crow laws; Military conscription in the United States; Navy, U.S.; Racial discrimination; Randolph, A. Philip; Truman, Harry S.; Tuskegee Airmen; White, Walter F.

■ Destroyers-for-bases deal

The Event The United States traded fifty World War I-vintage naval destroyers to Great Britain in return for valuable basing rights in eight British territories in the Western Hemisphere

Date Signed on September 2, 1940

The destroyers-for-bases deal marked the end of American neutrality in World War II. The destroyers increased the capabilities of the British Royal Navy in escorting and protecting the shipping of supplies from the United States across the Atlantic Ocean. The United States gained valuable military bases in the Western Hemisphere.

At the beginning of World War II, the United States pursued a policy of neutrality in the conflict between Nazi Germany and the West. However, on November 4, 1939, the Franklin D. Roosevelt administration passed the Neutrality Act of 1939, allowing the United States to carry out arms trades with nations at war on a cash-and-carry basis. This legislation favored trade with Great Britain and France in the war in Europe. As a result, German surface raiders attacked and sank British cargo ships transporting war goods from the United States to Britain. Throughout the early stages of the war, German attacks disrupted the vital supply lines to a point where, after the German invasion of France in May, 1940, Prime Minister Winston Churchill informed Roosevelt of the British need for American assistance in the war effort. He told Roosevelt that the immediate needs

of Britain included a loan of forty to fifty old naval destroyers to provide protection for British ships crossing the Atlantic. Roosevelt appreciated Britain's situation but had to consider American security in the Atlantic first, as well as congressional opposition from isolationists.

After the fall of France in June, 1940, the United States gradually began to support British war efforts. Americans began to view Britain as the first line of defense against the German threat to the Western Hemisphere. Negotiations took place during the height of the Battle of Britain between the Roosevelt administration and British ambassador Lord Lothian in Washington, D.C. The Destroyers-for-Bases Agreement was signed by U.S. secretary of state Cordell Hull and Lord Lothian on September 2, 1940. In the agreement, the United States would

Canadian naval personnel marching along the dock of a coastal port on their way to take possession of six destroyers acquired from the United States, on October 14, 1940. (AP/Wide World Photos)

provide Britain fifty old naval destroyers in exchange for the rights to build American bases in eight British territories in the western Atlantic and Caribbean region. Moreover, Britain pledged that the British fleet would never surrender to Germany. As a result, the U.S. Navy transferred forty-three destroyers to the British Royal Navy and seven more to the Canadian Royal Navy. The United States gained bases in Antigua, Bermuda, British Guiana, Jamaica, Saint Lucia, and Trinidad in the British West Indies, as well as Newfoundland and Labrador in Canada.

Impact The destroyers-for-bases deal had limited immediate impact. Many of the destroyers needed repair before they were considered operational for convoy duty. However, the deal had significant symbolic importance because it signified the start of closer cooperation between the United States and Britain. The destroyers-for-bases deal was one of the first steps that the United States took toward establishing a wartime alliance with Britain. It was followed by the Lend-Lease Agreement in March, 1941, followed by the Atlantic Charter in August and the Arcadia Conference in December.

William Young

Further Reading

Heinrichs, Waldo. *The Threshold of War: Franklin D. Roosevelt and American Entry into World War II.* New York: Oxford University Press, 1988.

Kimball, Warren F. *Forged in War: Roosevelt, Churchill, and the Second World War.* New York: William Morrow, 1997.

Reynolds, David. *The Creation of the Anglo-American Alliance, 1937-1941.* Chapel Hill: University of North Carolina Press, 1982.

_____. *From World War to Cold War: Churchill, Roosevelt, and the International History of the 1940's.* New York: Oxford University Press, 2006.

See also Atlantic Charter; Churchill, Winston; Foreign policy of the United States; Hull, Cordell; Lend-Lease; Navy, U.S.; Roosevelt, Franklin D.; Submarine warfare; World War II.

■ Dewey, Thomas E.

Identification New York governor and Republican presidential nominee in 1944 and 1948

Born March 24, 1902; Owosso, Michigan

Died March 16, 1971; Bal Harbour, Florida

Dewey governed the most populous state in the United States for most of the 1940's and was an active presidential candidate throughout the decade who nearly won in 1948.

Thomas E. Dewey was a lawyer whose public service began in 1931 as an assistant U.S. attorney in New York. His work investigating Dutch Schultz (who almost assassinated Dewey before being murdered himself) and Lucky Luciano (whom Dewey successfully convicted) brought fame, and he was elected Manhattan district attorney in 1937. He barely lost his first race for governor in 1938, at which point he resumed his work investigating racketeers.

Rising in Politics Dewey's antiracketeering success made him the strong leader in polls for the 1940 Republican nomination. Distrusted by party leaders, partly for his youth, inexperience, and personal stiffness, Dewey campaigned actively, relying heavily on primaries. He attacked President Franklin D. Roosevelt's New Deal for excessive spending, hostility to business, political cronyism, and failure to end the Great Depression. He urged stronger defense and blamed Roosevelt for failing to accomplish this, though his own foreign policy views were vague. His primary victories gave him an initial lead in convention delegates, but after the fall of France to Nazi Germany, he and longtime party rival Robert A. Taft fell to Wendell Willkie, whose nomination victory was fueled by media support and a blitz of telegrams, many of them spurious. Willkie lost to Roosevelt in the general election.

Dewey resumed district attorney work, prosecuting no more criminal bigwigs but many smaller fry, including tenement slumlords, and he did a major United Service Organizations (USO) tour in 1941. He decisively won the New York governorship in 1942. As governor, he supported free enterprise but not laissez-faire; pushed through various reforms, including long overdue legislative reapportionment; and avidly punished entrenched corruption. He accepted mild welfare state policies while opposing dependency and keeping careful watch on the budget. He worked hard to make sure that New York supported the war effort well while also preparing for postwar reconstruction, including unemployment compensation for returning veterans.

Governor Dewey again sought the nomination in 1944 on the basis of primary victories and popular support, which was strong enough this time to overcome the doubts of party regulars. He chose conservative Ohio governor John Bricker as his running mate and ran on a fiscally conservative and racially liberal platform vaguely committed to internationalism. The campaign proved rather nasty (Roosevelt detested Dewey), with organized labor playing a major role (and also a major Republican target). Dewey contrasted his youth and health to the tired, ailing Roosevelt. Allied success in World War II helped Roosevelt. Dewey intended to attack Roosevelt over Pearl Harbor after learning of the success of Magic, the American code-breaking project that intercepted Japan's cryptographic codes during the war. Dewey claimed that Roosevelt had known that the Japanese intended to bomb Pearl Harbor on December 7, 1941, but he reluctantly desisted from disclosing the project when told that the codes were still being used. However, he did criticize the lack of preparedness for war. Roosevelt's victory was his closest, winning about 53.5 percent of the popular vote to Dewey's 46 percent.

Party Leader   After the 1944 election, Dewey unsuccessfully sought a party policy charter. As governor, he supported a series of civil rights bills, and social welfare policies (such as emergency housing, a long-term antituberculosis program, and assistance for veterans) sufficiently modest to enable a large tax cut in 1946 while keeping the budget balanced. His support for reconversion of war plants minimized postwar disruption in New York. This enabled him to win another decisive victory in 1946, which led to another presidential campaign, advocating a staunchly activist internationalism that clearly separated him from the Taft wing despite compatible domestic policies.

In 1948, Dewey again relied on primaries to show himself a winner and to persuade Republican leaders to support him. His strongest rival was charismatic liberal Harold Stassen, whose Wisconsin and Nebraska victories threatened to supplant Dewey. In Oregon, the two debated the issue of banning the Communist Party; Dewey opposed it and won the primary. Dewey's rivals on both wings of the party tried to combine against him at the convention, but their differences and Dewey's "winner" image enabled him to succeed.

Harry S. Truman had his own problems, particularly the revolt of Democratic Party progressives, led by Henry A. Wallace, and (due to a powerful civil rights platform plank) revolt by Dixiecrats in the South, led by Strom Thurmond. Truman responded by calling the Republican-majority Congress back to pass legislation that he wanted and that the Republican platform promised. Congress chose to do little, which Truman used against Dewey in a mud-slinging class-warfare campaign that appealed particularly

New York attorney general Thomas E. Dewey (left) with John Hamilton, the chairman of the Republican National Committee, meeting shortly after Dewey announced his intention to seek the party's nomination for the U.S. presidency in 1940. Dewey failed to win the nomination that year but was the party's nominee in 1944 and 1948. (Library of Congress)

strongly to farmers. Dewey ran a mild, vague campaign, and even early favorable polls never showed him with the extra votes he needed over 1944 for a popular majority. The result was an embarrassing upset, with Truman triumphantly holding up the *Chicago Tribune* proclaiming Dewey the winner of the general election; Congress also changed hands.

After losing the presidency to Truman, Dewey went back to his governorship, being reelected for a third time in 1950. Upon retirement, he went into private practice but remained an active leader in the Republican Party, preferring centrists such as Richard Nixon in 1968.

Impact   By 1944, Dewey was the primary leader of the moderate wing of the Republican Party, which dominated party presidential politics until 1964. His views were more similar than Taft's to many of the conservatives who dominated the party after Lyndon B. Johnson's Great Society.

Timothy Lane

Further Reading

Karabell, Zachary. *The Last Campaign: How Harry Truman Won the 1948 Election.* New York: Alfred A. Knopf, 2000. Thorough study of the 1948 presidential election that looks at all four major candidates, the primaries, and the conventions, as well as the general election. Karabell sees Truman as the last successful traditional politician and Dewey as the first "packaged" candidate.

McCullough, David. *Truman.* New York: Simon & Schuster, 1992. Pulitzer Prize-winning popular biography, with extensive coverage of the 1944 and 1948 elections. Attributes Truman's win to the support of African Americans, white ethnics, farmers, and reverse coattails.

Patterson, James T. *Mr. Republican: A Biography of Robert A. Taft.* Boston: Houghton Mifflin, 1972. Full, family-authorized biography of Dewey's leading intraparty rival, with extensive coverage of Taft's relations with Dewey.

Ross, Irwin. *The Loneliest Campaign: The Truman Victory of 1948.* New York: New American Library, 1968. Good campaign account that attributes Truman's 1948 win to gains over 1944 in rural areas and especially small towns.

Smith, Richard Norton. *Thomas E. Dewey and His Times.* New York: Simon & Schuster, 1982. The only significant biography of Dewey. Full, de-

tailed, and authoritative. Blames the 1948 defeat on switchers and nonvoters in the Farm Belt.

See also   Elections in the United States: 1940; Elections in the United States: 1944; Elections in the United States: 1948; McCormick, Robert R.; Roosevelt, Franklin D.; Taft, Robert A.; Thurmond, Strom; Truman, Harry S.; Wallace, Henry A.; Willkie, Wendell.

■ Dieppe raid

The Event   Failed Allied operation resulting in significant Canadian casualties
Also known as   Operation Jubilee
Date   August 19, 1942
Place   Dieppe, France

The failure of the Dieppe raid taught the Allies valuable lessons about German defenses in continental Europe, while also convincing British prime minister Winston Churchill of the necessity of postponing the Allies' planned invasion of northern France—a delay that American military leaders opposed.

After the failed British landing at Dunkirk in mid-1940, the evacuated troops were returned to England, where they were joined by a steady influx of new troops from Canada. After 1941, American troops began joining them in anticipation of an eventual major invasion of northern France, which was occupied by Nazi Germany. Before the major invasion could be mounted, the Allied leaders wanted to gain some invasion experience in France, so they could learn as much as possible about German military strategy and possible German defensive actions against invasion. In early 1942, plans were made to launch a trial invasion at Dieppe, a port in northern France, to achieve these limited aims. They were code-named Rutter and planned by Combined Operations HQ and GHQ Home Forces, with Lieutenant General Bernard Montgomery in charge.

The force was initially conceived as consisting entirely of British troops. However, the Canadians waiting in England were growing restless at seeing no action, putting pressure on the British military. Eventually it was decided that the trial invasion should be made by a largely Canadian force, the Second Canadian Division under Major General John Hamilton Roberts. It would be accompanied by British commando units and a token force of Americans and Free French, using the British Royal Force and Royal Navy.

The date for the invasion was set for July 7, 1942, but bad weather on that day forced postponement. Montgomery wanted cancellation, but after his transfer to North Africa, his replacement, Vice Admiral Louis Mountbatten, was persuaded to continue the plan, now code-named Jubilee and scheduled for August 19.

The invasion was launched from five English ports and was aimed at hitting seven different beaches surrounding Dieppe, with covering air and naval operations. From the start, the operation went wrong. The element of surprise was lost when the convoy encountered German sea patrols in the early morning of the invasion. To the east, the British No. 3 Commando managed to knock out the Goebbels battery; to the west, the No. 4 Commando successfully destroyed the Hess battery and took the beaches.

In the center, however, around the port itself, the Canadians were pinned down by unexpectedly heavy gunfire. Their tanks could not get off the shingle beach, and one of the British destroyers was sunk by enemy batteries. In the air, Royal Air Force losses were much higher than those sustained by the Luftwaffe in their vain attempt to lay a smoke screen.

Around 11:00 A.M. the assault was called off. Some Canadian units had managed to penetrate a few miles inland, but they were met by German reinforcements. Evacuation proved difficult with the loss of many landing craft and was not fully effected until about 2:00 P.M. Eventually, of the original 6,086 soldiers, 3,623 were lost, killed, or captured, with the Canadians constituting the majority. By contrast, total German casualties amounted to fewer than 600. All twenty-seven Allied tanks used in the operation were lost.

Impact   The immediate impact of the failed operation was to make Winston Churchill and the other British leaders aware of the strength of the German defenses, especially around port areas. It was also clear that much more planning was needed for such combined operations. Many other more detailed lessons were learned. When the D-day landings in Normandy were planned in 1944, the mistakes at Dieppe were fully rectified.

David Barratt

Further Reading

Neillands, Robin. *The Dieppe Raid: The Story of the Disastrous 1942 Expedition.* Bloomington: Indiana University Press, 2005.

Thompson, R. W. *Dieppe at Dawn: The Story of the Dieppe Raid.* London: Hutchinson, 1956.

See also   Bulge, Battle of the; Canadian participation in World War II; D Day; Prisoners of war, North American; World War II.

■ DiMaggio, Joe

Identification   American baseball player
Born   November 25, 1914; Martinez, California
Died   March 8, 1999; Hollywood, Florida

In 1941, DiMaggio set a major-league record by hitting safely in fifty-six consecutive games. During the 1940's, with DiMaggio as their center fielder, the New York Yankees won four American League pennants and three World Series.

Joe DiMaggio kissing his bat after setting the major league record for consecutive baseball games with base hits in 1941. (Library of Congress)

A California native, Joe DiMaggio broke into Major League Baseball with the New York Yankees in 1936 and quickly established himself as one of the American League's most feared hitters, leading his league in both home runs and runs batted in during his second season. In 1939 and 1940, DiMaggio recorded his league's highest batting average, but his most significant baseball achievement came during the 1941 season. In every game from May 15 through July 16 of that season, DiMaggio recorded at least one hit—a record fifty-six-consecutive-game hitting streak that has never been broken; no other major-league player has had a hitting streak that reached fifty games. DiMaggio finished the 1941 season with a .357 batting average, and he won the American League's most valuable player award. Besides being a gifted hitter, DiMaggio became an excellent center fielder. He was nicknamed the "Yankee Clipper" for the graceful way that he glided across center field.

Like more than three hundred other major-league players, DiMaggio served in the armed forces during World War II and missed three baseball seasons. Twenty-seven years old and married when the United States entered the war in 1941, DiMaggio was entitled to a deferment from the military draft, but he joined the Air Force Cadets after the 1942 baseball season. He was stationed in California and Hawaii and was never engaged in combat. After the war, DiMaggio lost some of his hitting skills. In 1946, his seasonal batting average dropped below .300 for the first time in his career, and his seasonal home run totals in 1946 and 1947 dropped below thirty. He also missed some games during those two seasons with an assortment of injuries. In 1948, however, DiMaggio, healthy again, bounced back with one of his best seasons; he led the American League with thirty-nine homers and 155 runs batted in.

One of DiMaggio's career highlights occurred in 1949. DiMaggio, recovering from off-season surgery for the removal of bone spurs on his heel, missed the early months of the season. He was finally ready to play in late June, and he suited up for a key series against the Boston Red Sox at Fenway Park that commenced on June 28. Although he had not played in a game since the previous October, DiMaggio hammered Red Sox pitching. In the three-game series, all Yankee victories, he belted four home runs and drove in nine runs. He remained healthy for the rest

DiMaggio's Major League Statistics

Season	GP	AB	Hits	2B	3B	HR	Runs	RBI	BA	SA
1936	138	637	206	44	15	29	132	125	.323	.576
1937	151	621	215	35	15	46	151	167	.346	.673
1938	145	599	194	32	13	32	129	140	.324	.581
1939	120	462	176	32	6	30	108	126	.381	.671
1940	132	508	179	28	9	31	93	133	.352	.626
1941	139	541	193	43	11	30	122	125	.357	.643
1942	154	610	186	29	13	21	123	114	.305	.498
1946	132	503	146	20	8	25	81	95	.290	.511
1947	141	534	168	31	10	20	97	97	.315	.522
1948	153	594	190	26	11	39	110	155	.320	.598
1949	76	272	94	14	6	14	58	67	.346	.596
1950	139	525	158	33	10	32	114	122	.301	.585
1951	116	415	109	22	4	12	72	71	.263	.422
Totals	1,736	6,821	2,214	389	131	361	1,390	1,537	.325	.579

Notes: GP = games played; AB = at bats; 2B = doubles; 3B = triples; HR = home runs; RBI = runs batted in; BA = batting average; SA = slugging average

of the 1949 season and helped the Yankees win the American League pennant and the World Series.

Impact   DiMaggio's fifty-six-game hitting streak during the 1941 season is considered one of the greatest feats in baseball history. During the 1940's, the New York Yankees won five American League pennants and four World Series. (One Yankee pennant and World Series victory came in 1943, when DiMaggio was serving in the Air Force.) DiMaggio retired after the 1951 season and was voted into the Baseball Hall of Fame in 1955.

James Tackach

Further Reading

Allen, Maury. *Where Have You Gone, Joe DiMaggio: The Story of America's Last Hero*. New York: E. P. Dutton, 1975.

Cramer, Richard Ben. *Joe DiMaggio: The Hero's Life*. New York: Simon & Schuster, 2000.

Creamer, Robert W. *Baseball in '41: A Celebration of the "Best Baseball Season Ever"—in the Year America Went to War*. New York: Viking Press, 1991.

See also   Baseball; Gehrig, Lou; Gray, Pete; Paige, Satchel; Robinson, Jackie; Sports in the United States; Williams, Ted; World War II mobilization.

■ Dim-out of 1945

The Event   Federally mandated national reduction in lighting from dusk to dawn

Date   January 15, 1945-May 8, 1945

Place   Throughout the United States

To spare domestic energy for use in warfare, in which fuel was a strategic commodity, the Office of War Mobilization and Reconversion imposed a mandatory program reducing commercial consumption across America.

Blackouts were instituted voluntarily immediately following the attack on Pearl Harbor, out of fear of incoming enemy aircraft, which could use lights to hone in on targets. The necessity for such precautions became evident after Allied ships, silhouetted against bright East Coast cities, proved easy pickings for German U-boats. From early 1942, seaward lights remained extinguished at night. Lights also could be used by aerial bombers. Blackouts and dim-outs continued periodically on both coasts throughout the war.

Unlike previous programs, the dim-out of 1945 affected cities across the United States. Stores closed by dusk, restaurants and nightclubs shut down at midnight, neon signs remained dark, and street lighting was cut back. The dim-out was perceived as part of the patriotic cause rather than as a safety measure: The American military needed fuel to make the final push toward victory, and the dim-out was a conservation measure.

Impact   Though an inconvenience to businesses, the dim-out—particularly for cities on both coasts—was an improvement upon blackouts, during which accidents were commonplace and crime flourished. The day of the declaration of the end of the war in Europe (V-E Day), the dim-out was lifted. It was something of a precedent for the fuel conservation efforts in response to the energy crisis of the 1970's, which involved presidential pleas to use less energy for home heating and plans whereby automobile owners could buy gasoline only every other day.

Jack Ewing

Further Reading

Hoopes, Roy. *Americans Remember the Home Front*. New York: Berkeley Trade, 2002.

Lotchin, Roger W. *The Bad City in the Good War: San Francisco, Los Angeles, Oakland, and San Diego*. Bloomington: Indiana University Press, 2003.

Wagner, Margaret E., Linda Barrett Osborne, and Susan Reyburn. *The Library of Congress World War II Companion*. New York: Simon & Schuster, 2007.

See also   Daylight saving time; Economic wartime regulations; Office of War Mobilization; Submarine warfare; Wartime rationing; Wartime sabotage.

■ Diners Club

Definition   First general-purpose credit card organization

Diners Club revolutionized the American economy and consumer culture by creating a means of effecting cash-free transactions and providing consumers with ready access to credit.

The use of credit cards began in the 1920's, when department stores and gasoline retailers began issuing cards to their customers. By the 1930's, some companies had begun accepting cards from other businesses on a limited basis, yet until the establishment of Diners Club in 1950, no system existed by which a single credit card could be used at multiple businesses.

The event that led to the founding of Diners Club reportedly occurred in 1949, when its founder, Frank X. McNamara, was unable to pay for his dinner at a New York restaurant because he had forgotten his wallet. He subsequently resolved to devise a system by which consumers could pay for goods and services without cash by presenting a charge card that would allow member merchants to secure reimbursement from a central source. By 1950, Mc-Namara and his partner, Ralph Schneider, had established Diners Club, enrolling the restaurant at which McNamara conceived the idea as one of its first member merchants and adding more than twenty thousand cardholders to its rolls in its first year of operation.

Impact   At first little more than a small network of charge accounts, Diners Club quickly evolved into a sophisticated system of credit that set a precedent for the development of the modern credit card industry. Other credit card companies, such as American Express, Bank Americard (later Visa), and MasterCharge (later MasterCard), would follow the example of Diners Club in the 1950's and 1960's.

Michael H. Burchett

Further Reading

Evans, David, and Richard Schmalensee. *Paying with Plastic: The Digital Revolution in Buying and Borrowing.* Cambridge, Mass.: MIT Press, 1999.

Mandell, Lewis. *Credit Card Industry: A History.* Boston: Twayne, 1990.

See also   Business and the economy in the United States; Credit and debt.

■ Disney films

Definition   Popular films, chiefly animated, produced by the Walt Disney Studios

Having already attained prominence during the 1920's and 1930's, filmmaker Walt Disney continued his ascent to iconic status as a popular film producer during the 1940's with the release of some of his best-known animated features, among them Pinocchio, Fantasia, *and* Bambi.

Entering the 1940's, Walt Disney was already well established in the field of film animation. His cartoon characters Mickey Mouse, Donald Duck, Goofy, and Pluto had become household names, and his first full-length animated feature *Snow White and the Seven Dwarfs* (1937) had been a major success, both critically and at the box office. He moved into the 1940's with several major projects nearing completion and a growing level of popular appeal.

Disney began the new decade with the release of two new animated features—*Pinocchio*, in February of 1940, and *Fantasia* at the end of the year. The first followed the pattern established in *Snow White* in utilizing a well-known children's story as the basis for its plot and inspiration. Although the film was well received by critics, it was by no means the popular or financial success that *Snow White* had been three years earlier. The outbreak of war in Europe in 1939 and the drop in overseas distribution and revenue that resulted from it undoubtedly were key factors. The critical response to *Fantasia* was more mixed. Its concept, combining classical music (performed by the Philadelphia Orchestra under the direction of Leopold Stokowski) with animation, while considered by some to be bold and innovative, was seen by others as pretentious. Both films, however, proved sufficiently popular with theater audiences to bolster Disney's reputation. The next two years saw the release of three more animated features: *The Reluctant Dragon* and *Dumbo* in 1941, and *Bambi* in 1942.

The Reluctant Dragon, released in June of 1941, was seen largely as a means for Disney to acquire the financial resources necessary to advance other, more ambitious projects. It also marked an early experiment in combining real-life characters with animation: Popular humorist Robert Benchley visited Disney's studio and interacted with various Disney cartoon characters. In October of 1941, the more ambitious *Dumbo* was released. Based on a popular contemporary children's book, it also was financially successful and set the scene for the more artistically serious *Bambi*, the following year.

Like *Pinocchio*, *Bambi* was based on a well-known children's classic—a 1923 novel by Austrian writer Felix Salten. Work on it had been under way since before the release of *Snow White*. Part of the difficulty in bringing the film to completion was its more serious, realistic tone. Although the film marked an aesthetic advance for Disney, it proved to be out of sync with the times. Despite highly engaging characters

Walt Disney (left) studying cartoon storyboard sketches for the 1946 film Song of the South *with singer/songwriter Johnny Mercer.* (Getty Images)

such as Thumper the rabbit and Flower the skunk, the film failed to provide the escapism that film audiences desired during the war, and the work was neither well received critically nor a great success at the box office.

Bambi was followed by Disney's final full-length features of the war years—*Saludos Amigos* in 1942 and *The Three Caballeros*, which premiered in Rio de Janeiro on August 24, 1942, and was released in the United States on February 6, 1943. Both films were the outgrowth of a goodwill trip to South America made by Disney and several of his staff members under the auspices of the Office of the Coordinator of Inter-American Affairs in the summer of 1941. The works made use of a combination of animation and live action to create lively celebrations of Latin American life and were popular with both U.S. and Latin American audiences, while also serving to bring in much-needed revenue in the aftermath of *Bambi*'s lackluster financial performance.

Supporting the War Effort In addition to his full-length animated features produced during the wartime period, Disney also produced a number of films to support the war effort. The most ambitious of these was *Victory Through Air Power*, released to theater audiences in July of 1943. The film highlighted the ideas of Russian-born military figure Alexander de Seversky on the importance of air power in winning the war. It combined animation with footage of Seversky himself explaining his theories. The studio also produced a number of military training films as

Disney Films of the 1940's

- *Pinocchio* (1940)
- *Fantasia* (1940)
- *The Reluctant Dragon* (1941)
- *Dumbo* (1941)
- *Bambi* (1942)
- *Saludos Amigos* (1942)
- *The Three Caballeros* (1944)
- *Song of the South* (1946)
- *Make Mine Music* (1946)
- *Fun and Fancy Free* (1947)
- *Melody Time* (1948)
- *So Dear to My Heart* (1949)
- *The Adventures of Ichabod and Mr. Toad* (1949)

well as numerous wartime propaganda shorts, such as *Donald in Nutzi Land,* in which Donald Duck mocks Nazi leader Adolf Hitler.

After the war ended, Disney continued to produce a steady stream of full-length animated features. Many of them, however, were collections of shorter cartoons, such as *Melody Time* in 1948, which included the famous cartoon depictions of Johnny Appleseed and Pecos Bill. Perhaps the best-known and most ambitious (and also the most controversial) of the full-length features during this period was *Song of the South* in 1946. Drawing its inspiration from the "Uncle Remus" stories of nineteenth century southern writer Joel Chandler Harris, it combined live action and animation, and it starred black actor James Baskett in the role of Uncle Remus. Baskett won a special Academy Award for the film, which contained the highly popular and catchy tune "Zip-a-Dee-Doo-Dah." The work's positive depiction of slavery provoked protests by both film critics and civil rights groups during the early postwar period.

Although Disney's films of the 1940's focused on animation and mixtures of animation with live action, the company did produce a few non-animated films during the decade. *Seal Island* (1948), for ex-

ample, is a documentary made from film shot by Alfred and Elma Milotte, showing the seals of the Pribilof Islands of Alaska. It was the first of the True-Life Adventures series of nature documentaries.

Impact The 1940's saw Walt Disney adding significantly to his reputation as a leading figure in the field of film animation. Disney released several of his best-known and most ambitious works, and utilized his craft in the service of the United States during the war. The decade also saw Disney engendering controversy, particularly in the area of postwar race relations. His work during the 1940's laid the foundation for expansion of his company into a media and entertainment empire.

Scott Wright

Further Reading

Finch, Christopher. *The Art of Walt Disney: From Mickey Mouse to the Magic Kingdom.* New York: Harry N. Abrams, 1975. A richly illustrated study of the Disney Studios' artistic development.

Gabler, Neal. *Walt Disney: The Triumph of the American Imagination.* New York: Alfred A. Knopf, 2006. Probably the definitive Disney biography.

Schickel, Richard. *The Disney Version: The Life, Times, Art and Commerce of Walt Disney.* 3d ed. Chicago: Elephant Paperbacks, 1997. Originally published in 1968. Still stands as one of the best of the negative critiques of Disney and his work.

Thomas, Bob. *Walt Disney: An American Original.* New York: Hyperion Books, 1994. Originally published in 1972, this is a solidly written early biography.

Watts, Steven. *The Magic Kingdom: Walt Disney and the American Way of Life.* Columbia: University of Missouri Press, 1997. An excellent, balanced study of Disney and his place in American culture.

See also Academy Awards; Andy Hardy films; Animated films; Cowboy films; *Fantasia*; Film in the United States; Film serials; Latin America; *Miracle on 34th Street*; Wartime propaganda in the United States.

■ DNA discovery

The Event   Three molecular biologists demonstrated that the genetic transformation of bacteria is caused by deoxyribonucleic acid (DNA), providing direct evidence about the chemical nature of hereditary information. Their discovery, doubted at first, eventually led geneticists to understand that DNA carried life's genetic blueprints.

Until the Avery-MacLeod-McCarty experiment demonstrated that DNA is the hereditary chemical of life, most biologists believed that the substance responsible for heredity was protein because of its extensive diversity and variability. The Avery-MacLeod-McCarty discovery revolutionized the study of the biological sciences by focusing the study of living systems on molecular mechanisms and by changing the focus of the chemical nature of heredity from proteins to DNA.

Pneumococcus bacteria are categorized into various types (I, II, III, IV) based on the antigenic properties of their polysaccharide capsules. Under certain conditions, virulent, polysaccharide-encapsulated pneumococcus bacteria can grow into nonvirulent, unencapsulated bacteria. Colonies of encapsulated bacteria have a smooth surface (designated as *S*), while colonies of unencapsulated bacteria have a rough (*R*) surface. In 1928, geneticist Frederick Griffith discovered that although *R* bacteria are usually nonvirulent in mice, injection of *R* often caused death. Upon autopsy, *S* bacteria could be recovered. Griffith later demonstrated that heat-killed *S* bacteria could "transform" live *R* into live *S* bacteria.

Oswald Avery, a bacteriologist-immunologist at the Rockefeller Institute for Medical Research (now Rockefeller University), became interested in Griffith's results, which were confirmed by Henry Dawson in Avery's laboratory; later, at Columbia University, he and Richard Sia demonstrated transformation in vitro. In Avery's laboratory in the early 1930's, Lionel Alloway demonstrated transformation in vitro using cell-free bacterial extracts. Alloway introduced the use of ethanol to precipitate the active transforming principle from cell-free extracts.

Geneticist Colin MacLeod came to Avery's laboratory in 1934 and transformed type II *R* to type III *S* in vitro using the Alloway procedure. MacLeod used chloroform to precipitate and remove protein from the transformation preparation. By 1937, MacLeod had partially purified the transforming chemical and found that it was inactivated by ultraviolet (UV) light, the first indication that the transforming principle might be a nucleic acid. By 1941, MacLeod and Avery had refined the isolation and purification protocol by heat-killing the pneumococcus before using it to prepare a cell-free extract and by using ribonuclease to eliminate ribonucleic acid (RNA).

In 1941, geneticist Maclyn McCarty extended MacLeod's experiments by using an enzyme to digest the type III polysaccharide to remove it from the preparation. By early 1942, upon addition of alcohol to the preparation, a stringy, fibrous material precipitated. McCarty showed that all enzymes that degraded DNA destroyed the transforming principle, but inactivating these enzymes by heat eliminated their ability to destroy the transforming principle. By this time, the laboratory was convinced that the transforming and hereditary chemical was DNA. The manuscript describing the experiments and conclusions was published on February 1, 1944.

Impact   The Avery-MacLeod-McCarty experiment demonstrated that heredity could be explained in terms of chemistry. Many biologists, chemists, and physicists were inspired by the findings of the experiment and turned their attention to studying the molecular nature of living systems. Their work eventu-

---

"The Dream of Geneticists"

In a May 26, 1943, letter to his brother (also a bacteriologist), Oswald T. Avery revealed his own excitement and surprise at his discovery of the chemical nature of hereditary information:

But at last perhaps we have it . . . In short, this substance is highly reactive and on elementary analysis conforms very closely to the theoretical values of pure desoxyribose nucleic acid (thymus type). Who could have guessed it? . . . If we are right, and of course that's not yet proven, then . . . by means of a known chemical substance it is possible to induce predictable and hereditary changes in cells. This is something that has long been the dream of geneticists.

ally led to the discovery of the structure of DNA and the mechanism by which it encodes the structure of polypeptides. The year 1944 is often cited as the birth of molecular biology.

Charles L. Vigue

Further Reading

Avery, Oswald T., Colin M. MacLeod, and Maclyn McCarty. "Studies on the Chemical Nature of the Substance Inducing Transformation of Pneumococcal Types: Induction of Transformation by a Desoxyribonucleic Acid Fraction Isolated from Pneumococcus Type III." *Journal of Experimental Medicine* 79, no. 2 (February, 1944): 137-158.

McCarty, Maclyn. *The Transforming Principle: Discovering That Genes Are Made of DNA.* New York: W. W. Norton, 1985.

Tudge, Colin. *In Mendel's Footnotes: An Introduction to the Science and Technologies of Genes and Genetics from the Nineteenth Century to the Twenty-Second.* London: Jonathan Cape, 2000.

Watson, James D. *A Passion for DNA: Genes, Genomes, and Society.* Cold Spring Harbor, N.Y.: Cold Spring Harbor Laboratory Press, 2000.

See also Cancer; DNA discovery; Health care; Medicine; Science and technology.

■ Doolittle bombing raid

The Event First U.S. bombing attack on mainland Japan during World War II
Date April 18, 1942
Places Tokyo, Yokohama, Kobe, and Nagoya, Japan

Although the surprise attack resulted in little real damage, the Japanese were made to feel vulnerable, and the successful mission gave a much-needed morale boost to the Americans.

After their attack on Pearl Harbor on December 7, 1941, the Japanese made a series of other successful depredations in the Pacific and began to seem invincible to a dispirited American public. President Franklin D. Roosevelt, seeking a dramatic American victory to boost morale, called upon his military ad-

visers to plan an air raid on Tokyo. Colonel Jimmy Doolittle was chosen to lead the mission because he was a daring and experienced pilot. The volunteer force was assembled and trained in Florida.

The bombers to be used were B-25s, heavy twin-engine craft never intended for takeoffs from aircraft carriers. Nevertheless, the attack force of sixteen planes could fit on the flight deck of the USS *Hornet.* The planes were stripped of all unnecessary weight and loaded with extra fuel supplies. In order for the overloaded planes to take off, the carrier had to steam at full speed into a strong wind. It was not possible to land the large planes on the carrier after the raid, so the raiders would need to land in China.

On April 13, the *Hornet* met with other members of a task force in midocean: the USS *Enterprise,* commanded by Vice Admiral William F. Halsey, and four

Brigadier General Jimmy Doolittle after returning from Japan and receiving the Congressional Medal of Honor in May, 1942. He stands next to a new recruiting poster designed to capitalize on the success of the Tokyo bombing raid. (AP/Wide World Photos)

cruisers and eight destroyers. On April 18, these ships were about 650 miles from Tokyo when they encountered enemy trawlers, thus losing the element of surprise. The sixteen bombers took off that morning 150 miles short of their planned takeoff point. After four hours of flying at low altitude, the raiders reached Japan and bombed targets in Tokyo, Yokohama, Kobe, and Nagoya with a combination of high-explosive and incendiary bombs. After the raids, the planes tried to reach landing fields in China, with various degrees of success. Some landed in the sea; one landed in the Soviet Union. Doolittle himself found his way to Chungking with his crew and was repatriated to the United States.

Impact The raid did some damage to Japanese factories and ships but ultimately had mainly symbolic value. Doolittle became a hero and was promoted to lieutenant general. The American public was energized and soon began to enthusiastically support the war effort.

Embarrassed by the attack, the Japanese military diverted vital aircraft to protect the homeland from further assaults. Military leaders changed their war strategy, emphasizing their desire to destroy the American fleet. Part of their strategy was to attack Midway Island, which they did in June, 1942, resulting in a decisive American victory. This battle is often cited as the turning point of the war in the Pacific. After the Doolittle raid, Japanese troops searching for the bomber crewman murdered some 250,000 Chinese in revenge for helping the Americans.

John R. Phillips

Further Reading

Chun, Clayton K. S. *The Doolittle Raid, 1942: America's First Strike Back at Japan.* Illustrated by Howard Gerrard. New York: Osprey, 2006.

Doolittle, James H., with Carroll V. Glines. *I Could Never Be So Lucky Again.* New York: Bantam Books, 1991.

Nelson, Craig. *The First Heroes: The Extraordinary Story of the Doolittle Raid—America's First World War II Victory.* New York: Viking Press, 2002.

See also Air Force, U.S.; Aircraft carriers; Arnold, Henry "Hap"; Bombers; *Enola Gay*; Halsey, William F. "Bull"; Pearl Harbor attack; Strategic bombing.

■ Dorsey, Tommy

Identification American bandleader and trombonist

Born November 19, 1905; Shenandoah, Pensylvania

Died November 26, 1956; Greenwich, Connecticut

During the war years, Dorsey led what was arguably the most popular big band in America, making hundreds of impeccable recordings and presenting a well-tailored persona that contrasted with the boozy image Americans had of jazz musicians.

Tommy Dorsey was raised, with his clarinetist elder brother Jimmy, by his musician father. During the 1920's, the Dorsey brothers worked in various bands, leading their own group later that decade. The 1930's were fertile times, though a public feud between the brothers culminated in Tommy Dorsey forming his own band. In the course of the late 1930's, Dorsey's big band became legendary for its

Trombonist/bandleader Tommy Dorsey played himself in the 1941 film Las Vegas Nights. *(Redferns/Getty Images)*

ability to take newly written songs of uncertain value and produce brilliant, polished three-minute recordings. In 1940, Dorsey hired a young Frank Sinatra, and the pair became one of the most popular musical acts in America.

The 1940's were the years that Dorsey reached the height of popularity in American popular music. Dorsey, with Sinatra, made frankly commercial recordings, including the seventeen number one hits Dorsey compiled with his big band. "I'm Getting Sentimental Over You" had become his theme piece, and his performance on the recording displays an elegance and power unmatched by other trombonists. By the early 1950's, he had reconciled with brother Jimmy, and the two led a band until their deaths about a year apart.

Impact Dorsey's band was one of the most popular groups of the swing era, and he became the paradigmatic professional musician of the 1940's. Sinatra later credited Dorsey with influencing his singing style.

Jeffrey Daniel Jones

Further Reading

Levinson, Peter J. *Tommy Dorsey: Livin' in a Great Big Way—A Biography.* Cambridge, Mass.: Da Capo Press, 2005.

Stockdale, Robert L. *Tommy Dorsey: On the Side.* Metuchen, N.J.: Scarecrow Press, 1995.

See also Davis, Miles; Ellington, Duke; Goodman, Benny; Miller, Glenn; Music: Jazz; Music: Popular; Parker, Charlie; Recording industry; Sinatra, Frank.

■ *Double Indemnity*

Identification Film noir about murder and deception by a boorish insurance agent and the manipulative and seductive wife of a client

Director Billy Wilder (1906-2002)

Date Released on September 6, 1944

Though the term "film noir" would not be introduced until 1946, Double Indemnity *represents one of the earliest, and many say one of the best, examples of the cinematic style. Its techniques of characterization, narration, and lighting were widely imitated and became conventions of film noir.*

The difficulties of the Great Depression and World War II created an appetite for films with dark themes, so director Billy Wilder turned to James M. Cain's hard-boiled crime story *Three of a Kind* (1935) for his film *Double Indemnity.* To help write the screenplay, Wilder recruited Raymond Chandler, a novelist whose name became synonymous with hard-boiled crime fiction. Their simplified story line and Chandler's edgy dialogue gave the movie a moral ambiguity that became a trademark of film noir.

To accentuate the ambiguity, Wilder cast his leads against type: Fred MacMurray and Barbara Stanwyck, known for sympathetic and likeable characters, as seductive and deceitful murderers, and Edward G. Robinson, famous for portraying gangsters, as the film's moral center. Stanwyck's character seduces MacMurray's into killing her husband, but as their cover story falls apart, they turn against, and eventually kill, each other.

Impact *Double Indemnity* was nominated for seven Academy Awards, and though it won none, its erotic and brutal story line pushed the boundaries of the Motion Picture Production Code and paved the way for subsequent hard-boiled crime movies. The film's commercial success led Hollywood back to Cain's novels for two more successful pictures—*Mildred Pierce* (1945) and *The Postman Always Rings Twice* (1946)—and its critical success led film noir to be considered worthy of A-list actors and directors. Many such movies from the 1940's are among Hollywood's most revered films.

Devon Boan

Further Reading

Cain, James M. *Double Indemnity.* New York: Vintage Books, 1992.

Schickel, Richard. *Double Indemnity.* London: British Film Institute, 1992.

See also Chandler, Raymond; Crimes and scandals; Film in the United States; Film noir; *The Maltese Falcon; The Philadelphia Story;* Pulp magazines.

■ *Duncan v. Kahanamoku*

The Case   U.S. Supreme Court ruling on the power of military tribunals to try civilians

Date   Decided on February 25, 1946

The Supreme Court held that military tribunals did not have jurisdiction over civilians, even under martial law, if Congress had not given such authority.

After the Japanese attack on Pearl Harbor on December 7, 1941, the territorial governor of Hawaii, Joseph B. Poindexter, suspended the right of habeas corpus, placed Hawaii under martial law, and relinquished governmental authority to U.S. Army general Walter C. Short. He acted pursuant to the Hawaiian Organic Act of 1900, enacted by Congress to govern Hawaii during its territorial status. Short closed the civilian courts and instituted military tribunals to try all offenses against federal or territorial laws, or violations of orders from the military government. This regime would remain in effect until October of 1944.

Duncan was convicted before a military tribunal for public intoxication. In a majority opinion written by Justice Hugo L. Black, the Supreme Court held that such military tribunals were invalid because the Hawaii Organic Act of 1900 did not empower the territorial governor to transfer judicial authority to the military, even as it authorized martial law. The opinion rested solely on statutory grounds, avoiding constitutional issues of commander in chief powers of the president during war. Justices Harold H. Burton and Felix Frankfurter dissented.

Impact   The case was a significant break with the wartime cases of *Hirabayashi v. United States* (1943) and *Korematsu v. United States* (1944), as it reaffirmed the principle of civilian supremacy over the military, even during war. It also presaged controversies over military tribunals that would arise in the aftermath of the terrorist attacks on the World Trade Center and the Pentagon building in 2001.

John C. Hughes

Further Reading

Fisher, Louis. *Military Tribunals and Presidential Power: American Revolution to the War on Terrorism.* Lawrence: University Press of Kansas, 2005.

Hall, Kermit L. *The Oxford Companion to the Supreme Court.* New York: Oxford University Press, 1992.

See also   Civil rights and liberties; Pearl Harbor attack; Supreme Court, U.S.; World War II.

■ **Duplessis, Maurice Le Noblet**

Identification   Premier of Quebec, 1936-1939, 1944-1959

Born   April 20, 1890; Trois-Rivières, Quebec

Died   September 7, 1959; Schefferville, Quebec

Duplessis founded Quebec's influential Union Nationale political party and was the province's premier during the years when the environment of twentieth century Quebec politics changed irrevocably.

The rise of Maurice Duplessis to political prominence was rapid, and his stay at the center of Quebec politics was long; it lasted until his death while he served as Quebec's premier. He remains the only premier of Quebec to have won more than three consecutive majorities in the Quebec parliament. During his years in office, he tried simultaneously, and ultimately counterproductively, to develop his province's economy while preserving the rural and conservative nature of its political culture. In the end, the policies he chose tainted his personal reputation even as they gave birth to modern Québécois nationalism.

Duplessis's Politics and Policies   Born into public life as the son of a local politician and trained as a lawyer, Duplessis first won a seat in Quebec's provincial parliament as a candidate of the Conservative Party of Quebec in 1927. Five years later, amid turmoil in that party following its losses in the 1931 provincial election, he emerged as his party's leader. Three years after that, he fused together a coalition of his Conservative Party followers and dissident elements of other parties to create his own party, Union Nationale. In August of that same year, exploiting a corruption scandal inside the ruling Canadian Liberal Party, he led his new party to a landslide majority in the Quebec legislature that ended thirty-nine years of Liberal rule of the province and made Duplessis Quebec's premier.

At the time of Duplessis's rise to power, French-speaking Canada was struggling to keep its culture alive in a country in which 70 percent of the citizens spoke English and whose official (albeit ceremonial) head of state remained the British monarch. Those in Quebec committed to the province retaining its separate identity defined its Frenchness largely in terms of its native rural character and its strong commitment to Catholicism and the strong role of the Catholic clergy in the lives of its citizens. As a nationalist, Duplessis quickly allied his party with the interests of that clergy, and he retained that close alliance throughout most of his career. In return, he normally received the valuable endorsement of the church's officials in his political campaigns.

Duplessis was not, however, above making political miscalculations, and his one loss—in the 1939 elections—resulted from calling a snap election when England was at war with Germany, in order to exploit local resentment against the conscription of Quebecers to fight in the "English war." To his surprise, Quebec's voters generally rallied around the flag of Canada, complete with its miniature Union

Maurice Le Noblet Duplessis in 1937. (Getty Images)

Jack, and it was not until 1944 that Duplessis was returned to the premier's office, which he would hold for the remaining fifteen years of his life.

Promoting Quebec   Throughout his years in office, Duplessis continued to push a nationalist agenda vis-à-vis Quebec's autonomy from the rule of the federal government in Ottawa. In 1949, he successfully pushed for adoption as Quebec's flag the French fleur-de-lis pattern. Overall, his tenure can be characterized as conservative and antiprogressive rather than nationalistic. Union organizers and others who might have drawn Quebec's citizens into more liberal directions, for example, were frequently harassed, and provincial police often brutally broke up workers' strikes.

Corruption also crept gradually into Duplessis's administration, robbing him of the reformer image he had initially cultivated as he rose to power by attacking the corruption in the Liberal Party. Most damaging to his legacy is that his electoral successes often were built on a noticeable degree of election fraud. Although he succeeded in fostering substantial economic growth in Quebec during his years in office, Quebec's own citizens were not its primary beneficiaries. Rather, to avoid exposing French-speaking Quebecers to the liberalizing experiences of urban life, Duplessis encouraged English-speaking owners of capital to invest in Quebec and English-speaking workers to migrate to the new jobs being created in Montreal and elsewhere in the province.

Impact   Shortly after Duplessis's death, Quebec underwent its "Quiet Revolution," during which its political culture shifted in a predominantly secular and liberal as well as nationalist direction, as did its policies under the reinvigorated Liberal Party that took office in 1960. Consequently, Duplessis's long tenure was later often treated by French-Canadian historians as "the Great Blackness" (*la Grande Noirceur*). Duplessis's efforts to expand Quebec's economy, however, had much to do with ushering in these changes. French-speaking Quebecers, along with English-speakers, were drawn to the cities by the promise of better pay. Once there, however, they discovered their province's resources to be "foreign" (that is, English-owned) and their pay to be less than that earned by the workers imported from English-speaking Canada. The result was a nationalist reaction against both Quebec's rule by English-speaking

Canada and the conservative forces within Quebec with whom Duplessis was long allied.

Joseph R. Rudolph, Jr.

Further Reading

Black, Conrad. *Render unto Caesar: The Life and Legacy of Maurice Duplessis.* Toronto: Key Porter Books, 1998. A shortened, widely available edition of perhaps the best of the biographies on Duplessis.

Dyck, Rand. *Canadian Politics.* 4th ed. Scarborough, Ont.: Nelson Education, 2008. A standard book on the topic. Places Duplessis's Quebec into the broader context of the evolving patterns of Canadian politics in general and French Canada in particular.

Gauvreau, Michael. *The Catholic Origins of Quebec's Quiet Revolution, 1931-1959.* Montreal: McGill-Queen's University Press, 2008. An excellent treatment of the political awakening of once-conservative, Catholic French-speaking Quebec during the years of Duplessis's premierships.

Paulin, Marguerite, with Nora Alleyn, trans. *Maurice Duplessis: Powerbroker, Politician.* Staten Island, N.Y.: XYZ Publishing, 2005. A good translation of a solid study of Duplessis by an experienced biographer of Quebec political leaders, whose other work includes a popular biography of the founder of the Quebec nationalist party, Rene Levesque.

Roberts, Leslie. *The Chief: A Political Biography of Maurice Duplessis.* Toronto: Clarke, Irwin, 1963. One of the first biographies on Duplessis to appear after his death. Roberts's work stands the test of time in ably covering the man and his impact on Quebec politics.

See also Business and the economy in Canada; Canadian minority communities; Canadian nationalism; Canadian regionalism; Demographics of Canada; Elections in Canada; Foreign policy of Canada; Military conscription in Canada; Quebec nationalism; Religion in Canada; Urbanization in Canada.

E

■ Economic wartime regulations

Definition Regulations including rationing, various price controls, tax increases, and formal economic planning

The outbreak of war brought new stresses to an economy still not recovered from the Great Depression, prompting extensive federal regulation of economic matters, including rationing, wage and price controls, and other forms of government intervention. The controls provided lessons in economic policy, and some aspects of the controls persisted after the end of World War II.

When the United States entered World War II on December 8, 1941, the American economy had not yet recovered from the Great Depression. The demands of a war economy quickly changed the problems facing U.S. economic policy makers from coping with unemployment and insufficient demand to a tight labor market and inflationary pressures. For example, almost 10 percent of the labor force was still unemployed in 1941 on the eve of U.S. entry into World War II, but by 1943 unemployment was below 2 percent. At the same time, output soared. Aircraft production more than quadrupled between 1941 and 1943, shipbuilding increased more than fivefold, aluminum production tripled, and munitions manufacturing increased ninefold.

To address the economic problems this transformation posed, the federal government resorted to economic regulatory measures that were unprecedented even by the standards of the New Deal. These succeeded in holding inflation to the low single digits during the war, a considerable achievement given the double-digit inflation during World War I and immediately before World War II. At the same time, the economy was mobilized to produce sufficient war material to carry on a two-front war. The government undertook three main types of regulation: wage and price controls to restrain inflation, taxation to acquire revenue and to restrain inflation, and

economic planning to ensure that both civilian and military needs were met.

Wage and Price Controls World War II brought the most extensive set of wage and price controls the United States economy had ever experienced. Fearing inflation that might result from pressures to increase production, federal economic planners moved quickly to limit increases in both wages and prices. Congress passed the Emergency Price Control Act barely two months after the United States entered the war, and the newly created Office of Price Administration quickly issued sweeping regulations covering the prices of many consumer goods and war materials, limiting rent increases in areas around war plants, and limiting wage increases. Prices generally were held to their levels of March, 1942. Wages were allowed to rise by approximately 15 percent to cover equivalent increases in the cost of living,

The wartime controls are largely viewed as a success today, although some scholars are critical of their postwar impact, arguing that the extension of government controls deep into the economy led to postwar economic regulation that was unnecessary in the absence of wartime emergencies. Restrictions such as rationing constrained economic choices and led to hardships, and shortages even of rationed goods burdened consumers with queuing in long lines hoping to receive scarce commodities. Community boards' ability to increase individual rations sometimes led to charges of corruption and favoritism in allocations.

Perhaps the most significant failing of the wartime economic regulations was their inability to prevent a widespread black market from appearing. With price increases forbidden in legal markets and demand outstripping supply for goods from tobacco to gasoline, it is not surprising that Americans turned to unofficial markets to satisfy their needs.

Taxation Fighting on two fronts was expensive, and federal tax revenue soared during the war from 8

percent of gross domestic product (GDP) in 1941 to 20 percent in 1945. The most significant tax policy was the expansion of federal income taxation. Prior to World War II, the federal income tax was relatively small, affecting only four million taxpayers in 1939 and yielding under $8 billion. By 1945, forty-three million Americans were paying federal income tax, and the government took in more than $45 billion. Marginal tax rates for those earning $500 per year were 23 percent, and those earning more than $1 million paid a marginal rate of 94 percent.

The government worried that taxpayers would be unable to meet their tax liabilities and so instituted income tax withholding, both to ensure that wage earners could pay their tax bills when they filed their tax returns and to dampen inflationary pressures by reducing the amount of money wage earners had to spend. Ironically, a young Milton Friedman—later an outspoken advocate of free markets and limited government intervention in the economy—was one of the architects of the withholding scheme, something for which he later reported that his wife never forgave him.

Economic Planning Coordinating military and civilian needs, while bringing millions into the military and out of the civilian labor force, required considerable planning. The federal government established a wide range of agencies and boards to coordinate economic activity. For example, the War Production Board allocated steel, aluminum, and copper to industrial users; the War Manpower Commission controlled civilian labor markets and the flow of draftees into the military; the War Food Administration handled food supplies; and the Office of War Mobilization coordinated the other agencies. Building on the legacy of New Deal economic planning, these agencies extended government influence deep within previously private economic decision making.

Overall, the planning effort was successful in balancing civilian and military needs and allocating scarce resources between war industries and civilian needs. To accomplish this, wartime economic regulators used both price controls and quantity restrictions, primarily through rationing. Civilians were required to show ration coupons, issued by the government according to formulas reflecting relative need, for both goods critical to the war effort (such as gasoline) and luxury items (such as chocolate)

Late 1942 government poster encouraging Americans to economize on fuel by carpooling. (Getty Images)

whose production the government sought to restrict in an effort to shift inputs into more critical goods.

Postwar Developments Once the war was over, the government faced the problem of how to dismantle wartime controls without causing a sudden inflation in prices and wages, caused by pent-up demand for goods and services not available during the war. More than fifty leading economists, including free market advocates such as Henry Simons and Frank Knight, issued an open letter to Congress asking for the continuation of controls for a year after the war's end to give time for production to shift to meet peacetime demand for consumer goods. Inflation soared when controls were lifted, hitting an annual rate of 28 percent in the six months after June, 1946.

Impact All three major forms of economic controls used during World War II—wage and price controls, tax policy, and direct economic planning—contributed to the American war effort by preventing damaging inflation at home and by coordinating war and civilian production during the conflict. Although it is impossible to know how the American war effort would have succeeded without these measures, the consensus among historians and economists is that they largely succeeded in promoting mobilization of the economy to fight a truly global war on two fronts. Furthermore, all three played a major role in transforming American society, with much greater government intervention in economic matters, many more Americans paying federal income tax, and a larger degree of national economic planning at the end of the 1940's than at the start.

Perhaps the most long-lasting impact of wartime economic regulations was the creation of federal boards and agencies devoted to economic planning. For example, wartime cooperation between the petroleum industry and the government led to the postwar creation of the National Petroleum Council as a successor to the Petroleum Industry War Council that had coordinated oil industry efforts during the war. As industries organized to participate in such efforts, their associations and councils served as natural vehicles for lobbying the government for regulations they favored and for special consideration.

Andrew P. Morriss

Further Reading

Engerman, Stanley L., and Robert E. Gallman, eds. *The Twentieth Century*. Vol. 3 in *The Cambridge Economic History of the United States*. New York: Cambridge University Press, 2000. Includes a definitive survey of wartime economic measures.

Harrison, Mark, ed. *The Economics of World War II: Six Great Powers in International Comparison*. New York: Cambridge University Press, 2000. A somewhat technical, comparative look at how the great powers handled wartime economic issues.

Higgs, Robert. *Crisis and Leviathan: Critical Episodes in the Growth of American Government*. New York: Oxford University Press, 1987. A critical look at the growth of government through regulatory expansion during crises such as World War II.

Hixson, Walter L. *The American Experience in World War II*. New York: Taylor and Francis, 2003. A comprehensive social history of the war, with discussion of economic events.

Milward, Alan S. *War, Economy and Society, 1939-1945*. Berkeley: University of California Press, 1980. A comprehensive, accessible one-volume review of the economics of World War II, including how economic regulation affected the U.S. economy.

Rockoff, Hugh. *Drastic Measures: A History of Wage and Price Controls in the United States*. New York: Cambridge University Press, 1984. The definitive history of efforts to control prices, including extensive discussion of World War II efforts.

———. "Price and Wage Controls in Four Wartime Periods." *Journal of Economic History* 41, no. 2 (1981): 381-401. A concise survey of efforts to control inflation through economic regulations.

See also Business and the economy in the United States; Credit and debt; Income and wages; Keynesian economics; Labor strikes; New Deal programs; Presidential powers; Wartime rationing; Wartime seizures of businesses.

■ Education in Canada

World War II prompted Canadians to examine their society and its institutions, with education proving no exception. The war exposed the need for all Canadians to be literate and sufficiently educated to perform war-related responsibilities.

Historically, Canadians have considered education the responsibility of the provinces rather than the federal government. Provincial governments therefore controlled and supported most elementary, secondary, and postsecondary schools. World War II, however, increased the national government's role in education.

Other changes in Canadian education in the 1940's included consolidation of school districts in some provinces, commencement of educational broadcasting, withdrawal from progressivism, and integration of Native Canadian education into provincial education.

World War II   During the war, previous opposition to federal involvement in education lost momentum as wartime needs predominated. The federal government actively increased its jurisdiction over higher education to maximize the war effort. The national government guided universities on how to best use their resources of expertise and people to assist in the war. In 1939, the government counseled all male students of military age to remain in school or university until the nation's war effort was sufficiently coordinated, so that they could be employed to the best advantage. The next year, some groups of students of military age were deemed eligible for conscription. Others were at liberty to continue in college as long as they agreed to enroll in college military training units.

The federal government also influenced university academic programs during the war. To increase the numbers of scientists and engineers being produced by universities, in 1942 the federal government launched a student loan program for qualified young males who would not have otherwise been able to obtain a college education. The government influenced medical programs as well. To ensure an adequate number of doctors for the military, the ceiling on admission to medical programs was raised, and the curriculum was accelerated from six years to between four and five years.

Students' courses of study were affected by their apprehension about being drafted into the army. As the armed forces' requirements for manpower mounted rapidly in 1943 and 1944, with the opening of the Italian and African fronts and in preparation for the Normandy invasion, the programs of study of male students were assessed. Those in courses of study such as chemistry, physics, mathematics, and biology, which were considered indispensable to the execution of the war or the national interest, continued to be exempt from being called into active mili-

tary service until they had completed their degrees. Male students enrolled in arts courses such as fine arts, philosophy, history, language, and literature, however, would delay being conscripted into military service only if they ranked in the top half of their class. Proposals to severely contract arts studies were debated. The emphasis during the war on scientific and highly technical disciplines threatened to supplant the study of the liberal arts.

Throughout World War II, university enrollment remained steady. The decline in the number of men attending college due to their enlistment in the armed forces was offset by the increase in the numbers of women attending.

Primary and Secondary Schools   Primary and secondary schools were also employed to support the war effort. The classroom was used as a vehicle for teaching students about patriotism, democracy, citizenship, and other wartime matters. Numerous activities were encouraged both to promote an awareness of national responsibility and to assist in the war effort. Schools also had regular gas mask drills.

Secondary schools tailored their curricula and extracurricular activities to prepare high school students for war industries, the military, and community life. Educators stressed academic subjects according to their immediate wartime usefulness; therefore, mathematics, language training, science, and health gained a new emphasis in the high school curriculum. To address the rise in wartime juvenile delinquency, more time was allotted for religious education in the schools.

School sport and recreational activities were hampered by devotion to the war effort. Government officials, however, believed that physical training was an essential component of the war movement. This led the federal government in 1943 to pass the National Physical Fitness Act to promote physical fitness in schools and universities. As a result, physical fitness education was augmented.

Attendance at primary and secondary schools dropped during the war. The compulsory education laws produced few results before the mid-1940's. Children often were absent from school because they were needed to help on the farm or to bring in additional wages. Some teenagers opted to earn wartime wages rather than to attend school.

The Teaching Profession   One of the most significant problems arising from the war was the grave shortage of teaching staff. Some teachers' services were needed in other areas of the war effort; other teachers found higher paying jobs in industry. A number of schools were unable to open for lack of teachers. To offset this, the provinces reduced their already low standards for elementary teaching.

There were some significant positive developments in the teaching profession during the war. Financial enticements were offered to attract people into the teaching profession. With the shortage of teachers, salaries increased and better pension schemes were developed.

Progressive education emphasizes learning by doing, problem solving, group work, and exploration of questions rather than rote memorization. By the 1930's, progressivism had begun to influence Canadian education. Canada's leading exponent of progressivism was Donalda Dickie. Her book *The Enterprise in Theory and Practice* (1941) created a mild revolution in teaching methods throughout the country.

Just as this new educational approach was ready to be tried and tested, Canada became engaged in the war and its related concerns. Many of the teachers being enticed into the teaching profession during the war did not have the ability or background to handle the demands of the new education. Other factors also contributed to the withdrawal from progressive education. In the political climate of the period, progressive educators were sometimes labeled as being communistic. Canadians were also reading scathing denunciations by Americans of progressive education in the American press. The program of progressive education in Canada therefore was short-lived.

Postwar Developments   To avoid the displacement of current workers by returning soldiers, the federal government paid the living expenses and tuition of World War II veterans interested in pursuing higher education, through the Veterans Rehabilitation Act. In 1946, 34,000 veterans enrolled, doubling the student population. The resulting overload of classroom and housing facilities forced universities into a period of frantic improvisation. Veterans' enrollment increased over the next two years, then gradually dropped off as veterans completed their degrees.

Educational Broadcasting   Not all educational changes during the 1940's were connected to the

war. Technological advances also influenced education. The invention of television made educational broadcasting possible. It was inaugurated to provide equal educational opportunities for all young persons in Canada, whether they lived in a city or in a rural area. The first trans-Canada school television series was aired in 1942-1943.

Consolidation   The motor age of the 1920's, with its motor vehicles and improved highways, had made possible bus transportation of pupils to more distant schools, making more feasible the idea of consolidation of the schools from one-room schoolhouses and small school districts into larger units. Small units of school administration had led to inadequacy in the type and scope of the curriculum, as well as discrepancies in the level of teacher remuneration. School districts varied in whether, and how rapidly, they consolidated.

Prior to the 1940's, aboriginal Indian children had been educated in residential schools sponsored by the federal government separate from the provincial schools. Indian children had been removed from their homes and forced to attend residential schools that were often far from their communities. At school, they had been prevented from learning about their own culture and speaking their own language. Although many on the schools' staffs were dedicated and some students speak highly of their experience at the residential schools, many students suffered physical and sexual abuse as well as inferior education. By 1940, only a small percentage of Indian students were finishing elementary school and going on to high school. In 1945, there were only three hundred Canadian Indians in high schools.

After reviewing Indian education in the late 1940's, the federal government launched a policy of education integration. Federal funds were provided to make it possible for native children to attend provincial primary and secondary schools; in all residential schools, the provincial curriculum was to be used; and in all residential schools, certified teachers were to be employed instead of noncertified teachers. Enrollment in provincial schools grew quickly. By 1960, about 10,000 Indian students attended provincial schools off the reserves and 400 attended colleges and universities.

Impact   Perhaps the war's most significant long-term impact on education came from the increased involvement of the federal government. The success of the Veterans Rehabilitation Act, which awarded grants to veterans to complete a college education, disposed the federal government to continue its financial support of higher education. As a result of the large number of World War II veterans who completed university degrees, the numbers of educated, skilled, and productive Canadians increased. This served as a precursor to the increased wealth experienced by Canadians during the 1950's.

Chrissa Shamberger

Further Reading

Donald, Wilson J. *Canadian Education: A History.* Scarborough, Ont.: Prentice-Hall of Canada, 1970. Another useful comprehensive history.

Harris, Robin S. *A History of Higher Education in Canada, 1663-1960.* Toronto: University of Toronto Press, 1976. Comprehensive survey of education issues throughout Canadian history.

Jones, Giles, ed. *Higher Education in Canada: Different Systems, Different Perspectives.* New York: Garland, 1997. Different authors describe the higher education of each of the provinces; the last chapter provides a synthesis.

Manzer, Ronald. *Public Schools and Political Ideas: Canadian Educational Policy in Historical Perspective.* Toronto: Toronto University Press, 1994. Uses a thematic approach, but the individual chapters are related to historical stages in Canadian educational development.

Wilson, J. D., R. M. Stamp, and Louis-Philippe Audet, eds. *Canadian Education: A History.* Scarborough, Ont.: Prentice-Hall, 1970. Each chapter is by a different author, but each traces one of the stages in the evolution of Canada's schools.

See also Business and the economy in Canada; Canadian nationalism; Canadian participation in World War II; Canadian regionalism; Censorship in Canada; Demographics of Canada; Education in the United States; Literature in Canada; Radio in Canada; Women's roles and rights in Canada.

■ Education in the United States

During the 1940's, World War II influenced education as well as other areas of American society. The decade was also a time of transition. These years came between the dominance of progressivism in education and the reaction against progressivism. The late 1940's saw new federal support for higher education, and this helped to change public views on the goals of education at all grade levels.

The educational history of the 1940's was largely defined by World War II. The time just before the war and during the war saw a relative decline in attention to formal education, compared to the early years of the twentieth century and to the time immediately following the war. One of the reasons for this relative decline in attention was the shrinking pool of school-age children. The birth rate had gone down in the rapidly urbanizing United States during the 1920's and had then dropped even further during the Depression of the 1930's, so that a comparatively small proportion of the American population was of school age during the 1940's. In addition, the mobilization of the American economy for war that began even before the United States entered the conflict at the end of 1941 meant that Americans built few new schools and kept school spending to a minimum until the end of the war in 1945. The focus on military activities temporarily pulled Americans away from the more advanced years of schooling. High school attendance actually dropped during the war, as did college attendance. Young men who were eighteen, and frequently even seventeen, went into the military. Young women of these ages took places in assembly lines in factories or in other war-related activities.

Educational Trends By 1940, school attendance had become almost universal in the United States. Government census figures for that year showed that 95 percent of children aged seven to thirteen were enrolled in school and more than 93 percent of children aged fourteen were enrolled. However, formal education in early childhood and in late adolescence was much less common than it would become later in the twentieth century. Two-thirds of children were not in school by ages five and six. By age fifteen, 13 percent were out of school, and at sixteen and seventeen nearly one-third of Americans were not in school. Most Americans had not completed high school or gone on to college in 1940, even before the call of the military drew potential students away from high school and college during the war. Among people over twenty-five, only 29 percent had finished four years of high school, and a little over 5 percent had finished four years of college.

Ten years later, early childhood education had

become much more common, with most five- and six-year-olds (60 percent) in school. At the other end, three-fourths of sixteen- and seventeen-year-olds were in school by 1950. Most people still did not have diplomas or degrees, but the proportion of Americans over twenty-five who had completed four years of high school had gone up to over 36 percent. College was still a rarity, since only 6 percent of the American population had finished four years of higher education in 1950. This was beginning to change, though. While under 7 percent of those in the twenty to twenty-four age group were enrolled in an educational institution in 1940, 13 percent of this age group were enrolled in 1950. The late 1940's had begun a trend of increasing higher education that would continue throughout the twentieth century.

The rising rates of entry into higher education were largely the consequence of federal involvement, as discussed below. At the lower levels, the nation saw population changes during the 1940's that would change educational trends in future years. The birth rate increased dramatically beginning in 1946, but numbers of students entering primary and secondary schools only started to rise during the 1950's when children born after the war reached school age. However, the economic boom of the postwar period did make possible new spending on schools at all levels. Even more important, the new expectations for higher education that emerged during the late 1940's created changing attitudes toward education at the lower levels that would change American ideas about the purposes of primary and secondary education.

Perspectives on Education The 1940's came between two major trends in American educational perspectives: progressivism, which reached its high point at the end of the 1930's, and the reaction against progressivism, which began to gather momentum in the years following World War II and reached a peak during the early 1950's. During the early twentieth century, the progressive education movement came to dominate thinking about public education in the United States. Educational progressivism consisted of two main branches: life-adjustment education and education for social reform. Both of these came out of the work of educational thinkers such as the philosopher John Dewey, and both emphasized that schooling should be practical and be designed to address contemporary so-

cial situations. However, life-adjustment education emphasized socializing students to fit into a modern industrial society. Education for social reform emphasized using education to improve that society.

Life-adjustment education was generally prevalent among administrators and government policy makers. In 1935, the National Education Association (NEA), which had grown out of the progressive movement in education, created the Educational Policies Commission, charged with identifying the proper role of education in American society. In 1938, the commission recognized four purposes: self-realization, human relations, civic efficiency, and economic competence. All of these were ways in which students would be trained to fit into their society. As the 1940's opened, intellectual enhancement and mastery of a cultural tradition were educational goals that received comparatively little attention. Following the war, in 1946, the U.S. Office of Education created the National Commission on Life Adjustment Education. The commission recommended that for most high school students education should concentrate on helping students deal with issues of social adjustment, rather than on conveying vocational or academic skills.

A number of prominent educational theorists adhered to the view that the main purpose of education was to adjust American society to a set of ideals, rather than simply to adjust individuals to society as it was. In February, 1939, the theorist George S. Counts delivered an address to the Progressive Education Association in which he argued that the proper business of schooling was to create a more democratic society by cultivating the proper set of habits, attitudes, and loyalties among students. Counts agreed with the life-adjustment perspective that education should be mainly socialization but saw it as socialization for a desired future, rather than as socialization for the present. Later that same year, the address was published as a pamphlet entitled *The Schools Can Teach Democracy*. Harold Rugg, a curriculum expert in the same circle of thinkers as Counts, published a comprehensive approach to curriculum design soon after World War II. In *Foundations for American Education*, published in 1947, Rugg offered a scheme for the redesign of school curriculum that would bring together sociology, psychology, aesthetics, and ethics. He maintained that schooling should be part of a program of organized social planning.

At the time of the publication of Rugg's book, the popular and political reaction against both branches of progressivism was already spreading. In the Cold War atmosphere that followed World War II, many Americans saw socializing students for an ideal future as suspiciously similar to the educational ideology of socialism and even to have some resemblance to the type of schooling associated with America's great rival, the Soviet Union. In addition, the growing and technologically sophisticated American economy of the postwar years increased the demand for high levels of literacy and for specialized skills. Facing new opportunities for upward mobility that required training, the American public became skeptical of education aimed mainly at teaching interpersonal relations and adjustment to everyday life.

The Pledge of Allegiance in American schools   At the end of the nineteenth century, Francis Bellamy wrote a pledge to the U.S. flag. Bellamy intended this pledge first and foremost for students in public schools, and the practice of reciting it every day quickly became common practice in schools across the nation. However, some groups, especially religious denominations, objected to a practice that they saw as sacrilegious worship of the nation. During the 1930's, Joseph Rutherford, the head of Jehovah's Witnesses, compared the pledge and the salute to the flag to the salute to Adolf Hitler required by law in Nazi Germany. Since the American pledge at that time was performed with an upraised arm and open palm, this was an uncomfortable comparison for many Americans, and the stand of the Jehovah's Witnesses was not popular.

In 1940, the U.S. Supreme Court rendered a judgment on the constitutionality of requiring school children to say the pledge. In an 8-to-1 decision, with only Justice Harlan Fiske Stone dissenting, the Court ruled in *Minersville School District v. Gobitis* that local school districts did have the right to insist that public school pupils recite the pledge. According to Justice Felix Frankfurter, the pledge served a secular purpose of maintaining national unity and loyalty and that school boards had a legitimate interest in encouraging patriotic sentiments. Justice Stone argued, on the other side, that compulsion in thought and action violated the fundamental principle of civil liberty.

This ruling on school policy had consequences for life outside the schools. The publicity the case brought to the Jehovah's Witnesses resulted in a wave of persecution across the nation. According to a report of the American Civil Liberties Union to the U.S. Justice Department, more than 1,500 members of the denomination were physically attacked, and even more Witnesses suffered discrimination and mistreatment.

Although World War II brought an intensification of patriotic feeling to the United States, the Supreme Court actually reversed its position during the war. This may have been partly due to the fact that the country was at war with Nazi Germany, an enemy notorious for persecuting minority groups. It may also have been a reaction against the violence that followed the *Minersville* decision. In addition, Justice Stone, the dissenter and defender of the civil rights approach to the question, had become chief justice of the United States, and two new justices had joined the Court.

Following the reasoning of *Minersville* and immediately after entry of the United States into World War II, by early 1942 the West Virginia legislature had adopted new statutes that required programs of patriotic education in all schools and compelled participation in the pledge by students. Once again, families of Jehovah's Witnesses objected. When the case made its way to the Supreme Court, as *West Virginia State Board of Education v. Barnette* (1943), attorneys for West Virginia argued that the matter had already been settled by *Minersville*. However, this time the Supreme Court ruled in a 6-3 decision that forced unity of opinion was contrary to the values of the First Amendment to the Constitution. Justices Hugo L. Black and William O. Douglas had changed their opinions and joined Justice Stone and the two new justices. Now it was Justice Frankfurter's turn to write the dissent, repeating the views he had earlier stated in *Minersville*.

Ironically, during much of the time that the pledge had been imposed on American schools by public officials, the pledge itself had no official status. Its first formal adoption by the U.S. government came on January 22, 1942. A month and half after the Japanese attack on Pearl Harbor, the U.S. Congress included what it called the Pledge to the Flag in the United States Flag Code. In 1945, the recitation was officially designated the Pledge of Allegiance. The only change to this common school ritual after the 1940's would come in 1954, when the words "under God" were added.

Federal Support for Higher Education   After World War I, the sudden demobilization of America had resulted in a period of economic difficulty. American political leaders began to think about avoiding a similar situation at the end of World War II, even while American soldiers were still fighting the war. Frederic Delano, an uncle of President Franklin D. Roosevelt and head of the National Resources Planning Board, established a committee in mid-1942 to begin studying problems that might occur following demobilization. By 1943, the committee had concluded that putting so many soldiers back into the labor market would push the economy down. The Delano committee considered keeping servicemen in the military after the war and only discharging them gradually as the civilian job market grew sufficiently to absorb them. However, the committee decided that this would meet with opposition from the soldiers and from the families who were waiting to welcome them home. Therefore, the Delano committee decided that the best way to avoid massive unemployment was to send veterans to school.

The Servicemen's Readjustment Act of 1944, better known as the G.I. Bill, was intended to help reintegrate returning veterans into the American economy and to help keep that economy from plunging into recession as war spending decreased and former soldiers entered the labor market. The legislation provided guarantees for mortgages so that the veterans could buy houses, and it helped pay the costs of higher education. The G.I. Bill provided tuition and educational expenses to veterans who had served at least ninety days. These payments could cover the costs of even the nation's most elite institutions. In addition to tuition payments for American colleges, in 1946 the U.S. government also established the Fulbright fellowship program, which provided funds for advanced research and teaching abroad.

Some influential educators were concerned that the sudden expansion of higher education would lower the quality of American universities. Robert Maynard Hutchins, the president of the University of Chicago, objected that the bill would allow anyone to enter the nation's colleges and universities and would bring new students who had no qualifica-

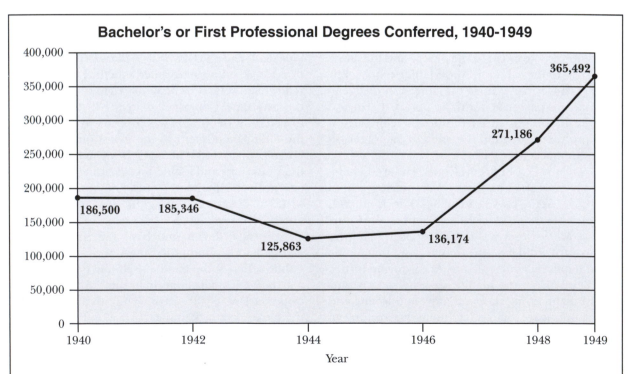

Bachelor's or First Professional Degrees Conferred, 1940-1949

Source: U.S. Office of Education , 1870-1953, *Biennial Survey of Education in the United States*, Statistics of Higher Education, biennial issues, and unpublished data.

tions other than unemployment. Harvard president James Bryant Conant worried that the tuition support would fail to distinguish between students who were able to benefit from college and those who were inadequately prepared. Despite such concerns, by most accounts returning veterans proved to be excellent students, and the American system of higher education, like the American economy, entered a boom period during the late 1940's.

The New College Population   One of the reasons that the dire predictions of Hutchins and Conant did not come to pass was that American higher education became more competitive and based more on meritocracy after World War II than it had been before. In addition, the highly motivated returned war veterans apparently did not lower the general standards of higher education but raised them. War veterans had higher rates of college completion than students who had not served.

By 1947, nearly half of those enrolled in American colleges were beneficiaries of the G.I. Bill. Nonveterans, including those who had been too young to serve and reached traditional college age only after the war, became more likely to set their sites on schooling beyond high school when they saw veterans of their own social backgrounds and from their own communities reaching advanced levels of schooling. As a result, schools across the nation became more likely to define their educational mission as college preparation. This helped to turn educational programs away from the life-adjustment approach, and it helped to turn higher education into mass education.

With growing numbers of students, colleges needed standardized means of ranking applicants on a large-scale basis. The Scholastic Aptitude Test (SAT) developed over the course of the early twentieth century, but it only began to be the main gateway to higher education at the end of the 1940's. The Educational Testing Service (ETS), which administered the SAT, opened on January 1, 1948. A decade later, more than 500,000 students were taking the test each year. This competition provided a ranking system for multitudes of newly entering college students. It also enabled elite schools, such as the University of Chicago and Harvard, to choose top scorers among high school graduates throughout the nation.

Impact   As a result of educational changes during the 1940's, the United States entered the second half

of the twentieth century with an educational system increasingly devoted to preparing students for higher education and for upward mobility in an expanding economy. The reaction against progressive education would last through the 1950's. Questions about the proper role of education in creating and maintaining political loyalty, which had come up in court cases about the Pledge of Allegiance, would take on new life as the Cold War with the Soviet Union followed World War II.

Carl L. Bankston III

Further Reading

Bankston, Carl L., and Stephen J. Caldas. *Public Education: America's Civil Religion—A Social History.* New York: Teachers College Press, 2009. History of public education from the nineteenth through the early twenty-first centuries. The chapters that deal with events during the 1940's are chapter 4, on public education between the two world wars, and chapter 5, on the education boom after World War II.

Bennett, Michael. *When Dreams Came True: The G.I. Bill and the Making of Modern America.* Washington, D.C.: Brassey's, 1996. Informative but informal history of the G.I. Bill and its impact on American society.

Lemann, Nicholas. *The Big Test: The Secret History of the American Meritocracy.* New York: Farrar, Straus and Giroux, 1999. History of the SAT test that explores its development before its establishment during the late 1940's as the main gateway to higher education and its broad influence after.

Mettler, Suzanne. *Soldiers to Citizens: The G.I. Bill and the Making of the Greatest Generation.* New York: Oxford University Press, 2005. Argues that the G.I. Bill promoted broad civic participation on the part of the generation that fought in World War II.

Ravitch, Diane. *Left Back: A Century of Battles over School Reform.* New York: Touchstone, 2000. Excellent examination of the rise and decline of the progressive education movement. It is highly critical of progressive education.

See also   Baby boom; Book publishing; Demographics of the United States; Education in Canada; Fulbright fellowship program; G.I. Bill; Great Books Foundation; Historiography; *West Virginia State Board of Education v. Barnette.*

■ Einstein, Albert

Identification German-born American physicist
whose work in theoretical physics made possible
the development of the atomic bomb

Born March 14, 1879; Ulm, Germany

Died April 18, 1955; Princeton, New Jersey

*Einstein not only developed the mathematics behind the
atomic bomb but also helped write a letter to President
Franklin D. Roosevelt that triggered work on the atomic
bomb; however, he later led opposition to the use of nuclear
weapons. He influenced work in both physics and philosophy and became the popular image and icon of a scientific
genius.*

Albert Einstein's famous equation $E = mc^2$, relating
energy to mass and based on his relativity theory, was
the basis of nuclear energy and weapons. Einstein
more directly jump-started the atomic bomb project
with a letter, codrafted with Leo Szilard and signed
by Einstein, sent to President Roosevelt. It warned of
German discoveries concerning nuclear chain reactions and the potential for a vastly powerful bomb in
the hands of Adolf Hitler. This led Roosevelt to fund
the Manhattan Project, the crash program to develop the atomic bomb.

Einstein became a U.S. citizen in 1940 but did not
have security clearance to participate in the project,
though it was based on his research and he had instigated it. Einstein's earlier pacifism (ended by the
rise of Hitler), his support for world government,
and his support of leftist causes, some backed by the
Communist Party, led J. Edgar Hoover, head of the
Federal Bureau of Investigation, to put him under
ongoing surveillance. Einstein's support for racial
integration of the Army and his public support for

*Albert Einstein (center) being sworn in as an American citizen at the federal courthouse in Trenton, New Jersey, on November 1, 1940. His
daughter, Margot Einstein, is taking the oath at his right, and his secretary, Helen Dukes, is at his left.* (New York Daily News via Getty
Images)

civil rights for African Americans earned him Hoover's identification as procommunist.

Einstein's personal research by the 1930's was on the unified field theory, an attempt to unify theoretical work on gravitational and electromagnetic forces that still had not been fully achieved. His research led him far from both mainstream nuclear physics and the sort needed for the atomic bomb. His opposition to the random aspect of the standard theory of subatomic physics led him still further from the popular topics of theoretical physics during the 1940's. Nevertheless, he was able to work on one wartime project unrelated to the bomb, using his earlier research. With the dropping of the atomic bomb on Japan, the end of World War II, and the beginning of the Cold War with the Soviet Union, Einstein became active in favor of nuclear disarmament.

Although Einstein did not believe in a personal God (he sometimes claimed belief in God as the universe but usually claimed to be an agnostic), he came more and more to identify himself culturally as a Jew after Hitler's persecution and extermination of the Jews of Europe. In 1948, he was offered the post of president of the newly formed state of Israel. He declined, not considering himself a politician. Nevertheless, he remained outspoken on political matters, supporting world government, criticizing governmental anticommunist investigations, and criticizing United States Cold War policy. He continued his search for the ultimate theory of the universe, but without success.

Impact   Einstein influenced later physics with his criticism of quantum mechanics and his goal of a unified theory. He was important in movements for peace, for disarmament, and for world government. His theories inspired later alternatives to the standard version of subatomic physics and inspired those who attempted to unify subatomic and cosmic physics through string theory. He stood as a beacon for later humanists, movements for tolerance, and the sense of wonder at and the attempt to comprehend the universe.

Val Dusek

Further Reading

Brian, Denis. *Einstein: A Life.* New York: John Wiley & Sons, 1996.
Cassidy, David. *Einstein and Our World.* 2d ed. New York: Humanity Books, 2004.
Isaacson, Walter. *Einstein: His Life and Universe.* New York: Simon & Schuster, 2007.

See also   Cold War; Fermi, Enrico; Hitler, Adolf; Hoover, J. Edgar; Israel, creation of; Jews in the United States; Manhattan Project; Oppenheimer, J. Robert; Roosevelt, Franklin D.

■ Eisenhower, Dwight D.

Identification   Supreme commander of the Allied forces during World War II
Born   October 14, 1890; Denison, Texas
Died   March 28, 1969; Washington, D.C.

Eisenhower commanded the invasions of North Africa in 1942, Sicily and Italy in 1943, and France in 1944, leading the American, British, and French armies to victory in World War II.

Dwight D. Eisenhower grew up in the small midwestern town of Abilene, Kansas, graduating from high school in 1909. When he learned that free education was available at West Point, he applied in 1911 despite the objections of his pacifist Mennonite parents, graduating in 1915.

After the United States entered World War I, Eisenhower was promoted to captain and put in charge of a tank training facility. On October 14, 1918, he was raised to lieutenant colonel (temporary) and given command of an armored unit, but the war ended before he could leave for France.

Eisenhower became a permanent major in 1920 and remained in that rank for sixteen years. During the 1920's, he served in the office of the secretary of war and attended elite Army postgraduate schools. General Douglas MacArthur took Eisenhower with him as chief of staff in 1935, when he left to organize the Philippine army. When Eisenhower returned to the United States in 1939, he expected to retire as a colonel. Seniority strictly governed all promotions until an officer reached that rank, and Eisenhower's West Point class would not be promoted to colonel until 1950. By that time, he would be sixty—too close to retirement age to anticipate further advancement.

Preparing for Battle   Everything changed in 1940, when the United States began a massive rearmament drive; the Army grew from 190,000 officers and men in 1939 to more than 5 million by 1942. Promotions came rapidly for Eisenhower. In March, 1941, he was raised to full colonel (temporary) and became chief of staff for the Third Army. When Eisenhower's battle plans helped the Third Army succeed in full-scale field maneuvers in September, 1941, he was promoted to brigadier general (temporary) and was ordered to Washington, D.C. Army Chief of Staff General George C. Marshall appointed Eisenhower the principal plans and operations officer for the War Department. In March, 1942, Marshall recommended his promotion to major general and set him to planning a cross-channel assault for spring, 1943.

In June, 1942, Marshall and President Franklin D. Roosevelt sent Eisenhower, with the rank of lieutenant general, to London to command American forces in Europe and prepare them for a 1943 invasion. Eisenhower's first press conference in England was widely reported and turned Eisenhower into a celebrity. He had a clear sense of what reporters and the public wanted to hear and how to present himself favorably. Stressing Allied unity in the struggle against Nazi Germany, he rapidly became an admired figure in Great Britain and the United States.

Into Battle Eisenhower expected Marshall to lead the invasion with Eisenhower as his chief of staff. The British insisted that a cross-channel invasion was too risky in 1942 and convinced the Americans to make French North Africa that year's target. Eisenhower received command to the reduced operation and created a combined U.S.-British staff to run the campaign.

The November, 1942, invasion became a diplomatic disaster when Eisenhower appointed fascist French admiral François Darlan governor of occupied Algeria. The American and British press and public opinion denounced the choice as a betrayal of the war against fascism, and the move increased Russian suspicions of Allied war aims. The admiral's assassination in December eased Eisenhower's problem. Eisenhower proved a cautious military leader, advancing his untried troops slowly, giving the Germans time to move an army into Tunisia, thereby delaying the Allied conquest of North Africa until late May.

Appointed to four-star rank and given command of the invasions of Sicily and Italy later that year, Eisenhower once more proved a careful leader. He was

again criticized for moving slowly, permitting the Germans to rush troops into Italy and to turn the campaign into a war of attrition. When Roosevelt decided to keep Marshall in Washington as his principal military adviser, Eisenhower received command of the 1944 cross-channel attack on Nazi-controlled Europe.

The invasion of France was Eisenhower's finest hour. He carefully prepared the way, engaging his troops in realistic training for the difficult landing on a heavily fortified coast. He demanded more landing craft, increasing the initial landing force from three to five divisions. He insisted that American and British bomber forces destroy the French railroad net, inhibiting movement of German reinforcements to Normandy. On June 5, the weather was poor, so Eisenhower decided to attack the following day, a move that caught enemy commanders by surprise. The successful organization and execution of what would become the greatest sea invasion in history led admirers to rank Eisenhower among the great generals of the world.

Once the armies broke through the Normandy defenses, Eisenhower's tanks ran rapidly across France, liberating Paris, and drove to the German border before literally running out of gasoline. In December, Eisenhower was promoted to the Army's highest rank, General of the Army. The invasion of Germany did not occur until March, 1945, when Eisenhower advanced into enemy territory along a broad front. He was criticized for not rushing to take Berlin before the Russians got there, but he preferred not to risk his troops attacking the heavily defended city for political reasons rather than for any compelling military advantage.

Peacetime After the surrender of all German forces on May 7, 1945, Eisenhower returned to the United States for an ecstatic welcome. Appointed head of the American Occupation Zone in Germany, Eisenhower enjoyed friendly relations with his Russian counterparts, cooperating easily with them. By 1947, as difficulties in Russian-American relations mounted, his view became much less favorable.

Eisenhower was recalled to Washington in November, 1945, to take over as Army chief of staff, a position he hated. He disliked fighting with the chiefs of the other armed services over unification of the armed forces and with Congress over demobilization and the size of the postwar Army. He retired on February 7, 1948, to assume the presidency of Columbia University, where he would remain uncomfortably until 1952, disliked by his faculty and struggling with university finances.

In 1947, leaders of both Democratic and Republican parties urged Eisenhower to become their candidate for president. He refused to run, but few believed his denials since he refused to say that he would never serve. He told his brother that he would accept the office if drafted, a highly improbable contingency, but one he preferred to keep open. As 1949 drew to a close, he was perhaps the most admired man in America and still widely considered a possible future president.

General Dwight D. Eisenhower acknowledging the crowds as rides in a motorcade through Manhattan on June 19, 1945. (AP/Wide World Photos)

Impact The defeat of Germany, for which Eisenhower's leadership deserves a significant degree of credit, was a necessary precondition for the massive economic expansion of the United States and Western Europe in the second half of the twentieth century. It also made possible the peaceful development of a European Union.

The quality of Eisenhower's leadership did not go unchallenged. Some British and American officers objected to serving under a soldier who had never led troops in combat. More serious were the claims that by failing to move more aggressively in North Africa and Italy, Eisenhower prolonged the campaigns and caused unnecessary loss of lives. Quick drives to Tunis and Rome would have been spectacular if successful, but Eisenhower believed that his careful approach increased the probability of victory while limiting troop losses. He thought the attempt to beat the Russians to Berlin an empty political gesture not worth what it would cost in men, since the city was assigned to the postwar Russian zone. That the Russians lost 100,000 men in the assault on Berlin would appear to validate his belief.

Eisenhower's major contribution to military victory was as an organizer. He created a combined Anglo-American command structure for the North African invasion that he held together despite all the friction caused by competing egos among his generals. He showed the same skills in organizing and leading the great cross-channel invasion, insisting that the air forces subordinate their bombing campaigns over Germany to the needs of the landing parties, and in convincing political leaders to provide the equipment necessary for success.

Despite Eisenhower's denial of any further ambition, he had created an aura and reputation that would carry him to the presidency of the United States (1953-1961) and yet another major role in world history.

Milton Berman

Further Reading

Ambrose, Stephen E. *Eisenhower: Soldier, General of the Army, President-Elect, 1890-1952.* New York: Simon & Schuster, 1983. First volume of the standard two-volume biography of Eisenhower.

Bischof, Gunter, and Stephen E. Ambrose. *Eisenhower: A Centenary Assessment.* Baton Rouge: Louisiana State University Press, 1995. Five scholarly articles examine Eisenhower's military career.

Brendon, Piers. *Ike: His Life and Times.* New York: Harper & Row, 1986. Portrait of Eisenhower that negatively assesses his career.

Chernus, Ira. *General Eisenhower: Ideology and Discourse.* East Lansing: Michigan State University Press, 2002. Argues that Eisenhower's public language was consciously manipulative.

Perret, Geoffrey. *Eisenhower.* New York: Harper & Row, 1999. Full-scale biography by an uncritical admirer.

Wukovits, John. *Eisenhower: A Biography.* New York: Palgrave Macmillan, 2006. A brief biography in Palgrave's Great Generals series.

See also D Day; Department of Defense, U.S.; Germany, occupation of; Italian campaign; Landing craft, amphibious; Marshall, George C.; North African campaign; Truman, Harry S.; V-E Day and V-J Day; World War II.

■ Elections in Canada

The Events National parliamentary and provincial government elections to choose members of Parliament

During the 1940's, the Canadian Liberal Party extended its dominance of the national political scene, winning three parliamentary elections with increasing majorities. The party, however, saw its influence diminished in the western provinces of Alberta and Saskatchewan as the Social Credit Party and the Cooperative Commonwealth Federation gained control of provincial governments and were elected to seats in the national parliament.

Much like the United States, the Canadian political system during the 1940's was dominated by a single political party that led the country through the Great Depression and World War II. The Canadian Liberal Party won three parliamentary elections in the decade, but while it racked up a large majority of seats, the party suffered from dwindling support in the western provinces and Quebec. Among the Liberals' regional opponents were the populist Social Credit Party in Alberta, a socialist-oriented party in Saskatchewan, and French separatists in Quebec.

National Politics The 1935 national election provided a Liberal Party majority under the leadership of William Lyon Mackenzie King, a liberal member from Prince Albert, Saskatchewan. When war struck in 1939, King and his party were popular with Canadians, and after the premier of Ontario sought a par-

liamentary vote condemning the Liberal Party's war effort, King called new elections. The war was a major issue in the campaign, and King was forced to appeal to the French Quebec vote as the western provinces turned from the Liberal Party. The prime minister promised not to introduce conscription, a promise popular with the antiwar French in Quebec. On March 26, 1940, the Liberals smashed their opponents, winning 181 seats, three times those of the opposition parties combined. The Progressive Conservative Party hobbled into the next parliament with only 40 members, the Alberta-based Social Credit Party had 10, and the new Cooperative Commonwealth Federation (CCF) won 9. Only in the west did the Liberals see losses, with King squeaking to a 1,000-vote victory in his Saskatchewan district. This weakness would haunt him in the next election.

The massive Liberal majority was chipped away by the smaller parties as the death or retirement of Liberal parliament members led to by-elections in August, 1943. Two provincial parties, the CCF and the Quebec Separatists, won seats formerly held by the Liberals. In 1942, King was forced to retract his campaign promise on conscription. The Canadian army suffered a shortage of volunteers, so that military need clashed with politics. The prime minister scheduled a plebiscite asking voters to release him from his promise while campaigning on the slogan "Conscription if necessary but not necessarily conscription." King was released from his promise with 63 percent of voters approving of his request, but the divisions in the country boded poorly for Canada. More than 80 percent of English-speakers approved, while nearly 73 percent of French-speakers in Quebec voted against conscription. A new party, the Bloc Populaire Canadien, was founded specifically to oppose King and conscription.

The 1945 Election The prime minister maintained the Liberal majority through the war, and in June, 1945, hoping to ride political victory on the coattails of military victory, King called another national election. The Liberal Party saw its massive majority cut to 127 seats, with the conservatives winning 68 and the CCF nearly tripling its seats to 29. The Social Credit Party managed to win 13 seats, all in Alberta. Even as his party was winning a third consecutive term in power, King suffered a shocking defeat in his own district.

In 1943, Saskatchewan Province had elected a

CCF government, with the Liberal Party being swept from power in King's Prince Albert parliamentary district. The loss was a warning to the prime minister, who had barely won reelection in 1940. The Liberal Party offered King a safe district in which to run for reelection, but the prime minister refused; instead he ran in his Prince Albert district even though he did not live there and rarely visited. With the odds against him, King campaigned hard, holding a lead on election night but then losing it when votes from soldiers came in favoring the CCF candidate, who won by 129 votes.

As a party without a leader, the Liberals quickly found a district in Glengarry, Ontario, that elected King, allowing him to serve as prime minister for a third consecutive term. King's popularity within the Liberal Party had declined, however, and at the party's 1948 leadership conference, he stepped aside to allow Louis St. Laurent to lead the Liberals during the 1949 election. Known as Uncle Louis because of his common touch, St. Laurent led the Liberals to another large victory, with 49 percent of the popular vote and 191 parliamentary seats, the most in Canadian history. The Progressive Conservatives lost ground, dropping to 41 seats. Postwar prosperity undermined the CCF's socialist message, and its seats fell by half, to 13.

National and Regional Parties   The Progressive Conservative Party, having lost power during the 1935 general election, struggled to remain an opposition force in Parliament. After their defeat in the 1940 election, the party ousted its leader, Robert Manein, but his chosen successor, Arthur Mayheim, was defeated in a by-election by a CCF candidate and could not serve. Leaderless, the Progressive Conservatives recruited John Bracken, a former liberal and former premier of Manitoba, to lead the party into the 1945 election. The Progressive Conservatives hoped that Bracken could lead a coalition of western conservatives and disgruntled liberal members to victory. The strategy failed, and the party lost two more national elections; it would not regain control of Parliament until 1957.

While the liberals were dominating national politics, they were losing support in the western provinces, where regional parties were gaining strength. In Alberta, the Social Credit Party won a provincial majority in the 1935 elections. The party was led by William "Bible Bill" Aberhart, who preached a popu-

list and nationalistic message for ending the Depression. The party supported a form of populist economics, deemed social credit, by which the government would distribute twenty-dollar certificates to every Albertan to be used for basic commodities and to raise living standards. The plan was never fully implemented, and Aberhart was unclear on how the certificates would be funded. In 1940, the party strengthened its control of the province by winning nearly two-thirds of the provincial seats. The victory came even as the conservatives, liberals, and independents joined in a fusion ticket, hoping to combine their votes to defeat the Social Credit Party.

Just to the east, Saskatchewan Province experienced its own third-party genesis. The CCF formed the first socialist government in the Western Hemisphere. The party won its first parliamentary seats in the 1940 national elections, then extended its influence by winning by-elections in 1943. One of the main platform items for the party was creating a province-wide health system for all of its citizens. The CCF's electoral success was noticed, and its policies were copied by the national Liberal Party, with Prime Minister King introducing legislation in 1944 to aid labor and start a national health service. The Liberal Party's success at co-opting the CCF's agenda weakened the CCF, which lost seats in the 1949 general election.

Impact   Liberal Party domination of Canadian politics during the 1940's saw the country's politics move to the left as the party tried to hold off provincial parties such as the Social Credit Party and the CCF. Louis St. Laurent led the Liberal Party to another victory in the elections of 1953. Under his leadership, Canada supported the United Nations actions in Korea and helped solve the Suez Crisis of 1956.

Douglas Clouatre

Further Reading

Bell, Edward. *Social Classes and Social Credit in Alberta.* Montreal: McGill-Queen's University Press, 1993. History of the philosophy and the leaders of the Social Credit Party in Alberta, its electoral successes, and its governing failures as the party sought to change the province's economic system.

Bothwell, Robert. *Penguin History of Canada.* London: Penguin Global, 2008. Brief history of Canada includes a section on Canadian politics and society during the war and the leadership of William Lyon Mackenzie King.

Clarkson, Stephen. *The Big Red Machine: How the Liberal Party Dominates Canadian Politics.* Seattle: University of Washington Press, 2006. Describes and analyzes the Canadian Liberal Party and its electoral success over the last sixty years. Includes discussion of the role of Liberal prime ministers.

Esberry, Joy. *Knight of the Holy Spirit: A Study of William Lyon Mackenzie King.* Toronto: University of Toronto Press, 1980. Full-length biography of King's political career, including his service as prime minister during World War II and his dominance of the political scene.

Rennie, Bradford Albert. *Premiers of the Twentieth Century.* Regina, Sask.: Canadian Plains Research Center, 2004. Listing and description of Alberta's provincial leaders, with a focus on the Social Credit Party, which controlled provincial government from 1935 to 1971.

Wardhaugh, Robert. *Mackenzie King and the Prairie West.* Toronto: University of Toronto Press, 2000. Having risen from the western provinces to become prime minister, King and his Liberal Party struggled to maintain their western base. This struggle included the prime minister's defeat in 1945 and gradual rejection of his party by western Canadians.

See also Canadian nationalism; Canadian participation in World War II; Canadian regionalism; Foreign policy of Canada; Military conscription in Canada; Quebec nationalism; Unemployment in Canada.

■ Elections in the United States: 1940

The Event Elections for federal and state offices that saw Franklin D. Roosevelt win an unprecedented third term as president

Date November 5, 1940

In a presidential election revolving around the American response to the tensions of World War II in Europe and Asia, Democrat Franklin D. Roosevelt won reelection to an unprecedented third consecutive term, defeating Republican Wendell Willkie. Voters retained an experienced president they had known through eight years of the Depression, reform, and international tensions, and the Democrats easily kept control of both houses of Congress.

World War II tensions formed the background for the 1940 presidential and congressional elections. American economic problems had overshadowed foreign policy in the 1932 and 1936 presidential elections. The German attack on Poland in September, 1939, shifted American attention from the Depression to the outbreak of World War II. The nation gradually moved from neutrality and isolationism to internationalism, sparking a fierce congressional and public debate over military aid to the Allies, short of war. Roosevelt originally had not planned to seek a third term, respecting the two-term tradition dating back to George Washington, and it is unclear when he changed his mind. The expanding European crisis in 1940, especially the fall of France, convinced him that the United States should not change leadership in midstream. He did not announce his candidacy officially but expected the Democratic Party convention delegates to draft him.

The Political Conventions France fell to Germany just two days before the Republican Party convention in Philadelphia in June. The Republican delegates were deadlocked for several ballots between Senator Robert A. Taft of Ohio, an adamant isolationist, and governor Thomas Dewey of New York. In perhaps the most dramatic, improbable surprise in American presidential politics since the Democratic nomination of Horace Greeley in 1872, the Republicans on the sixth ballot selected forty-eight-year-old Wendell Willkie of Indiana, the head of a public utility holding company, a former Democrat, and a political novice. Willkie had fought Roosevelt's Tennessee Valley Authority over the use of public power, but he backed most New Deal social legislation. He was a devout internationalist, supporting arms embargo repeal and American aid to Great Britain. Willkie selected Senator Charles McNary of Oregon as his running mate. Party leaders disliked Willkie, but he compensated for his political inexperience by being personable, enthusing younger followers, and portraying brash confidence.

Roosevelt, meanwhile, named two prominent Republicans to the cabinet on June 20. Frank Knox, a Chicago newspaper publisher, was selected as secretary of the Navy, while Henry Stimson, former secretary of state, was designated secretary of war. The appointments indicated Roosevelt's intention to seek bipartisan consensus in a time of crisis and split Republicans on aid to Great Britain, weakening the isolationists and Willkie. Roosevelt remained at the White House while Democrats gathered for their convention on July 15 in Chicago, choosing to respond at a distance to the expected call for his candidacy.

The presiding officer read a statement from Roosevelt freeing the delegates to vote for whomever they wished. Mayor Edward Kelly, the local Democratic Party boss, orchestrated a pro-Roosevelt floor demonstration, shouting through a microphone, "We want Roosevelt." The delegates, alarmed by the growing world crisis, drafted Roosevelt on the first ballot. Roosevelt's selection of his running mate sparked controversy—Henry A. Wallace, a former progressive Republican, liberal reformer, staunch New Dealer, and secretary of agriculture. Conservative delegates distrusted Wallace and considered rebellion. Roosevelt threatened to withdraw his name from consideration if the delegates rejected Wallace. Harry Hopkins and Eleanor Roosevelt persuaded disgruntled delegates to support Wallace.

The Fall Campaign   The presidential campaign revolved largely around foreign policy, but Willkie's internationalist sentiments and the Knox-Stimson appointments neutralized it as an issue for most of the campaign. Roosevelt and Willkie both backed the Selective Service Act of 1940, the nation's first peacetime draft. Roosevelt engineered the destroyers-for-bases deal, sending forty-three ships to the British Royal Navy and seven more to the Canadian Royal Navy, in exchange for British naval bases in the Western Hemisphere. Willkie mildly criticized Roosevelt for not giving the public sufficient time to debate the deal but assailed the bypassing of Congress as an arbitrary, dictatorial action. Willkie painted the Republican Party as the party of peace, inferred that Roosevelt wanted to get the United States involved in another foreign war, and attempted to link the New Deal with European totalitarianism. He labeled Roosevelt ambitious and authoritarian, portraying him as "the third term candidate." Willkie lost his poise in late October and showed increased political desperation, sharply criticizing Republican isolationists. He dropped the civility that had marked his early campaign statements, denouncing Roosevelt as a warmonger and vowing not to send American soldiers to Europe again.

The endorsements of Willkie by aviator Charles Lindbergh and United Mine Workers president John L. Lewis, coupled with the warmongering charge, shook Roosevelt's camp. Roosevelt stayed in the White House for most of the campaign, appearing presidential and statesmanlike. He joined the campaign trail, however, in late October when polls indicated that Willkie was gaining ground. Roosevelt reminded Boston voters on October 30 that Willkie belonged to the same party as isolationist representatives Joe Martin, Bruce Barton, and Hamilton Fish, and he worked the enthusiastic Democratic crowd with the chant "Martin, Barton, and Fish." He pledged, "Your boys are not going to be sent into any foreign war" and omitted a qualifying phrase he had used previously, indicating that the country would fight if attacked.

Roosevelt's pledge to remain out of war did not ultimately determine the election outcome. By election day, many voters had concluded that the United States would be drawn into war and preferred an experienced Roosevelt to lead them. Roosevelt reminded radio audiences in numerous cities that British weapons purchases had helped increase employment by 3.5 million since 1937 and had reduced the U.S. unemployment rate to 14.6 percent.

Roosevelt Wins Reelection   Roosevelt decisively won reelection, with 449 electoral votes to Willkie's 82. He triumphed by nearly 5 million votes (his narrowest winning margin yet), receiving 27.2 million popular votes to 22.3 million for Willkie. Roosevelt attracted 54.7 percent of the popular vote, less than his 57.4 percent in 1932 and 60.8 percent in 1936, and half a million fewer votes than in 1936. Willkie fared considerably better against Roosevelt than either Herbert Hoover in 1932 or Alf Landon in 1936, polling 5 million more votes than the latter. He carried 1,147 counties nationally, compared to only 459 for Landon.

The Democrats retained most of their urban support, as Roosevelt took every city with a population of more than 400,000 except Cincinnati. His plurality in New York City helped carry the Empire State, while Chicago gave him the measure of victory in Illinois, Cleveland in Ohio, and Milwaukee in Wisconsin. The swing of Polish American and Jewish voters, considered to be particularly vehement in hatred of Adolf Hitler, helped Roosevelt. City workers resoundingly backed Roosevelt, endorsing his labor and reform policies. Roosevelt won despite the defection of *The New York Times*, the *Cleveland Plain*

Republican presidential candidate Wendell Willkie in a motorcade through downtown Los Angeles on November 3, 1940—two days before the election. (AP/Wide World Photos)

Dealer, the Scripps-Howard newspaper chain, and other newspapers that had supported him in 1936. Willkie prevailed in just ten states, carrying the traditional Republican strongholds of Maine and Vermont, politically important Michigan and Indiana, and six western wheat and corn states—North Dakota, South Dakota, Iowa, Nebraska, Kansas, and Colorado. Willkie also fared well in areas with significant numbers of voters of Italian, German, or Irish birth or ancestry.

The Democrats still held a sizable majority in both the Senate and the House. They added 5 seats to their House majority, giving them 267 seats. The Republicans received fewer votes in the House races than in the presidential contest, dropping 7 seats to finish with 162. The Democrats lost 3 Senate seats but retained 66 and a two-thirds majority. The Re-

publicans made a net gain of 5 senators, for a total of 28. Republicans received fewer votes in the House races than in the presidential contest. Seventeen Republican governors were elected in 34 state contests for a net gain of 2, but the Democrats still held the majority there as well.

Impact With solid party majorities in both houses of Congress, Roosevelt—and the internationalists—controlled decision making. They still argued that American assistance to Allied nations would strengthen the defense of Western Europe and would help deter Hitler from invading the Western Hemisphere. The legislative branch in 1941 approved the Lend-Lease Act authorizing the president to sell, transfer, lend, or lease arms, equipment, and supplies to Great Britain and other allies. It also revised the 1939 Neutrality Act, authorizing Roosevelt to arm American merchant ships carrying supplies to belligerent European ports. Following the sudden Japanese attack on Pearl Harbor on December 7, 1941, Congress almost unanimously approved a war against Japan and thus sanctioned direct American involvement in World War II. Roosevelt and Willkie became political allies soon after the election. Willkie supported the administration's foreign policy and acted as a wartime emissary for Roosevelt, promoting political bipartisanship and national unity. Since Roosevelt, no president has served more than two terms. The Twenty-second Amendment, limiting later presidents to two terms in office, was passed by Congress on March 21, 1947, and ratified by the states on February 27, 1951.

David L. Porter

Further Reading

Burke, Robert F. "The Election of 1940." In *History of American Presidential Elections, 1789-1968*, edited by Arthur M. Schlesinger, Jr. Vol. 3. New York: Chelsea House, 1971. Describes the background to the 1940 presidential election, the Republican and Democratic Party conventions, the fall campaign, and the November elections, highlighting how foreign policy issues impacted the outcome.

Burns, James MacGregor. *Roosevelt: The Soldier of Freedom*. New York: Harcourt Brace Jovanovich, 1970. Second of a two-part Roosevelt biography that adeptly analyzes Roosevelt's political leadership and his approach toward critical foreign policy issues.

Donahoe, Bernard F. *Private Plans and Public Dangers: The Story of FDR's Third Nomination*. Notre Dame, Ind.: University of Notre Dame Press, 1965. Contends that the struggle between conservative and liberal Democrats from 1937 and 1940, not World War II, was the primary influence behind Roosevelt's choice to seek a third term in 1940. Argues that Roosevelt did not want to surrender party and national leadership to those he regarded as too conservative.

Moscow, Warren. *Roosevelt and Willkie*. Englewood Cliffs, N.J.: Prentice-Hall, 1968. Details the political contest between Roosevelt and Willkie, Willkie's surge in 1940, and his victory at the Republican convention. It provides a detailed description and astute analysis of the political and social situation in 1940.

Neal, Steve. *Dark Horse: A Biography of Wendell Willkie*. Lawrence: University Press of Kansas, 1989. Stresses Willkie's support of aid to the Allies, in contrast to Republican isolationists, and notes his personality, energy, and drive.

Parmet, Herbert S., and Marie B. Hecht. *Never Again: A President Runs for a Third Term*. New York: Macmillan, 1968. Points out the uniqueness of the 1940 presidential election, in which the Republicans chose an unorthodox candidate in an unusual manner and Roosevelt became the only president to run for a third consecutive term.

Peters, Charles. *Five Days in Philadelphia*. New York: Public Affairs, 2005. Shows that the five action-packed days of the Republican convention in Philadelphia produced the unlikeliest of presidential candidates in Willkie and argues that the selection of a nonisolationist candidate enabled Roosevelt to prepare the United States adequately for involvement in World War II.

See also   Elections in Canada; Elections in the United States: 1942 and 1946; Elections in the United States: 1944; Elections in the United States: 1948; Presidential powers; Presidential Succession Act of 1947; Roosevelt, Franklin D.; Willkie, Wendell.

■ Elections in the United States: 1942 and 1946

The Events   National elections for congressional seats held between presidential elections

Dates   November 3, 1942, and November 2, 1946

The Seventy-eighth and Eightieth Congresses, elected in 1942 and 1946 respectively, reflected the vastly different political landscapes during and after World War II.

Members of the U.S. House of Representatives serve two-year terms, and senators serve six-year terms. During midterm elections, therefore, all seats in the U.S. House of Representatives are up for reelection, while only one-third of the seats in the U.S. Senate are up for reelection in any given election year (presidential or midterm). Every U.S. election cycle has unique characteristics, and the American political environment can change very quickly. Two electoral forces present in every midterm cycle are economic performance in the year leading to the midterm election and presidential popularity. Specific campaign issues usually matter less than economic performance and what voters think of the incumbent president, even though the president is not running for reelection.

Midterm elections are important indicators of the political environment. Some electoral cycles produce such radical political changes that they are referred to as "realigning" elections. Cycles that produce considerable political change, but on a smaller scale, are referred to as "calibrating" elections. Drastic political shifts rarely are caused by world events or campaign issues; rather, they reflect shifts in broader political ideology and partisan philosophies within the political parties.

The midterm election cycles during the 1940's do not fit the profiles for realigning or calibrating elections; they are considered normal midterm elections despite the world events of the time. Despite the relative unity among Democrats and Republicans, however, the midterm elections of 1942 and 1946 did have unique and defining characteristics.

The 1942 Midterm Elections The 1942 midterm elections were the first national elections after the U.S. commitment to World War II. The political environment was transitioning from the Great Depression to a global conflict, and the American economy was transitioning to support the total war effort on the home front. President Franklin D. Roosevelt's Democratic Party had been in control of the government since 1933, when Roosevelt first took office. Roosevelt's political popularity helped the Democratic Party during the midterm elections of his presidency. In 1942, the Democrats maintained their political majority in both the House and the Senate. Along with Roosevelt's popularity, World War II likely also helped the Democrats. Polling data suggest that during national emergencies, such as wars, voters rarely change political leaders.

Although Roosevelt was still very popular in 1942, a slight political shift favored the Republican Party in the elections, but not enough to cost the Democrats their majorities in both houses of Congress. The Democrats maintained control of the U.S. House with the election of 222 candidates against the Republicans' 209 candidates. In the Senate, the Democrats fell from 66 seats to 47, while the Republicans increased their representation from 28 to 38 seats.

Several factors likely influenced the Republicans' gains in 1942. The war posed a period of political adjustment. The war effort on the home front brought on government sanctions and wartime controls on the domestic economy that included domestic rationing programs for various scarce resources and food items. Economic production was channeled into the wartime economy, causing shortages of many consumer goods. Labor-management disputes threatened wartime production schedules and the economy.

World War II was an influential context for the midterm elections of 1942, but in some different ways from what scholars and historians forecasted. As the electorate experienced the stresses associated with the war effort and various personal sacrifices, they remained united behind the Democratic Party. The issues expected to influence outcomes included the war effort, concerns about what would happen after the war, organized labor and how it would be allowed to operate, and international affairs. Voters were largely unified behind the president, however, and that general sentiment appeared to overwhelm concerns about specific issues.

Voter turnout on the whole decreased in 1942 from previous midterm elections. Of 60 million registered voters, 28 million voted in 1942. This turnout was down from 49.8 million voters in 1940, a presidential election year—and presidential elections tend to draw more voters—and also down from the 36.1 million voters in 1938. Low voter turnout was attributed to two specific factors. First, a large number of both men and women serving in the armed forces did not exercise their absentee voting privileges. Second, a large number of workers relocated for the war effort, and many did not register to vote in their new location or did not exercise an absentee vote.

1946 Elections and Republican Resurgence The midterm elections of 1946 marked major changes in the American political environment. In the first postwar national elections, the political party that had managed the Great Depression and World War II suffered considerable political losses. The political environment was much different from that of previous cycles. A major factor was the death of President Franklin D. Roosevelt while in office, in the spring of 1945, and the succession of Vice President Harry S. Truman to the presidency. The election was seen partly as a referendum on Truman as president, and his popularity was low. Another, more general, factor in the elections was that the transition from war to peace presented various challenges.

The Republican Party gained 55 seats in the U.S. House, for a total of 246; the Democrats lost 54, for a total of 188, thus losing their House majority. Republicans gained 13 seats in the Senate to hold 51, while Democrats lost 12 to hold 45, losing their majority there as well. The Republicans therefore held control of both houses of Congress for the first time since 1928. Losses by the Democratic Party were particularly heavy among liberal, progressive, northern Democrats; most southern Democrats held their seats.

The postwar transition was proving difficult, which hurt the Democratic Party, as the party in power. The switch from a wartime to a peace economy engendered an economic recession, but with high inflation; both inflicted considerable economic and financial burdens on an American population that already had suffered and sacrificed through the Great Depression and World War II. Labor tensions were high, with industry marked by protests for improved working conditions. Shortages of commodities continued to plague the economy, and many of the wartime controls remained in effect. After a prolonged economic depression, the war effort and its attendant sacrifices, and a postwar recession, voters were fatigued with the policies of the Democratic Party and voted many Democrats out of office.

The heavy Democratic losses in Congress prompted President Truman, a Democrat, to proactively surrender presidential powers that had been granted to Roosevelt during the war. Truman also made efforts to deregulate several private industries that had been heavily supervised by government agencies during the war. One of the first to be deregulated was the meatpacking industry.

The election of a Republican majority in both chambers of Congress signaled the decline of the New Deal era and its legislative agenda. The election of 1946 was the beginning of an era that saw dismantling of much of the New Deal's political infrastructure. Truman and the Republican-controlled Congress had a tumultuous political relationship. Congress challenged Truman's Fair Deal policy agenda, and Truman reciprocated with presidential vetoes to counter Republican legislative initiatives.

The Republican majority moved swiftly to implement postwar policies to rebuild the American economy and to supply aid to the allied nations most devastated by the war. Major legislative developments that came out of the Eightieth Congress included the Marshall Plan (postwar aid to Europe that began the U.S. policy of containment of communism); the National Security Act, which eventually created the Central Intelligence Agency; significant tax cuts; and the Taft-Hartley Act, which addressed labor-management tensions.

Social Changes   During the Great Depression, the New Deal altered many of the nation's domestic political and social structures. The country tended to be isolationist in its global outlook; entry into World War II was a major step out of that paradigm. After World War II, the United States held a large amount of political capital and goodwill with other allied nations; Congress recognized this and capitalized on it by enacting postwar aid policies. The Eightieth Congress thus laid the foundation for the growth of the United States into a political, as well as military, superpower.

The midterm election cycles of 1942 and 1946 put in place lawmakers who created policy agendas that became permanent fixtures in American society. Among these was expansion of the federal income tax. The Seventy-eighth Congress, elected in 1942, changed the federal income tax structure, so that both personal and corporate tax receipts increased. Before World War II, only 7 percent of the American workforce paid income taxes; that rose to 64 percent by the war's end.

The Eightieth Congress, elected in 1946, implemented many postwar measures designed to compensate for postwar strains on the economy. The Employment Act of 1946 created the Council of Economic Advisors, which assumed a role of overseeing the economy and advising the president. Labor laws were reorganized, largely more in favor of management, with the Taft-Hartley Act of 1947 standing as a major revision of government policy. Congress also established the National Science Foundation, a not-for-profit organization that funds social and scientific academic research. The Atomic Energy Act of 1946 was designed to regulate domestic atomic energy and its uses. The Legislative Reorganization Act of 1946 (also known as the Congressional Reorganization Act) strengthened the legislative branch and limited the powers of the executive branch. The G.I.

Bill funded educational expenses for returning soldiers, easing the transition of the economy back to peacetime and absorbing some of the shock to the labor market of servicemen returning to it.

Impact The Congresses elected in the midterm elections of the 1940's shaped major changes in U.S. society. In March, 1947, Congress approved the Twenty-second Amendment to the Constitution, limiting U.S. presidents to two terms in office, and sent it to the states for ratification, which was achieved in 1951. The National Security Act of 1947 established or consolidated several government departments related to national security, including the Central Intelligence Agency. Several notable political careers also were launched from the Eightieth Congress. Richard Nixon and John F. Kennedy both were elected to the U.S. House of Representatives in 1946; they competed for the U.S. presidency in 1960. Also in 1946, Senator Joseph McCarthy was elected to the U.S. Senate. He became infamous during the 1950's when he launched Senate committee investigations into communist influence within the United States.

Heather E. Yates

Further Reading

Busch, Andrew E. *Horses in Midstream: U.S. Midterm Elections and Their Consequences, 1894-1998.* Pittsburgh: University of Pittsburgh Press, 1999. Thoughtful study of the conduct and impact of midterm elections from the time of Benjamin Harrison's presidency through the late twentieth century.

Cantril, Hadley, and John Harding. "The 1942 Elections: A Case Study in Political Psychology." *Public Opinion Quarterly* 7, no. 2 (1943): 222-241. Contemporary analysis of the results of the 1942 elections. Harding also continued his study of the 1942 elections in another article in the first 1944 issue of *American Political Science Review.*

Kernell, Samuel. "Presidential Popularity and Negative Voting: An Alternative Explanation of the Midterm Congressional Decline of the President's Party." *The American Political Science Review* 71, no. 1 (1977): 44-66. Fascinating exploration of the tendency of American voters to turn against the party of the incumbent president in midterm elections.

Mayhew, David R. "Wars and American Politics." *Perspectives on Politics* 3, no. 3 (2005): 473-493. This essay on the interplay between election patterns and military conflicts is particularly relevant to the 1942 midterm elections.

Tufte, Edward R. "Determinants of the Outcomes of Midterm Congressional Elections." *American Political Science Review* 69, no. 3 (1975): 812-826. Brief but insightful overview of voting patterns in midterm elections.

See also Congress, U.S.; Conservatism in U.S. politics; Elections in the United States: 1940; Elections in the United States: 1944; Elections in the United States: 1948; Fair Deal; Inflation; Marshall Plan; New Deal programs; Presidential Succession Act of 1947.

■ Elections in the United States: 1944

The Event Presidential and congressional elections that saw President Roosevelt again reelected

Date November 7, 1944

Democratic president Franklin D. Roosevelt won an unprecedented fourth term, running against Republican Thomas E. Dewey, the governor of New York.

In the 1942 midterm elections, the Republican Party gained forty-seven seats in the House of Representatives and ten seats in the Senate. Those gains were not enough to gain control of either chamber, but they gave the Republicans hope for victory in the 1944 presidential election. Although many domestic issues needed to be resolved, the primary issue of concern was the country's involvement in World War II. In addition to raising concerns about the war, the Republican Party accused the Roosevelt administration of inefficiency and blamed the Democrats for the increased prices of food and overall inflation of prices. Conservatives hoped to bring an end to New Deal programs, and Democrats focused on winning the war and responding to labor union pressures.

The 1944 elections resulted in the Democrats gaining twenty seats in the House of Representatives and the Republicans losing eighteen. The Democrats thus maintained control of the House. The Democrats lost one seat in the Senate to the Republicans, maintaining a large majority.

The Presidential Candidates   Roosevelt faced little opposition from within the Democratic Party in his bid to be the party's candidate. At the Democratic National Convention in Chicago, only ninety delegates voted against his nomination. Vice president Henry A. Wallace, however, was perceived as too liberal and did not receive the southern vote at the Democratic convention. Roosevelt was forced to pick a new vice president and chose Harry S. Truman, a senator from Missouri. He selected Truman primarily because of his exemplary service in World War I, his voting record in the Senate, and the fact that Missouri was traditionally a swing state, so that a vice presidential candidate from that state might be the deciding factor in its presidential vote. Furthermore, Truman had served as the chairman of the Senate War Investigation Committee, which sought to reduce corruption and waste found in government contracts.

The Republican Party had numerous contenders for the presidential nomination. Wendell Wilkie, the Republican candidate in the 1940 election, quickly withdrew from the primaries after a poor showing in Wisconsin. Wilkie approved of many of Roosevelt's wartime programs, and that opened the path for Thomas Dewey to receive the nomination. Other contenders were wartime hero General Douglas MacArthur, former governor of Minnesota Harold E. Stassen, and Governor John W. Bricker of Ohio. MacArthur frequently spoke out against communism and many of the New Deal plans. Having proved himself as a special prosecutor and a district attorney, Dewey had been considered for the party nomination in 1940. He was elected governor of New York in 1942 and was popular throughout the state. His eventual nomination in 1944 reflected his strong voter base and the fact that he would most likely win the forty-seven electoral votes of New York, the most any state could offer.

At the Republican Convention, Dewey received all but one of the delegate votes. At forty-two years of age, he was the youngest man ever to win the Republican nomination and also the first to be born in the twentieth century. Dewey attempted to use his youth to his advantage and gain support of the younger voters. He was a full twenty years younger than Roosevelt and offered a stark contrast between his youthful energy and the declining health of Roosevelt. For his running mate, Dewey hoped to solidify the support of the conservative Republicans with his selection of Ohio's Governor Bricker. With the support of the Republican Party, Dewey and Bricker tried to influence voters by drawing their attention to anxiety about the war and resentment over domestic issues.

Coming into the elections, Roosevelt had proved to the American public his ability to serve during the twelve years of his presidential administration. The Republican Party and the press, however, questioned his health and continued ability to serve as president. Photographs circulated that showed Roosevelt looking old and ill. He ran a strong campaign nevertheless and was able to withstand or counter rumors about him.

Election Day Results   On election day, Roosevelt and Truman won with 53.4 percent of the popular vote, compared with 45.9 percent for Dewey and Bricker, representing an advantage of nearly 3.5 million votes. This was the narrowest victory of Roosevelt's four terms. The electoral vote favored Roosevelt 432 to 99; he needed only 266 electors to win. Roosevelt carried the entire South, most of the West Coast, and the eastern seaboard. His support came primarily from the New Deal coalition, labor unions, and absentee ballots from military personnel serving overseas. Dewey did well in the Midwest, winning in Indiana, Ohio, Wisconsin, Iowa, Nebraska, Kansas, and both North and South Dakota. He also won in Maine, Vermont, Colorado, and Wyoming. Other candidates were Norman M. Thomas of the Socialist Party and Claude A. Watson of the Prohibition Party. Thomas ran unsuccessfully as the Socialist presidential candidate in 1940, 1944, and 1948. In 1944, he received slightly more than 79,000 votes, primarily from New York, Pennsylvania, and Wisconsin. Watson had previously run as the vice presidential candidate for the Prohibition Party in 1936 and ran again as the presidential candidate in 1948. He received more than 74,000 votes in 1944, garnering support primarily from California and Indiana.

Impact   Roosevelt and Truman presided over an eventful administration. Roosevelt oversaw the Yalta Conference of world leaders from February 4 to February 11, 1945. Roosevelt died of a cerebral hemorrhage two months later, on April 12, and did not live to see the end of World War II.

When Truman took office following Roosevelt's death, he faced the continued pressures of World War II, though victory in Europe seemed assured. Germany offered unconditional surrender on May 8.

From July 17 to August 2, Truman met with the leaders of Great Britain and the Soviet Union at the Potsdam Conference. With Communist Party General Secretary Joseph Stalin of the Soviet Union, British prime minister Winston Churchill, and Churchill's successor, Clement Richard Attlee (whose election to the post was announced on July 26), he formulated plans to punish Germany for its aggressive actions. The conference also established policies for postwar order, settled issues of peace treaties, and made plans to counter the effects of the war.

After Japan refused the terms of unconditional surrender, Truman ordered that an atomic bomb be dropped on Hiroshima on August 6. Three days later, a second atomic bomb was dropped on Nagasaki.

Truman's administration also aided Turkey and Greece, both of which suffered from internal strife, providing funds to them in 1947 in an effort to contain communism. On March 12, 1947, Truman introduced the Truman Doctrine in a speech to Congress. The doctrine, based on the ideas of George Kennan (who had served as the deputy head of the U.S. mission in Moscow), outlined a policy for dealing with the Soviet Union and preventing the spread of communism to other countries. He pledged, in a policy of containment of communism, that the United States would provide political, military, and economic assistance to nations threatened by totalitarian forces, either internal or external.

Kathryn A. Cochran

Further Reading

Elston, Heidi. *Harry S. Truman.* Edina, Minn.: ABDO Publishing, 2009. As the vice presidential candidate, Truman played a critical role in the 1944 presidential election. This book examines Truman's life and impact on world events.

Evans, Hugh E. *The Hidden Campaign: FDR's Health and the 1944 Election.* Armonk, N.Y.: M. E. Sharpe, 2002. Discusses the impact of the presidency on Roosevelt's health and how his poor health affected the election. Argues that Roosevelt was in no physical condition to run for president in 1944.

Ferrell, Robert H. *Choosing Truman: The Democratic Convention of 1944.* Columbia: University of Missouri Press, 1994. Ferrell provides a detailed analysis of the 1944 Democratic Convention and the events that led to Truman receiving the vice presidential nomination.

Israel, Fred L. *Student's Atlas of American Presidential Elections, 1789 to 1996.* Washington, D.C.: Congressional Quarterly, 1997. Israel offers a brief look at the candidates, issues, and results of each presidential election for more than two centuries.

McCullough, David. *Truman.* New York: Simon & Schuster, 1992. Traces the life of Harry S. Truman from his youth in Independence, Missouri, to his time in the White House and beyond.

Mieczkowski, Yanek. *The Routledge Historical Atlas of Presidential Elections.* New York: Routledge, 2001. Coverage of all presidential elections from 1789 to 2000. Includes more than 70 maps and illustrations to facilitate interpretation of the data.

Morris-Lipsman, Arlene. *Presidential Races: The Battle for Power in the United States.* Minneapolis: Twenty-First Century Books, 2008. This book is filled with images from presidential campaigns, information about each race, and an explanation of how presidential races changed over the years.

Smith, Jean Edward. *FDR.* New York: Random House, 2007. More than half of the book deals with Roosevelt's four presidencies. Discusses his personal life in depth and evaluates his decisions as president. Though sympathetic to Roosevelt, Smith does not hesitate to discuss his flaws and questionable actions.

Truman, Harry S. *Dear Bess: The Letters from Harry to Bess Truman, 1910-1959.* Columbia: University of Missouri Press, 1998. A collection of more than six hundred letters that Truman wrote to his wife, Bess, chronicling the events in their lives.

See also Conservatism in U.S. politics; Dewey, Thomas E.; Elections in the United States: 1940; Elections in the United States: 1942 and 1946; Elections in the United States: 1948; MacArthur, Douglas; Presidential powers; Presidential Succession Act of 1947; Roosevelt, Franklin D.; Truman, Harry S.; Wallace, Henry A.

■ Elections in the United States: 1948

The Event Presidential and congressional elections

Date November 2, 1948

Following the death of Franklin D. Roosevelt from a cerebral hemorrhage on April 12, 1945, Harry S. Truman became president of the United States. In 1948, he ran for a full term against Republican candidate Thomas E. Dewey. Despite a divisive split within the Democratic Party and public opinion polls that predicted a landslide victory for Dewey, Truman persevered and won.

After the U.S. atomic bombing of Nagasaki and Hiroshima, World War II came to a fairly abrupt end. The economy that had thrived during the war was thrust into a recession, and the popularity of President Truman plummeted. Wages did not keep up with rising costs of living, and many necessities remained in short supply even after the end of wartime rationing. Labor strikes added to the economic turmoil affecting the steel, coal mining, and railroad industries. Truman could not solve the economic problems and was frequently portrayed by the media as unable to meet the challenges presented to him, making him politically vulnerable. The Republican Party was excited at the chance to reclaim the White House, and the Democratic Party felt doomed with Truman.

The Campaign The Republican Party selected New York governor Thomas E. Dewey as the party's nominee for president, as he had been in 1944. Dewey was a better orator than Truman, and his campaign seemed better organized. Former vice president Henry Wallace's decision to defect from the Democratic Party left the incumbent Truman hoping for the support of its splintered remains.

Truman began his campaign for reelection early. In his January, 1948, state of the union address, he promoted increases in the minimum wage, price supports for farmers, unemployment compensation, and an anti-inflation program designed to combat rising price levels. He also called for civil rights legislation. Both Truman and Dewey traveled extensively by railroad, crisscrossing the country, making speeches and appearances, and trying to gain support. Truman became quite adept at such whistle-stop campaigning and took an eighteen-state train tour under the guise of delivering a com-

mencement address at the University of California. His campaign realized that he faced an uphill battle but hoped and believed that he still had a chance to win. Clark Clifford, a White House counsel, and James Rowe, an adviser to Roosevelt, forecast the defection of Wallace to a third party and predicted Truman's eventual victory. They encouraged him to appeal to the Roosevelt coalition of labor, farmers, middle-class liberals, the South, and African Americans in the North. His campaign was long and tiresome, but effective. Dewey ran a more relaxed campaign, making fewer addresses than Truman and relying more on the radio time the Republican Party was able to purchase.

Also in the running were Governor Strom Thurmond of South Carolina, who ran for the States' Rights Party, and Wallace, who upset the Democratic Party when he declared his candidacy for the newly formed Progressive Party. Thurmond appeared to have widespread support in the South and with the Democrats who were unwilling to take on civil rights issues. Wallace was likely to garner support from the Northeast and parts of the Midwest. The Progressive Party platform called for repaired diplomatic relations between the United States and the Soviet Union, the destruction of all atomic bombs, an end to segregation, and an end to the Marshall Plan.

Throughout the campaign, numerous public opinion polls were taken to predict the presidential winner. In August of 1948, Gallup polls showed Dewey 11 points ahead of Truman (48 percent to 37 percent). As the two continued to campaign, more citizens came to see Truman, but Dewey found fewer people at his rallies. Journalists did not recognize the significance of the increasing crowds that turned out to see Truman speak, discounting this as mere curiosity and not support. The final polls for the election by both Gallup and Crossley showed Dewey in the lead with about 49 percent and Truman trailing at 44 percent. On the evening of election night, newspapers began to print their editions for the next day, declaring Dewey the winner. In perhaps the most famous picture of the election, Truman was photographed holding a copy of the *Chicago Daily Tribune* with a banner headline declaring "Dewey Defeats Truman."

The Election Day Upset The election saw one of the biggest political upsets in American history. Truman received 49.5 percent of the popular vote, topping

President Harry S. Truman gleefully holding up a newspaper that prematurely proclaimed his opponent the winner of the 1948 presidential election. (Library of Congress)

the Senate to recapture the majority. The Democrats' gain of 75 seats in the House brought their total to 263, against the Republicans' 171.

Impact Truman pledged continued support for the United Nations, which was formed in 1945. He spoke adamantly against what many saw as communist aggression and vowed to continue the Marshall Plan in Europe. Furthermore, in his inaugural address, Truman proposed aid for underdeveloped countries, hoping to contain the spread of communism. He also sent troops into South Korea to help resist an invasion from North Korea. On April 11, 1951, Truman dismissed World War II hero General Douglas MacArthur from his role in the military oversight of Japan, largely as a result of MacArthur's disagreements with Truman over handling of the Korean War. In April of 1952, he seized U.S. steel mills to prevent a labor strike, but that action was found unconstitutional in the case of *Youngstown Sheet and Tube Co. v. Sawyer* (1952). This decision, by a U.S. Supreme Court composed entirely of judges appointed by Truman and Roosevelt, was one of the major defeats of Truman's presidency. Truman is also recognized for desegregating the military.

Kathryn A. Cochran

Dewey's 45.1 percent. A major reason for the discrepancy between the predicted and the actual results was that many of the polls ended in mid-October and they did not account for the last-minute decisions of voters. The difference in the candidates' popular votes was magnified in the electoral college, where Truman received 303 votes to Dewey's 189, with 266 being enough for victory. Wallace and Thurmond each received about 2.4 percent of the national total. Thurmond won 39 electoral votes with the support he gained in his home state of South Carolina, Alabama, Mississippi, and Louisiana; he also earned one electoral vote from Tennessee. Wallace did not earn any electoral college votes. Socialist candidate Norman Thomas and Prohibition candidate Claude A. Watson each received less than 0.4 percent of the popular vote.

Congressional Results The Eightieth Congress (1947-1949) had seen the loss of Democratic control in the Senate. In the 1946 elections for the House of Representatives, Republicans had picked up 55 seats and the majority. The Republican Party thus gained control of Congress for the first time since 1930. In the 1948 elections, the electorate turned its support back to the Democratic Party, which gained 9 seats in

Further Reading

Israel, Fred L. *Student's Atlas of American Presidential Elections, 1789 to 1996.* Washington, D.C.: Congressional Quarterly, 1997. Offers a quick look at the candidates, issues, and results of each U.S. presidential election over the course of more than two centuries.

McCullough, David. *Truman.* New York: Simon & Schuster, 1992. Traces Harry S. Truman's life from his early years in Independence, Missouri, to his time in the White House and beyond. Offers a look at Truman's personality and experiences that shaped his political decisions.

Mieczkowski, Yanek. *The Routledge Historical Atlas of*

Presidential Elections. New York: Routledge, 2001. Coverage of all presidential elections from 1789 to 2000. Includes more than 70 maps and illustrations to facilitate interpretations of the data and comparisons among elections and candidates.

Morris-Lipsman, Arlene. *Presidential Races: The Battle for Power in the United States.* Minneapolis: Twenty-First Century Books, 2008. Filled with images from presidential campaigns, information about each race, and explanations of how presidential elections have changed since the first one in 1789.

Ross, Irwin. *The Loneliest Campaign: The Truman Victory of 1948.* New York: New American Library, 1968. Looks at the challenges facing the Truman team and the difficulties that they had to overcome to achieve Truman's surprising victory in 1948.

Schlesinger, Arthur M., Jr., with Fred L. Israel and David J. Frent, eds. *The Election of 1948 and the Administration of Harry S. Truman.* Broomall, Pa.: Mason Crest, 2003. This short book (128 pages) for younger readers discusses the election and Truman's second administration. Based on source documents.

Truman, Harry S. *Dear Bess: The Letters from Harry to Bess Truman, 1910-1959.* Columbia: University of Missouri Press, 1998. This collection of more than six hundred letters Truman wrote to his wife, Bess, offers a personal perspective on the events in their lives.

See also   Conservatism in U.S. politics; Elections in the United States: 1940; Elections in the United States: 1942 and 1946; Elections in the United States: 1944; Roosevelt, Franklin D.; Socialist Workers Party; Truman, Harry S.; Wallace, Henry A.

Electronic Numerical Integrator and Computer.
See **ENIAC**

■ Eliot, T. S.

Identification   American-born English poet, playwright, critic, and Nobel laureate
Born   September 26, 1888; St. Louis, Missouri
Died   January 4, 1965; London, England

With his profound themes of disillusionment and decadence reflective of the periods in which he wrote, Eliot was one of the pioneers of modern poetry. His Waste Land *(1922) and* Four Quartets *(1943) are two of the most celebrated literary works of the twentieth century.*

Thomas Stearns Eliot was born in Missouri into a prominent family with New England roots. From his family, he inherited but often struggled with the legacy of his upbringing: moral rigor, a sense of duty, an acute conscience, and an emotionally constricted rationalism. After entering Harvard University in 1906, he was influenced by the humanism of Irving Babbitt and discovered the French Symbolist poets of the nineteenth century, who would have a great impact on his own poetry. As part of his graduate work in philosophy, Eliot studied in Paris and, briefly, in Germany. The outbreak of World War I in 1914 sent him to England, where he befriended poet Ezra Pound, and his literary career began in earnest. In 1927, he became a British subject.

By the 1940's, Eliot had written his way through two decades. He had produced "The Love Song of J. Alfred Prufrock" (1915), the poem a reflection of the bleakness of his earlier urban years and later marriage and a response to the physical and spiritual disillusionment of the individual and the culture at large. He had also delivered the work often considered the most influential poem of the twentieth century—*The Waste Land* (1922), a social and psychological commentary in response to World War I that extended the themes of disenfranchisement through what Eliot once called his "grouse against life." In 1943, he published the *Four Quartets*, a poetical work that was a culmination of not only his best place memories but also his melancholy and alarm at the economic Depression, the rise of Nazism, and World War II.

In *Four Quartets* and other works of that period, Eliot began conveying a sense of peace with, satisfaction over, or acceptance of place in the context of time and history. Both his personal aesthetics and poetic authority continued to some extent to be preoccupied with and motivated by themes of time and its impact on aging, fragmentation, and dissociation. Eliot was under the pressure of a weakening marriage to an artist's daughter, Vivian Haigh, whose neuroses competed with his own interpersonal issues. He also faced the unrelenting pressures of sustaining his writing and banking careers, which were in conflict with each other by their very nature and demands on his time.

Meanwhile, Eliot met with criticisms of his work

ranging from its having repetitious imagery to being simply boring. Nevertheless, his efforts at synthesizing, or reconciling, spiritual fragmentation proved successful by the 1940's. For a time, *Four Quartets* would come to be regarded as being as influential and celebrated as *The Waste Land* had been during the 1920's.

Impact In most respects, Eliot was regarded an archetype of the intellectual literati of the 1940's. In 1948, he was awarded the Nobel Prize in Literature for his "outstanding, pioneer contribution" to the poetry of the period. Despite the mixed responses to his poetry and other writings, Eliot was also typically respected for his sensitivity to the surrounding oppressions of the period and for having an accurate grasp of the tone of the times: the Depression, the disaster of war, and the disillusionment of displacement.

Roxanne McDonald

Further Reading

Cooper, John Xiros. *The Cambridge Introduction to T. S. Eliot.* New York: Cambridge University Press, 2006.

Eliot, T. S. *The Complete Poems and Plays, 1909-1950.* London: Faber & Faber, 2004.

Raine, Craig. *T. S. Eliot.* New York: Oxford University Press, 2006.

See also Auden, W. H.; Literature in the United States; Nobel Prizes; Pound, Ezra; World War II.

■ Ellington, Duke

Identification Jazz pianist and bandleader

Born April 29, 1899; Washington, D.C.

Died May 24, 1974; New York, New York

Ellington was a brilliant pianist, composer-arranger, and bandleader. Renowned for his good business sense, polished appearance, and great rapport with audiences, he was able to build a successful musical career starting in the 1920's that carried on until

his death. By the 1940's, Ellington had established himself through radio broadcasting, recording, and touring extensively in the United States and abroad.

During the 1940's, Edward Kennedy "Duke" Ellington and his band struggled to overcome the fading popularity of the swing-era big bands and to stay afloat in a wartime economy that restricted unnecessary travel. The band also experienced a large turnover in personnel due to the loss of several band members. Ellington adapted to these conditions by relentlessly composing new music, while still performing his most popular tunes in all possible venues. Despite the recording ban of 1942-1944, Ellington achieved success with hits such as "Don't Get Around Much Anymore" and "Do Nothing 'Til You Hear from Me."

Ellington also expanded his musical vocabulary with more serious compositions. The band made its Carnegie Hall debut in 1943 with the performance of Ellington's jazz suite entitled *Black, Brown, and Beige.* Although the three-part extended work did not receive much critical acclaim initially, it was the beginning of Ellington's exploration of larger forms, and it was essential in establishing that jazz could be a sophisticated art form.

Duke Ellington (left) and Louis Armstrong at a 1941 recording session. (AP/Wide World Photos)

Impact   With more than one thousand works attributed to Duke Ellington, his music has become an important component of the jazz repertoire. At the beginning of the twenty-first century, he remained a world-renowned figure in American music.

Staci A. Spring

Further Reading

Ellington, Edward K. *Music Is My Mistress*. New York: Da Capo Press, 1980.

Howland, John. *Ellington Uptown: Duke Ellington, James P. Johnson, and the Birth of Concert Jazz*. Ann Arbor: University of Michigan Press, 2009.

Tucker, Mark, ed. *The Duke Ellington Reader*. New York: Oxford University Press, 1993.

See also   Davis, Miles; Dorsey, Tommy; Goodman, Benny; Music: Classical; Music: Jazz; Music: Popular; Parker, Charlie; Recording industry.

■ Emergency Price Control Act of 1942

The Law   Federal statute to control prices during World War II

Date   Enacted on January 30, 1942

The act established a comprehensive set of price and rent controls in an effort to prevent wartime inflation from weakening the U.S. economy.

During World War I, the United States experienced significant inflation. Thus, when the United States entered World War II in 1941, inflation became an immediate concern. The inflation fears stemmed from three effects of the war effort. First, it effectively ended unemployment, as men joined the armed forces and war production needs boosted civilian employment. Second, war spending pumped enormous amounts of money into the economy, increasing the money supply. Third, the focus on production for the war effort and the rationing of essential goods meant that war plant employees and the families of soldiers had few places to spend the wages they were receiving. With more cash chasing fewer goods, inflation was a serious economic danger.

Inflation posed a serious threat to the war effort. If prices for the limited consumer goods available, housing, and food rose significantly, workers in war plants would insist on wage increases and could engage in industrial actions such as strikes that would curtail production of essential war goods. Increasing wages in an effort to keep up with rising prices, however, would force additional price increases as producers passed on the higher cost of labor. To prevent wartime inflation from undermining both the economic recovery that the war brought and the war effort itself, Congress passed the Emergency Price Control Act of 1942 to contain both wages and prices.

Statutory Provisions   The act established the Office of Price Administration, to which it delegated the authority to select the specific maximum amounts for both wages and prices. To aid in enforcement, the statute required businesses to maintain records of sales for the agency to inspect. The agency also had authority to fix rents in areas near defense plants. Crucially, those affected by the agency's regulations had only a brief time to object to the price ceilings after they were put in place and had to do so in a special court, greatly limiting opportunities to mount legal challenges.

Those persons charging prices higher than authorized were subject to six months imprisonment and fines of $1,000 (about $13,000 in 2009 dollars). The conviction in early 1942 of two Massachusetts butchers and their employer for violating the price controls on wholesale meat led to the landmark Supreme Court case of *Yakus v. United States* (1944), which upheld the statute against both the nondelegation doctrine and due process challenges.

Impact   The act had two major effects during the 1940's. First, in large part because of the price controls, wartime inflation during World War II was held to just over 2 percent, a sharp contrast to the more than 16 percent inflation experienced during World War I. This low inflation rate was a significant aid to the war effort. Second, the Supreme Court's decision upholding the act firmly entrenched the government's power to regulate the economy, ending any hope that the nondelegation doctrine would serve as a limit on expanding government intervention.

Andrew P. Morriss

Further Reading

Mayer, Kenneth R. *With the Stroke of a Pen: Executive Orders and Presidential Power*. Princeton, N.J.: Princeton University Press, 2002.

Rockoff, Hugh. *Drastic Measures: A History of Wage and Price Controls in the United States.* New York: Cambridge University Press, 1984.

Rozell, Mark J., and William D. Pederson. *FDR and the Modern Presidency: Leadership and Legacy.* Westport, Conn.: Greenwood Press, 1997.

See also Black market; Business and the economy in the United States; Economic wartime regulations; Labor strikes; Office of Price Administration; Wartime rationing.

■ ENIAC

Identification The world's first general-purpose electronic computer

Completed in 1946, the ENIAC marked the dawn of modern computer science and the twilight of analog computing.

The Electronic Numerical Integrator and Computer (ENIAC) was built during a time when the idea of an all-electronic computer was virtually inconceivable. In the early 1940's, it was commonly held that analog computational devices, such as the differential analyzer (which used wheel-and-disc mechanisms to perform integrations), were the wave of the future. When, in 1942, University of Pennsylvania professor John William Mauchly proposed to the directors of his institution a plan to build a vacuum-tube-based calculator, his idea was immediately dismissed.

If not for the demands of World War II, computing would have followed a vastly different path. To be used effectively, the large artillery pieces employed by the U.S. Army needed firing tables: exhaustive charts showing how to make aiming adjustments for factors including humidity, windage, and ground softness. The Ballistics Research Laboratory at Aberdeen Proving Ground (APG) in Maryland employed both human mathematicians and differential analyzers for this purpose, but they could not produce tables quickly enough. APG's impatience

---

What Is ENIAC?

The U.S. Army Ordnance Department and the Moore School of Electrical Engineering at the University of Pennsylvania published A Report on the Eniac (Electronic Numerical Integrator and Computer) *on June 1, 1946, introducing the ENIAC computer:*

What the ENIAC Does

The Electronic Numerical Integrator and Computer (ENIAC) is a high-speed electronic computing machine which operates on discrete variables. It is capable of performing the arithmetic operations of addition, subtraction, multiplication, division, and square rooting on numbers (with sign indication) expressed in decimal form. The ENIAC, furthermore, remembers numbers which it reads from punched cards, or which are stored on the switches of its so-called function tables, or which are formed in the process of computation, and makes them available as needed. The ENIAC records its results on punched cards from which tables can be automatically printed. Finally, the ENIAC is automatically sequenced, i.e., once set-up . . . to follow a routine consisting of operations in its repertoire, it carries out the routine without further human intervention. When instructed in an appropriate routine consisting of arithmetic operations, looking up numbers stored in function tables, etc., the ENIAC can carry out complex mathematical operations such as interpolation and numerical integration and differentiation.

The speed of the ENIAC is at least 500 times as great as that of any other existing computing machine. The fundamental signals used in the ENIAC are emitted by its oscillator at the rate of 100,000 per second. . . .

---

with these methods led it to take a gamble and hire Mauchly and John Presper Eckert, a fellow instructor at the University of Pennsylvania's Moore School of Electrical Engineering and champion of Mauchly's all-electronic idea, to head the creation of ENIAC in 1943.

Impact Completed in 1946 and used in many experiments thereafter, including the first computerized weather forecasts, ENIAC came too late to provide any support during the war. However, its accuracy and speed did conclusively prove the superiority of electronic computing to mechanical computing, paving the way for subsequent smaller digital computers. ENIAC consisted of forty nine-foot-tall cabinets, weighed thirty tons, and used decimal notation instead of the binary notation used by modern computers.

Abram Taylor

Further Reading

Hally, Mike. *Electronic Brains: Stories from the Dawn of the Computer Age.* Washington, D.C.: Joseph Henry Press, 2005.

McCartney, Scott. *ENIAC: The Triumphs and Tragedies of the World's First Computer.* New York: Walker, 1999.

See also Army, U.S.; Binary automatic computer; Computers; Science and technology; Wartime technological advances.

■ *Enola Gay*

Identification B-29 bomber that dropped the first atomic bomb on Japan

Date Dropped the bomb on August 6, 1945

Place Hiroshima, Japan

The successful atomic bombing of Hiroshima by the Enola Gay, *combined with the bombing of Nagasaki three days later by the* Bockscar, *contributed to the conclusion of World War II. The* Enola Gay *became a symbol of atomic warfare viewed with pride by some and with remorse by others.*

The B-29 Superfortress bomber was a long-range, high-altitude, four-engine, propeller-driven bomber used in firebombing missions over Japan near the end of World War II. As part of the Manhattan Project, some B-29s were modified so that their bomb bays and bomb doors could accommodate atomic bombs. These modified bombers became known as the Silverplate B-29. Twenty-nine of these planes were assigned to the 509th Composite Group during World War II, and fifteen were prepared for use in atomic bombings. The *Enola Gay*, named after the mother of the plane's pilot, Paul Tibbets, was a Silverplate.

In May of 1945, the *Enola Gay* was constructed in Bellevue, Nebraska, on an assembly line run by the Glenn L. Martin Company. Tibbets, commander of

Pilot Paul Tibbets waving from the cockpit of the Enola Gay *before taking off on his flight to Hiroshima.* (National Archives)

the 509th Composite Group, selected the plane. The U.S. Army Air Forces accepted Tibbets's selection on May 18; the plane was flown on June 14 to Wendover, Utah, where the 509th Composite Group was training. Two weeks later, the plane went to Guam for modifications of the bomb bay. On July 6, the plane flew to Tinian, the Pacific island that served as the point of departure for the mission over Hiroshima, Japan.

Transportation of the components for the atomic bomb was done in two phases. Portions of the bomb were shipped aboard the cruiser USS *Indianapolis* and arrived in Tinian on July 26. Also arriving aboard the *Indianapolis* were several crew members of the *Enola Gay*, who armed the nuclear weapon during flight. Three C-54 aircraft brought target rings for the bomb on July 28.

After leaving Tinian, the *Indianapolis* sailed for Guam and then to Leyte Gulf, on the east coast of the Philippines. Before reaching the gulf, the *Indianapolis* sustained massive damage from torpedoes fired by a Japanese submarine. The ship sank swiftly, and the surviving crew of almost 900 sailors was cast into the sea. Because of faulty communications, for the next four days crew members desperately struggled to survive. Finally, rescue ships arrived and recovered 317 survivors. Thus, the ship that had delivered the atomic bomb to the point of departure for the *Enola Gay* went down disastrously only days before the bombing of Hiroshima.

On August 6, at 8:15 A.M., the *Enola Gay* dropped the uranium bomb "Little Boy" on Hiroshima. On August 9, the plutonium bomb "Fat Man" was dropped on Nagasaki. Approximately 100,000 people died at Hiroshima out of a population of 400,000, and about 50,000 more died at Nagasaki. Japan surrendered on August 15.

Impact The *Enola Gay*'s mission contributed to the ending of World War II, and the plane became a focal point for the debate about the morality of atomic weapons. Tibbets never regretted his actions, but he did face criticism. Rather than have his grave become a site for protests, he chose to be cremated.

In 1995, controversy arose when the National Air and Space Museum of the Smithsonian Institution planned an exhibit to mark the fiftieth anniversary of the bombing of Japan. The script for the exhibit, some said, portrayed the Japanese as victims without paying adequate attention to Japanese atrocities or to justifications for the use of atomic weapons under the circumstances. An exhibit based on revised plans opened on June 28 and displayed components of the *Enola Gay*, a video featuring Captain Tibbets, and information about the development of the B-29 Superfortress. This exhibit closed on May 17, 1998, but the fully restored *Enola Gay* went on permanent display at the National Air and Space Museum's Steven F. Udvar-Hazy Center in December, 2003.

William T. Lawlor

Further Reading

Campbell, Richard H. *The Silverplate Bombers: A History and Registry of the Enola Gay and Other B-29 Bombers Configured to Carry Atomic Bombs.* Jefferson, N.C.: McFarland, 2005. Background on the development of the B-29.

Newman, Robert P. *Enola Gay and the Court of History.* New York: Peter Lang, 2004. Discussion of moral questions following the bombing of Japan.

Thomas, Gordon, and Max Morgan Witts. *Enola Gay: The Bombing of Hiroshima.* Old Saybrook, Conn.: Konecky & Konecky, 2006. A presentation of interviews and historical documents.

Tibbets, Paul. *The Tibbets Story.* New York: Stein & Day, 1982. The pilot's personal account of the Hiroshima bombing mission.

See also Air Force, U.S.; Aircraft design and development; Atomic bomb; Bombers; Doolittle bombing raid; *Hiroshima*; Hiroshima and Nagasaki bombings; World War II.

■ Everson v. Board of Education of Ewing Township

The Case U.S. Supreme Court ruling that upheld bus fare reimbursements for private parochial school students

Date Decided on February 10, 1947

The Everson *decision held that states were limited by the establishment clause of the First Amendment, which was given its initial robust interpretation.*

The Bill of Rights originally limited only the federal government, not the states. The *Everson* decision marked the first application of the establishment clause of the First Amendment, "Congress shall make no law respecting an establishment of religion," to a state.

New Jersey reimbursed parents for part of the cost of bus transportation to and from public and private schools, including Roman Catholic parochial schools. Arch R. Everson challenged the program as a subsidy of religious education in violation of the First Amendment.

Although all the Supreme Court justices agreed on the principles of the First Amendment, the Court split on their application to this case. A state's policy must have a secular purpose, and its primary effect could not aid or burden religion. However, since all government activity aided religion to some degree, the Court permitted secondary benefits, those enjoyed by religious persons or institutions in common with all members of organized society. Denial of such ordinary benefits would constitute hostility to religion—also a violation of the First Amendment.

While the majority upheld New Jersey's law as aiding only a secular purpose of transporting children to and from school, four dissenting justices found the program to be an unconstitutional subsidy of religious education.

Impact   The *Everson* decision was the first case to interpret the establishment clause of the First Amendment. Subsequently, in *Lemon v. Kurtzman* (1971), the Court would add the requirement that state policy avoid excessive church-state entanglements.

John C. Hughes

Further Reading

Hall, Kermit L., ed. *The Oxford Companion to the Supreme Court.* New York: Oxford University Press, 1992.

Pfeffer, Leo. *Church, State, and Freedom.* Boston: Beacon Press, 1967.

See also   Civil rights and liberties; Education in the United States; *Illinois ex rel. McCollum v. Board of Education*; Religion in the United States; Supreme Court, U.S.

■ Executive Order 8802

The Law   Presidential order that prohibited racial discrimination in government and in the defense industry

Date   Signed on June 25, 1941

Prior to Executive Order 8802, African Americans were often excluded from employment by private corporations under contract with the federal government to produce goods for military use by Great Britain at the beginning of World War II. As a result of this law, companies were required to hire more African Americans or risk loss of their contracts at a time when American corporations had not fully recovered from the Depression and were in need of business opportunities that the government alone could provide.

In 1941, Congress approved military production contracts for the Lend-Lease program to support the Allied war effort, resulting in the creation of thousands of American jobs. Most companies, however, refused to hire fully qualified African Americans for skilled jobs; instead, African Americans were considered fit only for positions as janitors. Black leaders such as A. Philip Randolph were incensed about this discrimination. Although Eleanor Roosevelt communicated Randolph's complaint to her husband, President Franklin D. Roosevelt, nothing was done in response. Accordingly, African American leaders began to organize a March on Washington to protest racial discrimination and to demand that hiring be done in a nondiscriminatory way.

On June 18, 1941, Randolph met President Roosevelt in the White House, insisting that an executive order be issued to prohibit employment discrimination by military contractors. When Randolph informed the president that 100,000 protesters were ready to march if the order were not signed, the president agreed to the executive order.

Executive Order 8802 required federal agencies and departments responsible for military production to monitor vocational and training programs so that those enrolled would be selected without discrimination on the basis of "race, creed, color, or national origin." Defense contracts had a similar provision prohibiting discrimination in employment.

A Fair Employment Practices Commission was established by Executive Order 8802 within the Office of Production Management. The commission had responsibility to investigate allegations of discrimination and was empowered "to take appropriate steps to redress grievances that it finds to be valid." The commission also reviewed developments within the industry through site visits and other fact-finding actions in order to develop recommendations on the most effective measures to promote compliance.

Impact   The threatened March on Washington was suspended after Executive Order 8802 was issued.

Extract from Executive Order 8802

Now, therefore, by virtue of the authority vested in me by the Constitution and the statutes, and as a prerequisite to the successful conduct of our national defense production effort, I do hereby reaffirm the policy of the United States that there shall be no discrimination in the employment of workers in defense industries or government because of race, creed, color, or national origin, and I do hereby declare that it is the duty of employers and of labor organizations, in furtherance of said policy and of this order, to provide for the full and equitable participation of all workers in defense industries, without discrimination because of race, creed, color, or national origin.

Subsequently, President Harry S. Truman signed Executive Order 9981 in 1948, which expanded on Roosevelt's order. In the same vein, stronger executive orders were issued by later presidents, the most comprehensive of which was Executive Order 11246, signed by Lyndon B. Johnson in 1965.

African Americans were indeed hired throughout World War II on military contracts. In 1943, after a fistfight broke out in Detroit because whites resisted the hiring of African Americans at one of the automobile companies, a large-scale race riot developed. In response, military contractors agreed to hire African Americans on every work crew, sometimes on the basis of "hire now, train later." Executive Order 8802 set the stage for the eventual development of affirmative action plans for all federal contractors, not just military contractors, from the 1960's to the present.

Michael Haas

Further Reading

Goodwin, Doris Kearns. *No Ordinary Time: Franklin and Eleanor Roosevelt: The Home Front in World War II.* New York: Simon & Schuster, 1994.

Miller, Calvin Craig. *A. Philip Randolph and the African-American Labor Movement.* Greensboro, N.C.: Morgan Reynolds, 2005.

Milleson, Debra A. "W(h)ither Affirmative Action: The Future of Executive Order 11,246." *University of Memphis Law Review* 29 (Spring/Summer, 1999): 679-737.

See also Executive orders; Lend-Lease; National Association for the Advancement of Colored People; Racial discrimination; Randolph, A. Philip; Roosevelt, Eleanor; Roosevelt, Franklin D.

■ Executive orders

Definition Directives and regulations issued by presidents of the United States

Many executive orders are issued for administrative purposes in the president's capacity as chief executive. Others, ordinarily implementing an act of Congress, a treaty, or a provision of the Constitution, have the force of law and can affect the rights and liberties of the general public.

The best-known executive orders of President Franklin D. Roosevelt's first two terms, in the 1930's,

helped shape the New Deal's response to the Great Depression. Before the bombing of Pearl Harbor in December, 1941, executive orders played a major role in U.S. efforts to avoid going to war but preparing for it, just in case. Executive Order 8926 (October 28, 1941) established the Office of Lend-Lease Administration, through which the United States provided future allies with billions of dollars in food and military equipment, including the Liberty ships. Executive Order 8802 (June 25, 1941), to head off a major civil rights protest in Washington, D.C., created a temporary Fair Employment Practices Commission to combat racial discrimination in federal employment. Eventually, Congress followed suit and established a permanent commission. Roosevelt's most notorious executive order was Executive Order 9066 (February 19, 1942), which authorized the Army to exclude Japanese Americans from the West Coast and intern them in concentration camps throughout World War II. This led to the landmark Supreme Court case of *Korematsu v. United States* (1944), in which the Court upheld the constitutionality of the executive order.

Roosevelt used executive orders to stabilize the economy. On July 30, 1941, he established the Economic Defense Board to use economic controls to strengthen national defense. This later became the Board of Economic Warfare, which played an important part in World War II. On August 6, 1941, Roosevelt ordered the Federal Reserve Board to combat the inflationary pressures of prewar production by curbing installment buying. Arguably, his most important order was one he never issued. Widely expected in August, 1941, to issue economic orders stabilizing wages and prices to fight inflation, Roosevelt decided to leave the issue to the democratic process and instead urged Congress to legislate controls, which it did in the Economic Stabilization Act of 1942.

Both Roosevelt and Harry S. Truman used executive orders, with congressional authority, to put down strikes or seize defense plants threatened by labor action during the war. In 1952, when Truman seized steel mills during the Korean War without congressional authority, the Supreme Court declared the seizures unconstitutional.

Truman used executive orders to combat racial discrimination. On December 5, 1946, he created the first Presidential Committee on Civil Rights (Executive Order 9808) and, on July 26, 1948, caught

Congress and the public by surprise with a pair of orders designed to end segregation in federal employment (Executive Order 9980) and in the military (Executive Order 9981).

After the National Security Act of 1947 reorganized the military establishment and created the Central Intelligence Agency (CIA), Truman utilized executive orders to shape the development of the intelligence community and the new Defense Department. Truman's Loyalty Order (March 21, 1947), responding to Republican charges that the Democrats were soft on communism, launched years of security investigations of millions of federal employees in a prelude to the McCarthy era. Executive Order 9857 (May 22, 1947) provided for military and economic aid to Greece and Turkey to help them fight communist insurgencies, implementing the Truman Doctrine of Soviet containment and laying the groundwork for the Cold War.

Impact Executive orders helped set the tone for Roosevelt's and Truman's presidencies. Roosevelt used them to establish the New Deal and combat the Great Depression and to prepare for and conduct World War II. Truman used them to enhance national security early in the Cold War and to combat racial discrimination when he thought that Congress was not moving quickly enough.

William V. Dunlap

Further Reading

McCullough, David G. *Truman*. New York: Simon & Schuster, 1992.

McElvaine, Robert S. *Franklin Delano Roosevelt*. Washington, D.C.: CQ Press, 2002.

Warber, Adam L. *Executive Orders and the Modern Presidency: Legislating from the Oval Office*. Boulder, Colo.: Lynne Rienner, 2006.

See also Desegregation of the U.S. military; Emergency Price Control Act of 1942; Executive Order 8802; Japanese American internment; Lend-Lease; Loyalty Program, Truman's; New Deal programs; Presidential powers; Roosevelt, Franklin D.; Truman, Harry S.; Wartime seizures of businesses.

F

■ Fads

Definition   Fashions, products, ideas, interests, and behaviors that are intensely popular for brief periods of time

With major societal changes and the development of new technologies, the 1940's was a pivotal decade for fads. Reflecting both wartime living and postwar optimism, fads heralded a new global consumer culture.

Seven million Americans became newly employed during World War II. Older citizens, traditional housewives, and teenagers acquired more earning and spending power. With fathers at war and mothers working outside the home, young people became more independent. Women worked in formerly all-male jobs. There was a booming war economy, but the government had to impose rationing of materials and foods in order to support military needs. Research produced new materials and technologies. These social, economic, and technological developments led to creative and often radical fads in the 1940's.

Fashion and Hairstyles   The most famous clothing fad of the early 1940's was the zoot suit, which consisted of an oversized jacket with broad, padded shoulders and tapered waist, and baggy pants with neat, pegged cuffs. This suit was popular among urban youth, especially African American and Mexican American teens. However, when the U.S. War Production Board restricted the fabric that could be used in clothing, this oversized suit represented an unpatriotic extravagance. The violent zoot-suit riots of 1943 also hastened the end of this fad.

Bobby socks and saddle shoes were fashion fads popularized by teenage girls. Bobby socks had their tops folded over to form a cuff above the ankles. They were worn with saddle shoes—low shoes laced over the instep, with a saddle of contrasting color, usually brown. Adolescent girls became known as "bobby-soxers."

With men serving in the military, a third of all women went to work, often in traditionally male jobs. For these women, symbolized by "Rosie the Riveter," slacks became acceptable clothing. Prior to the war, American fashion followed French styles, but during the war America had to create its own fashion styles. Because of restrictions on the use of fabric, dye, buttons, and hosiery, women's clothing was simple and practical. The faddish "convertible suit" consisted of a boxy daytime jacket with padded shoulders, short skirt, and plain blouse. This suit could be worn for both daytime activities and evening dancing. After the war, French design was popular again, as designer Christian Dior introduced a new fashion fad, the "New Look," which was a feminine style with softer shoulders, a longer full skirt with layers of petticoat underneath, and a belted waist. Postwar men's fashion also took advantage of more plentiful materials. Colorful Hawaiian shirts and trench coats were fashion fads.

In the early 1940's, exotic film star Carmen Miranda wore hats topped with plastic tropical fruits. She inspired the "tutti-frutti" fad, which used artificial fruit in jewelry, hats, and home decor.

During the 1940's, women often wore long hair parted on the side, with rolls or many curls, such as pin and ringlet curls. Also popular was the omelet fold, with hair parted in the back and crisscrossed to create folds, and soft curls at the top. Factory workers favored the chignon bun style, with hair pinned into a knot at the nape of the neck, and worn with a scarf. However, the most famous hairstyle fad of the 1940's was film star Veronica Lake's "sheepdog," or "peekaboo," style. Her shoulder-length blond hair was parted on the left and fell in front to hide her right eye. This style was glamorous but dangerous for women working with machinery, so Lake changed her trademark cascading hairstyle.

Food   In the early 1940's, gourmet food and entertaining became popular. In 1940, James Beard published his first book, *Hors d'Oeuvre and Canapés*. In January, 1941, a new magazine, *Gourmet*, began publication. A restaurant dessert in the 1930's, crêpe suzette, was the chic fad dessert of the 1940's. The February, 1943, issue of *Gourmet* published a poem in honor of crêpe suzette, and Beard included his own recipe in *The Fireside Cook Book*, published in 1949.

However, the war years were generally a time of food rationing, substitutions, and making do with fewer ingredients. Since food was needed to feed soldiers, there was a shortage of food supplies for civilian consumers. In 1942, the U.S. Office of Price Administration introduced rationing of food supplies. Home-cooked dishes without meat, sugar, or eggs became common. The government encouraged citizens to cultivate "victory gardens," also known as "war gardens," which boosted morale among the populace and reduced the pressure on the food supply, providing needed produce and saving money. These gardens were vegetable, fruit, and herb gardens planted on vacant lots, in backyards, on rooftops, and in some public parks. Even the Franklin D. Roosevelt White House had a victory garden. During the war, nearly 20 million Americans planted victory gardens, which accounted for 40 percent of all vegetable consumption in the country.

In 1943, the Canadian government gave official approval for victory gardens. *Canadian Horticulture and Home* published articles on victory gardening, the National Film Board of Canada produced films on nutrition, and seed companies promoted the idea in their advertisements. The public was enthusiastic, and by the end of 1943 there were 209,200 victory gardens, each producing an average of 550 pounds of vegetables.

Military Culture In 1939, a mysterious graffiti phrase, "Kilroy was here!" started appearing on ships and in military ports. Accompanied by a line drawing of a bald creature with a long nose and two big round eyes peeking over a wall, and fingers gripping the top of the wall, this popular phrase was an obsessive fad throughout the 1940's and into the early 1950's. Appearing wherever American troops went, it signified that the American G.I. had already been somewhere, including unlikely places such as the torch of the Statue of Liberty and the Arc de Triomphe in Paris. The graffiti even appeared in the bathroom used exclusively by Harry S. Truman, Clement Attlee, and Joseph Stalin during the Potsdam Conference in the summer of 1945.

Kilroy variations included the British Chad, the Australian Mr. Foo, and the Canadian Clem. Some Clem phrases were "Clem's pub," "Clem had chow here," and "Clem sweated out his last queue here." After the war, the American Transit Association (ATA) sponsored a nationwide contest on their *Speak to America* radio program to solve the Kilroy mystery. The ATA concluded that the originator was James J. Kilroy, a ship inspector in Quincy, Massachusetts, who used to write the phrase in yellow crayon on bulkheads in newly constructed ships to indicate rivet holes he had already inspected.

Another popular fad among soldiers was the "pinup girl," a term which first appeared in the April 30, 1943, issue of *Yank*, a military newspaper. Soldiers posted these pictures of scantily clad women inside their helmets, lockers, and even on the noses of fighter planes. The most famous pinup girl was Betty Grable, whose best-known pinup photo shows her wearing a white swimsuit and glancing back over her right shoulder. Other celebrated "forties girls" were film stars Ava Gardner, Lana Turner, and Rita Hayworth. Pinup girl Chili Williams was called the "Polka-Dot Girl" because of her bathing suit pattern. Pinup girls quickly became a national phenomenon and appeared on the covers of *Time* and *Life* magazines. Until banned by the postmaster general, Alberto Vargas's provocative paintings of women appeared in *Esquire*.

During the 1940's, a special candy was created for American soldiers. Forrest Mars and Bruce Murrie developed M&M's, small rounds of milk chocolate covered in a hard candy coating so that the chocolate did not melt in the hands. Production started in 1940, and in 1941 M&M's were introduced to soldiers and became a popular part of their rations.

Soldiers also helped stimulate the book club fad. While in the military and later as civilians, they were avid book readers. During the 1940's, previous hardcover best sellers were reprinted as paperbacks for the mass market, and book clubs printed millions of copies. At the height of book club mania, membership totaled 3 million.

Entertainment and Leisure During the 1940's, social dancing was popular. The most important dance fad was the jitterbug, a new form of swing dance that was carefree and improvisational. This dance used a six-count basic step, with a loose body posture, bent knees, and a low center of gravity. Allowing unusual

Boy holding a Slinky in 1946. (Getty Images)

flips and moves, the jitterbug was popular, especially among soldiers and teenagers.

From the 1930's through the late 1940's, comic books were hugely popular. During this "golden age," the modern superhero was born. Superman (1938), Captain America (1940), Batman (1940), and Wonder Woman (1941) all battled the forces of evil. Because of its wartime ban on American comic books, Canada created its own comic books, the "Canadian Whites," and superheroes, including Nelvana, Johnny Canuck, and Canada Jack.

The most celebrated toy invention of the decade was the Slinky, eighty-seven feet of flat wire coiled into three-inch-wide circles and standing two inches high. Invented by shipbuilder Richard James, Slinky could open and close like an accordion and could be turned end over end to "walk" down stairs. In 1945, more than fifty thousand Slinkys were sold during the toy's first two months on the market.

Introduced in Al Capp's classic comic strip *Li'l Abner* in August, 1948, the Shmoo was one of the greatest fads of the decade. This lovable and gentle pear-shaped creature had eyebrows, whiskers, and round feet, but no nose, ears, or arms. It produced eggs, butter, and milk. It asexually reproduced and loved to be eaten by humans. However, before the literary demise of this creature, Shmoo marketing from 1948 to 1952 was phenomenally successful. Seventy different manufacturers produced nearly one hundred licensed products, including plastic dolls, ashtrays, baby rattles, comic books, and jewelry.

Commercial television began in 1947 with sixteen stations and ended the decade with 107 stations. The advent of "kiddie TV" enabled profitable spin-off toy fads. On December 27, 1947, the *Howdy Doody* show premiered, and an estimated one-third of American children became fans. Fads included Howdy Doody sleeping bags, records, and dolls. *Kukla, Fran, and Ollie* premiered on November 29, 1948, and it had six million viewers and dozens of toy fads by 1950. On June 24, 1949, *Hopalong Cassidy* premiered, introducing television's first cowboy hero. The show generated fads such as "Hoppy" bicycles, peanut butter, hats, and cowboy outfits. Before the show ended in 1953, Hoppy fads had spread to France, Italy, England, Sweden, and Mexico.

Impact Fads of the 1940's reflected and influenced all areas of popular culture. Many eventually entered mainstream culture, while others had revivals. The Christian Dior fad began the trend toward designer-named labels. The Veronica Lake hairstyle staged a comeback at designer fashion shows in 2007. Slinky and M&M's continued to be best sellers into the twenty-first century. Renewed interest in victory gardens led to the cultivation of gardens in public places, including one at the Barack Obama White House in 2009.

Many fads of the 1940's showed the global potential of mass media marketing. Television and comic books had created beloved characters and superheroes capable of generating profitable fads. The rise of the teenage consumer also helped define future consumerism.

Alice Myers

Further Reading

Giordano, Ralph G. *Social Dancing in America.* Westport, Conn.: Greenwood Press, 2007. Comprehensive, two-volume history covers social dance movements in the United States from 1607 through 2000, including swing and the jitterbug. Illustrated. Bibliography and index.

Hoffman, Frank, and William G. Bailey. *Fashion and Merchandising Fads.* New York: Haworth Press, 1994. Entertaining stories about 140 fads, including several from the 1940's. Illustrated. Bibliography and index.

Lovegren, Sylvia. *Fashionable Food: Seven Decades of Food Fads.* Chicago: University of Chicago Press, 2005. This collection of anecdotes and faddish recipes covers the 1940's in a chapter entitled, "The forties: Oh, what a hungry war!" Illustrated. Bibliography and index.

Panati, Charles. *Panati's Parade of Fads, Follies, and Manias: The Origins of Our Most Cherished Obsessions.* New York: HarperPerennial, 1991. Comprehensive and entertaining history of a century of popular culture, including 1940's fads. Photos and bibliography.

Sickels, Robert. *The 1940's.* Westport, Conn.: Greenwood Press, 2004. Scholarly work covering everyday America, the world of youth, and all aspects of popular culture during the 1940's. Illustrated. Bibliography and index.

Steele, Valerie. *Fifty Years of Fashion: New Look to Now.* New Haven, Conn.: Yale University Press, 1997. Beautifully illustrated with photographs from the Museum at the Fashion Institute of Technology, this history covers both wartime and postwar fashions, including the New Look. Bibliography and index.

Walford, Jonathan. *Forties Fashion: From Siren Suits to the New Look.* London: Thames & Hudson, 2008. A thorough study of world fashion, including practical wartime and glamorous postwar styles. Illustrated. Bibliography and index.

See also   Comic books; Comic strips; Dance; Fashions and clothing; Hairstyles; Jitterbug; M&M candies; Recreation; Zoot-suit riots; Zoot suits.

■ Fair Deal

Identification   President Harry S. Truman's policy program for bolstering civil rights and domestic social policy

Date   Launched in September, 1945; articulated in January, 1949

The Fair Deal achieved neither the success nor the lasting notoriety of Franklin D. Roosevelt's New Deal. However, President Truman did achieve some positive changes for African American citizens, particularly those living in poor urban areas. The program also institutionalized the model of a bigger federal government created by Roosevelt.

Following Roosevelt's death in April, 1945, Harry S. Truman assumed the presidency, looking to affirm his former boss's conception of America as a progressive liberal democracy. Truman's activist proposals met with more limited success than the policy work of Roosevelt and that of later, fellow big-government Democrats John F. Kennedy and Lyndon B. Johnson. Truman was repeatedly stymied in Congress—first by a group of Democratic moderates and later by the heavy weight of the unpopular Korean War. The president from Missouri was, however, direct and tenacious as always, and was able to claim victory on at least a handful of policy fronts.

The Mixed Success of the Fair Deal   Scholars have noted the failures of the Fair Deal, while pointing out a few of its unlikely successes. Decades later, it became safe to pronounce the legislative effort of President Truman as a mixed bag containing both slow defeat and surprising change. In September, 1945, fewer than six months after assuming office, Truman sent a twenty-one-point domestic policy plan to Congress. It included both renewed funds for New Deal programs, such as rural electrification and public housing, as well as more innovative policies such as broad education grants and robust agricultural support. However, his plan was flawed by being overly vague and conciliatory in tone. At this point, the plan did not have a name; the "Fair Deal" moniker came in January, 1949, at the start of his second term.

Truman was not the gifted, aggressive policy leader that Roosevelt had been. His approach to the Fair Deal was to negotiate with Congress to achieve its passage. He wanted the legislative branch to take the lead. As a former senator, Truman believed in the legislative process as the prime mover of federal law. He strove personally to frame the conversation regarding America's conversion from a wartime footing to a peacetime footing, but he wanted to leave the details to Congress. This was perhaps a noble nod to the intent of the Framers of the Constitution, but the method failed to produce strong legislative outcomes during the mid- and late 1940's.

Truman's first priority was to support organized labor with greater unemployment compensation, reduced taxes, national health insurance, and full unemployment legislation. All of these efforts failed despite Truman's best efforts at charming members of Congress. These failures caused Truman's reputation to suffer in the public eye, and he consequently lost some of his influence in Washington, particularly within his own cabinet, whose holdovers from Roosevelt's New Dealers did not hold him in high regard. The New Deal coalition was certainly not strongly behind Truman, who was expected to lose the 1948 presidential election. To the surprise of most prognosticators, however, Truman won a second term. Nevertheless, although he was energized by his electoral victory, he did not make much more progress with his Fair Deal agenda in the second term.

The Fair Deal and Civil Rights   The aspect of Truman's Fair Deal proposals that experienced the greatest success was civil rights, even though most of his ideas failed. Truman envisioned a permanent commission to deal with civil rights, a new civil rights division within the Justice Department, measures against discrimination in employment and lynching, as well as the strengthening of federal civil rights protections already in the books. These ideas would not come to fruition for another twenty years.

Where Truman most succeeded was in pointing out the continuing ills left by slavery in post-World War II America. Although American slavery had long been legally dead, Truman recognized that its effects lingered. Truman's efforts to address racial segregation in public restrooms, schools, and transportation did not get through Congress.

Stymied by Congress, Truman used his presidential power to issue executive orders to achieve some of his goals and achieved what are perhaps his most lasting accomplishments in domestic policy.

On December 5, 1946, he used Executive Order 9808 to create the first Presidential Committee on Civil Rights. On July 26, 1948, he issued Executive Order 9980 to end segregation in federal employment and Executive Order 9981 to abolish segregation in the military. Breaking down these racial barriers would help set the stage for further civil rights actions in the 1960's.

At this period in American history, southern Democratic politicians did not support the equal treatment of African Americans. Truman recognized this but persisted to win them over nonetheless. In the end, he never did.

Impact   In retrospect, the Fair Deal did not have the grand impact of the New Deal. Nevertheless, it is impressive that Truman achieved as much as he did even though he inherited a cabinet that was not personally loyal to him and had to work with a hostile Congress. Southern congressmen opposed every progressive move he made.

The looming crisis of the Great Depression was over, as was any real sense of urgency about drastically changing American society. During his second term, Truman faced the mighty challenges of the Korean War, the rise of communist China, and McCarthyism. In the end, he was able to continue to fund Roosevelt's programs such as old age insurance and unemployment benefits. Whenever and wherever he could, Truman supported organized labor and minorities. Perhaps most important of all, he changed the terms of the national debate after World War II. The genius in the Fair Deal, to the extent that it was a political masterstroke, was not in the details of specific policies. The lasting impact of the Fair Deal lies in how it kept issues regarding the most disadvantaged citizens in the public spotlight for later change.

R. Matthew Beverlin

Further Reading

Gardner, Michael M. *Harry Truman and Civil Rights: Moral Courage and Political Risks.* Carbondale: Southern Illinois University Press, 2002. Using the actual speeches and executive orders of Truman as a narrative structure, this sweeping work is a great place to begin study of this president and his civil rights platform.

Hamby, Alonzo L. *Beyond the New Deal: Harry S. Truman and American Liberalism.* New York: Columbia University Press, 1973. A noted Truman scholar takes up the topic of Truman and his time guiding the American experiment in liberal democracy. It focuses on not only the Fair Deal program but also on his foreign policy work.

_____. *Man of the People: A Life of Harry S. Truman.* New York: Oxford University Press, 1995. Informative, thick one-volume work on Harry Truman, covering his birth through his post White House years back in Missouri.

_____, ed. *Harry S. Truman and the Fair Deal.* Lexington, Mass.: D. C. Heath, 1974. A respectable collection of academic writings and original texts concerning the Fair Deal. The entry by Truman staffer Neustadt is particularly insightful.

Woods, Randall Bennett. *Quest for Identity.* New York: Cambridge University Press, 2005. Well-written general work of history that covers the time of the Fair Deal to the present. Provides information on which direction the country followed after Truman's policy initiatives in the 1940's.

See also   Civil rights and liberties; Loyalty Program, Truman's; New Deal programs; Presidential powers; Truman, Harry S.

■ Fair Employment Practices Commission

Identification   Federal executive branch agency created by an executive order

Date   Operated 1941-1946

The Fair Employment Practices Commission (FEPC) was created to enforce a presidential order prohibiting discrimination on the basis of race or religion in defense-related companies having contracts with the federal government.

In January, 1941, as war between the United States and Germany appeared likely, A. Philip Randolph, the dynamic leader of the Brotherhood of Sleeping Car Porters, joined with other civil rights activists in announcing the March on Washington movement, which planned to bring 100,000 demonstrators to the nation's capital to protest racial discrimination in the military and the defense industry. President Franklin D. Roosevelt was worried that the march might result in violence, and on June 18, he discussed the matter with Randolph and Walter White, the executive secretary of the National Association for the Advancement of Colored People. The two African American leaders offered to call off the march if the president would issue an executive order banning discrimination in the defense industries and the military. Roosevelt was adamantly opposed to desegregation of the armed forces, but he authorized members of his administration to work out a compromise on defense industries with the two men.

On June 25, 1941, Roosevelt signed Executive Order 8802, which created the Committee on Fair Employment Practices (FEPC), declaring that there should be no discrimination in the employment of workers in defense industries or government "because of race, creed, color, or national origin." The FEPC was empowered to investigate complaints of discrimination and to take appropriate action to eliminate discriminatory practices in any company selling products to the government. In 1942, Roosevelt restricted the FEPC's funding and placed it under the authority of the War Manpower Commission. After the head of the commission, Paul V. McNutt, failed vigorously to enforce the antidiscrim-

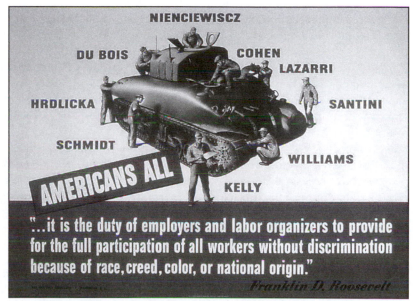

Late 1942 War Manpower Commission poster calling attention to the contributions made to the war effort by Americans of diverse national heritages. (Getty Images)

ination mandate, Randolph renewed his plans to organize a march on Washington.

Yielding to the threat of a mass demonstration for a second time, Roosevelt strengthened the FEPC in 1943 with Executive Order 9346, which reorganized the committee's membership and placed it under the Office of Emergency Management. The order further required all government contracts to contain a nondiscrimination pledge, it created regional offices, and it significantly increased the commission's budget. Although enforcement of the order was uneven, the FEPC sometimes demonstrated its seriousness in upholding the nondiscrimination principle. In 1944, for example, it successfully coerced white workers to end a strike they had called to protest the promotions of eight African Americans at the Philadelphia Transit Company.

The FEPC had a significant impact on northern industries. By 1945, African Americans held almost 9 percent of the jobs in defense industries, compared with about 2.5 percent in 1941. In addition, the number of African Americans working for the federal government more than tripled. However, the FEPC never attempted to challenge segregation in the southern states, and efforts to enforce the executive order led to a number of "hate strikes" in the Midwest and border states. Even in the more liberal states of the Northeast, nevertheless, a significant percentage of African Americans were segregated into relatively low-paying jobs and restricted in their right to participate in labor unions.

The FEPC was unpopular with the majority of white citizens as well as with most members of Congress. With the return of peace in 1945, President Harry S. Truman appeared content to allow its termination. Liberal members of Congress tried but failed to pass legislation that would have continued the FEPC. In the election year of 1948, Truman supported a bill to reestablish it as a permanent government agency, but the bill attracted little support. In 1950, a majority of the members of the U.S. House of Representatives voted in favor of resurrecting the committee, but in the Senate, southern Senators utilized the filibuster to kill the measure. After the outbreak of the Korean War in June, the Truman administration became too absorbed in foreign policy to devote much attention to the issue.

Impact The FEPC was the first agency that the federal government created to oppose employment discrimination. It inspired five northern states—New York, New Jersey, Massachusetts, Connecticut, and Washington—to establish their own antidiscrimination agencies. Historian Louis Ruchames wrote that the FEPC "brought hope and confidence" into the lives of African Americans. Its provisions and language provided a precedent for the later enactment of the Civil Rights Act of 1964.

Thomas Tandy Lewis

Further Reading

Collins, William J. "Race, Roosevelt, and Wartime Production: Fair Employment in World War II Labor Markets," *American Economic Review* 91 (March 2001): 272-286. Quantitative study concluding that the FEPC had some positive effects on African American employment throughout the 1940's.

Garfinkel, Herbert. *When Negroes March: The March on Washington Movement in the Organizational Politics for FEPC.* New York: Athenaeum, 1969. Focuses on how Randolph's threat to bring a large demonstration to Washington led to creation of the FEPC.

Kersten, Andrew E. *Race, Jobs, and the War: The FEPC in the Midwest, 1941-1946.* Urbana: University of Illinois Press, 2000. Detailed account arguing that the commission was moderately successful in some cities and unsuccessful in others, depending on the attitudes of workers and labor leaders.

Pfeffer, Paula F. *A. Philip Randolph: Pioneer of the Civil Rights Movement.* Baton Rouge: Louisiana State University Press, 1996. Detailed and insightful biography arguing that Randolph's ideas and strategies provided the blueprint for the later civil rights movement.

Reed, Merl E. *Seedtime for the Modern Civil Rights Movement: The President's Committee on Fair Employment Practice, 1941-1946.* Baton Rouge: Louisiana State University Press, 1991. Favorable account of the founding, activities, efficiency, and impact of the FEPC.

Ruchames, Louis. *Race, Jobs, and Politics: The FEPC.* New York: Columbia University Press, 1953. Written before the achievements of the Civil Rights movement, this book emphasizes the value of the FEPC and advocates that it be made a permanent agency.

See also African Americans; American Negro Exposition; Civil rights and liberties; Executive orders; Jim Crow laws; National Association for the Advancement of Colored People; Racial discrimination; Randolph, A. Philip; Universal Declaration of Human Rights; White, Walter F.

■ *Fantasia*

Identification Animated film set to classical music
Producer Walt Disney (1901-1966)
Date Released on November 13, 1940

The intention behind this Disney film was to create a new medium in which visual elements would bring to life great music. Release of the film coincided with broader aesthetic movements during the 1940's that attempted to educate the public in fine art. Although the film was never a commercial success, it would eventually be hailed as a classic.

The first version of *Fantasia* was conceived for formal theatrical engagements, and was over two hours in length. Its music director, conductor, and arranger, Leopold Stokowski, led the Philadelphia Orchestra when the film's musical selections were recorded. Music critic Deems Taylor introduced each piece, providing narrative voiceovers on various aspects of the music, including the composer intent. Each musical selection was performed over visually dramatic animated sequences designed to convey the spirit and energy of the music. For example, audiences listened to Johann Sebastian Bach's *Toccata and Fugue in D Minor* (1703-1707) being played while watching abstract patterns of light and color move across the screen.

Other selections in the film included Peter Ilich Tchaikovsky's *Nutcracker Suite* (1891), choreo-graphed to personify the seasons. In one of the most memorable sequences, Mickey Mouse struggles with a magic broom in a castle to to the sound of Paul Dukas's *The Sorcerer's Apprentice* (1897). Igor Stravinsky's *The Rite of Spring* (1913) is the musical backdrop to the extinction of dinosaurs. Another dramatic episode creates a demoniac scene to the thundering music of Modest Mussorgsky's *Night on Bald Mountain* (1886). In a lighter mood, comical animals dance to Amilcare Ponchielli's "Dance of the Hours" from his opera *La Gioconda* (1876).

The film opened to mixed critical reviews and failed to attract large audiences, leaving Walt Disney in financial distress. Believing that its length was the reason for the film's failure, the Radio-Keith-Orpheum (RKO) studio reedited the film, reducing

---

The Music of Fantasia

Fantasia *includes several major works of Western music, two of which—*Bach's Toccata and Fugue in D Minor *and Mussorgsky's* Night on Bald Mountain*—were adapted for the film by Leopold Stokowski.*

- Johann Sebastian Bach, Toccata and Fugue in D Minor, BWV 565 (1703-1707): Stokowski adapted this piece for performance by an orchestra; in the film, this music accompanies a series of abstract images.
- Peter Ilich Tchaikovsky, *Nutcracker Suite*, Op. 71a (1891): In the film, this music frames a series of dances performed by characters such as fairies, mushrooms, and fish.
- Paul Dukas, *The Sorcerer's Apprentice* (1897): In the famous "sorcerer's apprentice" sequence, Mickey Mouse plays the role of the apprentice.
- Igor Stravinsky, *The Rite of Spring* (1913): This music accompanies a depiction of Earth's history, including the extinction of the dinosaurs.
- Ludwig van Beethoven, Sixth Symphony in F, *Pastorale*, Op. 68 (1808): In this memorable scene, centaurs, fauns, and other mythological creatures relax and play together.
- Amilcare Ponchielli, *La Gioconda: Dance of the Hours* (1876): As it was originally, this piece is performed as a ballet, but here the dancers are elephants, ostriches, hippos, and alligators.
- Modest Mussorgsky, *Night on Bald Mountain* (1886): In one of the film's final scenes, the demon Chernabog and other malevolent creatures wreak havoc until Franz Schubert's "Ave Maria" (1825) signals the breaking of day and the entrance of monks.

its running time to eighty-one minutes. After the film was rereleased in January, 1942, it finally achieved commercial success. Subsequent releases of *Fantasia* restored some of its deleted footage, and it eventually became one of the highest-grossing films of the 1940's.

Impact Although *Fantasia* did not herald the beginning of a new art form, as Walt Disney had hoped, the film advanced the art of animation by freeing it from strict plot and character limits. Moreover, its mixtures of live and animated elements within the same frames led to other films following suit. It also influenced sound recording technologies as the first major film released in a state-of-the-art stereophonic sound ("Fantasound") created by Bell Laboratories.

Richard R. Bunbury

Further Reading

Barrier, Michael. *Hollywood Cartoons: American Animation in Its Golden Age.* New York: Oxford University Press, 1999.

Finch, Christopher. *The Art of Walt Disney.* Rev. ed. New York: Harry N. Abrams, 2004.

Maltin, Leonard. *The Disney Films.* 4th ed. New York: Disney Editions, 2000.

Taylor, Deems. *Walt Disney's "Fantasia."* New York: Simon & Schuster, 1940.

See also Animated films; Disney films; Film in the United States; Music: Classical.

■ Farmer, Frances

Identification American film star
Born September 19, 1913; Seattle, Washington
Died August 1, 1970; Indianapolis, Indiana

A popular film star, Farmer wrecked her career by opposing the obtrusive control of Hollywood studios during the 1930's and 1940's. Two highly publicized arrests led to her involuntary commitment to mental hospitals. Now best known for sensational accounts of her life, Farmer has become the subject of books, films, dramas, songs, and articles.

A University of Washington drama graduate, Frances Farmer was awarded a seven-year contract with Paramount Pictures in 1935 and was soon acclaimed as a rising star. She had unchallenging roles in the fourteen mostly B movies she made for Paramount,

Frances Farmer after being taken from her home to the Santa Monica, California, city jail in January, 1943. (AP/Wide World Photos)

but performance in *Come and Get It* (1936) was critically praised. Meanwhile, Farmer considered herself a serious actor and rebelled against her studio bosses. She left Hollywood in 1937 and accepted New York City's Group Theatre offer for her to appear in a stage production of *Golden Boy* by playwright Clifford Odets, with whom she had an affair. Despite receiving good reviews for her performance, Farmer was not chosen for the play's London engagement, so she later returned to Hollywood.

By 1940, Farmer's erratic work habits and developing alcoholism were damaging Farmer's career. Her marriage to actor Leif Erikson had ended. In 1942, she was arrested for driving in a blackout zone at a time when the West Coast was fearing a Japanese invasion. Accused of abusive behavior, she was placed on probation and subsequently imprisoned for parole violation and aggressive behavior in court—events that the press sensationalized. From

1944 to 1950, she was in and out of mental institutions. Placed under her mother's guardianship, Farmer was eventually sent to a Washington State institution until she was released in 1950, and her full civil rights were legally restored.

Impact Although Farmer is regarded as a fine actor, her reputation is clouded by the scandals arising from her legal and mental problems during the 1940's. Thanks to a renewal of public interest during the 1950's, she made a comeback in her acting career and appeared on television shows and dramas and acted in one final film, *The Party Crashers*. While living in Indianapolis from 1958 to 1964, she hosted a successful daily television show, *Frances Farmer Presents*, in which she presented feature films.

Christian H. Moe

Further Reading

Arnold, William. *Frances Farmer: Shadowland*. New York: Berkley Books, 1983.

Farmer, Frances. *Will There Really Be a Morning? An Autobiography*. New York: G. P. Putnam's Sons, 1972.

See also Civil rights and liberties; Crimes and scandals; Film in the United States; Psychiatry and psychology; Theater in the United States.

■ Fashions and clothing

Definition Styles and trends in clothing that reflected wartime shortages and sentiments in the first half of the decade

World War II forced adjustments in fashion; in particular, some fabrics became rare because they were needed for the war effort, and women moved into the workforce to take jobs left by men who joined the armed forces, sparking demand for utilitarian clothing for women. After the war, Dior's New Look became the prevalent silhouette for women, featuring longer skirts and emphasis on the waist, and men, tired of the conformity of their military uniforms, adopted more casual and expressive clothing styles.

Clothing fashions during the war years of the 1940's were characterized by utility and practicality. As men left for the war, women found themselves stepping into industrial roles and requiring clothing that fit new workplaces and that lasted longer, because replacements were not as easy to acquire. Civilian menswear did not change as dramatically, but like women's clothing, it was simpler and often used less fabric.

Womenswear, 1940-1945 Fabric was rationed in the United States and Canada during World War II, and partly as a result, skirts generally became shorter in the first half of the 1940's than they had been during the 1930's, though still not as short as during the flapper years of the 1920's. Shorter skirts allowed women to save fabric for the war effort: Nylon was needed for parachutes and wool for uniforms, and silk was no longer available because most of it had come from Japan. Pencil skirts economized fabric.

Women also found themselves reusing former outfits and making or remaking clothing at home. *McCall's* magazine published patterns to help women take old dresses and form them into clothing for children. Husbands who went off to war were no longer in need of the suits in their closets, and women altered those suits into feminine forms. *Vogue* even featured a trouser suit on its cover in 1941, and movie stars such as Lauren Bacall helped popularize wearing what had formerly been considered male clothing.

Women's tops featured broad, square shoulders inspired by the military uniforms of the day. Blouses went without ruffles, though some featured a bow at the neckline. Mixing and matching colors became a prominent part of 1940's fashion. Coordinating separates allowed women to stretch their wardrobes further, creating the illusion of having more outfits, and mixing and matching colors provided a way to use smaller pieces of material for those coordinates.

The nylon stocking was introduced to the United States in 1940. Soon, however, these stockings were virtually unavailable to women in the United States or Canada because the nylon to make them was required for parachutes. The United States also issued restrictions on women's clothing in 1942, specifying limits on using silk and wool through the L-85 order to save 15 percent of domestic fabric production for the war effort. To create the illusion of wearing stockings, some women applied makeup on their bare legs to tint them tan and drew lines along the backs of their legs with special paint to re-create the color and seams of nylon stockings. Teenage girls wore bobby socks rather than nylon stockings, often with penny loafers or shoes in the "Mary Jane" style. Other clothing also was rationed, and many outfits were designed with year-round wear in mind to make them more versatile.

Women also found themselves wearing trousers to work. These trousers, as well as work coveralls, were made from long-lasting materials such as denim. The character Rosie the Riveter (created in a 1942 song of the same name, with the character later adopted to promote women working for the war effort) popularized the bandanna as a means to protect the bobs and shoulder-length hairstyles that were popular at the time, in part because long hair could be dangerous in a factory setting. Some film stars cut their hair to encourage other women to do so. Women with long hair who worked around dangerous machinery wore hairnets or snoods.

The occupation of Paris cut off France from the rest of the world, leaving world fashion couture without leadership from its traditional center. American and Canadian designers, rather than continuing to copy French designs, were forced to create their own, and to do so under government restrictions on clothing. More ready-to-wear clothing was manufactured because women who were working for the war effort no longer had time to make their own clothing. Women who chose to create their own clothing often found themselves knitting their clothing because yarn was easier to acquire than fabric. Patterns abounded for knitting, and knitted goods not only were worn at home but also were sent abroad to wounded soldiers and sailors.

American designer Claire McCardell began designing clothes for everyday use that could be mass-produced. One of her first designs was a bias-cut dress, with the fabric cut diagonally across the weave, allowing a soft, flowing shape. McCardell also invented the popover dress, a comfortable garment that moved easily and was meant to be worn around the house. McCardell's designs, which were both simple and practical, became known as the American Look. The style spread to sportswear, winter wear, outerwear, and even swimsuits.

Women's undergarments became more relaxed during the war as well. Girdles, which often had been required to achieve the desired look of fashions popular before the war, no longer were available because the rubber in them was needed for the war effort. A few enterprising designers attempted to create rubberless girdles, but dresses that would have required girdles mostly disappeared from the fashion industry. Zippers became less common, to preserve metal for the war, and fewer buttons were sewn into garments. Even shoes adapted to rationing, as heels could not be made more than one inch in height.

Rather than create a wedding dress that used voluminous skirts, wartime brides often married in a

Neiman Marcus model wearing a 1945 suit with the heavily padded shoulders characteristic of early 1940's fashions. (Time & Life Pictures/Getty Images)

simple suit, with a veil as a nod to tradition, while grooms often wore their service uniforms. Some women who were serving in the armed forces married in their uniforms as well. The poofy Gibson sleeves of the 1930's disappeared in favor of slim sleeves, and those who had wedding dresses reused them, either wearing them as they were or revamping them into entirely new garments.

Women who volunteered for military auxiliaries had their own specific uniforms. American fashion designer Main Rousseau Bocher, of the Mainbocher label, closed up shop in Paris at the beginning of the war and returned to the United States, where he designed the uniform for the Women's Red Cross. Women's military uniforms were made in drab colors to provide camouflage if needed, though women were not on the front lines, and usually featured a skirt rather than trousers. Otherwise, female military uniforms were similar to male uniforms. They did offer more options for individualization, such as different ways to wear hats and options for some elements of the design. Because practicality was more important than style, women tended more often to wear flat, sturdy shoes for comfort.

To counter the blandness of their civilian outfits, women accessorized with handbags, small hats, and gloves. Dickeys, rather than full blouses, were worn under dresses, saving fabric and offering an easy-to-use, interchangeable garment to freshen up an otherwise tired ensemble. Hats were easy to make and accessorize at home with bits of leftover fabric or even fresh flowers.

Film stars continued to provide a more glamorous view of fashion, and women attempted to mimic their look. Because it was difficult to purchase the fabric to create a glamorous dress and such fashions were not widely available for purchase, women sought glamorous looks through use of cosmetics and through hairstyles. Women, especially nurses, wore red victory lipstick (which came in tubes made of paper, plastic, or wood to conserve metal) to raise morale both of the public and of soldiers. Mascara helped accentuate the eyes, and a small amount of blush put pink into the cheeks of women.

Hairstyles were practical, though still feminine. Hair was often shoulder length or shorter, and waved or permed into soft curls. Some women used peroxide to bleach their hair blond. Women often covered their hair with turbans, bandannas, or tied head scarves because many of them working for the war effort had little time to style their hair, and such headwear hid dirty or unruly hair. Hats were smaller, often created from felt, and new styles were influenced by military designs.

Menswear, 1940-1945   Menswear also needed to adapt to the shortage of fabric. Men's suits more often were made out of synthetic blends rather than pure wool. Trousers were made without pleats or cuffs to save fabric, and double-breasted suits no longer were worn with vests. Also to conserve on fabric, jackets were cut shorter and trousers were cut more narrowly; even the top flaps for jacket pockets were eliminated. Fewer buttons were used on shirts and jackets. To make up for the austerity in color, ties became more brightly colored and more intricately designed, often using a geometric pattern. The fedora became one of the most popular hats for men. Suspenders also became popular, as leather for belts was redirected toward the war effort.

Zoot suits, introduced in the late 1930's, became more popular, especially with minority groups. Cab Calloway wore one in the film *Stormy Weather* (1943), which featured a mostly African American cast. These baggy suits with long jackets were made in bright colors. After clothing restrictions were passed during rationing, those wearing zoot suits, particularly Mexican Americans, found themselves under close and disapproving scrutiny. Servicemen in Los Angeles carried out numerous attacks against Mexican Americans, whom they identified partly by this clothing, during the zoot-suit riots of 1942.

Womenswear, 1945-1949   After the end of the war, less practical fashions reemerged as men came home and women left the factories. Despite the liberation of Paris in 1944, French fashions remained largely absent from the United States until 1947, when Christian Dior introduced his New Look to the world, a look that was immediately copied in the United States and Canada. The New Look featured a classic, feminine hourglass figure, characterized by rounded shoulder designs, as opposed to the boxy, padded shoulders of the early decade; full skirts, rather than pencil skirts; and tiny waistlines and bodices. Skirts, while falling only to mid-calf, were created from yards of fabric, a lavish move after the rationing of the war era, and supported by petticoats or crinolines, which also used large amounts of fabric. The New Look was also characterized by the return of high heels and nylon stockings, and hats and gloves became common accoutrements. The New Look brought French fashion back to the United States and Canada, and it made Paris the center of the fashion world once again—at least for couture. The United States remained the leader when it came to creating sportswear.

The tiny waists of the New Look brought a need for more elaborate undergarments as well; corsets were once again fashionable, and petticoats were required to create the full New Look skirt. The new corsets were called waspies, for the tiny "waists" of wasps. Nylon made these undergarments easier to create and easier to wear. These tiny waists were also accentuated by the peplum jacket, which was trim at the waist but then expanded outward over the hips to create a type of overskirt. Girdles returned when rubber once again became available, assisting in creating the hourglass silhouette.

The two-piece swimsuit was debuted in France by two separate designers. Jacques Heim called his the *Atome*, for its small size, and Louis Réard called his two-piece swimsuit the bikini. Heim's design had originally covered the wearer's navel, but Réard's was cut much lower. Some fashion historians believe that Réard's design was called the bikini because it was expected to create the same kind of shock and excitement from people as had the atomic tests at Bikini Atoll in 1946; other historians believe that it was because Réard's design split the *Atome*, another reference to the atomic bomb.

The war effort left behind a legacy of mass production of clothing, which remained much more common than before the war. It allowed designers to provide new fashions for women in large quantities all across the country, rather than up-to-date fashion being the province of clothing produced by hand in limited quantities. Every woman could have a copy of the designer garments she saw in films.

Women had adopted cosmetics to a greater extent during the war and continued to use them during the latter half of the decade, still relying on mascara and lipstick to accentuate facial features. Hairstyles became somewhat longer but continued with the soft waves that had popularized such coifs in the first part of the decade. Hair was often pinned up to be out of the way, and elegant chignons were often seen paired with formal wear.

Menswear, 1945-1949 When men returned from the war, they were tired of their uniforms. The only uni-

form item that remained fashionable after the war was the leather bomber jacket worn by pilots. These jackets quickly became a fashionable item for both men and women, especially for teenage boys. Pleats were once again used in men's trousers, though cuffs remained absent from all but the most formal wear.

Fashion designers created the "teddy boy" style, modeled after Edwardian fashion. The fashion's suit jackets were much longer than the jackets worn during the war and were known as drape jackets. These jackets ranged in color from the drab sorts used during the war to the bright ones of zoot suits. Trousers were thinner and more tapered at the ankle. Double-breasted suits returned, complete with vests. Bright ties featured more than geometric designs; they also featured landscapes, cityscapes, and even pinup girls. The utilitarian clothing developed during the war was used by men returning to factory work. Socks, which had been shortened during the war to save wool, remained shorter than prior to the war. T-shirts, used as uniform undershirts during the war, became common as casual sportswear. Also in the realm of casual wear, men returning from the Pacific brought Hawaiian styled shirts, featuring bold patterns.

A jacket no longer was required for a man to look respectable, and an untucked shirt was far from the norm. America began to take the lead in sportswear design and use, while Europe remained the center for couture.

Impact The 1940's brought a measure of gender equality into fashion when trousers became acceptable for women as well as men. During the war years, practicality became a more important element of design. The advent of the bikini was part of a new level of sensuality in both fashion and culture, and Dior's New Look created the classic hourglass shape that has come to epitomize femininity in fashion. The 1940's also brought cosmetics into wider and more acceptable use.

Emily Carroll Shearer

Further Reading

Arnold, Rebecca. *The American Look: Sportswear, Fashion, and the Image of Women in 1930s and 1940s New York*. New York: I. B. Tauris, 2008. Discusses the American Look created for women during the 1930's and 1940's.

Baker, Patricia. *Fashions of a Decade: The 1940's*. New York: Facts On File, 1992. Presents an illustrated overview of fashions during the 1940's.

Dior, Christian. *Dior by Dior: An Autobiography of Christian Dior.* London: Victoria and Albert Museum, 2007. Gives an inside look at the war years of fashion and how the creation of the New Look changed the fashion industry forever.

Gourley, Catherine. *Rosie and Mrs. America: Perceptions of Women in the 1930's and 1940's.* New York: Twenty-First Century Books, 2007. Discusses how fashion affected women's perceptions of themselves during the 1930's and 1940's.

Walford, Jonathan. *Forties Fashion: From the Siren Suit to the New Look.* London: Thames & Hudson, 2008. Provides a look at fashions worldwide during the 1940's. Discusses children's clothing and the postwar resurgence of French fashion.

Waller, Linda. *Knitting Fashions of the 1940's: Styles, Patterns and History.* Ramsbury, Marlborough, England: Crowood Press, 2007. Provides an interesting overview of knitting during the 1940's and discusses how women knitted clothing not only for themselves but also to provide garments for the troops.

Watson, Linda. *Vogue Fashion.* London: Condé Nast, 2002. An illustrated history of the fashions featured in *Vogue* magazine in the twentieth century.

See also Hairstyles; Nylon stockings; *Stormy Weather*; Wartime rationing; Women's roles and rights in Canada; Women's roles and rights in the United States; Zoot suits.

■ Faulkner, William

Identification Nobel Prize-winning American author

Born September 25, 1897; New Albany, Mississippi

Died July 6, 1962; Byhalia, Mississippi

Although most of his novels were out of print by the mid-1940's, Faulkner persevered as a writer and regained literary prominence during the decade. He continued to mine the richness of his native Mississippi for artistic purposes. His legendary Yoknapatawpha County gave his fiction a distinct sense of place with worldwide appeal.

William Faulkner began the decade with the publication of *The Hamlet* (1940), the first novel of a trilogy depicting the rise of the Snopes clan in Mississippi society and politics. The Snopes's rise to power during the mid-twentieth century South poses a seri-

---

Burying Mannie

In William Faulkner's Go Down, Moses *(1942), Rider is a sawmill worker helping to bury his dead wife Mannie. The manner in which he partakes in the ritual reveals a profound, but stoic, sadness. He never overcomes his grief.*

He stood in the worn, faded clean overalls which Mannie herself had washed only a week ago, and heard the first clod stride the pine box. Soon he had one of the shovels himself, which in his hands (he was better than six feet and weighed better than two hundred pounds) resembled the toy shovel a child plays with at the shore, its half cubic foot of flung dirt no more than the light gout of sand the child's shovel would have flung. Another member of his sawmill gang touched his arm and said, "Lemme have hit, Rider." He didn't even falter. He released one hand in midstroke and flung it backward, striking the other across the chest, jolting him back a step, and restored the hand to the moving shovel, flinging the dirt with that effortless fury so that the mound seemed to be rising of its own volition, not built up from above but thrusting visibly upward out of the earth itself, until at last the grave, save for its rawness, resembled any other marked off without order about the barren plot by shards of pottery and broken bottles and old brick and other objects insignificant to sight but actually of a profound meaning and fatal to the touch, which no white man could have read. Then he straightened up and with one hand flung the shovel quivering upright in the mound like a javelin and turned and began to walk away, walking on even when an old woman came out of the meagre clump of his kin and friends and a few old people that had known him and his dead wife both since they were born, and grasped his forearm. She was his aunt. She had raised him. He could not remember his parents at all.

ous threat to the genteel aristocracy that Faulkner knew so well in his own life and literature. Two years later, Faulkner published a collection of thematically unified stories titled *Go Down, Moses* (1942). He dedicated this book to Caroline Barr ("Mammie Callie"), the African American woman who helped raise him. The collection includes "The Bear," which explores young Isaac "Ike" McCaslin's coming of age under the tutelage of Sam Fathers, the son of a Chickasaw Indian chief, who teaches Ike reverence for the wilderness. This story was included in *The Portable Faulkner* (1946), edited by literary critic Malcolm Cowley, a publication that brought Faulkner back to the public's attention.

Throughout the 1940's, Faulkner divided his time between Oxford, Mississippi, and Hollywood, California, where he worked as a scriptwriter for Metro-Goldwyn-Mayer (MGM). He contributed to screenplays for two film adaptations of novels that became popular movies, *To Have and Have Not* (1945; based on Ernest Hemingway's 1937 novel) and *The Big Sleep* (1946; adapted from Raymond Chandler's 1939 novel). MGM also paid Faulkner $50,000 for the rights to his novel *Intruder in the Dust* (1948). Filmed in Oxford, the story depicts the friendship between a white adolescent, Charles "Chick" Mallison, and a middle-aged African American, Lucas Beauchamp, who is charged and ultimately cleared of a crime he did not commit.

The decade concluded with Faulkner receiving two prestigious awards and publishing *Knight's Gambit* (1949), a collection of short stories set in the South during the Civil War. In 1948, he was elected to the American Academy of Arts and Letters, and in 1950 he traveled to Sweden with his daughter Jill to deliver his acceptance speech for the 1949 Nobel Prize in Literature.

Impact In creating his imaginary Yoknapatawpha County and grounding it in his understanding of southern history and culture, Faulkner made his "little postage stamp of native soil" famous. As a modernist writer, Faulkner used his distinct style of writing, including stream-of-consciousness techniques, to examine themes of race, class, and gender as well as rites of passage, the receding American wilderness, and the Civil War. Faulkner was the twentieth century American novelist most often compared to canonical writers Gustave Flaubert, Joseph Conrad, James Joyce, and Virginia Woolf. Moreover, his writ-

ing style and subject matter influenced subsequent Nobel laureates Gabriel García Márquez and Toni Morrison. Each July, scholars and devotees alike gather in Oxford for the annual Faulkner and Yoknapatawpha Conference, which began in 1973. His fiction has secured his critical and popular reputation into the twenty-first century.

Kevin Eyster

Further Reading

Parini, Jay. *One Matchless Time: A Life of William Faulkner.* New York: HarperCollins, 2004.

Williamson, Joel. *William Faulkner and Southern History.* New York: Oxford University Press, 1993.

See also Book publishing; Chandler, Raymond; Film in the United States; Halsey, William F. "Bull"; Lynching and hate crime; Nobel Prizes; Wright, Richard.

■ Federal Bureau of Investigation

Identification Chief federal law-enforcement agency in the United States
Also known as FBI
Date Founded on July 26, 1908

The Federal Bureau of Investigation is tasked with protecting and defending the United States against foreign threats while upholding and enforcing countless federal criminal and civil laws of the United States. Although the agency has been in existence for more than a century, it was during the 1940's that the bureau, under the leadership of J. Edgar Hoover, truly expanded its investigative authority.

With the outbreak of World War II in 1939, the responsibilities of the traditional Federal Bureau of Investigation (FBI) were greatly expanded under the watchful eye of Director J. Edgar Hoover. For example, a 1939 presidential directive further strengthened the FBI's authority to investigate known subversives in the United States. In addition, Congress passed the Smith Act in 1940, which outlawed advocacy of a violent overthrow of the government. During this time, Hoover's agents investigated tens of thousands of both known and suspected subversives and radicals. Although agents were tasked with new investigative areas involving national security, they continued to train in general intelligence collection. In fact, the FBI developed a strong network of

FBI special agents training with rifles in June, 1942. (AP/Wide World Photos)

informational sources, frequently using members of fraternal or veterans' organizations. Following leads developed by these intelligence sources, agents investigated countless potential threats to the U.S. government.

As the war in Europe continued, Great Britain found itself alone after the defeat of France by Germany. U.S. government officials became increasingly concerned that further Axis victories abroad could threaten democracy at home. Although the United States had signed neutrality agreements, the government began to offer aid to Great Britain and France in 1940-1941. In late 1940, on the brink of war, Congress reestablished the draft, giving the FBI an additional responsibility of locating draft dodgers and deserters. Also in 1940, the FBI Disaster Squad was established when the FBI's Identification Division was asked to identify some bureau employees who had died as a result of a plane crash in Lovettsville, Virginia.

After the Germans attacked Russia in June, 1941, the FBI refocused its security efforts on numerous and potentially problematic German, Italian, and Japanese nationals as well as many native-born Americans whose ideologies and activities offered aid to Axis Powers. In particular, the FBI's technical laboratory, staffed with some of the world's best scientists, analysts, code breakers, and engineers, played a crucial role in this process. Sabotage investigations also fell under the auspices of the FBI. In June, 1942, the FBI proved itself to the American public when it captured eight Nazi-trained saboteurs in Amagansett, Long Island, and Ponte Vedra Beach, Florida.

U.S. Entry into War and an Expanded FBI Before the United States entered the war, the FBI uncovered another major espionage ring, commonly referred to as the Frederick Duquesne spy ring. The FBI was assisted by a loyal American citizen with German relatives who acted as a double agent to uncover Nazi war plans. For nearly two years, the FBI manned a radio station for the double agent, learning specific details of what Germany was sending to its American spies while controlling the information that was being conveyed back to the Nazis. This particular investigation ended with the arrest of thirty-three known spies.

On December 7, 1941, Japanese forces attacked U.S. ships and facilities at Pearl Harbor, Hawaii. The United States immediately declared war on Japan. By 9:30 P.M. that day, the FBI was prepared to assist the military in any capacity. FBI headquarters and all fifty-four field offices were placed on twenty-four-hour, round-the-clock working schedules. Within forty-eight hours, the FBI arrested previously identified aliens who posed potential immediate threats to national security. Those arrested by the FBI were immediately turned over to military or immigration authorities for detention and further questioning. On December 8, Germany and Italy declared war on the United States. In order to deal with the mounting workload, Hoover opted to enhance his agent force with those National Academy graduates who had taken an abbreviated training course. Thus, from 1941 to 1943, the total number of FBI employees increased from 7,400 to over 13,000, including approximately 4,000 agents. Although war-focused investigations were considered to be a necessity for the FBI, agents continued to carry out their regular enforcement duties dealing with violations of criminal and civil laws.

One of the most egregious acts of discrimination ever to take place on U.S. soil occurred during World War II. President Franklin D. Roosevelt, under the advice of the attorney general and his top military cabinet members, called for the internment of all Japanese nationals and American citizens of Japanese descent living on the West Coast. Since the FBI was responsible for arresting individuals whom it considered security threats, it was also given this direct assignment by Roosevelt. Although Hoover did not agree with the idea of confining Japanese Americans, he obediently carried out this charge. As a result, the FBI became responsible for arresting both Japanese curfew and evacuation violators.

While most FBI agents and staff worked on traditional war-related or criminal and civil cases, one group of highly trained field agents, known as the Special Intelligence Service (SIS), were assigned to special missions throughout Latin America. This elite team was established in 1940 at the request of the president. The major goals of the SIS were to gather detailed information on Axis activities in Latin America and to destroy its intelligence and propaganda infrastructure. Thousands of Germans, German descendants, and Japanese lived in South America, some of whom provided pro-Axis cover for enemy communications facilities. By 1944, the SIS had agents in every South American country who were responsible for destroying and quelling any sympathy and support for the Axis war efforts.

Postwar Years The postwar years provided the FBI with new challenges. The United States had now become a dominant world superpower—an idea that many communist countries held in great disdain. In 1946, the United States and other world democratic leaders anxiously listened to Joseph Stalin's public address in which he implied that future wars were certain until capitalism was replaced by communism. Several events in Europe and North America convinced U.S. leaders that Stalin would stop at nothing to achieve his goal. By 1947, substantial evidence was collected indicating that Soviet supporters had infiltrated various facets of the American government. In fact, two years prior in 1945, the FBI had raided the offices of *Amerasia*, a publication dedicated to issues dealing with the Far East. During the raid, agents discovered countless classified State Department documents.

Months later, Canadian police arrested twenty-two people who were attempting to steal atomic secrets. U.S. government leaders now feared that they were not the only country to have perfected the atomic bomb. This fear became a reality when the Soviets detonated their own bomb in 1949. After the news of the detonation reached the United States, all levels of the federal government refocused their efforts on defeating communist expansion both home and abroad. A new war was brewing, a Cold War focusing on conflicting government ideologies and atomic weaponry.

In the United States, the Communist Party USA,

which worked through front organizations and secret groups, became the new concern of the FBI. In fact, the FBI's authority to conduct background investigations of current and prospective government employees expanded dramatically. With the passage of the 1946 Atomic Energy Act, the FBI was given the task of determining the loyalty of individuals who had access to U.S. atomic secrets. In addition, executive orders from Presidents Harry S. Truman and Dwight D. Eisenhower gave the FBI responsibility for investigating all allegations of disloyalty among federal employees from all branches of government. For these special cases, the FBI only conducted the investigation and reported the result to the agency that had requested the actual inquiry. Some of the most notorious spies in U.S. history were in fact federal employees. Thus, comprehensive background investigations were considered to be crucial for the security of the nation throughout the end of the 1940's.

Impact   Throughout the turbulent 1940's, the FBI played a crucial role in the security of the United States. Aside from being tasked with investigating regular federal offenses, the bureau had its role expanded to help support the war efforts abroad by investigating any Axis sympathizers found in the United States. Additionally, they were also tasked with the tracking, identification, investigating, and, if need be, arresting of countless members of various communist groups located in the United States.

Paul M. Klenowski

Further Reading

Federal Bureau of Investigation, comp. *FBI: A Centennial History, 1908-2008*. Washington, D.C.: U.S. Department of Justice, 2008. Pays special attention to the 1940's and the role the FBI played during the war years and the Second Red Scare.

Gentry, Curt. *J. Edgar Hoover: The Man and the Secrets.* New York: W. W. Norton, 2001. Provides a unique look at the former longtime director of the FBI, offering a detailed examination of Hoover's accomplishments spanning five decades and ten presidents. Examines the role that Hoover's bureau played during the 1940's, especially its security efforts during World War II.

Holden, Henry. *FBI One Hundred Years: An Unofficial History*. Minneapolis, Minn.: Zenith Press, 2008. Written by a former law-enforcement officer, this work provides an excellent overview of the FBI's history. In particular, it shows how the FBI expanded its mission and investigative capabilities during the turbulent war years of the 1940's.

Jeffreys-Jones, Rhodri. *The FBI: A History*. New Haven, Conn.: Yale University Press, 2008. Composed by an academic, this work offers a comprehensive historical overview of the FBI and chronicles each decade of the FBI's existence, highlighting its ever-evolving mission. Of great relevance is the section regarding the FBI's role in assisting the military with the investigation, control, and prompt arrests of those who posed an immediate threat to the United States during World War II.

Kessler, Ronald. *The Bureau: A Secret History of the FBI*. New York: St. Martin's Press, 2003. Written from a journalist's perspective, this work presents a layperson's look at the FBI.

Theoharis, Athan. *The FBI: A Comprehensive Reference Guide*. Phoenix, Ariz.: Oryx Press, 1999. This encyclopedia provides one of the most comprehensive overviews of the FBI.

See also   Anticommunism; Central Intelligence Agency; Communist Party USA; Crimes and scandals; Hobbs Act; Hoover, J. Edgar; Lynching and hate crime; National Security Act of 1947; Organized crime; Pornography.

■ Federal Tort Claims Act

The Law   Legislation recognizing the federal government's liability for numerous torts
Date   Enacted on August 2, 1946

The Federal Tort Claims Act allowed private parties to sue the federal government for a number of specified torts— harmful actions or injuries—committed by individuals acting on behalf of the government.

According to the ancient doctrine of sovereign immunity, a government cannot be sued without its consent. Throughout American history, many citizens have believed that this doctrine was unjust. Before passage of the Federal Tort Claims Act (FTCA) in 1946, members of Congress sometimes introduced private relief bills for constituents who had suffered injuries because of government actions or negligence. These bills resulted in great inconsistencies in monetary relief. The Tucker Act of 1887 permitted individuals to sue the government for non-tort claims based on the U.S. Constitution or federal legislation.

During the 1920's, Congress began to debate whether or not to wave its immunity from tort liability. Support for such a waver increased in 1945, after a B-25, a military aircraft, crashed into the seventy-ninth floor of the Empire State Building on July 28, killing fourteen people and injuring many others. When families of the victims of the crash were unable to initiate tort lawsuits against the government, the resulting publicity prompted Congress to enact the FTCA. The law was enacted in 1946 but was made retroactive to the preceding year so that persons harmed by the aircraft accident might seek monetary damages.

The FTCA authorized a federal district judge, sitting without a jury, to render a judgment in circumstances in which a private person would be liable for "damage, loss, injury, or death in accordance with the law of the place where the act or the omission took place." The burden of proof, as in all tort actions, was on the plaintiff. The statute recognized the U.S. government's liability for most injuries committed by federal law-enforcement officers, including assault, false imprisonment, and wrongful death. The government, however, continued to have immunity for a number of intentional torts, including libel, misrepresentation, and interference with contracts. One of the FTCA's most important provisions was its "discretionary function exception," which disallowed any claims based on the performances or omissions of discretionary functions by federal agencies or employees. A large percentage of governmental services are not required by the Constitution and are therefore classified as discretionary.

Impact   The impact of the Federal Tort Claims Act turned out to be more limited than many lawyers expected. Since 1946, the U.S. Supreme Court has interpreted the statute in numerous cases, and these interpretations have generally increased the hurdles that plaintiffs face when pursuing tort suits against the government. In the controversial ruling of *Feres v. United States* (1950), for example, the Court held that the FTCA was not applicable to persons injured while on active duty in the military. In another case with broad implications, *Dalehite v. United States* (1953), the Court interpreted the statute's discre-

tionary function exception broadly to exclude the government's liability for negligence in the certification of an aircraft. Under the FTCA, however, plaintiffs have often obtained significant awards when they have been able to demonstrate unjustifiable injuries by federal law-enforcement officers.

Thomas Tandy Lewis

Further Reading

Colligan, Ben V. *Federal Torts Reform: Claims and Liability.* Hauppauge, N.Y.: Nova Science, 2009.

Lester, Urban, and Michael Noone, eds. "The Federal Tort Claims Act." In *Litigation with the Federal Government.* 3d ed. Philadelphia: American Law Institute, 1994.

Levine, James R. "The Federal Tort Claims Act: A Proposal for Institutional Reform." *Columbia Law Review* 100 (October, 2000): 1,538-1,571.

Shapo, Marshall. *Principles of Tort Law.* St. Paul: West Books, 2003.

Wright, William B. *The Federal Tort Claims Act Analyzed and Annotated.* New York: Central Books, 1957.

See also   Fair Deal; National Security Act of 1947; Presidential Succession Act of 1947; Supreme Court, U.S.

■ Fender, Leo

Identification   Inventor and manufacturer of electric guitars
Born   August 10, 1909; Anaheim, California
Died   March 21, 1991; Fullerton, California

Fender spent the late 1940's developing what would become the first mass-produced, solid-body electric guitar. Named the Esquire and the Broadcaster before being famously renamed the Telecaster in 1951, this classic instrument is still widely used in the twenty-first century.

Throughout the late 1930's and early 1940's, Clarence Leonidas "Leo" Fender ran his own repair shop, Fender's Radio Service, in Fullerton, California. As the 1940's developed, he realized that there was a much stronger demand for instrument manufacturing than for repair work, and in 1946 he launched Fender Manufacturing. After renaming the company the Fender Electric Instrument Company in 1947, he first introduced a highly successful line of tweed-covered amplifiers in 1948. In the same year, Fender began work on a two-pickup solid-body electric guitar known as the Esquire, which was completed in 1949 and advertised in 1950. Soon to be reconstructed with a single pickup, however, the original two-pickup Esquire model was renamed the Broadcaster and entered full production in late 1950. The Broadcaster was ultimately renamed the Fender Telecaster in February, 1951, and was readily available in April that year.

Impact   With the wide release of the simply constructed, easy-to-play Fender Telecaster, the guitar quickly became the first choice of countless country, rhythm-and-blues, and rock-and-roll guitarists looking to take advantage of its powerful tone. Through Fender's research and development during the 1940's, his company played an essential role in defining the new electric sound of American music during the 1950's and beyond.

Eric Novod

Further Reading

Bacon, Tony. *Six Decades of the Fender Telecaster: The Story of the World's First Solidbody Electric Guitar.* San Francisco: Backbeat Books, 2005.

White, Forrest. *Fender: The Inside Story.* San Francisco: GPI Books, 1994.

See also   Music: Popular; Radio in the United States; Recording industry.

■ Fermi, Enrico

Identification   Italian American physicist
Born   September 29, 1901; Rome, Italy
Died   November 28, 1954; Chicago, Illinois

Fermi's atomic reactor showed the possibility of a controlled chain reaction in the fission of uranium and was a prototype of the reactors that produced plutonium for the nuclear weapons that helped to end World War II.

Enrico Fermi was born and raised in Rome, where he attended local schools and the Ginnasio Liceo Umberto I. He entered university at Pisa, where he held a fellowship at the Scuola Normale Superiore, and graduated with a doctorate in physics in 1922. Following postdoctoral work in Göttingen and Leiden, he returned to Italy and by 1926 held the post of professor of physics at the University of Rome. It was there that he pursued his studies of neutrons and

their interaction with various chemical elements. He realized that slow neutrons are more easily captured by the atomic nucleus, and he developed techniques of slowing down, or "moderating," the neutrons emitted by radioactive sources.

For his discoveries in the field of neutron reactions and artificial isotopes, Fermi was awarded the 1938 Nobel Prize in Physics. He and his family attended the prize ceremony in Sweden. When they left Sweden, they did not go back to Italy, with its fascist politics, but instead to the United States, where they settled permanently.

In 1939, Otto Hahn and Fritz Strassmann reported fission of uranium. Fermi was by then a professor of physics at Columbia University in New York, and he began work to determine if a fission chain reaction could be maintained with uranium. Neutron moderation was important in this work because fission occurs best with slow neutrons. It was decided to use graphite as a moderator, and construction of a fission experiment, or "pile," began at Columbia. Later, the work on this experiment was shifted to the University of Chicago's Metallurgical Laboratory.

By 1942, plans were made to acquire the needed quantities of graphite and uranium, and construction of the pile (code named CP-1) began in a large space under Stagg Field that had been a squash court. On December 2, 1942, the experiment was complete, and the pile went critical. The fission reaction was controlled by inserting cadmium rods into the pile (cadmium absorbs neutrons that otherwise might cause fission). This experiment proved the possibility of controlled nuclear fission. The pile itself could be used as a neutron source and for the production of plutonium.

When the Manhattan Project began, Fermi went to Los Alamos, New Mexico, where he was a valued member of the team that created the first atomic bomb. After the war, Fermi returned to the University of Chicago, where he did research on cosmic rays and various aspects of particle physics. He died of cancer in 1954.

Impact   The course of world history was changed by the atomic bomb and by the peaceful uses of atomic energy. Fermi contributed in a major way to the use of the atom. Many of his discoveries are important for the design of nuclear reactors. World War II came to an end as a result of the atomic bomb. The bomb was a team effort, and no single individual can claim credit for it, but Fermi was a major contributor.

John R. Phillips

Further Reading

Cronin, James W. *Fermi Remembered*. Chicago: University of Chicago Press, 2004.

Fermi, Laura. *Atoms in the Family: My Life with Enrico Fermi*. Chicago: University of Chicago Press, 1954.

Libby, Leona Marshall. *The Uranium People*. New York: Crane, Russak, 1979.

See also Atomic bomb; Einstein, Albert; Groves, Leslie Richard; Hanford Nuclear Reservation; Hiroshima and Nagasaki bombings; Manhattan Project; Oppenheimer, J. Robert; Plutonium discovery; Science and technology; Synchrocyclotron.

■ Fields, W. C.

Identification American comedian and entertainer

Born January 29, 1880; Darby, near Philadelphia, Pennsylvania

Died December 25, 1946; Pasadena, California

Fields was one of the most influential entertainers in vaudeville and early Hollywood, establishing several archetypal characters.

By 1940, comic legend W. C. Fields was slowing down. No comedian stays on top for long, and the reigning kings of comedy from the previous decade, the Marx Brothers and Fields, were being pushed aside as the 1940's dawned by a new group of funnymen, led by former vaudeville stars Bud Abbott and Lou Costello. Like a proud heavyweight fighter, Fields refused to go down quietly and made several of his greatest films near the end of his career.

Fields's first film of the decade for Universal, his new studio, was *My Little Chickadee* (1940), with Mae West. The set was a battle of ad-libs and one-upmanship, but the resulting film did well at the box office, earning nearly $2 million in gross receipts. Fields received good critical reviews. His next film was the *The Bank Dick* (1940), in which he assumed his classic role as a henpecked husband. Approaching the age of sixty-one as the movie was being filmed, Fields was wearing down from a life of drink. At four o'clock every afternoon, he would need his "pill"—a drink of

Actor W. C. Fields at a horse race in May, 1944. (Time & Life Pictures/Getty Images)

orange juice and rum. Although *The Bank Dick* was lauded by critics and eventually became one of his best-known films, it did poorly at the box office.

His next film began as *The Great Man*, then morphed into *Never Give a Sucker an Even Break* (1941). His energy flagging, Fields rarely worked a full day and stayed in his dressing room when not on camera to conserve his strength. The film was a critical and commercial failure. The film was Fields's last starring vehicle. After the film's failure, Universal dropped Fields.

In early 1942, Fields shot a segment with Margaret Dumont at Fox for an episodic film titled *Tales of Manhattan* (1942). Even though he lost weight for the role, he was still without energy on the set. Although enthusiastically received by preview audiences, the sequence was mysteriously cut from the film.

The death of his good friend John Barrymore on May 29, 1942, further depressed Fields. His face was marred by a skin condition, and the comedian by that time freely admitted the drinking that for years he had gone to great pains to deny. In September,

1942, he was diagnosed with liver disease. Arthritis in his fingers robbed him of his legendary juggling ability. He lived in a rundown house with a lawn so unkempt that his housekeeper was frightened to get the evening paper.

Late in 1943 and into early 1944, Fields filmed short appearances in three musical films. He had difficulty remembering his lines and had to have them written on blackboards just off camera. Thereafter, except for appearing on radio shows in which he could keep scripts directly in front of him, Fields worked little.

In the waning months of 1945, in the advanced stages of cirrhosis, Fields checked into Las Encinas Sanatorium in Pasadena, California, where he remained for the rest of his life. The following summer, Fields gave his final performance, recording a spoken word album with Les Paul. He died on Christmas Day, 1946, of a stomach hemorrhage.

Impact   Fields was a unique comic genius whose style and characterizations would be copied and repeated by succeeding generations, though his brand of comedy was going out of style. His characterizations remained known and loved by legions of fans, and many of his films became minor classics.

Russell Roberts

Further Reading

Curtis, James. *W. C. Fields*. New York: Alfred A. Knopf, 2003.

Louvish, Simon. *Man on the Flying Trapeze: The Life and Times of W. C. Fields*. New York: W. W. Norton, 1997.

Taylor, Robert Lewis. *W. C. Fields: His Follies and Fortunes*. New York: Signet, 1967.

See also   Abbott and Costello; Benny, Jack; Berle, Milton; Film in the United States; Recording industry.

■ Film in Canada

During the 1940's, the film industry in Canada was shaped by government initiatives, from the creation of the National Film Board of Canada to the implementation of the Canadian Cooperative Project. The cultural and geographic proximity to the United States facilitated the promotion of Hollywood feature films in Canada. Documentary, animation, and French-language features were established as the primary genres of Canadian film.

In 1939, the Canadian parliament passed the National Film Act, effectively creating the National Film Board of Canada (NFB). Under the direction of the first film commissioner, John Grierson, the NFB released more than five hundred films, produced two propaganda series (*The World in Action* and *Canada Carries On*), and nurtured internationally renowned departments for animation (led by Norman McLaren, who came to the NFB in 1941) and documentary film (influenced by Grierson, Stuart Legg, and Tom Daly). In 1941, the NFB production *Churchill's Island*, directed by Legg, won the Academy Award for best documentary film. Grierson left the NFB in 1945 after suspicions of his communist affiliations threatened to hurt the organization as a whole. Largely because of Grierson's influence over the early direction of the NFB, documentary and animation have remained strong components of Canadian film.

The two major theater chains in Canada—Odeon (started by MGM cofounder N. L. Nathanson and sold to Britain's Rank Organization in 1945) and Famous Players (a subsidiary of the U.S.-based Paramount Pictures)—exhibited primarily Hollywood feature films and neglected some of the unique requirements within the Canadian population: first, the need for French-language films for the distinct French Canadian audiences; and second, the large number of rural communities without access to commercial theaters. The German occupation of France during World War II stopped the distribution of French-language films to Canada. While the NFB produced some French documentaries and animations, the French-language feature film industry flourished in Quebec throughout the 1940's, producing the first Québécois sound film, *À la croisée des chemins* (1943), followed by the commercially successful *Le Père Chopin* (1944) and *Un homme et son péché* (1949), and the first bilingual feature film, *La forteresse/Whispering City* (1947).

Because large landmasses separated isolated communities in Canada, the NFB instituted a nontheatrical-based distribution system using the preexisting agricultural networks established in rural Canada during the 1920's and 1930's. Films (typically NFB productions) were screened in schools, churches, and/or community halls. In 1941, there were thirty film circuits in Canada reaching twenty different rural communities; by 1945, the distribution system expanded to include ninety-two circuits, reaching a quarter-million rural Canadians per month.

The NFB and government legislatures did not always work congruously. In the post-World War II era, the NFB, along with private studios and other interested parties within the Canadian commercial film industry, pushed for legislation limiting American film exhibition in Canada. Instead, the Canadian minister of trade and commerce, C. D. Howe, and the Motion Picture Association of America signed the Canadian Cooperative Project in 1948. The Canadian Cooperative Project promised the distribution of NFB films in the United States, the production of Hollywood films in Canada, and more references to Canada in American feature films in exchange for the continuation of unrestricted profits for the Famous Players Canadian Corporation and terminating the rumored threats of a restricted exhibition quota—that is, by legislating Canadian content mandates. While the U.S. Supreme Court declared vertical and horizontal integration illegal in 1948, no such measures were taken in Canada. The major theaters in Canada continued cartel-like practices, exclusively booking Hollywood films. Few references were added to Canada in Hollywood films, and the distribution of Canadian film in the United States continued to be minimal at best.

Impact While the intention may have been to promote Canada stateside, the actuality of the Canadian Cooperative Project simply reinforced Hollywood's hegemony in Canada. In 1951, influenced by the struggle for a Canadian cinema, the Royal Commission on National Development in the Arts, Letters and Sciences (commonly known as the Massey Commission) recommended state-funded cultural development in Canada, which would lead to the creation of the Canada Council of the Arts and influence Canadian content regulations over the production and exhibition of television programming.

Kelly Egan

Further Reading

Leach, Jim. *Film in Canada.* New York: Oxford University Press, 2006.

Madger, Ted. *Canada's Hollywood: The Canadian State and Feature Films.* Toronto: University of Toronto Press, 1993.

See also Academy Awards; Canadian nationalism; Demographics of Canada; Film in the United States; Film serials; Films about World War II; Foreign policy of Canada; Radio in Canada; Wartime propaganda in Canada.

■ Film in the United States

At its apex during the mid-1940's, the film industry dominated American culture, not only drawing in actors from the New York stage and abroad but also enticing the talents of great composers, writers, and other world-renowned figures. As the war ended, however, the American public began to reconsider the trends of the war years, and the film industry struggled to maintain its preeminence in the fraught atmosphere of Cold War controversies.

The Hollywood film industry entered the decade of the 1940's at the height of its prestige and prosperity. The year 1939 alone saw the popular and critical successes *Gone with the Wind, Stagecoach, The Wizard of Oz, Mr. Smith Goes to Washington, Ninotchka, Dark Victory, Destry Rides Again, The Women,* and *Wuthering Heights.* These films not only enhanced the stardom of figures such as Clark Gable, John Wayne, Judy Garland, James Stewart, Greta Garbo, Bette Davis, and Joan Crawford but also represented the finest efforts of legendary directors such as Victor Fleming, John Ford, Frank Capra, and William Wyler. No area of American life and its culture and heritage seemed beyond the scope of the cinema. Thus, the Civil War, America's place in the world, the country's frontier and Western experience, contemporary politics, domestic life, the lives of children, and the relationships between men and women all received riveting treatment on a weekly basis for audiences that averaged between fifty and sixty million strong. It would have been difficult to believe in 1940 that in less than a decade, Hollywood's hegemony as a cultural institution would be challenged and that the authority of its studios would begin to disintegrate.

Prewar Hollywood The 1940's began with a continuation of the types of films that had proven so successful during the 1930's. Musicals, dominated by the team of Fred Astaire and Ginger Rogers during the 1930's, continued with Astaire, Gene Kelly, and two new female stars—Betty Grable and Rita Hayworth—in *Down Argentine Way* (1940), *Moon over*

Miami (1941), *You Were Never Lovelier* (1942), and *Cover Girl* (1944). Both Grable and Hayworth were glamorous stars who became "pinup girls" for American soldiers during the war. Grable was the indisputable box office star, perhaps because she exuded not only beauty but also a very open cheerfulness that seemed to epitomize American optimism, whereas Hayworth, the more glamorous figure and a stunning dancer, also, like Lana Turner, exuded a more complicated sexuality verging on a troubled eroticism, best evidenced in the postwar film *Gilda* (1946).

Hollywood at War   Business as usual did not change for the film industry until the Japanese attack on Pearl Harbor (December 7, 1941). American films suddenly confronted a new, vital, major subject as well as a problem for a studio system that depended, in large part, upon youthful, virile, male stars. Clark Gable, James Stewart, Henry Fonda, and Tyrone Power, for example, were eager to join the armed forces, but these were the very actors their studios wanted to use as exemplary heroes in their war films. Power managed to make a war film, *Crash Dive* (1943), but for the most part a new generation of stars such as Dana Andrews, Van Johnson, and Robert Mitchum took on the burden of fighting the war on screen, in such films as *The Purple Heart* (1944), *Wing and a Prayer* (1944), *Thirty Seconds over Tokyo* (1944), and *A Walk in the Sun* (1945)—to name four of the better productions of this period. Although prewar stars such as John Wayne played war heroes, the emphasis in many war films was not on the individual but on American men of different races, creeds, and ethnicities banding together to fight for the cause of freedom.

Other films of the 1940's emphasized America's faith in its great ally, the Soviet Union. Thus, *The North Star* (1943), *Song of Russia* (1944), and *Mission to Moscow* (1943) idealized and sentimentalized Soviet farmers, workers, and leaders. Such productions were a blatant form of propaganda, obviously aimed at promoting war aims and presenting an ally in the best possible light. That no criticism of an ally was permitted in these films led to considerable controversy during the late 1940's, when the U.S. political climate changed and Hollywood (along with other cultural institutions) was subject to charges that it had been infiltrated by communist agents intent on subverting American values and, indeed, the American government itself.

Postwar Trauma and the Advent of Film Noir   The war meant an upheaval in American society, not only in terms of a wartime economy in which millions of women joined the workforce as their husbands and boyfriends went into the armed services but also in terms of the subject matter and style of the movies. Beginning with *The Maltese Falcon* (1941) and *Laura* (1944), the mystery thriller took on a psychological complexity largely absent from earlier detective/mystery films. In place of the breezy *Another Thin Man* (1939), which featured the happily married duo of Nick and Nora Charles (played by William Powell and Myrna Loy), Humphrey Bogart's Sam Spade and Dana Andrews's Mark McPherson played men encountering fascinating women who called into question the normal male prerogatives. The ambiguous relationships between men and women

As this elaborate marquee for the 1944 film Kismet *suggests, motion pictures remained big business through the war years, and film openings were important events.* (Time & Life Pictures/Getty Images)

Films Nominated for Best Picture Oscars in the 1940's

Asterisks indicate winners.

All the King's Men* (1949)
All This, and Heaven Too (1940)
Anchors Aweigh (1945)
Battleground (1949)
The Bells of St. Mary's (1945)
The Best Years of Our Lives* (1946)
The Bishop's Wife (1947)
Blossoms in the Dust (1941)
Casablanca* (1943)
Citizen Kane (1941)
Crossfire (1947)
Double Indemnity (1944)
For Whom the Bell Tolls (1943)
Foreign Correspondent (1940)
Forty-ninth Parallel (1942)
Gaslight (1944)
Gentleman's Agreement* (1947)
Going My Way* (1944)
The Grapes of Wrath (1940)
The Great Dictator (1940)
Great Expectations (1947)
Hamlet* (1948)
Heaven Can Wait (1943)
The Heiress (1949)

Henry V (1946)
Here Comes Mr. Jordan (1941)
Hold Back the Dawn (1941)
How Green Was My Valley* (1941)
The Human Comedy (1943)
In Which We Serve (1943)
It's a Wonderful Life (1946)
Johnny Belinda (1948)
Kings Row (1942)
Kitty Foyle (1940)
The Letter (1940)
A Letter to Three Wives (1949)
The Little Foxes (1941)
The Long Voyage Home (1940)
The Lost Weekend* (1945)
Madame Curie (1943)
The Magnificent Ambersons (1942)
The Maltese Falcon (1941)
Mildred Pierce (1945)
Miracle on Thirty-fourth Street (1947)
The More the Merrier (1943)
Mrs. Miniver* (1942)

One Foot in Heaven (1941)
Our Town (1940)
The Ox-Bow Incident (1943)
The Philadelphia Story (1940)
The Pied Piper (1942)
The Pride of the Yankees (1942)
Random Harvest (1942)
The Razor's Edge (1946)
Rebecca* (1940)
The Red Shoes (1948)
Sergeant York (1941)
Since You Went Away (1944)
The Snake Pit (1948)
The Song of Bernadette (1943)
Spellbound (1945)
Suspicion (1941)
The Talk of the Town (1942)
The Treasure of the Sierra Madre (1948)
Twelve O'clock High (1949)
Wake Island (1942)
Watch on the Rhine (1943)
Wilson (1944)
Yankee Doodle Dandy (1942)
The Yearling (1946)

were portrayed in dim lighting, in a world of shadows and of interiors with light broken by venetian blinds, suggesting that reality had become occluded.

Social issues such as racism and anti-Semitism that had largely been ignored during the war years came to the fore in message pictures such as *Gentleman's Agreement* (1947), *Pinky* (1949), and *Crossfire* (1947), which made Robert Ryan a star playing an American veteran who murders a Jewish man in the mistaken notion that he is a Jewish war profiteer (in fact, he is a decorated veteran). Similar films, such as *Out of the Past* (1947), also linked the returning veteran's problematic readjustment to civil society with the brooding atmosphere of film noir, a term French critics coined to express American cinema's increasingly dark view of a society torn by psychological, social, and sexual tensions.

Postwar Politics and Cold War Controversies Beginning in the 1920's, Hollywood studios battled against the efforts of writers, actors, and film technicians to organize themselves into unions to negotiate for proper compensation and job security. Until the late 1930's, the studios held the upper hand, blunting the effectiveness of most unionizing efforts, but the political atmosphere changed during the Franklin D. Roosevelt administration, when laws were passed guaranteeing the right to organize. During the 1940's, the government sought court judgments that would force the Hollywood studios to divest their ownership of movie theaters, thus weakening the control film producers had over the distribution of their films. By the end of the decade, the industry's most important film stars were beginning to organize their own production companies and to make deals with television networks.

During the late 1940's, a resurgent Republican Party that had gained control of Congress used the House Committee on Un-American Activities (also known as the House Un-American Activities Committee, or HUAC) to investigate the role of leftists and communists in the American film industry. Suddenly films such as *Mission to Moscow* became suspect, and writers, directors, and actors whose leftist political sympathies were public knowledge were summoned to Washington, D.C., to testify about their knowledge of communist infiltration in labor unions and in film production.

The Hollywood Ten became a cause célèbre when a group of writers refused to testify about their political beliefs before HUAC. At first, these writers enjoyed considerable support in Hollywood, and they expected the weight of public opinion to be on their side, reasoning that it was unconstitutional to force American citizens to testify about their beliefs. From 1947 to the end of the decade, however, with the American government now in a Cold War with the Soviet Union, and with charges surfacing that Soviet spies had stolen military and diplomatic secrets from the federal government, Hollywood executives deemed it prudent to ask their employees to publicly profess their loyalty to the United States and to deny membership in the Communist Party. When the Hollywood Ten and others refused to make such public declarations, they found themselves on a blacklist, making them no longer employable in Hollywood.

The Hollywood Ten were screenwriters and directors who, on November 24, 1947, were cited for contempt of Congress for refusing to testify before HUAC. The ten were screenwriter Alvah Bessie, screenwriter and director Herbert Biberman, screenwriter Lester Cole, director Edward Dmytryk, screenwriter Ring Lardner, Jr., screenwriter John Howard Lawson, screenwriter Albert Maltz, screenwriter Samuel Ornitz, producer and screenwriter Adrian Scott, and screenwriter Dalton Trumbo.

Thus, a form of political censorship pervaded Hollywood films well beyond the 1940's. Censorship in itself was not new, since matters of sexuality, for example, had been censored in Hollywood films since the advent of the Hays Code in 1930. Not until the film studios began to disintegrate during the 1950's, because of competition with television and with film

stars who began to form their own production companies, did the effects of the blacklist finally dissipate.

Impact   During the early part of the decade, Hollywood adjusted to a world at war, consenting to the federal government's desire to produce films that would inspire and sustain the war effort. At the same time, Hollywood cultivated a new generation of stars to continue making many of its popular genres of films such as Westerns, detective stories, musicals, dramas, and comedies. After the war, Hollywood found it increasingly difficult to maintain its huge weekly audiences because of the free entertainment provided by television, which now allowed families to view their favorite shows at home and organize their leisure activities without having to attend movie theaters, as they regularly did during the 1930's and early 1940's.

By the late 1940's, Hollywood's impact on American culture began to weaken as its films were attacked for their political content, which was deemed insufficiently critical of communist ideology that was said to undermine American values. Hollywood responded with a number of films, such as *The Iron Curtain* (1948) and *I Was a Communist for the FBI* (1951), that confronted head-on charges of Soviet espionage and showed America's former ally as now an untrustworthy partner. Even when the content of Hollywood films was not overtly political, studios were careful to present stories that in no way could be viewed as undermining national ideals.

Carl Rollyson

Further Reading

Dixon, Wheeler Winston, ed. *American Cinema of the 1940s: Themes and Variations.* New Brunswick, N.J.: Rutgers University Press, 2006. Essays on war films, national identity, postwar recovery, Cold War politics, communist subversion, and the American family. Includes an introduction and a list of works cited.

Friedrich, Otto. *City of Nets: A Portrait of Hollywood in the 1940's.* New York: Harper & Row, 1986. One of the classic accounts of this period, written in a lively, engaging style. Friedrich provides a good explanation of the rise of labor unions in Hollywood, the exile of stars such as Charles Chaplin because of Cold War politics, and the fate of the Hollywood Ten and the development of the blacklist.

Jewell, Richard. *The Golden Age of Cinema: Hollywood, 1929-1945.* New York: Wiley-Blackwell, 2007. Chapters on historical events and social phenomena that have shaped Hollywood films, the studio system and how films were distributed, the role of censorship, narrative and style, genres, and stars and the star system. Includes bibliography and index of film titles.

McClelland, Doug, ed. *Forties Film Talk: Oral Histories of Hollywood, with 120 Lobby Posters.* Jefferson, N.C.: McFarland, 1992. Part 1 consists of interviews with actors, and part 2 of discussions of genre films (biographies, comedies, dramas, epics, fantasies, horror films, melodramas, musicals, political films, religious films, war films, and Westerns). Includes bibliography.

Ragan, David. *Movie Stars of the '40's: A Complete Reference Guide for the Film Historian or Trivia Buff.* Englewood Cliffs, N.J.: Prentice Hall, 1985. Succinct biographies of all the important actors in this period, with lists of their most significant films.

See also Academy Awards; Andy Hardy films; Animated films; Cowboy films; Disney films; Film in Canada; Film noir; Film serials; Films about World War II; Maisie films.

■ Film noir

Definition Atmospheric, moody crime films stressing moral ambiguities and the psychological states of their characters

While earlier crime and mystery films emphasized societal conflicts and the solving of crimes, film noir took a more pessimistic and stylized approach.

Film noir, a term popularized by French critics beginning in the 1950's, emphasizes darkness, both in the chiaroscuro lighting of the films and in the dark sides of their protagonists. Whether police officers, detectives, or ordinary citizens, these characters always find obstacles, if not bodies, blocking their paths. They recognize the thin line separating them from villains and are tormented by their flaws. They are usually men who find more danger than love in their duplicitous women. The influences of Freudian psychology and existentialism are often on display in these nihilistic films.

The anxieties of World War II, following the aus-terity and social concerns of the Great Depression, contributed to the development of film noir. Early examples of the genre reflected the psychological pressures and emotional uncertainties experienced as a result of the war. The effects of different pressures—including the adjustment to civilian life by servicemen and worries over the atomic bomb, the Cold War, and America's new role as the leader of the free world—can be construed in later films.

Pulp Predecessors and European Influences Film noir could not have existed without hard-boiled pulp writers such as W. R. Burnett, James M. Cain, Raymond Chandler, David Goodis, Dashiell Hammett, and Cornell Woolrich. In addition to the many films based on the short stories and novels of these writers, Burnett cowrote the screenplay for *This Gun for Hire* (1942), and Chandler wrote the script *The Blue Dahlia* (1946) and cowrote the screenplay for *Double Indemnity* (1944), derived from Cain's novella *Three of a Kind* (1935).

Film noir themes and visual styles were strongly influenced by German expressionistic films such as Fritz Lang's *M* (1931). After coming to Hollywood, Lang made several influential films noirs, including *Scarlet Street* (1945). Many other Austrian, French, German, and Hungarian directors made significant contributions to film noir, including Robert Siodmak with *Phantom Lady* (1944), Billy Wilder with *Double Indemnity,* Otto Preminger with *Laura* (1944), Michael Curtiz with *Mildred Pierce* (1945), Edgar G. Ulmer with *Detour* (1945), Jacques Tourneur with *Out of the Past* (1947), and Max Ophüls with *The Reckless Moment* (1949).

Evolution of Noir Many authorities cite director John Huston's *The Maltese Falcon* (1941) as the first true noir, with private investigator Sam Spade (Humphrey Bogart) bending the rules to catch the killer of his partner. Others point to *Stranger on the Third Floor* (1940), in which a murder witness (John McGuire) begins to question the validity of his own testimony. Many films from the early 1940's have strong noir aspects without encompassing all the criteria of the genre. For example, *I Wake Up Screaming* (1941), presenting a wrongly accused man (Victor Mature) who tries to prove his innocence in the face of hostility from a cop (Laird Cregar) who loved the murder victim, is darker than *The Maltese Falcon* and also introduced the flashback to the genre.

The first film in which all the noir elements fell into place may be *Double Indemnity*, with its femme fatale (Barbara Stanwyck) manipulating a weak-willed man (Fred MacMurray) into murder. *Double Indemnity* begins with Mac-Murray's character bleeding from a gunshot and speaking into a Dictaphone to explain how he came to these circumstances, as flashbacks are added to the voice-over narration so important to the genre.

Out of the Past (1947) is often cited as the best written, directed, and acted film of the genre, with flashbacks, voice-over narration, and some of the strongest sexual content of the era. Gas-station owner Jeff Bailey (Robert Mitchum) falls deeper and deeper into a moral morass despite himself. When femme fatale Kathie Moffat (Jane Greer) warns him that she may not be trustworthy, he replies, "Baby, I don't care."

Orson Welles and Rita Hayworth in the famous hall-of-mirrors scene in the 1948 noir classic The Lady from Shanghai. *(Getty Images)*

Visual Style and Budgetary Restraints   The visual style of film noir emphasizes contrasts between light and dark with shadows and smoke. Especially popular are shadows cast by venetian blinds. Images are diffused as reflections on windows and pools of water, and light shimmers on skin. Flashing neon lights illuminate the energy and vulgarity of the noir world. Tilted camera angles underscore the chaos and uncertainty of the milieu.

The stylized look of film noir was often the result of the restraints of time and money imposed on the filmmakers. The restrictions were even greater for directors working for small studios. *Detour*, in which two hitchhikers (Tom Neal and Ann Savage) become caught up in blackmail and murder, is generally considered the masterpiece of low-budget noir, with Ulmer using his limited resources to their utmost.

Impact   American crime films would never be the same after film noir made psychological realism and moral ambiguity acceptable. Police, private detectives, and criminals would never again be portrayed in the black-and-white terms seen during the 1930's.

Film noir's popularity slowly declined during the 1950's as American audiences began seeking lighter entertainment. Nevertheless, the genre began to have an enormous impact on foreign crime films. Ironically, by the 1990's American crime films were strongly influenced by those from France, Japan, and Hong Kong, which were heavily indebted to the American noir films of the 1940's and early 1950's, and the subgenre of neo-noir began to flourish.

Michael Adams

Further Reading

Biesen, Sheri Chinen. *Blackout: World War II and the Origins of Film Noir.* Baltimore, Md.: Johns Hopkins University Press, 2005. Traces the political and social conditions of Hollywood during the war that led to the rise of film noir.

Borde, Raymond, and Étienne Chaumeton. *A Panorama of American Film Noir, 1941-1953.* Translated by Paul Hammond. San Francisco: City Lights Books, 2002. An influential study of the genre, originally published in 1955.

Hirsch, Foster. *The Dark Side of the Screen: Film Noir.* New York: Da Capo Press, 2001. Explains the evolution of noir in detail.

Muller, Eddie. *Dark City: The Lost World of Film Noir.* New York: St. Martin Press, 1998. Addresses how films noirs differ in setting and psychology.

Naremore, James. *More than Night: Film Noir in Its Contexts.* Rev. ed. Berkeley: University of California Press, 2008. Details how modernism, politics, censorship, and media have affected noir.

Silver, Alan, and Elizabeth Ward, eds. *Film Noir: An Encyclopedic Reference to the American Style.* 3d ed. Woodstock, N.Y.: Overlook Press, 1992. Includes credits, summaries, and analyses of 137 noir films from the 1940's.

See also Bogart, Humphrey; Chandler, Raymond; *Double Indemnity*; Faulkner, William; Film in the United States; Hayworth, Rita; Hitchcock, Alfred; *Laura*; *The Maltese Falcon.*

■ Film serials

Definition Feature-length films, almost exclusively action-adventures, divided into single-reel "chapters"

Because film serials were packaged with major-studio feature films in the local theaters, many B-film actors in these chapter plays reached an audience potentially as large as those of Hollywood's top stars. Drawing from other popular culture media such as radio and comic books helped give film serials a presold audience. Only three studios—Republic, Columbia, and Universal—produced all ninety serials that appeared between 1940 and 1949.

By 1940, the film serial was already a standard part of a theater's offering in America. While film serials date back to Thomas Alva Edison's *What Happened to Mary* (1912), the 1935 merger of several small studios in Hollywood's "Poverty Row" to form Republic Pictures is generally recognized as the catalyst that formed the serial style of the 1940's. At that time, the only major (A-picture) studio actively producing serials was Universal Studios, which had been cranking them out since the advent of the talkie in 1929. When Columbia Pictures entered the arena in 1937 with *Jungle Menace*, starring animal trainer "Bring-'em-back-alive" Frank Buck, the stage was set for the three-studio competition that would characterize the 1940's serial.

Republic Pictures Serials Republic had already produced sixteen serials by 1940, mostly Dick Tracy, Zorro, Lone Ranger, and various other adventure titles. The studio's success with Dick Tracy, and the popularity of Universal's comic-strip-based serials during the late 1930's, led Republic to seek comics that it could profitably transfer to the screen. The comic-book superhero was itself only two years old: Superman's first comic-book appearance was in 1938; early in 1939, the character debuted in the newspapers, and in February, 1940, on radio. Republic negotiated with Superman's creators, Jerry Siegel and Joe Shuster, for a serialized Man of Steel, but when the pair demanded control of the script, Republic turned to another costumed hero, Captain Marvel, in 1941. With Tom Tyler in the title role, the dozen episodes of *Adventures of Captain Marvel* became Republic's most popular adventure serial, finishing a close second to Universal's *Flash Gordon* series.

The same year, 1941, Republic hit again with Frances Gifford in *Jungle Girl.* In the early days of the movie serial, during the silent era, female adventurers followed the example of Pearl White in *The Perils of Pauline* (1914), but once sound came in, film serial heroes tended to be exclusively male—until Republic's *Jungle Girl.* Universal and Independent Studios had been producing *Tarzan* serials since 1929, but the female characters had all been helpless victims for Tarzan to rescue. *Jungle Girl*'s Nyoka Meredith, played by Gifford, changed all of that. Nyoka hatched the plans to catch the villains, swung from the trees, and rescued the (often male) good guys. The Nyoka character was popular enough for a sequel, but Gifford had moved on to the "A" list at Radio-Keith-Orpheum (RKO Pictures), then Paramount and Metro-Goldwyn-Mayer (MGM). Thus, she was replaced in *Perils of Nyoka* (1942) by Kay Aldridge as the Jungle Girl.

In 1944, another comic-book hero, Captain America, hit big for Republic, but the rest of the decade saw mostly Westerns and G-Men in their serials. Clayton Moore, who would later become television's Lone Ranger, emerged as a star in *Jesse James Rides Again* (1947), *Adventures of Frank and Jesse James* (1948), and *Ghost of Zorro* (1949).

Universal Studios Serials Universal, which had dominated the serial market with its *Flash Gordon* and *Buck Rogers* science-fiction films (both title characters played by Buster Crabbe), opened the 1940's with its last *Flash* serial, *Flash Gordon Conquers the Universe* (1940). The same year, Universal discovered a property that would become an unlikely success in the serials: the Dead End Kids. Samuel Goldwyn had seen these juvenile actors on Broadway in *Dead End* (pr. 1935) and hired them to do a movie version of the play (1937). MGM sold the boys' contract to Warner Bros. in 1938, and Universal borrowed them to make three serials, *Junior G-Men* (1940), *Sea Raiders* (1941), and *Junior G-Men of the Air* (1942).

By the middle of the decade, however, Universal knew that the market for serials was drying up. The few dollars a theater was willing to pay for twelve or fifteen episodes were not enough to cover even the low-budget production expenses, and Universal closed down its serials line in 1946.

Children watching a serial at a Saturday matinee in 1948. Weekly serials—especially those with exciting cliff-hanging endings—kept children returning to the theaters every weekend. (Michael Ochs Archives/Getty Images)

Columbia Pictures Serials Columbia began the 1940's by filming radio's most popular adventure program, *The Shadow*, in 1940, then scored with other comic-book successes, *The Batman* and *The Phantom*, both in 1943. Tom Taylor, who had been popular as Republic's Captain Marvel, donned a mask to play the Phantom for Columbia. Other comic and radio characters who became Columbia serials in the 1940's included Brenda Starr (1945), Hop Harrigan (1946), Jack Armstrong (1947), and, finally, Superman (1948). The Man of Steel did not prove to be worth the wait: production budgets were too small by 1948 to afford the effects necessary to make *Superman* believable.

Impact Though the commercial success of television brought the end of the serial era—Republic closed its line in 1955, and Columbia the following year—it also created a new market for the old serials. Television stations repackaged the "chapter plays" as feature-length films or kept the serial format for once-daily or one-weekly segments on children's shows. The success of the *Batman* television show in 1965 caused Columbia to rerelease *The Batman* more than twenty years after it was filmed. Half a century later, DVD sales gave a third life to the great serials of the 1940's.

John R. Holmes

Further Reading

Barbour, Alan G. *Days of Thrills and Adventure.* New York: Macmillan, 1970. An analysis of American film serials from 1929 to 1956, with more than one hundred photos and a complete filmography.

Bifulco, Michael J. *Heroes and Villains: Movie Serial Classics.* Woodland Hills, Calif.: Bifulco Books, 1989. Detailed synopses of four superhero serials of the 1940's, along with one hundred frame blow-ups and lobby cards from the films, and an introduction on the nature of the costumed-hero serial.

Cline, William C. *Serials-ly Speaking: Essays on Cliffhangers.* Jefferson, N.C.: McFarland, 1994. Collection of Cline's columns in the film fan magazine *Big Reel* between 1984 and 1991, reflecting on the adventure serials of the 1940's.

Rainey, Buck. *Serial Film Stars: A Biographical Dictionary, 1912-1956.* Jefferson, N.C.: McFarland,

2005. Details on the lives and films of nearly 450 stars in 863 pages.

Zinman, David. *Saturday Afternoon at the Bijou*. New York: Castle Books, 1973. A thorough treatment of serials, though including some series films that were never issued as installments.

See also   Andy Hardy films; *Brenda Starr*; Comic books; Comic strips; Cowboy films; Film in the United States; Maisie films.

■ Films about World War II

Definition   Films about North American involvement in World War II made during and after the war

After the United States entered World War II in December, 1941, the American film industry embraced the Allied war effort and became a central transmitter of wartime policy, with a goal of inspiration for the war effort added to the traditional mandate of entertainment. By mid-1942, one-third of all features in production explicitly referenced the war, and Americans flocked to movie theaters for stories of valor and hope.

During the early 1940's, each Hollywood genre adapted its formulas to war themes. Musicals continued to headline stars, such as Paramount's popular team of Bob Hope and Bing Crosby. In *Star Spangled Rhythm* (1943), the duo continued their typical patter and music, with a focus on war goals. Hollywood studios efficiently delivered popular revues to movie audiences by filming military stage shows. Warner Bros. bought the rights from the War Department to film the 1942 Broadway show *This Is the Army*, with music by Irving Berlin. An enormous success on both stage and screen, the 1943 film, featuring many soldiers who had been actors in civilian life, ran without interruption throughout the war years. Betty Grable, a musical star at Twentieth Century-Fox, became the quintessential pinup girl of the war as the gal with the "million-dollar legs" (insured by Lloyd's of London for that amount).

Comedy production continued, with military topics inspiring amusing situations. The team of Bud Abbott and Lou Costello, who were ranked fifth among stars in the war years, appeared in eleven quickly produced wartime comedies. Director Preston Sturges adapted sophisticated screwball comedy

formulas to war themes. The talented satirist worked against the Hollywood grain of boosterism by questioning the fidelity of women on the home front in *The Miracle of Morgan's Creek* (1944) and by mocking hero worship in *Hail the Conquering Hero* (1944).

Thrillers turned their attention to spy plots, stories of resistance fighters, and dramas about mysterious men living in dangerous circumstances. In three films—*Casablanca* (1942), *Passage to Marseille* (1944), and *To Have and Have Not* (1944)—Warner Bros. star Humphrey Bogart played a reluctant patriot; in each film, his ultimate conversion to the war effort forms the climax.

The adventure and action of big-budget Westerns transferred into combat pictures, and the emotional intensity and focus on female protagonists of "women's pictures" transferred into home-front dramas. Many early features with military themes focused on fliers, including *Cavalcade of Aviation* (1942), *Eagle Squadron* (1942), *Flying Tigers* (1942), and *Thunder Birds* (1942). *Wake Island* (1942) was one of the first of scores of films that dramatized ground-war heroics. Production of combat films quickly accelerated, with about 60 percent of war-related films in this subgenre by 1945 (in contrast to a decline in espionage films, which were dominant during the early 1940's). Most combat films shifted the traditional Hollywood spotlight on the exploits of a single hero to the actions of a disparate group of combatants, led by an appealing individual. These idealized "melting pot" units, brought together by the circumstances of war in films such as *Gung Ho!* (1943), *Bataan* (1943), and *Pride of the Marines* (1945), put aside differences of class, ethnicity, region, religion, and (most unrealistically) race to defeat the enemy. Although Army soldiers occupied the most military positions on screen (as well as off), all branches of the military appeared in Hollywood films. The combat film *Corvette K-225* (1943; released in the United Kingdom as *The Nelson Touch*) saluted the Canadian Navy.

"Women's pictures" continued to emphasize women making sacrifices, but with a new emphasis on how the war caused separation from husbands, sweethearts, and sons. Working-girl dramas such as *Tender Comrade* (1943), starring the dynamic and much-loved Ginger Rogers, and *Since You Went Away* (1944) showed the physical and moral strength of female workers in industrial plants, while *So Proudly We Hail!* (1943) honored the military nurses who worked and sometimes died in combat zones. Often the struggle between duty and romance drove these films, with female protagonists inevitably choosing wartime duty. John Ford's memorable drama *They Were Expendable* (released in 1945, after the war's end) featured a combat nurse as a figure of goodness who sacrifices romance for military necessity.

By 1944, 80 cents of every dollar spent on "spectator amusement" in the United States went for movie tickets. The military movie audience was also massive. Called "two-hour furloughs," screenings of Hollywood features boosted morale and entertained troops. By 1945, approximately 2,400 nightly shows occurred in the European and Mediterranean theaters.

Nonfeature Films In addition to theatrical features released by Hollywood during the war years, studios also produced war-related serials, newsreels, live-action shorts, and cartoons. The first war-related animations, produced by Disney and Warner Bros., appeared in January, 1942, only a month after the United States entered the war. A patriotic Donald Duck not only starred in many cartoons but also was featured in more than 400 official military insignia designed by Disney animators. Bugs Bunny and Daffy Duck served the war effort in the Warner Bros. animation unit, while Popeye fought the good fight at Paramount and Mighty Mouse battled the Axis forces for Twentieth Century-Fox. MGM's combative Tom and Jerry won an Academy Award for the Hanna-Barbera unit with *The Yankee Doodle Mouse* (1943).

The U.S. government also engaged in filmmaking during the 1940's, enlisting the assistance of a contingent of top Hollywood directors. In 1942, director Frank Capra took command of the 834th Signal Service Photographic Detachment. Under Major Capra's leadership, the unit produced a

seven-part series of orientation films that became required viewing during military training. The *Why We Fight* films (1942-1945) were the most widely viewed of the wartime documentaries (sometimes perceived as propaganda) and became landmarks of documentary history. Each of the films wove together a variety of source materials, combining clips from old Hollywood films, newsreels, and documentaries (including several made in Germany and Japan) with originally produced maps, illustrations, and special scenes. An emotional, aggressive voice-over delivered a history lesson and an argument for "why we fight." Three of the films—*Prelude to War*

Sheet music for a song from the Oscar-winning Donald Duck cartoon Der Fuehrer's Face. *(Getty Images)*

(1942), which won an Academy Award for best documentary, *The Battle of Russia* (1943), and *War Comes to America* (1945)—were offered free to exhibitors and played in movie theaters stateside, while the entire series was screened in many noncommercial venues. Another War Department orientation film made under Capra's supervision, *The Negro Soldier* (1944), was required viewing for all soldiers and was shown in theaters stateside (but not in the South).

The Battle of Midway (1942), directed by John Ford, was the first and most influential of the government-sponsored combat reports, although atypically, it was shot in color. Ford, who had enlisted in the Navy, won an Academy Award for this endeavor. The Office of War Information (OWI) was far less pleased with the trilogy of documentaries directed by John Huston. *Report from the Aleutians* (1943) had a sorrowful tone and provoked a lukewarm response from the small audiences who saw it. The mood of regret also permeated *The Battle of San Pietro* (1945). Shot in central Italy, the documentary showed the great loss of life among American and German troops; in addition, two of the fourteen cameramen were killed and all but two were wounded during the making of the film. The OWI attached an introduction by General Mark Clark to the film in which he claimed that the deaths presented were "not in vain." The third Huston film, *Let There Be Light* (1946), was suppressed from distribution until 1981 on the basis of privacy concerns regarding the veterans shown receiving care at an Army psychiatric treatment center. A masterful combat report, William Wyler's *The Memphis Belle* (1944), documented (in Technicolor) the twenty-fifth and final mission of a storied flight crew.

John Grierson, a Scot who was the film commissioner of Canada during the war years, oversaw production of the influential Canadian series *The World in Action*. He also acted as spokesman for the effectiveness of films in the propaganda war.

War Films in the Postwar Years   New depictions of the war by Hollywood all but ended after V-J Day (August 15, 1945). Despite the tremendous success of *The Best Years of Our Lives* (1946), a sensitive drama of postwar adjustment that earned seven Academy Awards, including those for best director for William Wyler and best supporting actor for disabled veteran Harold Russell, only two of 369 features produced in Hollywood in 1947 had war-related themes. After al-

most three years of avoiding the war, and during the confusion of the Korean War, Hollywood returned to the certainties of World War II, with films such as *Battleground* (1949) and *The Sands of Iwo Jima* (1949; rereleased in 1954) celebrating American heroism. The most decorated soldier in World War II, Audie Murphy, played himself in a Cinemascope reenactment of his bravery in *To Hell and Back* (1955). During the 1960's, several epic films, including *The Longest Day* (1962) and *Battle of the Bulge* (1965), memorialized successful American campaigns in Europe.

A significant shift in tone concerning the war occurred during the late 1960's and into the 1970's, when Hollywood reflected a national attitude of questioning the legitimacy of war. Two films based on best-selling novels set in World War II—*Catch-22* (1970, from Joseph Heller's 1961 novel of the same title) and *Slaughterhouse-Five* (1972, from Kurt Vonnegut, Jr.'s 1969 novel *Slaughterhouse-Five: Or, The Children's Crusade, a Duty-Dance with Death*)—dramatized the absurdity of war. *Tora! Tora! Tora!* (1970) told the story of the attack on Pearl Harbor from both American and Japanese perspectives, *Hell in the Pacific* (1973) reduced the Pacific theater to a struggle of wills between a surviving Marine and his Japanese counterpart, and *Patton* (1970), a biopic of the flamboyant general, played to Oscar-winning perfection by George C. Scott, opened itself to interpretations attractive to both hawks and doves in a nation polarized by the Vietnam War.

Many of the best contemporary directors have turned to "the good war" as a thematic source and a forum to consider issues of morality. Sam Fuller, himself a veteran of the D-day landing on Omaha Beach, directed *The Big One* (1980), re-creating his memories of confusion and terror. Terrance Malick set his meditative film *The Thin Red Line* (1998) in Pacific jungles to explore the interior emotions of combatants in a natural environment of great beauty and terrible violence. Steven Spielberg has directed several films set in the war years, including his memorable *Saving Private Ryan* (1998), which earned him an Academy Award for best director. Framed by a contemporary visit to the commanding officer's grave in France, this widely successful film acknowledges the role of memory while presenting skillfully produced combat sequences of enormous visceral power.

Filmed on an enormous budget of $150 million, with full military cooperation and expert use of computer-generated imagery, *Pearl Harbor* (2001) returned to traditional storytelling, with war heroics surrounding the personal stories of men whose lives were changed forever by the December, 1941, attack. In sharp contrast, Clint Eastwood directed a pair of films that explore the role of memory in contrasting history and the distortions of myth making. *Flags of Our Fathers* (2006) shows how memories of their buddies' deaths haunt veterans for a lifetime, while a companion film, *Letters from Iwo Jima* (2006), tells the story from a Japanese perspective, with English subtitles. Critics uniformly praised this thoughtful diptych, but even with modest production budgets by Hollywood standards, each of the films lost money.

A stream of documentaries about U.S. involvement in World War II has been produced since the war years; many of them have aired on the History Channel. None has been more ambitious than the seven-part, fourteen-hour series *The War* (2007), codirected and produced by Ken Burns and broadcast on public television to a huge audience. The series focuses on the impact of the war on the lives of families living in four different parts of the United States, spotlighting the recollections of average Americans rather than depending on the opinions of historians.

Impact   World War II was the most thoroughly documented event in history. During the war years, many Hollywood studio heads, stars, and studio personnel enlisted in the armed services; those who stayed stateside directed their efforts toward producing pictures that would help to win the war while still entertaining audiences. During the 1940's and ever since, representations of "the good war" and its key events, effects, and influences have captivated filmmakers and audiences in the United States and beyond.

Carolyn Anderson

Further Reading

Basinger, Jeanine. *The World War II Combat Film: Anatomy of a Genre.* Middletown, Conn.: Wesleyan University Press, 2003. Includes an extensive annotated filmography by Jeremy Arnold. An excellent genre study of films made between 1941 and 2002.

Doherty, Thomas. *Projections of War: Hollywood, American Culture, and World War II.* New York: Columbia University Press, 1999. Thorough survey of war films and their political and industrial contexts. Appendixes list most popular films from 1941 to 1945 as well as "victory films" released in the same period. This revised edition considers relatively recent films about World War II.

Eberwein, Robert. *The War Film.* New Brunswick, N.J.: Rutgers University Press, 2005. Essays, five focused on World War II, are organized by topics of genre, race, gender, and history.

O'Brien, Kenneth Paul, and Lynn Hudson Parsons, eds. *The Home-Front War: World War II and American Society.* Westport, Conn.: Greenwood Press, 1995. Essays by nine scholars on domestic issues during the war.

Shull, Michael S., and David Edward Wilt, comps. *Hollywood War Films, 1937-1945.* Jefferson, N.C.: McFarland, 1996. Exhaustive, useful filmography.

Suid, Lawrence H. *Guts and Glory: The Making of the American Military Image in Film.* Lexington: University Press of Kentucky, 2002. Research based on hundreds of interviews by the author. Provides detailed information (including the extent of military cooperation) on more than two hundred films. Outstanding resource.

See also   Animated films; *The Best Years of Our Lives*; Capra, Frank; *Casablanca*; Censorship in the United States; Disney films; Film in Canada; Film in the United States; Film serials; Pinup girls; *They Were Expendable*.

■ Fiscus rescue attempt

The Event   Struggle to save the life of a three-year-old girl who had fallen down an abandoned well

Date   April 8-10, 1949

Place   San Marino, California

Although the effort to save Kathy Fiscus's life failed, the event captured national attention and demonstrated the power of on-the-spot, live television news coverage of dramatic events.

Early on Friday evening, April 8, 1949, three-year-old Kathy Fiscus fell into an abandoned water well while playing with her sister and cousins in an empty lot in San Marino, California. Emergency workers and volunteers dug shafts around and toward the narrow well in the hope of rescuing Kathy. After fifty-two hours, they reached her on Sunday evening, only to find that she had died shortly after she fell.

The rescue effort was covered by newspapers and radio as well as two local television stations, KTTV and KTLA. KTLA canceled all scheduled programming and broadcast live from the scene for 27.5 hours. Two years earlier, KTLA had broadcast live coverage of an industrial explosion, but at that time there were fewer than four hundred television sets within the station's range. By 1949, there were an estimated twenty thousand televisions in the area, and the story therefore reached a far greater number of people.

Impact Television had always provided news reports, but not extended live coverage of exciting and dramatic events. Because of the Fiscus tragedy, people realized that television could provide more than entertainment or sports coverage; it could inform an entire community and unite thousands over a single event.

Maureen Puffer-Rothenberg

Rescue workers at the moment Kathy Fiscus is found to be dead. (AP/Wide World Photos)

Further Reading

Chambers, Stan. *KTLA's News at Ten: Sixty Years with Stan Chambers.* Lake Forest, Calif.: Behler, 2008.

Morrison, Patt. "The Little Girl Who Changed Television Forever." *Los Angeles Times,* January 31, 1999, p. 9.

See also Television; Water pollution.

■ Fish and Wildlife Service, U.S.

Identification Federal government agency
Date Established on June 30, 1940

Although the Fish and Wildlife Service had relatively low priority during World War II, it was the principal wildlife research agency in the United States during the 1940's and was actively involved in fish and mammal conservation. The agency also established a migratory bird management program and helped create many opportunities for public sport fishing and wildlife hunting.

As part of a move to improve federal efficiency in 1939, the U.S. Congress established the Fish and Wildlife Service by consolidating the Bureaus of Fisheries and Biological Survey in the Department of the Interior. As the 1940's began, the service was active in studying birds and mammals, managing wildlife refuges, eliminating predators, protecting habitats for fish and wildlife, enforcing wildlife laws, and managing migratory waterfowl hunting.

The service was the principal wildlife research agency during the 1940's. Field biologists working for the service were responsible for investigating the effects of the pesticide DTT on wildlife. The service also conducted research on fish parasites and developed captive breeding techniques that were still in use into the twenty-first century and have played a role in protecting rare species such as the whooping crane. In 1947, the service worked to improve migratory waterfowl hunting by developing a program that recognized North America's four migratory bird flyways. After the end of World War II, the service began to publish quarterly reports that summarized the results of its biological research and management techniques.

By 1946, many water-based projects were causing damage to fish and wildlife habitats, and Congress responded with amendments to the Fish and Wildlife Coordination Act, which had been passed in 1934. Under the act, the service was responsible for evaluating the impact of water resource development on fish and wildlife resources. In response to the amendments, which required developers to consult with the service concerning development on bodies of water controlled or to be modified by federal agencies, the service created the River Basins Study program. The Tennessee Valley Authority, however, was exempt from the act.

Impact   Through its research, the Fish and Wildlife Service has played a major role in conserving fish, birds, and wildlife and enhancing fishing and hunting opportunities during the 1940's and afterward. The federal Aid in Sport Fish Restoration Act (Dingell-Johnson Act), passed in 1950, helped improve fishery resources, and several pieces of legislation were adopted after the 1940's to improve upon refuge management and public use, including some that called for creation of numerous wilderness areas and national wildlife refuges and fish hatcheries. The National Wildlife Refuge System Improvement Act of 1997, which requires a comprehensive plan for every wildlife refuge, carries on the mission of the service to achieve the proper balance between fish, wildlife, and habitat conservation and public use.

Further reorganization of the Fish and Wildlife Service, including a name change to the United States Fish and Wildlife Service in 1956, resulted in the creation of two new bureaus—Commercial Fisheries and Sport Fisheries and Wildlife. The Bureau of Commercial Fisheries was transferred to the Department of Commerce in 1970 and was renamed the National Marine Fisheries Service. Congress passed the Endangered Species Act in 1973 to protect endangered plants and animals and assigned administrative responsibilities to the United States Fish and Wildlife Service and the newly created National Marine Fisheries Service.

Carol A. Rolf

Further Reading

Harmon, Will, and Matthew McKinney. *The Western Confluence: A Guide to Governing Natural Resources.* Covelo, Calif.: Island Press, 2004.

Schweiger, Larry J. *Last Chance: Preserving Life on Earth.* Golden, Colo.: Fulcrum, 2009.

Taylor, Joseph E. *Making Salmon: An Environmental History of the Northwest Fisheries Crisis.* Seattle: University of Washington Press, 2001.

See also   Bureau of Land Management; National parks; Natural resources; Recreation; Water pollution; Water Pollution Control Act.

■ Fluoridation

The Event   Introduction of fluoride into the public water supply to reduce tooth decay

Date   Began in 1945

Fluoride was first introduced into the water of Grand Rapids, Michigan, and Newburgh, New York, in an experiment designed to eliminate or significantly reduce tooth decay in those communities. The introduction of fluoride into water supplies in the United States succeeded in reducing dental caries (tooth decay), but it raised serious questions about how much leeway the government should be permitted in imposing medical experiments upon the public.

Fluoride, a chemical element, exists naturally in many water supplies. Before the 1940's, it had been recognized that people who drank from these naturally fluoridated water sources had a much lower occurrence of dental caries than the general population. It was also observed that some of those who had ingested quantities of fluoride in water supplies that contained more than one part per million exhibited conditions that came to be associated with excesses of fluoride. Among these conditions, the most obvious was, despite an absence of dental caries, a discoloration and mottling of the teeth.

It was also determined that in laboratory rats who ingested two or three parts per million of fluoride in their water, the bones became brittle and were often subject to breaking. Even when the amount of fluoride ingested is in acceptable quantities, some people display conditions associated with higher intakes of the chemical. People suffering from kidney disease may also experience urinary problems when they are exposed to fluoride in supposedly acceptable quantities.

Fluoridating Water Supplies   Despite the problems associated with treating a whole community's water supply with chemicals, in 1945 fluoridation was introduced in Newburgh, New York, and Grand Rapids, Michigan. Initial public outcries against fluoridation were overcome because enthusiastic support came from distinguished public health officials. Their support was vindicated in the eyes of many because people living in Newburgh and in Grand Rapids experienced an almost immediate decline in dental caries.

By the end of the decade, the fluoridation of water was broadly adopted by communities across the United States. The American Dental Association and the American Medical Association both advocated adding fluoride to public water supplies in acceptable quantities of one part per million or less, as did the prestigious World Health Organization, although few foreign countries rushed to fluoridate their public water sources.

Tooth decay occurs largely because the enamel that covers the teeth, which is porous and crystalline, absorbs elements from the food and drink of which people partake. Decay takes place when acid and plaque enter the microscopic holes on the surface of the teeth.

Fluorine, which belongs to the halogen group of chemicals, contains fluorides and fluorocarbons, both of which, because of their low friction, are used commercially as lubricants. The fluorine used in water fluoridation fills the minute holes in the enamel of the teeth, making them impervious to penetration by substances that cause decay.

Objections to Fluoridation   Although fluoridation is now used in water supplies throughout the United States, many people have serious reservations about its use, citing cases in which fluoride, which accumulates in both the bones and teeth, has caused some people with a sensitivity to fluoride to be more subject to broken bones than the general population or to experience urinary problems associated with the ingestion of fluoride.

Some religious groups have strong objections to governmental imposition of medical mandates upon the public. Thus far, these objections have been overcome because public health officials have touted the substantial benefits of controlling dental caries as effectively as fluoridation does.

Impact   The overall impact of water fluoridation has been a substantial reduction in dental problems and tooth decay in the general populations of communities that add fluoride to their water. The cost of fluoridation is dramatically less than the cost of treating tooth decay.

Fluoridation has been particularly effective in young children, whose teeth are developing and whose bones and teeth absorb fluoride in substantial quantities. Fluoride in the teeth increases among people who drink fluoridated water until, at some point between ages thirty and forty, the absorption of it levels off.

R. Baird Shuman

Further Reading

Diamond, Richard. *Dental First Aid for Families.* Ravensdale, Wash.: Idyll Arbor, 2000. Aimed at general readers, this book presents the pros and cons of using fluoride in both water supplies and in toothpastes and mouthwashes to reduce dental caries.

Harris, Norman O., and Franklin Garcia-Godoy, eds. *Primary Preventive Dentistry.* 6th ed. Upper Saddle River, N.J.: Pearson Prentice Hall, 2004. Chapters 8 and 9 focus on water fluoridation and on topical fluoride therapy. This is a standard work in the field of dentistry and is highly recommended.

McClure, Frank J. *Water Fluoridation: The Search and the Victory.* Bethesda, Md.: National Institute of Dental Research, 1970. A useful account of the initial problems that those advocating water fluoridation faced and how they overcame these problems, clearing the way for widespread water fluoridation in the United States.

Mittelman, Jerome, Beverly Mittelman, and Jean Barillo. *Healthy Teeth for Kids: A Preventive Program—Prenatal Through the Teens.* New York: Twin Stream, 2001. A practical approach directed at parents. Chapter 10, "Fluoride: How Safe? How Effective?" is particularly relevant.

Murray, John J., A. J. Rugg-Gunn, and G. N. Jenkins. *Fluorides in Caries Prevention.* 3d ed. Oxford, England: Butterworth-Heinemann, 1991. Perhaps the most impressive presentation of the topic of fluorides in dentistry. Very thorough coverage.

National Research Council. *Health Effects of Ingested Fluoride.* A comprehensive assessment of the effects fluoride has when ingested based on extensive experiments both with laboratory animals and with humans. Quite technical but highly significant.

Pine, Cynthia, ed. *Community Oral Health*. Oxford, England: 1997. Chapter 7 focuses on the use of fluoride to prevent tooth decay, discussing the benefits of water fluoridation but also mentioning possible dangers and limitations of the process.

See also   Health care; Medicine; World Health Organization.

■ Flying saucers

Definition   Term initially used in media reportage for "unidentified flying objects" (UFOs) following a widely publicized sighting that initiated sudden and widespread public interest in such phenomena

The sighting of a group of flying objects near Mount Rainier by a pilot in a small plane became the basis for one of the most widespread and extensively elaborated items of modern mythology. It engendered military interest, cosmological speculation and conspiracy theories on a remarkable scale, and controversy of a remarkable intensity.

When businessman Kenneth Arnold landed in Yakima, Washington, on June 24, 1947, he reported seeing a mysterious group of nine flying objects near Mount Rainier, apparently traveling at 1,200 miles per hour. The news was passed on by the airport manager and spread like wildfire. In subsequent interviews, Arnold compared the objects' motion to saucers being skimmed over a lake; that description was then compacted into the term "flying saucer," which caught on during the remarkable surge of public interest that followed, although "flying disks" was initially used with greater frequency.

Reports of strange objects in the sky were by no means new—many newspaper clippings relating to such objects had been collated two decades earlier by the indefatigable chronicler of the unusual, Charles Fort—but the Arnold sighting touched a raw nerve irritated by anxieties related to the recent advent of the atom bomb and the initial stirrings of the Cold War. Other witnesses soon came forward to support Arnold's testimony, including the crew of a United Airlines flight, who reported having seen

similar objects over Idaho on July 4. A further group was photographed on July 12 over Tulsa, Oklahoma. The Army Air Forces Directorate of Intelligence felt compelled to investigate; its initial investigators concluded that the objects had been real but made no judgment as to their nature.

Roswell Incident   Ten days before the Arnold sighting, a rancher in Roswell, New Mexico, had found some debris on his land; as soon as the publicity regarding mysterious flying objects reached him, he began to speculate publicly as to whether he had found one. On July 8, the Roswell Army Air Field (RAAF) issued a press release advertising the wreckage as that of a "flying disk," but the commanding general of the Eighth Air Force promptly issued another press release stating that the wreckage was that of a weather balloon—an explanation accepted at the time. In 1978, however, one of the officers from RAAF who had collected the debris, Jesse Marcel, gave an interview alleging that the debris had been that of an alien spacecraft but that the truth had been concealed by the Air Force.

When Marcel was subsequently interviewed by the *National Enquirer,* his story was further elaborated to allege that the Air Force had removed similar debris from ten other crash sites to a secret military facility (subsequently named as "Area 51"). In 1989, an ex-mortuary worker, Glen Dennis, added the further elaboration that alien corpses had been autopsied at Roswell, completing the incident's belated elevation to a central position in UFO mythology, which it continued to occupy into the twenty-first century.

Military Investigations   A formal investigation of UFO sightings, code-named Project Sign, was initiated by Lieutenant General Nathan F. Twining, the head of Air Materiel Command, in 1948. Its most notable inquiries included one into a crash near Franklin, Kentucky, on January 7, 1948, in which Air Force pilot Thomas Mantell had been killed after attempting to pursue "a large metallic object," and one into a sighting by two airline pilots over Montgomery, Alabama, on July 24, 1948, of a glowing "rocket-shaped" UFO that appeared to have a row of portholes. Skeptical members of the investigating team suggested that what Mantell had actually seen was the planet Venus and that what the pilots had seen was another airplane, but some of their fellows were more credulous. The project's report concluded that the objects were real, but of unknown origin; those members who favored the hypothesis that UFOs were extraterrestrial were not allowed to include that assertion.

Project Sign was followed in February, 1949, by Project Grudge, which reported in December that there was no reliable evidence that any of the sightings involved real objects, and that most had arisen from perceptive errors or from deliberate deceptions. There was, however, widespread suspicion that the investigators had been instructed in advance to reach that conclusion, and that the entire project was merely an element of a "military cover-up." The controversy was by then unstoppable, and subsequent negative reports were widely attributed by believers to be exercises in deception.

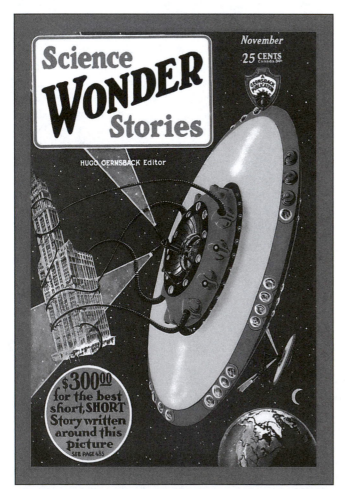

After "flying saucers" were first described during the late 1940's, saucer-shaped alien spacecraft quickly became a science-fiction staple. (Getty Images)

Flying Saucers in Science Fiction   One rapid and particularly excited reaction to Arnold's report was that of Ray Palmer, editor of the pulp science-fiction magazine *Amazing Stories*, who had published numerous works in the previous two years by Richard S. Shaver alleging that dire events on the world's surface were mostly caused by underground-dwelling "deros" (detrimental robots) descended from servants left behind when rival races of immortal giants abandoned Earth. These had proved successful enough to prompt Palmer to begin picking up other items of Fortean reportage to offer as evidence in its favor; his editorial in the October, 1947, issue of *Amazing* hailed the Arnold sighting as "proof" of Shaver's claims and asked for reports of further sightings of "flying discs" [sic]. He claimed to have received tens of thousands of responses to this contention.

Arnold's sightings were then given pride of place on the cover of the first issue of *Fate*, a new magazine devoted to occult and Fortean subjects launched by Palmer in 1948. The headline article was Arnold's "The Truth About Flying Saucers," and the cover showed a flying disk looming over a civilian aircraft. Other science-fiction editors and writers remained skeptical, and many were horrified by Palmer's championship of the most bizarre interpretations of flying saucers. The notion became a generic cliché regardless, rapidly incorporated into comic-book and movie imagery, where UFO sightings were routinely represented as "proof" that the genre's anticipations regarding extraterrestrial life had been accurate. The willingness of Americans to believe in nightmares of alien invasion had already been demonstrated before the outbreak of World War II by Orson Welles's Mercury Theatre radio dramatization of *The War of the Worlds* on October 30, 1938, to which the flying saucer panic was a sequel of sorts.

Impact   The elaboration of flying saucer mythology in the wake of the sightings of the late 1940's took several new directions, translated into autobiographical fantasy in such works as George Adamski's *Flying Saucers Have Landed* (1953), imitations of which eventually gave rise to a large number of accounts of "alien abduction," often featuring memories recovered under hypnosis after allegedly having been suppressed. A similar paranoia was reflected in the elaboration of the "cover-up" myth to encompass mysterious "men in black" charged with visiting people who experienced "close encounters" with aliens and their craft. Even more remarkable was the rapid adoption of flying saucer mythology by religious cults as signs of imminent apocalypse and potential avenues of salvation—an appropriation that encouraged Carl Jung's intepretation of flying saucers as expressions of yearning sprung from the archetypes of the collective unconscious. Within the wide bounds set by these seemingly lunatic fringes, thousands of people became involved in practical "ufology," hunting for UFOs, studying reports of sightings, and speculating prolifically as to what might lie behind them.

Brian Stableford

Further Reading

Bloecher, Ted. *Report on the UFO Wave of 1947*. Washington, D.C.: National Investigations Committee on Aerial Phenomena, 1967. A detailed retrospective compilation of reported sightings, made by a believer, assembled with the relentless assiduity that only believers can muster.

Curran, Douglas. *In Advance of the Landing: Folk Concepts of Outer Space*. Rev. ed. New York: Abbeville Press, 2001. An account of UFO-related lore and legend in the United States. Although its central concern with flying saucer cults means that its main focus is on the second half of the twentieth century, its account of the 1940's prelude sets those events in a context markedly different from the other sources cited.

Dolan, Richard M. *UFOs and the National Security State: An Unclassified History—Volume One, 1941-1973*. New York: Keyhole, 2000. A balanced account of UFO sightings and investigations in the context of anxiety about national security, broadly based on the investigations carried out by the military.

Jacobs, David M., ed. *UFOs and Abductions: Challenging the Borders of Knowledge*. Lawrence: University Press of Kansas, 2000. A significant collection of academic essays; the most relevant items to the 1940's are Michael D. Swords's "UFOs, the Military and the Early Cold War" and Thomas E. Bullard's "UFOs: Lost in the Myths."

Jung, Carl. *Flying Saucers: A Modern Myth of Things Seen in the Sky*. Translated by R. F. C. Hull. London: Routledge, 1959. A psychoanalytic account of the possible significance of the sudden flare-up in UFO sightings, based on the assumption that their real "source" is the human collective unconscious.

See also Air Force, U.S.; Astronomy; Cold War; Fads; Pulp magazines.

■ Flying Tigers

Identification Volunteer American flying group that flew combat missions for China during World War II
Also known as American Volunteer Group
Date Operated from 1941 to 1942

After Japan's attack on Pearl Harbor on December 7, 1941, three squadrons of the American Volunteer Group were the only modern air force available to counter Japanese threats to China and Burma. Japan had to expend valuable resources to deal with the Flying Tigers at a critical time during its invasion. When the United States entered World War II, the Flying Tigers were integrated into the U.S. Twenty-third Fighter Group.

After retiring from the U.S. Army Air Corps, Captain Claire Chennault was hired in 1937 by Nationalist Chinese leader Chiang Kai-shek to establish and train an air force to fight the invading Japanese as well as the Chinese communist forces of Mao Zedong waging civil war. A lack of suitable trainees, modern facilities, and aircraft prevented Chennault from accomplishing his task, forcing him to take a different approach. In spring, 1941, Chennault returned to the United States with a plan to build a Chinese air force with recruited pilots, mechanics, and logistical support from the U.S. military; his plan was supported by powerful Chinese lobbyists and Secretary of the Navy Frank Knox.

In April, 1941, President Franklin D. Roosevelt issued an unpublished executive order authorizing reserve officers and enlisted men to resign from the military if they agreed to join the Chennault's American Volunteer Group (AVG) and fight in China. As the United States was not at war, this order in effect established a covert U.S. air force. Chennault was able to recruit 90 pilots and 150 ground crewmen, but in part because the executive order was unpublished, it would be the basis of much animosity toward the AVG, whose volunteers were branded as soldiers of fortune. The mercenary stigma centered on pay: Word got out that AVG salaries ranged three to seven times that of military enlisted men. In addition, AVG pilots received an under-the-table bonus of $500 for every confirmed aircraft downed.

After intense training at Toungoo, Burma, the AVG attacked the Japanese throughout the fall and winter of 1941. Never having more than fifty P-40 fighter aircraft in action at any time, the Flying Tigers held the skies above the Burma Road while tons of vital supplies were rushed into China, and they defended Chinese cities against aerial attacks. In the seven months after Pearl Harbor, the Flying Tigers destroyed nearly 300 enemy airplanes with an additional 160 probable kills. The Flying Tigers maintained a 25:1 aircraft kill ratio and a 92:1 airmen loss ratio against the Japanese.

Flying Tiger pilots posing by one of their planes. (Time & Life Pictures/Getty Images)

Impact The Flying Tigers were praised for their courage and heroic actions against overwhelming odds, and their shark-faced painted planes became cultural icons of World War II. Later in the war, Walt Disney Studios would design the Flying Tigers' winged tiger symbol.

Although most of the volunteers of the Flying Tigers came from the U.S. military, they were considered mercenaries during World War II and for nearly fifty years after. In 1991, a U.S. Air Force inquiry concluded that all pilots and ground crews of the AVG had fought on behalf of the United States, making them eligible for veterans' benefits. In 1996, the Air Force awarded all AVG pilots the Distinguished Flying Cross and AVG ground crews the Bronze Star for their service.

Randall L. Milstein

Further Reading

Bond, Charles, and Terry Anderson. *A Flying Tiger's Diary.* College Station: Texas A&M University Press, 1993.

Ford, Daniel. *Flying Tigers: Claire Chennault and His American Volunteers, 1941-1942.* Washington, D.C.: Smithonian Books, 2007.

Lopez, Don. *Into the Teeth of the Tiger.* Washington, D.C.: Smithsonian Books, 1997.

Samson, Jack. *The Flying Tiger: The True Story of General Claire Chennault and the U.S. Fourteenth Air Force in China.* Guilford, Conn.: Lyons Press, 2005.

See also Air Force, U.S.; China and North America; China-Burma-India theater; Stilwell, Joseph Warren; War heroes; World War II.

■ Flynn, Errol

Identification Australian-born film star
Born June 20, 1909; Hobart, Tasmania, Australia
Died October 14, 1959; Vancouver, British
    Columbia, Canada

In his film roles and in his publicized personal life, Flynn embodied the concept of gallantry in its various senses of valiant selflessness, nonchalance, and random amorousness. His films dramatized the first two senses; his publicized antics evoked the third sense, giving the public a salacious slant to the phrase "in like Flynn."

During the 1940's, Errol Flynn reflected the distinction he had achieved as a film star during the 1930's, when he had played the romantically adventurous swashbuckler in *Captain Blood* (1935) and *The Prince and the Pauper* (1937); the gallant, self-sacrificing military hero in *The Charge of the Light Brigade* (1936) and *The Dawn Patrol* (1938); the righteously gallant and lighthearted outlaw of *The Adventures of Robin Hood* (1938); and a lighthearted but serious-minded lawman in *Dodge City* (1939). His portrayal of a tragically gallant Robert Devereaux, Earl of Essex, in *Elizabeth and Essex* (1939) has come to be recognized as a masterly performance.

It was during the 1940's that Flynn's recognition as a Hollywood star and his reputation as an off-screen rakehell combined to produce an image of invincible charm and flamboyant sensuality. He appeared, during this decade, in twenty-two films, seven of which fully captured and sustained the essence of his stardom: *The Sea Hawk* and *Santa Fe Trail* (both in 1940), *Dive Bomber* (1941), *They Died with Their Boots On* and *Gentleman Jim* (both in 1942), *Objective Burma!* (1945), and, in the role he had become considered as born to play, *The Adventures of Don Juan* (1949).

Off-screen, Flynn's marital changes during this period were punctuated by a sensational trial. His marriage to the volatile Lili Damita, who bore him a son, Sean, ended in 1942. In November of that year, Flynn was accused of statutory rape. The charge was made by seventeen-year-old Betty Hansen, who claimed to have been violated by Flynn during a party at a Bel Air mansion. A concurrent charge, by sixteen-year-old Peggy LaRue Satterlee, held that Flynn had forced her into sexual intercourse twice aboard his yacht. Jerry Giesler, Flynn's defense attorney, convinced a jury of nine women and three men that both plaintiffs were, despite their youth, sophis-

ticated pleasure-seekers and fortune-hunters. Flynn was fully acquitted in February, 1943. Then, during the following October, twenty-one-year-old Shirley Evans Hassau brought a paternity suit against him. Three years earlier, Flynn had paid Hassau and her mother $2,000 to settle a sexual assault case that the mother had initiated. He denied fathering Hassau's two-year-old daughter; the case, after intermittent proceedings, was dropped ten years later.

After the rape trial, Flynn married Nora Eddington, who bore him two daughters, Deirdre and Rory. This marriage ended in 1949. In 1950, Flynn married his third and last wife, the film star Patrice Wymore; she presented him with his third daughter, Arnella. He sought a divorce from Wymore in 1958, reportedly to be free to wed the seventeen-year-old Beverly Aadland. However, Wymore, avoiding this action, soon became his widow.

In *Errol Flynn: The Untold Story* (1980), Charles Higham attempts to expose Flynn as a bisexual (having affairs with, for example, Truman Capote and Tyrone Power) and as a spy for the Nazi Gestapo. Attorney Marvin Belli filed suit against Higham on behalf of Flynn's daughters, and Wymore described Higham's charges as ludicrous. Tony Thomas convincingly repudiates and disproves Higham's contentions in *Errol Flynn: The Spy Who Never Was* (1990).

The darker side of Flynn's gallantry is apparent from his critically praised roles, each as an unregenerate but noble drunk, in *The Sun Also Rises* (1957), *Too Much Too Soon* (1958), and *The Roots of Heaven* (1958).

Impact In *The Two Lives of Errol Flynn* (1978), Michael Freeland analyzes the legendary impact created by Flynn through "raucous high living and cinematic heroism." One must go on to note that the combination of Flynn's effortless nobility of character in the seven films he made with Olivia De Havilland and the three he made with Alexis Smith and the perverse amorousness and willful bibulousness of his personal life came to be received in America not as contradictory but as stimulatingly complementary.

Roy Arthur Swanson

Further Reading

Aadland, Florence, with Lisa Janssen. *The Beautiful Pervert.* Chicago: Novel Books, 1965.
Freeland, Michael. *The Two Lives of Errol Flynn.* New York: William Morrow, 1978.

Thomas, Tony, ed. *From a Life of Adventure: The Writings of Errol Flynn.* Secaucus, N.J.: Citadel Press, 1980.

Valenti, Peter. *Errol Flynn: A Bio-Bibliography.* Westport, Conn.: Greenwood Press, 1984.

See also Bogart, Humphrey; Crimes and scandals; Film in the United States; Film noir; Films about World War II.

■ Food processing

Definition Techniques used to transform such plant and animal foodstuffs as grains, vegetables, fruits, meats, and fish into marketable goods appropriate for human consumption

By the 1940's, the American food-processing industry had become big business, with annual sales of hundreds of billions of dollars and a gigantic labor force. During the first half of the 1940's, food-processing companies had to reduce production for civilians in order to supply military personnel, but the postwar era began a period of phenomenal growth in productivity and profitability resulting in part from new technologies and products.

During the first half of the twentieth century, the American food-processing industry was well on its way to becoming a trillion-dollar enterprise. Much of food processing already had migrated from homes and small-town businesses to large factories, where food scientists in research facilities created such products as canned soups and meats, cake mixes, gelatin desserts, fruit juices, and nonalcoholic drinks. During the 1920's and 1930's, technological innovations such as the rapid heating or cooling of foods helped preserve their nutritional content and flavor.

Because the average American consumed more than a thousand pounds of food each year, an increasing proportion of which was processed, many food-processing companies proved to be relatively recession-proof. The Great Depression actually saw greater declines in sales of raw foods than of processed ones, and some food companies increased their profitability between 1929 and 1939. By 1940, more than two-thirds of all American food passed through some stage of processing.

Agricultural and Food-Processing Productivity Some scholars believe that because of the unprecedented expansion of farm productivity during the 1940's, this period deserves the designation of a modern agricultural revolution. With the help of growth in scientific knowledge and the new technologies developed in previous decades, during the five years from 1939 to 1944, the output of plant and animal foodstuffs grew to double the average level of the twenty years from 1919 to 1939. Harvests per acre increased 44 percent, and yields per worker-hour rose 210 percent. This meant that much larger amounts of corn, wheat, livestock, milk, and eggs were available to food processors.

After World War II began in Europe in 1939, American exports of raw and processed foods initially declined, to a level more than 30 percent below the average of the ten years of the Depression. One of the reasons for this decline was the sinking of merchant ships by German submarines. The 1941 Lend-Lease Act helped not only Britain and other European countries fighting Nazi Germany but also American farmers and food processors, because a provision of this law allowed the U.S. government to purchase food surpluses and ship them to the Allies. By the end of 1941, American farm income had recovered from the Great Depression, with an average value higher than at any time since 1929. Many U.S. farms were now large, specialized, and highly efficient, and food-processing companies were making a large variety of products desired by domestic and foreign consumers.

World War II and the Food-Processing Industry After the surprise Japanese attack on Pearl Harbor in December, 1941, and the American entrance into the war, the Franklin D. Roosevelt administration accelerated the conversion of industry into a new system designed for the mass production of goods that would be needed to achieve victory. The food-processing industries were a large part of this plan, helping to feed the vast numbers of armed forces and support staff. Furthermore, because the war was being fought on two fronts, both at great distances from the United States, new foods had to be developed that were lightweight, nutritious, and good-tasting and that would not spoil during long periods of shipment and storage.

Even before the United States entered the war, the government had made efforts to mobilize the nation for a possible conflict. Some of these efforts affected food processing. For example, in 1941, President Roosevelt's Nutrition Conference for Defense made important recommendations for the inclusion of essential nutrients in processed foods. One early war directive created a program to enrich wheat flower with various vitamins and iron. American entry into the war rapidly led to a series of laws establishing various agencies, some of which directly affected food processing. For example, the government instituted price controls on such commodities as meat, butter, and sugar, and the Office of Price Administration introduced rationing of these and other products such as canned goods and coffee, with the goal of equitably distributing precious food supplies (as well as such commodities as rubber and gasoline).

Leaders of governmental agencies proclaimed that "food will win the war" and encouraged farmers, ranchers, and homemakers as well as workers and managers in the food-processing industries to increase efficiency, productivity, and use and creation of substitutes for foods that were in short supply. Although the War Production Board (WPB) was largely concerned with weapons, ammunition, and chemicals, its officials also were interested in the processing of food. Besides encouraging the production of certain foods, such as canned chicken, the WPB also had the power to interfere with manufacturers producing items deemed unessential to the war. For example, La Choy Food Products Company suffered when the government ruled that Chinese food was not essential for feeding Americans at home or overseas.

Processed Foods for the Military and Civilians The U.S. Quartermaster Corps oversaw the development of meat, dairy, poultry, and fish products for military personnel, as well as the development of such specialized items as C-rations and K-rations. C-rations were canned or precooked foods intended to be used when fresh foods or foods prepared in field kitchens were impractical or unavailable. K-rations were compact and lightweight processed foods designed to be carried in a soldier's backpack and consumed mainly in combat. These rations were developed during the war. Another processed food, SPAM, had been introduced during the 1930's but proved an ideal wartime ration because it was durable and easily transportable. By 1943, Hormel was

producing 15 million cans of the processed ham product each week for troops.

The Campbell Soup Company also participated in the war effort by manufacturing special canned products for the Army and Navy. Despite food shortages, Campbell was also able to create new products for civilians, such as Franco-American macaroni and its first dry soup. Because of the need for hot foods for front-line soldiers, researchers in the canning industry developed a two-can device for which piercing the outer can would create a chemical reaction that heated the contents of an inner can.

Food processors introduced other new products for the armed forces and civilians, including dehydrated potatoes, frozen dinners, frozen juice concentrates, nonfat powdered milk, and powdered coffee creamers. Some new products, such as M&M® coated chocolate candy and Cheerios® cereal, would become successful after the war, as did Tootsie Rolls®, first introduced in 1942 in ration kits.

The sugar shortage led to the success of packaged cake mixes among consumers. Processed fish products, an excellent source of protein, became popular with the American military and consumers.

Transition from War to Peace Many food products developed during the war became successful in the postwar period. For example, millions of American servicemen tasted instant (or soluble) coffee for the first time during the war; by 1946, more than thirty brands of instant coffee had reached civilian markets. The Research Corporation of Boston had perfected a high-vacuum process for manufacturing penicillin, and the U.S. Army requested that this company adapt its process to making an orange-juice powder for troops. The company formed a subsidiary, Vacuum Foods Corporation (later called the Minute Maid Company), which built a pilot plant in Florida, but the war ended before its orange-juice powder could be used. When the powder was put on the market in 1945, it failed, but a frozen orange-juice concentrate proved a great success the next year. By 1950, 15.3 million gallons of Minute Maid orange-juice concentrate were being sold annually.

Similarly, precooked rice had been developed for the U.S. Army as a field ration. Military leaders wanted a product that required no cooking, and General Foods developed a process for manufacturing precooked rice. In 1946, "Minute Rice" was first sold to civilians; it soon became popular. Because

General Foods' process was protected by patent, the company was able to develop other easy-to-prepare foods. Other companies used dehydration techniques to create powdered soups, potatoes, and eggs, and some of these found a niche in the postwar marketplace.

Postwar Food Processing From 1945 to 1950, the size and variety of food-processing operations escalated. Though annual variations occurred, farm production of plant and animal foodstuffs generally increased, and the processing of these raw foods also accelerated. Part of this increase reflected the lift of rationing and consumers' return to products that had been unavailable. European countries added to American food sales because their agricultural and industrial infrastructures, damaged by the war, were unable to meet consumers' demand. In the

The modern fast-food restaurant industry may be said to have originated in this first McDonald's hamburger stand, which opened in San Bernadino, California, in 1948. (AP/Wide World Photos)

half decade after the war, the American population boomed, and companies manufactured products to meet the growing population's need for traditional and new foods.

In attempts to increase efficiency and lower costs, processing facilities were built near where fruits, vegetables, and livestock were produced. Mergers of companies also contributed to the growth and efficiency of food processing. For example, some large companies involved in dairy product processing acquired more than a thousand small farms. Food processors increased their ownership of farms, and fish canners added to their fishing fleets. Some processors also acquired stores, supermarkets, and retail chains. Consumers could see the results of this oligopolization of the food industry as products created by small firms became less common on supermarket shelves.

A good example of these trends is the Campbell Soup Company, which, with the removal of war restrictions, resumed full production aimed at civilians. With a new company president and the introduction of new soup varieties, Campbell began a period of rapid expansion. In 1948, Campbell acquired the V8 brand from Standard Brands, and its researchers improved the quality, uniformity, and taste of this blend of juices, which became a great success. The company also reinvigorated its Franco-American line and entered the baby-food market. By the early 1950's, Campbell was third in sales among food processors, behind General Foods and Standard Brands.

In addition to the competition among these large companies, rivalries grew out of different methods of processing foods, such as freezing, freeze-drying, and dehydrating. Lyophilization, or freeze-drying, was developed during World War II for blood plasma and other biological substances, but after the war it was used successfully for foods. Drying foods without raising their temperature helped to preserve flavor. The development of quick-freezing techniques helped in the expansion of the frozen-foods industry, with the concomitant spread of many cold-storage locker plants and booming sales of home freezers. Food scientists were now creating thousands of new processed foods each year, although the intense competition that characterized the food-processing industry meant that some of these products did not last long in the marketplace.

Impact The decade of the 1940's was a time of transformational, even revolutionary, change in the food-processing industry. Building on the new products and processes developed for the military during World War II, food processors during the postwar years diversified their product lines and expanded production to meet the needs and desires of both domestic and foreign consumers. Mass-production techniques lowered costs even for perishable items, and improved transportation meant that even perishable foods and beverages could be transferred efficiently from countryside to cities.

Trends that began in the 1940's continued through the remainder of the twentieth century as companies improved traditional products and engineered new ones to maximize consumer choice and convenience. Americans consumed more processed foods, both in their homes and, increasingly, in fast-food restaurant chains. Critics pointed out the negative health and environmental effects of fast foods. They also criticized pesticide residues in processed foods as well as such chemical additives as artificial flavors and colors. *The Chemical Feast* (1970), by James S. Turner, a member of Ralph Nader's consumer advocacy group, attacked both the American food industry and the Food and Drug Administration. Industry representatives responded that they had actually improved the nutritional value of many processed foods by adding essential vitamins and minerals. Members of the organic-foods movement also challenged food processors by urging consumers to eat fresh fruits and vegetables rather than processed foods. Some food processors reacted by introducing products with reduced amounts of fat, sugar, salt, and cholesterol. Whether these changes will lead to another food revolution remains unresolved.

Robert J. Paradowski

Further Reading

Collins, Douglas. *America's Favorite Food: The Story of Campbell Soup Company.* New York: Harry N. Abrams, 1994. This lavishly illustrated volume details the history of the Campbell Soup Company from its nineteenth century origins to the end of the twentieth century. The author analyzes the roles played by chemists as well as cooks in developing various successful convenience foods; he also probes the marketing and advertising practices that helped create a giant in the food industry. Chronology and index.

Hempe, Edward C., Jr., and Merle Wittenberg. *The Lifeline of America: Development of the Food Industry.* New York: McGraw-Hill, 1964. The authors intend their book, a thematic history of the food industry, for "everyone who is interested" in their subject. They treat the 1940's in America in such chapters as "The Fourth Agricultural Revolution," "Food Processing: Catalyst to Mankind," and "Canning: Breakthrough to Mass Distribution." Illustrated with figures, maps, and photographs. Selected bibliography and index.

Levenstein, Harvey A. *Paradox of Plenty: A Social History of Eating in Modern America.* Rev. ed. Berkeley: University of California Press, 2003. This new edition of a book originally published by Oxford University Press in 1993 centers on the interactions between American consumers and the businesses that supplied them with processed foods in the period from 1930 to the early twenty-first century. Illustrated, with notes and an index.

Nestle, Marion. *Food Politics: How the Food Industry Influences Nutrition and Health.* Rev. ed. Berkeley: University of California Press, 2007. Seen by reviewers as a major contribution to the understanding of how politics and science interact in the food industry, this book shows how food processors have affected the lives of most Americans in the twentieth century. An appendix on "Issues in Nutrition and Nutrition Research," notes, and an index.

Turner, James S. *The Chemical Feast: Ralph Nader's Study Group Report on the Food and Drug Administration.* New York: Viking Press, 1970. Though this book is primarily concerned with a critical analysis of the Food and Drug Administration, the author also analyzes the American food-processing industry, especially its policies and products that he claims have harmed consumers. Notes and index.

See also Advertising in the United States; Agriculture in Canada; Agriculture in the United States; Business and the economy in the United States; Economic wartime regulations; Natural resources; Science and technology; Wartime technological advances.

■ Football

Definition   Popular spectator and participant sport that saw declines as a result of World War II but nevertheless had many memorable moments

The 1940's both changed and challenged the sport of American football, more so than virtually any previous decade. For four years of World War II, both collegiate and professional football teams were caught in the struggle to keep the sport alive for the benefit of institutions, players, spectators, and the nation as a whole.

The 1941 championship contest between the Chicago Bears and the Washington Redskins of the National Football League could be called the battle of the Georges. George Marshall, the owner of the Redskins, and George Halas, the owner of the Bears, had little affection for each other, and the Redskins had defeated the Bears 3-0 during the regular season. The title game was played before a sellout crowd in Washington, D.C.'s Griffith Stadium. Utilizing the T formation, the Bears, with Sid Luckman at quarterback, buried the Redskins in a record-setting 73-0 defeat. The game was overshadowed by an event of the previous day, the December 7, 1941, attack on Pearl Harbor that signaled the beginning of American battles of a very different sort.

Collegiate football had some unforgettable moments in the immediate prewar era, particularly the 1940 game between Cornell and Dartmouth. With its eighteen-game winning streak on the line, Cornell trailed Dartmouth 3-0 in the waning minutes of the game. An error by the officials gave Cornell an extra down, allowing it to score a touchdown and an extra point. A later film review verified the official's error. Cornell sent a telegram to Dartmouth offering to forfeit the game, and the offer was accepted, thus ending Cornell's winning streak. These games in some ways set the stage for a decade that would be filled with excitement in the sport, even though the war would see its dramatic decline.

College Football   By the opening of the 1940's, collegiate football had already shaped and reshaped itself over the years from the initial battle between Rutgers and Princeton in 1869 through the Knute Rockne era at Notre Dame and through the growth of traditional rivalries and conferences across the country. By the 1940's, most large colleges and uni-

versities had teams. As the sounds of war echoed from Europe, the 1940 season proceeded mostly as usual. The Associated Press ranked Minnesota, Stanford, Michigan, Tennessee, and Boston College as the top five teams. The 1941 season saw coach Bernie Bierman and his Gophers repeating as Associated Press champion, followed by Duke, Notre Dame, Texas, and Michigan. Many of the schools that made up the remainder of the top twenty in these two years would be relatively unfamiliar to football fans of the twenty-first century. The modern competition that pits major football schools against each other in terms of recruiting and facilities was yet to develop, though the latter part of the 1940's offered some hints that it was on its way.

With the exception of the bowl games, the 1941 season was essentially completed prior to the bombing of Pearl Harbor. As a precaution against possible Japanese attacks on the Pacific coast, the Rose Bowl game was shifted to Duke University's stadium at Durham, North Carolina, where Oregon State defeated Duke, 20-16.

The wartime draft greatly reduced male enrollment at colleges and universities across the country, forcing schools to do their best to keep collegiate athletics alive. Many colleges introduced or expanded specific training programs to prepare officers for the Army and the Navy, and many of the participants in these programs came with previous academic and athletic experience at both the collegiate and high-school levels. Many of these programs organized football teams to compete with each other and with the teams of colleges and universities that still maintained their own programs.

The 1943 season, for example, saw five service teams ranked among the top twenty in the nation: Iowa Pre-Flight was number two, Great Lakes Naval Training Station was six, Del Monte Pre-Flight was eight, March Field was ten, and Bainbridge Naval Training Station was seventeen. Because they were able to recruit from other schools and could keep their players for up to three years (the reduced length of study during the war), the two military academies—Army and Navy—also fared well in the rankings. In 1943, Navy ranked third and Army ranked eleventh. The next season found coach Red Blaik's Army team blessed with two all-time great players, halfback Glenn Davis ("Mr. Outside") and fullback Doc Blanchard ("Mr. Inside"). The team's nine-win season, including a 59-0 rout of defending champion Notre Dame, catapulted Army to the championship.

To ease the strain on players that essentially all college teams faced, the rules committee decided to allow players to enter a game at any time, instead of only once a quarter. It also allowed unlimited substitutions on changes of possession. Instrumental in this rule change was Fritz Chrysler, a successful coach with a record of 116 victories, 32 defeats, and 9 ties at the University of Michigan. Although these changes were rescinded in 1953, they provided the basis for the return of platoon football in 1965. Another liberalizing change in 1945 allowed forward passes to be thrown from anywhere behind the line of scrimmage, thus giving the T formation a boost.

Professional Football   The teams from the National Football League (NFL) were not as fortunate as the college football teams in retaining player rosters. The same can be said for professional football in Canada, which canceled games for the duration of the war. Although the NFL had come far, it still lagged behind collegiate football in fan acceptance. With weaker rosters and many potential fans serving in the armed forces, attendance at games dwindled. Commissioner Elmer Layden, who had been one of Notre Dame's famed Four Horsemen, worked hard to keep the league afloat. In one unique move, the Pittsburgh Steelers and the Philadelphia Eagles were combined for the 1943 season; the team, formally called the Eagles, often was referred to as the "Steagles." The end of the war not only brought back

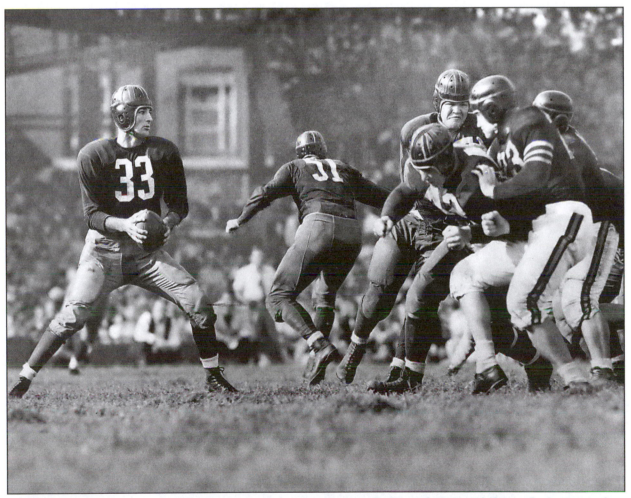

Washington Redskins quarterback Sammy Baugh dropping back to pass against the Chicago Bears in a 1942 game. During an era of two-way players, Baugh not only set passing records on offense, he also played safety on defense and punted. (AP/Wide World Photos)

NFL All-Decade Team (1940's)

Name	Position	Team(s)
Jim Benton	End	Cleveland/Los Angeles Rams, Chicago Bears
Jack Ferrante	End	Philadelphia Eagles
Ken Kavanaugh	End	Chicago Bears
Dante Lavelli	End	Cleveland Browns
Pete Pihos	End	Philadelphia Eagles
Mac Speedie	End	Cleveland Browns
Ed Sprinkle	End	Chicago Bears
Al Blozis	Tackle	New York Giants
George Connor	Tackle	Chicago Bears
Frank "Bucko" Kilroy	Tackle	Philadelphia Eagles
Buford "Baby" Ray	Tackle	Green Bay Packers
Vic Sears	Tackle	Philadelphia Eagles
Al Wistert	Tackle	Philadelphia Eagles
Bruno Banducci	Guard	Philadelphia Eagles, San Francisco 49ers
Bill Edwards	Guard	New York Giants
Garrard "Buster" Ramsey	Guard	Chicago Cardinals
Bill Willis	Guard	Cleveland Browns
Len Younce	Guard	New York Giants
Charley Brock	Center	Green Bay Packers
Clyde "Bulldog" Turner	Center	Chicago Bears
Alex Wojciechowicz	Center	Detroit Lions, Philadelphia Eagles
Sammy Baugh	Quarterback	Washington Redskins
Sid Luckman	Quarterback	Chicago Bears
Bob Waterfield	Quarterback	Cleveland/Los Angeles Rams
Tony Canadeo	Halfback	Green Bay Packers
Bill Dudley	Halfback	Pittsburgh Steelers, Detroit Lions, Washington Redskins
George McAfee	Halfback	Chicago Bears
Charley Trippi	Halfback	Chicago Cardinals
Steve Van Buren	Halfback	Philadelphia Eagles
Byron "Whizzer" White	Halfback	Pittsburgh Pirates (now Steelers), Detroit Lions
Pat Harder	Fullback	Chicago Cardinals, Detroit Lions
Marion Motley	Fullback	Cleveland Browns, Pittsburgh Steelers
Bill Osmanski	Fullback	Chicago Bears

Note: Team picked by members of the Pro Football Hall of Fame Selection Committee.

a multitude of players but also saw the creation of a new rival league in 1946, the All-America Football Conference.

Two Great College Coaches   At the collegiate level, the 1940's saw a plethora of notable teams and coaches. Sports network ESPN has ranked Army (1945), Michigan (1947), and Notre Dame (1947) as the best college football teams of all time. Frank Leahy of Notre Dame fame, though he coached for only fourteen years, stands out as one of college football's great coaches and was inducted into the College Football Hall of Fame in 1970. With a win-loss-tie record of 107-13-9 in twenty-four years of coaching, Leahy guided Notre Dame to national championships in 1943, 1946, 1947, and 1949. Leahy had played tackle for Knute Rockne at Notre Dame from 1928 to 1930. After nine years at the assistant-coaching level, Leahy went to Boston College as head coach and led the Eagles to a 20-2 record, including a Sugar Bowl victory in 1940. When Notre Dame called after one year, he broke his contract with the Eagles to begin his outstanding career with the Fighting Irish. The Irish roared to a record of 8-0-1 in 1941 and, after instituting the T formation, went 7-2-2 in 1942. Following a stint in the Navy, Leahy returned to Notre Dame for the 1946 season, in which the team won a national championship and began a winning streak of thirty-nine games (including two ties) that ran through 1949. His overall record at Notre Dame was 87-11-9.

Paul Brown left his indelible trademark on three levels of football—high school, college, and professional. After high school and college careers as a diminutive quarterback, he was hired in 1932, at the age of twenty-four, to rebuild the football program at Washington High School in Massillon, Ohio. From 1933 through 1940, Brown led the Massillon Tigers to a 62-5-1 record and was instrumental in having a 20,000-seat stadium built for the team. In 1940, Brown's final season, the Tigers romped through an undefeated national championship season with ten wins, outscoring opponents 477-6. In 1941, Brown moved to Ohio State, where his three-year record of 18-8-1 included a national championship in 1942. After a year at the Great Lakes Naval Training Station in 1945, Brown was ready to make his move into professional football.

The latter part of the 1940's saw important changes for both collegiate and professional foot-

ball. The new All-America Football Conference (AAFC) was formed to begin play in 1946. At the urging of team owner Arthur McBride, Paul Brown signed on as part owner and coach of the Cleveland Browns. Brown wasted no time in putting together a football team that would literally crush the other teams in the new league. Led by quarterback Otto Graham, the Browns, in the four years prior to the merging of the AAFC with the NFL in 1950, compiled a 47-4-5 record with four championships. In 1946, Brown helped to break the color barrier in pro football by signing two black players, Marion Motley and Bill Gillis. After the merger of the two leagues, the Browns were to remain a force for several years in the enlarged NFL. Brown would also later found the Cincinnati Bengals franchise.

Canadian Football   Though Canadian professional football players and coaches were less publicized than those in the United States, they were poised at the end of the 1940's to make football a rival of ice hockey as a spectator sport. Some American players who were unable to find good places in the NFL went north, taking with them a high level of play that Canadian players would soon parallel. The Winnipeg Blue Bombers, for example, were led by quarterback "Indian" Jack Jacobs during the late 1940's. Pageantry also would become part of the games. The Calgary Stampeders introduced saddle horses and chuck wagons in a 1948 Grey Cup game.

Impact   Football at both the collegiate and professional levels was ready to move into the second half of the twentieth century. The NFL would continue expansion, and colleges and universities were well into defining and redefining their rules and styles of play. Various collegiate teams established, or reestablished, powerful football programs. The latter half of the 1940's saw numerous major undefeated teams: Notre Dame, Army, Georgia, and UCLA in 1946; Notre Dame, Michigan, Southern Methodist University, and Penn State in 1947; Michigan, Notre Dame, North Carolina, and California in 1948; and Notre Dame, Oklahoma, California, and Army in 1949.

Football at all levels became more vibrant and more exciting for players and fans alike. The game on the field, however, was only part of the picture. Tightening recruiting rules for colleges, fine-tuning the draft of players for the professional teams, building gigantic stadiums, and televising games would all play significant roles in the development of football in the decades following the 1940's.

Wilton Eckley

Further Reading

Algeo, Matthew. *Last Team Standing.* Cambridge, Mass.: Da Capo Press, 2006. Shows how professional football teams dealt with problems caused by World War II.

The College Game. Indianapolis: Bobbs-Merrill, 1974. An overview of college football from its origins. Many pictures, including special photography by Malcolm Emmons.

Fleder, Rob, ed. *The College Football Book.* New York: Sports Illustrated Books, 2008. Covers college football from its beginnings, with illustrations and many stories of interest.

MacCambridge, Michael, ed. *College Football Encyclopedia.* New York: Hyperion, 2005. Contains myriad statistics along with stories of teams and individuals.

Morgan, John. *Glory for Sale.* Baltimore: Bancroft, 1997. Covers the move of the Cleveland Browns to Baltimore and describes how professional football operates behind the scenes.

Walsh, Christopher J. *Who's #1? 100-Plus Years of Controversial National Champions in College Football.* New York: Taylor Trade Publishers, 2007. Excellent coverage of college football, with team rankings and controversies.

See also Baseball; Basketball; Baugh, Sammy; Davis, Glenn; *Knute Rockne: All American*; Robinson, Jackie; Sports in Canada; Sports in the United States.

■ *For Whom the Bell Tolls*

Identification Novel set during the Spanish Civil War

Author Ernest Hemingway (1899-1962)

Date Published in 1940

This best-selling novel set during the Spanish Civil war of the 1930's spoke to the apprehensions of the United States as World War II began in Europe, and it also was a subtle critique of isolationism and inspirational in its affirmation of heroic sacrifice, passion, democracy, and duty.

Based on Ernest Hemingway's experiences as a journalist during the Spanish Civil War, *For Whom the Bell Tolls* centers on the character of Robert Jordan, an American engineer who, in 1937, joins a left-wing Republican militia in the mountains near Segovia as it battles the right-wing fascist supporters of dictator Francisco Franco. The entirety of the action takes place in only three tension-filled days, in which the possibility of death is imminent for everyone in the guerrilla group. The title of the novel, taken from a poem by John Donne that references a tolling bell's death knell, reinforces this theme of facing death and also indicates the way in which the novel moves beyond the political to the existential. Mortal danger in fact contributes to the importance of these three days in Jordan's life, as he considers issues of meaning and value.

Jordan, a former loner, falls in love with Maria, a young Spanish girl who has been violently raped by fascist soldiers. Their passionate romance has a healing effect on Maria and revives Jordan's own dormant emotional life, pulling him out of his psychological isolation. Jordan is also affected by the charismatic Pilar, a mystic gypsy woman whose world is peopled with good and evil spirits; evil spirits are especially present in this novel in the form of the prevalent violence, the atmosphere of profanation suggested by the rape of Maria, the selfish and cowardly behavior of some of the soldiers, and the obscenities that surface in the conversation of the rebels. Despite his dwindling idealism, however, Jordan loyally detonates a bridge. As Pilar predicted, however, it was his destiny to be wounded in the process; alone but steady, he waits for death at the hands of the fascists as the rest of the group flees to safety.

Throughout the narrative, Jordan demonstrates fortitude, loyalty, and a stoic composure in the face of danger and disillusionment. Even as he develops deep reservations with regard to the communist ideologues and self-serving insurgents with whom he must work on behalf of the Republican cause, he remains devoted with his whole heart to Maria, who becomes a symbol of Spain itself; similarly, Pilar awakens spiritual intuitions, and a fellow soldier, Anselmo, stands as an example of integrity and nobility. Ultimately, Jordan finds meaning in working for a cause and a community: Through participation in the struggle and in his sacrificial death, he at last becomes part of something greater than himself.

Impact *For Whom the Bell Tolls* immediately became a best seller. The 1943 film of the novel was its year's most popular film and garnered nine Academy Award nominations, winning one, for the Greek actress Katina Paxinou who portrayed Pilar. The Pulitzer Prize committee and Pulitzer Board recommended the book for the Pulitzer Prize, but Nicholas Murray Butler, president of Columbia University, overrode both, with the result that no award was presented for 1941. The novel returned Hemingway to literary prominence and is considered one of his masterpieces.

Margaret Boe Birns

Further Reading

Josephs, Allen. *For Whom the Bell Tolls: Ernest Hemingway's Undiscovered Country.* New York: Twayne, 1994.

Perez, Janet, and Aycock Wendell. *The Spanish Civil War in Literature.* Lubbock: Texas Tech University Press, 2007.

Sanderson, Rena, ed. *Blowing the Bridge: Essays on Hemingway and "For Whom the Bell Tolls."* New York: Greenwood Press, 1992.

See also Academy Awards; Films about World War II; Literature in the United States.

■ Ford, John

Identification American film director
Born February 1, 1894; Cape Elizabeth, Maine
Died August 31, 1973; Palm Desert, California

One of the most significant directors in American film, Ford won four Academy Awards—two for best director and two for best documentary—during the 1940's.

Born in Maine during the last decade of the nineteenth century, John Ford was the youngest son of Irish immigrants. He was named John Martin Feeney at birth but changed his name to Ford when he moved to Hollywood in 1914. Ford's older brother Francis, who was a successful actor and director, helped him land small film roles, including a small part as a Klansman in D. W. Griffth's *The Birth of a Nation* (1915). In 1917, Ford directed his first Hollywood film, *The Tornado,* and by 1925, he had shot fifty-four silent films. Many of his early films were Westerns and featured stars such as Harry Carey and Tom Mix. During the 1920's and 1930's, Ford made a name for himself with classic films such as *The Iron Horse* (1924), *Arrowsmith* (1931), *The Lost Patrol* (1934), *The Informer* (1935), and *Stagecoach* (1939). He won his first of six Oscars for *The Informer.*

Ford began the 1940's with tremendous success, winning back-to-back best director Academy Awards for *The Grapes of Wrath* (1940) and *How Green Was My Valley* (1941). In addition to directing films, Ford was an avid sailor and a member of the Naval Reserves. As World War II approached, Ford founded the Field Photographic Unit, a branch of the Office of Strategic Services that was charged with making documentaries for the military and morale-boosting, informational films for a nation at war. His first documentary, *Sex Hygiene,* was viewed by all recruits as a reminder of the dangers of venereal disease. After the Japanese attack on Pearl Harbor, Ford and his unit filmed the aftermath of the assault on the Hawaiian Islands. He was later at Midway Island when the American and Japanese navies clashed in June, 1942, and was wounded while capturing film coverage of Japanese planes strafing the island. Ford used the footage from Pearl Harbor and Midway to create two documentaries: *The Battle of Midway* (1942) and *December 7th* (1943). He won Academy Awards for both documentaries.

Ford made a number of other documentaries during the war, but after D Day the Navy released him from active duty so that he could direct *They Were Expendable* (1945), a film that recounted the heroics of young naval officers during the fall of the Philippines in 1942. Ford used the proceeds from this film to fund the Field Photo Home, a club for the veterans of his beloved Field Photographic Unit. In 1946, he returned to his roots and began filming Westerns. Ford strove for authenticity in his Westerns and thus shot many of his films in Monument Valley. He worked with the biggest stars of the day, including Henry Fonda in *My Darling Clementine* (1946) and *The Fugitive* (1947) and John Wayne in *They Were Expendable, Fort Apache* (1948), and *She Wore a Yellow Ribbon* (1949).

Ford went on to make another twenty-three films after the 1940's, including classic Westerns such as *The Searchers* (1956) and *The Man Who Shot Liberty Valance* (1962). By the 1960's, with social upheavals produced by the Civil Rights movement and the war in Vietnam, the public lost interest in Ford's Westerns that depicted rugged individualism. After retiring from Hollywood, Ford became something of a recluse. He died on August 31, 1973, in Palm Desert, California.

Impact   Ford directed 136 films during a Hollywood career that spanned almost fifty years. Although only fifty-four of his films were Westerns, his name is synonymous with the Western genre. During the 1940's, he won four of his six Academy Awards and launched the Western genre to new levels with films shot in Monument Valley and starring John Wayne and Henry Fonda.

Mark R. Ellis

Further Reading

Davis, Ronald L. *John Ford: Hollywood's Old Master.* Norman: University of Oklahoma Press, 1995.

Eyman, Scott. *Print the Legend: The Life and Times of John Ford.* New York: Simon & Schuster, 1999.

Ford, Dan. *Pappy: The Life of John Ford.* Englewood Cliffs, N.J.: Prentice Hall, 1979.

See also   Capra, Frank; Cowboy films; Film in the United States; Films about World War II; *The Grapes of Wrath*; Midway, Battle of; *They Were Expendable.*

■ Ford Motor Company

Identification   Automotive company

Date   Established on June 16, 1903

In addition to maintaining its automotive division, Ford was one of the largest U.S. providers of defense products during the war. The company's Willow Run plant alone manufactured more than five hundred B-24 bombers per month during World War II.

Early in the decade, the Ford Motor Company jumped into manufacturing defense products. The aircraft division was developed partially in response to a government-ordered cut in automobile production. Ultimately, the company became the fourth largest defense contractor in the United States. Its Willow Run plant, opened in 1942, mass-produced warplanes in an unprecedented use of the assembly line system. The main product was the B-24 Liberator Bomber, a four-engine, long-range aircraft. Exaggerated advertising efforts gained the company both positive feedback and critical commentary as a result of promotions with inflated estimates of production. The plant struggled to produce the aircraft in its first years. Only fifty-six B-24s were completed in 1942, with the first one rolling off the line on September 10. The following year, the plant was able to increase production, with 31 Liberators produced in January, 75 in February, 148 in April, and 190 in June. In 1943, the Liberator was advertised with a slogan that would be remembered for years afterward: "Watch the Fords Go By!" Ford was also building M-I tank destroyers, gliders, and aircraft engines. By 1944, Willow Run had produced five thousand bombers.

In another direction, the Ford Motor Company's sponsorship of the *Sunday Evening Hour* radio broadcast on the Columbia Broadcasting System (CBS), begun during the 1930's, came to a close on January 16, 1942, as the company cited a "war article" in the contract. Loss of advertising during the programming made the decision to cease the sponsorship fis-

Henry Ford II posing with three generations of Ford automobiles: a 1949 sedan, a late 1920's-early 1930's Model A, and a 1910's-early 1920's Model T. (Time & Life Pictures/Getty Images)

cally responsible. Prior to this point, the company had been the foremost radio advertiser, contributing to public knowledge about Ford products, Henry Ford himself, and Ford dealerships, in turn leading to growth in car sales.

The company also underwent a number of personnel changes during the decade. The ongoing personality conflicts between Henry and his son Edsel Ford increased with Henry's support of Harry Bennett, head of the company's security department, and Edsel's growing friendship with Charles Sorensen, the Ford Motor Company manager in charge of defense contracts.

Henry Ford's 1941 stroke resulted in mental problems that made his continued leadership questionable. Edsel Ford was suffering from physical problems as well. Edsel was diagnosed with stomach cancer and died on May 26, 1943. In his grief, Henry Ford retook control of his company and was re-elected president on June 1, 1943. However, his increasingly poor decisions led to Bennett stepping up as acting head of the company. In this role, Bennett went on a firing spree, removing management-level officials previously supported by Edsel Ford and Sorensen. Sorensen resigned in March, 1944, after pressure from Henry Ford and Harry Bennett, but not before he was able to help Henry Ford II take a larger role in the company. Henry Ford's 1945 stroke ended his leadership, and he was pressured by family to instate Henry II as president. Henry II immediately fired Bennett.

As the decade drew to a close, Henry Ford II dealt with labor strikes and price controls. He gained popular support through lowering prices, undercutting the company's competition.

Impact   Ford Motor Company's production of wartime aviation products provided hope to American citizens and Allied soldiers during the war. The assembly line system of manufacturing airplanes produced unprecedented numbers of defense products efficiently and illustrated how a peacetime producer of consumer products could switch fairly quickly to producing war material.

Theresa L. Stowell

Further Reading
Lewis, David L. *The Public Image of Henry Ford: An American Folk Hero and His Company.* Detroit: Wayne State University Press, 1976.
Segal, Howard P. *Recasting the Machine Age: Henry Ford's Village Industries.* Amherst: University of Massachusetts Press, 2005.
Watts, Steven. *The People's Tycoon: Henry Ford and the American Century.* New York: Alfred A. Knopf, 2005.

See also   Advertising in the United States; Aircraft design and development; Automobiles and auto manufacturing; Bombers; General Motors; Labor strikes; Radio in the United States; Wartime industries.

■ Foreign policy of Canada

During the 1940's, Canada found itself projected into World War II, from which it emerged as possessing one of the largest armies and air forces in the world. It then disarmed and regained its prosperity far quicker than any of the other wartime combatants other than the United States. It thus was able to play a key role in world economic recovery during the postwar period, as well as a formative part in various international organizations set up to keep the peace.

At the beginning of the decade, Canadian foreign policy came under the direct aegis of Prime Minister William Lyon Mackenzie King, who acted as minister for external affairs. Despite some initial reluctance during the 1930's to commit itself to any future European war, Canada had declared war on Germany within a week of the British declaration of war in September, 1939. King's own position was centered on the British Commonwealth, with its political and economic center in London, England, with only a secondary emphasis on a wider commitment to continental defense and trade. King's Canadian Liberal Party came with him into the war, as long as there was a commitment to no conscription, which had been a strong source of division in World War I, especially in Francophone Canada. King was content to let first the British and later the main Allied leaders—Britain, the United States, and the Soviet Union—dictate the course of the war and Canada's role in it.

World War II   The first half of the decade saw Canada's foreign policy equate with the war aims of the Allies. The five years can be divided into the period before the United States and the Soviet Union joined the war as combatants in the later part of 1941, and the period of invasion and conquest between 1942 and 1945.

By May, 1940, Canada and the other Commonwealth countries were standing almost alone with Britain in the fight against Nazi Germany and Fascist Italy. Canada had sent units of its small army to Britain almost at once, but too late to be sent to engage in the Nazi invasion of France. Over the next eighteen months, it built its army up in southern England into an effective fighting force, though its first action, in 1942 at Dieppe, northern France, was a disaster.

More effectively, Canada offered sites and finances for the British Commonwealth Air Training Plan, through which, throughout the war, Commonwealth pilots and air personnel trained. Canadian pilots at first integrated with Britain's Royal Air Force (RAF) but then gradually, and against RAF policy, formed their own squadrons of the Royal Canadian Air Force. Ships of the Royal Canadian Navy were given escort responsibilities in the North Atlantic from the start, operating out of Halifax.

American neutrality had posed a problem for Canada. At first, this was solved by King and President Franklin D. Roosevelt meeting at Ogdenburg in August, 1940, to formulate a joint North American defense policy. When the United States began its lend-lease program to Britain, Canada was allowed to be one of the suppliers, though the United States still demanded a licensing system. Other trade and military aid agreements were formulated at the Hyde Park agreement of April, 1941.

From 1942, a much more formulated supply program could be operated, with an open border and free trade for American and Canadian war supplies and production. Canada operated a centralized supply system under the ministry of munitions and supplies, promoting greater efficiencies and avoiding overlap.

In the military arena, the Canadian army was impatient to see action, having reached, under General A. G. L. McNaughton, a strength of five divisions, three infantry and two armored, together with two tank brigades. In 1943, it was decided that Canadian troops should see action in the invasion of Sicily, and then form part of the British/Commonwealth Eighth Army working its way up the Adriatic side of Italy. The main part of the Canadian Army was to be held in readiness for the June, 1944, invasion of Normandy under General H. D. G. Crerar of the First Canadian Army.

The Canadian Army was allocated to one of the five beachheads, the most easterly, and the Canadians made the quickest gains on landing. They found themselves against crack German units at Caen, however. Finally, the German army was surrounded, and the Canadian troops then fought their way along the coast to Antwerp and the Scheldt Estuary by the end of 1944. At the beginning of 1945, they were joined by the Italian contingents that had managed to reach the plains of northern Italy, and they became part of the final push into Germany. They also mopped up the remaining German units in the Netherlands.

Postwar Period, 1945-1950 Unlike the other Allied nations, Canada had no wish to remain in Europe. Within a year, it had withdrawn all forces and demobilized most of them. Conscription had been a problem in 1944, when the issue threatened the Liberal government, but King had found a compromise. Still, apart from the military itself, no one wanted to see a Canadian military presence to keep the peace.

Canadian foreign policy instead became directed toward trade, particularly restarting trade with Europe. Canada realized its prosperity had always come from trade and wanted to avoid that trade being absorbed into the much bigger United States trade. At first, it sought to support free trade agreements, but in the light of American reluctance, it settled for a General Agreement on Tariffs and Trade (GATT). Canada's role in the setting up of GATT was invaluable, managing to assuage American suspicions of the Commonwealth preference scheme. Canada also negotiated a long-term wheat deal with the United Kingdom, along with providing large loans to the mother country to help the shattered British economy.

Immediately after the war, Canada realized that it was a middle power and saw its foreign role as being a broker and fixer, especially within the newly formed United Nations organization. It welcomed developments within the British Empire of granting independence to India and Pakistan. Gradually, however, these idealistic notions changed in the light of continued European bankruptcy and the threat of the Soviets in Central Europe.

King realized that external affairs needed its own minister, and he appointed Louis St. Laurent. When

King retired in 1949, St. Laurent, the new prime minister, appointed the extremely capable Lester Pearson as minister of external affairs. Pearson was to become a leading formulator of Canada's foreign policy on the world stage well into the 1950's.

The Gouzenko affair awoke many Canadians to the Soviet threat. Igor Gouzenko was a defector from the Russian embassy in Ottawa who brought details of a large spy ring within Canada. The spy ring focused on Canada's atomic program, developed alongside the British program over the closing stages of the war.

Canada's response was to begin discussions with the new British prime minister, Clement Attlee, over a defense treaty to cover Atlantic countries from the Soviet threat to northern Europe. Eventually, the North Atlantic Treaty Organization (NATO) was set up in 1949, with Canada contributing finances but no military

Canadian foreign minister Lester B. Pearson. (Library of Congress)

forces. Not until the Korean conflict during the early 1950's was Canadian military strength restored. Canadian policy wanted to make NATO more than just a military organization and thought this was agreed to in principle; in practice, this did not happen, and the European and American economies grew apart.

Impact The decade was one of great contrasts. In the first half, Canada contributed in major ways to the Allied war effort through finance, production, and military force. After the war, it sought to assist in reconstructing the Western world through loans, trade, and diplomacy. Its foreign policy continued to reflect its dual identity of being North American and a member of the British Commonwealth. In the establishment of NATO, Canada's diplomacy bore a long-lasting significance in the eventual outcome of the Cold War and the breaking of the Iron Curtain. In its generous trade terms with the United Kingdom, it certainly helped to bring about the recovery and future prosperity of the mother country. By the end of the decade, Canadian diplomacy was recog-

nized as a new and independent force on the world stage.

David Barratt

Further Reading

Black, J. L., and Martin Rudner. *The Gouzenko Affair: Canada and the Beginnings of Cold War Counter-Espionage.* East Lansing: Michigan State University Press, 2006. Traces the spy affair that made Canada aware of the Cold War and turned its foreign policy around.

Bothwell, Robert, Ian Drummond, and John English. *Canada, 1900-1945.* Toronto: University of Toronto Press, 1987. One of the most complete historical accounts of Canada's development through the first half of the twentieth century, covering its foreign policy along with other aspects of government.

_____. *Canada Since 1945.* Rev. ed. Toronto: University of Toronto Press, 1989. Continuation of the above volume, looking in some detail at Canada's changing foreign policy in the late 1940's.

Harrison, W. E. C. *Canada in World Affairs, 1949-1950.* New York: Oxford University Press, 1957. Important source material for these two years; part of a series.

Melakopides, Costas. *Pragmatic Idealism: Canadian Foreign Policy, 1945-1995.* Montreal: McGill-Queen's University Press, 1998. Defends Canada's foreign policy against charges of subservience to U.S. policy or enlightened self-interest. Makes a sustained case for Canada's policy of middle-power internationalism.

Spencer, Robert A. *Canada in World Affairs: From UN to NATO, 1946-1949.* New York: Oxford University Press, 1959. Like other volumes in this scholarly series, this book contains important source materials.

See also Alaska Highway; Atlantic, Battle of the; Canada and Great Britain; Canadian nationalism; Canadian participation in World War II; Cold War; Elections in Canada; Immigration to Canada; North Atlantic Treaty Organization; Wartime propaganda in Canada.

■ Foreign policy of the United States

The 1940's was a pivotal decade in United States foreign policy—one in which the country entered World War II, irrevocably abandoned its traditional isolationistic approach to the outside world after the war, and implemented foreign policies that altered not only its future but also the shape of much of the late twentieth century world.

In his 1797 farewell address, President George Washington counseled his countrymen on the wisdom of adopting a strategy of tactical isolationism as an approach to foreign policy, given the world as it was and the new country as it found itself in the mid-1790's. Because his new country was weak and had little in common with the conflict-causing interests of European states, Washington advised his countrymen to take advantage of its "detached and distant situation" to concentrate on its domestic development to the point where it could someday "choose peace or war, as our interest, guided by justice, shall counsel."

One hundred years later, the United States had that luxury. It had absorbed most of the land between the Atlantic and Pacific Oceans, and between the Mexican and Canadian borders, into statehood, and it had combined its rich resource base with the immigrants it drew from throughout Europe to become one of the world's rising industrial powers. It did not, however, redefine its foreign policy to fit its new status. Instead, the country drifted into a war with Spain that left it with an unintended empire and nearing a world war ostensibly fought to make the world safe for democracy. That war ended instead by making the world a larger playground for its European allies, who, at the postwar Versailles Conference, carved up the former Ottoman Empire for themselves.

All of this, to the American public, seemingly confirmed the earlier wisdom of avoiding the world. Thus, during the interwar period, the U.S. Congress essentially legislated isolationism in the form of neutrality laws that bound the hands of American presidents even as Europe drifted toward war. This isolationism ended only when the Japanese bombed the country back into the world on December 7, 1941, with their sudden attack on Pearl Harbor.

Final Days of American Isolationism On the eve of Germany's invasion of Belgium and resultant war with Britain and France, a respected polling firm asked the American public what the United States should do if Germany were to attack Belgium and trigger a war in Europe. Of those surveyed, 96 percent favored doing nothing at all. One year later, opinion was gradually changing, but Republican presidential candidate Wendell Willkie was still able to reduce the size of his loss in the 1940 presidential election by accusing President Franklin D. Roosevelt of plotting to lead the nation into the war. To protect himself against that charge, Roosevelt was forced to promise during the campaign that he would "not send American boys into any foreign wars." In January of the following year, however, Roosevelt already was discussing, with Russian and British leaders, means of otherwise assisting them in their war efforts.

Wartime Planning Conferences The wartime conferences at Tehran (November, 1943), Casablanca (January, 1943), Yalta (February, 1945), and Potsdam (July, 1945) understandably have received considerable attention because they were the gatherings personally attended by the leaders of the principal countries fighting against Adolf Hitler's Germany,

Benito Mussolini's Italy, and Imperial Japan. They were, however, only four of the nearly two dozen, often extended, meetings among some of the heads of these countries, their personal designates, or their military leaders. The series began with the meeting of high-ranking American, British, and Canadian military officers in Washington at the end of January in 1941. That meeting ran for nearly two months and focused on the circumstances under which the United States would enter the war.

Most of the conferences were concerned with the conduct of the war itself. The pre-Pearl Harbor Moscow Conference, for example, convened on September 29, 1941, focused on the Allies funneling aid to a Soviet Union that had been invaded by Germany on June 22 and was in desperate need of assistance. The First Washington Conference—also knwon as the Arcadia Conference—held from December 22, 1941, to January 14, 1942, was the first meeting of the American and British heads of state following U.S. entry into the war, and it produced the decision to focus fully on the war in Europe first, and to concentrate on the Pacific war against Japan only after victory in the European theater.

Some of these conferences had immediate battlefield importance, such as the secret conference in Cherchell, Algeria, between American general Mark Clark and French officers of German-occupied Vichy France, in which the latter agreed not to fight in the planned Allied invasion of North Africa. Perhaps the most famous of all the wartime meetings, the Casablanca Conference involving Roosevelt, British prime minister Winston Churchill, and French general Charles de Gaulle, also falls under the category of military strategy, discussing as it did the invasion of Italy; a spring, 1944, invasion of northern Europe across the English Channel; and the Allies' intent to fight until its enemies accepted an "unconditional surrender."

As the war in Europe continued to be pursued successfully, these conferences also turned to considering the postwar world and the role that the United States would play in it. The Bretton Woods Conference in July, 1944, for example, focused on establishing an International Monetary Fund and an International Bank for Reconstruction and Development in the postwar world, and the Dumbarton Oaks conference the following month laid the foundation for establishing a United Nations organization after the war, in which the United States

would be a sponsoring member. Similarly, before the year was over Roosevelt and Churchill had met in Quebec to consider a postwar plan for the future of Germany.

When the war ended and the United States fulfilled its promise to join the United Nations and remain an active participant in world affairs, the United States also began a very rapid demobilization of its military presence around the world, which shrank from approximately 12 million in uniform when the war ended in Europe to less than 2 million the following year. Moreover, the demobilization process was organized around a points system that effectively stripped units of their personnel most experienced in combat.

The Birth of Containment   In the fourth Moscow meeting, held in October of 1944, Churchill and Soviet leader Joseph Stalin discussed the future of Eastern Europe and the Balkans without the United States present. A scheme of spheres of influence subsequently was agreed upon that was to leave Romania and Bulgaria in Moscow's orbit in return for the Soviets agreeing to leave Greece under Britain's influence. The two wartime allies were to have equal influence in Hungary. When World War II ended, however, the Red Army occupied a great deal more territory in Eastern Europe than anticipated by that agreement. With the rapid withdrawal of United States forces from Europe, even had there been a will, there would have been little way to prevent the consolidation of Moscow's control over Poland, Czechoslovakia, Hungary, Romania, and Bulgaria, as well as eastern Germany. Stalin, nonetheless, wanted more, and in response to his reach there emerged a tenet of U.S. foreign policy that remained central for more than two generations: the containment of communist expansionism.

The containment policy did not emerge immediately, but rather gradually in the form of United States responses to three developments. First came the Soviet effort to establish a proxy government in northern Iran, which the United States took to the United Nations for action before Stalin bowed to diplomatic pressure and withdrew his troops. Next came the Soviet demand that Turkey cede to it joint control over the Dardanelles area linking the Black Sea and Mediterranean Sea, which prompted Washington to dispatch to the Mediterranean, in a show of support for Turkey, the USS *Missouri*. It was the first U.S. warship to enter those waters in peacetime since President Thomas Jefferson had dispatched the navy to destroy the Barbary Coast pirates in 1803; additionally, as the battleship upon which the Japanese had unconditionally surrendered the previous year, it was the physical embodiment of American military power at a time when the United States had a nuclear monopoly. The point was not lost on Stalin, who promptly dropped his demands on Turkey.

The third major issue was the war in Greece between the elected government and communist insurgents who had fought the Germans during World War II and who were now waging a civil war to gain control of the country. In late 1946, the British government, which until then had been aiding the government in Athens, informed the U.S. government that because of Britain's own need to rebuild at home, it would not be able to continue to aid Greece's government after March 31 of the following year. In response, President Harry S. Truman sought military and economic assistance from Congress to aid postwar Greece and Turkey. Solidifying what had been a practice of piecemeal U.S. responses to Soviet probes into policy, Truman stated that henceforth it would be American policy to help free peoples to maintain their free institutions and national integrity against direct or indirect aggression by totalitarian regimes, a policy stance called the Truman Doctrine. Although he had to make a strong case to achieve broad public support for the policy, that commitment effectively ended any possibility of a postwar return to the isolationism of the past.

Building Peace in the Postwar World Apart from security challenges, posed by Stalin's Russia, confronting some of the United States' wartime allies, the end of World War II brought a consequent need for the United States to refine its approach to the world so as to reflect its new status and the state of the world in 1945. The United States and the Soviet Union were the only major countries that emerged from World War II stronger than when they entered it, and the economic and military capacities of the United States dwarfed those of the Soviet Union in all but the size of conventional military forces.

The world at that time differed greatly from the one that preceded the war. The great colonial powers of Europe needed to rebuild, and they would soon, voluntarily or otherwise, give up their empires

in Asia and Africa. Nationalism was at a low ebb in Europe, with the exception of Britain. France had succumbed to Nazi occupation in six weeks, at large cost to nationalist spirit, while in Germany and Italy the excesses of nationalism were blamed for having plunged the world into World War II. In short, the era demanded a bold foreign policy reappraisal. The United States met the challenge and helped reshape the world.

The containment of communism became the cornerstone of U.S. foreign policy. Over the decades of the Cold War, the policy was militarized in Korea and given a global application by presidents Dwight D. Eisenhower and Lyndon B. Johnson. At its inception, however, it was only an integral part of the foreign policies that the United States undertook between 1947 and 1950. Over the Soviet Union's opposition, in 1948 the United States chose to unify and rebuild Germany, and to strengthen it in every capability but military as a part of democratic Western Europe. When the Soviet Union refused to cooperate, the United States persuaded the French and British to merge their three sectors of West Germany into the Federal Republic of Germany and set it free of allied occupation. The decision to do the same thing with their sectors of Berlin ushered in one of the more dangerous moments in the Cold War: Stalin responded by freezing ground access to the portions of Berlin located within Soviet-occupied East Germany, so as to make Berlin dependent upon Soviet supply lines. The United States and its allies responded by airlifting to West Berlin the supplies that the city needed, for more than three hundred tense days (June 24, 1948-May 11, 1949), before the Soviet Union relented and reopened rail and roadway access to the city.

Meanwhile, elsewhere in Europe, countries tried to rebuild their debilitated social and economic landscapes with few resources and often little success. Three months after announcing the Truman Doctrine, the Truman administration announced the Marshall Plan (more officially, the European Recovery Program)—a broad plan for the economic rebuilding of Europe. Although autonomous from Cold War issues in its goal (that is, the economic recovery of Europe as opposed to containing the forceful spread of communism), the Marshall Plan did correctly foresee that by rebuilding the economic health of Western Europe, it would make communism less appealing. As the economies of these countries improved, the electoral fortunes of their local communist parties did in fact generally wane.

The signing of the North Atlantic Treaty on April 4, 1949, and the strengthening of the North Atlantic Treaty Organization (NATO) in response to North Korea's attack on South Korea in June, 1950, also indirectly tied the Marshall Plan to the containment of Soviet expansionism. NATO, the United States' first peacetime entangling alliance, provided the countries of Europe with a military-security shield behind which they could concentrate on their recovery and devote large sums of money to economic and social programs rather than costly arms buildups.

Austrian farmworkers loading hay onto a machine labeled "Marshall" because it came to Austria through the U.S. Marshall Plan. (Getty Images)

Also tied to both the evolving world order and the Cold War, in his inaugural address in January, 1949, President Truman proposed a program for economically aiding the poorer countries in the developing world (the Point Four Program). As European countries began to divest themselves of the empires that they could no longer maintain, poverty increased in many of these countries. As the Cold War intensified, countries important to the containment doctrine, such as Iran, were added to the list of potential aid recipients, and although the program lost presidential support during the Eisenhower administration because of the leftist and/or neutralist orientations of many developing states, it became the lineal predecessor of the Agency for International Development that continued to be an important part of U.S. operations in the economically and politically developing world.

Impact   Much of the modern world still bears witness to the success of policies established during the 1940's. In his 1969 memoir, *Present at the Creation*, President Truman's longtime secretary of state Dean Acheson described the postwar world as being malleable, like clay, and U.S. foreign policies during the 1947-1950 era as the hands of a sculptor molding that world. The United States sought to halt Soviet expansion, based on the reasoning of George Ken-

nan that if it did not expand, its communist government eventually would implode. Kennan's time framework was unclear; however, there is no denying that the policy eventually worked, or at least contributed to the 1989-1991 fall of communism in both the Soviet Union and its Central European empire.

Likewise, it was the American goal that someday Europe would unite. The enticement and administration of the Marshall Plan encouraged Europeans to consider their recovery in a unified framework. This, coupled with American encouragement of the growth of supranational institutions in postwar Europe, set Europe on the path that produced the European Union. Subsequent policies have built on those of the 1947-1950 era. The Peace Corps, for example, gave a human face to the economic assistance programs for developing countries that President Truman envisioned, and efforts by the United States to help the postcommunist countries of Europe liberalize their economies and democratize can trace their roots to the postwar Marshall Plan, as well as to the postwar efforts to rebuild Germany and someday integrate it into the Western world.

Joseph R. Rudolph, Jr.

Further Reading

Acheson, Dean. *Present at the Creation: My Years in the State Department*. New York: Norton, 1969. Widely available and immensely valuable, this autobiography by President Truman's longtime secretary of state provides critical insights into U.S. foreign policy thinking during the formative years of the Cold War.

Birdwell, Michael E. *Celluloid Soldiers: The Warner Brothers Campaign Against Nazism.* New York: New York University Press, 1999. A valuable glimpse of both the capacity of the entertainment industry to influence opinion and the strength of isolationist sentiment in the United States during the 1930's.

Braverman, Jordan. *To Hasten the Homecoming: How Americans Fought World War II Through the Media.* New York: Madison Books, 1996. Broader than Birdwell's study, an intriguing analysis of the role of the entertainment, informational, and advertising industries in the home front mobilization of support for the war.

Foster, H. Schuyler. *Activism Replaces Isolationism: U.S. Public Attitudes, 1940-1975.* Washington, D.C.: Foxhall Press, 1985. The title tells it all. The 1940's was the critical decade as the Truman administration took the lead in promoting international activism to the postwar American public.

Hook, Steven W., and John W. Spanier. *American Foreign Policy Since World War II.* Washington, D.C.: CQ Press, 2006. One of the more recent editions of a standard survey text for courses in U.S. foreign policy. Basic reading on U.S. foreign policy, from the postwar era through President George W. Bush's war on terrorism.

Kennan, George. *American Diplomacy.* Expanded ed. Chicago: University of Chicago Press, 1984. Lectures and writings by the architect of the containment doctrine. Kennan's analysis of the United States' cyclical, often moralistic approach to foreign policy remains relevant to contemporary U.S. foreign policy fifty years after he first presented the material.

LeFeber, Walter. *America, Russia, and the Cold War, 1945-2006.* 10th ed. Boston: McGraw-Hill, 2008. A standard text in college courses for more than a generation, Lefeber's work densely covers the origins and subsequent evolution of the Cold War. Widely available in university libraries. Valuable reading.

McCauley, Martin. *Origins of the Cold War, 1941-1949.* 3d ed. New York: Longman, 2008. One of the most reliable studies of U.S.-Soviet relations, and of the various explanations of the origins of the Cold War.

Morgenthau, Hans J. *In Defense of the National Interest: A Critical Examination of American Foreign Policy.* Washington, D.C.: University Press of America, 1982. Postwar American foreign policy approached the world from the perspective of *realpolitik* (political realism), and no one made a stronger case for that approach than the author of this basic reading, originally published in 1951.

See also Arcadia Conference; Cairo Conference; Casablanca Conference; Isolationism; Marshall Plan; North Atlantic Treaty Organization; Point Four Program; Potsdam Conference; Roosevelt, Franklin D.; Tehran Conference; Truman, Harry S.; Truman Doctrine; Yalta Conference.

■ Forrestal, James

Identification U.S. secretary of the Navy, 1944-1947, and secretary of defense, 1947-1949
Born February 15, 1892; Matteawan, New York
Died May 22, 1949; Bethesda, Maryland

As the last secretary of the Navy, Forrestal oversaw the racial integration of the Navy; as the first secretary of defense, he campaigned for the integration of all the armed services. He presided over the end of World War II and in 1949 committed suicide under what some consider suspicious circumstances.

A former naval aviator, James Vincent Forrestal entered New York state politics after World War I, making friends with future president Franklin D. Roosevelt. In 1940, Roosevelt named Forrestal a special administrative assistant, and then undersecretary of the Navy. Forrestal replaced Secretary of the Navy Frank Knox upon the latter's death in 1944, and he saw out the end of World War II in that position, promoting peaceful negotiations with Japan in an effort to end the war in the Pacific. He also headed the Navy during the difficult years of demobilization.

In 1947, President Harry S. Truman named Forrestal to the new position of secretary of defense. Forrestal promoted a full racial integration of the armed services, which was accomplished in 1949. As defense secretary, he argued against a partition of Palestine in 1947-1948 and strongly opposed the spread of communism and Soviet power after the war. He also fought against reductions in defense spending during the Truman administration.

Forrestal's service as defense secretary was short-lived. After privately meeting with New York governor Thomas E. Dewey, the Republican presidential candidate expected to defeat Truman in the 1948 election, Forrestal became the target of syndicated columnist Drew Pearson, who revealed Forrestal's meetings with Dewey. As a result, Truman asked Forrestal to resign his position as secretary of defense. Forrestal subsequently entered into psychiatric care at Bethesda Naval Hospital, where Navy captain George N. Raines was the chief psychiatrist. Forrestal's official condition was announced as exhaustion, though Raines privately diagnosed him with depression.

Though Forrestal seemed to be recovering, on May 22, 1949, his body was found on the roof of the third floor at the hospital. (Forrestal's room was on the sixteenth floor.) The Navy convened an official review board that concluded only that Forrestal had died from the fall. The general consensus, however, was that Forrestal had committed suicide. Conspiracy theories abounded about Forrestal's death and were magnified by the fact that the Navy did not release any of its findings until 2004. Some of these theories hypothesized that Forrestal had been assassinated by Palestinian or Zionist extremists or by Soviets.

Impact Forrestal's greatest impact was the racial integration of the armed forces years before the Civil Rights movement began. As the first secretary of defense, Forrestal also presided over the creation of the Department of Defense, which unified the armed forces. Forrestal's influence on the Navy resulted in the naming of the *Forrestal* class aircraft carriers.

Emily Carroll Shearer

Further Reading

Hoopes, Townsend, and Douglas Brinkley. *Driven Patriot: The Life and Times of James Forrestal.* Annapolis, Md.: Naval Institute Press, 2000.
Simpson, Cornell. *The Death of James Forrestal.* Boston: Western Islands, 1966.

See also Anticommunism; Department of Defense, U.S.; Desegregation of the U.S. military; Dewey, Thomas E.; Foreign policy of the United States; Israel, creation of; Navy, U.S.; Roosevelt, Franklin D.; Truman, Harry S.; World War II.

■ "Four Freedoms" speech

The Event President Franklin D. Roosevelt's annual message to the U.S. Congress that proclaimed four fundamental human freedoms

Date Delivered on January 6, 1941

The speech provided a clear statement of the war aims that would guide the United States in opposing Axis aggression in World War II.

Speaking at a time when Great Britain was battling Nazi Germany in Europe, China was fighting Japanese aggression, and isolationists were still vocal in the United States, President Franklin D. Roosevelt sought to rally the American public behind a program of material support for those countries fighting the Axis Powers. After describing the grave threat that would face the United States should the Axis forces win in Europe, Africa, and the Far East, he called for an escalation of defense production and concluded by revisiting a theme he had mentioned to the press in July, 1940, the four essential freedoms that would be preserved by defeating the Axis: freedom of speech and expression, freedom of religion, freedom from want, and freedom from fear.

Impact Roosevelt's Four Freedoms were incorporated (absent freedom of religion) into the Atlantic Charter in August, 1941. In January, 1942, they were recognized in a proclamation of the United Nations that bound together the United States, Great Britain, and the Soviet Union. Commonly used as a theme in U.S. propaganda, in 1943 they were immortalized in popular culture by Norman Rockwell's illustrations in the *Saturday Evening Post.* The Allied victory in 1945 did not, however, fulfill the wartime promise that these freedoms held out to all peoples.

Larry Haapanen

Further Reading

Davis, Kenneth. *FDR: The War President, 1940-1943.* New York: Random House, 2000.
Podell, Janet, and Steven Anzovin, eds. *Speeches of the American Presidents.* New York: H. W. Wilson, 1988.
Smith, Jean Edward. *FDR.* New York: Random House, 2007.

See also "Arsenal of Democracy" speech; Atlantic Charter; Rockwell, Norman; Roosevelt, Franklin D.; *Saturday Evening Post*; Wartime propaganda in the United States; World War II.

■ France and the United States

Good Franco-American relations during the 1940's were essential to defeating Germany and establishing a free Europe. They were also important in building a working partnership between the United States and Europe both during the war and after.

At the beginning of the 1940's, the United States had begun to move away from its long-established policies of isolationism and protectionism. The country had opened up trade with European nations through the 1936 Reciprocal Trade Act during the late 1930's. By the early 1940's, the United States had entered into bilateral trade agreements with several European countries. The United States, however, still viewed itself as distinctly separate from and independent of Europe.

General Charles de Gaulle at a ceremony by Paris's tomb of the unknown soldier, next to the Arc de Triomphe, on August 27, 1944—only a few days after Allied troops liberated the city from German occupation. (Popperfoto/Getty Images)

Hitler Comes to Power in Germany   When Adolf Hitler came to power in Germany, the United States perceived the threat that he posed. American leaders saw it as a threat primarily to Europe and attempted to convince Great Britain and France of its seriousness. When Hitler began his invasion of Europe on May 10, 1940, Great Britain was content to follow a policy of appeasement. France believed its own army invincible and defensive action sufficient to contain Hitler's army. Consequently, once France's Maginot Line was in place, the country tended to consider the conflict as a *drôle de guerre* (silly little war). The United States continued to emphasize the potential danger of Hitler and expressed willingness to sell war supplies to Great Britain and France, but it continued to consider the conflict a European war and wished to remain neutral.

U.S. Relations with Vichy France   The French government underwent several changes of leadership, with Marshall Henri-Philippe Pétain becoming prime minister on June 16, 1940. Germany had occupied much of France after the evacuation of Dunkirk by Allied forces at the end of May and beginning of June. Pétain established the Vichy government in southern France early in July and sought collaboration with Germany. The United States recognized the Vichy government as the official government of France and maintained cordial diplomatic relations with Vichy.

Even though the United States knew about Vichy's collaboration with Germany, it needed to interact with Vichy to have as much influence as possible on the decisions made by the regime and to acquire as much intelligence information as possible. It was essential to the United States for Germany not to gain control of the French fleet, which would have given Hitler the ability to interfere with Atlantic shipping and possibly threaten the American East Coast. The United States also wanted the French government to remain on European soil rather than move into the French North African colonies, believing that a transfer of the government from France to Africa would draw Hitler's attention to conquest outside Europe and impair American intelligence work.

General Charles de Gaulle   The United States refused to recognize General Charles de Gaulle and his resistance fighters as representatives of the French government and nation. It was with Pétain, not de Gaulle, that the United States military had worked to win World War I. De Gaulle was relatively unknown to American diplomats and politicians. He and his government in exile did not inspire the confidence that Pétain did, nor did the United States believe that he had a significant number of supporters in France. Unlike the United States, Great Britain refused to recognize the Vichy government and instead recognized de Gaulle as the leader of Free France on June 28, 1940. De Gaulle went to London, where he made radio broadcasts encouraging the French to continue the fight and attempted to organize a unified French Resistance.

On May 30, 1943, de Gaulle moved to Algeria and established the French Committee of National Liberation (FCNL). On May 26, 1944, he declared the FCNL the provisional government of the French Republic. This announcement incurred the displeasure of both British prime minister Winston Churchill and U.S. president Franklin D. Roosevelt, neither of whose governments recognized de Gaulle's provisional government at that time. Churchill and Roosevelt decided not to include him in the planning for the Allied invasion of France known as Operation Overlord. Some European countries did recognize the FCNL, however. As a result, the United States and Great Britain agreed that de Gaulle would be able to assist in the administration of liberated areas of France. De Gaulle and his forces entered France on August 20, and he and his soldiers entered Paris with the American soldiers on August 25. De Gaulle still was not accepted as the official governmental representative of France and was not invited to attend the Yalta Conference, although he did sign the final documents for France regarding the surrender of Germany.

Marshall Plan and the Cold War   After the war, the United States was eager to help rebuild Europe and to stop the spread of communism. The Marshall Plan provided financial aid to the war-torn countries, enabling them to rebuild their economies. France received a major portion of this aid, and soon its economy had recovered to the prewar level. During the Cold War, France aligned itself with the United States, Great Britain, and the other noncommunist countries.

Impact   The relations that the United States maintained with France during the 1940's were important in enabling the Allies to defeat Germany. The policies of cooperation and aid developed during the 1940's laid the foundation for the later relationship of interdependence and mutual assistance that the United States established not only with France but also with the European Community.

Shawncey Webb

Further Reading

Black, Conrad. *Franklin Delano Roosevelt: Champion of Freedom*. Cambridge, Mass.: Perseus Books, 2005. Good for understanding Roosevelt's diplomacy and why he maintained relations with Vichy.

Crowdy, Terry. *French Resistance Fighter: France's Secret Army*. London: Osprey, 2007. Interesting look at the development of the French Resistance.

Jackson, Julian. *Charles De Gaulle*. London: Haus, 2003. Excellent for understanding de Gaulle's attitudes about France and how they shaped his actions during the 1940's.

Langer, William L. *Our Vichy Gamble*. New York. W. W. Norton, 1947. Explains why the author believes U.S. maintenance of relations with Vichy was the right choice.

Paxton, Robert O. *Vichy France*. Reprint. New York: Columbia University Press, 2001. Thorough explanation of how Vichy functioned and how it affected France.

See also   D Day; "Four Freedoms" speech; Hull, Cordell; Lend-Lease; Marshall Plan; *President Roosevelt and the Coming of the War*; Roosevelt, Franklin D.; V-E Day and V-J Day; World War II; Yalta Conference.

■ Freeways

Definition   Limited-access highways with the lanes that move traffic in opposite directions separated by a median or concrete divider

Freeways permitted rapid toll-free travel by car through congested areas, particularly useful as Detroit began producing larger and more powerful automobiles in the postwar era.

Through most of America's existence, the history of its roads was one of evolutionary development. The

Southern California's Arroyo Seco Parkway in 1940. (Caltrans)

earliest roads were animal trails followed by various Native American peoples and subsequently widened by European settlers, particularly the English and Spanish, for use by wagons and stagecoaches. When the railroad came, roads fell into decline for cross-country travel, relegated largely to carrying people and goods from a train station to their final destination.

It was only with the development of first the safety bicycle and then the automobile that there was a real push for improved roads. Even these roads still followed the old trade paths originally carved through the landscape by original inhabitants and early settlers. They went through the heart of each small town they passed, so that people on long-haul trips had to slow down for each town. They wound their way through the landscape with sharp turns and blind hills that could be hazardous at high speeds. In general, they were good for local traffic but not for long trips.

A New Kind of Road   The idea of a new kind of road in the United States began to develop during the 1930's, as word came across the Atlantic of Germany's new system of superhighways, the autobahn. Intended by Nazi dictator Adolf Hitler as a combination of a public works project and a military transportation system, it featured wide lanes and gentle curves, with the lanes bearing oncoming traffic separated, generally with an unpaved median. Instead of intersections, there were ramps and overpasses that permitted traffic to move from one road to another without stopping and with minimal slowing down.

Some American leaders proposed a similar project to President Franklin D. Roosevelt both because such roadways seemed to make sense and as a way to create jobs and inject money into the economy, much as the Tennessee Valley Authority (TVA) was doing. The first sections of the Los Angeles Freeway, a six-mile section called the Arroyo Seco Parkway, were laid out between Los Angeles proper and Pasadena, and the freeway opened in 1940. When America was drawn into World War II, all nonessential projects were shelved while the country concentrated on defeating two aggressive industrialized enemies at once, so freeway construction halted.

Speeding up the Country　In 1945, following the defeat first of Nazi Germany and then of Japan, the United States moved back onto a peacetime footing, and the production of consumer goods resumed in earnest. Among the goods being produced in record numbers to satisfy the long-deferred appetites of American consumers were powerful new models of automobile that seemed fairly designed to roar down open roads.

The Arroyo Seco Parkway, which originally had been planned as an attractive boulevard in which the dividing median was primarily a green space, was rapidly transformed along the lines of a German autobahn, becoming a fully divided highway with limited access. It was renamed the Pasadena Freeway, with "free" simultaneously invoking the fact that one did not need to pay a toll (unlike the superhighways of the East such as the Pennsylvania Turnpike, with their tollbooths) and the free movement of cars at high speed along it, unimpeded by stoplights. Concept of what constituted a good road changed from beauty to practicality, allowing cars to drive as rapidly as possible.

Even during the war, when gas was rationed and tires were almost impossible to come by, Angelenos drove enough that a temperature inversion in the Los Angeles basin trapped enough pollutants in the area that the air turned foul with smog. As the postwar economic boom led to an ever-expanding number of cars on the freeway system, air quality in the Los Angeles basin took a downturn.

Impact　The immediate effect of freeways was to enable drivers to get places far more rapidly than ever dreamed possible. In sprawling Los Angeles, commute times were cut significantly because drivers could avoid stoplights for a large portion of their drive. The success of early freeways of the 1940's helped President Dwight D. Eisenhower to make his case during the 1950's for the Interstate Highway System, which would cross the entire nation with a network of such high-speed highways. Most of the early freeways were incorporated into the interstate system.

In the long term, the effects of the freeway were more complex, including demographic shifts as crowded city interiors were spurned by the middle class in favor of suburbs and exurbs that previously took too long to reach on a daily commute. As shopping and new housing moved into the suburbs, however, poorer neighborhoods became cut off. Poverty changed from being largely a temporary situation of immigrants, whose children assimilated into the American mainstream, and increasingly a multigenerational trap as poor people remained in their neighborhoods.

Leigh Husband Kimmel

Further Reading

Goddard, Stephen B. *Getting There: The Epic Struggle Between Road and Rail in the American Century.* New York: Basic Books, 1994. Places the development of the freeway in the larger context of the competition between railroad companies and automobile manufacturers.

Lewis, Tom. *Divided Highways: Building the Interstate Highways, Transforming American Life.* New York: Viking, 1997. Discusses the Interstate Highway System, including its cultural antecedents.

Schwantes, Carlos Arnaldo. *Going Places: Transportation Redefines the Twentieth-Century West.* Bloomington: Indiana University Press, 2003. Focuses on the role of transportation, including freeways and the Interstate Highway System, in making the western wilderness accessible.

Smith, Claude Clayton. *Lapping America: A Man, a Corvette, and the Interstates.* Short Hills, N.J.: Burford Books, 2006. Reminiscences of a man who watched the birth of the modern freeway and fell in love with the freedom of the open road it afforded.

See also　Air pollution; Auto racing; Automobiles and auto manufacturing; Ford Motor Company; General Motors.

■ Freezing of Japanese assets

The Event　President Franklin D. Roosevelt's issuance of an executive order to freeze Japanese assets in the United States

Date　July 26, 1941

The United States issued a series of economic sanctions against Japan between 1938 and 1941, as a reaction to

Japan's expansion into East and Southeast Asia. A freeze of all Japanese assets in the United States was one of these sanctions. Although the intent was to gain a form of control over Japan without military conflict, this economic act was unsuccessful in preventing the outbreak of war in the Pacific.

Japan's invasion of China began with an incident near Beijing in July, 1937. This was the beginning of a long-lasting conflict between Japan and China, the second Sino-Japanese War, although both counties did not declare the war until December, 1941. Japan soon occupied Shanghai, and this expansion became a great concern for countries of the West, particularly the United States, the United Kingdom, and France.

In July, 1938, the U.S. government issued an oral embargo on the export of airplanes and aircraft parts against countries that were using these materials to attack civilian populations. Japan was among those countries. This moral embargo was extended to materials for building airplanes, such as molybdenum, aluminum, and nickel, in December, 1939. President Franklin D. Roosevelt restricted export licenses for selling iron, heavy scrap steel, lubricating oil, and aviation gasoline to Japan on July 26, 1940. Because Japan had relied on imports from the United States, this restriction made it difficult to continue the war against China.

In September, 1940, Japan occupied the northern part of French Indochina to hinder China from the import of arms and fuels by the United States and Britain. Japan also signed a military alliance with Germany and Italy on September 27, 1940. Although Japan demanded from the Dutch East Indies an increase of oil export to Japan, the negotiations ended unsuccessfully.

In July, 1941, the Japanese military began invading the southern part of French Indochina to build air and naval bases under an agreement with the French Vichy government. As retaliation for the Japanese occupation, President Roosevelt issued an executive order to freeze Japanese assets in the United States on July 26, 1941. Britain and the Dutch East Indies followed. This was a serious blow to Japan because the order not only restricted Japanese economic activity in the United States but also affected Japanese trade with Latin America and Europe, because those transactions were settled in the United States. On August 1, the United States announced an embargo on exports of oil to Japan. As a result, Japan lost access to nearly 90 percent of imported oil. Japan's oil supply would last three years, and only one and half years if it went to war.

Impact   The last and most harsh economic sanctions against Japan, the freezing of Japanese assets and the oil embargo, left Japan with two options: either withdraw its occupation troops from Southeast Asia and negotiate the release of the sanctions, or initiate war against the United States. On December 7, 1941, the Japanese navy conducted a strike against the United States naval base at Pearl Harbor, prompting U.S. entrance into World War II.

Fusako Hamao

Further Reading

Cashman, Greg, and Leonard C. Robinson. *An Introduction to the Causes of War: Patterns of Interstate Conflict from World War I to Iraq.* Lanham, Md.: Rowman & Littlefield, 2007.

Thompson, Robert S. D. *Empires on the Pacific: World War II and the Struggle for the Mastery of Asia.* New York: Basic Books, 2001.

Utley, Jonathan G. *Going to War with Japan, 1937-1941.* Knoxville: University of Tennessee Press, 1985.

See also   Asian Americans; China and North America; China-Burma-India theater; Executive orders; Japan, occupation of; Japanese American internment; Pearl Harbor attack; Roosevelt, Franklin D.; World War II.

■ Fulbright fellowship program

Identification   The largest U.S. international exchange program of grants for students, scholars, educators, and professionals to undertake graduate study, advanced research, and teaching practice

Date   Established on August 1, 1946

Since its creation in 1946, the Fulbright fellowship program has promoted peace and understanding through educational exchange, fostering better relationships with the global community and gaining allies and support for the United States.

In 1945, Senator J. William Fulbright of Arkansas introduced a bill in the U.S. Congress that called for the use of surplus war property to fund the "promotion of international good will through the exchange of students in the fields of education, culture, and science." As a mainstay of America's public-diplomacy efforts in the aftermath of World War II, the Fulbright program has fostered bilateral relationships with other countries and governments.

On August 1, 1946, President Harry S. Truman signed the bill into law, and Congress created the Fulbright program. The J. William Fulbright Foreign Scholarship Board (FSB) was created by Congress to supervise the program. Its board has twelve members appointed by the president of the United States, each serving a three-year term. The intent of Congress in creating the board was to establish an impartial and independent body that would ensure the respect and cooperation of the academic world for the educational exchange program, particularly in the selection of grantees and of educational institutions qualified to participate. The FSB was to set policies and procedures for administration of the Fulbright program, having final authority for selection of all grantees and for supervision of the conduct of the program both in the United States and abroad.

On March 23, 1948, the Fulbright commission established its first program, the Philippine-American Educational Foundation (PAEF); this program was fully funded by war reparations and foreign loan repayments to the United States. Other programs followed quickly, as for example the US-UK Fulbright Commission, which was created on September 22, 1948. The primary source of funding for the Fulbright program is an annual appropriation by the U.S. Congress to the Department of State; however, participating governments and host institutions in foreign countries and in the United States also contribute financially through cost-sharing.

Impact   The Fulbright program has promoted understanding between the United States and other nations by giving its participants an opportunity to explore each other's political, economic, and cultural institutions and to exchange ideas. With more than 300,000 participants chosen during its history for their leadership potential, from hundreds of countries, the Fulbright program is the largest U.S. exchange program, with 1,500 grants annually in all fields of study. The Fulbright program is one of the

> ## Global Educational Exchange
>
> *In his foreword to* The Fulbright Program *(1965), Senator J. William Fulbright explained the importance of educational exchange among nations:*
>
> There is nothing obscure about the objectives of educational exchange. Its purpose is to acquaint Americans with the world as it is and to acquaint students and scholars from many lands with America as it is—not as we wish it were or as we might wish foreigners to see it but exactly as it is—which by my reckoning is an "image" of which no American need be ashamed.

most prestigious awards programs in the world; more Fulbright alumni have won Nobel Prizes than those of any other academic program.

Concepcion Saenz-Cambra

Further Reading

Gayner, Jeffrey B. *The Fulbright Program After Fifty Years: From Mutual Understanding to Mutual Support.* Washington, D.C.: Capital Research Center, 1996.

Johnson, Walter, and Francis J. Colligan. *The Fulbright Program: A History.* Chicago: University of Chicago Press, 1965.

Woods, Randall Bennett. *Fulbright: A Biography.* Cambridge, England: Cambridge University Press, 2006.

See also   Congress, U.S.; Education in the United States; Foreign policy of the United States.

■ Fuller, R. Buckminster

Identification   American engineer, inventor, designer, and philosopher
Born   July 12, 1895; Milton, Massachusetts
Died   July 1, 1983; Los Angeles, California

An advocate for environmentally friendly design and forward-thinking technology, Fuller was one of the greatest American visionary thinkers of the twentieth century. He was an active inventor, best known for the development of the geodesic dome and the Dymaxion house.

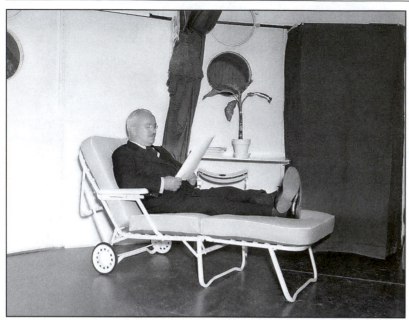

R. Buckminster Fuller relaxing inside of a unit of a Dymaxion house set up as an exhibit at New York's Museum of Modern Art in October, 1941. (AP/Wide World Photos)

R. Buckminster "Bucky" Fuller changed the world of architecture by creating designs that were efficient and eco-friendly and employed leading technology. His first design to attain international acclaim was the Dymaxion house, a single-family dwelling that was suspended from a central mast that could be erected quickly. The Dymaxion was inexpensive, mobile, and could be mass-produced.

Fuller's best-known creation, the geodesic dome, was invented in 1947. The structure embodied Fuller's concept of "maximum gain of advantage from minimum energy output" and relied on a structural design principle that he called "energetic-synergetic geometry." He designed domes all over the world, including in the United States, Antarctica, Moscow, and Paris. His motto, "more for less," embraced designs that would benefit the largest number of people while using a minimum of resources.

Impact Fuller espoused his global philosophy in many publications that focused on the technological betterment of humankind and the world. It was through his designs that this message was spread, inspiring generations of artists, architects, engineers, environmentalists, and mathematicians.

Amanda J. Bahr-Evola

Further Reading

Hays, K. Michael, and Dana A. Miller. *Buckminster Fuller: Starting with the Universe.* New York: Whitney Museum of American Art, 2008.

Sieden, Lloyd. *Buckminster Fuller's Universe: His Life and Work.* New York: Basic Books, 2000.

See also Architecture; Housing in the United States; Inventions; Philosophy and philosophers; Science and technology; Wright, Frank Lloyd.

G

■ G.I. Bill

Identification Federal law providing war veterans with readjustment benefits such as unemployment compensation, loan guarantees for purchases of homes, farms, and businesses, and tuition and subsistence for education and training

Also known as Servicemen's Readjustment Act; G.I. Bill of Rights

Date Signed into law on June 22, 1944

The U.S. Congress enacted this legislation to help the nation reabsorb millions of veterans returning home after fighting in World War II. Passage of the law showed that lawmakers had learned from the mistakes made by the U.S. government in the way World War I veterans had been treated.

The G.I. Bill put higher education within the reach of millions of veterans of World War II and later military conflicts. Taking its name, "G.I." from "government issue," a term used by soldiers, the law created a comprehensive package of benefits designed to help veterans readjust to civilian life. The bill boosted American confidence and changed the way individuals lived, worked, and learned.

Harry W. Colmery, a former national commander of the American Legion and former Republican National Party chairman, is credited with drawing up the first draft of the G.I. Bill. It was introduced in the House on January 10, 1944, and in the Senate the following day. Both chambers approved their own versions of the bill. However, the bill almost died when Senate and House members met to iron out differences between their versions of the new legislation. Both groups agreed on the need for education and home loan benefits but were deadlocked on the bill's provisions for unemployment insurance. Finally, Representative John Gibson of Georgia cast the tie-breaking vote. The Senate approved the final form of the bill on June 12, and the House followed the next day. President Franklin D. Roosevelt signed it into law on June 22, 1944. When Roosevelt signed the G.I. Bill, he remarked that the bill substantially carried out most of the recommendations he had made in a speech on July 28, 1943, and in his messages to Congress later that same year.

Provisions of the Law The Veterans Administration (VA) was responsible for carrying out the law's key provisions. Through the VA, the bill provided financial aid for veterans' hospitals; school and college tuition; building of and building materials for VA hospitals; for purchases of homes, farms, and

Many war veterans enjoying the educational benefits of the G.I. Bill are among these University of Iowa students in 1947. (Time & Life Pictures/Getty Images)

Roosevelt Signs the G.I. Bill

U.S. president Franklin D. Roosevelt signed the Servicemen's Readjustment Act, known as the G.I. Bill, in 1944. The act provided benefits for veterans returning from service in World War II. Roosevelt outlined these benefits in the following public statement made the same day he signed the bill into law:

1. It [the G.I. Bill] gives servicemen and women the opportunity of resuming their education or technical training after discharge, or of taking a refresher or retrainer course, not only without tuition charge up to $500 per school year, but with the right to receive a monthly living allowance while pursuing their studies.
2. It makes provision for the guarantee by the Federal Government of not to exceed 50 percent of certain loans made to veterans for the purchase or construction of homes, farms, and business properties.
3. It provides for reasonable unemployment allowances payable each week up to a maximum period of one year, to those veterans who are unable to find a job.
4. It establishes improved machinery for effective job counseling for veterans and for finding jobs for returning soldiers and sailors.
5. It authorizes the construction of all necessary additional hospital facilities.
6. It strengthens the authority of the Veterans Administration to enable it to discharge its existing and added responsibilities with promptness and efficiency.

With the signing of this bill a well-rounded program of special veterans' benefits is nearly completed. It gives emphatic notice to the men and women in our armed forces that the American people do not intend to let them down.

By prior legislation, the Federal Government has already provided for the armed forces of this war: adequate dependency allowances; mustering-out pay; generous hospitalization, medical care, and vocational rehabilitation and training; liberal pensions in case of death or disability in military service; substantial war risk life insurance, and guaranty of premiums on commercial policies during service; protection of civil rights and suspension of enforcement of certain civil liabilities during service; emergency maternal care for wives of enlisted men; and reemployment rights for returning veterans.

This bill therefore and the former legislation provide the special benefits which are due to the members of our armed forces—for they "have been compelled to make greater economic sacrifice and every other kind of sacrifice than the rest of us, and are entitled to definite action to help take care of their special problems." While further study and experience may suggest some changes and improvements, the Congress is to be congratulated on the prompt action it has taken.

businesses; low-interest mortgages and small-business loans; job training; job relocation assistance; special hiring privileges; and cash stipends to unemployed veterans of twenty dollars per week for fifty-two weeks. It also had a provision for reviewing veterans' dishonorable discharges from the services. Although veterans eagerly embraced the bill's education and loan benefits, few collected on one of the bill's most controversial provisions—unemployment pay. Less than 20 percent of funds set aside for the purpose were used for unemployment benefits.

The central purpose of the G.I. Bill was to do a better job of helping veterans return home from war than had been done after the conclusion of World War I in 1918. Veterans were so shamefully neglected after that war that thousands of them would eventually march on the nation's capital to demand the government keep the promises it had made to them. The end of World War I also brought an economic slowdown that legislators did not want to see repeated after World War II. Assisting veterans to improve their educations, get jobs, and become homeowners were seen as ways to help avert an economic slump.

Educational Benefits   After the G.I. Bill was signed into law, veterans began receiving grants for higher education and vocational training, mortgage loan guarantees, and cash payments for those who were unemployed. In providing help for more than 3.5 million home mortgages, the bill was instrumental in encouraging the rapid growth of suburbia after 1945. Between 1944 and 1952, the VA backed nearly 2.4 million home loans. During its peak year, 1947, about 40 percent of all housing starts in the nation were funded by loans made under the G.I. Bill.

About 7,800,000 World War II veterans—more than one-half of all veterans eligible for the bill's educational benefits—eventually used them to help restart their civilian careers. The resulting boost in new college students helped postwar college enrollments to swell by 70 percent over prewar levels. By 1947, almost half of all college students were military veterans. New facilities had to be constructed to accommodate expanding enrollments.

The increasing numbers of veterans in higher education also helped bring other kinds of changes to college and university campuses. New types of programs evolved that were geared more to the vocational and professional needs of the veterans. A primary reason for the program's success was the flexibility that it gave to veterans, who were allowed to spend their tuition money on a wide range of options. Many veterans became some of the most academically successful of all college students during the late 1940's. Moreover, their presence on college campuses provided proof that colleges and universities were no longer the exclusive preserves of the sons and daughters of the elite.

One of the initial projections between the G.I. Bill that proved wrong was the expectation that a larger proportion of returning veterans would want to enter the job market immediately. Only a few hundred thousand veterans were expected to opt for higher education. Instead, more than 1 million of them enrolled in institutions of higher education in both 1946 and 1947, and more than 900,000 more enrolled in 1948. These veterans took very active roles in college. Many of them joined fraternal groups and neighborhood and community organizations and got involved in local politics.

Impact   Despite its clear successes, the G.I. Bill also had its failures. In contrast to similar legislation in Canada and European nations, it did not address broader domestic agenda that would have provided fuller health care, child care, job training and education to members of the families of veterans and their survivors. Nevertheless, the nation earned back many times its investment, through increased tax revenues of better educated and more prosperous veterans.

The G.I. Bill proved the ability of the federal government could promote social and economic advancement through educational attainment and training, and changed and empowered the lives of millions of veterans following the completion of their military service. The successes of the G.I. Bill encouraged legislators to create educational opportunities for individuals in these groups as a means of redressing past social and economic inequities.

Ursula Goldsmith

Further Reading

Ballard, Jack Stokes. *The Shock of Peace: Military and Economic Demobilization After World War II*. Washington, D.C.: University Press of America, 1983. Well-researched narration of U.S. demobilization efforts during and after World War II. Places the G.I. Bill in context with other readjustment measures.

Blum, John Morton. *V Was for Victory: Politics and American Culture During World War II*. New York: Harcourt Brace Jovanovich, 1976. Excellent account of mobilization on the home front. Discusses the G.I. Bill in the light of congressional politics, the weakening of New Deal reforms, and Roosevelt's 1944 "Economic Bill of Rights."

Greenberg, Milton. *The G.I. Bill: The Law That Changed America*. Foreword by Bob Dole. New York: Lickle, 1997. Companion volume to a documentary aired on public television; explains the broad effects of the G.I. Bill—both intended and unintended—in American history.

Mettler, Suzanne. *Soldiers to Citizens: The G.I. Bill and the Making of the Greatest Generation*. New York: Oxford University Press, 2005. Focuses on the role of the G.I. Bill in shaping the economy, culture, and identity of Americans in the decades following World War II.

Olson, Keith W. *The G.I. Bill, the Veterans, and the Colleges*. Lexington: University Press of Kentucky, 1974. Excellent study of educational aspects of the G.I. Bill, with topical chapters.

Ross, Davis R. B. *Preparing for Ulysses: Politics and Veter-*

ans During World War II. New York: Columbia University Press, 1969. Comprehensive analysis of veterans' benefits, including mustering-out pay, the G.I. Bill, demobilization, reconversion, and housing.

Severo, Richard, and Lewis Milford. *The Wages of War: When America's Soldiers Came Home—from Valley Forge to Vietnam*. New York: Simon & Schuster, 1989. Comprehensive review of the postwar treatment of military veterans over the sweep of U.S. history, helping to place the exceptional positive case of World War II veterans in proper historical perspective.

See also Army, U.S.; *The Best Years of Our Lives*; Credit and debt; Education in the United States; Military conscription in the United States; Navy, U.S.; Women in the U.S. military; World War II.

■ Gambling

The 1940's was a comparatively quiet era for gambling. The most important developments during the decade were an expansion of pari-mutuel betting on horse races and the beginnings of the legal casino industry in Nevada.

The gambling boom that would eventually transform Las Vegas, Nevada, into one of the tourist capitals of the world began during the 1940's. Much of this development was funded by organized crime bodies looking for alternative investments after the end of Prohibition during the early 1930's had taken away the huge profits they had made from bootlegging liquor.

In 1931, Nevada became the first state to legalize casino gambling in an effort to revitalize its state's declining economy by attracting tourists from out of state—particularly from neighboring California. Despite the fact that Nevada would remain the only state with legal casino gambling for nearly fifty years, its tourist industry was slow to develop. Reno, a town in the most densely populated part of the state, near Lake Tahoe, became the first Nevada city to develop a significant tourist industry.

The Rise of Las Vegas At that time, Las Vegas was barely more than a village in a comparatively desolate area near the state's southwestern border with California. Construction of Boulder Dam on the nearby Colorado River during the 1930's enhanced Las Vegas's attractiveness by creating Lake Mead, which would develop into a major recreational area. Sensing Las Vegas's potential, developers started building hotels offering entertainment there during the early 1940's. In 1945, the state of Nevada began requiring casinos to have licenses and started taxing casino profits and setting standardized fees.

In 1946, William Harrah built the first lavish casino resort in Reno, Nevada, and used buses to transport tourists in from thirty-one cities. The following year, mobster Bugsy Siegel opened the Flamingo Hotel and Casino in Las Vegas. Siegel's casino was initially so unprofitable that it had to close down, leaving many of Siegel's mob associates suspecting him of having embezzled from them. He was murdered in June, 1947. Shortly thereafter, the Flamingo reopened and began to flourish. It proved so successful that other casino hotels were soon added to the Las Vegas district that would become known as The Strip. Thanks to organized crime's investments in the Hollywood film industry, celebrities frequented Las Vegas—both as guests and as entertainers, adding to the attractiveness of Las Vegas as a place to visit.

Another major area of legalized gambling during the 1940's was horse racing. Pari-mutuel betting at racetracks was legal in eleven states, but a great deal of illegal off-track betting also occurred and was managed by organized crime.

Impact In a 1951 essay, historian Herbert Bloch wrote that gambling was opposed by religious groups because of its perceived negativity. However, the position of religious groups during the 1940's was inconsistent. While they opposed some forms of gambling, they seemingly endorsed others—most notably bingo, sometimes even in jurisdictions where bingo was illegal. In 1949, New Hampshire became the second state, after Rhode Island, to legalize bingo. Bloch went on to observe other apparently contradictory attitudes that Americans had about gambling. For example, he pointed out that many people disapproved of casino gambling while regarding stock market speculations which offered similar odds to be legitimate forms of behavior. He concluded class distinctions accounted for some of the differences in public attitudes toward gambling: Anyone might play a game of cards, but not all had access to the stock market and not all could place bets with illicit bookmakers. He went on to argue that media contests offering prizes for nothing fostered a gambling mentally during the 1940's.

Camille Gibson

Further Reading

Bloch, Herbert A. "The Sociology of Gambling." *American Journal of Sociology* 57, no. 3 (1951): 215-221.

Haugen, David M. *Library in a Book: Legalized Gambling.* New York: Facts On File, 2006.

Reuter, Peter. *Disorganized Crime.* Cambridge: Massachusetts Institute of Technology Press, 1983.

See also Business and the economy in the United States; Crimes and scandals; Organized crime; Recreation; Siegel, Bugsy; Sinatra, Frank; Travel in the United States.

■ Gamow, George

Identification   Russian-born American physicist
Born   March 4, 1904; Odessa, Russia
Died   August 19, 1968; Boulder, Colorado

Gamow made important contributions to nuclear and atomic physics, cosmology, and molecular biology. He wrote a series of books for general audiences that explained many complex, difficult physics concepts in a simple way.

George Gamow moved to the United States in 1934 and served as a professor of physics at George Washington University from 1934 until 1954. During the 1940's, he advocated the big bang theory as the model for the creation of the universe. He suggested that the universe expanded from a very dense mixture of neutrons, electrons, and protons held together by high-energy radiation to form nuclei and eventually elements. In 1944, he postulated that there should be a certain level of remnant, background radiation from the big bang, which was discovered nearly twenty years later. In 1948, he published a paper in which he developed equations for the mass and radius of a primordial galaxy.

Among the many books that Gamow authored, the most famous is his Mr. Tompkins series. Gamow used the Mr. Tompkins character, a rather odd man, to explain science to the layperson. *Mr. Tompkins in Wonderland* (1940) explains the theory of relativity. *Mr. Tompkins Explores the Atom* (1944) discusses modern theories of the atom. In 1947, Gamow published

One, Two, Three . . . Infinity, a work that integrates concepts of mathematics, physics, and biology.

Impact   Gamow introduced nuclear theory into cosmology and laid the foundations for research dealing with the formation of the elements from the big bang. He also participated in the development of the hydrogen bomb. His writings helped laypersons understand the complexities of science.

Alvin K. Benson

Further Reading

Barbour, Julian. *The End of Time: The Next Revolution in Physics.* New York: Oxford University Press, 2001.

Singh, Simon. *Big Bang: The Origin of the Universe.* New York: Fourth Estate, 2005.

See also Astronomy; Big bang theory; Fermi, Enrico; Nuclear reactors; Oppenheimer, J. Robert; Science and technology.

■ Garland, Judy

Identification   American singer and film star
Born   June 10, 1922; Grand Rapids, Minnesota
Died   June 22, 1969; London, England

Judy Garland made an impact with her singing and acting and during the 1940's became known as one of Metro-Goldwyn-Mayer's brightest stars.

Judy Garland starred in nearly two dozen movies through the 1940's. She received an Academy Juvenile Award in 1940 for her role in *The Wizard of Oz* (1939) and went on to become one of the most acclaimed stars of the Metro-Goldwyn-Mayer (MGM) studio with her exceptional singing voice and unique acting ability. The 1944 film *Meet Me in St. Louis* showed her outstanding singing ability with "The Trolley Song" and "Have Yourself a Merry Little Christmas," which received rave reviews.

Garland was married twice during the 1940's: to Dave Rose from 1941 to 1944 and to Vincente Minnelli from 1945 to 1951. In 1946, she gave birth to daughter Liza Minnelli, who, like her mother, would go on to stardom in both acting and singing.

The overworked star suffered greatly near the end of the 1940's, going through periods of deep depression and making a suicide attempt. The 1940's started out as a promising decade for her, but follow-

Judy Garland (center) dancing in the 1946 film The Harvey Girls. *(Getty Images)*

ing numerous problems in her work, she was suspended by MGM in 1950.

Impact   Garland became one of Hollywood's most promising young stars with her singing and acting during the 1940's. Although her life was troubled during the decade, she produced beautiful work in numerous films including *Meet Me in St. Louis, The Harvey Girls* (1946), in which she sang the Oscar-winning "On the Atchison, Topeka and the Santa Fe," and *The Pirate* (1948). Following the 1940's, she continued her singing career with concerts on stage and also made memorable films, including a remake of *A Star Is Born* (1954). On June 22, 1969, she was found dead from an accidental overdose of barbiturates.

Timothy Sawicki

Further Reading

Clarke, Gerald. *Get Happy: The Life of Judy Garland.* Miami, Fla.: Warner Bros. Publications, 2000.

Coleman, Emily R. *The Complete Judy Garland.* New York: Harper & Row, 1990.

Fricke, J., and Lorna Luft. *Judy Garland: A Portrait in Art and Anecdote.* New York: Bulfinch Press, 2003.

See also   Andy Hardy films; Crosby, Bing; Kelly, Gene; *Meet Me in St. Louis*; Rooney, Mickey; Sinatra, Frank.

■ Garner, Erroll Louis

Identification   African American jazz pianist and composer

Born   June 15, 1921; Pittsburgh, Pennsylvania

Died   January 2, 1977; Los Angeles, California

Known primarily for his 1940's trio work, Garner developed a unique style of piano playing that involved the use of

block chords in a steady rhythmic pattern. He had a profound influence on later musicians.

Perhaps best remembered as the composer of "Misty," Erroll Garner was a completely self-taught musician who never even learned to read music. Consequently, he developed an idiomatic style that stands apart from mainstream jazz piano playing. He began his long musical career at an early age while growing up in Pittsburgh, Pennsylvania, the city of his birth. There he performed on radio programs at the age of seven and was playing the piano on local riverboats when he was eleven. When he was in his teens, he was playing professionally and beginning to extend his contacts among the jazz musicians of the East Coast.

Garner began his recording career during the late 1940's, and he would eventually build a substantial library of records for five different labels, including Mercury, Columbia, Verve, Blue Note, and London. Although some of his early recordings are illustrative of the Harlem stride piano patterns with an alternating bass note-mid-range-chord left hand, Garner already had a distinct style. He had developed a characteristic four-beat pulse of block chords by the late 1940's. Against this, he embellished the melodic content with brilliant octave passages and incisive, single-note flourishes that were reminiscent of one of his distinguished mentors, Earl "Fatha" Hines. The rhythmic nature of Garner's approach was both inventive and compelling. His tremendous hand independence allowed him to juxtapose his harmonic and melodic ideas against each other, thus creating a staggering sense of swing as the melody lagged behind the pulse by as much as a semiquaver.

After releasing six albums during the 1940's, Garner went on to record steadily through the remaining years of his life. He toured frequently, both in the United States and in other countries. Along the way he became noted for his contributions to moving jazz into the musical mainstream and was much revered by the time he died in 1977.

Impact　Garner's impact on the history and tradition of jazz is evidenced by his legacy. His orchestral approach to the piano, one in which he exploited the entire range of the instrument, was steeped in the swing tradition, yet he was open to the harmonic and rhythmic complexities of bebop. This methodology was adopted by subsequent generations of jazz

pianists. Exponents such as Jimmy Rowles, Ahmad Jamal, and Dave Brubeck adapted his approach to fit their own musical conceptions.

Michael Conklin

Further Reading

Doran, James M. *Erroll Garner: The Most Happy Piano.* Metuchen, N.J.: Scarecrow Press, 1985.

See also　Ellington, Duke; Holiday, Billie; Music: Jazz; Music: Popular; Parker, Charlie.

■ Garson, Greer

Identification　British-born film star
Born　September 29, 1904; London, England
Died　April 6, 1996; Dallas, Texas

A major 1940's film star who embodied dignified female strength and honor, Garson was nominated for best actress Oscars every year from 1941 through 1945.

Greer Garson earned bachelor's degrees from King's College, London, in 1926 in eighteenth century literature and French. A member of the Birmingham Repertory Theatre for two years until illness made her resign, she debuted on the London stage in 1934. In 1937, Louis B. Mayer signed her to a seven-year contract with Metro-Goldwyn-Mayer (MGM). Considering herself a leading actor, she balked at the small part of Mrs. Chipping in 1939's *Goodbye, Mr. Chips.* However, wanting to return to England, where the movie would be filmed, she agreed to the role, which earned her the first of her seven Academy Award nominations for best actress. This was followed by other honored films, including *Pride and Prejudice* (1940), *Blossoms in the Dust* (1941), *Mrs. Miniver* (1942), *Random Harvest* (1942), *Madame Curie* (1943), and *Mrs. Parkington* (1944).

Impact　Garson's greatest impact came from her role in *Mrs. Miniver,* a propaganda film aimed at changing American isolationist attitudes toward World War II. It depicts the wartime struggles of average Britons. Middle-class housewife Mrs. Kay Miniver faces danger with humor and strength, bridging social classes, comforting her children, confronting Nazis, and dealing with the domestic problems of war. The film's quiet pride and dignity so touched American moviegoers that many were inspired to purchase war bonds. Concluding with a speech urging all to join the war against Germany, *Mrs. Miniver* still ranks as one of the most socially significant American films.

Leslie Neilan

Further Reading

Troyan, Michael. *A Rose for Mrs. Miniver: The Life of Greer Garson.* Lexington: University Press of Kentucky, 1999.

Turner Classic Movies. *The Fifty Most Unforgettable Actresses of the Studio Era.* San Francisco: Chronicle Books, 2006.

See also Academy Awards; *The Best Years of Our Lives*; Davis, Bette; Film in the United States; Films about World War II.

■ Gehrig, Lou

Identification American baseball player
Born June 19, 1903; New York, New York
Died June 2, 1941; New York, New York

Gehrig is best remembered for his consistency, symbolized by his record 2,130 consecutive games played between 1925 and 1939, and for the courage with which he faced the fatal neuromuscular disease that ended his career.

Born to poor German immigrants, New York Yankees Hall of Fame first baseman Lou Gehrig was an outstanding player by any account. However, it was only after his diagnosis with the then-obscure amyotrophic lateral sclerosis—now frequently known as Lou Gehrig's disease—and his subsequent death from the disease that Gehrig, the "Iron Horse," became an American icon.

Somewhat shy, Gehrig was easily overshadowed by his colorful teammate, Babe Ruth, throughout much of his playing career. However, he was given an emotional public tribute at Yankee Stadium soon after the 1939 an-nouncement of his illness, which was later echoed in the news media's reports of his passing two years later. It was the 1942 Frank Capra-like film based on Gehrig's life and death, *The Pride of the Yankees* (directed by Sam Wood and starring Gary Cooper), that produced the heroic image of Gehrig that has most endured.

Impact With his diagnosis and death occurring in the transitionary years between the Great Depression and World War II, Gehrig represented a heroic everyman who, for many, came to symbolize cherished "American values" of both eras: hard work, moral decency, and self-sacrifice.

William C. Bishop

Further Reading

Eig, Johnathan. *Luckiest Man: The Life and Death of Lou Gehrig.* New York: Simon & Schuster, 2005.

Robinson, Ray. *Iron Horse: Lou Gehrig in His Time.* New York: W. W. Norton, 1990.

See also Baseball; Capra, Frank; DiMaggio, Joe; Film in the United States; Gray, Pete; Immigration to the United States; Paige, Satchel; Robinson, Jackie; Sports in the United States; Williams, Ted.

Lou Gehrig sliding into home plate in a New York Yankees game. (Library of Congress)

■ General Agreement on Tariffs and Trade

The Treaty   International agreement that set basic rules under which open and nondiscriminatory trade could be conducted among nations

Also known as   GATT

Date   Preliminary agreement signed on October 30, 1947; final agreement signed on January 1, 1948

The General Agreement on Tariffs and Trade (GATT) was an international agreement under which signatory nations agreed to provide equal treatment in trade to all member nations, engage in multilateral negotiations to reduce tariffs, and abolish import quotas. Through its forty-seven years of existence, according to GATT officials, 123 different agreements were reached, involving tariffs on thousands of products.

GATT was a treaty, or series of agreements, first proposed in 1946 during considerations to create the International Trade Organization (ITO). The ideas behind ITO and, indirectly, GATT had their beginnings in the Bretton Woods Conference of 1944. The ITO was never ratified by the United States, so GATT ended up being a tariff-reduction treaty that was initially signed by twenty-three nations, including Canada and the United States. The concept upon which GATT was based was that free trade makes the entire world better off. The provisions of GATT were based on the "most favored nation" principle, which meant that the tariff rates that applied to the most favored nation would also apply to all signatories to GATT.

Initially, the agreement applied to 45,000 different products. Later amendments (called "rounds") to the treaty added thousands more products and resulted in even lower tariffs. Although the U.S. Congress was not willing to support the establishment of the ITO, it had given the U.S. president the authority to negotiate treaties governing international trade when it voted in 1945 to extend the 1934 Reciprocal Trade Agreements Act. President Harry S. Truman therefore had the authority to approve the GATT agreement. Although GATT was technically not an international institution, it did have a secretariat that was eventually headquartered in Geneva, Switzerland, to administer complaints that arose among member countries.

In attempts to further reduce tariffs and trade barriers, GATT members met regularly in what came to be called "negotiating rounds." The initial round, known as the Geneva Round, started in April, 1947, and met for seven months; the result was 45,000 tariff concessions. The April, 1949, Annecy Round, lasting five months, added an additional 5,000 tariff concessions. These and future rounds were designed to further reduce tariffs that countries could impose on other GATT members. The success of these meetings is evidenced by the fact that tariffs averaged about 35 percent before the creation of GATT but had been reduced to 6.4 percent by the start of the Uruguay Round in 1986.

Nondiscrimination Provisions   The success of the GATT agreements was based on the founding principles of nondiscrimination and reciprocity. Reciprocity refers to the process whereby one country offers to reduce a trade barrier or reduce a tariff and a second country reciprocates by offering to reduce its barriers or tariffs on another product. Basically, companies swap tariff concessions. The nondiscrimination provision means that if a trade benefit is offered to one member of GATT, it also must be offered to every other signatory country. Thus, what starts out as a reciprocal trade agreement between two countries becomes a benefit to all members of GATT. The result is freer trade and a more efficient world economy.

Some exceptions to the general rules allow the use of discriminatory tariffs under special circumstances. One such exception to the nondiscrimination rules concerns regional trade agreements. The GATT agreements allow for regional trade agreements and customs unions. These exceptions often were controversial, but the level of controversy tended to fall over time as tariff rates fell. Another exception allowed by the GATT agreements is known as Administered Trade Protection, which is a temporary discriminatory tariff such as an antidumping duty, a countervailing duty, a safeguard measure, or a tariff intended to help a country solve its balance-of-payments problems. Although some arguments support these exceptions, the exceptions provide countries with a temptation to cheat on the GATT agreements.

Impact   The GATT secretariat was replaced by the World Trade Organization (WTO) on January 1, 1995, though GATT principles and agreements became part of the WTO. During its nearly half century of existence, GATT reduced or eliminated tariffs on more than 50,000 items among 146 nations. The WTO took over mediation and settling disputes among countries that have agreed to abide by GATT and WTO rules. When a country is found to be in violation, it can either amend its laws to be in compliance or keep its laws in place and be subject to measured retaliation from aggrieved trading partners.

From 1986 through 1994, a new round of trade negotiations—the Uruguay Round—was launched. This round was prompted by the fact that textiles and agricultural commodities were generally exempt from GATT rules. The goals of the Uruguay Round were more ambitious than had been the case with earlier rounds; the overall objective was to introduce major reforms into the international trading system. The result was a 1994 treaty that established the WTO, which superseded GATT. Tariffs were reduced by an additional 40 percent. In addition, the Uruguay Round reduced agricultural subsidies, allowed full access for textiles and clothing from developing countries, and extended GATT provisions to intellectual property rights. The intellectual property rights provisions applied to such disparate products as films, computer software, and patents on pharmaceutical products.

By the early twenty-first century, about 97 percent of world trade was covered by GATT and WTO agreements. Nondiscrimination in tariff policy is meant to ensure that the world's resources are allocated to their most productive and efficient uses; trading on an equal basis is meant to ensure that no country creates an unfair advantage through tariff policy and thereby attract resources that would be better used elsewhere.

Dale L. Flesher

Further Reading

Bagwell, Kyle, and Robert W. Staiger. *Multilateral Trade Negotiations, Bilateral Opportunism and the Rules of GATT.* Cambridge, Mass.: National Bureau of Economic Research, 1999.

Beane, Donald G. *The United States and GATT: A Relational Study.* Amsterdam, N.Y.: Pergamon Press, 2000.

Kirshner, Orin, ed. *The Bretton Woods-GATT System: Retrospect and Prospect After Fifty Years.* Armonk, N.Y.: M. E. Sharpe, 1996.

See also Bretton Woods Conference; Business and the economy in Canada; Business and the economy in the United States; Economic wartime regulations; International trade; Keynesian economics; Truman, Harry S.

■ General Motors

Identification Largest American manufacturer of automobiles and trucks and a major defense contractor during World War II

Also known as GM

Date Established on September 16, 1908

Throughout the twentieth century, the General Motors Corporation was the epitome of American big business. Because it was the world's largest automobile manufacturer, many people believe that the American economy was reflected in its success. The company's leaders were viewed as spokespersons for American industry as a whole. During World War II, the company maintained its leadership in industry, as it switched from manufacturing automobile to manufacturing military vehicles and equipment.

When the United States entered World War II at the end of 1941, General Motors (GM) controlled 41 percent of the entire U.S. automobile market. However, civilian auto production dropped to zero in 1942 as factories turned their efforts to supplying equipment for the U.S. war effort. Armored tanks and other military vehicles soon replaced automobiles on GM factory floors. After the war ended in 1945, GM's automobile market quickly grew. Its newly designed cars of the late 1940's lifted the company's car sales to a 54 percent market share by the early 1950's.

In 1923, Alfred P. Sloan became president and chief executive officer of GM, and he held the latter position until 1956. Much of the company's growth occurred under his leadership, but he did not act alone; credit can also be accorded to the company's chief financial officer through those years—Donaldson Brown, who applied his return-on-investment formula to every department within GM. A knowledge of the rate of return on investment was important at GM because the company was among the first to use discounted-cash-flow analysis to evaluate investment alternatives.

Working under Sloan and Brown was Ernest R. Breech, who was to become the chief aviation expert at GM during the war years. Breech had been the executive in charge of several of GM's aviation divisions through the prewar years. These divisions included North American Aviation and Bendix Aviation. Despite its reputation for being in the automotive business, GM management had diversified into airplanes during the 1920's under the mistaken belief that eventually every American family would own a small aircraft. GM wanted to be in a position to fulfill all transportation needs of consumers, even if the preferred form of transportation became personal airplanes. The coming of the war gave GM the opportunity to profit from those early investments in aviation manufacturing. Although GM could have profited extensively from its defense businesses, management elected instead to voluntarily return a portion of profits to the federal government to help fight the war.

GM even provided the government with manpower to help fulfill the country's needs for war supplies. William Knudsen, the GM president, was appointed by President Franklin D. Roosevelt in 1940 to chair the wartime Office of Production Management. Alternatively, however, GM's German subsidiary became an important part of the Nazi war effort. GM took a tax deduction for the loss of its German factories and later received reparations payments after those factories were bombed by the Allies.

After the war, consumer optimism in the future and a growing for need for new cars led to unprecedented demand for automobiles. GM quickly retooled with designs that proved popular in the marketplace. Innovations included the industry's first V-8 engines in 1948. Despite facing new competitors, GM took back its old market share and even expanded that percentage.

Impact   Because of GM's efforts during the war, Detroit became known as the "Arsenal of Democracy." GM was the major American car manufacturer before the war; it became the major defense contractor during the war, and it came out of the war even stronger than it had been at the start. A later GM president, Charles E. Wilson, summarized the role of GM succinctly with a statement that what benefited the country also benefited GM, and vice versa.

Dale L. Flesher

Further Reading

Koistinen, Paul A. C. *Arsenal of World War II: The Political Economy of American Warfare, 1940-1945*. Lawrence: University Press of Kansas, 2004.

Nelson, Donald M. *Arsenal of Democracy: The Story of American War Production*. New York: Harcourt, Brace, 1946.

Sloan, Alfred P. *My Years with General Motors*. Garden City, NY: Doubleday, 1964.

Wright, J. Patrick. *On a Clear Day You Can See General Motors: John Z. De Lorean's Look Inside the Automotive Giant*. Grosse Pointe, Mich.: Wright Enterprises, 1979.

See also   Aircraft design and development; Auto racing; Automobiles and auto manufacturing; Business and the economy in the United States; Ford Motor Company; Wartime industries; Wartime technological advances.

■ Geneva Conventions

The Treaties   Several international agreements, collectively known as the Geneva Conventions, that specified and clarified the internationally accepted laws of warfare

Date   Adopted on August 12, 1949

The Geneva Conventions of 1949 stipulated how warfare would be conducted so as to prevent egregious practices. Prior Geneva Conventions had provided a framework for armed hostilities and military occupation of other countries, but these were notoriously violated by World War II aggressors Nazi Germany and Imperial Japan.

The Axis powers of Nazi Germany, Italy, and Imperial Japan engaged in acts of unprovoked aggression that began World War II. Although Canada supported Britain, which was under attack, American troops were not dispatched to join those forces. After Japan attacked Pearl Harbor on December 7, 1941, the United States entered the war, joining the Allied powers, with the intention of abiding by the then-current Geneva Conventions.

Contrary to the Geneva Conventions, the aggressors engaged in indiscriminate, unannounced attacks on undefended military targets. Neither the Geneva nor the Hague conventions, however, prohibited attacks from airplanes. In addition, during the war both sides mercilessly bombed civilian targets, including Dresden, London, and Tokyo, with the war eventually ending following the atomic bombing of Hiroshima and Nagasaki.

As the war progressed, soldiers were captured by

enemy forces and held as prisoners of war (POWs). Allied armies scrupulously observed the Geneva Conventions in their POW camps. Nazi Germany and Imperial Japan pretended to follow suit but in fact used some POW camps for interrogation, contrary to the Geneva Convention requirement that soldiers were required to provide only their names, ranks, and serial numbers to their captors. Some POWs were tortured, and medical experiments were performed on them. Germany also murdered about half of its Soviet POWs. Japan ordered American and Philippine soldiers on a death march after assuming control of the Philippines, a possession of the United States.

While occupying several countries militarily, Germany and Japan violated Geneva Conventions guidelines about the rules of occupation, notably diverting civilian facilities and expending civilian funds for military purposes and leaving many in the occupied population without necessities of life. Germany and Japan undertook wholesale reprisals against entire towns and villages, and their captured citizens were forced to work for the aggressors' war effort. One notorious practice was forcing captives to work as "comfort women" for Japanese soldiers, providing sexual services.

Officials of Nazi Germany and Imperial Japan faced judgment for violations of the Geneva Conventions in war crimes trials conducted soon after the war at Nuremberg, Tokyo, and elsewhere. Many were convicted in a series of trials from 1945 to 1949.

The four Geneva Conventions adopted in 1949 were designed with the excesses of World War II in mind. The First and Second Geneva Conventions focused on the conduct of warfare, including aerial warfare. These were known as the First Geneva Convention for the Amelioration of the Condition of the Wounded and Sick in Armed Forces in the Field, an update of an 1864 convention, and the Second Geneva Convention for the Amelioration of the Condition of Wounded, Sick and Shipwrecked Members of Armed Forces at Sea, an update of a 1906 convention. The Third Geneva Convention Relative to the Treatment of Prisoners of War, an update of a 1929 convention, banned interrogation camps and medical experiments on POWs, and it otherwise tightened the requirements of how prisoners were to be treated in time of war. The Fourth Geneva Convention Relative to the Protection of Civilian Persons in Time of War provided extensive guidelines for civil-military occupation.

Impact Although the U.S. military incorporated provisions of the four new Geneva Conventions in the training of soldiers, both in training manuals and in the Uniform Code of Military Justice, Congress has been slow in passing laws to implement provisions of the Geneva Conventions. Whereas the military has engaged in courts-martial to enforce the Geneva Conventions, relevant cases in civilian courts have been insufficient to provide clear precedents. The Fourth Geneva Convention guided the United States as an occupying power of a portion of Germany during 1949 and most of Japan until 1952.

Violations of the Geneva Conventions occurring during military conduct of the Vietnam War resulted in several courts-martial but not in the prosecution of military or civilian leaders. The U.S. war in Iraq also generated complaints of violations of the Geneva Conventions, particularly with regard to the detainment camp at the Guantánamo naval station in Cuba. A Supreme Court ruling in 2006 required observance of article 3, common to all four Geneva Conventions, but violations of other provisions continued even after the inauguration of President Barack Obama in 2009.

Geneva Convention Provision Against Torture

Article 32 of the Fourth Geneva Convention, reproduced below, prohibits the use of torture and other forms of physical abuse of individuals in protective custody.

The High Contracting Parties specifically agree that each of them is prohibited from taking any measure of such a character as to cause the physical suffering or extermination of protected persons in their hands. This prohibition applies not only to murder, torture, corporal punishments, mutilation, and medical or scientific experiments not necessitated by the medical treatment of a protected person, but also to any other measures of brutality whether applied by civilian or military agents.

The Geneva Conventions have been updated by several protocols. Protocol I (1977) relates to the Protection of Victims of International Armed Conflicts. Protocol II (1977) relates to the Protection of Victims of Non-International Armed Conflicts. Protocol III (2005) relates to the Adoption of an Additional Distinctive Emblem, so that providers of medical services can be more clearly identified.

Michael Haas

Further Reading

Best, Geoffrey. *War and Law Since 1945.* New York: Oxford University Press, 1994. Reviews the origins of the theory and concept of war crimes, the barbarities of World Wars I and II, the reconstruction of the law of warfare by the United Nations and the 1949 Geneva Conventions, and the additions to the law of warfare since 1950.

Gutman, Roy, David Rieff, and Kenneth Anderson, eds. *Crimes of War: What the Public Should Know.* New York: W. W. Norton, 1999. Uses journalistic accounts of major war crimes to illustrate the law of international warfare.

Haas, Michael. *George W. Bush, War Criminal? The Bush Administration's Liability for 269 War Crimes.* Westport, Conn.: Praeger, 2009. Uses the Geneva Conventions and other documents to compile a list of specific war crimes committed by the Bush administration.

Heaton, Colin D. *Occupation and Insurgency: A Selective Examination of the Hague and Geneva Conventions on the Eastern Front, 1939-1945.* Edited by Steve Greer. New York: Algora, 2008. Discusses Nazi policy regarding the territories Germany conquered and occupied from 1941 to 1944. Relates how Germany willfully disregarded international laws and treaties regarding the conduct of warfare, thus setting the stage for the Geneva Conventions.

Trombly, Maria. *Reference Guide to the Geneva Conventions.* Indianapolis: Society of Professional Journalists, 2000. An e-book that provides links to the relevant treaties.

See also   Casualties of World War II; Germany, occupation of; Japan, occupation of; Nuremberg Trials; Prisoners of war, North American; Red Cross; War crimes and atrocities; World War II.

■ *Gentleman's Agreement*

Identification   Film about anti-Semitism
Director   Elia Kazan (1909-2003)
Date   Premiered on November 11, 1947

One of the first post-World War II films to engage the subject of anti-Semitism, Gentleman's Agreement *helped stimulate discussion about American discrimination against Jews.*

Based on the book by Laura Hobson that shares the same title, *Gentleman's Agreement* is one of the most influential motion pictures about anti-Semitism in the twentieth century. The film stars Gregory Peck as journalist Philip Green, who has recently moved to New York City with his son Tommy (Dean Stockwell) and mother (Anne Revere). Asked by magazine publisher John Minify (Albert Dekker) to write

(Getty Images)

an article about anti-Semitism, Philip decides to assume the identity of a Jewish man, Phil Greenberg. He subsequently meets Minify's niece Kathy (Dorothy McGuire), and the two soon begin dating. At this time, Philip and his son begin to experience a series of discriminatory acts because of their new identity.

The majority of the film focuses on Kathy's appeasing her anti-Semitic friends in Connecticut rather than confronting their bigotry. For instance, when Philip's Jewish friend Dave Goldman (John Garfield) has difficulty finding housing, Philip asks Kathy to rent her Connecticut cottage to Dave. When Kathy refuses for fear of alienating her anti-Semitic friends and neighbors, Philip decides to break off their engagement. At the end of the film, Kathy has a change of heart on the subject and the two ultimately reconcile.

Impact   *Gentleman's Agreement* was generally met with both popular and critical success. The high-grossing picture earned an Academy Award for best picture in 1947. The film, with its overtly liberal message, also drew the attention of the House Committee on Un-American Activities (HUAC), which brought in several of the film's cast members and staff to present testimony. This eventually led to the Hollywood blacklisting of John Garfield and Anne Revere for their failure to testify.

Brion Sever

Further Reading

Ceplair, Larry, and Steven Englund. *The Inquisition in Hollywood: Politics in the Film Community, 1930-1960.* Urbana: University of Illinois Press, 2003.

Hobson, Laura. *Gentleman's Agreement.* New York: Simon & Schuster, 1947.

See also   Film in the United States; Hollywood blacklisting; House Committee on Un-American Activities; Jews in the United States.

■ German American Bund

Identification   Pro-German organization based in the United States

Date   Established in March, 1936

The principal pro-Nazi organization in the United States during the 1930's and 1940's, the German American

Bund was formed to promote positive views of Nazi Germany and Adolf Hitler within the United States. However, the organization had such a negligible impact that even Hitler's government disavowed it.

A small National Socialist Association of Teutonia existed during the 1920's but had no influence. After Adolf Hitler came to power in Germany in 1933, his Nazi Party's foreign department looked for ways to mobilize Germans abroad. It created an association in the United States called the Friends of the New Germany, comprising mainly immigrants, but by late 1935, the regime found this organization embarrassing and withdrew its support. In March, 1936, the remnants of the organization gathered around Fritz Julius Kuhn to form the German American Bund with him as its national leader.

Born in Munich in 1896, and a veteran of World War I, Kuhn had studied chemical engineering and worked as an industrial chemist in Mexico. After 1927, he worked for the Ford Motor Company in Detroit, Michigan, and became an American citizen in 1934. He joined the Detroit branch of Friends of New Germany, worked his way to its top post, and continued as head of the new Bund. In 1936, he went to Berlin, where he posed for a picture with Hitler, and claimed—falsely—that he had Hitler's blessing for his American organization.

Kuhn's group held rallies filled with swastikas, Nazi salutes (at the time similar to the U.S. flag salute), and German songs, and it vigorously promoted anti-Semitism. It established recreational camps on Long Island, New York; New Jersey; Wisconsin; and California and created an American version of the Hitler Youth to indoctrinate children in German language and history and Nazi philosophy. The uniformed organization also had its own goon squad to protect meetings and harass protesting demonstrators.

As exaggerated rumors about the Bund's growing membership spread, the Federal Bureau of Investigation began monitoring its activities, and the House Committee on Un-American Activities held hearings about it. However, it never had more than about six thousand members. Its high point came during a spectacular rally at New York's Madison Square Garden in February, 1939.

In 1938, the German government acknowledged the Bund's ineffectiveness by barring German citizens from joining the organization and forbidding the organization itself from using Nazi emblems and symbols. Afterward, the Bund quickly declined. Kuhn was jailed for embezzling Bund funds, and the U.S. government banned the organization after the United States entered World War II at the end of 1941. In 1944, some of its leaders were tried for sedition.

Impact Although the Bund was a noisy, attention-getting organization, it had no influence on American policy. Kuhn himself was deported back to Germany where he died in obscurity in 1951, at the age of fifty-five.

Richard V. Pierard

Further Reading

Canedy, Susan. *America's Nazis: A Democratic Dilemma—A History of the German American Bund.* Menlo Park, Calif.: Markgraf Publications Group, 1990.

Diamond, Sander. *The Nazi Movement in the United States, 1924-1941.* Ithaca, N.Y.: Cornell University, 1974.

MacDonnell, Francis. *Insidious Foes: The Axis Fifth Column and the American Home Front.* New York: Oxford University Press, 1995.

Van Ells, Mark D. "Americans for Hitler" *America in World War II* 3, no. 2 (August, 2007): 44-49.

See also America First Committee; Germany, occupation of; Hitler, Adolf; Wartime espionage in North America; Wartime propaganda in the United States; Wartime sabotage.

■ Germany, occupation of

The Event Military occupation of Germany by the United States after World War II

Date 1945-1949

Place Germany

Following World War II, the United States and other countries maintained troops in Germany to monitor the country.

In 1943, in Casablanca, Morocco, President Franklin D. Roosevelt demanded Nazi Germany's unconditional surrender during World War II. Aside from occasional flippant remarks about Germans, however, the president gave no clear instructions on what to do about a nation that was responsible for the war and for the mass murder of Jews and other "undesirables." The president's close friend Henry Morgenthau, the secretary of the Treasury, was outraged by the Holocaust and suggested a radical solution. He believed in collective German guilt and thought that the military's "Handbook for Military Government in Germany," which he examined in August, 1944, was much too soft because it advocated restoring a German civilian government and economy.

At the Second Quebec Conference, in early September, 1944, President Roosevelt and British prime minister Winston Churchill adopted Morgenthau's "Program to Prevent Germany from Starting a World War III," which advocated the complete deindustrialization of Germany. Within weeks, Roosevelt changed his mind because of growing opposition to a plan that the *Wall Street Journal* called "Carthaginian." The president died on April 12, 1945, before final occupation plans could be issued. His successor, Harry S. Truman, signed occupation policy JCS (Joint Chiefs of Staff) 1067, which incorporated much of Morgenthau's plan. This policy guided the American military government in Germany until it was replaced in 1947 by the more moderate JCS 1779, which facilitated the economic and political reconstruction of West Germany and ended the military government in 1949.

U.S. Military Occupation Policies, 1945-1947 At a conference at Potsdam on August 2, 1945, the Allies adopted plans for the occupation of Germany based on previous wartime agreements. For administrative purposes, Germany west of the Oder-Neisse line was divided into four zones, with a similar arrangement made for Berlin. The United States zone included Bavaria, Hesse, Baden-Württemberg, and an enclave around Bremen including a port to accommodate American shipping needs. General Dwight D. Eisenhower was the first American military governor, but his deputy, General Lucius D. Clay, a 1918 West Point graduate who became head of military procurement in 1942, was primarily responsible for military government long before he took official control over the occupation army in March, 1947. President Truman rarely interfered with Clay's actions.

Clay initially accepted German collective guilt for war crimes. He supported the 4D's: de-Nazification, demilitarization, de-cartelization, and democratization. The German General Staff and military institutions were abolished. Clay suggested Nuremberg for

U.S. Occupied Germany, 1944

DENMARK

North Sea

Baltic Sea

POLAND

Hamburg

Elbe

Oder River

NETHERLANDS

GERMANY

Hanover

★ Berlin

Leipzig

Dresden

Koln

Bonn

Rhine

BELGIUM

River

Wiesbaden • Frankfurt

Mainz

LUXEMBOURG

CZECHOSLOVAKIA
(now Czech Republic
and Slovakia)

• Nürnberg

Regensburg

Stuttgart

Danube River

FRANCE

• Augsburg

Munich

AUSTRIA

SWITZERLAND

Note: Shaded regions designate American-occupied areas.

the trial of major German war criminals and subsequent trials of German organizations implicated in war crimes. He also supported a massive de-Nazification program, part of which involved collecting millions of documents and questionnaires that were turned over to the German courts in March, 1946, for use in war crimes trials. Clay was also the first Western military governor and introduced free local elections in January, 1946, followed later that year by elections to three state constituent assemblies.

A major problem Clay faced in instituting de-industrialization was that it would limit German ability to pay for imports, particularly of food. In 1946, American taxpayers paid for 90 percent of German imports. Clay gradually reduced the dismantling of German industry. Of 1,210 plants scheduled to be closed, only 24 were shut down by May, 1946. In that same month, Clay stopped reparations payments from the American Zone. To improve economic conditions, on January 1, 1947, Clay's zone was combined with the British occupation zone as a Bizone.

1947-1949   In January, 1947, President Truman appointed George C. Marshall as secretary of state. Marshall replaced JCS 1067 with a new policy, JCS 1779, which acknowledged that Europe could not recover without a productive Germany. In June, 1947, he announced the Marshall Plan, which promised massive U.S. financial aid to Europe. The formation of the Trizone and the introduction of German currency reform in West Berlin in June, 1948, caused the Soviets to blockade all land access to Berlin on June 24, 1948. Clay was determined to ensure the survival of West Berlin, and he won the support of Truman. On June 26, the Berlin airlift was launched, which supplied West Berlin until the Soviet blockade was lifted in May, 1949. West Berliners honored Clay by naming a major avenue after him.

May, 1949, also saw the creation of a new West German government (formally the Federal Republic of Germany), which ended the American (and French and British) military occupation and created an Allied High Commission. The Occupation Statute of September 21, 1949, continued Allied rights to intervene in German affairs. Clay was replaced by the U.S. high commissioner John J. McCloy (1895-1989), assistant secretary of war during World War II. McCloy played a key role in the creation of a new German military, which was totally integrated

into the North Atlantic Treaty Organization (NATO) in 1955. Although German sovereignty was gradually restored by 1952, the high commissioners did not fully end the occupation status and grant West Germany full sovereignty until May 5, 1955.

Effect on the United States and the U.S. Military   After the defeat of Nazi Germany and Japan, the American military government in Germany was challenged by numerous problems, ranging from increasing cases of venereal disease to thefts by American personnel. In December, 1945, *The New York Times* described "homesick Americans," and in January, 1946, three thousand American soldiers demonstrated at the headquarters of General Joseph McNarney, demanding to go home.

American soldiers ignored nonfraternization orders, particularly in actions involving women and children. Polls in the United States in the fall of 1945 revealed that a majority of Americans opposed fraternization in Germany. Despite official policy, many serious relationships had developed between G.I.'s and German women, including marriages. The nonfraternization rule was ended in October, 1945, and in December, 1946, the marriage ban was lifted. By June, 1950, more than fourteen thousand German women married to American soldiers were living in the United States.

African Americans serving in Germany were often treated better by Germans than by their own military authorities. Freda Utley, a newspaper reporter, noted Jim Crow practices in occupied Germany. Leon Standifer and David Brion Davis, a member of the military constabulary force in occupied Germany, recalled the abysmally racist attitudes of the white American military police, particularly when the police confronted black G.I.'s with white German girlfriends. African American newspapers and civil rights organizations in the United States monitoring the treatment of black soldiers in Germany reported that the former enemy German population treated blacks better than many white American officers and soldiers did, and they used that argument effectively to support their fight for civil rights and integration of the U.S. military.

Impact   In 1945, a sign at the entrance of the major U.S. building in Nuremberg prohibited entry to Germans and dogs. By 1947, however, a Gallup poll revealed that a majority of Americans were friendly toward Germans, and two years later two-thirds of

Americans felt that Germans had been punished enough. Although growing anti-Soviet sentiments in the United States played a role in changing American attitudes toward Germans, the increasing interaction between American occupation forces and Germans was equally important.

Clay's support of local and state democratic government, as well as his efforts to unite the three Western zones of Germany, played a key role in establishing the basis for a durable new democratic system in West Germany. U.S. support for German reunification within NATO was one important factor leading to the Moscow treaty of September 12, 1990, between the four major World War II Allies and the two German states (the Federal Republic of Germany and the German Democratic Republic, known as East Germany). This treaty officially ended all Allied occupation rights in Germany and Berlin and led to German unity one month later. Soviet troops left former East German territory by the end of 1994, while American troops are still welcome in a Germany that has been cured of its past militarism.

Johnpeter Horst Grill

Further Reading

Beschloss, Michael. *The Conquerors: Roosevelt, Truman, and the Destruction of Hitler's Germany, 1941-1945*. New York: Simon & Schuster, 2002. Essential for understanding the debate generated by Henry Morgenthau's plan. Insightful notes, bibliography.

Goedde, Petra. *GIs and Germans: Culture, Gender, and Foreign Relations, 1945-1949*. New Haven, Conn.: Yale University Press, 2003. Argues that the interaction of G.I.'s with German women and children was crucial for the rapprochement of Germany and the United States. Bibliography and index.

Peterson, Edward N. *The American Occupation of Germany: Retreat from Victory*. Detroit: Wayne State University Press, 1978. A chronological survey. Suggests that the military government left a conservative power structure. Exhaustive notes, bibliography.

Schroer, Timothy L. *Recasting Race After World War II: Germans and African Americans in American-Occupied Germany*. Boulder: University Press of Colorado, 2007. Part of a growing literature on the experience of African American soldiers in Germany and its impact on American racial attitudes. Bibliography.

Schwartz, Thomas Alan. *America's Germany: John J. McCloy and the Federal Republic of Germany*. Cambridge, Mass.: Harvard University Press, 1991. Academic survey of McCloy's actions as U.S. high commissioner in Germany. Scholarly bibliography.

Smith, Jean Edward. *Lucius D. Clay: An American Life*. New York: Henry Holt, 1990. Uses extensive interviews with Clay to explain his German policy. Extensive notes, bibliography.

See also Berlin blockade and airlift; Casablanca Conference; Eisenhower, Dwight D.; German American Bund; North Atlantic Treaty Organization; Nuremberg Trials; Patton, George S.; Potsdam Conference; Quebec Conferences; Unconditional surrender policy.